Frommer's®

W9-CHT-553

POSTCARDS

FROM

WASHINGTON, D.C.

If these walls could talk. . . See chapter 7 for information on how to visit the White House.
© Kindra Clineff Photography.

At the Capitol, our elected representatives debate bills, pass laws, and barrel pork. See chapter 7. © Kelly/Mooney Photography.

Viewing this stark memorial to America's Vietnam War dead is a powerful and poignant experience. See chapter 7. © Wolfgang Kaehler Photography.

Washington is at its most beautiful in the spring, when the cherry blossoms bloom along the Tidal Basin. See chapter 7. © John Skowronski/Folio, Inc.

WE ARE THE SHOES, WE ARE THE LAST WITNESSES.
WE ARE SHOES FROM GRANDCHILDREN AND GRANDFATHERS,
FROM PRAGUE, PARIS, AND AMSTERDAM,
AND BECAUSE WE ARE ONLY MADE OF FABRIC AND LEATHER
AND NOT OF BLOOD AND FLESH, EACH ONE OF US AVOIDED THE HELLFIRE.

MOSES SCHULSTEIN (1911–1981),
YIDDISH POET

This display of thousands of shoes collected at Nazi concentration camps is one of many harrowing and evocative exhibits at the United States Holocaust Memorial Museum. See chapter 7. © Phoebe Bell/Folio, Inc.

A bit of memorial revisionism: FDR sans wheelchair and cigarette. See chapter 7. © Michael Ventura/ Folio, Inc.

At the hands-on Capital Children's Museum, your kids won't have to resist the urge to touch the exhibits. See chapter 7 for more attractions that children will love. © Catherine Karnow Photography.

A walk along the C&O Canal in Georgetown reveals a quainter side of Washington. See chapter 7 for neighborhood walking tours. © Tom Dietrich/Tony Stone Images.

The Folger Shakespeare Library houses the world's largest collection of the Bard's printed works. See chapter 7. © Catherine Karnow Photography.

Painstakingly restored to its former glory, stunning Union Station is not only a gateway to D.C., but an attraction itself, with great dining and shopping. See chapters 6, 7, and 8. © Catherine Karnow Photography.

The memorial to America's third president and original Renaissance man, Thomas Jefferson, is even more beautiful at night. See chapter 7. © Robert Shafer/Tony Stone Images.

The Changing of the Guard ceremony at the Tomb of the Unknown Soldier in Arlington National Cemetery. See chapter 7. © Jeff Greenberg/Folio, Inc.

The National Air & Space Museum, the most visited museum in the world, chronicles the story of flight, from Kitty Hawk to outer space. See chapter 7. © John Neubauer Photography.

The Capitol dome at night. See chapter 7. © Robert Shafer/Folio, Inc.

Washington natives go "Hog" wild for their Redskins. See chapter 7 for information on sporting events. © Catherine Karnow Photography.

Influential wheelers-and-dealers who gathered in the Willard's spectacular lobby were the original "lobbyists." See chapter 5 for other historic hotel choices. © Catherine Karnow Photography.

The dignified simplicity of Arlington National Cemetery. See chapter 7. © Christie Parker/ Dave G. Houser Photography.

The domed Main Reading Room of the Library of Congress is the epicenter of the world's largest library. Visit it for the exquisite architecture or to peruse one of its 113 million items. See chapter 7. © Jake Rajs Photography/Tony Stone Images.

Mount Vernon, George Washington's Virginia estate. See chapter 10 for this and other side trips from D.C. © Walter Bibikow/Folio, Inc.

The National Museum of American History's First Ladies exhibit is one of the few D.C. attractions to focus on the achievements of women. See chapter 7. © John Neubauer Photography.

Lincoln was sitting in this box at Ford's Theatre when he was shot by John Wilkes Booth. See chapter 7. © Catherine Karnow Photography.

The streets extending out from Dupont Circle are jumping with all-night bookstores, great restaurants and nightspots, movie theaters, and Washingtonians at play. See chapter 9. © Michael Ventura/Folio, Inc.

EQUAL JUSTICE UNDER LAW

The Supreme Court: where the country's brightest minds get to wear robes to work. If you plan carefully, you may get to see the Court in action. See chapter 7. © Kelly/Mooney Photography.

Frommer's® 2000

Washington, D.C.

by Elise Hartman Ford

With Online Directory by Michael Shapiro

IDG Books Worldwide, Inc.
An International Data Group Company
Foster City, CA • Chicago, IL • Indianapolis, IN • New York, NY

About the Author

Elise Hartman Ford has been a freelance writer in the Washington, D.C., area since 1985. She contributes regularly to such newspapers as the *Washington Post,* and to *Washingtonian* and other magazines. In addition to this guide, she is the author of two books about places to rent for special events and meetings: *Unique Meeting, Wedding and Party Places in Greater Washington,* now in its fourth edition, and *Unique Meeting Places in Greater Baltimore.*

For my husband, Jim, my most reliable source, who not only keeps me informed of the latest hot spots around town, but is ready to stay out all night trying them.

IDG Books Worldwide, Inc.

An International Data Group Company
919 E. Hillsdale Blvd.
Suite 400
Foster City, CA 94404

Find us online at **www.frommers.com**

ISBN 0-02-863053-X
ISSN 0899-3246

Editor: Justin Lapatine
Production Editor: Tammy Ahrens
Photo Editor: Richard Fox
Design by Michele Laseau
Staff Cartographers: John Decamillis, Roberta Stockwell
Page Creation by Sean Monkhouse, Kendra Span, and Julie Trippetti
Front cover photo: The Washington Monument

Special Sales

For general information on IDG Books Worldwide's books in the U.S., please call our
Consumer Customer Service department at 1-800-762-2974. For reseller information,
including discounts, bulk sales, customized editions, and premium sales, please call our
Reseller Customer Service department at 1-800-434-3422.

Manufactured in the United States of America

5   4   3   2   1

Contents

List of Maps

AN INVITATION TO THE READER

In researching this book, we discovered many wonderful places—hotels, restaurants, shops, and more. We're sure you'll find others. Please tell us about them, so we can share the information with your fellow travelers in upcoming editions. If you were disappointed with a recommendation, we'd love to know that, too. Please write to:

Frommer's Washington, D.C. 2000
IDG Travel
1633 Broadway
New York, NY 10019

AN ADDITIONAL NOTE

Please be advised that travel information is subject to change at any time—and this is especially true of prices. We therefore suggest that you write or call ahead for confirmation when making your travel plans. The authors, editors, and publisher cannot be held responsible for the experiences of readers while traveling. Your safety is important to us, however, so we encourage you to stay alert and be aware of your surroundings. Keep a close eye on cameras, purses, and wallets, all favorite targets of thieves and pickpockets.

WHAT THE SYMBOLS MEAN

✪ Frommer's Favorites

Our favorite places and experiences—outstanding for quality, value, or both.

The following abbreviations are used for credit cards:

AE	American Express	EURO	Eurocard
CB	Carte Blanche	JCB	Japan Credit Bank
DC	Diners Club	MC	MasterCard
DISC	Discover	V	Visa
ER	EnRoute		

FIND FROMMER'S ONLINE

Arthur Frommer's Budget Travel Online (**www.frommers.com**) offers more than 6,000 pages of up-to-the-minute travel information—including the latest bargains and candid, personal articles updated daily by Arthur Frommer himself. No other Web site offers such comprehensive and timely coverage of the world of travel.

Introducing Washington, D.C.

You're standing on the steps of the Lincoln Memorial, where the wind is having its way with your hair. It's often breezy here, a park ranger tells you, just as another gust lifts the cap off the head of the tourist right next to you. You reach for it, and then it's gone, and as you scan the landscape, you find yourself looking across to the Reflecting Pool and beyond that, to the Washington Monument, presiding on its own hill nearly a mile away. The monument looks rather odd, but impressive nonetheless, encased in a shroud of scaffolding as its restoration progresses. You hope to tour there today, you're thinking. But you want to visit the Capitol, too, and you snake your way left across the crowded step to view the Capitol hiding behind the Washington Monument and—what's this? A noisy commotion has broken out, down below you on 23rd Street. A stream of black sedans and limos, the largest bearing little American flags on its front fenders, is sweeping through an intersection cleared by police cars and motorcycles. "The President's out on an official visit," you hear someone behind you say.

It's your capless fellow tourist, who thanks you for trying to catch his hat. He's from Louisiana, it turns out, which compels you to tell him about the excellent Southern restaurant where you dined the night before. He in turn enthuses about the free nightly concerts at the Kennedy Center; a zydeco band is playing tonight as it happens. "You know, you can see the Kennedy Center from here," he says, and together you stroll to the back platform of the Lincoln Memorial to admire the gorgeous view of Memorial Bridge and the Potomac River, which swerves gracefully past the Kennedy Center, sure enough, to Georgetown. A handful of other tourists have discovered this picturesque spot, including a sunburned British family, whose patriarch is attempting to pose his brood for a family photo portrait.

In another few minutes, you will be back among the hordes of other tourists visiting the Smithsonian, boarding a tour bus, standing in line at the Capitol. And by day's end, back at the hotel, you will be regretting that you didn't wear sunscreen, and resolving to rise earlier the next day to secure a ticket to tour the White House. Right now, though, you're enjoying the moment, and the view, and the possibilities of this monumental day in the nation's capital.

A visit to Washington promises countless adventures, some planned for, others not. Using this book you can pick a theme—art, architecture, science, history, politics, food, drama, music, nightlife, outdoor activity, the millennium—and design your tour accordingly. But, use this book also to throw your itinerary a curve from time to time. Choose the road less taken: Leave the crowds behind and head straight to the third floor of the National Museum of American History, for example, and you will have the exhibits on ceramics, textiles, military memorabilia, musical instruments, and popular culture (this is where Dorothy's ruby slippers are on display) mostly to yourself. Walk from the museums on the Mall to a downtown restaurant (believe me, if you care about what you eat, it's worth it) and observe the fashions, ways, and wiles of Washingtonians.

Finally, leave room for the chance encounter. In this city, whose population is as culturally diverse as those who tour here, you may find yourself forging connections with people from halfway around the world—or from your own hometown—and these experiences may become your fondest memories of the city. As the nation's capital and the home of our democratic government, Washington, like no other city, holds a certain place in the world, as it represents all the freedoms and ideals that Americans hold dear. Against the backdrop of the White House, the Capitol, and the Supreme Court, a little small talk between strangers creates opportunities for understanding differences. It'll make a good story when you get home, too.

1 Frommer's Favorite Washington Experiences

- **Attending the Kennedy Center Open House.** In late September/early October, the weather almost always cooperates for this fun, free, mostly outdoor celebration of the arts. Diplomats and office drones alike can't resist shimmying to the music played by top Washington musicians on the terraces. Call ☎ **800/ 444-1324** or 202/467-4600. See chapter 2.
- **Sipping Afternoon Tea at the Top of Washington National Cathedral.** On Tuesday and Wednesday afternoons at 1:30pm, you can tour the world's sixth largest cathedral, then succumb to tea, scones, and lemon tarts served on the seventh floor of the West tower, whose arched windows overlook the city and beyond to the Sugarloaf Mountains in Maryland. It's $18 a person; reserve as far in advance as possible (☎ **202/537-8993**). See chapter 6.
- **Visiting the Lincoln Memorial After Dark.** During the day, hordes of rambunctious schoolchildren may distract you; at night, the experience is infinitely more moving. See chapter 7.
- **Taking a Monument and Memorials Walking Tour.** Have a hearty breakfast, then take the Metro to Foggy Bottom, and when you exit, turn right on 23rd Street NW and follow it to Constitution Ave. NW. Cross the avenue, make a left, walk past Henry Bacon Drive, and follow the signs to the Vietnam and Lincoln Memorials; cross Independence Ave., and follow the cherry tree–lined Tidal Basin path to the FDR Memorial and further to the Jefferson Memorial; and finish your tour at the Washington Monument. This is a long but beautiful hike; afterward, head up 15th St. NW to the charming Old Ebbitt Grill (make reservations in advance) for a strength-restoring lunch, or eat at the food court in the nearby Shops at National Place. See chapter 7.
- **Rambling through Rock Creek Park.** A good place to ride a bike, run, or even work out. A paved bike/walking path extends 11 miles from the Lincoln Memorial to the Maryland border. You can hop on the trail at many spots throughout the city—it runs past the National Zoo, behind the Omni Shoreham Hotel in Woodley Park, near Dupont Circle, and across from the Watergate/Kennedy Center complex. You can rent a bike from Big Wheel Bikes at 1034 33rd St. NW (☎ **202/337-0254**) in Georgetown, and from the Thompson Boat Center

(☎ **202/333-4861**), located on the path across from the Kennedy Center. For a really long bike ride, trek to the Lincoln Memorial, get yourself across the busy stretch that connects the parkway to the Arlington Memorial Bridge, and cross the bridge to the trail on the other side; this path winds 19 miles to Mount Vernon. See chapter 7.

• **Spending the Day in Alexandria.** Just a short distance (by Metro, car, or bike) from the District is George Washington's Virginia hometown. Roam the quaint cobblestone streets, browse charming boutiques and antique stores, visit the boyhood home of Robert E. Lee and other historic attractions, and dine in one of Alexandria's fine restaurants. See chapter 10.

• **Weighing in Judgement.** If you're in town when the Supreme Court is in session (October through late April; call ☎ **202/479-3000** for details), you can observe a case being argued; it's thrilling to see this august institution at work. See chapter 7.

• **Admiring the Library of Congress.** The magnificent Italian-Renaissance–style Thomas Jefferson Building of the Library of Congress—filled with murals, mosaics, sculptures, and allegorical paintings—is one of America's most notable architectural achievements. Be sure to take the tour detailed in chapter 7.

• **Seeing the Earth Revolve.** The Foucault Pendulum at the National Museum of American History provides empirical evidence that the earth is revolving; don't miss it. See chapter 7.

• **Spending a Morning on the Mall.** Arrive at about 8:30am (take the Metro to the Smithsonian station), when the Mall is magical and tourist-free. From the station, walk east (toward the Capitol Building) along Jefferson Drive to the Smithsonian Information Center (the Castle) and stroll through the magnolia-lined parterres of the beautiful Enid A. Haupt Garden. Return to Jefferson Drive, walk further east to the Hirshhorn, ducking in, on your way, for a look at the lovely Ripley Garden, before crossing the street to tour the Hirshhorn's sunken Sculpture Garden. Climb back to street level and cross the Mall to another sculpture garden, the new and enchanting National Gallery Sculpture Garden, at 7th Street and Madison Drive. Stop at the outdoor cafe there for refreshment, or, if it's a Sunday, retrace your steps to the Smithsonian Castle, which serves brunch from 11am to 3pm in the dining room, styled in 12th-century Norman design. (For details call ☎ **202/357-2957** before 10am and after 3pm.) See chapter 7.

• **Debarking at Union Station.** Noted architect Daniel H. Burnham's turn-of-the-century beaux arts railway station is worth a visit even if you're not trying to catch a train. Dawdle and admire its coffered 96-foot-high ceilings, grand arches, and great halls, modeled after the Baths of Diocletian and the Arch of Constantine in Rome. Then shop and eat: The station's 1988 restoration filled the tri-level hall with everything from Ann Taylor and Crabtree & Evelyn to a high-quality food court and the refined B. Smith's restaurant. See chapter 7.

• **Enjoying an Artful Evening at the Phillips Collection.** Thursday evenings (September through mid-July) from 5 to 8:30pm, you pay $5 to tour the mansion-museum rooms filled with Impressionist, post-Impressionist, and modern art, ending up in the paneled Music Room, where you'll enjoy jazz, blues, or other musical combinations performed by fine local musicians, topped off by an artful lecture. It's a popular mingling spot for singles (there's a cash bar and sandwich fare). Call ☎ **202/387-2151** for information. See chapter 9 for more nightlife.

• **Strolling Along Embassy Row.** Head northwest on Massachusetts Avenue from Dupont Circle. It's a gorgeous walk along tree-shaded streets lined with beaux arts mansions. Built by fabulously wealthy magnates during the Gilded Age, most of these palatial precincts today are occupied by foreign embassies. See chapter 7.

- **People-Watching at Dupont Circle.** One of the few "living" circles, Dupont's is the all-weather hangout for mondo-bizarre biker-couriers, chess players, street musicians, and lovers. Sit on a bench and be astounded by the passing scene. See chapter 7.
- **Viewing Washington from the Water.** Cruise the Potomac River aboard one of several sightseeing vessels and relax from foot-weary sightseeing. River cruises not only offer a pleasant interval for catching a second wind, they treat you to a marvelous perspective of the city. See chapter 7.
- **Cutting a Deal at the Georgetown Flea Market.** Pick up a latte at the Starbucks across the street and spend a pleasant Sunday browsing through the castoffs of wealthy Washingtonians, handpainted furniture by local artists, and a hodgepodge of antiques and collectibles. Everybody shops here at one time or another, so you never know who you'll see or what you'll find. Wisconsin Avenue NW at S Street NW in Georgetown; open March to December, Sunday from 9am to 5pm. See chapter 8 for more shopping.
- **Shopping at Eastern Market.** Capitol Hill is home to more than government buildings; it's a community of old townhouses, antique shops, and the veritable institution, Eastern Market. Here, the locals barter and shop on Saturday mornings for fresh produce and baked goods, and on Sunday for flea market bargains. At 7th Street SE, between North Carolina Avenue and C Street SE. See chapter 8 for more shopping.
- **Ordering Drinks on the Rooftop Terrace of the Hotel Washington.** Posher bars exist, but none with this view. The experience is almost a cliche in Washington: When spring arrives, make a date to sit on this outdoor rooftop terrace, sip a gin and tonic, and gaze at the panoramic view of the White House, Treasury Building, and the monuments. Open from the end of April through October, for drinks and light fare (☎ 202/347-4499). See chapter 9.

2 Frommer's Best Hotel Bets

- **Best Historic Hotel:** The grande dame of Washington hotels is the magnificent **Renaissance Mayflower**, 1127 Connecticut Ave. NW (☎ 800/228-7697 or 202/347-3000), which, when it was built in 1925, was considered not only the last word in luxury and beauty, but also "the second-best address" in town. Harry S. Truman preferred it over the White House.
- **Best Location:** The **Willard Inter-Continental**, 1401 Pennsylvania Ave. NW (☎ 800/327-0200 or 202/628-9100), is within walking distance of the White House, museums, theaters, downtown offices, good restaurants, and the Metro. It's also a quick taxi ride to Capitol Hill.
- **Best Place to Stay During an Inauguration:** For the best views of the inaugural parade, book rooms at the **J. W. Marriott**, 1331 Pennsylvania Ave. NW (☎ 800/228-9290 or 202/393-2000), or the **Hotel Washington**, 15th St. and Pennsylvania Ave. NW (☎ 800/424-9540 or 202/638-5900). Be sure to specify a room with a view of Pennsylvania Avenue. Also, the best inaugural parties are inevitably held at the Willard Inter-Continental (see "Best Location," above).
- **Best Place for a Romantic Getaway:** The posh **Jefferson**, 16th and M streets NW (☎ 800/368-5966 or 202/347-2200), is just enough off the beaten track, but still conveniently downtown, to feel like you've really escaped. Because the service, bar, and restaurant (see chapter 6 for a review of the Restaurant at the

Jefferson) are outstanding, you have no need to leave the premises. The restaurant itself has one of the most romantic nooks in the city.

- **Best Moderately Priced Hotel:** The **Lincoln Suites Downtown Hotel,** 1823 L St. NW (☎ **800/424-2970** or 202/223-4320) is located downtown, within easy walking distance of the White House, Dupont Circle, and Foggy Bottom. Its rates are outstanding for the clean, newly renovated, spacious suites, one third of which have full kitchens. Free use of a nearby health spa and complimentary homemade cookies and milk each evening will win you over.

- **Best Inexpensive Hotel:** The boutique hotel, the **Doyle Normandy,** 2118 Wyoming Ave. NW (at Connecticut Ave.) (☎ **800/424-3729** or 202/483-1350), charges $79 to $155 for rooms that are small but charming, and for service that's personable; extras like exercise room, pool, and restaurant are available at its sister hotel around the corner.

- **Best Inn:** The stunning **Morrison-Clark Historic Inn,** Massachusetts Avenue and 11th Street NW (☎ **800/332-7898** or 202/898-1200), housed in two beautifully restored Victorian townhouses, has exquisite rooms and an acclaimed restaurant.

- **Best B&B: Swann House,** 1808 New Hampshire Ave. NW (☎ **202/265-7677**) is remarkably pretty and comfortable, in a great neighborhood (Dupont Circle), and not outrageously priced.

- **Best Service:** The staff at **The Four Seasons,** 2800 Pennsylvania Ave. NW (☎ **800/332-3442** or 202/342-0444), pampers you relentlessly and greets you by name. The hotels also offers an "I Need It Now" program that delivers any of 100 or more left-at-home essentials (tweezers; batteries; cuff links; electric hair curlers; and so on) to you in three minutes, at no cost.

- **Best Place to Hide If You're Embroiled in a Scandal:** Lovely as it is, the **Doyle Normandy,** 2118 Wyoming Ave. NW (☎ **800/424-3729** or 202/483-1350), remains unknown to many Washingtonians—a plus if you need to lay low. The neighborhood teems with embassies, in case your trouble is of the I-need-a-foreign-government-to-bail-me-out variety. (And a bargain besides—see listing above for "Best Inexpensive Hotel.")

- **Best for Business Travelers:** If money's no object, **The Jefferson,** 16th and M streets NW (☎ **800/368-5966** or 202/347-2200), is a stand-out hotel, with its in-room fax machines; morning delivery of newspaper of choice; 24-hour room, butler, and multilingual concierge service; and graciously solicitous staff. Robert Rubin lived here during his tenure as treasury secretary. Across town, the newly remodeled **Swissôtel Washington—The Watergate,** 2650 Virginia Ave. NW (☎ **800/424-2736** or 202/965-2300), offers a pretty good array of amenities for the business traveler: 24-hour room service, an extensive fitness center, a business center with Internet access, same day dry cleaning, daily delivery of your choice of newspaper, complimentary limo service weekday mornings to nearby offices, fax machine and writing desk in each room, post office and drugstore within complex, early check-in and express checkout, a large ballroom and lots of meeting space.

- **Best Hotel Restaurant:** The inventive French fare at sumptuous **Lespinasse,** in the St. Regis Hotel, 923 16th St. NW (☎ **202/879-6900**), competes with the creations of **Michel Richard's Citronelle,** in the Latham Hotel, 3000 M St. NW (☎ **202/625-2150**). Other top picks are the new American cuisine served at the **Restaurant at the Jefferson,** in the Jefferson Hotel (☎ **202/833-6206;** see "Best for a Romantic Getaway," above); and the San Francisco-influenced menu of **Brighton,** in the Canterbury Hotel, 1733 N St. NW (☎ **202/296-0665**).

- **Best Health Club:** The **Fitness Company West End Center,** at the Washington Monarch Hotel, 2401 M St. NW (☎ **877/222-2266** or 202/429-2400), is a 17,500-square-foot center offering classes in yoga and aerobics; seminars in stress management and weight loss; and equipment that includes virtual-reality bike machines, stair climbers with telephones and TV/VCR units, NordicTraks, rowing machines, exercise bikes with telephones, and more. The health club also has squash and racquetball courts; a swimming pool; a steam room; a whirlpool; saunas; and a minispa. Personal trainers, fitness evaluation, and workout clothes are available.
- **Best Views:** The **Hay-Adams,** 16th and H streets NW (☎ **800/424-5054** or 202/638-6600), has such a great, unobstructed view of the White House that the Secret Service comes over regularly to do security sweeps of the place.
- **Best for Travelers with Disabilities: Courtyard by Marriott Convention Center** (☎ **202/638-4600**) has four rooms equipped for disabled guests, two with roll-in showers; wider than normal corridors and entryways; its reception area includes a check-in desk, rather than a counter, for guests in wheelchairs; hearing impaired services and visual alert systems available in each room; and most of all, a staff trained to respond graciously to individual requests for assistance.

3 Frommer's Best Dining Bets

- **Best Spot for a Romantic Dinner:** Just ask for the "snug" (tables 39 and 40) at **The Restaurant at The Jefferson,** 1200 16th St. NW (at M St.) (☎ **202/ 833-6206**). Two cozy, banquette seating areas in alcoves are secluded from the main dining room. Follow your sumptuous dinner with drinks in front of the fireplace in the adjoining lounge.
- **Best Spot for a Business Lunch: La Colline,** 400 North Capitol St. NW (☎ **202/737-0400**), is conveniently located near Capitol Hill, has a great bar, four private rooms, high-backed leather booths that allow for discrete conversations, and, last but not least, consistently good food. A perfect spot for the Washington breakfast meeting or fundraiser.
- **Best Spot for a Celebration: Café Atlantico,** 405 8th St. NW (☎ **202/ 393-0812**), will give you reason to celebrate even if you didn't arrive with one. The restaurant is pure fun, with charming waiters, seating on three levels, colorful wall-size paintings by Latin and Caribbean artists, fantastic cocktails, and unusual but not trendy Latin/Caribbean food.
- **Best Decor: The Willard Room** (☎ **202/637-7440**), in the Willard Inter-Continental Hotel, is decorated in such a grand manner—with paneling, velvet, and silk—that it's been used more than once for a movie shoot, including the upcoming *The Hollow Men.* (Consider this another contender for most romantic.)
- **Best View:** Washington Harbour is the setting for **Sequoia,** 3000 K St. NW (☎ **202/944-4200**), where a multilevel garden terrace offers a panoramic vista of the Potomac and verdant Theodore Roosevelt Island beyond; if you're dining inside, ask for the bar-level alcove overlooking the Potomac—the best seat in the house.
- **Best Wine List:** At **Michel Richard's Citronelle,** in the Latham Hotel, 3000 M St. NW (☎ **202/625-2150**), the extensive, 8,000-bottle wine cellar is on display behind glass in the dining room. If you're serious about wine, come here; but check your wallet first. Citronelle is probably the city's most expensive restaurant and wines costing in the three-digits predominate. The food is excellent.

- **Best for Kids:** The **Austin Grill,** 2404 Wisconsin Ave. NW (☎ **202/ 337-8080**), is a friendly, chattering place with a children's menu, unspillable cups, and an atmosphere that will please everyone. Go before 9pm.
- **Best American Cuisine: Kinkead's,** 2000 Pennsylvania Ave. NW (☎ **202/ 296-7700**), concentrates on seafood, but always offers meat and poultry on each menu; at any rate, you could eat here every day and not go wrong.
- **Best Chinese Cuisine: Full Kee,** 509 H St. NW (☎ **202/371-2233**), in the heart of Chinatown, is consistently good and a great value.
- **Best French Cuisine:** For upscale, contemporary French, **Lespinasse,** in the St. Regis Hotel, 923 16th St. NW (☎ **202/879-6900**), is the place to go. The luxuriously decorated dining room is a fitting backdrop for the divinely prepared creations of chef Sandro Gamba. For French staples served with great enthusiasm and charm in a more relaxed setting, head for **Bistrot Lepic,** at 1736 Wisconsin Ave. NW (☎ **202/333-0111**).
- **Best Italian Cuisine:** Roberto Donna's **Galileo,** 1110 21st St. NW (☎ **202/ 293-7191**), does fine Italian cuisine best, preparing exquisite pastas, fish, and meat dishes with savory ingredients. For more traditional (and affordable) classic Italian fare, Donna's **Il Radicchio** does the trick. At several locations, including 1211 Wisconsin Ave. NW (☎ **202/337-2627**); 1509 17th St. NW (☎ **202/ 986-2627**); and on Capitol Hill, 233 Pennsylvania Ave. SE (☎ **202/547-5114**).
- **Best Seafood: Pesce,** 2016 P St. NW. (☎ **202/466-3474**), offers reasonably priced, perfectly grilled or sautéed seafood in a convivial atmosphere.
- **Best Southern Cuisine: Vidalia,** 1990 M St. NW (☎ **202/659-1990**). Chef Jeff Buben calls his cuisine "provincial American," a euphemism for fancy fare that includes cheese grits and biscuits in cream gravy.
- **Best Southwestern Cuisine:** It doesn't get more exciting than **Red Sage,** 605 14th St. NW (☎ **202/638-4444**), where superstar chef Mark Miller brings contemporary culinary panache to traditional southwestern cookery; keep his Café and Chili Bar in mind for Red Sage cuisine and ambience at lower prices.
- **Best Steakhouse:** After 24 years **The Prime Rib,** 2020 K St. NW (☎ **202/ 466-8811**), is still going strong, putting out what carnivores consider the best steaks and prime ribs in town, despite some awesome competition.
- **Best Tapas:** The upbeat **Gabriel,** 2121 P St. NW (☎ **202/956-6690**), where you can graze on chef Greggory Hill's ambrosial little dishes; they range from black figs stuffed with Spanish chorizo to crunchy fried calamari with fiery harissa sauce and lemony thyme aioli.
- **Best Pizza:** At **Pizzeria Paradiso's,** 2029 P St. NW (☎ **202/223-1245**), peerless chewy-crusted pies are baked in an oak-burning oven and crowned with delicious toppings; you'll find great salads and sandwiches on fresh-baked focaccia here, too.
- **Best Desserts:** No frou-frou desserts served at **Café Berlin,** 322 Massachusetts Ave. NE (☎ **202/543-7656**); these cakes, tortes, pies, and strudels are the real thing.
- **Best Healthy Meal:** At **Legal Sea Foods,** 2020 K St. NW (☎ **202/496-1111**), follow up a cup of light clam chowder (made without butter, cream, or flour) with an entree of grilled fresh fish and vegetables and a superb sorbet for dessert.
- **Best Late-Night Dining:** To satisfy a yen for Chinese food, go to **Full Kee,** 509 H St. NW in Chinatown (☎ **202/371-2233**), open until 3am on weekends; for more comfortable surroundings and good old American cuisine, try the **Old Ebbitt Grill,** 675 15th St. NW (☎ **202/347-4801**), whose kitchen stays open until 1am on weekends.

Presidential Scandals

As you will recall, public and media reaction to the revelation in 1998 of the affair between President Bill Clinton and the 20-something White House intern, Monica Lewinsky, was rather intense. So it may surprise you to know that presidential scandals, real or imagined, have been in the news ever since George Washington maintained an innocent friendship with Sally Fairfax. Granted, the president's dalliance with Lewinsky was a scandal nonpareil because of its high sleaze quotient; because the president was combating accusations of sexual misconduct, lying under oath, and obstructing justice while still in office; and most of all, of course, because he was impeached, albeit acquitted by the Senate. To some extent, however, we have been here before.

Sometimes allegations are politically provoked or arise solely from conjecturing troublemakers. Anti-federalist and British journalists were never able to prove anything unseemly about Washington's friendship with Fairfax. Our 17th president, Andrew Johnson, was the only other president to be impeached, and the reasons were political: Congress found Johnson guilty of "high crimes and misdemeanors" because members believed the president had violated the law in his constant exercise of veto power and in his firing of Edwin M. Stanton, his secretary of war.

Alas, some presidential scandals prove to be the real thing. In 1998, a few months after DNA testing of a stain on Lewinsky's famous blue dress proved conclusively that, indeed, this was a semen stain, and that, indeed, the semen came from the president, we also learned that scientists, again using DNA testing, had found a genetic match between Thomas Jefferson's family line and a descendant of Jefferson's slave, Sally Hemings; in other words, our third president had fathered a child with Hemings.

Warren Gamaliel Harding, our 29th president, offers another example. Harding, himself, was suspected but never implicated in the Teapot Dome Case, in which several of his cabinet members were exposed for accepting bribes in return for arranging the private development of federal oil reserve lands. But a more salacious scandal surfaced after Harding's death. (He died in office, after serving less than 3 years.) Harding, a debonair fellow with an eye for the ladies, had carried on several affairs during his unhappy marriage, and one, with the much-younger Nan Britton, overlapped his time in the White House. So passionate were the couple that they once made love in a hidden part of Central Park. That was before he became president. Later, Harding had Secret Service agents smuggle Britton into the White House, where, on one occasion, they cuddled together in a coat closet to evade detection by the prowling Mrs. Harding. It may have been this tryst that produced Elizabeth Ann, Britton's daughter. Though the Harding estate never recognized the child, Harding was indeed her father, Britton revealed in her book, *The President's Daughter.*

Though he never came right out and admitted it, our 22nd president, Grover Cleveland, probably fathered a child out of wedlock, giving his girlfriend's son his last name, paying for his support, and arranging for his adoption. Cleveland was a bachelor at the time and his affair with the woman, a widow, occurred in 1874, 10 years before Cleveland ran for president. During Cleveland's presidential campaign in 1884, newspapers made the most of the disclosure, portraying him as a drunk and a frequenter of "harlots." Republicans taunted the Democratic candidate with the cry, "Ma, Ma, Where's my pa? Gone to the White House, ha, ha, ha." But the incident only served to play up Cleveland's honesty, for which voters rewarded him by voting him into office.

Andrew Jackson committed adultery, but not on purpose, he claimed. Jackson married his wife Rachel in 1791, when both believed that Rachel's divorce from her first husband was legal, which it was not. The couple legally remarried in 1794, but accusations of adultery surrounded them all their lives. In 1806, Jackson fought a duel and killed his accuser, Charles Dickinson, over the matter, although not before Dickinson had fired a bullet into Jackson that landed so close to his heart, that doctors were never able to remove it. The adultery became such an issue when Jackson ran for president in 1828 that he credited Rachel's sudden death just after he won the election to the stress of her having to deal constantly with vituperative comments. This embittering experience effected a rather unexpected turn of events. When President Jackson was putting his cabinet together, he appointed his good friend and supporter, John Eaton, as secretary of war, disregarding the rumors that swirled around Eaton's beautiful wife Peggy, said to be a woman of low morals. Jackson believed that society's vitriolic attacks on Peggy Eaton's character were as baseless as those made on his wife. Jackson's support for the Eatons divided his Cabinet and society as he tried to force his administration, and their wives, to treat the Eatons properly. (At parties, the women would scram as soon as Peggy and John arrived.) In 1831, Jackson was compelled to dissolve his cabinet, make new appointments, and dispatch the Eatons to Spain, where John served as minister and Peggy found herself welcome, by the queen, no less.

Scholars disagree about the nature of the relationship between Woodrow Wilson and Mary Hulbert Peck. Wilson met Peck, a divorcee, in Bermuda, where he was vacationing (without his wife, Ellen) during a break from his job as president of Princeton University. Some believe that Wilson paid her off so that she'd not talk of their affair. The press never got wind of the friendship, which lasted, in correspondence anyway, until Wilson died. Wilson caused a bit of a scandal while President, though, remarrying only 16 months after his first wife died. Journalists relentlessly followed Wilson's whirlwind romance with Edith Galt. The *Washington Post* (a Republican bastion at the time) caused a sensation one day by reporting that "The President spent last evening entering Mrs. Galt." A typo, the newspaper apologized; the word "entering" should have read "entertaining."

Much has been made of John F. Kennedy's escapades with women, from Marilyn Monroe to Judith Exner, while occupying the White House and married to the beautiful Jacqueline. But, like Harding's infidelities, Kennedy's affairs did not become public until after his death. Franklin Delano Roosevelt, too, has been linked romantically with many women, most notably Lucy Mercer Rutherfurd, Eleanor Roosevelt's social secretary. Letters and papers document genuine affection, but not the existence of a sexual relationship.

Until Bill Clinton's presidency, history books would have recorded Richard Nixon's tenure as the most scandalous of the 20th century. Facing impeachment proceedings in 1974 for his knowledge of and participation in the 1972 burglary of Democratic National Committee headquarters in the Watergate apartment-office complex, Nixon chose to resign.

Makes one wonder: What scandals does the millennium hold? Stay tuned.

- **Best Outdoor Dining: Les Halles,** 1201 Pennsylvania Ave. NW (☎ **202/347-6848**), so much fun inside, carries the party outside in warm weather to its partly covered sidewalk cafe, excellently located for people watching and sightseeing (the Capitol lies down the street; the Old Post Office Pavilion is directly across the avenue).
- **Best Afternoon Tea:** With lush plantings and windows overlooking the C&O Canal, the **Garden Terrace** at the Four Seasons Hotel, 2800 Pennsylvania Ave. NW (☎ **202/342-0444**), provides soothing piano music during afternoon tea Monday through Saturday from 3 to 5pm and Sunday from 3:30 to 5pm. For $18 ($9 for kids) you can enjoy a selection of finger sandwiches, fresh fruit tartlets, assorted English tea breads and biscuits, a Scottish sultana scone with double Devonshire cream and homemade preserves, and a pot of fresh-brewed tea. Vintage ports, sherries, and champagne are also available.
- **Best Brunch:** Go to **Georgia Brown's,** 950 15th St. NW (☎ **202/393-4499**), Sunday from 11:30am to 2:30pm to enjoy live jazz and a part buffet/part à la carte menu featuring such dishes as biscuit-batter french toast with maple-pecan syrup, country ham, buttermilk-fried chicken, omelets made to order, and a host of other items. This brunch ($21.95 per person) is popular, so be sure to make a reservation.
- **Best for Pretheater Dinner:** How could you do better than **701**'s $22 three-course bargain and its prime location, right around the corner from the Shakespeare Theater and a few blocks from the National and Warner theaters? At 701 Pennsylvania Ave. NW (☎ **202/393-0701**).

4 Washington Today

Headlines from the *Washington Post* over the past year say it all: "Momentum Is Building in Downtown Revival"; "District Mayor Scores on Shape-Up Goals"; "From Offices to Hotels, Projects Roll."

Washington's future is looking pretty good, and it's about time. After years of Mayor Marion Barry's mismanagement, to the point that Congress had to step in and appoint a financial control board to oversee the city, Washington is getting back on its own two feet. The turnaround is due to the booming economy; rising investments by local entrepreneurs, like Washington businessman/Wizards owner/MCI Center developer Abe Pollin; funding from Congress; and the energy of the city's new mayor, Anthony A. Williams, who took office January 2, 1999. Williams won because he had already proven himself. As chief financial officer of the congressionally appointed control board he had worked a miracle in 1997–1998 by whipping the city's finances into shape. Mayor Williams hopes to work similar miracles in other areas, from repairing

My God! What have I done to be condemned to reside in such a city!
—A French diplomat in the early days

potholes to restructuring the District's government so that it will run like a corporation.

Evidence of the District's revival is everywhere. The roads are improved. Major gateways into the city, like New York Avenue, are being cleaned up, beautified, and altered to provide easier access. But most remarkable is the rebirth of the downtown section bounded by Pennsylvania and Massachusetts avenues, between 5th and 15th streets NW. Here, construction cranes hover over the skyline, as 30 or more building projects progress—hotels; office buildings; shops; a 22-screen, 5,000-seat, stadium-style movie theater; a new convention center. Encouraged by the continuing success of hip restaurants like Café Atlantico, Coco Loco, and Jaleo, other restaurateurs are setting up shop in this once-forsaken area: The Mark, District Chophouse & Brewery, Austin Grill, to name a few.

Old office buildings, especially along the 7th Street corridor, have been refurbished to hold art galleries. Within a few short blocks are at least five theaters, including the National, Warner, and Shakespeare. Nightclubs, always loyal to the heart of the city, are prospering here and along the U Street strip, further north.

A transformation is occurring, but it isn't happening overnight. Construction takes time, which means you may find parts of this neighborhood a mess, with sidewalks closed, equipment blocking traffic, and the noise level during the day hard to take. In another four years or so, city and business leaders hope the downtown will be as lively day and night as Georgetown, Dupont Circle, Adams-Morgan, Capitol Hill, and other favorite neighborhoods. The key, they say, is housing: People need to live downtown to provide the city the vibrancy and character that only residents can bestow upon a place. To that end, community leaders are pushing for the development of more apartment buildings and condos along these streets. A nonprofit organization of business leaders has banded together to form the Downtown Business Improvement District (BID), which uses funds raised privately from downtown property owners to keep city streets clean and safe, thereby attracting visitors, businesses, and prospective city dwellers, all. (Look for the telltale red uniforms of BID's Downtown SAMs, the Safety and Maintenance team employees who roam the downtown simply to help anyone needing directions, information, or safety assistance.)

Washington's community of business and government leaders want everyone to know the city is changing, and in 1999 announced a new slogan to spread the word: "Washington, DC: The American Experience." Not exactly earthshaking, the slogan nevertheless conveys the essential uniqueness of the city. As the nation's capital and a city in its own right, Washington today welcomes visitors from all over the nation and the world to revel in American history and culture, while enjoying the particular attractions of this town on the Potomac.

2 Planning a Trip to Washington, D.C.

Locals tend to find out the hard way about the inconveniences and idiosyncrasies of their particular town, whether it's how far ahead you have to call to get a table at the hot, new restaurant or how long you can expect to wait in line at a popular tourist attraction in high season. My job is to give you the benefit of this learned wisdom in Washington, amplified by further research, to help you enjoy your stay here without the least hint of hassle. A little advance preparation on your part is recommended, however, and that's what this chapter nails down. Read on to discover everything you need to know about planning a trip to Washington, including how best to get here, upcoming events, what weather to expect, and how to obtain advance tickets for entry into various tourist attractions.

1 Visitor Information

Before you leave, contact the **Washington, D.C. Convention and Visitors Association,** 1212 New York Ave. NW, Washington, DC 20005 (☎ **202/789-7000;** www.washington.org), and ask them to send you a free copy of the *Washington, D.C. Visitors Guide,* which details hotels, restaurants, sights, shops, and more. They'll also be happy to answer specific questions.

Also call the **D.C. Committee to Promote Washington** (☎ **800/422-8644**), and request free copies of brochures listing additional information about Washington.

For the latest information about specific tourist spots, check out the National Park Service's www.nps.gov/nacc (the National Park Service maintains Washington's monuments, memorials, and other sites), and the Smithsonian Institution's www.si.edu.

Most helpful is the *Washington Post* Web site, **www.washingtonpost. com,** which gives you up-to-the-minute news, weather, visitor information, restaurant reviews, and nightlife insights, and features live, online discussions on specific subjects and at scheduled times daily, with local experts and *Post* journalists answering questions submitted by people over the web. For example, Thursdays at noon, the *Post*'s restaurant critic, Phyllis Richman takes questions about dining out in Washington.

Another good site is *Washington Flyer* magazine, at **www. washingtonflyermag.com**. You can pick up the magazine for free in

Trip Tips

Washington, D.C., always a popular destination, is experiencing a boom in tourism. Hotels, the Smithsonian museums, and restaurants are reporting higher numbers of visitors than they've seen since the 1980s. All the more reason to plan ahead.

The earlier you book your room, the greater your chance of finding the best rate at your preferred hotel. If dining at a hot new or favorite old restaurant is important, why not play it safe by calling in advance (2 weeks is realistic) to reserve a table.

A number of sightseeing attractions permit you to obtain tickets as far as 6 months in advance. Here's how to avoid the wait of a long line or the ultimate disappointment of missing a tour altogether:

Based on ticket availability, senators and/or representatives can provide their constituents with advance tickets for tours of the Capitol, the White House, the FBI, the Bureau of Engraving and Printing, the Supreme Court, and the Kennedy Center. (See chapter 7 for detailed touring information about each site.) This is no secret. Thousands of people know about it and do write, so make your request as far in advance as possible—even 6 months ahead is not too early—specifying the dates you plan to visit and the number of tickets you need. Their allotment of tickets for each site is limited, so there's no guarantee you'll secure them, but it's worth a try. (Advance tickets are not necessary to tour an attraction; they just preclude a long wait.)

Address requests to representatives as follows: name of your congressperson, U.S. House of Representatives, Washington, DC 20515; or name of your senator, U.S. Senate, Washington, DC 20510. Don't forget to include the exact dates of your Washington trip. When you write, also request tourist information and literature. You can also correspond by email; check out the Web sites www.senate.gov and www.house.gov for email addresses, individual member information, legislative calendars and much more. You also might try calling a senator or congressperson's local office; in some states you can obtain passes by phone. The phone numbers for Congress are: ☎ **202/224-3121** (Senate) and ☎ **202/225-3121** (House).

One other tip: If you have acquaintances who work at any of the sites, or within a related organization, by all means, contact them. For example, an employee of the Justice Department may be able to obtain FBI tour tickets for you, hassle-free.

Ronald Reagan Washington National and Washington Dulles International airports, but you may want to look at it online in advance, since it often talks about airport and airline news and upcoming events in Washington—things you'd want to know before you got here. The Metropolitan Washington Airports Authority publishes the magazine, which carries a comprehensive flight guide for National and Dulles airports in each issue. If you don't have access to the Internet, you can subscribe to the bimonthly; the rate is $15 for six issues, or $3 for one. The phone number is ☎ **202/331-9393.**

2 Money

Maybe because so many of Washington's attractions—the Smithsonian museums, the monuments, even nightly concerts at the Kennedy Center—are either free or inexpensive, it may come as a shock to see the high price of lodging or a meal at a fine restaurant. It makes sense to have some cash on hand to pay for incidentals, but it's not necessary to carry large sums around. After all, even some Metro farecard

---

---

machines are accepting credit cards now. At any rate, it's unlikely you'll find yourself in a pinch in the capital, whose merchants accept cash, traveler's checks, and credit cards (but seldom personal checks from out-of-towners).

ATMS

Automated Teller Machines (ATMs) are everywhere, from the National Gallery of Art's giftshop, to Union Station, to the bank at the corner. Because ATMs link local banks with a national network, you can leave your cash at home and just get it at ATMs throughout the city as you need it. Before you leave for Washington, though, you may want to make sure your bank at home connects with the ATM networks most prevalent in the capital, and to check out Washington locations of your bank's affiliated ATMs. **Cirrus** (☎ 800/424-7787; www.mastercard.com/atm/) and **Plus** (☎ 800/843-7587; www.visa.com/atms) are the two most popular networks; check the back of your ATM card to see which network your bank belongs to. Use the toll-free numbers or Web sites to locate ATMs in Washington. Be sure to check the daily withdrawal limit before you depart.

TRAVELER'S CHECKS

These days, traveler's checks seem less necessary because of all the 24-hour ATMs that allow visitors to withdraw small amounts of cash as needed—and thus avoid the risk of carrying a fortune around an unfamiliar environment. But, as in most cities, Washington banks impose a fee (anywhere from $1 to $3) every time you use a card at an ATM not affiliated with your hometown bank. If you're withdrawing money every day, you might be better off with traveler's checks—provided that you don't mind showing identification every time you want to cash a check.

You can get traveler's checks at almost any bank. **American Express** offers denominations of $10, $20, $50, $100, $500, and $1,000. You'll pay a service charge ranging from 1 to 4 percent. You can also get American Express traveler's checks over the phone by calling ☎ 800/221-7282; by using this number, Amex gold and platinum cardholders are exempt from the 1 percent fee. AAA members can obtain checks without a fee at most AAA offices. (AAA has a downtown Washington office at 701 15th St. NW, not far from the White House.)

Visa offers traveler's checks at Citibank locations nationwide, as well as at several other banks. The service charge ranges between 1.5 and 2%; checks come in denominations of $20, $50, $100, $500, and $1,000. **MasterCard** also offers traveler's checks. Call ☎ 800/223-9920 for a location near you.

CREDIT CARDS

Credit cards are invaluable when traveling. They are a safe way to carry money and provide a convenient record of all your expenses. You can also withdraw cash advances from your credit cards at any bank (though you'll start paying hefty interest on the advance the moment you receive the cash, and you won't receive frequent-flyer miles on an airline credit card). At most banks, you don't even need to go to a teller; you can get a cash advance at the ATM if you know your PIN (personal identification

For the latest information about millennium events in Washington as the New Year opens, call ☎ **1-888-294-2100.**

number). If you've forgotten your PIN or didn't even know you had one, call the phone number on the back of your credit card and ask the bank to send it to you. It usually takes five to seven business days, though some banks will provide the number over the phone if you tell them your mother's maiden name or pass some other security clearance.

THEFT   Almost every credit-card company has an emergency 800-number that you can call if your wallet or purse is stolen. They may be able to wire you a cash advance off your credit card immediately, and in many places, they can deliver an emergency credit card in a day or two. The issuing bank's toll-free number is usually on the back of the credit card—although of course that doesn't help you much if the card was stolen. The toll-free information directory will provide the number if you dial ☎ **800/ 555-1212.** Citicorp Visa's U.S. emergency number is ☎ **800/336-8472.** American Express cardholders and traveler's check holders should call ☎ **800/221-7282** for all money emergencies. MasterCard holders should call ☎ **800/307-7309.**

If you opt to carry traveler's checks, be sure to keep a record of their serial numbers, separately from the checks of course, so you're ensured a refund in just such an emergency.

Odds are that if your wallet is gone, the police won't be able to recover it for you. However, after you realize that it's gone and you cancel your credit cards, it is still worth informing them. Your credit-card company or insurer may require a police report number.

3 When to Go

Washington, these days, is one of the country's top tourist destinations, and there's seldom a lull in visitors. The city's peak-peak seasons coincide generally with two activities: the sessions of Congress and springtime, starting with the appearance of the cherry blossoms along the Potomac. Specifically, when Congress is "in," from about the second week in September until Thanksgiving, and again from about mid-January through June, hotels are quite full with guests whose business takes them to Capitol Hill or to conferences. The period April through June traditionally is the most frenzied season, when families and school groups descend upon the city to see the cherry blossoms and enjoy Washington's sensational spring. Hotel rooms are at a premium and airfares tend to be higher.

If crowds turn you off, consider visiting Washington at the end of August/early September, when Congress is still "out," and families return home to get their children back to school, or between Thanksgiving and mid-January, when Congress leaves again and many people are ensconced in their own holiday-at-home celebrations. Hotel rates are cheapest at this time, too, and many offer attractive packages.

You might also consider visiting in July and August, but be forewarned: The weather is very hot and humid. Also, if you're a theater buff, you should know that many of Washington's stages go dark in summer, although outdoor arenas and parks pick up some of the slack by featuring concerts, festivals, parades and more (see chapter 9 for details about performing arts schedules). There's something doing almost every night and day. And, of course, Independence Day (July 4th) in the capital is a spectacular celebration.

THE WEATHER

Try to check the *Washington Post*'s Web site (see above) for weather forecasts.

Season by season, here's what you can expect of the weather in Washington.

Fall: This is my favorite season. The weather is often warm during the day, and if you're here in early fall, it may seem entirely too warm. But it cools off, getting even a bit crisp, at night. And all the greenery that Washington is famous for changes to fall foliage colors. The stream of tourists tapers off.

Winter: People like to say that Washington winters are mild—and yes, if you're from Minnesota, you will find Washington warmer, no doubt. But our winters are unpredictable, bitter cold one day, an ice storm the next, followed by a couple of days of sun and higher temperatures. Pack for all possibilities.

Spring: Spring weather is delightful, and, of course, there are those cherry blossoms. Along with autumn, it's the nicest time to enjoy D.C.'s outdoor attractions, to visit museums in comfort, and to laze away an afternoon or evening at the ubiquitous Washington street cafes. But this is when the city is most crowded with visitors and school groups.

Summer: Throngs remain in summer, and anyone who's ever spent a summer in D.C. will tell you how hot and steamy it can be. Though the buildings are air-conditioned, many of Washington's attractions, like the memorials, monuments, and organized tours, are outdoors, and the heat can quickly enervate you. Make sure you stop frequently for drinks (vendors are everywhere).

Average Temperatures (°F) in Washington, D.C.

	Jan	Feb	Mar	Apr	May	June	July	Aug	Sept	Oct	Nov	Dec
Avg. High	42	46	57	67	76	85	89	87	80	70	59	47
Avg. Low	27	29	38	46	57	67	71	70	63	50	41	32

Average Monthly Rainfall (in inches) in Washington, D.C.

Jan	Feb	Mar	Apr	May	June	July	Aug	Sept	Oct	Nov	Dec
2.72	2.71	3.17	2.71	3.66	3.38	3.8	3.91	3.31	3.2	3.12	3.12

Washington Calendar of Events

Washington's most popular annual events are the Cherry Blossom Festival in spring, the Fourth of July celebration in summer, the Taste of D.C. food fair in the fall, and the lighting of the National Christmas Tree in winter. But special events are going on daily year-round around town. As it welcomes in the new millennium, though, the city is jumping with even more activities. The Washington D.C. Millennium Alliance has coordinated with the White House Millennium Council to orchestrate a year-long schedule of millennium festivities, starting July 1999 and running through July 2000. Check the Washington, D.C. Convention & Visitors Association Web site, **www.washington.org,** to keep up with the schedule. In the meantime, look over this list of major, mostly annual, events.

About information phone numbers—they seem to change constantly. I have done my best to provide the most accurate contact information, but if the number you try doesn't get you the details you need, call the Washington, D.C. Convention & Visitors Association at ☎ **202/789-7000.** When in town, grab a copy of the *Washington*

Post, especially the Friday "Weekend" section. The Smithsonian Information Center, 1000 Jefferson Dr. SW (☎ **202/357-2700**), is another good source. For annual events in Alexandria, see chapter 10.

January

- **Presidential Inauguration.** On the Capitol steps. After the swearing-in, the crowd lines the curbs as the new or re-elected president proceeds down Pennsylvania Avenue to the White House. The event is heralded by parades, concerts, parties, plays, and other festivities. For details, call ☎ **202/619-7222.** January 20 in years following a national election.
- **Martin Luther King, Jr.'s Birthday.** Events include speeches by prominent civil rights leaders and politicians; readings; dance, theater, and choral performances; prayer vigils; a wreath-laying ceremony at the Lincoln Memorial; and concerts. Many events take place at the Martin Luther King Memorial Library, 901 G St. NW (☎ **202/727-0321**). Call ☎ **202/789-1111** for further details. Third Monday in January.

February

- **Chinese New Year Celebration.** A friendship archway, topped by 300 painted dragons and lighted at night, marks Chinatown's entrance at 7th and H streets NW. The celebration begins the day of the Chinese New Year and continues for 10 or more days, with traditional firecrackers, dragon dancers, and colorful street parades. Some area restaurants offer special menus. For details, call ☎ **202/638-1041.** Early February.
- **Black History Month.** Features numerous events, museum exhibits, and cultural programs celebrating the contributions of African Americans to American life. For details check the *Washington Post* or call ☎ **202/357-2700.** For additional activities at the Martin Luther King Library, call ☎ **202/727-0321.**
- **Abraham Lincoln's Birthday.** Lincoln Memorial. Marked by the laying of a wreath and a reading of the Gettysburg Address at noon. Call ☎ **202/619-7222.** February 12.
- **George Washington's Birthday.** Washington Monument. Similar celebratory events. Call ☎ **202/619-7222** for details. Both presidents' birthdays also bring annual citywide sales. February 22. Mount Vernon also marks Washington's birthday with free admission and activities that include music and military performances on the bowling green. Call ☎ **703/780-2000.** President's Day, third Monday in February.

March

- **St. Patrick's Day Parade.** On Constitution Avenue NW from 7th to 17th streets. A big parade with all you'd expect—floats, bagpipes, marching bands, and the wearin' o' the green. For parade information, call ☎ **301/879-1717.** The Sunday before March 17.
- **Smithsonian Kite Festival.** A delightful event if the weather cooperates—an occasion for a trip in itself. Throngs of kite enthusiasts fly their unique creations on the Washington Monument grounds and compete for ribbons and prizes. To compete, just show up with your kite and register between 10am and noon. Call ☎ **202/357-2700** or 202/357-3030 for details. A Saturday mid or late March, or early April.

April

- **Cherry Blossom Events.** Washington's best-known annual event: the blossoming of the 3,700 famous Japanese cherry trees by the Tidal Basin in Potomac

Park. Festivities include a major parade (marking the end of the festival) with floats, concerts, celebrity guests, and more. There are also special ranger-guided tours departing from the Jefferson Memorial. For information, call ☎ 202/547-1500. Early April (national news programs monitor the budding).

- **Easter Sunrise Services.** Memorial Amphitheater at Arlington National Cemetery. Free shuttle buses travel to the site from the cemetery's visitors center parking lot. Call ☎ 703/607-8052 or 202/789-7000 for details. Easter Sunday.
- **White House Easter Egg Roll.** The biggie for little kids. In past years, entertainment on the White House South Lawn and the Ellipse has included clog dancers, clowns, Ukrainian egg-decorating exhibitions, puppet and magic shows, military drill teams, an egg-rolling contest, and a hunt for 1,000 or so wooden eggs, many of them signed by celebrities, astronauts, or the president. Note: Attendance is limited to children ages 3 to 6, who must be accompanied by an adult. Hourly timed tickets are issued at the National Parks Service Ellipse Visitors Pavilion just behind the White House at 15th and E streets NW beginning at 7am. Call ☎ 202/456-2200 for details. Easter Monday between 10am and 2pm; enter at the southeast gate on East Executive Avenue, and arrive early.
- **Thomas Jefferson's Birthday.** Jefferson Memorial. Celebrated with a wreath-laying, speeches, and a military ceremony. Call ☎ 202/619-7222 for time and details. April 13.
- **White House Spring Garden Tours.** These beautifully landscaped creations are open to the public for free afternoon tours. Call ☎ 202/456-2200 for details. Two days only, in mid-April.
- **Shakespeare's Birthday Celebration.** Folger Shakespeare Library. Music, theater, children's events, food, and exhibits are all part of the afternoon's hail to the Bard. Call ☎ 202/544-7077. Free admission. Mid-April.
- **Filmfest DC.** The year 2000 marks the 14th occurrence of this annual international film festival, which presents as many as 75 works by filmmakers from around the world. Screenings are staged throughout the festival at movie theaters, embassies, and other venues. Tickets are usually $7 per movie; some events are free. Call ☎ 202/628-FILM; www.capaccess.org/filmfestdc. Two weeks in mid-to-late April.
- **Taste of the Nation.** An organization called Share Our Strength (SOS) sponsors this fundraiser for which 70 to 90 major restaurants and many wineries set up tasting booths at Union Station and offer some of their finest fare. For the price of admission, you can do the circuit, sampling everything from barbecue to bouillabaisse; wine flows freely, and there are dozens of great desserts. The evening also includes a silent auction. Tickets are $65 if purchased in advance, $75 at the door, and 100% of the profits go to feed the hungry. To obtain tickets call ☎ 800/955-8278. Late April.
- **The Smithsonian Craft Show.** National Building Museum, 401 F St. NW. Features one-of-a-kind limited-edition crafts by more than 100 noted artists (it's a juried show) from all over the country. There's an entrance fee of about $10 per adult, $7 per child, each day. For details, call ☎ 202/357-2700 (TDD 202/357-1729) or 202/357-4000. Four days in late April.

May

- **Georgetown Garden Tour.** View the remarkable private gardens of one of the city's loveliest neighborhoods. Admission (about $18) includes light refreshments. Some years there are related events such as a flower show at a historic home. Call ☎ 202/244-0381 for details. Early to mid-May.

- **Washington National Cathedral Annual Flower Mart.** Cathedral grounds. Includes displays of flowering plants and herbs, decorating demonstrations, ethnic food booths, children's rides and activities (including an antique carousel), costumed characters, puppet shows, and other entertainment. Admission is free. Call ☎ **202/537-6200** for details. First Friday and Saturday in May.
- **Memorial Day.** At 11am, a wreath-laying ceremony takes place at the Tomb of the Unknowns in Arlington National Cemetery, followed by military band music, a service, and an address by a high-ranking government official (sometimes the president); call ☎ **202/685-2851** for details. There's also a ceremony at 1pm at the Vietnam Veterans Memorial, including a wreath-laying, speakers, and the playing of taps (call ☎ **202/619-7222** for details), and activities at the U.S. Navy Memorial (call ☎ **202/737-2300**). On the Sunday before Memorial Day, the National Symphony Orchestra performs a free concert at 8pm on the West Lawn of the Capitol to officially welcome summer to Washington; call ☎ **202/ 619-7222** for details.

June

- **Dupont-Kalorama Museum Walk Day.** This year marks the 16th annual celebration of collections by six museums and historic houses in this charming neighborhood. Free food, music, tours, and crafts demonstrations. Call ☎ **202/ 667-0441.** Early June.
- **Shakespeare Theatre Free For All.** This free theater festival presents a different Shakespeare play each year, for a 2-week run at the Carter Barron Amphitheatre in upper northwest Washington. Tickets required but are free. Evenings, mid-June. Call ☎ **202/547-3230.**
- **Smithsonian Festival of American Folklife.** A major event with traditional American music, crafts, foods, games, concerts, and exhibits. Folklife Festival 2000 highlights the 200th anniversary of Washington, D.C., with activities on the National Mall and throughout the city, as well as a program on children's toys and play. All events are free; most events take place outdoors. Call ☎ **202/ 357-2700,** or check the listings in the *Washington Post* for details. For 5 to 10 days, always including July 4.

July

- **Independence Day.** There's no better place to be on the Fourth of July than in Washington, D.C. The festivities include a massive National Independence Day Parade down Constitution Avenue, complete with lavish floats, princesses, marching groups, and military bands. There are also celebrity entertainers and concerts. (Most events take place on the Washington Monument grounds.) A morning program in front of the National Archives includes military demonstrations, period music, and a reading of the Declaration of Independence. In the evening the National Symphony Orchestra plays on the west steps of the Capitol with guest artists (for example, Leontyne Price). And big-name entertainment also precedes the fabulous fireworks display behind the Washington Monument. You can also attend an 11am free organ recital at Washington's National Cathedral. Consult the *Washington Post* or call ☎ **202/789-7000** for details. July 4, all day.
- **Bastille Day.** This Washington tradition honors the French Independence Day with live entertainment and a race by tray-balancing waiters and waitresses from Les Halles Restaurant to the U.S. Capitol and back. Free, mais bien sur. 12th Street and Pennsylvania Avenue NW. Call ☎ **202/347-6848.** July 14.
- **Latino Festival.** Pennsylvania Avenue, between 9th and 14th streets NW. Latin American bands from Miami, New York, and L.A. entertain the crowds who come

to celebrate the music, food, and culture of Latin America. Free admission, purchase tickets for food. Late July.

September

- **National Frisbee Festival.** Washington Monument grounds. See world-class Frisbee champions and their disk-catching dogs at this noncompetitive event. Labor Day Weekend.
- **Labor Day Concert.** West Lawn of the Capitol. The National Symphony Orchestra closes its summer season with a free performance at 8pm; call ☎ 202/619-7222 for details. Labor Day. (Rain date: same day and time at Constitution Hall.)
- **International Children's Festival.** Wolf Trap Farm Park in Vienna, Virginia. At this 2-day arts celebration, the entertainment—all of it outdoors—includes clowns, musicians, mimes, puppet shows, and creative workshops from 10am to 4:30pm each day. Admission is charged. For details, call ☎ 703/642-0862. Late September.
- **Washington National Cathedral's Open House.** Celebrates the anniversary of the laying of the foundation stone in 1907. Events include demonstrations of stone carving and other crafts utilized in building the cathedral; carillon and organ demonstrations; and performances by dancers, choirs, strolling musicians, jugglers, and puppeteers. This is the only time visitors are allowed to ascend to the top of the central tower to see the bells; it's a tremendous climb, but you'll be rewarded with a spectacular view. For details, call ☎ 202/537-6200. A Saturday in late September or early October.
- **Black Family Reunion.** National Mall. Performances, food, and fun are part of this celebration of the African American family and culture. Free. Call ☎ 202/737-0120. Mid-September.
- ✪ **Kennedy Center Open House Arts Festival.** A day-long festival of the performing arts, featuring local and national artists on the front plaza and river terrace (which overlooks the Potomac), and throughout the stage halls of the Kennedy Center. Past festivals have featured the likes of Los Lobos, Mary Chapin Carpenter, and Washington Opera soloists. Kids' activities usually include a National Symphony Orchestra "petting zoo," where children get to bow, blow, drum, or strum a favorite instrument. Admission is free, although you may have to stand in a long line for the inside performances. Check the *Washington Post* or call ☎ 800/444-1324 or 202/467-4600 for details. A Sunday, in early to mid-September, noon to 6pm.

October

- **Taste of D.C. Festival.** Pennsylvania Avenue, between 9th and 14th streets NW. Dozens of Washington's restaurants offer food-tastings, along with live entertainment, dancing, storytellers, and games. Admission is free; purchase tickets for tastings. Call ☎ 202/724-5347 for details. Three days, including Columbus Day weekend.
- **White House Fall Garden Tours.** For two days, visitors have an opportunity to see the famed Rose Garden and South Lawn. Admission is free. A military band provides music. For details, call ☎ 202/456-2200. Mid-October.
- **Marine Corps Marathon.** More than 16,000 runners compete in this 26.2-mile race (the fourth-largest marathon in the United States). It begins at the Marine Corps Memorial (the Iwo Jima statue) and passes major monuments. Call ☎ 800/RUN-USMC or 703/784-2225 for details. Anyone can enter; register up to a week ahead. Fourth Sunday in October.

- **Halloween.** There is no official celebration, but costumed revels are on the increase every year. Giant block parties take place in the Dupont Circle area and Georgetown. Check the *Washington Post* for special parties and activities. October 31.

November

- **Veterans Day.** The nation's war dead are honored with a wreath-laying ceremony at 11am at the Tomb of the Unknowns in Arlington National Cemetery followed by a memorial service. The president of the United States or a very high-ranking government personage officiates. Military music is provided by a military band. Call ☎ 202/685-2951 for information. At the Vietnam Veterans Memorial (☎ 202/619-7222), observances include speakers, a wreath-laying, a color guard, and the playing of taps. November 11.

December

- **Christmas Pageant of Peace/National Tree Lighting.** Northern end of the Ellipse. The president lights the national Christmas tree to the accompaniment of orchestral and choral music. The lighting inaugurates the 3-week Pageant of Peace, a tremendous holiday celebration with seasonal music, caroling, a Nativity scene, 50 state trees, and a burning Yule log. Call ☎ 202/619-7222 for details. A select Wednesday or Thursday in early December, at 5pm.
- **White House Candlelight Tours.** On three evenings after Christmas from 5 to 7pm, visitors can see the president's Christmas holiday decorations by candlelight. String music enhances the tours. Lines are long; arrive early. Call ☎ 202/456-2200 for dates and details.

4 Insurance

There are three kinds of travel insurance: trip cancellation, medical, and lost luggage coverage. Trip cancellation insurance is a good idea if you have paid a large portion of your vacation expenses up front. The other two types of insurance, however, don't make sense for most travelers. Rule number one: Check your existing policies before you buy any additional coverage.

Your existing health insurance should cover you if you get sick while on vacation (though if you belong to an HMO, you should check to see whether you are fully covered when away from home). For independent travel health-insurance providers, see below. Your homeowner's insurance should cover stolen luggage. The airlines are responsible for $1,250 on domestic flights if they lose your luggage; if you plan to carry anything more valuable than that, keep it in your carry-on bag. (An airline passengers' rights bill under discussion in Congress may up the amount of money airlines must pay to compensate a passenger for lost luggage, as well as require compensations for other inconveniences suffered.)

The differences between travel assistance and insurance are often blurred, but in general the former offers on-the-spot assistance and 24-hour hotlines (mostly oriented toward medical problems), while the latter reimburses you for travel problems (medical, travel, or otherwise) after you have filed the paperwork. The coverage you consider will depend on how much protection is already contained in your existing health insurance or other policies. Some credit- and charge-card companies may insure you against travel accidents if you buy plane, train, or bus tickets with their cards. Before purchasing additional insurance, read your policies and agreements over carefully. Call your insurers or credit/charge-card companies if you have any questions.

Some credit cards (American Express and certain gold and platinum Visa and MasterCards, for example) offer automatic flight insurance against death or dismemberment in case of an airplane crash.

If you do require additional insurance, try one of the companies listed below. But don't pay for more than you need. For example, if you need only trip cancellation insurance, don't purchase coverage for lost or stolen property. Trip cancellation insurance costs approximately 6% to 8% of the total value of your vacation. The reputable issuers of travel insurance are:

America, 6600 W. Broad St., Richmond, VA 23230 (☎ **800/284-8300**);

Travel Guard International, 1145 Clark St., Stevens Point, WI 54481 (☎ **800/826-1300**);

Travel Insured International, Inc., P.O. Box 280568, East Hartford, CT 06128 (☎ **800/243-3174**);

Travelex Insurance Services, P.O. Box 9408, Garden City, NY 11530-9408 (☎ **800/228-9792**).

5 Tips for Travelers with Special Needs

As the nation's capital, Washington is equipped to handle visitors of every stripe. Within each category below, you'll find general tips for planning your trip, followed by specific information about Washington you might find helpful to know ahead of time.

FOR TRAVELERS WITH DISABILITIES

Washington, D.C., is one of the most accessible cities in the world for travelers with disabilities. But before you arrive you have to get here. A lot of resources are available to help you plan a trip to Washington or anywhere.

A World of Options, a 658-page book of resources for disabled travelers, covers everything, costs $35 ($30 for members), and is available from **Mobility International USA,** P.O. Box 10767, Eugene, OR 97440 (☎ **541/343-1284,** voice and TDD; www.miusa.org). Annual membership for Mobility International is $35, which includes its quarterly newsletter, *Over the Rainbow.* In addition, **Twin Peaks Press,** P.O. Box 129, Vancouver, WA 98666 (☎ **360/694-2462**), publishes travel-related books for people with disabilities.

The Moss Rehab Hospital (☎ **215/456-9600**) has been providing friendly and helpful phone advice and referrals to disabled travelers for years through its **Travel Information Service** (☎ **215/456-9603;** www.mossresourcenet.org).

You can join **The Society for the Advancement of Travel for the Handicapped (SATH),** 347 Fifth Ave. Suite 610, New York, NY 10016 (☎ **212/447-7284;** fax 212/725-8253; www.sath.org) for $45 annually, $30 for seniors and students, to gain access to their vast network of connections in the travel industry. They provide information sheets on travel destinations and referrals of tour operators that specialize in traveling with disabilities. Their quarterly magazine, *Open World for Disability and Mature Travel,* is full of good information and resources. A year's subscription is $13 ($21 outside the U.S.).

Many of the major car rental companies now offer hand-controlled cars for disabled drivers. **Avis** can provide such a vehicle at any of its locations in the U.S. with 48-hour advance notice; **Hertz** requires between 24 and 72 hours advance notice at most of its locations. **Wheelchair Getaways** (☎ **800/873-4973;** www.blvd.com/wg.htm) rents specialized vans with wheelchair lifts and other features for the disabled in more than 100 cities across the U.S.

Travelers with disabilities may also want to consider joining a tour that caters specifically to them. One of the best operators is **Flying Wheels Travel,** 143 West Bridge (P.O. Box 382), Owatonna, MN 55060 (☎ **800/535-6790**). They offer various escorted tours and cruises, with an emphasis on sports, as well as private tours in minivans with lifts. Other reputable specialized tour operators include **Access Adventures** (☎ **716/889-9096**), which offers sports-related vacations; **Accessible Journeys** (☎ **800/TINGLES** or 610/521-0339), for slow walkers and wheelchair travelers; **The Guided Tour, Inc.** (☎ **215/782-1370**); **Wilderness Inquiry** (☎ **800/728-0719** or 612/379-3858); and **Directions Unlimited** (☎ **800/533-5343**).

You can obtain a copy of *Air Transportation of Handicapped Persons* by writing to Free Advisory Circular No. AC12032, Distribution Unit, U.S. Department of Transportation, Publications Division, M-4332, Washington, DC 20590. When making your flight reservations, ask the airline or travel agent where your wheelchair will be stowed on the plane and if seeing or hearing guide dogs can accompany you.

Amtrak's (☎ **800/USA-RAIL;** www.amtrak.com) services for disabled passengers includes redcap service at Washington's Union Station, wheelchair assistance, and special seats with 24 hours' notice. Passengers with disabilities are also entitled to a discount of 15% off the lowest available rail fare at the time of booking. Documentation from a doctor or an ID card proving your disability is required. Amtrak also provides wheelchair-accessible sleeping accommodations on long-distance trains, and service animals are permitted and travel free of charge. Amtrak publishes a handbook called "Access Amtrak," which tells you all you need to know about traveling on Amtrak when you have a disability; call the 800 number to order it and allow 7 to 10 days for delivery. Amtrak's TDD number is ☎ **800/523-6590.**

If you are traveling by **Greyhound Bus,** you should know that a companion can accompany a person with a disability at no charge aboard a Greyhound bus (you must inform Greyhound in advance); call ☎ **800/231-2222** for details, or visit www. greyhound.com. Call ☎ **800/752-4841** at least 24 hours in advance to discuss other special needs. Greyhound's TDD number is ☎ **800/345-3109.**

Vision-impaired travelers should contact the **American Foundation for the Blind,** 11 Penn Plaza, Suite 300, New York, NY 10001 (☎ **800/232-5463**), for information on traveling with seeing-eye dogs.

You can call ahead for general information about special arrangements that various Washington sites make for people with disabilities. The Washington, D.C. Convention & Visitors Association publishes a fact sheet detailing general accessibility of Washington hotels, restaurants, shopping malls, and attractions. For a free copy, call ☎ **202/789-7093** or write to WCVA, 1212 New York Ave. NW, Suite 600, Washington, DC 20005.

The Washington Metropolitan Transit Authority also publishes a free guide on Metro's bus and rail system accessibility for the elderly and physically disabled. Call ☎ **202/962-0128** to order the guide, or check out Metro's Web site at www. wmata.com. Each Metro station is equipped with an elevator (complete with braille number plates) to train platforms, and rail cars are fully accessible. Metro is now installing 24-inch sections of punctuated rubber tiles leading up to the granite-lined platform edge to warn visually impaired Metro riders that they are nearing the tracks. Train operators make station and on-board announcements of train destinations and stops. Most of the District's Metrobuses have wheelchair lifts and kneel at the curb (the number will increase as time goes on). The TDD number for Metro information is ☎ **202/638-3780.** For other questions about Metro services for travelers with disabilities, call ☎ **202/962-6464.** In fact, it's probably a good idea to call this number to verify that the elevators are operating at the stations you'll be traveling to.

Regular **Tourmobile** trams (see "Organized Tours" in chapter 7 for info about this sightseeing company) are accessible to visitors with disabilities. The company also operates special vans for immobile travelers, complete with wheelchair lifts. Tourmobile recommends that you call a day ahead to ensure that the van is available for you when you arrive. For information, call ☎ **202/554-5100.**

All Smithsonian museum buildings are accessible to wheelchair visitors. A comprehensive free publication called Smithsonian Access lists all services available to visitors with disabilities, including parking, building access, sign language interpreters, and more. To obtain a copy, call ☎ **202/357-2700** or TTY 202/357-1729. You can also use the TTY number to obtain information on all Smithsonian museums and events.

You may also find it helpful to know about the arrangements available at these specific sites:

For tours of the White House, visitors in wheelchairs should come to the East Visitors's Gate (along East Executive Avenue) between 10:30am and noon, and you will be allowed to go to the head of the line; visitors arriving in wheelchairs, and their companions (up to four people) by the way, do not need tickets. For details, call ☎ **202/456-2322.**

The Lincoln, Jefferson, and Vietnam Memorials and the Washington Monument are also equipped to accommodate visitors with disabilities and keep wheelchairs on the premises. There's limited parking for visitors with disabilities on the south side of the Lincoln Memorial. Call ahead to other sightseeing attractions for accessibility information and special services: ☎ **202/619-7222** or TDD 202/619-7083.

Call your senator or representative to arrange wheelchair-accessible tours of the Capitol; they can also arrange special tours for the blind or deaf. If you need further information on these tours, call ☎ **202/224-4048.**

Shoppers should know that places well equipped with wheelchair ramps and other facilities for visitors with disabilities include Union Station, the Shops at National Place, the Pavilion at the Old Post Office, and Georgetown Park Mall.

And if you're a theater-goer, be assured that Washington theaters are handily equipped: The John F. Kennedy Center for the Performing Arts provides headphones to hearing-impaired patrons at no charge. A wireless, infrared listening enhancement system is available in all theaters. Some performances offer sign-language and audio description. A public TTY is located at the Information Center in the Hall of States. Large print programs are available at every performance; a limited number of braille programs are available from the house manager. All theaters in the complex (except the Terrace) are wheelchair accessible. The 1997 renovation of the Concert Hall has made it the most accessible venue in the city; improvements include ingenious wheelchair seating, increased to 4% of the seats, and enhanced acoustics. To reserve a wheelchair, call ☎ **202/416-8340.** For other questions regarding patrons with disabilities, including information about half-priced tickets (you will need to submit a letter from your doctor stating that your disability is permanent), call ☎ **202/416-8727.** The TTY number is ☎ **202/416-8728.**

The Arena Stage (☎ **202/554-9066**) has a wheelchair lift and is otherwise accessible. It offers audio description and sign interpretation at designated performances as well as infrared and audio loop assisted-listening devices for the hearing-impaired, plus program books in braille and large-print. The TTY box office line is ☎ **202/484-0247.** You can also call ahead to reserve handicapped parking spaces for a performance.

Ford's Theatre is wheelchair-accessible and offers listening devices as well as special signed and audio-described performances. Call ☎ **202/347-4833** for details. The TTY number is ☎ **202/347-5599.**

The National Theatre is wheelchair-accessible and features special performances of its shows for visually and hearing-impaired theatergoers. To obtain amplified-sound earphones for narration, simply ask an usher before the performance. The National also offers a limited number of half-price tickets to patrons in wheelchairs; seating is in the orchestra section and you may receive no more than 2 half-price tickets. For details, call ☎ **202/628-6161.**

FOR GAY & LESBIAN TRAVELERS

The **International Gay & Lesbian Travel Association (IGLTA)** (☎ **800/448-8550** or 954/776-2626; fax 954/776-3303; www.iglta.org) links travelers up with the appropriate gay-friendly service organization or tour specialist. With around 1,200 members, it offers quarterly newsletters, marketing mailings, and a membership directory that's updated quarterly. Membership often includes gay or lesbian businesses but is open to individuals for $150 yearly, plus a $100 administration fee for new members. Members are kept informed of gay and gay-friendly hoteliers, tour operators, and airline and cruise-line representatives. Contact the IGLTA for a list of its member agencies, who will be tied into IGLTA's information resources.

General gay and lesbian travel agencies include **Family Abroad** (☎ **800/999-5500** or 212/459-1800; gay and lesbian); **Above and Beyond Tours** (☎ **800/397-2681;** mainly gay men); and **Yellowbrick Road** (☎ **800/642-2488;** gay and lesbian).

There are also two good, biannual English-language gay guidebooks, both focused on gay men but including information for lesbians as well. You can get the ***Spartacus International Gay Guide*** or ***Odysseus*** from most gay and lesbian book stores, or order them from **Giovanni's Room** (☎ **215/923-2960**), or **A Different Light Bookstore** (☎ **800/343-4002** or 212/989-4850). Both lesbians and gays might want to pick up a copy of ***Gay Travel A to Z*** ($16). **The Ferrari Guides** (www.q-net.com) is yet another very good series of gay and lesbian guidebooks.

Out and About, 8 W. 19th St. #401, New York, NY 10011 (☎ **800/929-2268** or 212/645-6922) offers guidebooks and a monthly newsletter packed with good information on the global gay and lesbian scene. A year's subscription to the newsletter costs $49. ***Our World,*** 1104 North Nova Rd., Suite 251, Daytona Beach, FL 32117 (☎ **904/441-5367**) is a slicker monthly magazine promoting and highlighting travel bargains and opportunities. Annual subscription rates are $35 in the U.S., $45 outside the United States.

Washington, D.C., has a strong gay and lesbian community, the complete source for which is ***The Washington Blade,*** a comprehensive weekly newspaper distributed free at about 700 locations in the District. Every issue provides an extensive events calendar and a list of hundreds of resources, such as crisis centers, health facilities, switchboards, political groups, religious organizations, social clubs, and student activities; it puts you in touch with everything from groups of lesbian bird-watchers to the Asian Gay Men's Network. Gay restaurants and clubs are, of course, also listed and advertised. You can subscribe to the Blade for $45 a year or pick up a free copy at: Olsson's Books/Records, 1307 19th St. NW; Borders, 18th and L streets; and Kramerbooks, 1517 Connecticut Ave. NW, at Dupont Circle. Call the Blade office at ☎ **202/797-7000** for other locations. One final source: Washington's gay bookstore, Lambda Rising, 1625 Connecticut Ave. NW (☎ **202/462-6969**), also informally serves as an information center for the gay community, which centers in the Dupont Circle neighborhood.

FOR SENIORS

Rule of thumb: Mention the fact that you are a senior citizen when making your travel arrangements and carry identification that shows your date of birth. Discounts abound for seniors, beginning with the 10%-off-your-airfare deal that most airlines offer to anyone 62 or older. In addition, a number of airlines have clubs you can join and coupon books you can buy that may or may not increase your savings beyond that base 10% discount, depending upon how often you travel, where you are going, and how long you're going to stay. Airlines with clubs include United, Continental, Delta and American; these same airlines also sell coupon books, along with Northwest, Trans World Airlines, and US Airways.

Both **Amtrak** (☎ 800/USA-RAIL; www.amtrak.com) and **Greyhound** (☎ 800/752-4841; www.greyhound.com) offer discounts to persons over 62. And many hotels offer seniors discounts; in Washington, the Clarion Hampshire Hotel is a **Choice Hotels** property, which means that if you're over 50 you get 30 percent off the hotel's published rates if you book your room through the nationwide toll-free reservations number, rather than directly through the hotel or through a travel agent. Many hotels in Washington offer senior discounts, as do theaters, museums, stores, even the Metro. Available from the D.C. Office on Aging, 441 Fourth St. NW, 9th floor South, Washington, DC 20001 (☎ 202/724-5622) is the free **Goldmine Directory** of Washington-area restaurants, stores and facilities that offer discounts to people 60 and older.

Members of the **American Association of Retired Persons (AARP)**, 601 E St. NW, Washington, DC 20049 (☎ 800/424-3410 or 202/434-2277; www.aarp.org), get discounts not only on hotels but on airfares and car rentals, too. AARP offers members a wide range of special benefits, including *Modern Maturity* magazine and a monthly newsletter.

The National Council of Senior Citizens, 8403 Colesville Rd., Suite 1200, Silver Spring, MD 20910 (☎ 301/578-8800), a nonprofit organization, offers a newsletter six times a year (partly devoted to travel tips) and discounts on hotel and auto rentals; annual dues are $13 per person or couple.

Mature Outlook, P.O. Box 9390, Des Moines, IA 50306 (☎ 800/336-6330), began as a travel organization for people over 50, though it now caters to people of all ages. Members receive discounts on hotels and receive a bimonthly magazine. Annual membership is $19.95, which often also entitles members to free coupons for discounted merchandise from Sears.

Golden Companions, P.O. Box 5249, Reno, NV 89513 (☎ 702/324-2227), helps travelers 45-plus find compatible companions through a personal voice-mail service. Contact them for more information.

The Mature Traveler, a monthly 12-page newsletter on senior citizen travel is a valuable resource. It is available by subscription ($30 a year) from GEM Publishing Group, Box 50400, Reno, NV 89513-0400. GEM also publishes *The Book of Deals,* a collection of more than 1,000 senior discounts on airlines, lodging, tours, and attractions around the country; it's available for $9.95 by calling ☎ 800/460-6676. Another helpful publication is *101 Tips for the Mature Traveler,* available from Grand Circle Travel, 347 Congress St., Suite 3A, Boston, MA 02210 (☎ 800/221-2610 or 617/350-7500; fax 617/346-6700).

SAGA International Holidays, 222 Berkeley St., Boston, MA 02116 (☎ 800/343-0273), offers inclusive tours and cruises for those 50 and older. In Washington, D.C., SAGA sponsors a 7-night Smithsonian Odyssey Tour that offers a behind-the-scenes look at several museum and other major D.C. institutions. For this specific program, call ☎ 800/258-5885.

If you want something more than the average vacation or guided tour, try **Elder-hostel** (☎ 877/426-8056; www.elderhostel.org), a national nonprofit organization that offers low-cost educational programs for people 55 or older and their adult companions. In Washington, D.C., Elderhostel sponsors weeklong residential programs, some of which focus on government and American history, others on art, literature, and more. Cost averages $450 to $500 per person, including meals, room, and classes.

Among specialty books on the market are three that provide good general advice and contacts for the savvy senior traveler. Thumb through *The 50+ Traveler's Guidebook* (St. Martin's Press), *The Seasoned Traveler* (Country Roads Press), or *Unbelievably Good Deals and Great Adventures That You Absolutely Can't Get Unless You're Over 50* (Contemporary Books). Also check out your newsstand for the quarterly magazine *Travel 50 & Beyond.*

FOR FAMILIES

Field trips during the school year and family vacations during the summer keep Washington, D.C., crawling with kids all year long. As the nation's capital, Washington is a natural place for families to visit. Still, you may be surprised at just how much there is to do. More than any other city, perhaps, Washington is crammed with historic buildings, arts and science museums, parks, and recreation sites to interest young and old alike. Some of the museums, like the National Museum of Natural History and the Daughters of the American Revolution (DAR) Museum, have hands-on exhibits for children. Many more sponsor regular, usually free, family-oriented events, such as the Corcoran Gallery of Art's "Family Days" and the Folger Shakespeare Library's seasonal activities. It's worth calling or writing in advance for schedules from the sites you're thinking of visiting (see chapter 7 for addresses and phone numbers). Truly, there is something here for everyone, and the fact that so many attractions are free is a boon to the family budget.

Hotels, more and more, are doing their part to make family trips affordable, too. At many of the hotels, children under a certain age (usually 12) sleep free in the same room with their parents. Hotel weekend packages often offer special family rates. An excellent resource for family travel, including information about hotel deals for families, is *Family Travel Times,* a bimonthly newsletter published by FTT Marketing. To subscribe or get information, contact Family Travel Times, call toll-free ☎ 888/822-4388, or 212/477-5524. For $39 per year you get six issues of the newsletter, discounts on other publications and back issues, and weekly call-in service for advice.

Family Travel Forum, 891 Amsterdam Ave., New York, NY 10025 (☎ 888/383-6786; www.familytravelforum.com) is another helpful source of information for families planning trips. You can receive a newsletter in the mail and/or access information online to read tips on traveling with children, staff-written travel articles, and members' first-hand accounts of experiences in various destinations. Each issue of the newsletter focuses on a specific theme, from traveling with teens to intergenerational travel. A comprehensive annual membership is $48, or you can subscribe simply to the online service for $28 annually, or $2.95 monthly.

Restaurants throughout the Washington area are growing increasingly family-friendly, as well: Many provide kids menus or charge less for children's portions. The best news, though, is that families are welcome at all sorts of restaurants these days and need no longer seek out the hamburger/french fries eateries.

Washington, D.C., is easy to get around with children. The Metro covers the city and it's safe. Children under 4 ride free. Remember, however, that eating or drinking on the subway or in the station is prohibited.

Once you arrive, get your hands on a copy of the most recent *Washington Post* "Weekend" section, published each Friday. The section covers all possible happenings in the city, with a weekly feature, "Saturday's Child," and a column, "Carousel," devoted to children's activities.

FOR STUDENTS

The best resource for students is the **Council on International Educational Exchange,** or CIEE. It can set you up with an ID card (see below), and its travel branch, **Council Travel Service** (☎ **800/226-8624;** www.ciee.com), is the biggest student travel agency operation in the world. It can get you discounts on plane tickets, railpasses, and the like. Ask them for a list of CTS offices in major cities so you can keep the discounts flowing (and aid lines open) as you travel.

From CIEE you can obtain the $18 **International Student Identity Card (ISIC).** It's the only officially acceptable form of student identification, good for cut rates on railpasses, plane tickets, and other discounts. It also provides you with basic health and life insurance and a 24-hour help line. If you're no longer a student but are still under 26 you can get a GO 25 card from the same people, which will get you the insurance and some of the discounts (but not student admission prices in museums).

Also call **STA Travel** (☎ **800/781-4040**), or look at it's Web site, www.sta-travel. com, to take advantage of student airfares on both domestic and international flights. You can also use the Web site to obtain travel insurance and the ISIC, read planning tips, and exchange travel information.

Washington theaters, museums, and the Metro accord students the same discounts as seniors and the disabled, so always ask and be ready to present a student ID when gaining admission to these places.

6 Getting There

BY PLANE
D.C.'s AREA AIRPORTS

Washington, D.C., has three airports serving the area: Ronald Reagan Washington National (formerly named Washington National), Washington Dulles International ("Dulles"), and Baltimore-Washington International (BWI). Dulles is in the midst of a grand expansion, to be completed in stages in the decades to come; currently, it is the most confusing of the three airports, and it is also the one experiencing the most growth. (You can blame Sen. John McCain, chairman of the Senate Commerce Committee, for much of the debacle. For more than two years, the senator blocked money for improvements to Dulles and held up confirmation of federal appointees to the regional airport authority, who were needed for the funding process to flow. The senator schemed to hold up funding for Dulles until Congress passed legislation adding flights to National Airport, including new flights to the senator's own state of Arizona.) General information follows that should help you determine which airport is your best bet; for more details about individual airport services and transportation into the city from each, see chapter 4.

Ronald Reagan Washington National Airport (everyone still calls it National) lies across the Potomac River in Virginia, about 20 minutes from downtown in non-rush hour traffic. Nineteen major airlines and shuttles operate at this airport. If you are arriving from a city that is within 1,250 miles of National, this may be your airport; by law only short- and medium-haul flights use National.

Built in 1941, National was long due for an overhaul, and the recently completed, $1-billion project has vastly improved the airport, without increasing the number of flights or passengers it can handle. Enhancements include a new terminal; ticket counters that provide access to passengers with disabilities; 24 restaurants and 38 shops; more parking space; and climate-controlled pedestrian bridges that connect the terminal directly to the Metro station, whose Blue and Yellow lines stop here. For airport information, call ☎ **703/419-8000;** the airport's Web site is www.metwashairports. com. For Metro information, call ☎ **202/637-7000.**

Washington Dulles International Airport (Dulles) lies 26 miles outside the capital, in Chantilly, VA, a 35- to 45-minute ride to downtown in non-rush hour traffic. The expansion, to be finished over the course of the next few decades, will eventually add an underground "moving sidewalk" to replace the inconvenient and unwieldy mobile lounges that, for now, transport travelers to and from the main and midfield terminals. Both domestic and international carriers use Dulles. Call ☎ **703/419-8000** for airport information; the airport's Web site is the same as National's, above.

Last but not least is Baltimore-Washington International Airport (BWI), which is located about 45 minutes from downtown, a few miles outside of Baltimore. Often overlooked by Washingtonians, BWI's bargain fares make it worth considering. Call ☎ **410/859-7111** for airport information; www.baltwashintlairport.com.

THE MAJOR AIRLINES

Domestic airlines with scheduled flights into all three airports include American (☎ **800/433-7300;** www.aa.com); Continental (☎ **800/525-0280;** www.fly continental.com); Delta (☎ **800/221-1212;** www.deltaairlines.com); Northwest (☎ **800/225-2525;** www.nwa.com); TWA (☎ **800/221-2000;** www.twa.com); United (☎ **800/241-6522;** www.ual.com); and US Airways (☎ **800/428-4322;** www.usairways.com). In the spring of 1999, United Airlines was boasting that it offers more nonstops from more destinations to Washington than any other airline: 350 flights a day, including its United Express shuttle service (see below).

International airlines with scheduled flights into National are Air Canada (☎ **800/ 776-3000;** www.aircanada.ca) and Canadian Airlines (☎ **800/426-7000;** www.cdnair.ca). International airlines with scheduled flights into BWI include Air Canada, British Airways (☎ **800/247-9297;** www.british-airways.com), El Al Israel (☎ **800/223-6700;** www.elal.co.il), and Icelandair (☎ **800/223-5500;** www. icelandair.com). International airlines with scheduled flights into Dulles include Air Canada, Air France (☎ **800/237-2747;** www.airfrance.com), All Nippon Airways (☎ **800/235-9262;** www.allnipponairways.com), British Airways, KLM Royal Dutch (☎ **800/374-7747;** www.klm.nl); Lufthansa (☎ **800/645-3880;** www. lufthansa.com); Saudi Arabian Airlines (☎ **800/472-8342;** www.saudiarabian-airlines.com), Swissair (☎ **800/221-4750;** www. swissair.com), and Virgin Atlantic (☎ **800/862-8621;** fly.virgina.com).

SHUTTLES BETWEEN WASHINGTON AND BOSTON, CHICAGO AND NEW YORK

Delta, US Airways, and United airlines are competing to dominate the lucrative shuttle service, so much a large part of travel to Washington. As a result, all three airlines operate hourly shuttle service weekdays between Boston's Logan Airport and Washington, and New York's La Guardia Airport and Washington. Both the Delta Shuttle (☎ **800/221-1212**) and the US Airways Shuttle (☎ **800/428-4322**) fly into and out of Ronald Reagan Washington National Airport. By the time you read this,

US Airways will probably have expanded its shuttle service to include hourly Dulles to Boston and Dulles to New York flights. United Airlines has a joint venture with Atlantic Coast Airlines to run a shuttle called United Express that offers hourly service daily between La Guardia Airport and Dulles Airport, and between Boston's Logan Airport and Dulles. United Express also offers frequent service to and from Atlanta, Orlando, L.A., San Francisco, and Chicago. Southwest Airlines offers nearly hourly service daily between Chicago's Midway Airport and BWI. In addition, low-fare airlines are increasing service between Washington and these—and other—major cities; see below.

FLYING FOR LESS: TIPS FOR GETTING THE BEST AIRFARES

The first thing you want to do is find out whether a low fare carrier travels between your city and Washington. Low fare airlines are on the rise and offer great deals, especially up and down the East Coast, and west to Chicago. If you can do without frills, find out whether any of the following low-fare airlines fly from your city to Washington: Delta Express (☎ 800/325-5205; www.deltaairlines.com), US Airways' MetroJet (☎ 888-METROJET; www.flymetrojet.com), Midway Airlines (☎ 800/446-4392; www.midwayair.com), AirTran (formerly ValuJet) (☎ 800/247-8726; www.airtran.com), Southwest Airlines (☎ 800/435-9792; www.southwest.com), and United Express (☎ 800/241-6522). MetroJet flies into Dulles and BWI, Delta Express and AirTran fly into Dulles, Midway flies into National and BWI, Southwest flies into BWI, and, as mentioned earlier, United Express flies into Dulles.

It always helps to be flexible. If you can purchase your ticket long in advance, don't mind staying over Saturday night, or are willing to travel on a Tuesday, Wednesday, or Thursday after 7pm, you'll pay a fraction of the full fare. Here are a few other easy ways to save.

1. **Special rates.** Periodically, airlines lower prices on their most popular routes. Check your newspaper for advertised discounts or call the airlines directly and ask if any promotional rates or special fares are available; whether seniors, children, and students receive reduced rates; and if the airline offers money-saving packages that include such essentials as hotel accommodations, car rentals, and tours with your airfare (see section on package tours at the end of this chapter). Read the Sunday travel sections of the *New York Times* and the *Washington Post;* their weekly columns ("Fly Buys" in the *Post* and "Lowest Air Fares for Popular Routes" in the *Times*) highlight bargain airfares.

   You'll almost never see a sale during the peak summer vacation months of July and August, or during the Thanksgiving or Christmas seasons. If you don't mind traveling on Christmas Day or Thanksgiving Day, itself, however, you might snag a cheaper fare (most people would rather not be on an airplane on the actual holiday). If your schedule is flexible, ask if you can secure a cheaper fare by staying an extra day or by flying midweek. (Many airlines won't volunteer this information.) If you already hold a ticket when a sale breaks, it may even pay to exchange your ticket, which usually incurs a $50 to $75 charge. Note, however, that the lowest-priced fares are often nonrefundable, require advance purchase of 1 to 3 weeks and a certain length of stay, and carry penalties for changing dates of travel.

2. **Consolidators,** also known as bucket shops, are a good place to find low fares, but you must expect the most basic seating. Consolidators buy seats in bulk from the airlines and then sell them back to the public at prices below even the airlines' discounted rates. Their small ads usually run in the Sunday travel section at the bottom of the page. Before you pay, however, ask for a confirmation number from the consolidator and then call the airline itself to confirm your seat. Be prepared

to book your ticket with a different consolidator—there are many to choose from—if the airline can't confirm your reservation. Also be aware that bucket shop tickets are usually non-refundable or rigged with stiff cancellation penalties, often as high as 50% to 75% of the ticket price. Contact the Better Business Bureau in the consolidator's home city to see whether complaints have been registered against it. One way to choose a consolidator is to check with professional organizations whose members, including consolidators, must satisfy certain solid requirements. For example, the United States Tour Operators Association includes a number of tour operators who also handle consolidator business; all USTOA members are listed on its Web site, www.ustoa.com. (This Web site is also useful if you're looking into package tours; see that section further in this chapter.) Also, when using a consolidator, try booking your ticket through a travel agent experienced with consolidators and always use a credit card to pay.

Council Travel (☎ **800/226-8624;** www.counciltravel.com) and **STA Travel** (☎ **800/781-4040;** www.sta.travel.com) cater especially to young travelers, but their bargain basement prices are available to people of all ages. **Travel Bargains** (☎ **800/AIR-FARE;** www.1800airfare.com) was formerly owned by TWA but now offers the deepest discounts on many other airlines, with a four-day advance purchase. Other reliable consolidators include **1-800-FLY-CHEAP** (www.1800flycheap.com); **TFI Tours International** (☎ **800-745-8000** or 212/736-1140), which serves as a clearinghouse for unused seats; or "rebators" such as **Travel Avenue** (☎ **800/333-3335** or 312/876-1116) and the **Smart Traveller** (☎ **800/448-3338** in the U.S., or 305/448-3338), which rebate part of their commissions to you.

3. **Book a seat on a charter flight.** Discounted fares have pared the number available, but they can still be found. Most charter operators advertise and sell their seats through travel agents, thus making these local professionals your best source of information for available flights. Before deciding to take a charter flight, however, check the restrictions on the ticket: You may be asked to purchase a tour package, to pay in advance, to be amenable if the day of departure is changed, to pay a service charge, to fly on an airline you're not familiar with (this usually is not the case), and to pay harsh penalties if you cancel—but be understanding if the charter doesn't fill up and is canceled up to 10 days before departure. Summer charters fill up more quickly than others and are almost sure to fly, but if you decide on a charter flight, seriously consider cancellation and baggage insurance.

4. **Travel Clubs.** Join a travel club such as **Moment's Notice** (☎ **718/234-6295;** www.moments-notice.com) or **Sears Discount Travel Club** (☎ **800/433-9383,** or 800/255-1487 to join), which supply unsold tickets at discounted prices. You pay an annual membership fee to get the club's hotline number. Of course, you're limited to what's available, so you have to be flexible.

5. **Web bargains.** Finally, if you're at home in cyberspace, check out last-minute discounted fares posted by airlines on the Internet. See **Frommer's Online Directory** in the back of the book for descriptions of Web sites that can help you find cheap rates for airfare, lodging, car rental, and other travel items.

BY TRAIN

Amtrak offers daily service to Washington from New York, Boston, Chicago, and Los Angeles (you change trains in Chicago). At the end of 1999, Amtrak unveiled its high-speed Acela trains, which travel as fast as 150 miles per hour, along the Northeast Corridor, linking Boston, New York and Washington. The Acela cuts up to 30 minutes off the usual 4-hour ride between New York and Washington, and as much as an hour off the trip between Boston and Washington.

Amtrak trains arrive at historic Union Station, 50 Massachusetts Ave. NE, a turn-of-the-century beaux arts masterpiece that was magnificently restored in the late 1980s. Offering a three-level marketplace of shops and restaurants, this stunning depot is conveniently located and connects with Metro service. There are always taxis available there. For rail reservations, contact Amtrak (☎ **800/USA-RAIL;** www.amtrak.com). (For more on Union Station, see chapters 7 and 8.)

Like the airlines, Amtrak offers several discounted fares; although not all are based on advance purchase, you have more discount options by reserving early. The discount fares can be used only on certain days and hours of the day; be sure to find out exactly what restrictions apply. Tickets for children ages 2 to 12 cost half the price of a regular coach fare. And Amtrak recently got into the Internet bargain fares act, introducing Rail Sale, an on-line service that allows you to purchase reserved tickets at great discount, for designated one-way coach seats. This program is only available on Amtrak's Web site, www.reservations.amtrak.com, and when you charge your tickets by credit card.

Also inquire about money-saving packages that include hotel accommodations, car rentals, tours, and so on with your train fare. Call ☎ **800/321-8684** for details.

Metroliner service—which costs a little more but provides faster transit and roomier, more comfortable seating—is available between New York and Washington, D.C., and points in between. Note: Metroliner fares are substantially reduced on weekends. The most luxurious way to travel is First Class Club Service, available on all Metroliners as well as some other trains. For a hefty additional fee, passengers enjoy more spacious and refined seating in a private car; complimentary meals and beverage service; and Metropolitan Lounges (in New York, Chicago, Philadelphia, and Washington) where travelers can wait for trains in a comfortable setting while enjoying free snacks and coffee.

BY BUS

Greyhound buses connect almost the entire United States with Washington, D.C. They arrive at a terminal at 1005 1st St. NE at L Street (☎ **800/231-2222;** www.greyhound.com). The closest Metro stop is Union Station, four blocks away. The bus terminal is in an edgy neighborhood, so if you arrive at night, it's best to take a taxi. If you're staying in the suburbs, you should know that Greyhound also has service to Silver Spring, MD, and Arlington and Springfield, VA.

The fare structure on buses is not necessarily based on distance traveled. The good news is that when you call Greyhound to make a reservation, the company will always offer you the lowest fare options. Call in advance and know your travel dates, since some discount fares require advance purchase.

BY CAR

Major highways approach Washington, D.C., from all parts of the country. Specifically, these are I-270, I-95, and I-295 from the north; I-95 and I-395, Route 1, and Route 301 from the south; Route 50/301 and Route 450 from the east; and Route 7, Route 50, I-66, and Route 29/211 from the west. No matter what road you take, there's a good chance you will have to navigate some portion of the Capital Beltway (I-495 and I-95) to gain entry to D.C. The Beltway girds the city, 66 miles around, with 56 interchanges or exits, and is nearly always congested, but especially weekdays, during the morning and evening rush hours, roughly between 7 to 9am and 3 to 7pm.

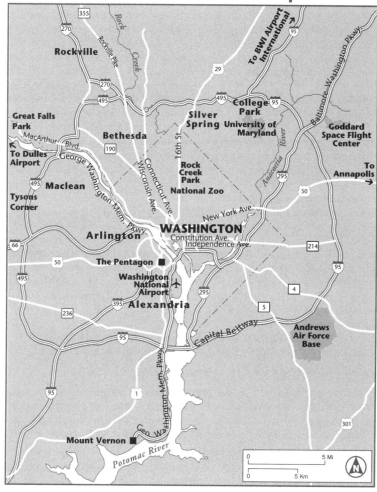

Commuter traffic on the Beltway now rivals that of major L.A. freeways, and drivers can get a little crazy, weaving in and out of traffic.

Note: A couple of major access roads into Washington are currently undergoing major reconstruction. If you are coming from a point south of Washington and planning to drive into the city via I-95 to I-395, you should find an alternate route; an enormous highway construction project along this route, at the point where I-395 and I-495 meet, near Springfield, is closing lanes and diverting traffic, and will continue to do so for about 8 years. If you must come this way, do not travel the I-395 portion at rush hour (see times above), unless you want to add hours to your trip. The alternate route I would recommend is Route 1: From I-95, take exit 161, Route 1 North, marked "Fort Belvoir/Mt. Vernon." Continue north about 6 miles along a traffic light-controlled drive until you reach Rte. 235 North, where you turn right. This route, which now becomes quite picturesque, puts you on the George Washington Memorial Parkway, and takes you past Mount Vernon, alongside the Potomac

River, through Old Town Alexandria (where the parkway is called Washington Street), and past Ronald Reagan Washington National Airport; see directions from the airport into the city, listed in chapter 4.

The other access road undergoing construction is New York Avenue NE. Repair work will continue throughout the year 2000 on precisely that portion of New York Avenue linking the Baltimore-Washington Parkway, so you might consider avoiding I-295 altogether. Instead, if you're coming from north of Washington, take I-95 toward Washington and when you see the signs for I-495, move into one of the right-most lanes and pick up I-495 in the direction of Silver Spring/Bethesda. Stay on I-495 until you reach the Chevy Chase/Kensington exit. Stay left as you exit and take a left at the bottom of the ramp, onto Connecticut Avenue. Follow Connecticut Avenue about 7 miles south, straight into the District; the avenue finally deadends at Lafayette Square, across from the White House. You'll want to ask your hotel for directions from Connecticut Avenue and K Street NW.

If you're planning to drive to Washington, get yourself a good map before you do anything else. The American Automobile Association (AAA) (☎ **800/222-4357** or 703/222-6000) provides its members with maps and detailed Trip-Tiks that give travelers precise directions to a destination, including up-to-date information about areas of construction. AAA also provides towing services should you have any car trouble during your trip. If you are driving to a hotel in D.C. or its suburbs, contact the establishment to find out the best route to the hotel's address, and other crucial details concerning parking availability and rates. See "Getting Around," in chapter 4 for information about driving in D.C.

The District is 240 miles from New York City, 40 miles from Baltimore, 700 miles from Chicago, nearly 500 miles from Boston, and about 630 miles from Atlanta.

PACKAGE TOURS VS. ESCORTED TOURS

Before you start your search for the lowest airfare, you may want to consider booking your flight as part of a travel package such as an escorted tour or a package tour. What you lose in adventure, you'll gain in time and money saved when you book accommodations, and maybe even food and entertainment, along with your flight.

ESCORTED TOURS   Packaged travel may not be the option for you if you like to navigate strange places at whim. If you like to plan your coordinates in advance, however, many package options will enable you to do just that—and save you money in the process.

Some people love escorted tours. They let you relax and take in the sights while a bus driver fights traffic for you; they spell out your costs up front; and they take you to the maximum number of sites in the minimum amount of time with the least amount of hassle. If you do choose an escorted tour, you should ask a few simple questions before you buy:

1. **What is the cancellation policy?** Do they require a deposit? Can they cancel the trip if they don't get enough people? Do you get a refund if they cancel? If you cancel? How late can you cancel if you are unable to go? When do you pay in full?
2. **How busy is the schedule?** How much sightseeing do they plan each day? Do they allow ample time for relaxing by the pool, shopping, or wandering?
3. **What is the size of the group?** The smaller the group, the more flexible the itinerary, and the less time you'll spend waiting for people to get on and off the bus. Tour operators may be evasive about this, because they may not know the exact size of the group until everybody has made their reservations; but they should be

able to give you a rough estimate. Some tours have a minimum group size and may cancel the tour if they don't book enough people.

4. **What is included in the price?** Don't assume anything. You may have to pay for transportation to and from the airport. A box lunch may be included in an excursion, but drinks might cost extra. Beer might be included, but wine might not. Can you opt out of certain activities, or does the bus leave once a day, with no exceptions? Are all your meals planned in advance? Can you choose your entree at dinner, or does everybody get the same chicken cutlet?

Note: If you choose an escorted tour, think strongly about purchasing travel insurance from an independent agency, especially if the tour operator asks you to pay up front. One final caveat: Since escorted tour prices are based on double occupancy, the single traveler is usually penalized.

PACKAGE TOURS   Package tours are not the same thing as escorted tours. They are simply a way to buy airfare and accommodations at the same time. For popular destinations like Washington, they can be a smart way to go, because they may save you a lot of money. In many cases, a package that includes airfare, hotel, and transportation to and from the airport will cost you less than just the hotel alone would have, had you booked it yourself. That's because packages are sold in bulk to tour operators—who resell them to the public at a cost that drastically undercuts standard rates.

Packages, however, vary widely. Some offer a better class of hotels than others. Some offer the same hotels for lower prices. Some offer flights on scheduled airlines, while others book charters. In some packages, your choice of accommodations and travel days may be limited. Some packages let you choose between escorted vacations and independent vacations; others will allow you to add on just a few excursions or escorted day trips (also at lower prices than you could locate on your own) without booking an entirely escorted tour. Each destination usually has one or two packagers that are cheaper than the rest because they buy in even greater bulk. If you take the time to shop around, you will save in the long run.

FINDING A PACKAGE DEAL, ESCORTED AND UNESCORTED   The best place to start your search is the travel section of your local Sunday newspaper. Also check the ads in the back of national travel magazines like *Travel & Leisure, National Geographic Traveler,* and *Conde Nast Traveler.* If you're having no luck finding package deals to Washington, you can try the sources that follow, of course, or you can simply go to an established travel agent. Many tour companies require you to book through a travel agent, anyway. If you think you've found a good package deal, you can make sure the company is dependable by finding out if it holds membership in one or both of the two major trade organizations, the U.S. Tour Operators Association (☎ **800/468-7862;** www.ustoa.com) or the National Tour Association (☎ **800/682-8886;** www.ntaonline.com). The USTOA lists its members on-line; the NTA does not, but it does allow you to enter the name of your destination and read about packages offered by its various member companies for that location.

A good resource for unescorted tour packages is the airlines themselves, which often package their flights together with accommodations. Among the airline packagers with deals in Washington are **American Airlines Vacations** (☎ **800/321-2121;** www.aavacations.com), **Delta Dream Vacations** (☎ **800/872-7786;** www.deltavacations.com), **US Airways Vacations** (☎ **800/455-0123;** www.usairways.com), **United Airlines** (☎ **800/328-6877,** www.ual.com; click on "reservations," then "United Vacations"), and **Northwest Airlines** (☎ **800/800-1504,** www.nwa.com; click on "vacation packages"). These Web sites are often extremely frustrating to navigate. The best of the bunch, in my opinion, both for ease in using and for lowest hotel package offered (from $108 per person, double occupancy for 2 nights, including hotel tax), is Northwest. Something else that's great about Northwest is its Cyber Saver alerts, posted every Wednesday and listing special hotel rates, package deals, and discounted airlines.

It's good to remember as you work each of these airline Web sites that Baltimore might also be listed as a destination; Baltimore-Washington International Airport, as explained at the beginning of this chapter, also serves Washington, and many airlines fly into that airport, as well as the two others.

Amtrak's **Amtrak Vacations** program (☎ 800/321-8684) offers package deals. In 1999, the program advertised a Boston-to-Washington package starting at a rate of $245 per person, based on double occupancy, and including two nights lodging in Washington, round-trip fare between Boston and Washington, and a narrated trolley tour. (Washington packages from Chicago and San Francisco were also available.)

The biggest hotel chains sometimes offer package deals. If you already know where you want to stay, call the hotel itself and ask if it can offer land/air packages. You can also look at the Washington Convention & Visitors Association Web site at www.washington.org, and click on "Special Packages," to find out about deals being offered by individual hotels, sometimes in conjunction with the WCVA or with a tour operator, and sometimes including extras, like city tours or a boat cruise.

Here's a short list of the major tour operators offering package deals in Washington, and sample packages and prices available in 1999. Prices go up if you choose a higher class hotel or reserve additional nights.

- **Liberty Travel** (toll-free ☎ 888/271-1584; www.libertytravel.com), or check your local directory for one of its many local branches nationwide. One of the biggest packagers in the Northeast, Liberty usually boasts a full-page ad in Sunday papers. You won't get much in the way of service, but you will get a good deal. In 1999, Liberty's (unescorted) package started at $205 per person double occupancy, for 3 nights lodging at the Quality Hotel Downtown, including hotel tax and a 4-hour sightseeing tour.

- **Globus and Cosmos** (www.globusandcosmos.com). If you want to make Washington, D.C., part of a multi-city tour, try this company, which is a member of both the US Tour Operators Association and the National Tour Association. These are all escorted tours. Cosmos handles the budget packages; in 1999 these included one 6-day tour that traveled by private air-conditioned motorcoach from New York City to Niagara Falls to Lancaster, PA, to Washington. The cost was about $500 per person, for a double room (in D.C., the hotel was the Holiday Inn Downtown) based on double occupancy, and included hotel tax, service charges, tips for baggage handling, and a number of sightseeing tours. Globus, the upscale end of the company, offered in 1999 an 8-day package that started in Washington and traveled to Williamsburg, Charlottesville, Gettysburg, and Philadelphia, and back to Washington. The cost per person, double occupancy, at the Doubletree Park Terrace, including the tax, service and tip charges, seven breakfasts, five 3-course dinners, and visits to historic sites was about $1,000.

- Another big name in multi-city escorted travel is **Maupintour** (☎ 800/255-4266; www.maupintour.com), also a member of both the USTOA and the NTA. In 1999, Maupintour offered an 8-day tour that took in Williamsburg, Charlottesville, and Washington for $1,595 per person, double occupancy (in D.C., the hotel was the Renaissance Mayflower, one of Washington's finest), a night tour of the capital, 16 meals, and gratuities.

- **Yankee Holidays** (☎ 800/225-2550; www.yankee-holidays.com) has been offering individual city packages and customized group tour packages for about 28 years. The company is a National Tour Association member. 1999 trips to Washington included a 2-night, 3-day Capitol Experience with lodging and a 1-day sightseeing pass for $132 to $374 (per person, double occupancy), depending on your choice of lodging and season you travel. The Washington Diplomat tour (4 days and 3 nights) included lodging, dinner at the Hard Rock Cafe, a day of sightseeing, and a choice of tours, from $269 to $632, per person, double occupancy. Other tours and additional nights are available. Groups of 20 or more should call ☎ 800/343-6768.
- **Globetrotters** (☎ 800/999-9696; www.globetrotters.com), a USTOA member, offered in 1999 a 2-night package to Washington for $389 per person, double occupancy of a room at Swissôtel Washington—The Watergate, including taxes and a night-time tour of the monuments. If any service is not delivered as described in the brochure, Globetrotters will issue an appropriate refund. The company also offers a Price Match Guarantee that will honor any competitor's published price at the same hotel, same room category, same length of stay, same travel dates, and comparable flights.

3

For Foreign Visitors

When Americans travel abroad, they are often reassured that language will not be a problem, because "everybody speaks English." If you are one who does speak English, naturally, you will have an easy time of it in Washington, D.C. But even if you do not speak the language, I can reassure you that Washington offers many forms of foreign language assistance.

Flip briefly to chapter 4 and read the section "Arriving by Plane" to find out how you can get immediate help communicating as soon as you arrive. Of the three airports, Washington Dulles International probably has the best foreign language assistance setup, because an arm of **Meridian International Center** is stationed here. The Meridian International Center (☎ **202/667-6800**) offers its multilingual services daily at the number listed above for help with sightseeing and other tourist needs, and at its information desk at Dulles (☎ **703/572-2536**). The center has on call a bank of volunteers who, together, speak more than 400 languages.

In Washington, D.C., several major attractions (the White House, the Kennedy Center, the Library of Congress, and the Smithsonian Institution) offer free brochures in several languages. The Smithsonian also welcomes international visitors at its Information Center with a multilingual slide show and audio phones. You can obtain Metro maps in French, German, Japanese, and Spanish by calling ☎ **888/METRO-INFO (888/638-7646)** and requesting that Metro send you a Visitor's Kit that includes a map in the specific language that you need. In addition, you'll discover multilingual staff at hotels, multilingual audio tapes provided on guided tours of the city or for rent at museums, and staff at your own country's embassy ready to handle your questions.

Here's more information to help you prepare for your trip to Washington.

1 Preparing for Your Trip

ENTRY REQUIREMENTS

Immigration laws are a hot political issue in the United States these days, and the following requirements may have changed somewhat by the time you plan your trip. Check at any U.S. embassy or consulate for current information and requirements. You can also plug into the **U.S. State Department** site at **www.state.gov**.

VISAS   The U.S. State Department has a **Visa Waiver Pilot Program** allowing citizens of certain countries to enter the United States without a visa for stays of up to 90 days. At press time these included Andorra, Argentina, Australia, Austria, Belgium, Brunei, Denmark, Finland, France, Germany, Iceland, Ireland, Italy, Japan, Liechtenstein, Luxembourg, Monaco, the Netherlands, New Zealand, Norway, San Marino, Slovenia, Spain, Sweden, Switzerland, and the United Kingdom. Citizens of these countries need only a valid passport and a round-trip air or cruise ticket in their possession upon arrival. If they first enter the United States, they may also visit Mexico, Canada, Bermuda, and/or the Caribbean islands and return to the United States without a visa. Further information is available from any U.S. embassy or consulate. Canadian citizens may enter the United States without visas; they need only proof of residence.

Citizens of all other countries must have (1) a valid passport that expires at least 6 months later than the scheduled end of their visit to the United States, and (2) a tourist visa, which may be obtained without charge from any U.S. consulate.

Obtaining a Visa   To obtain a visa, the traveler must submit a completed application form (either in person or by mail) with a 1½-inch-square photo, and must demonstrate binding ties to a residence abroad. Usually you can obtain a visa at once or within 24 hours, but it may take longer during the summer rush from June through August. If you cannot go in person, contact the nearest U.S. embassy or consulate for directions on applying by mail. Your travel agent or airline office may also be able to provide you with visa applications and instructions. The U.S. consulate or embassy that issues your visa will determine whether you will be issued a multiple- or single-entry visa and any restrictions regarding the length of your stay.

British subjects can obtain up-to-date passport and visa information by calling the **U.S. Embassy Visa Information Line** (☎ **0891/200-290**) or the **London Passport Office** (☎ **0990/210-410** for recorded information).

Immigration Questions   Telephone operators will answer your inquiries regarding U.S. immigration policies or laws at the **Immigration and Naturalization Service's Customer Information Center** (☎ **800/375-5283**). Representatives are available from 9am to 3pm, Monday through Friday. Also, access the Web site at www.ins.usdoj.gov.

MEDICAL REQUIREMENTS   Unless you're arriving from an area known to be suffering from an epidemic (particularly cholera or yellow fever), inoculations or vaccinations are not required for entry into the United States. If you have a disease that requires treatment with narcotics or syringe-administered medications, carry a valid signed prescription from your physician to allay any suspicions that you may be smuggling narcotics (a serious offense that carries severe penalties in the United States).

The Immigration and Naturalization Service receives so many questions about U.S. policy regarding HIV-positive visitors that the public affairs office has issued a fact sheet on the subject:

"HIV Infection: Inadmissibility and Waiver Policies": "Section 212(a)(1)(A)(i) of the Immigration and Nationality Act renders inadmissible any applicant for a visa or admission who is found, according to regulations published by the Secretary of Health and Human Services (HHS), to have a communicable disease of public health significance, which includes HIV infection. However, in view of humanitarian and family unity concerns, the law also provides waivers of inadmissibility, which are discretionary and granted on a case-by-case basis.

Two specific waiver policies have been implemented for applicants seeking admission as **nonimmigrants** (for a temporary period of time), who are inadmissible due to HIV infection:

- **Routine HIV Waiver Policy.** Nonimmigrants may be granted a waiver for admission to the United States for 30 days or less to attend conferences, receive medical treatment, visit close family members, or conduct business. The applicant must demonstrate that he or she is not currently afflicted with symptoms of the disease; there are sufficient assets, such as insurance, that would cover any medical care that might be required in the event of illness while in the United States; the proposed visit to the United States is for 30 days or less; and that the visit will not pose a danger to public health in the United States.
- **The "Designated Event" Policy.** This policy facilitates the admission of HIV-positive persons to attend certain "designated events," which are considered to be in the public interest, such as academic and educational conferences and international sports events. To initiate the process, HHS writes a letter to the Department of State (DOS) regarding a specific event. DOS recommends the event to the Attorney General, who "designates" the event and authorizes a blanket waiver. This blanket waiver allows HIV-positive applicants—seeking admission to the US specifically to participate in the "designated event"—to be admitted for the duration of the event without being questioned about their HIV status."

For up-to-the-minute information concerning HIV-positive travelers, contact the Center for Disease Control's **National Center for HIV** (☎ 404/332-4559; www.hivatis.org) or the **Gay Men's Health Crisis** (☎ 212/367-1000; www.gmhc.org).

DRIVER'S LICENSES   Foreign driver's licenses are mostly recognized in the United States, although you may want to get an international driver's license if your home license is not written in English.

PASSPORT INFORMATION

Safeguard your passport in an inconspicuous, inaccessible place like a money belt. If you lose it, visit the nearest consulate of your native country as soon as possible for a replacement. Passport applications are downloadable from the Internet sites listed below.

For Residents of Canada

You can pick up a passport application at one of 28 regional passport offices or most travel agencies. The passport is valid for five years and costs $60. Children under 16 may be included on a parent's passport but need their own to travel unaccompanied by the parent. Applications, which must be accompanied by two identical passport-sized photographs and proof of Canadian citizenship, are available at travel agencies throughout Canada or from the central **Passport Office, Department of Foreign Affairs and International Trade,** Ottawa, Ont. K1A 0G3 (☎ 800/567-6868; www.dfait-maeci.gc.ca/passport). Processing takes 5 to 10 days if you apply in person, or about three weeks by mail.

For Residents of the United Kingdom

To pick up an application for a regular 10-year passport (the Visitor's Passport has been abolished), visit your nearest passport office, major post office, or travel agency. You can also contact the London Passport Office at ☎ 020/7271-3000 or www.open.gov.uk/ukpass/ukpass.htm. Passports are 21£ for adults and 11£ for children under 16.

CUSTOMS
WHAT YOU CAN BRING IN

Every visitor over 21 years of age may bring in, free of duty, the following: (1) 1 liter of wine or hard liquor; (2) 200 cigarettes, 100 cigars (but not from Cuba), or 3 pounds of smoking tobacco; and (3) $100 worth of gifts. These exemptions are offered to travelers who spend at least 72 hours in the United States and who have not claimed them within the preceding 6 months. Foreign tourists may bring in or take out up to $10,000 in U.S. or foreign currency with no formalities; larger sums must be declared to U.S. Customs on entering or leaving, which includes filing form CM 4790.

You may bring in certain food products, such as bakery items and all cured cheeses. To bring fruits, vegetables, plants, cuttings, seeds, unprocessed plant products, and certain endangered plant species into the country, you must obtain an import permit, or else you will not be allowed to carry those things into the United States. The only meat you may bring in is canned meat that the inspector can determine has been commercially canned, cooked in the container, hermetically sealed, and requires no refrigeration; you are otherwise prohibited or restricted from bringing any other meat, livestock, poultry, or their by-products into the country.

For more specific information regarding U.S. Customs, call your nearest U.S. embassy or consulate, or the **U.S. Customs** office at ☎ **202/927-1770** or www.customs.ustreas.gov. Ask for copies of "Visiting the United States," which offers travelers more information about what U.S. Customs allows you to bring in. You can also call the U.S. Department of Agriculture's Animal and Plant Health Inspection Service (☎ **301/734-8455**) and ask for a copy of "Traveler's Tips," which provides detailed information on bringing food, plant, and animal products into the United States.

WHAT YOU CAN TAKE HOME

U.K. citizens returning from the United States have a customs allowance of: 200 cigarettes; 50 cigars; 250g of smoking tobacco; 2 liters of still table wine; 1 liter of spirits or strong liqueurs (over 22% volume); 2 liters of fortified wine, sparkling wine or other liqueurs; 60cc (ml) perfume; 250cc (ml) of toilet water; and 145£ worth of all other goods, including gifts and souvenirs. People under 17 cannot have the tobacco or alcohol allowance. For more information, contact HM Customs & Excise, Passenger Enquiry Point, 2nd floor Wayfarer House, Great South West Road, Feltham, Middlesex TW14 8NP (☎ **020/8910-3744;** from outside the U.K. 44/181-910-3744), or at www.open.gov.uk.

For a clear summary of Canadian rules, write for the booklet *I Declare,* issued by **Revenue Canada,** 2265 St. Laurent Blvd., Ottawa K1G 4KE (☎ **613/993-0534**). Canada allows its citizens a $500 exemption, and you're allowed to bring back duty-free 200 cigarettes, 2.2 pounds of tobacco, 40 imperial ounces of liquor, and 50 cigars. In addition, you're allowed to mail gifts to Canada from abroad at the rate of Can$60 a day, provided they're unsolicited and don't contain alcohol or tobacco (write on the package "Unsolicited gift, under $60 value"). All valuables should be declared on the Y-38 form before departure from Canada, including serial numbers of valuables you already own, such as expensive foreign cameras. *Note:* The $500 exemption can only be used once a year and only after an absence of seven days.

INSURANCE

Although it's not required of travelers, health insurance is highly recommended. Unlike many European countries, the United States does not usually offer free or low-cost medical care to its citizens or visitors. Doctors and hospitals are expensive, and in most cases will require advance payment or proof of coverage before they render their services. Policies can cover everything from the loss or theft of your baggage and trip cancellation to the guarantee of bail in case you're arrested. Good policies will also cover the costs of an accident, repatriation, or death. See "Insurance" in chapter 2 for more information. Packages such as **Europ Assistance** in Europe are sold by automobile clubs and travel agencies at attractive rates. **Worldwide Assistance Services, Inc.** (☎ **800/821-2828**) is the agent for Europ Assistance in the United States.

Though lack of health insurance may prevent you from being admitted to a hospital in nonemergencies, don't worry about being left on a street corner to die: The American way is to fix you now and bill the living daylights out of you later.

INSURANCE FOR BRITISH TRAVELERS   Most big travel agents offer their own insurance and will probably try to sell you their package when you book a holiday. Think before you sign. **Britain's Consumers' Association** recommends that you insist on seeing the policy and reading the fine print before buying travel insurance. **The Association of British Insurers** (☎ **020/7600-3333**) gives advice by phone and publishes the free *Holiday Insurance,* a guide to policy provisions and prices. You might also shop around for better deals: Try **Columbus Travel Insurance Ltd. (☎ 020/ 7375-0011)** or, for students, **Campus Travel (☎ 020/7730-2101)**.

INSURANCE FOR CANADIAN TRAVELERS   Canadians should check with their provincial health plan offices or call **HealthCanada (☎ 613/957-2991)** to find out the extent of their coverage and what documentation and receipts they must take home in case they are treated in the United States.

MONEY

CURRENCY   The U.S. monetary system is painfully simple: The most common bills (all ugly, all green) are the $1 (colloquially, a "buck"), $5, $10, and $20 denominations. There are also $2 bills (seldom encountered), $50 bills, and $100 bills (the last two are usually not welcome as payment for small purchases). Note that a newly redesigned $100 and $50 bill were introduced in 1996, and a redesigned $20 bill in 1998. Expect to see redesigned $10 and $5 notes in the year 2000. Despite rumors to the contrary, the old-style bills are still legal tender.

There are six denominations of coins: 1¢ (1 cent, or a penny); 5¢ (5 cents, or a nickel); 10¢ (10 cents, or a dime); 25¢ (25 cents, or a quarter); 50¢ (50 cents, or a half dollar); and, prized by collectors, the rare $1 piece (the older, large silver dollar and the newer, small Susan B. Anthony coin). A new gold $1 piece will be introduced by the year 2000.

Note: It's best not to change foreign money (or traveler's checks denominated in a currency other than U.S. dollars) at a small-town bank, or even a branch in a big city; in fact, leave any currency other than U.S. dollars at home—it may prove a greater nuisance to you than it's worth.

TRAVELER'S CHECKS   Though traveler's checks are widely accepted, make sure that they're denominated in U.S. dollars, as foreign-currency checks are often difficult to exchange. The three traveler's checks that are most widely recognized—and least likely to be denied—are **Visa, American Express,** and **Thomas Cook.** Be sure to record the numbers of the checks, and keep that information separately in case they get lost or stolen. Most businesses are pretty good about taking traveler's checks, but you're better off cashing them in at a bank (in small amounts, of course) and paying in cash. Remember: you'll need identification, such as a driver's license or passport, to change a traveler's check.

CREDIT CARDS & ATMS   Credit cards are the most widely used form of payment in the United States: **Visa** (BarclayCard in Britain), **MasterCard** (Eurocard in Europe, Access in Britain, Chargex in Canada), **American Express, Diners Club, Discover,** and **Carte Blanche.** You must have a credit or charge card to rent a car. There are, however, a handful of stores and restaurants that do not take credit cards, so be sure to ask in advance. Most businesses display a sticker near their entrance to let you know which cards they accept. (*Note:* Often businesses require a minimum purchase price, usually around $10, to use a credit card.)

It is strongly recommended that you bring at least one major credit card. Hotels, car-rental companies, and airlines usually require a credit-card imprint as a deposit against expenses, and in an emergency a credit card can be priceless. You'll find automated teller machines (ATMs) on just about every block—at least in almost every town—across the country. See chapter 2 for more information about use of credit cards and ATMS.

SAFETY

GENERAL SAFETY SUGGESTIONS   While tourist areas are generally safe, crime is on the increase everywhere, and U.S. urban areas tend to be less safe than those in Europe or Japan. You should always stay alert. It is wise to ask your hotel front-desk staff or the city's tourist office if you're in doubt about which neighborhoods are safe.

Avoid deserted areas, especially at night, and don't go into public parks at night unless there's a concert or similar occasion that will attract a crowd.

Avoid carrying valuables with you on the street, and don't display expensive cameras or electronic equipment. If you are using a map, consult it inconspicuously—or better yet, try to study it before you leave your room. In general, the more you "look" like a tourist, the more likely someone will try to take advantage of you. If you're walking, pay attention to who is near you as you walk. If you are attending a convention or event where you wear a name tag, remove it before venturing outside. Hold onto your pocketbook, and place your billfold in an inside pocket. In theaters, restaurants, and other public places, keep your possessions in sight.

Remember also that hotels are open to the public, and in a large hotel, security may not be able to screen everyone entering. Always lock your room door.

DRIVING SAFETY   Question your rental agency about personal safety and ask for a traveler-safety brochure when you pick up your car. Obtain written directions—or a map with the route clearly marked—from the agency showing how to get to your destination. (Many agencies now offer the option of renting a cellular phone for the duration of your car rental; check with the rental agent when you pick up the car.) And, if possible, arrive and depart during daylight hours.

Recently, more and more crime has involved cars and drivers. If you drive off a highway into a doubtful neighborhood, leave the area as quickly as possible. If you have an accident, even on the highway, assess the situation or wait until the police arrive before you get out of the car. If you're bumped from behind on the street or are involved in a minor accident with no injuries and the situation appears to be suspicious, motion to the other driver to follow you. Handle the situation at the nearest police precinct, well-lit service station, or 24-hour store.

Always try to park in well-lit and well-traveled areas if possible. Never leave any packages or valuables in sight. If someone attempts to rob you or steal your car, don't try to resist—report the incident to the police department immediately by calling ☎ **911.**

2 Getting to the U.S.

BY AIR   International airlines with scheduled flights into National are Air Canada (☎ **800/776-3000;** www.aircanada.ca) and Canadian Airlines (☎ **800/426-7000;** www.cdnair.ca). International airlines with scheduled flights into BWI include Air Canada, British Airways (☎ **800/247-9297;** www.british-airways.com), El Al Israel (☎ **800/223-6700;** www.elal.co.il), and Icelandair (☎ **800/223-5500;** www. icelandair.com). International airlines with scheduled flights into Dulles include Air Canada, Air France (☎ **800/237-2747;** www.airfrance.com), All Nippon Airways (☎ **800/235-9262;** www.allnipponairways.com), British Airways, KLM Royal Dutch

(☎ **800/374-7747;** www.klm.nl); Lufthansa (☎ **800/645-3880;** www.lufthansa. com); Saudi Arabian Airlines (☎ **800/472-8342;** www.saudiarabian-airlines.com), Swissair (☎ **800/221-4750;** www.swissair.com), and Virgin Atlantic (☎ **800/ 862-8621;** www.fly.virgin.com).

Read Frommer's Online Directory in the back of the book for tips on using the Internet to find a good airfare. If you are coming from Europe, you will want to know about Discount Tickets, www.discount-tickets.com, a Web site operated by the European Travel Network, which offers discounts on airfares, accommodations, car rentals and tours. It deals with flights between the United States and other countries, so it's most useful for travelers coming to Washington from abroad.

Travelers from overseas can take advantage of the APEX (advance purchase excursion) fares offered by all the major U.S. and European carriers.

BY TRAIN   Amtrak (☎ 800/USA-RAIL; www.amtrak.com) operates two trains between Canada and Washington: The Vermonter travels from Montreal to Washington and Washington to Montreal daily, stopping in Vermont, Massachusetts, Connecticut, New York, and so on; the Maple Leaf operates in both directions, Washington to Toronto and Toronto to Washington daily, via stops in New York State, Philadelphia, and Ontario. See chapter 2 "Getting There," for more information on train travel.

3 Getting Around the U.S.

BY PLANE   Some large American airlines, for example, American, Northwest, United, and Delta, offer travelers on their trans-Atlantic or trans-Pacific flights special discount tickets allowing travel between U.S. destinations at minimum rates. (Two such programs are American's **Visit USA** and Delta's **Discover America.**) These tickets are not on sale in the United States and must, therefore, be purchased before you leave your foreign point of departure. This arrangement is the best, easiest, and fastest way to see the United States at low cost. You should obtain information well in advance from your travel agent or the office of the airline concerned, since the conditions attached to these discount tickets can be changed without advance notice.

If you are arriving by air, allow lots of time to make connections between international and domestic flights—an average of two to three hours at least.

In contrast, air travelers from Canada, Bermuda, and some places in the Caribbean can sometimes go through Customs and Immigration at the point of departure, which is much quicker and less painful.

BY TRAIN   International visitors, except Canadians, can buy a **USA Railpass,** good for 15 or 30 days of unlimited travel on Amtrak (☎ 800/USA-RAIL). The pass is available through many foreign travel agents. Prices in 1999 for a 15-day pass were $285 off-peak, $425 peak; a 30-day pass cost $375 off-peak, $535 peak. (With a foreign passport, you can also buy passes at some Amtrak offices in the United States, including locations in Chicago, New York, Boston, and Washington, D.C.) Reservations are generally required and should be made for each part of your trip as early as possible.

If your travel plans include visiting both the United States and Canada, you need to purchase a **North American Railpass.** Also available through Amtrak is an **Airail** pass, a joint venture of United Airlines and Amtrak that's available as part of **Amtrak Vacations** packages (☎ **800/321-8684**) (see chapter 2 for information on package deals). The pass allows you to arrive in Washington (from a location within the U.S.) by one mode, plane or rail, and return via the other. During the train portion of your trip, you can make up to three stops along the way at no extra charge.

BY BUS   Although bus travel is often the most economical form of public transit for short hops between U.S. cities, it can also be slow and uncomfortable—certainly not an option for everyone (particularly when Amtrak, which is far more luxurious, offers similar rates). **Greyhound/Trailways** (☎ 800/231-2222), the sole nationwide bus line, offers an **Ameripass** for unlimited travel for 7 days at $199, 15 days at $299, 30 days at $409, and 60 days at $599. Passes must be purchased at a Greyhound terminal. Special rates are available for senior citizens and students.

Fast Facts: For the Foreign Traveler

Automobile Organizations   Auto clubs will supply maps, suggested routes, guidebooks, accident and bail-bond insurance, and emergency road service. The **American Automobile Association (AAA)** is the major auto club in the United States. If you belong to an auto club in your home country, inquire about AAA reciprocity before you leave. You may be able to join AAA even if you're not a member of a reciprocal club; to inquire, call AAA (☎ **800/763-9900**). In the Washington, D.C. area, AAA's emergency road service telephone number is ☎ **800/AAA-HELP.**

Business Hours   See "Fast Facts" in chapter 4.

Climate   See "When to Go" in chapter 2.

Currency   See "Entry Requirements" and "Money" under "Preparing for Your Trip," above.

Currency Exchange   In addition to the currency exchange desks at each of the three airports, you will find a Thomas Cook currency exchange office (☎ **800/ CURRENCY**) at Union Station, opposite Gate G on the train concourse, at the Crestar Bank, 1445 New York Ave. NW (☎ **202/879-6000**), and at the Riggs Bank, 800 17th St. NW (☎ **301/887-6000**).

Drinking Laws   See "Liquor Laws" in Fast Facts, chapter 4.

Electricity   Like Canada, the United States uses 110 to 120 volts AC (60 cycles), compared to 220 to 240 volts AC (50 cycles) in most of Europe. If your small appliances use 220 to 240 volts, you'll need a 110-volt transformer and a plug adapter with two flat parallel pins to operate them here. Downward converters that change 220–240 volts to 110–120 volts are difficult to find in the United States, so bring one with you.

Embassies & Consulates   All embassies are located in Washington, D.C., since it's the nation's capital, and many consulates are located here, as well. Here are several embassy addresses: Australia, 1601 Massachusetts Ave. NW (☎ **202/ 797-3000;** www.austemb.org); Canada, 501 Pennsylvania Ave. NW (☎ **202/ 682-1740;** www.cdnemb-washdc.org); France, 4101 Reservoir Rd. NW (☎ **202/944-6000;** www.info-france-usa.org); Germany, 4645 Reservoir Rd. NW (☎ **202/298-4000;** www.germany-info.org); Ireland, 2234 Massachusetts Ave. NW (☎ **202/462-3939;** www.irelandemb.org); Japan, 2520 Massachusetts Ave. NW (☎ **202/238-6700;** www.embjapan.org); Netherlands, 4200 Linnean Ave. NW (☎ **202/244-5300;** www.netherlands-emb.org); New Zealand, 37 Observatory Circle, NW (☎ **202/328-4800;** www.emb.com/nzemb); and the United Kingdom, 3100 Massachusetts Ave. NW (☎ **202/462-1340;** www. britain-info.org). You can obtain the telephone numbers of other embassies and consulates by calling information in Washington, D.C. (dial ☎ **411** within D.C. and its metropolitan area). Or consult the phone book in your hotel room.

Emergencies Call ☎ **911** to report a fire, call the police, or get an ambulance anywhere in the United States. This is a toll-free call (no coins are required at public telephones). See chapter 4 for more information.

Gasoline (Petrol) Petrol is known as gasoline (or simply gas) in the United States, and petrol stations are known as both gas stations and service stations. Gasoline costs about half as much here as it does in Europe (about $1.05 per gallon at press time), and taxes are already included in the printed price. One U.S. gallon equals 3.8 liters or .85 Imperial gallons.

Holidays Banks, government offices, post offices, and many stores, restaurants, and museums are closed on the following legal national holidays: January 1 (New Year's Day), the third Monday in January (Martin Luther King, Jr. Day), the third Monday in February (Presidents' Day, Washington's Birthday), the last Monday in May (Memorial Day), July 4 (Independence Day), the first Monday in September (Labor Day), the second Monday in October (Columbus Day), November 11 (Veterans' Day/Armistice Day), the fourth Thursday in November (Thanksgiving Day), and December 25 (Christmas). Also, the Tuesday following the first Monday in November is Election Day and is a federal government holiday in presidential-election years (held every four years, and next in 2000).

Legal Aid The foreign tourist will probably never become involved with the American legal system. If you are pulled over for a minor infraction (for example, speeding), never attempt to pay the fine directly to a police officer; this could be construed as attempted bribery, a much more serious crime. Pay fines by mail, or directly into the hands of the clerk of the court. If accused of a more serious offense, say and do nothing before consulting a lawyer. Here the burden is on the state to prove a person's guilt beyond a reasonable doubt, and everyone has the right to remain silent, whether he or she is suspected of a crime or actually arrested. Once arrested, a person can make one telephone call to a party of his or her choice. Call your embassy or consulate.

Mail If you want your mail to follow you on your vacation and you aren't sure of your address, your mail can be sent to you, in your name, c/o General Delivery at the main post office of the city or region where you expect to be. The addressee must pick it up in person and produce proof of identity (for example, driver's license, credit or charge card, or passport). In Washington, the main post office is located at 900 Brentwood Rd. NE, Washington, DC 20066-9998, USA (☎ **202/636-1532**). It's open Monday to Friday 8am to 8pm, Saturday 8am to 6pm, and Sunday noon to 6pm.

Generally found at intersections, mailboxes are blue with a red-and-white stripe and carry the inscription U.S. MAIL. If your mail is addressed to a U.S. destination, don't forget to add the five-digit postal code (or ZIP code), after the two-letter abbreviation of the state to which the mail is addressed. At press time, domestic postage rates were 20¢ for a postcard and 33¢ for a letter. For international mail, a first-class letter of up to one-half ounce costs 60¢ (46¢ to Canada and 40¢ to Mexico); a first-class postcard costs 50¢ (40¢ to Canada and 35¢ Mexico); and a preprinted postal aerogramme costs 50¢.

Newspapers & Magazines National newspapers include the *New York Times,* the *Washington Post, USA Today,* and the *Wall Street Journal.* There are also a great many national newsweeklies including *Newsweek, Time,* and *U.S. News and World Report.* For information on local Washington, D.C., periodicals, see "Newspapers/Magazines" in "Fast Facts: Washington, D.C." in chapter 4. To find newspapers and magazines from your own country, head to The Newsroom at

1753 Connecticut Ave. NW, just above Dupont Circle (☎ **202/332-1489**); it's open 7 days a week. South of the Newsroom is another store that sells newspapers and magazines from around the world: News World, 1001 Connecticut Ave. NW (☎ **202/872-0190**).

Taxes In the United States there is no value-added tax (VAT) or other indirect tax at the national level. Every state, county, and city has the right to levy its own local tax on all purchases, including hotel and restaurant checks, airline tickets, and so on.

The sales tax on merchandise is 5.75% in the District, 5% in Maryland, and 4.5% in Virginia. The tax on restaurant meals is 10% in the District, 5% in Maryland, and 7.5% in Virginia.

In the District, you pay 14.5% hotel tax. The hotel tax in Maryland varies by county but averages 12%. The hotel tax in Virginia also varies by county, averaging about 9.75%.

Telephone, Telegraph, Telex & Fax The telephone system in the United States is run by private corporations, so rates, especially for long-distance service and operator-assisted calls, can vary widely. Generally, hotel surcharges on long-distance and local calls are astronomical, so you're usually better off using a public pay telephone, which you'll find clearly marked in most public buildings and private establishments as well as on the street. Convenience grocery stores and gas stations always have them. Many convenience groceries and packaging services sell prepaid calling cards in denominations up to $50; these can be the least expensive way to call home. Many public phones at airports now accept American Express, MasterCard, and Visa credit cards. Local calls made from public pay phones cost 35¢. Pay phones do not accept pennies, and few will take anything larger than a quarter.

Most long-distance and international calls can be dialed directly from any phone. For calls within the United States and to Canada, dial ☎ 1 followed by the area code and the seven-digit number. For other international calls, dial ☎ 011 followed by the country code, city code, and the telephone number of the person you are calling. Calls to area codes 800, 888, and 877 are toll-free. However, calls to numbers in area codes 700 and 900 (chat lines, bulletin boards, dating services, and so on) can be very expensive—usually a charge of 95¢ to $3 or more per minute, and they sometimes have minimum charges that can run as high as $15 or more.

For reversed-charge or collect calls, and for person-to-person calls, dial ☎ 0 (zero, not the letter "O") followed by the area code and number you want; an operator will then come on the line, and you should specify that you are calling collect, or person-to-person, or both. If your operator-assisted call is international, ask for the overseas operator. For local directory assistance (information), dial ☎ 411; for long-distance information, dial ☎ 1, then the appropriate area code and 555-1212.

Telegraph and telex services are provided primarily by Western Union. You can bring your telegram into the nearest Western Union office (there are hundreds across the country) or dictate it over the phone (☎ **800/325-6000**). You can also telegraph money or have it telegraphed to you, very quickly over the Western Union system, but this service can cost as much as 15% to 20% of the amount sent.

Most hotels have fax machines available for guest use (be sure to ask about the charge to use it), and many hotel rooms are even wired for guests' fax machines. A less expensive way to send and receive faxes may be at stores such as Mail Boxes

Etc., a national chain of packing service shops (look in the Yellow Pages directory under "Packing Services").

There are two kinds of telephone directories in the United States. The so-called White Pages list private households and business subscribers in alphabetical order. The inside front cover lists emergency numbers for police, fire, ambulance, the Coast Guard, poison-control center, crime-victims hot line, and so on. The first few pages will tell you how to make long-distance and international calls, complete with country codes and area codes. Government numbers are usually printed on blue paper within the White Pages. Printed on yellow paper, the so-called Yellow Pages list all local services, businesses, industries, and houses of worship according to activity with an index at the front or back.

Time The continental United States is divided into four time zones: eastern standard time (EST), central standard time (CST), mountain standard time (MST), and Pacific standard time (PST). Alaska and Hawaii have their own zones. For example, noon in **Washington, D.C. (EST)** is 11am in Chicago (CST), 10am in Denver (MST), 9am in Los Angeles (PST), 8am in Anchorage (AST), and 7am in Honolulu (HST). Daylight saving time is in effect from 1am on the first Sunday in April through 1am the last Sunday in October, except in Arizona, Hawaii, part of Indiana, and Puerto Rico. Daylight saving time moves the clock 1 hour ahead of standard time. On the last Sunday in October, everyone (except those living in the areas mentioned above) sets the clocks back 1 hour.

Tipping Tipping is so ingrained in the American way of life that the annual income tax of tip-earning service personnel is based on how much they should have received in light of their employers' gross revenues. Accordingly, they may have to pay tax on a tip you didn't actually give them. Here are some rules of thumb: In hotels, tip bellhops at least $1 per bag ($2 to $3 if you have a lot of luggage) and tip the chamber staff $1 per day. Tip the doorman or concierge only if he or she has provided you with some specific service (for example, calling a cab for you or obtaining difficult-to-get theater tickets). Tip the valet parking attendant $1 every time you get your car.

In restaurants, bars, and nightclubs, tip service staff 15% to 20% of the check, tip bartenders 10% to 15%, tip checkroom attendants $1 per garment, and tip valet-parking attendants $1 per vehicle. Tip the doorman only if he has provided you with some specific service (such as calling a cab for you). Tipping is not expected in cafeterias and fast-food restaurants.

Tip cab drivers 15% of the fare.

As for other service personnel, tip skycaps at airports at least $1 per bag ($2 to $3 if you have a lot of luggage) and tip hairdressers and barbers 15% to 20%.

Toilets You won't find public toilets or rest rooms on the streets in most U.S. cities, but they can be found in hotel lobbies, bars, restaurants, museums, department stores, railway and bus stations, or service stations. Note, however, that restaurants and bars in heavily visited areas may reserve their rest rooms for the use of their patrons. You can avoid arguments by paying for a cup of coffee or a soft drink, which will qualify you as a patron. Large hotels and fast-food restaurants are probably the best bet for good, clean facilities. If possible, avoid the toilets at parks and beaches, which tend to be dirty.

Getting to Know Washington, D.C. **4**

With its skyscraper-less skyline, Washington enables even the first time visitor to gain a general sense of direction in the city: All you have to do is look for the buildings that stand out—the Washington Monument, the U.S. Capitol, the Washington National Cathedral—and you can often figure out which way to go. But how to get from here to there is another question. And what are the safest, quickest, and most pleasant routes? And what will you see along the way? And what are the neighborhoods you'll be passing through? The information in this chapter should help you find your answers.

1 Orientation

ARRIVING
BY PLANE

Baltimore-Washington International Airport (BWI) lies about 30 miles north of Washington along a route (the busy I-95) that will take you a good 45 minutes to travel into downtown. The airport itself, however, makes up for the inconveniences of traffic and location, by providing exemplary customer services. These services include two information desks located on the upper level near the ticket counters, and one information desk on the lower (baggage claim) level, near the international arrivals gates (☎ **800/435-9294** for information and paging); two Travelers Aid desks (☎ **410/859-7207**), on the upper level, one at pier C, the other at pier D; foreign language assistance in French, Spanish, German and Arabic (you must use one of the courtesy phones located throughout the airport and dial ☎ **410/859-7111**); several locations for buying insurance and exchanging currency (☎ **410/859-5997**); two automated teller machines (ATMs), near the ticket counters on the upper level; plenty of public phones, including those next to the Burger King on the upper level, between piers C and D, which have computerized instructions in German, French, and Spanish, as well as Telecommunications Device for the Deaf (TDD) services and voice relay phones; many rest rooms, restaurants, and bars; a romper room for kids and a small aviation museum.

BWI offers the most convenient **car rental** arrangement of the three area airports, with reservation desks located inside the airport, near baggage claim carousels. Upon confirming your reservation and obtaining your key, you simply walk from the terminal a few yards to the on-site lot, where all rental cars are held; on-site rental agencies include **Avis** (☎ 410/859-1680), **Alamo** (☎ 410/850-5011), **Budget** (☎ 410/ 859-0850), **Dollar** (☎ 410/684-3316), **Hertz** (☎ 410/850-7400), **National** (☎ 410/859-8860), and **Thrifty** (☎ 410/859-1136). (For car rental companies' toll-free 800 numbers and Web sites, consult the appendix at the back of the book.

Other useful phone numbers are: lost and found (☎ **410/859-7387**), police (☎ **410/859-7040**), and parking lots and garage (☎ **410/859-9230**); the airport's Web site is http://www.bwiairport.com.

If you are not renting a car, transportation from BWI to downtown Washington is via taxi, shuttle van, Amtrak and MARC (Maryland Rural Commuter) trains, and limousine, all of which depart from the lower level, outside the baggage claim area. Expect a trip by **taxi** (☎ **410/859-1100** for information) to cost $45 and take 45 minutes. **SuperShuttle** (☎ **800/258-3826**) operates seven-passenger blue vans that provide shared-ride, door-to-door service between the airport and downtown and suburban locations; expect to pay $28 to $30 one way ($5 for each additional passenger in your party), with the van departing from BWI within 60 minutes of your request at the SuperShuttle desk in the baggage claim area. SuperShuttle also runs scheduled departures from BWI to the downtown area, every 30 minutes from 6am to 11:30pm, for $21 one-way. **Amtrak** (☎ **800/872-7245**) and the **Maryland Rural Commuter** service (☎ **800/325-7245**) travel between the BWI Railway Station and Washington's Union Station, about a 30-minute ride. Amtrak's is daily service ($14 per person, one-way), while MARC's is weekdays only ($5 per person, one-way). A courtesy shuttle runs every 15 minutes or so between the airport and the train station; stop at the desk near the baggage claim area to check for the next departure time of both the shuttle bus and the train. Trains depart about every 30 minutes during morning and evening rush hours, about every 50 minutes the rest of the day.

Airport area hotels and motels operate free shuttle service from BWI to their properties; ask for details when you book your stay at one of these hotels. (See chapter 5 for a description of airport hotels.)

Finally, you can arrange for door-to-door **limousine** service by calling ☎ **202/ 737-2600;** the fare for a ride to K Street NW in downtown Washington will run you $63 for the car, plus $9.45 driver gratuity.

If you rent a car, here's how you reach Washington: Look for signs for I-195 and follow I-195 west until you see signs for Washington and the Baltimore-Washington Parkway (I-295); head south on I-295. When I-295 forks, one direction leading to Bladensburg Road, the other to Route 50/New York Avenue, bear right and follow the Route 50/New York Avenue lanes, which lead right into the District. New York Avenue will take you right into the downtown; ask your hotel for specific directions from New York Avenue NE.

Note: Because of repair work underway throughout the year 2000 on precisely that portion of New York Avenue linking the Baltimore-Washington Parkway, please consider this alternate route: From BWI Airport, take I-195 to I-95, headed south toward Washington; when you see the signs for I-495, move into one of the right-most lanes and pick up I-495 in the direction of Silver Spring/Bethesda. Stay on I-495 until you reach the Chevy Chase/Kensington exit. Stay left as you exit and take a left at the bottom of the ramp, onto Connecticut Ave. Follow Connecticut Avenue about 7 miles south, straight into the District; the avenue finally deadends at Lafayette Square, across from the White House. You'll want to ask your hotel for directions from Connecticut Avenue and K Street NW.

Ronald Reagan Washington National Airport (☎ **703/417-8000**) is just across the Potomac River from Washington, in Arlington, Virginia. Newly renovated to the tune of $1 billion, the airport is improved in nearly every way. You'll arrive on the second level; ticket counters are on the third level, baggage claim and ground transportation on the first level. The second, or concourse, level is where you'll get your questions answered: at either end of the new main concourse are both a general information desk and a customer service center (☎ **703/417-3200** or 3201), where you can exchange currency, purchase insurance, even recharge batteries. An enclosed passageway connects the main concourse to "historic Terminal A," where another general information desk operates, as well as a Travelers Aid desk (☎ **703/417-3972**). You should seek Travelers Aid assistance if you need foreign language or crisis help; a second Travelers Aid desk (☎ **703/417-1807**) operates on the baggage claim level of the main concourse. You'll find ATMs located near the customer service centers on the concourse level, and next to the Travelers Aid desk on the baggage claim level.

Hotel and car rental phone centers in the baggage claim areas are available to call for courtesy transportation to nearby motels and hotels (these are all Virginia properties—no District hotels offer airport transportation service), and for transportation to off-site car rental lots. Public phones located at gates 15 to 22 include data ports for laptops. Each bank of two or more phones has a telecommunications device for the deaf (TDD).

Most of the **car rental** agencies are located in parking garage A, which you get to by taking the complimentary Airport Shuttle (look for the sign posted at curbside outside the terminal). On site agencies include **Alamo** (☎ 703/684-0086), **Avis** (☎ 703/419-5815), **Budget** (☎ 703/920-3360), **Hertz** (☎ 703/419-6300), and **National** (☎ 703/783-1590). **Thrifty** (☎ 703/658-2200) is off-airport, but you still must go to garage A to catch a Thrifty shuttle. If you've rented from **Dollar** (☎ 703/519-8700) or **Enterprise** (☎ 703/553-7744), use a courtesy phone in the baggage claim area to call for a van and then head up one level to the arrivals curb, where the van will pick you up. (See appendix for toll-free numbers and Web sites.)

Other useful phone numbers are lost and found (☎ **703/417-8560**), parking lots and garage (☎ **703/417-4300**), and police (☎ **703/417-8560**); the airport's Web site is www.metwashairports.com/National.

The best way to get into the city is by **Metrorail** (☎ **202/637-7000**), whose Yellow and Blue lines stop at the airport and connect via an enclosed walkway to level 2, the concourse level, of the main (new) terminal. If yours is one of the airlines that still uses the old terminal (Midway, Northwest, TWA, and TW Express), or the connector (Continental, Continental Express), you will have a longer walk to reach the Metro station, and signs pointing the way can be confusing; ask an airport employee if you're headed in the right direction or, better yet, head out to the curb and hop a shuttle bus to the station, but be sure to ask the driver to let you know when you've reached Metro (it may not be obvious, and drivers don't announce the stops). **Metrobuses** (☎ **703/638-3780**) also serve the area, should you be going somewhere off the Metro route. But Metrorail is fastest, about a 20-minute, nonrush hour ride to downtown. It is safe, convenient, and cheap, costing $1.10 nonrush hour, $1.40 during rush hour.

Taxi service is available at the exits of Terminal A from the upper level roadway, and along the lower level roadway to Terminals B and C (just look for the signs); taxis cost about $9 and take about 20 minutes to reach downtown. **SuperShuttle** buses (☎ **800/258-3826**) offer shared-ride, door-to-door service between the airport and your destination, whether in the District or in a suburban location; fares are based on ZIP code, so expect to pay about $8 to reach downtown, and about $25 for Maryland and Virginia suburbs. To get ground transportation questions answered, visit the ground transportation information centers, located near baggage claim, or call ☎ **703/685-1400**.

To get downtown by car, follow the signs out of the airport for the George Washington Parkway. Stay on the GW Parkway until you see signs for I-395 North to Washington. Take the I-395 North exit to the 12th Street exit, which puts you at 12th Street and Constitution Avenue NW; ask your hotel for directions from that point. Or, take the more scenic route, always staying to the left on the GW Parkway as you follow the signs for Memorial Bridge; you'll be driving alongside the Potomac River, with the monuments in view across the river, then, as you cross over Memorial Bridge, you're greeted by the Lincoln Memorial. Stay left coming over the bridge, swoop around to the left of the Memorial, take a left on 23rd Street NW, a right on Constitution Avenue, and then left again on 15th Street NW (the Washington Monument will be to your right), if you want to be in the heart of downtown.

Washington Dulles International Airport (☎ 703/572-2700) is the least fun airport in which to arrive, thanks to a major renovation often held up by funding fights in Congress. Most flights arrive at midfield terminals B and C/D, where you follow the crowd to the mobile lounges, which you board and ride (for about 7 minutes) to reach the main terminal. The satellite terminals are actually rather attractive and offer decent shopping; the main terminal is another story. The number of open customer service, information and currency exchange desks is ever in a state of flux, and as you walk through the main terminal, you'll see entire walls boarded up. You can count on getting help from the Travelers Aid folks (☎ 703/572-8296, or 703/260-0175 for TDD service). Phone numbers for other help desks include ☎ 703/572-2536 and 703/572-2537 for international visitors information desk; ☎ 703/572-2963, 703/572-2969 for general service, foreign currency exchange, and insurance purchases. Restaurant offerings are sparse and the facilities tiny for such a large airport. ATMs, rest rooms, stamp vending machines, and phones, are plentiful, however.

At ground level in the main terminal are the baggage claim areas. A couple of tips: The most reliable source for finding out the number of the baggage carousel handling your flight's luggage is the "Arrivals" monitors you'll see posted throughout the terminal as you make your way to the baggage claim level. It has been my experience that the actual "Baggage Claim" monitors in the baggage claim area post the carousel numbers for every flight but the one on which you have arrived. Also, don't assume that because your flight is a domestic one that your luggage will not be found on an international arrivals baggage carousel; Dulles uses its international arrivals area for handling domestic flight luggage, too.

Baggage in hand, you're ready to tackle ground transportation. Head down the ramps from baggage claim, and you will find banks of monitors displaying information in eight languages for contacting airport area hotels and car-rental locations. A number of nearby hotels offer free shuttle service. Car-rental lots are located on the National Service Road, near satellite parking. These include **Alamo** (☎ 703/260-0182), **Avis** (☎ 703/661-3505), **Budget** (☎ 703/920-3360), **Dollar** (☎ 703/661-6630), **Enterprise** (☎ 703/661-8800), **Hertz** (☎ 703/471-6020), and **National** (☎ 703/471-5278). To reach the lots, head outside to the second curb, where car rental shuttle buses stop; shuttles come by every 5 minutes or so for each lot. **Thrifty** (☎ 703/471-4544) operates a lot separate from the airport; call them from the airport to request a pickup outside baggage claim. (See appendix for agencies' toll-free 800 numbers and Web sites.)

Other useful numbers: police ☎ 703/572-2950, lost and found ☎ 703/572-2954, and skycap and wheelchair services ☎ 703/661-8151 or 703/661-6239; the airport's Web site is www.metwashairports.com/Dulles.

To reach downtown Washington from Dulles by car, exit the airport and stay on the Dulles Access Road, which leads right into I-66 East. Follow I-66 East to exit 73, Rosslyn/Key Bridge. Ask your hotel for directions from this point.

Washington Flyer (☎ **703/685-1400**) maintains exclusive transportation service from Dulles. Go to one of the dispatchers on duty at the east and west ramps, down from baggage claim to arrange for transportation by taxi, SuperShuttle van, or Express bus. A **taxi** will cost about $40 to the downtown area, 26 miles from the airport. **Buses** run between the Dulles and downtown and between Dulles and National Airports. Fares to/from Dulles, to either downtown or National are $16 one way, $26 round-trip. Children 6 and under ride free. Service between Dulles and downtown runs in each direction about every 30 minutes weekdays, less frequently weekends. Service between the airports runs hourly weekdays, less frequently weekends. At the downtown terminal, near the convention center, you can board a free loop shuttle that goes to eight Washington hotels: the Washington Marriott Wardman Park, Omni Shoreham, Washington Hilton, Renaissance Mayflower, Washington Renaissance, Grand Hyatt, J. W. Marriott, and Hotel Harrington.

As at National Airport, Washington Flyer's **SuperShuttle** buses (☎ **800/ 258-3826**) offer shared-ride, door-to-door service between Dulles Airport and your destination, whether in the District or in a suburban location; fares are based on ZIP code, so expect to pay about $20 to reach downtown.

Finally, you can take public transportation, though it's a little cumbersome. Here's what you do: Go to the Washington Flyer desk and purchase a ticket for a Washington Flyer Express Bus, board where directed, and get off at the West Falls Church Metro station, where you board a **Metro** Orange line train. The Orange line will make stops in Arlington and Rosslyn in Virginia before it reaches the District. If you want to get to the heart of downtown, you probably want to go as far as Metro Center, which is the major transfer point to other Metro lines and stops throughout the city. The cost for the bus is $8, add $2.20 (rush hour) or $1.60 (nonrush hour) for the Metro ride; the trip will take you about an hour.

BY TRAIN

Amtrak (☎ **800/USA-RAIL;** www.amtrak.com) trains arrive at historic Union Station (☎ **202/371-9441**), 50 Massachusetts Ave. NE, a magnificently restored turn-of-the-century beaux arts masterpiece. Offering a three-level marketplace of shops and restaurants, this stunning depot is conveniently located and connects with Metro service; you'll see signs directing you to the Metro's Red Line station even before you reach the main hall of Union Station. Union Station is a stone's throw from Capitol Hill, within walking distance of a number of hotels (see the Capitol Hill section of chapter 5), and a short cab or Metro ride to central downtown and other parts of the city. Proceed through the grand arcade straight out through its front doors and you'll be looking right at the Capitol Building; there are always taxis here. The central information desk is in the main hall at the front of the building. You'll find ATMs in the gate area, another near the side doors of the building (near the outdoor escalator to the Metro), and on the lower level, at the end of the Food Court. In the gate area are a Thomas Cook Currency Exchange office (☎ **202/371-9219**) across from gate G and a Travelers Aid desk (☎ **202/546-3120**) near gate K. A number of car rental agencies operate lots here (see "Car Rentals," further along in this chapter for specific names and phone numbers). For security, lost and found, and other help or information, call the main number ☎ **202/371-9441.**

VISITOR INFORMATION

INFORMATION CENTERS   If you haven't already called ahead for information from the Washington, D.C., Convention & Visitors Association (☎ **202/789-7038**), stop in at their headquarters, 1212 New York Ave. NW, Suite 600, Monday to Friday, 9am to 5pm.

More convenient and accessible is the new **DC Chamber of Commerce Visitor Information Center** (☎ **202/328-4748**), inside the Ronald Reagan Building and International Trade Center, open daily (subject to change during nontourist season), 8am to 6pm Monday to Saturday, noon until 5pm Sunday. This very large and just-completed structure at 1300 Pennsylvania Ave. NW occupies space on the ground floor of the building, off the Wilson Plaza entrance, near the Federal Triangle Metro. Right next door is the building that houses the White House Visitor Center (see below). For more information, access the DC Chamber of Commerce Web site, www.dcchamber.org.

There are two other excellent tourist information centers in town, and though each focuses on a specific attraction, they can also provide information about other popular Washington sights.

The **White House Visitors Center,** on the first floor of the Herbert Hoover Building, Department of Commerce, 1450 Pennsylvania Ave. NW (between 14th and 15th streets), is open daily 7:30am to 4pm (call ☎ **202/208-1631,** or 202/456-7041 for recorded information).

The **Smithsonian Information Center,** in the "Castle," 1000 Jefferson Dr. SW (☎ **202/357-2700,** or TTY 202/357-1729; www.si.edu), is open every day but Christmas, 9am to 5:30pm. For a free copy of the Smithsonian's "Planning your Smithsonian Visit," which is full of valuable tips, write to Smithsonian Institution, VIARC, SI Building, Room 153, MRC 010, Washington, DC 20560, or stop at the Castle for a copy. A calendar of Smithsonian exhibits and activities for the coming month appears the third Friday of each month in the *Washington Post*'s "Weekend" section.

Try to visit both facilities when you're in town to garner information and see interesting on-site exhibits. Further details are provided in chapter 7.

The **American Automobile Association (AAA)** has a large central office near the White House, at 701 15th St. NW, Washington, DC 20005-2111 (☎ **202/ 331-3000**). Hours are 9am to 6pm, Monday through Friday.

The **Travelers Aid Society** is a nationwide network of volunteer nonprofit social-service agencies providing help to travelers in difficulty. This might include anything from crisis counseling to straightening out ticket mix-ups, not to mention reuniting families accidentally separated while traveling and helping retrieve lost baggage (sometimes at the wrong airport). The society operates desks at all three airports and at Union Station—see "Arriving" earlier in this chapter for these specific locations.

NEWSPAPERS   If you've arrived at the airport, pick up a free copy of *Washington Flyer.* This magazine is handy as a planning tool (see chapter 2), since it carries so much news about coming events, from transportation to restaurant openings, in Washington. Check out the magazine's Web site at www.washingtonflyermag.

Washington has two daily newspapers: the *Washington Post* and the *Washington Times.* The Friday "Weekend" section of the *Post* is essential for finding out what's going on, recreation-wise. *City Paper,* published every Thursday and available free at downtown shops and restaurants, covers some of the same material but is a better guide to the club and art gallery scene. If you're staying in the suburbs, the Friday *Journal* papers (one for each area county) provide comprehensive coverage of activities beyond the downtown.

Also on newsstands is *Washingtonian,* a monthly magazine with features, often about the "100 Best" this or that (doctors, restaurants, and so on) in Washington; the magazine also offers a calendar of events, restaurant reviews, and profiles of Washingtonians.

HELPFUL TELEPHONE NUMBERS AND WEB SITES

- **National Park Service** (☎ **202/619-7222;** www.nps.gov/nacc). You reach a real person and not a recording when you call the phone number with questions about the monuments, the National Mall, national park lands, and activities taking place at these locations. National Park Service information kiosks are located near the Jefferson, Lincoln, Vietnam Veterans, and Korean War memorials, and at several other locations in the city.
- **Dial-A-Park** (☎ **202/619-7275**). This is a recording of information regarding park service events and attractions.
- **Dial-A-Museum** (☎ **202/357-2020;** www.si.edu). This recording informs you about the locations of the 14 Washington Smithsonian museums and of their daily activities.
- **Recreation and Parks** (☎ **202/673-7660**). This is the number for the D.C. Department of Recreation and Parks, who maintain city parks and recreation areas not under federal jurisdiction.

CITY LAYOUT

Pierre Charles L'Enfant designed Washington's great sweeping avenues crossed by numbered and lettered streets. At key intersections he placed spacious circles. Although the circles are adorned with monuments, statuary, and fountains, L'Enfant also intended them to serve as strategic command posts to ward off invaders or marauding mobs. After what had happened in Paris during the French Revolution—and remember, that was current history at the time—his design views were quite practical.

The U.S. Capitol marks the center of the city, which is divided into quadrants: **northwest (NW), northeast (NE), southwest (SW),** and **southeast (SE).** If you look at your map, you'll see that some addresses—for instance, the corner of G and 7th streets—appear in all quadrants. Hence you must observe the quadrant designation (NW, NE, SW, or SE) when looking for an address.

MAIN ARTERIES & STREETS   From the Capitol, North Capitol Street and South Capitol Street run north and south, respectively. East Capitol Street divides the city north and south. The area west of the Capitol is not a street at all, but the National Mall, which is bounded on the north by Constitution Avenue and on the south by Independence Avenue.

The primary artery of Washington is **Pennsylvania Avenue,** scene of parades, inaugurations, and other splashy events. Pennsylvania runs northwest in a direct line between the Capitol and the White House—if it weren't for the Treasury Building, the President would have a clear view of the Capitol—before continuing on a northwest angle to Georgetown.

Since May 1995, Pennsylvania Avenue between 15th and 17th streets NW has been closed to cars, for security reasons. H Street is now one-way eastbound between 19th and 13th streets NW; I Street is one-way westbound between 11th and 21st streets NW.

Constitution Avenue, paralleled to the south most of the way by Independence Avenue, runs east-west flanking the Capitol and the Mall. If you hear Washingtonians talk about the "House" side of the Hill, they're referring to the part of the Capitol that holds Congressional House offices and the House Chamber, on the Independence Avenue side, in other words; the "Senate" side is the part of the Capitol that holds Senate offices and the Senate Chamber, on the Constitution Avenue side.

Washington, D.C. at a Glance

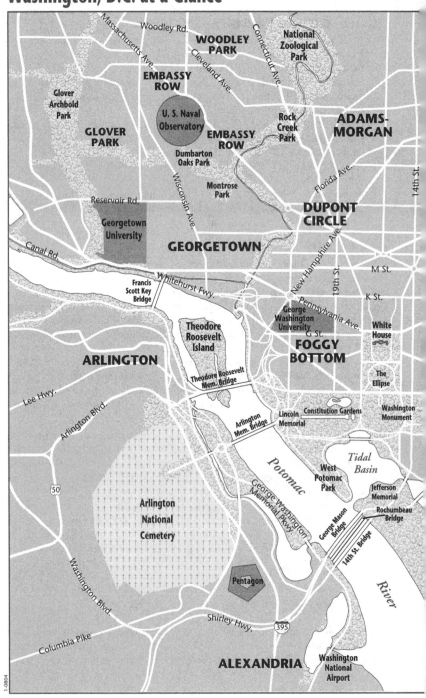

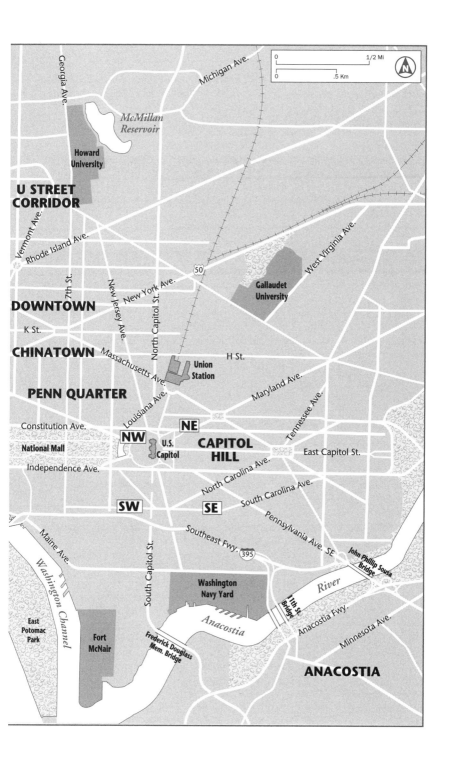

If Washington should ever grow to be a great city, the outlook from the Capitol will be unsurpassed in the world. Now at sunset I seemed to look westward far into the heart of the continent from this commanding position.

—Ralph Waldo Emerson

Washington's longest avenue, **Massachusetts Avenue,** runs north of and parallel to Pennsylvania. Along the way, you'll find Union Station and then Dupont Circle, which is central to the area known as Embassy Row. Farther out are the Naval Observatory (the vice-president's residence is on the premises), Washington National Cathedral, American University, and eventually, Maryland.

Connecticut Avenue, which runs more directly north, starts at Lafayette Square, intersects Dupont Circle, and eventually takes you to the National Zoo, on to the charming residential neighborhood known as Cleveland Park, and into Chevy Chase, Maryland, where you can pick up the Beltway to head out of town. Downtown Connecticut Avenue, with its posh shops and clusters of restaurants, is a good street to stroll.

Wisconsin Avenue originates in Georgetown and intersects with M Street to form Georgetown's hub. Antique shops, trendy boutiques, discos, restaurants, and pubs all vie for attention. Wisconsin Avenue basically parallels Connecticut Avenue; one of the few irritating things about the city's transportation system is that the Metro does not connect these two major arteries in the heart of the city. (Buses do, and, of course, you can always walk or take a taxi from one avenue to the other.) In fact, Metro's first stop on Wisconsin Avenue is in Tenleytown, a residential area. Follow the avenue north, and you land in the affluent Maryland cities, Chevy Chase and Bethesda.

FINDING AN ADDRESS   Once you understand the city's layout, it's easy to find your way around. As you read this, have a map handy.

Each of the four corners of the District of Columbia is exactly the same distance from the Capitol dome. The White House and most government buildings and important monuments are west of the Capitol (in the northwest and southwest quadrants), as are important hotels and tourist facilities.

Numbered streets run north-south, beginning on either side of the Capitol with First Street. Lettered streets run east-west and are named alphabetically, beginning with A Street. (Don't look for a B, a J, an X, Y, or Z Street, however.) After W Street, one-syllable, two-syllable, and three-syllable street names come into play; the more syllables in a name, the farther the street will lie from the Capitol.

Avenues, named for U.S. states, run at angles across the grid pattern and often intersect at traffic circles. For example, New Hampshire, Connecticut, and Massachusetts avenues intersect at Dupont Circle.

With this in mind, you can easily find an address. On lettered streets, the address tells you exactly where to go. For instance, 1776 K St. NW is between 17th and 18th streets (the first two digits of 1776 tell you that) in the northwest quadrant (NW). *Note:* I Street is often written Eye Street to prevent confusion with 1st Street.

To find an address on numbered streets, you'll probably have to use your fingers. For instance, 623 8th St. SE is between F and G streets (the sixth and seventh letters of the alphabet; the first digit of 623 tells you that) in the southeast quadrant (SE). One thing to remember: You count B as the second letter of the alphabet even though no B Street exists today (Constitution and Independence avenues were the original B streets), but since there's no J Street, K becomes the 10th letter, L the 11th, and so on.

Neighborhoods in Brief

Adams-Morgan   This ever-trendy, multiethnic neighborhood is about the size of a postage stamp, though crammed with boutiques, clubs, and restaurants. Everything is located on either 18th St. NW or Columbia Rd. NW. You won't find any hotels here, although there are a couple of B&Bs; nearby are the Dupont Circle and Woodley Park neighborhoods, each of which has several hotels (see below). Parking during the day is OK, but forget it at night. But you can easily walk (be alert; the neighborhood is edgy) to Adams-Morgan from the Dupont Circle or Woodley Park Metro stops, or taxi here for a taste of Malaysian, Ethiopian, Spanish, or some other international cuisine. Friday and Saturday nights, the hot nightlife here rivals Georgetown and Dupont Circle.

Capitol Hill   Everyone's heard of "the Hill," the area crowned by the Capitol. When people speak of Capitol Hill, they refer to a large section of town, extending from the western side of the Capitol to the D.C. Armory going east, bounded by H Street NE and the Southwest Freeway north and south. It contains not only the chief symbol of the nation's capital, but the Supreme Court building, the Library of Congress, the Folger Shakespeare Library, Union Station, and the U.S. Botanic Garden. Much of it is a quiet residential neighborhood of tree-lined streets and Victorian homes. There are many restaurants in the vicinity and a smattering of hotels, mostly close to Union Station.

Downtown   The area roughly between 7th and 22nd streets NW going east to west, and P Street and Pennsylvania Avenue going north to south is a mix of the Federal Triangle's government office buildings, K Street ("Lawyer's Row"), Connecticut Avenue restaurants and shopping, historic hotels, the city's poshest small hotels, and the White House. You'll also find the Historic Penn Quarter (see profile in box), a part of downtown that is taking on new life with the opening of the MCI Center, trendy new restaurants, and art galleries. The total downtown area takes in so many blocks and attractions that I've divided discussions of accommodations (chapter 5) and dining (chapter 6) into two sections: "Downtown, 16th Street NW and west," and "Downtown, east of 16th Street NW." 16th Street and the White House form a natural point of separation.

Dupont Circle   My favorite part of town, Dupont Circle is fun day or night. It takes its name from the traffic circle minipark, where Massachusetts, New Hampshire, and Connecticut avenues collide. The streets extending out from the circle are lively with all-night bookstores, really good restaurants, wonderful art galleries and art museums, nightspots, movie theaters, and Washingtonians at their loosest. It is also the hub of D.C.'s gay community. There are plenty of hotels, from the small and charming Hotel Normandy to the chain blockbuster, the Washington Hilton.

Foggy Bottom   The area west of the White House to the edge of Georgetown, Foggy Bottom was Washington's early industrial center. Its name comes from the foul fumes emitted in those days by a coal depot and gasworks, but its original name, Funkstown (for owner Jacob Funk), is perhaps even worse. There's nothing foul about the area today. This is a low-key part of town, enlivened by the presence of the Kennedy Center, George Washington University, small and medium-size hotels, and a mix of restaurants on the main drag, Pennsylvania Avenue, and on residential side streets.

Georgetown   This historic community dates from colonial times. It was a thriving tobacco port long before the District of Columbia was formed, and one of its attractions, the Old Stone House, dates from pre-Revolutionary days. Georgetown action

Historic Penn Quarter

From Pennsylvania Avenue north to Chinatown, and stretching from 6th Street west to 10th Street is this neighborhood within a neighborhood (the downtown), where Washington's identity as the nation's capital merges nicely with its identity as its own city. In the past, your main motivation for visiting this part of town would have been to tour the **FBI Building** on E Street NW, **Ford's Theatre** and the **Petersen House** on 10th Street, and the two fantastic Smithsonian museums, the **National Portrait Gallery** on F Street and the **National Museum of American Art,** on G Street. These days, you'll want to keep those stops on your itinerary, but allow time for other Penn Quarter sites. Start at the new **MCI Center** at 601 F St. NW and proceed to the **Discovery Channel Retail Store** to view the 15-minute film, "Destination DC," shown every half-hour on the fourth floor. (Tickets are $2.50 per adult, $1.50 per child.) Follow the film with a **DC Heritage Tour** ($7.50 per adult, $5 per child), which departs from the MCI Center weekdays at 10:30am and Saturday and Sunday at 1:30pm; you should call ahead to reserve: ☎ **202/639-0908.** During this walking tour, a costumed guide whisks you in and out of historic spots for 90 minutes, as she offers a view of 19th-century Washington, revealing on her way the house where John Wilkes Booth plotted Lincoln's assassination, the halls where Walt Whitman cared for the Civil War wounded, and so on.

From there, you're on your own: You can tour **Chinatown;** pop in and out of **art galleries,** like the Zenith on 7th Street NW; eat at one of the best **restaurants** in the city, like Cafe Atlantico (on 8th Street NW); experience the offbeat **Bead Museum** at 400 7th St. NW; take a ride (maybe) in the oldest working elevator in the world (hand-operated by Mr. Litwin, in his Merchants of Antiques and Fancy Furniture store, at 637 Indiana Ave. NW; take in a Shakespeare play at the **Lansburgh Theatre** (7th Street NW); or **shop** for gorgeous, glazed Italian pottery at the Corso De-Fiori boutique in Market Square, 8th and D streets NW. Downtown Washington has never seemed so alive!

centers on M Street and Wisconsin Avenue NW, where you'll find the luxury Four Seasons hotel and less expensive digs, numerous boutiques (see chapter 8 for details), chic restaurants, and popular pubs (lots of nightlife here). But get off the main drags and see the quiet tree-lined streets of restored colonial row houses, stroll through the beautiful gardens of Dumbarton Oaks, and check out the C&O Canal. Georgetown is also home to Georgetown University and its lively students.

Glover Park   Mostly a residential neighborhood, this section of town, just above Georgetown and just south of the Washington National Cathedral, is worth mentioning because of the increasing number of good restaurants opening along its main stretch, Wisconsin Avenue NW, and because the few hotels here tend to offer lower rates than you might expect for its location. Glover Park sits between the campuses of Georgetown and American Universities, so there's a large student presence here.

The Mall   This lovely tree-lined stretch of open space between Constitution and Independence avenues, extending for 2½ miles from the Capitol to the Lincoln Memorial, is the hub of tourist attractions. It includes most of the Smithsonian Institution museums and many other visitor attractions. The 300-foot-wide Mall is used by natives as well as tourists—joggers, food vendors, kite-flyers, and picnickers among them. As you can imagine, hotels and restaurants are located on the periphery.

U Street Corridor   D.C.'s newest nightlife neighborhood between 12th and 15th streets NW is rising from the ashes of nightclubs and theaters frequented decades ago by African Americans. At the renovated Lincoln Theater, where Duke Ellington, Louis Armstrong, and Cab Calloway once performed, patrons today can enjoy performances by popular black artists. The corridor offers at least six alternative rock and contemporary music nightclubs and several restaurants (see chapter 9 for details). Go here to party, not to sleep—there are no hotels along this stretch.

Woodley Park   Home to Washington's largest hotel (the Washington Marriott Wardman Park—formerly known as the Sheraton Washington) and the Omni Shoreham, Woodley Park boasts the National Zoo, many good restaurants, and some antique stores. Washingtonians are used to seeing conventioneers wandering the neighborhood's pretty residential streets with their name tags still on.

2 Getting Around

Washington is one of the easiest U.S. cities in which to get around. Only New York rivals its comprehensive transportation system, but Washington's clean, efficient subways put the Big Apple's underground nightmare to shame. A complex bus system covers all major D.C. arteries, as well, and it's easy to hail a taxi anywhere at any time. But because Washington is of manageable size and marvelous beauty, you may find yourself shunning transportation and getting around on foot.

BY METRORAIL

It must be said: After 20-odd years in operation, Metrorail has begun to show its age. Stations are still cool, clean and attractive. Cars are still air-conditioned and comfortable, fitted with upholstered seats; rides are still quiet. But service has deteriorated a little as trains break down more frequently. Metro's management became alarmed enough in the spring of 1999 to authorize an "Emergency Rail Rehabilitation Plan," which should return service back to the standards we spoiled patrons are used to: frequent enough so that one usually can get a seat, at least during off-peak hours (basically weekdays 10am to 3pm, weeknights after 7pm, and all day weekends).

Some things will not change: Expect lines at farecard machines and very crowded platforms and trains during peak hours and peak seasons. If you don't want to risk the ire of commuters, be sure to follow these guidelines: Stand to the right on the escalator so that people in a hurry can get past you on the left; and when you reach the train level, don't puddle at the bottom of the escalator blocking the path of those coming behind you, but move down the platform. As mentioned earlier, eating, drinking, and smoking are strictly prohibited on the Metro and in the station.

Metrorail's 75 stations and 92.3 miles of track (83 stations and 103 miles of track are the eventual goal) include locations at or near almost every sightseeing attraction and extend to suburban Maryland and northern Virginia. If you're in Washington even for a few days, you'll probably have occasion to use the system; but if not, create an excuse. The Metro is a sightseeing attraction in its own right.

There are five lines in operation—Red, Blue, Orange, Yellow, and Green—with extensions planned for the future. The lines connect at several points, making transfers easy. All but Yellow and Green Line trains stop at Metro Center; all except Red Line trains stop at L'Enfant Plaza; all but Blue and Orange Line trains stop at Gallery Place/Chinatown.

Metro stations are indicated by discreet brown columns bearing the station's name and topped by the letter M. Below the M is a colored stripe or stripes indicating the line or lines that stop there. When entering a Metro station for the first time, go to the

Major Metro Stops

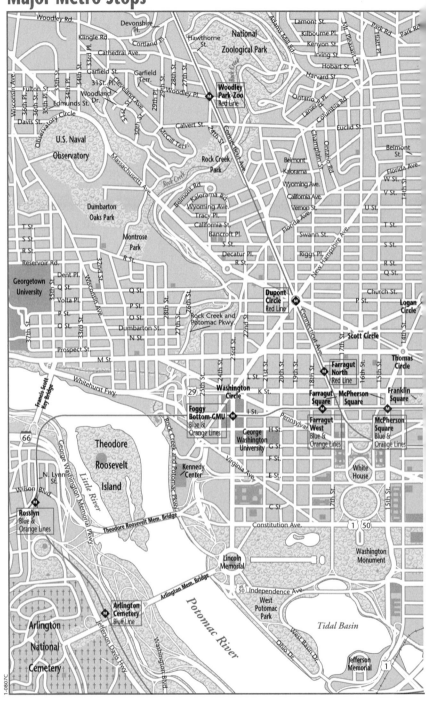

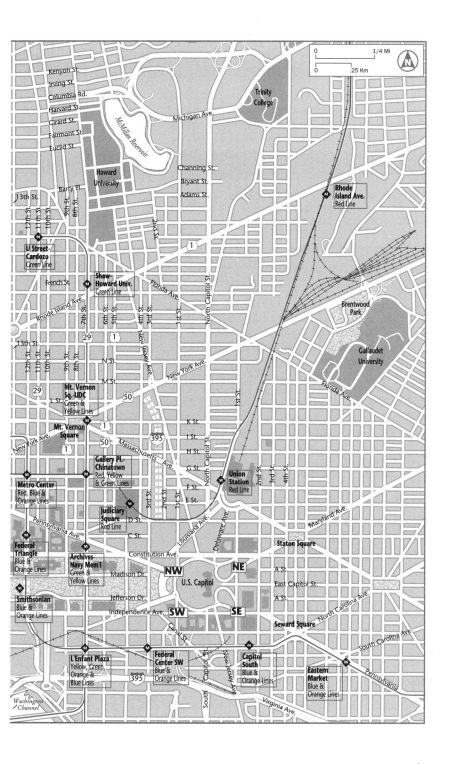

kiosk and ask the station manager for a free "Metro System Pocket Guide" (available in English, German, Spanish, Korean, Japanese, and French). It contains a map of the system, explains how it works, and lists the closest Metro stops to points of interest. The station manager can also answer questions about routing or purchase of farecards. At some Metro stations, Union Station and Ronald Reagan Washington National Airport among them, riders can use touch-screen computers to determine the best routes to take to reach a particular destination, obtain copies of maps and schedules of bus service, and find out answers to other transportation-related queries.

To enter or exit a Metro station, you need a computerized farecard, available at vending machines near the entrance. The minimum fare to enter the system is $1.10, which pays for rides to and from any point within 7 miles of boarding during non-peak hours; during peak hours (Monday to Friday 5:30am to 9:30am and 3pm to 7pm), $1.10 takes you only 3 miles. The machines take nickels, dimes, quarters, and bills from $1 to $20; they can return up to $4.95 in change (coins only). If you plan to take several Metrorail trips during your stay, put more value on the farecard to avoid having to purchase a new card each time you ride. There's a 10% bonus on all fare-cards of $20 or more. Up to two children under 5 can ride free with a paying passenger. Senior citizens (65 and older) and people with disabilities (with valid proof) ride Metrorail and Metrobus for a reduced fare.

Discount passes, called "One-Day Rail passes," cost $5 per person and allow you unlimited passage for the day, after 9:30am weekdays, and all day on a Saturday, Sunday, or holiday. You can buy them at most stations; at Washington Metropolitan Area Transit Authority, 600 5th St. NW (☎ **202/637-7000;** www.wmata.com); at Metro Center, 12th and G streets NW; or at a Giant or Safeway grocery store.

When you insert your card in the entrance gate, the time and location are recorded on its magnetic tape, and your card is returned. Don't forget to snatch it up and keep it handy; you have to reinsert it in the exit gate at your destination, where the fare will automatically be deducted. The card will be returned if there's any value left on it. If you arrive at a destination and your farecard doesn't have enough value, add what's necessary at the Exitfare machines near the exit gate.

Metrorail operates Monday to Friday from 5:30am to midnight, weekends and holidays from 8am to midnight. Call ☎ **202/637-7000,** or visit www.wmata.com, for information on Metro routes. *Warning:* The line is often busy, so just keep trying.

BY BUS

While a 10-year-old can understand the Metrorail system, the **Metrobus** system is considerably more complex. The 15,800 stops on the 1,489-square-mile route (it operates on all major D.C. arteries as well as in the Virginia and Maryland suburbs) are indicated by red, white, and blue signs. However, the signs tell you only what buses pull into a given stop, not where they go. For routing information, call ☎ **202/ 637-7000.** Calls are taken Monday to Friday from 6am to 10:30pm, weekends and holidays from 8am to 10:30pm. This is the same number you call to request a free map and time schedule, information about parking in Metrobus fringe lots, and for locations and hours of those places where you can purchase bus tokens.

Travel Tip

If you're on the subway and plan to continue your travel via Metrobus, pick up a transfer at the station when you enter the system (not your destination station). Transfer machines are on the mezzanine levels of most stations. It's good for a discount on bus fares in D.C. and Virginia. There are no bus-to-subway transfers.

Base fare in the District is $1.10; bus transfers cost 10¢. There are additional charges for travel into the Maryland and Virginia suburbs. Bus drivers are not equipped to make change, so be sure to carry exact change or tokens. If you'll be in Washington for a while and plan to use the buses a lot, consider buying a $20 2-week pass, also available at the Metro Center station and other outlets.

Most buses operate daily almost around the clock. Service is quite frequent on weekdays, especially during peak hours. On weekends and late at night, service is less frequent.

Up to two children under 5 ride free with a paying passenger on Metrobus, and there are reduced fares for senior citizens (☎ **202/962-7000**) and people with disabilities (☎ **202/962-1245** or 202/962-1100; see chapter 2 for discussion of "Tips for Travelers with Special Needs" for travelers with disabilities). If you should leave something on a bus, train, or in a station, call Lost and Found at ☎ **202/962-1195.**

BY CAR

More than half of all visitors to the District arrive by car, but my advice is don't use it for getting around. Metrorail is definitely the easiest way to go. If you must drive, be aware that traffic is always thick during the week, parking spaces often hard to find, and parking lots ruinously expensive. The garages around the MCI Center on F Street NW, at 7th Street NW, charge outrageously high prices, especially when there's an event on at the center. (For information about parking garage/lot locations and costs in and around Washington, look up the www.parkingguide.com Web site, or call ☎ **301/262-9197** and ask for a copy of the monthly publication, *Parking Guide Magazine.*)

Watch out for the traffic circles. Traffic law states that the circle traffic has the right of way. No one pays any attention to this rule, however, which can be frightening (cars zoom into the circle without a glance at the cars already there). The other thing you will notice is that while some circles are easy to figure out (Dupont Circle, for example), others are nerve-wrackingly confusing (Thomas Circle, where 14th Street NW, Vermont Avenue NW, and Massachusetts Avenue NW come together, is to be avoided at all cost).

Sections of certain streets in Washington become one-way during rush hour: Rock Creek Parkway, Canal Road, and 17th Street NW are three examples. Other streets during rush hour change the direction of some of their traffic lanes: Connecticut Avenue NW is the main one. In the morning, traffic in four of its six lanes travels south to downtown and in late afternoon/early evening, downtown traffic in four of its six lanes heads north; between the hours of 9am and 3:30pm, traffic in either direction keeps to the normally correct side of the yellow line. Lit-up traffic signs alert you to what's going on, but pay attention. Unless a sign is posted prohibiting it, a right-on-red law is in effect.

Road rage, when an aggressive driver, acting out of impatience and intolerance for others on the road, has tried to force another driver out of the way, has caused severe injury and even fatalities on local highways and on the George Washington Parkway in the past two years. Should you find yourself in such a threatening situation, forget any inclination to stand up to this kind of driver, but change lanes and move out of the way as safely and quickly as you can.

To keep up with street closing and construction information, grab the day's *Washington Post,* pull out the Metro section and turn to page 3, where the column "Metro, In Brief" tells you about potential traffic and routing problems in the District and suburban Maryland and Virginia. The paper also publishes a regular column in the Metro section called "Dr. Gridlock," which addresses traffic questions.

CAR RENTAL   Outside of the city, you will want a car to get to most attractions in Virginia and Maryland. All the major car-rental companies are represented here, including Alamo, Avis, Budget, Dollar, Enterprise, Hertz, National, and Thrifty. Consult the appendix for each rental company's toll-free 800 number and Web site, and refer to the information about area airports, at the beginning of this chapter for phone numbers for each of these companies' airport locations. Within the District, car-rental locations include: **Avis,** 1722 M St. NW (☎ 202/467-6585) and 4215 Connecticut Ave. NW (☎ 202/686-5149); **Budget,** Union Station (☎ 703/920-3360); **Enterprise,** 1015 Wisconsin Ave. NW (☎ 202/338-0015); **Hertz,** 901 11th St. NW (☎ 202/628-6174); **National,** Union Station (☎ 202/842-7454); and **Thrifty,** 12th and K streets NW (☎ 202/783-0400) and 1310 Wisconsin Ave. NW (☎ 202/338-9500).

Saving Money on a Rental Car   Car rental rates vary even more than airline fares. The price you pay will depend on the size of the car, where and when you pick it up and drop it off, the length of the rental period, where and how far you drive it, whether you purchase insurance, and a host of other factors. A few key questions could save you hundreds of dollars.

- Are weekend rates lower than weekday rates? Ask if the rate is the same for pickup Friday morning, for instance, as it is for Thursday night.
- Is a weekly rate cheaper than the daily rate? Even if you only need the car for four days, it may be cheaper to keep it for five.
- Does the agency assess a drop-off charge if you don't return the car to the same location where you picked it up? Is it cheaper to pick up the car at the airport compared to a downtown location?
- Are special promotional rates available? If you see an advertised price in your local newspaper, be sure to ask for that specific rate; otherwise you may be charged the standard cost. Terms change constantly.
- Are discounts available for members of AARP, AAA, frequent flyer programs, or trade unions? If you belong to any of these organizations, you may be entitled to discounts of up to 30%.
- How much tax will be added to the rental bill? Local tax? State use tax? Local taxes and surcharges can vary from location to location, even within the same car company, which can add quite a bit to your costs.
- What is the cost of adding an additional driver's name to the contract?
- How many free miles are included in the price? Free mileage is often negotiable, depending on the length of your rental.
- How much does the rental company charge to refill your gas tank if you return with the tank less than full? Though most rental companies claim these prices are "competitive," fuel is almost always cheaper in town. Try to allow enough time to refuel the car yourself before returning it.

Some companies offer "refueling packages," in which you pay for an entire tank of gas up front. The price is usually fairly competitive with local gas prices, but you don't get credit for any gas remaining in the tank. If a stop at a gas station on the way to the airport will make you miss your plane, then by all means take advantage of the fuel purchase option. Otherwise, skip it.

Package Deals   Many packages are available that include airfare, accommodations, and a rental car with unlimited mileage. Compare these prices with the cost of booking airline tickets and renting a car separately to see if these offers are good deals.

Arranging Car Rentals on the Web   Internet resources can make comparison shopping easier. Frommer's Online Directory, in the back of this book, reviews a number of car-rental sites. (For more tips on renting cars, check out www.bnm.com/tips.htm.)

BY TAXI

District cabs operate on a zone system instead of meters. By law, basic rates are posted in each cab. If you take a trip from one point to another within the same zone, you pay just $4.00, regardless of the distance traveled. So it would cost you $4.00 to travel a few blocks from the U.S. Capitol to the National Museum of American History, but the same $4.00 could take you from the Capitol all the way to Dupont Circle. They're both in Zone 1, as are most other tourist attractions: the White House, most of the Smithsonian, the Washington Monument, the FBI, the National Archives, the Supreme Court, the Library of Congress, the Bureau of Engraving and Printing, the Old Post Office, and Ford's Theatre. If your trip takes you into a second zone, the price is $5.50, $6.90 for a third zone, $8.25 for a fourth, and so on.

So far, the fares seem modest. But here's how they could add up: There's a $1.50 charge for each additional passenger after the first, so a $4.00 Zone 1 fare can become $8.50 for a family of four (though one child under 5 can ride free). There's also a rush-hour surcharge of $1 per trip between 7 and 9:30am and 4 and 6:30pm weekdays. Surcharges are also added for large pieces of luggage and for arranging a pickup by telephone ($1.50). Try Diamond Cab Company (☎ **202/387-6200**), Yellow Cab (☎ **202/544-1212**), or Capitol Cab (☎ **202/546-2400**).

The zone system is not used when your destination is an out-of-District address (such as an airport); in that case, the fare is based on mileage covered—$2 for the first half mile or part thereof and 70¢ for each additional half mile or part. You can call ☎ **202/ 331-1671** to find out the rate between any point in D.C. and an address in Virginia or Maryland. Call ☎ **202/645-6018** to inquire about fares within the District.

It's generally easy to hail a taxi, although the *Washington Post* has reported that taxi cabs, even those driven by black cabbies, often ignore African Americans to pick up white passengers; African-American friends corroborate that this is so. Unique to the city is the practice of allowing drivers to pick up as many passengers as they can comfortably fit, so expect to share (unrelated parties pay the same as they would if they were not sharing). To register a complaint, note the cab driver's name and cab number and call (☎ **202/645-6010**). You will be asked to file a written complaint either by fax (☎ **202/ 889-3604**) or mail (Commendations/Complaints, District of Columbia Taxicab Commission, 2041 Martin Luther King, Jr. Ave. SE, Room 204, Washington, DC 20020).

Fast Facts: Washington, D.C.

Airports   See "Getting There" in chapter 2, and "Arriving," earlier this chapter.

American Express   There's an American Express Travel Service office at 1150 Connecticut Ave. NW (☎ **202/457-1300**) and another in upper northwest Washington at 5300 Wisconsin Ave. NW, in the Mazza Gallerie (☎ **202/ 362-4000**). Each office functions as a full travel agency and currency exchange; of course, you can also buy traveler's checks here.

Area Code   Within the District of Columbia, it's 202. In suburban Virginia, it's 703. In suburban Maryland, it's 301.

Baby-sitters   Most hotels can arrange for sitters. If your hotel does not offer a baby-sitting service, you can contact White House Nannies (☎ **301/652-8088**) yourself. In business since 1985, this company checks their "caregivers'" qualifications, child-care references, and personal histories, including driving and social security records. Each caregiver has been trained in CPR and first aid training. Rates are $10 to $12 per hour (4-hour minimum), plus a one-time referral fee of $25.

Business Hours   Banks are open weekdays from 9am to 2 or 3pm, with some open on Friday until 6pm and on Saturday morning. Most banks provide 24-hour access to their automated teller machines (ATMs), usually set in the bank's outside wall; other ATM locations include grocery stores, airports, shopping malls, and some sightseeing attractions.

Generally, public and private offices are open weekdays 9am to 5pm. Stores are open 6 days a week, with many open on Sunday, too; department stores usually stay open until 9pm at least 1 day (usually Thursday) a week. Some grocery stores and drugstores are open for 24 hours. Most bars close at 2am weekdays, 3am weekends.

Car Rentals   See "Getting Around," earlier in this chapter.

Climate   See "When to Go" in chapter 2.

Congresspersons   To locate a senator or congressional representative, call the Capitol switchboard (☎ 202/224-3121). Or access the Web sites, www.senate.gov and www.house.gov, to contact individual senators and congressional representatives by e-mail, find out what bills are being worked on and the calendar for the day, and more.

Doctors/Dentists   Prologue (☎ 800/DOCTORS) can refer you to any type of doctor or dentist you need. Its roster includes just about every specialty. Hours are Monday through Friday, 8:30am to 6pm and Saturday 9am to 4pm. The **Washington Hospital Center** (☎ 202/877-DOCS) referral service operates weekdays 8am to 6pm, and will point you to a nearby doctor. **Physicians Home Service,** Suite 401, 2311 M St. NW (☎ 202/331-3888) will come to your hotel if you are staying in the District (for a hefty fee of $250 to $300, which insurance companies do not reimburse), or will treat you in its downtown office during regular hours; PHS accepts credit cards, traveler's checks, local personal checks with adequate identification, and cash.

Driving Rules   See "Getting Around," earlier in this chapter.

Drugstores   **CVS,** Washington's major drugstore chain (with more than 40 stores), has two convenient 24-hour locations: 14th Street and Thomas Circle NW, at Vermont Avenue (☎ 202/628-0720), and at Dupont Circle (☎ 202/785-1466), both with round-the-clock pharmacies. Check your phone book for other convenient locations.

Embassies   See "Fast Facts: For the Foreign Traveler" in chapter 3.

Emergencies   Dial ☎ 911 to contact the police or fire department or to call an ambulance. See also "Hospitals," below.

Hospitals   In case of a life-threatening emergency, call ☎ 911. If you don't require immediate ambulance transportation but still need emergency-room treatment, call one of the following hospitals; be sure to get directions: Children's Hospital National Medical Center, 111 Michigan Ave. NW (☎ 202/884-5000 for general information and 202/884-5203 for the emergency room); George Washington University Hospital, 901 23rd St. NW (entrance on Washington Circle; ☎ 202/994-3211 for emergency room or 202/994-1000 for general information); Georgetown University Hospital, 3800 Reservoir Rd. NW (☎ 202/784-3111 for emergency room or 202/687-2000 for general information); Howard University Hospital, 2041 Georgia Ave. NW (☎ 202/865-1141 for emergency room or 202/865-6100 for general information).

Hot lines   To reach a 24-hour poison control hot line, call ☎ 202/625-3333, to reach a 24-hour crisis line, call ☎ 202/561-7000, and to reach the drug and alcohol abuse hot line, which operates 24 hours daily, call ☎ 888/294-3572.

Internet Access You have free Internet access at the **Martin Luther King, Jr. Memorial Library,** 901 G St. NW (☎ **202/727-0321**), but time is limited because of high demand. Or try **Myth.com** (☎ **202/625-6984**) at 3241 M St. NW in Georgetown; rates here are $10 an hour or pro-rated amounts for portions of an hour.

Liquor Laws The minimum drinking age is 21. Establishments can serve alcoholic beverages from 8am to 2am Monday to Friday, until 3am Saturday, and 10am to 3am Sunday. Liquor stores are closed on Sunday. District gourmet grocery stores, mom-and-pop grocery stores, and 7-Eleven convenience stores often sell beer and wine, even on Sundays.

Maps Free city maps are often available at hotels and throughout town at tourist attractions. You can also contact the Washington, D.C., Convention and Visitors Association, 1212 New York Ave. NW, Washington, DC 20005 (☎ **202/789-7000**).

Newspapers/Magazines See "Visitor Information," earlier in this chapter.

Police In an emergency, dial ☎ **911.** For a nonemergency, call ☎ **202/ 727-1010.**

Post Office If you want your mail to follow you on your vacation and you aren't sure of your address, your mail can be sent to you, in your name, c/o General Delivery at the main post office of the city or region where you expect to be. The addressee must pick it up in person and produce proof of identity (for example, driver's license, credit or charge card, or passport). In Washington, the main post office is located at 900 Brentwood Rd. NE, Washington, DC 20066-9998, USA (☎ **202/636-1532**). It's open Monday to Friday 8am to 8pm, Saturday 8am to 6pm, and Sunday noon to 6pm. This is not a convenient location. Other post offices are located throughout the city, including the one in the National Postal Museum building, opposite Union Station at 2 Massachusetts Ave. NE (at G and North Capitol streets) (☎ **202/523-2628**). It's open Monday to Friday 7am to midnight, and on weekends until 8pm.

Safety In Washington, you're quite safe throughout the day in all the major tourist areas described in this book, and you can also safely visit the Lincoln Memorial after dark. Riding the Metro is quite safe. U Street Corridor, Adams-Morgan, and Capitol Hill are the least safe neighborhoods, but it's really at nighttime that you should be especially careful. Although, at nighttime, be alert anywhere you go in Washington. In addition, follow the safety tips provided in chapter 3 under "General Safety Suggestions."

Salons See box in chapter 8, "Primping for a Night on the Town: Salons"; the best ones are in Georgetown, but you'll need to call ahead for an appointment.

Taxes See "Fast Facts: For the Foreign Traveler" in chapter 3.

Taxis See "Getting Around," earlier in this chapter.

Time Washington is in the eastern standard time zone. To find out what time it is, call ☎ **202/844-2525.**

Transit Information See "Getting There" in chapter 2 and "Getting Around," earlier in this chapter.

Weather Call ☎ **202/936-1212.**

5 Where to Stay in Washington, D.C.

If a destination's popularity can be measured by the number of new hotels opening or in the works, than Washington's star is indeed on the rise. The Hotel George on Capitol Hill, the Doyle Washington at Dupont Circle, and the Courtyard by Marriott Convention Center, downtown, are among the latest to open (all are described in this chapter). At least six more hotels are scheduled for completion by or within the year 2000, from a fancy-schmancy Ritz-Carlton in the West End, to the more conventional Hilton Garden Inn at 14th and H streets, downtown.

So business is booming. More hotels are being built because more of you are visiting the capital, filling up the 24,061 rooms in 103 hotels that are already here. A number of hotels are looking like new after undergoing massive, million-dollar renovations. These include upgrades at the Omni-Shoreham, the Marriott Wardman Park and Towers, and the Washington Monarch, and the addition of 60 luxury suites and a state-of-the-art health spa at the Four Seasons.

But, as anyone in the hotel business will tell you, hotels are ever in a state of self-improvement as they try to maintain their properties and keep pace with travelers' trends. You'll notice how many of the hotels listed here now offer an exercise room, or provide guests with passes to a nearby health club. Coffeemakers, hair dryers, in-room safes, and computer dataports are almost de rigueur, at even the least expensive properties. And thanks to the Americans with Disabilities Act, hotels are becoming increasingly more accessible to those with disabilities, although standards seem to differ widely from hotel to hotel.

All of these improvements come at a price: Rates are higher, with the average cost of an overnight stay in a D.C. hotel at $138.43. And then, there are taxes: In the District, in addition to your hotel rate, you pay a 14.5% hotel tax. Rates quoted for each hotel do not include this tax, so don't forget to calculate it. Be sure, too, to add in other costs, like parking, which can be hefty.

If it's April and you've waited until the last minute to reserve a room, yes, you're going to pay every cent of the top price quoted for a hotel, assuming you're able to get a reservation at all. But, with a little planning, there are a multitude of ways to get yourself a rate you can live with.

HOW TO GET THE BEST RATE

Here's the deal: It pays to know what you want and to do some research. Call around. Surf the Internet. Talk to friends. Contact reservations services. Pin people down. You may be surprised at the vast array of rates available to you, and you'll find they often differ substantially from the published rack rates. One point that hotel staff like to emphasize however, is that **discounted rates and packages are offered** *subject to availability.*

As you peruse this chapter, keep these thoughts in mind.

- Consider all the hotels, no matter the rate category. The accepted wisdom is that one can often pay less than the advertised "rack" rate. Even the best and most expensive hotels may be ready to negotiate and often offer bargain rates at certain times or to guests who are members of certain groups, and you may be eligible.
- If you can be flexible about the time you are traveling, all the better. Try booking during Washington's less busy periods: on weekends, in July, August and early September, and between Thanksgiving and early January.
- As a rule, when you call a hotel, you should ask whether there are special promotions or discounts available. Most hotels offer discounts of at least 10% to members of the American Automobile Association (AAA) and the American Association of Retired Persons (AARP). The magnificent Willard Hotel, for instance, offers 50% off its published rates for guests older than 65—on a space available basis. Many hotels in Washington, like the Hotel Lombardy, discount rates for government, military, or embassy-related guests (a discounted rate of $139 was quoted in spring 1999). Long-term rates, corporate rates, holiday rates, and rates or perks for "frequent guest" members are also possibilities.
- Ask about family rates: Families often receive special rates, as much as 50% off on a room adjoining the parents' room (Hyatt is one chain that offers this, based on availability), or perhaps free fare in the hotel's restaurant (many Holiday Inns, including the Holiday Inn on the Hill, let kids 12 and under eat free from children's menus year-round). Every hotel (but not necessarily inns or bed-and-breakfasts) included in this chapter allows children under a certain age, usually 12 or 18, to stay free in the parents' room.
- Dial direct. When booking a room in a chain hotel, call the hotel's local line, as well as the toll-free number, and see where you get the best deal. A hotel makes nothing on a room that stays empty. The clerk who runs the place is more likely to know about vacancies and will often grant deep discounts in order to fill up.
- Avoid excess charges, like those imposed for parking or for telephone use.
- Watch for coupons and advertised discounts.
- Consider a suite. If you are traveling with your family or another couple, you can pack more people into a suite (which usually comes with a sofa bed), and thereby reduce your per-person rate. Remember that some places charge for extra guests, some don't.
- Book an efficiency. A room with a kitchenette allows you to grocery shop and eat some meals in. Especially during long stays with families, you're bound to save money this way.
- Investigate reservation services, both national and local. These outfits usually work as consolidators, buying up or reserving rooms in bulk, and then dealing them out to customers at a profit. They do garner special deals that range from 10% to 50% off; but remember, these discounts apply to rack rates, that is, the published higher prices. You're sometimes better off dealing directly with a hotel, but if you don't like bargaining, this is certainly a viable option. Most of them offer online reservation services as well. Among the national reservations services are:

  Hotel Reservations Network (☎ **800/964-6835;** www.hoteldiscount.com), which allows you to compare properties and book your reservation online, is known for finding rooms when the city is booked (one to keep in mind during inaugural celebrations).

Quikbook (☎ 800/789-9887; www.quikbook.com), is a good one to consider when you want a break on a top-drawer hotel.

Central Reservations Services (☎ 800/548-3311; www.reservation-services. com), is adept at finding mid-to-low-priced accommodations.

The best local reservations services are:

Capitol Reservations; 1730 Rhode Island Ave. NW, Suite 1114, Washington, DC 20036 (☎ 800/VISIT-DC or 202/452-1270; fax 202/452-0537; www.hotelsdc.com). Capitol will find you a hotel that meets your specific requirements and is within your price range, and they'll do the bargaining for you. Capitol Reservations listings begin at about $70 a night for a double. The 16-year-old service works with about 75 area hotels, all of which have been screened for cleanliness, safe locations, and other desirability factors; you can check rates and book online.

Washington D.C. Accommodations, 2201 Wisconsin Ave. NW, Suite C110, Washington, DC 20007 (☎ 800/554-2220 or 202/289-2220; fax 202/338-4517; www.dcaccommodations.com). D.C. Accommodations has been in business for 15 years and, in addition to finding hotel accommodations, this service can advise you about transportation and general tourist information and even work out itineraries.

U.S.A. Groups (☎ 800/872-4777 or 202/861-1900; fax 703/440-9705). If you're planning a meeting, convention, or other group function requiring 10 rooms or more, contact this free service representing hotel rooms at almost every hotel in the District and suburban Virginia–Maryland region, in all price categories.

Bed and Breakfast Reservations Services. If a stay in a private home, apartment, or small inn appeals to you, you may want to consider the specific inns I've listed in this chapter, or try calling these two services: **The Bed and Breakfast League/Sweet Dreams and Toast,** P.O. Box 9490, Washington, DC 20016 (☎ 202/363-7767; fax 202/363-8396; e-mail: bedandbreakfast-washingtondc@ erols.com), represents more than 65 B&Bs in the District. The accommodations are screened, and guest reports are given serious consideration. All listings are convenient to public transportation. There's a 2-night minimum-stay requirement and a booking fee of $10 (per reservation). American Express, Diners Club, MasterCard, and Visa are accepted.

A similar service, **Bed & Breakfast Accommodations Ltd.,** P.O. Box 12011, Washington, DC 20005 (☎ 202/328-3510; fax 202/332-3885; www. bnbaccom.com), has more than 80 homes, inns, guest houses, and unhosted furnished apartments in its files. American Express, Diners Club, MasterCard, Visa, and Discover are accepted.

• Negotiate a cyber deal. You can use the online reservations services above, or check out Frommer's Online Directory, in the back, to read about Web sites that cover all travel needs, including hotel rooms.

You can book rooms by calling up the home pages of various chain hotels, such as Holiday Inn's **www.holiday-inn.com**. A few of these chains post special rates on the Internet that you wouldn't otherwise know about. Radisson (**www.radisson.com**), for instance, publishes its "Hot Deals" only on the Web. For a complete listing of hotel chain Internet addresses, see the Appendix.

But many hotels that are not part of a chain now have individual home pages, and sometimes those posted rates are amazingly lower than the ones they'll quote you. In

Landing the Best Room

Somebody has to get the best room in the house. It might as well be you.

Always ask for a corner room. They're usually larger, quieter, and closer to the elevator. They often have more windows and light than standard rooms, and they don't always cost more. Also, try calling direct to the hotel, rather than the 800 number, and ask for the "rooms manager," to request a specially situated room.

Remember that smaller hotels tend to be more personal, more likely to rely on staff, rather than computers, to handle special requests and reservations.

Though most hotels will tell you that check-in time is at 3pm, in fact, hotels often have rooms available before then; if you arrive early ask what rooms are available and take your pick.

When you make your reservation, ask if the hotel is renovating; if it is, request a room away from the renovation work. Many hotels now offer no-smoking rooms; if smoke bothers you, by all means ask for one. Inquire, too, about the location of the restaurants, bars, discos and ice machines in the hotel—these could all be a source of irritating noise. If you aren't happy with your room when you arrive, talk to the front desk. If they have another room, they should be happy to accommodate you, within reason.

spring of 1999, the St. James Suites, for instance, was offering online rates as low as $79 (for a weekend night in July), much different from the $109 weekend low rate the hotel publishes.

Another possibility is a service like **Travelweb,** at **www.Travelweb.com**. This Web site gives you access to the hotel industry's reservations system, where you may stumble upon last-minute offerings posted by Hilton, Hyatt, Sheraton, and other chains. Still another site, Aaron's Hotel and Motel Directory, at **www.hotel-intl.com**, gives you access to a comprehensive listing of properties for a particular town or zip code and other helpful travel information. If you are more in the mood to stay at an inn, try **www.innsandouts.com**.

1 Capitol Hill/The Mall

VERY EXPENSIVE

✪ **The Hotel George.** 15 E St. NW, Washington, DC 20001. ☎ **800/576-8331** or 202/347-4200. Fax 202/347-4213. www.hotelgeorge.com. 147 units. A/C MINIBAR TV TEL. Weekdays $225–$245 double, weekends $149 double; $375–$500 suite. Ask about seasonal and corporate rates. Extra person $20. Children under 14 stay free. AE, CB, DC, DISC, MC, V. Parking $18. Metro: Union Station.

Posters throughout this fairly new (opened in 1998) hotel, housed in a 1928 building, depicting a modern-day George Washington, sans wig, set the tone for this hotel. Rather than stick to old-style traditions, this place brings a hip attitude to Washington à la 2000. The lobby isn't fancy, but it's comfortable, and the decor is "cool retro." The large rooms are bright and white and offer modern amenities: hair dryers, coffeemakers, interactive cable TV with on-demand movies, irons and ironing board, two-line telephones with data port and voice mail, and granite-topped executive desks. I especially love the spacious, mirrored, marble bathrooms, with a speaker that broadcasts TV sound from the other room. The hotel attracts groups, Hill-ites waiting to make their mark on Capitol Hill, and stars like Alanis Morissette.

Dining/Diversions: The hotel's immensely popular restaurant, Bistro Bis, serves French bistro food. Chef Jeff Buben co-owns Bis and the acclaimed Vidalia with his wife, Sallie. (See chapter 6 for reviews of both Bistro Bis and Vidalia.)

Amenities: 24-hour concierge, overnight shoe shine, weekday delivery of *Washington Post,* laundry and valet, room service during restaurant hours, express checkout, VCR and CD player rentals, cigar-friendly billiard room, business/secretarial services, 1,600 square feet of meeting/banquet space, 24-hour fitness center with men's and women's steam rooms.

EXPENSIVE

Phoenix Park Hotel. 520 N. Capitol St. NW, Washington, DC 20001. ☎ **800/824-5419** or 202/638-6900. Fax 202/393-3236. phoenixpark@worldnet.att.net. 150 units. A/C MINIBAR TV TEL. Weekdays $189–$219 double, weekends starting from $89 double; $199–$799 suite. Extra person $20. Children under 16 stay free. AE, DC, DISC, MC, V. Parking $19. Metro: Union Station.

The Phoenix Park is one of a cluster of hotels across from Union Station and two blocks from the Capitol. What distinguishes this one is its popular and authentic Irish pub, the Dubliner, which attempts to set the tone for the entire property. This well-worn, wood-paneled pub, which offers Irish fare, ale, and entertainment, attracts a number of Irish and Irish-American guests, stages a number of Ireland-related events in its ballroom, and attempts an Irish air of hospitality—which, frankly, fails outside the doors of the pub. The rooms are attractive but cramped with furnishings. Each room is equipped with computer connections and iron and ironing board. Irish linens and toiletries are in the bathroom, along with coffeemakers and hair dryers.

Dining/Diversions: The hotel's pub, the Dubliner, attracts drinkers and guests from all over—see description above and in chapter 9.

Amenities: Room service until 11pm, voice mail, some secretarial services (faxing, copying), a small fitness center; daily delivery of the *Washington Post.*

MODERATE

Capitol Hill Suites. 200 C St. SE, Washington, DC 20003. ☎ **800/424-9165** or 202/543-6000. Fax 202/547-2608. 152 units. A/C TV TEL. $89–$199 double. Extra person $20. Rates include continental breakfast. Children under 18 stay free. AE, CB, DC, DISC, MC, V. Valet parking $18. Metro: Capitol South.

This well-run all-suite property (on the House side of the Capitol) comprises two converted apartment houses on a residential street near the Library of Congress, the Capitol, and Mall attractions. Photographs of the numerous congresspeople who stay here are displayed in the pleasant lobby. Accommodations are looking a little worn these days, but are clean and include full kitchens or kitchenettes and dining areas. Most units are efficiencies, with the kitchenette (humming refrigerator, sink, two gas burners, toaster), bed, and sofa all in the same room. The best are the one-bedroom units that have a full kitchen and a living room separate from the bedroom. A third option is the "studio double," with two double beds, a sofa, and a full, separate kitchen, but no living room area. Every suite has a coffeemaker, iron and ironing board, and hair dryer. Bathrooms are small, some tiny.

A food market and more than 20 nearby restaurants (many of which deliver to the hotel) compensate for the lack of on-premises dining facilities. Complimentary continental breakfast is offered daily in the first floor "salon." The *Washington Post* is available daily in the lobby. There are coin-operated washers and dryers, and guests enjoy free use of extensive facilities at the nearby Washington Sports and Health Club.

ⓘ Family-Friendly Hotels

Holiday Inn on the Hill *(see below)*   Children receive a free toy and book on arrival during summer promotions. Kids 12 and under eat free in the restaurant with an adult who's dining. The hotel is near Union Station, Capitol Hill, and the Mall and Smithsonian museums. Connecting rooms are available. Kids ages 4 to 11 can participate in the hotel's free Discovery Zone program of activities 4 to 10pm daily in summer and weekends the rest of the year. The hotel has a rooftop outdoor pool.

Omni Shoreham *(see p. 103)*   Adjacent to Rock Creek Park, the Omni is also within walking distance of the zoo and Metro and is equipped with a large outdoor pool and kiddie pool.

St. James Suites *(see p. 102)*   You're three Metro stops on the Blue line away from the Smithsonian museums and within walking distance of Georgetown. Reserve a one-bedroom suite, and the kids can sleep on the pullout sofa in the living room. Your kitchen is fully equipped, and continental breakfast is included in your room rate. There's an outdoor pool, too.

Washington Hilton & Towers *(see p. 92)*   A large, heated outdoor pool; a wading pool; three tennis courts; shuffleboard; and bike rental—what more does a kid need?

INEXPENSIVE

✪ **Holiday Inn on the Hill.** 415 New Jersey Ave. NW. ☎ **800/638-1116** or 202/638-1616. Fax 202/638-0707. www.holiday-inn.com/hotels/wasch. 343 units. A/C TV TEL. $89–$189 (Mon and Tues are most expensive days). Extra person $20. Children under 19 stay free, children 12 and under eat free. AE, CB, DC, DISC, MC, V. Parking $15. Metro: Union Station.

Refurbished in 1999, this hotel has put new bedspreads, drapes, shower curtains, TVs with Nintendo, individually controlled thermostats, and other items in every room; expanded its 24-hour fitness center; and upgraded the overall look and feel of the place. The staff aims to make you feel at home. Rooms are standard size, though the bathrooms are larger than expected, with a small vanity ledge just outside the bathroom for overflow counter space. Each room has a coffeemaker, hair dryer, iron and ironing board.

Clientele are mostly people with business on the Hill, especially "labor" folks, that is, people who have business with one of the several labor union headquarters located nearby. This place is good for families: In addition to the Holiday Inn–wide program that allows children 12 and under to eat free in the restaurant when an adult orders a meal, the hotel has an outdoor pool. Best of all is the Discovery Zone program—open 4pm to 10pm, daily in summer and on weekends the rest of the year—which is staffed by teachers and offers fun, but educational, activities for children ages 4 to 11. At this writing, the Discovery Zone is free. To get the best deals and perks, ask about summer promotions, the "Great Rates" package, and the hotel's "Priority Club" frequent guest membership. The hotel restaurant, Senators Grille, serves American food; room service is available 6am to 11pm daily. The hotel has eight meeting rooms, the second largest ballroom on Capitol Hill, and eight rooms equipped for the disabled, including two with a roll-in shower.

Georgetown,
West End, Downtown & Capitol Hill Accommodations

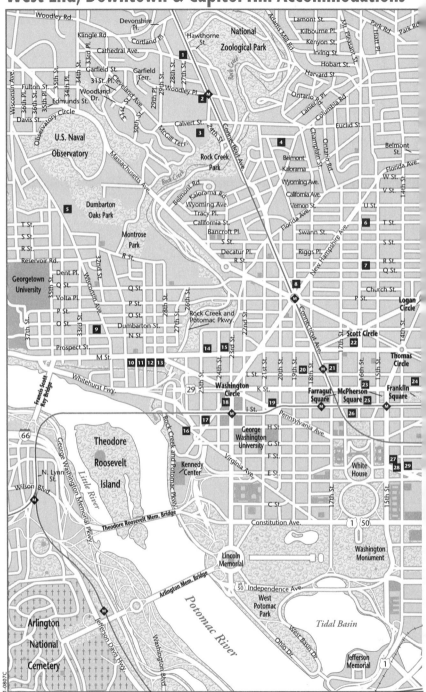

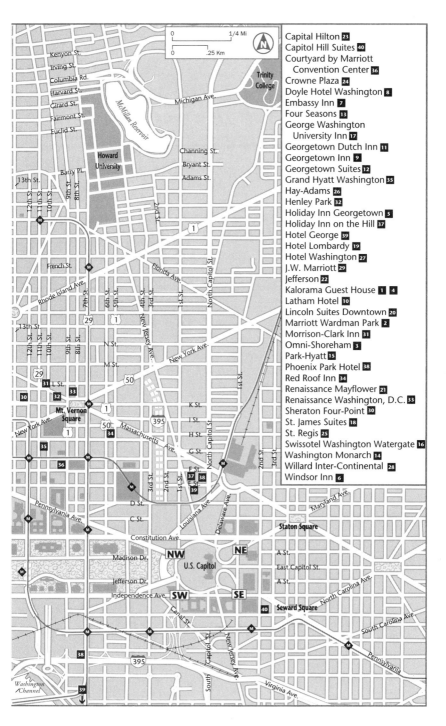

Capital Hilton **23**
Capitol Hill Suites **40**
Courtyard by Marriott
    Convention Center **36**
Crowne Plaza **24**
Doyle Hotel Washington **8**
Embassy Inn **7**
Four Seasons **13**
George Washington
    University Inn **17**
Georgetown Dutch Inn **11**
Georgetown Inn **9**
Georgetown Suites **12**
Grand Hyatt Washington **35**
Hay-Adams **26**
Henley Park **32**
Holiday Inn Georgetown **5**
Holiday Inn on the Hill **37**
Hotel George **39**
Hotel Lombardy **19**
Hotel Washington **27**
J.W. Marriott **29**
Jefferson **22**
Kalorama Guest House **1** **4**
Latham Hotel **10**
Lincoln Suites Downtown **20**
Marriott Wardman Park **2**
Morrison-Clark Inn **31**
Omni-Shoreham **3**
Park-Hyatt **15**
Phoenix Park Hotel **38**
Red Roof Inn **34**
Renaissance Mayflower **21**
Renaissance Washington, D.C. **33**
Sheraton Four-Point **30**
St. James Suites **18**
St. Regis **25**
Swissotel Washington Watergate **16**
Washington Monarch **14**
Willard Inter-Continental **28**
Windsor Inn **6**

2 Downtown, East of 16th Street NW

VERY EXPENSIVE

Grand Hyatt Washington. 1000 H St. NW, Washington, DC 20001. ☎ **800/233-1234** or 202/582-1234. Fax 202/637-4781. www.washington.grand.hyatt.com. 900 units. A/C MINIBAR TV TEL. Weekdays $305 double, weekends $119–$139 double. Extra person $25. Children under 18 stay free. AE, CB, DC, DISC, MC, V. Parking $12. Metro: Metro Center.

Hotel as circus, that's the Grand Hyatt. There's always something going on in the vast lobby—whose atrium is 12 stories high and enclosed by a glass, mansard-style roof. The hotel's waterfalls, baby grand piano floating on its own island in the 7,000-square-foot "lagoon," catwalks, 22-foot-high trees, and an array of bars and restaurants on the periphery will keep you permanently entertained. Should you get bored, head to the nearby nightspots and restaurants, or hop on the Metro, to which the Hyatt has direct access. The hotel is across from the Convention Center, between Capitol Hill and the White House, and two blocks from the MCI Center.

Guest rooms seem tame, by comparison, which is probably a good thing. They are attractive and comfortable, but don't have much personality. Each room has cable TV with free HBO service, hair dryers, irons, and ironing boards. Among the potpourri of special plans and packages available is one for business travelers: Pay an extra $15 and you stay in an 8th- or 9th-floor room equipped with a large desk, fax machine, computer hookup, and coffeemaker; have access to printers and other office supplies on the floor; and complimentary continental breakfast. Tourists should ask about package deals, like the "Grand Romance," All Around the City," and the "Via Pacifica dinner package."

Dining/Diversions: On site are three restaurants: The Zephyr Deli, the informal Grand Cafe, and the smaller Via Pacifica, which features Italian and Asian cuisine. There are three bars: the lobby Via Bar, the large Grand Slam sports bar, and Butlers—The Cigar Bar.

Amenities: Concierge, room service (Monday through Thursday 6am to 1am, Friday through Saturday 6am to 2am), dry cleaning/laundry service, twice daily maid service, express checkout, courtesy car available on a first come, first served basis to nearby destinations; two-story health club with Jacuzzi, lap pool, exercise room, steam and sauna room, and aerobics program; two large ballrooms, a 102-seat theater, and 40,000 square feet of meeting space; and American Express Travel Center for traveler's checks and ticketing.

✪ **Willard Inter-Continental.** 1401 Pennsylvania Ave. NW, Washington, DC 20004. ☎ **800/327-0200** or 202/628-9100. Fax 202/637-7326. www.interconti.com. 341 units. A/C MINIBAR TV TEL. Weekdays $410–$470 double, weekends $199–$299 double; $900–$3,500 suite. Extra person $30. Children under 18 stay free. AE, DC, DISC, JCB, MC, V. Parking $20. Metro: Metro Center.

If you're lucky enough to stay here, you'll be a stone's throw from the White House and the Smithsonian museums, in the heart of downtown near plenty of excellent restaurants, down the block from the National Theater, and down the avenue from the Capitol. Rooms are sumptuous, spacious, and furnished with Edwardian and Federal-period reproductions. Half of the Willard's 12 floors are no-smoking. And, because of the many heads of state (more than 100 in the last decade) who bunk here, the hotel offers the 6th floor as "Secret Service–cleared." Eight rooms are outfitted to accommodate guests with disabilities. Ten of the suites have kitchenettes. The rooms with the best views are the oval suites overlooking Pennsylvania Avenue to the Capitol, the rooms fronting Pennsylvania Avenue and, if it's quiet you're after, those facing the courtyard. The best room is the "Jenny Lind" suite perched in the curve of the 12th floor's southeast corner—a round "bull's eye" window captures glimpses of the Capitol. If you're here on a weekend you may choose one from five complimentary options, including an upgrade to a suite, or valet parking. Rooms have phones with dual lines, voicemail, and data-port plugs, and cable TVs with pay-movie channels, video message, and retrieval/checkout. Each room has an in-room safe, an iron, and an ironing board. In the oversize, marble bathrooms are a hair dryer, scale, phone, and TV speaker.

The Willard's designation as a National Historic Landmark in 1974 and magnifi-cent restoration in the 1980s helped revitalize Pennsylvania Avenue and this part of town. Stop in at the Round Robin Bar to hear bartender and manager Jim Hewes spin tales about the history of the 1901 Willard and its predecessor, the City Hotel, built on this site in 1815. The Willard's spectacular lobby and restaurant makes it a favorite location for movie and TV show shoots (look for it in the recent Harrison Ford release, *Random Hearts*). Most guests are corporate travelers.

Dining/Diversions: The Willard Room (the term power lunch originated here) is stunning (see chapter 6 for a review). The circular Round Robin Bar is where Henry Clay mixed the first mint julep in Washington (see "Behind Hotel Bars" in this chapter, for more about the Round Robin and bartender Jim Hewes). The Café Espresso (open until 3pm) offers croissant sandwiches, pastas, pastries, and vintage wines by the glass.

Amenities: Twice-daily maid service, 24-hour room service, currency exchange, airline/train ticketing, express checkout, newspaper delivery, fax and cellular phone rental, full business center, meeting rooms, complete fitness center, upscale boutiques.

EXPENSIVE

Crowne Plaza Washington, D.C. 14th and K sts. NW, Washington, DC 20005. ☎ **800/ 2CROWNE** or 202/682-0111. Fax 202/218-7600. www.crowneplazawashingtondc.com. 318 units. A/C TV TEL. Weekdays $189–$269 double, weekends $129–$239 (lower rates may be available—always ask); from $329 suite. Ask about the breakfast-included package for $139–$189 weekends, holidays and off-season, based on availability. Extra person $20. Chil-dren under 12 stay free. AE, CB, DC, DISC, MC, V. Parking $19. Metro: McPherson Square.

If the lobby were less grand and large, the room you're shown to might seem less plain and small. That said, standard guest rooms are clean and adequate, each equipped with iron and ironing board, computer outlet, safe, coffeemaker, two phones and voice mail, and beds with semi-firm mattresses; a hair dryer, cosmetic mirror, and Lord & Mayfair toiletries complete the bathroom. Tips for ensuring a good stay: Ask for a room on the K Street side, which overlooks Franklin Park and, if you're on an upper floor, views of the city skyline. Consider paying about $30 more to reserve a club-level (12th and 14th floors) room, for the better view (K Street side), in-room fax machine, complimentary continental breakfast and evening hors d'oeuvres, and complimentary delivery of the *Washington Post*.

Located 4 blocks from the White House and near many good restaurants, the hotel attracts a business clientele weekdays, tourists on weekends.

Dining/Diversions: The hotel's restaurant, the Franklin Exchange, is popular with local officeworkers because of its $12.95 lunch buffet featuring house-made soup, fresh salads, rotisserie items, and French pastries.

Amenities: Health club, room service, business center and meeting space.

✪ **Henley Park.** 926 Massachusetts Ave. NW (at 10th St.), Washington, DC 20001. ☎ **800/222-8474** or 202/638-5200. Fax 202/638-6740. 95 units. A/C MINIBAR TV TEL. Weekdays $145–$225 double, summer and weekends $98 double; $315 junior suite, $395–$475 1-bedroom suite, $725 Ambassador Suite. Senior discounts. Extra person $20. Children under 14 stay free. AE, CB, DC, DISC, MC, V. Parking $16. Metro: Metro Center, Gallery Place, or Mt. Vernon Square.

This is an intimate, English-style hotel housed in a converted 1918 Tudor-style apartment house with 119 gargoyles on its facade. The lobby, with its exquisite Tudor ceiling, archways, and leaded windows, is particularly evocative of the period. Luxurious rooms make this a good choice for upscale romantic weekends, although these lodgings fill up with corporate travelers weekdays. Rooms are decorated in the English country house mode, with Hepplewhite-, Chippendale-, and Queen Anne–style furnishings, including lovely period beds. Bathrooms have phones, cosmetic mirrors, and luxury toiletries, and in-room amenities include terry-cloth robes and, in some rooms, fax machines. All the suites have kitchenettes. The hotel has one room equipped for disabled travelers.

Dining/Diversions: The hotel's restaurant, Coeur de Lion, serves classic continental cuisine; the menu highlights seafood and the wine list is excellent. Marley's, a delightful cocktail lounge, is the setting for piano bar entertainment (and complimentary hors d'oeuvres) weeknights, live jazz nightly, and dancing Friday and Saturday. Afternoon tea (reservations required) is served daily between 4 and 6pm in the octagonal Wilkes Room, a charming parlor with a working fireplace.

Amenities: 24-hour concierge and room service, *Washington Post* delivery each weekday morning, complimentary shoe shine, complimentary weekday 7:30 to 10am limo service to downtown and Capitol Hill locations, access to a fitness room in the Morrison-Clark Historic Inn (see listing below) across the street.

✪ **Hotel Washington.** 515 15th St. NW (at Pennsylvania Ave. NW), Washington, DC 20004. ☎ **800/424-9540** or 202/638-5900. Fax 202/638-1594. www.hotelwashington.com. 350 units. A/C MINIBAR TV TEL. Weekdays $179–$245 double; weekends $145–$185; $438–$680 suite. Subject to availability, certain bargain rates apply: weekends $135 double; $174 corporate rate, weekdays, double; family plan of $106 for family of 4, with children under 14, including breakfast. Extra person $18. Children under 14 stay free. AE, DC, MC, V. Parking $20. Metro: Metro Center.

Built in 1918, this hotel is the oldest continuously operating hotel in Washington. Renovations throughout the years play up the historic angle. The wooden moldings, crystal chandeliers, and marble floors in the two-story lobby are reconstructed originals. Decor in the guest rooms is traditional, with lots of mahogany furnishings and historically suggestive print fabrics and wall coverings.

People choose to stay at the Hotel Washington because of its location and views. From its corner perch at Pennsylvania Avenue and 15th Street, the 12-story hotel surveys the avenue, monuments, Capitol, and the White House. No other hotel in town can top a more panoramic spectacle than its Rooftop Terrace where, from late April through October, you can have drinks and light fare. Guest rooms on the Pennsylvania Avenue side have great views, as do the first-floor meeting rooms.

Dining/Diversions: The hotel's main restaurant, the Two Continents, is on the lobby level and serves American cuisine. In the lobby Corner Bar, complimentary coffee is provided daily and free hors d'oeuvres, nuts, and fruit are put out weekdays after 3:30pm during the winter. At the Rooftop Terrace, you can soak up the views while enjoying light fare.

Amenities: Room service (7am to 11pm), dry cleaning and laundry, express checkout, valet parking, business center and meeting rooms, fitness center, sauna, tour desk (for Old Town Trolley), gift shop.

✪ **J. W. Marriott.** 1331 Pennsylvania Ave. NW (at E St.), Washington, DC 20004. ☎ **800/228-9290** or 202/393-2000. Fax 202/626-6991. www.marriott.com. 772 units. A/C TV TEL. Weekdays $244–$274 double, $254 for city view, $264 for concierge-level, $274 for concierge-level with view. Weekends $149–$244 double. Extra person free. AE, DC, DISC, JCB, MC, V. Parking $20. Metro: Metro Center.

The best thing about this hotel is its location: situated on Pennsylvania Avenue, adjacent to the National Theater, one block from the Warner Theater, two blocks from the White House, and within walking distance of the Washington Monument, the Smithsonian museums, and lots of restaurants. The best rooms on the 7th, 12th, 14th, and 15th floors overlook Pennsylvania Avenue and the monuments (floors 14 and 15 are concierge levels). Corporate types and conventioneers make up much of the clientele, with tourists (including families) filling in the rest.

This is a busy place and the rooms are pretty standard. They are furnished with desks and armoires, many of them cherry-wood pieces. You'll find an iron and full-size ironing board in your room, as well as a cable TV that offers HBO and On-Command videos, video checkout and message center. For best value, book around the Christmas holidays or on weekends.

Dining/Diversions: The hotel's main dining room is Celadon, which serves American/continental cuisine. Allie's American Grille overlooks Pennsylvania Avenue and serves American fare. A pianist plays during Sunday brunch and after 6pm nightly in the skylit Garden Terrace.

Amenities: Concierge and 24-hour room service, laundry and dry cleaning, weekday delivery of *USA Today,* baby-sitting, express checkout, a connecting mall with 80 shops and restaurants, complete health club (with indoor swimming pool and whirlpool), video games, full business center, gift shop.

Renaissance Washington, D.C. Hotel. 999 9th St. NW (at K St.), Washington, D.C. 20001. ☎ **800/228-9898** or 202/898-9000. Fax 202/289-0947. www.renaissancehotel.com. 801 units. A/C TV TEL. Weekdays $199–$229 double; weekends $109–$129 double; club level $229–$249 double; $295–$2,000 suite. Extra person $25. Children under 18 stay free. AE, CB, DC, DISC, MC, V. Parking $15. Metro: Gallery Place.

Directly across the street from the D.C. Convention Center and 1 block away from the MCI Center, this hotel caters primarily to conventioneers and business travelers, so much so that the hotel is adding another 550 rooms, to be completed by 2003, just in time for the opening of the new convention center.

A renovation completed in 1997 transformed guest rooms from contemporary to traditional decor, with oak furnishings and earth tones. Rooms offer remote-control TVs (with cable stations, pay-movie options, and video message retrieval/checkout) and phones with voicemail and computer jacks. The hotel has 16 rooms for guests with disabilities, including two with roll-in showers. The Renaissance Club, a 15-story tower with 153 rooms, has concierge-level amenities, such as free use of the health club and complimentary hors d'oeuvres served in the club room every evening.

Dining/Diversions: Mahogany-paneled and crystal-chandeliered, The Tavern features American regional cuisine; a bar adjoins. The less formal Café Florentine offers reasonably priced buffets and à la carte meals with a Mediterranean flair. The Caracalla prepares classic Italian cuisine. And the Plaza Gourmet offers take-out sandwiches, salads, and fresh-baked pastries.

Amenities: 24-hour room service and concierge; dry-cleaning and laundry service; daily delivery of *USA Today;* express checkout; valet parking; gift shop; full business center including 72,000 square feet of meeting space; 10,000-square-foot health club ($8 a day, or $14 for your whole stay), including pool, sauna, extensive exercise equipment, and aerobics floor.

MODERATE

✪ **Courtyard by Marriott Convention Center.** 900 F St. NW (at 9th St. NW), Washington, DC 20004. ☎ **800/321-2211** or 202/638-4600. Fax 202/638-4601. www.courtyard.com. 188 units. A/C TV TEL. Weekdays $129–$189, weekends $99–$129; from $165 suites. Extra

Behind Hotel Bars: The Willard's Round Robin Bartender Tells All

A good hotel bar is a haven. Whether you are a woman alone, a couple in love, old friends catching up with each other, colleagues talking business, or a journalist interviewing a subject, a hotel bar can offer a comfortable, relaxing place for quiet conversation and a well-mixed drink or glass of wine. In Washington, exceptional bars include those at the **Jefferson, St. Regis, Westin Fairfax, Hay-Adams, Mayflower, Canterbury,** and the **Tabard.**

The **Willard Hotel's Round Robin Bar** is in a class of its own, largely because of its legendary bartender. Jim Hewes, who, with colleagues Carol Randall and Shawn Carey, has bartended at the Round Robin since the renovated Willard reopened in 1986, is steeped in nearly 2 centuries' worth of knowledge of presidential drink preferences and Washington political and social life. A cast of characters from Hewes's stories are depicted in the black-and-white portraits that line the green felt–covered walls of the bar: Charles Dickens, Samuel Clemens, Warren Harding, and Abraham Lincoln are just some of the many famous people who have stopped in or stayed at the Willard. If you care for an easy and amiable history lesson, along with that classic gin and tonic, grab a stool at the round mahogany bar and let the ponytailed Hewes regale you.

"In the old days, everything took place within 10 blocks of the White House. The center of activity was supposed to be the Capitol, but it was really around here, and the Willard, starting in the 1840s and 1850s, gained a reputation as a meeting place. Presidents Zachary Taylor, Millard Fillmore, James Buchanan, Calvin Coolidge, Warren Harding, and Abraham Lincoln each lived or stayed for a time at the Willard. Washington Irving brought Charles Dickens (a port, brandy, and wine drinker) here for a drink. Samuel Clemens (better known as

person $10. Children under 17 free. AE, CB, DC, DISC, MC, V. Parking $16. Metro: Gallery Place or Metro Center.

Downtown Washington needs a place like this: A conveniently situated, moderately priced, medium-size property with a better than average restaurant on site. The hotel only just opened in late spring of 1999, but the eight-story building with its handsome stonework and many arches is a historic landmark, constructed in 1891 to house a bank. Rooms have two double beds or a king-size bed, firm mattresses, a chair and ottoman, large desk, two-line phones with voicemail and data ports, good-size bathrooms, hair dryer, iron and ironing board, coffeemaker, and lots of windows with views of downtown (best views—including glimpses of the Washington Monument and the Capitol—are on the 9th Street side, the higher up the better). There's a fitness center, small pool, and meeting space for 35 (including a boardroom, the bank's restored safe-deposit vault with its original 2-foot-thick circular door). Seven of the suites have a Jacuzzi, four rooms are designed for disabled guests, including two with roll-in showers. You're across the street from the MCI Center, the National Museum of American Art and the National Portrait Gallery, around the corner from Ford's Theatre, one block from the FBI, and 2½ blocks from the convention center. Nick's Fish Market occupies the marble-floored, columned space that was once the bank's lobby. Word is that this hotel is striving to be the most customer service-oriented property in the Courtyard by Marriott domain.

Mark Twain) palled around with Senator Stewart from Nevada, imbibing bourbon at the bar. Walt Whitman wrote a poem about the Willard bar. Nathaniel Hawthorne, in the capital to cover the Civil War for *The Atlantic* magazine, wrote 'You adopt the universal habit of the place, and call for a mint-julep, a whiskey-skin, a gin cocktail, a brandy smash, or a glass of pure old Rye, for the conviviality of Washington sets in at an early hour and, so far as I have had the opportunity to observe, never terminates at any hour.'"

"Throughout the 19th century, and up until World War I, people drank constantly throughout the day," says Hewes. "Popular in the 1840s was the Mamie Taylor, a potent mix of Scotch whiskey, lime juice, and ginger soda that was invented in Washington to honor Old Rough and Ready's sweetie, a hard-drinking, corn-cob-smoking first lady," notes Hewes. The mint julep, introduced at the Round Robin by statesman Henry Clay in 1850, quickly caught on and has been associated with the Round Robin ever since. (For the past few Kentucky Derby Days, Hewes has discussed the history of the mint julep for National Public Radio's *All Things Considered*.) Ulysses S. Grant was among the presidents to enjoy the julep.

"President Clinton is a Tanqueray and tonic man, and he likes his beer, though usually he'll have what the others in his party are having. Bush liked martinis. Reagan, and Nixon, too, introduced the city to California wines and Schramsburg sparkling wine," says Hewes.

And Hewes's favorite drink? "A good Irish whiskey, or a beer," he says. If you're intent on hitting the Round Robin when Hewes is tending bar, better call ahead (☎ **202/637-7348**) since he's not there everyday.

☼ **Morrison-Clark Historic Inn.** 1015 L St. NW (at 11th St. and Massachusetts Ave. NW), Washington, DC 20001. ☎ **800/332-7898** or 202/898-1200. Fax 202/289-8576. 54 units. A/C MINIBAR TV TEL. Weekdays $155–$185 double, weekends $99–$129 double; $175–$205 suite. Rates include continental breakfast. Extra person $20. Children under 16 stay free. AE, CB, DC, DISC, MC, V. Parking $15. Metro: Metro Center or Mt. Vernon Square.

This magnificent inn, occupying twin 1865 Victorian brick townhouses—with a newer wing in converted stables across an interior courtyard—is listed in the National Register of Historic Places. Guests enter via a turn-of-the-century parlor, with velvet- and lace-upholstered Victorian furnishings and lace-curtained bay windows. A delicious continental breakfast is served in the adjoining Club, which boasts an original white marble fireplace and 13-foot windows flanking gilded mirrors. In warm weather, you can breakfast in the lovely, two-level, brick-paved courtyard, enclosed by the inn and neighboring buildings.

High-ceilinged guest rooms are individually decorated with original artworks, sumptuous fabrics, and antique or reproduction 19th-century furnishings. Most popular—and the grandest—are the Victorian-style rooms, with new chandeliers and bedspreads added in the past year. Four Victorian rooms have private porches; many other rooms have plant-filled balconies. All have two phones (bed and bathroom) equipped with computer jacks and hair dryers.

Room service is available from the inn's highly acclaimed restaurant (see chapter 6 for a review). Other amenities include twice-daily maid service, complimentary *Washington Post* weekdays, business services, and fresh flowers in every room. A tiny fitness center is on the premises.

INEXPENSIVE

✪ **Red Roof Inn.** 500 H St. NW, Washington, DC 20001. ☎ **800/THE-ROOF** or 202/ 289-5959. Fax 202/682-9152. www.redroof.com. 197 units. A/C TV TEL. Weekdays $89–$119 double, weekends $69–$119 double. Children under 18 stay free. AE, CB, DC, DISC, MC, V. Parking $9.50. Metro: Gallery Place.

Reserve early. This popular hotel, with considerate staff, sits in the heart of Chinatown, within walking distance of many attractions, including the National Building Museum and the MCI Center, and super restaurants and nightlife. The neighborhood is still a little shaky, but looking better all the time: This is the part of town that's undergoing a renaissance. Rooms in the 10-story hotel are attractively decorated and have coffeemakers, irons and ironing boards, hair dryers, and TVs with free Showtime and Nintendo. Bathrooms have surprisingly generous counter space. There's a reasonably priced cafe open 6:30am to 2pm and 5:30 to 10pm weekdays, breakfast-only on weekends. On-premises facilities include coin-operated washers and dryers and a sunny 10th-floor exercise room with sauna. *USA Today* is free at the front desk. Eight rooms are equipped for disabled guests, including one with roll-in shower.

Sheraton Four-Point Downtown. 1201 K St. NW, Washington, DC 20005. ☎ **800/ 562-3350** or 202/842-1020. Fax 202/289-0336. 219 units. A/C TV TEL. Weekdays $99–$145 double, weekends $89–$135 double. Extra person $15. Children under 12 stay free. AE, CB, DC, DISC, MC, V. Parking $16. Metro: McPherson Square or Metro Center.

Note: This hotel is undergoing a renovation until March 2000, at least. Much of the information provided here may change, but I include the property because it will still probably be a less expensive option for those seeking a central downtown address.

Proximity to the Convention Center and MCI Center makes this eight-floor hotel a perfect choice for visitors attending events there. A small rooftop pool will appeal to families with young children. Rooms are clean, cheerfully decorated and equipped with satellite TVs in armoires, hair dryers, and coffeemakers. On the top two "executive floors," guests get king-size beds; minifridges; microwaves; views of the Capitol (corner room 919 is probably best); and access to the Executive Club, with a computer, TV, continental breakfast, and kitchen. Rooms are split between smoking and no-smoking. Four rooms are equipped for wheelchair accessibility.

The lobby is always crowded with conventioneers checking in, along with families during the summer. The facility has 12,000 square feet of meeting space, a full-service restaurant, and adjoining lounge. Additional amenities include room service (7am to 10pm), a small fitness center, and a coin-operated laundry; a car-rental agency is just across the street. City tours depart from the lobby. Complimentary shuttle service operates weekdays within a 5-mile radius of the hotel.

3 Downtown, 16th Street NW & West

VERY EXPENSIVE

✪ **Hay-Adams.** 16th and H sts. NW, Washington, DC 20006. ☎ **800/424-5054** or 202/ 638-6600. Fax 202/638-3803. www.hayadams.com. 143 units. A/C MINIBAR TV TEL. Weekdays $300–$520 double, weekends $220–$370. (The more expensive rooms are the ones with White House views.) Extra person $30. Children under 16 stay free. AE, CB, DC, JCB, MC, V. Parking $22. Metro: Farragut West or McPherson Square.

Reserve a room on the 6th through 8th floors, H Street side of the hotel, pull back the curtains from the windows, and enjoy a full frontal view of the White House—with the Washington Monument behind it. One block from the president's abode, the Hay-Adams offers the best vantage point in town. Between the hotel and the White House is Lafayette Square, another landmark. (Actually, in winter, when trees in Lafayette Park are bare, you can view the White House from rooms on the 2nd floor and up, H-street-side).

The Hay-Adams is one in the triumvirate of exclusive hotels built by Harry Wardman in the 1920s (the Jefferson and the St. Regis are the other two). Its architecture is Italian Renaissance, and the building's interior has walnut wainscoting, arched alcoves, and intricate Tudor and Elizabethan ceiling motifs. The hotel is working to improve other of its older, less charming features: rattling pipes and thin windows and walls. Among the hotel's first guests were Amelia Earhart, Sinclair Lewis, Ethel Barrymore, and Charles Lindbergh. Today's guests tend to be socialites, foreign dignitaries, and power elite lawyers and business leaders (but the staff won't divulge names).

The high-ceilinged guest rooms are individually furnished with antiques and superior appointments that might include 18th-century-style furnishings, silk-covered walls hung with botanical prints, a molded plaster ceiling, and French silk floral-print bedspreads and upholstery. Many rooms have ornamental fireplaces. All rooms have plush bathrobes, hair dryers, and three two-line phones with data ports and voicemail. Check out special packages on the hotel's Web site, like the $199 deal, which offers an overnight with a choice of full American breakfast for two, afternoon tea for two, or valet parking.

Dining/Diversions: The sunny Lafayette Restaurant (overlooking the White House) is an exquisite dining room that serves contemporary American/continental fare, plus afternoon tea. The adjoining lounge features nightly piano-bar entertainment. Off the Record is the hotel's bar.

Amenities: 24-hour room and concierge service, daily delivery of *Washington Post,* complimentary shoe shine, access to a local health club, secretarial and business services, in-room fax on request, meeting rooms, complimentary morning sedan service.

✪ **The Jefferson.** 1200 16th St. NW (at M St.), Washington, DC 20036. ☎ **800/368-5966** or 202/347-2200. Fax 202/331-7982. www.camberley.com. 100 units. A/C MINIBAR TV TEL. Weekdays $319–$339 double, $350–$1,200 suite; weekends $189 double; from $289 suite. Extra person $25. Children under 12 stay free. AE, CB, DC, JCB, MC, V. Parking $20. Metro: Farragut North.

Opened in 1923 just 4 blocks from the White House, the Jefferson is one of the city's three most exclusive venues (along with the Hay-Adams and the St. Regis), proffering discreet hospitality to political personages, royalty, literati, and other notables. With a very high staff-to-guest ratio, the Jefferson puts utmost emphasis on service; if you like, a butler will unpack your luggage and press clothes wrinkled in transit.

Set foot in the lobby and you won't want to leave. An inviting sitting room with a fireplace at the rear of an extended vestibule draws you past green-velvet loveseats placed back-to-back down the middle and enclosed terraces opening off each side. A fine art collection, including original documents signed by Thomas Jefferson, graces the public area as well as the guest rooms.

Each antique-filled guest room evokes a European feel. Yours might have a four-poster bed with plump eyelet-trimmed comforter and pillow shams (many are topped with canopies), or a cherry-wood bookstand from the Napoleonic period filled with rare books. In-room amenities include two-line speaker phones; fax machines (you get your own fax number when you check in); VCRs; CD players; and, in the bathrooms, terry robes, hair dryers, and phones.

Dining/Diversions: Off the lobby is The Restaurant at the Jefferson, one of the city's premier dining rooms (see chapter 6 for a review) and a cozy bar/lounge. In the paneled lounge, whose walls are hung with framed letters and documents written by Thomas Jefferson, you can sink into a red leather chair and enjoy a marvelous high tea daily from 3 to 5pm, or cocktails anytime—the bar stocks a robust selection of single-malt scotches and a fine choice of Davidoff cigars.

Amenities: 24-hour butler service, overnight shoe shine, morning delivery of *Washington Post* or any other major newspaper, 24-hour room and multilingual concierge service, video and CD rentals, express checkout, business/secretarial services, meeting rooms, and for a fee of $20, guests have access to full health club facilities (including pool) at the University Club across the street.

✪ **Renaissance Mayflower.** 1127 Connecticut Ave. NW (between L and M sts.), Washington, DC 20036. ☎ **800/228-7697** or 202/347-3000. Fax 202/466-9082. www.marriott.com. 738 units. A/C MINIBAR TV TEL. Weekdays $265–$315, weekends $139–$189. Extra person $25. Children under 18 stay free. AE, CB, DC, DISC, JCB, MC, V. Parking $12. Metro: Farragut North.

Superbly located in the heart of downtown, the Mayflower is the hotel of choice for guests as varied as Monica Lewinsky and jazz genius Wynton Marsalis. The lobby, which extends an entire block from Connecticut Avenue back to 17th Street, is always active, since Washingtonians tend to use it as a shortcut in their travels.

The hotel is imbued with history: The Mayflower was the site of Calvin Coolidge's inaugural ball in 1925, the year it opened. (Coolidge didn't attend—he was mourning his son's death from blood poisoning.) President-elect FDR and family lived in rooms 776 and 781 while waiting to move into the White House, and this is where FDR penned the words, "The only thing we have to fear is fear itself." A major restoration in the 1980s uncovered large skylights and renewed the lobby's pink marble bas-relief frieze and spectacular promenade.

Graciously appointed guest rooms have high ceilings, cream moiré wall coverings, and mahogany reproduction furnishings (Queen Anne, Sheraton, Chippendale, Hepplewhite). Amenities include ironing board and iron; three phones; terry robe; hair dryer; and a small color TV in the bathroom. Inquire about "summer value rates."

Dining/Diversions: Washington lawyers and lobbyists gather for power breakfasts in the Café Promenade. Under a beautiful domed skylight, the restaurant is adorned with Edward Laning's murals, crystal chandeliers, marble columns, and lovely flower arrangements. A full English tea is served here afternoons Monday through Saturday. The clubby, mahogany-paneled Town and Country is the setting for light buffet lunches and complimentary hors d'oeuvres during cocktail hour. Bartender Sambonn Lek has quite a following and as much for his conversation as for his magic tricks. The Lobby Court, a Starbucks espresso bar just opposite the front desk, serves coffee and fresh-baked pastries each morning, and becomes a piano bar serving cocktails later in the day.

Amenities: Coffee, tea, or hot chocolate and *USA Today* with wake-up call, 24-hour room service, twice-daily maid service, complimentary overnight shoe shine, concierge, courtesy car takes you within a 3-mile radius, express checkout, valet parking, business center, full on-premises fitness center, florist, gift shop.

The St. Regis. 923 16th St. NW, Washington, DC 20006. ☎ **800/562-5661** or 202/638-2626. Fax 202/638-4231. www.luxurycollection.com. 192 units. A/C MINIBAR TV TEL. Weekdays $345–$460 double, weekends $285–$405 double; $600–$2,500 suite. Children under 10 stay free. AE, CB, DC, DISC, JCB, MC, V. Parking $24. Metro: Farragut West or McPherson Square.

Ah, luxury! Guest rooms are quietly opulent and decorated in tastefully coordinated colors, with duvets on the beds, desks set in alcoves, a mirror-covered armoire, and creamy silk moiré wall coverings. The marble bathrooms have hair dryers, lighted makeup mirrors, and designer toiletries by Bijan. Other amenities include three direct dial telephones with voicemail and modem capabilities; personal safes; and fax machines. Guests have included everyone from Queen Elizabeth to the Rolling Stones.

You may just want to hang out in the lobby, designed to resemble a Milan palazzo, with Palladian windows hung with rich damask draperies, elaborately gilded ceilings, Louis XVI chandeliers, plush green oversized sofas, and cozy chairs.

Dining/Diversions: Lespinasse is quite the elegant restaurant (see chapter 6 for a review). The Library Lounge, which might be the best hotel bar in Washington, has a working fireplace and paneled walls lined with bookcases. High tea is offered daily in the posh lobby.

Amenities: 24-hour concierge and room service, pressing service, complimentary coffee or tea with wake-up call, complimentary newspaper of your choice weekdays, complimentary shoe shine, complimentary bottled water with turndown service, no charge for credit-card calls and local faxes, 24-hour state-of-the-art fitness room and access to a complete health club (at the University Club), 10,000 square feet of meeting space, ballroom.

EXPENSIVE

The Capital Hilton. 1001 16th St. NW (between K and L sts.), Washington, DC 20036. ☎ **800/HILTONS** or 202/393-1000. Fax 202/639-5784. www.capital.hilton.com. 543 units. A/C MINIBAR TV TEL. Weekdays $126–$275 double, add $30 more for Tower units; weekends (including continental breakfast) $133 double, $155 Tower. Extra person $25. Children under 12 stay free. AE, CB, DC, DISC, JCB, MC, V. Parking $22. Metro: Farragut West, Farragut North, or McPherson Square.

This longtime Washington hotel has hosted every American president since FDR, and the annual Gridiron Club Dinner and political roast takes place in its ballroom. The Hilton's central location (2 blocks from the White House) makes it convenient for tourists, and business travelers appreciate the Tower's concierge floors (10, 11, 12, and 14) and extensive facilities.

The rooms are decorated in Federal-period motif with Queen Anne– and Chippendale-style furnishings. Each room has three two-line phones with dataports. Standard Hilton features include a hair dryer, iron and ironing board, and coffeemaker. Ask about special rates for AAA members, senior citizens, military, and families, or ask about the "Hilton Bounce-back" weekend rate ($129 to $159, you get a room and continental breakfast).

Dining/Diversions: Steak and seafood are the menu highlights at Fran O'Brien's Steakhouse, an upscale sports-themed restaurant named for its owner, a former Redskin. American regional fare is served at the sunny, gardenlike Twigs and the more elegant Twigs Grill, which adjoins. The Bar is the hotel's lobby lounge.

Amenities: 24-hour room service, concierge (7am to 11pm), full business center with conference rooms, daily delivery of *USA Today,* tour and ticket desk, unisex hair dresser, gift shop, facial salon, shoe-shine stand, ATM with foreign-currency capabilities, and airline desks (American, Continental, Northwest). In 1999, the hotel opened a $2.4 million, two-level, 10,000-square-foot health club and spa, offering everything from massage therapy to personal trainers. (Hotel guests pay a small fee to use it.)

MODERATE

✪ **Lincoln Suites Downtown.** 1823 L St. NW, Washington, DC 20036. ☎ **800/ 424-2970** or 202/223-4320. Fax 202/223-8546. www.lincolnhotels.com. 99 suites. A/C TV

TEL. Weekdays $129–$159 suite, weekends $99–$129 suite. Children under 16 stay free. AE, DC, DISC, MC, V. Parking $14 (in adjoining garage). Metro: Farragut North or Farragut West.

Lots of long-term guests stay at this all-suite, 10-story hotel in the heart of downtown, just 5 blocks from the White House. A multimillion dollar renovation was completed in May 1997, refurbishing the large, comfortable suites and sprucing up hallways. About 27 suites offer full kitchens; others have refrigerators, wet bars, coffeemakers, and microwaves. Rooms are fairly spacious, well-kept, attractive, and equipped with hair dryers and irons and ironing boards. The property also has a coin-operated washer and dryer and a small meeting room.

The hotel is connected to Mackey's, an Irish pub, next door. Mackey's features reasonably priced Irish food. Luigi's, an Italian restaurant around the corner, provides room service for lunch and dinner. Complimentary copies of the *Washington Post* are delivered to your door Monday through Saturday (and are for sale in the lobby on Sunday). The hotel serves complimentary milk and homemade cookies each evening, and complimentary continental breakfast weekend mornings in the lobby. Guests enjoy free use of the well-equipped Bally's Holiday Spa nearby.

INEXPENSIVE

Embassy Inn. 1627 16th St. NW (between Q and R sts.), Washington, DC 20009. ☎ **800/423-9111** or 202/234-7800. Fax 202/234-3309. 38 units. A/C TV TEL. Weekdays $79–$159 double, weekends $59 double. Rates include continental breakfast, evening sherry, and snacks. Smoking rooms on lower level. Extra person $10. Children under 14 stay free. AE, CB, DC, MC, V. Metro: Dupont Circle.

This four-story 1910 brick building, a former inn, was rescued from demolition some years back, spruced up, and restored as a quaint, homey, small hotel. Its Federal-style architecture harmonizes with other turn-of-the-century townhouses along this block, within a district designated "historic" in 1964. Both the Embassy and its sister property, the Windsor (see below), are located near lots of restaurants and just a few streets over from Connecticut Avenue, which forms the center of the Dupont Circle neighborhood.

Accommodations are comfortable, clean, and a little quirky in design: The sink is in the bedroom, not the bathroom; bathrooms have only shower stalls; and middle rooms have no windows. Cable TV with free HBO and hair dryers, are unexpected perks. The lobby doubles as a parlor where breakfast (including fresh-baked muffins and croissants) is served daily and fresh coffee brews all day. You can pick up maps and brochures, read a complimentary *Washington Post,* or request sundries you may have forgotten (toothbrush, razor, and the like). *Note:* There is no elevator, and there's street parking only.

Windsor Inn. 1842 16th St. NW (at T St.), Washington, DC 20009. ☎ **800/423-9111** or 202/667-0300. Fax 202/667-4503. 47 units. A/C TV TEL. Weekdays $79–$129 double; $129–$159 suite; weekends $59. Rates include continental breakfast, evening sherry, and snacks. Smoking rooms on lower level. Extra person $10. Children under 14 stay free. AE, CB, DC, MC, V. Metro: Dupont Circle.

Under the same ownership and just a couple of blocks north of the above-mentioned Embassy Inn, the Windsor Inn occupies two brick buildings, side by side but with separate entrances. The Windsor annex has slightly larger rooms and more charming features, such as the occasional bay window or arched ceiling. Some of the public areas are done in art deco motif. All rooms are neat and comfortable, and a few have sofas and/or decorative fireplaces. The Windsor offers cable TV with free HBO and hair dryers in each room. Six of the 39 rooms have tub and shower in bathrooms, the rest have only showers. Suites offer the greatest value, are very roomy and attractively furnished, and cost much less than you'd usually pay in Washington. Lower-level rooms (the smoking floor) face a skylit terrace with lawn furnishings and colorful murals. Continental breakfast, which includes croissants and muffins, is served in the lobby. Ice machines, a refrigerator, and a handsome conference room are available to guests. The very friendly multilingual staff is a big plus. *Note:* There is no elevator, and parking is on the street.

4 Georgetown

VERY EXPENSIVE

✪ **The Four Seasons.** 2800 Pennsylvania Ave. NW, Washington, DC 20007. ☎ **800/ 332-3442** or 202/342-0444. Fax 202/944-2076. www.fourseasons.com. 260 units. A/C MINIBAR TV TEL. Weekdays $370–$465 double; $775–$3,500 suite; weekends $285 double, from $575 suite. Extra person $40. Children under 16 stay free. AE, DC, JCB, MC, V. Parking $22. Metro: Foggy Bottom.

Set just at the mouth of Georgetown, this hotel is where the rich and famous stay. And the reason is the service. Staff are trained to know the names, preferences, even allergies of guests, and repeat clientele rely on this discreet attention.

Accommodations, many of them overlooking Rock Creek Park or the C&O Canal, have a residential atmosphere: walls hung with gilt-framed antique prints; beds outfitted with down-filled bedding, dust ruffles, and scalloped spreads; and large desks and plump cushioned armchairs with hassocks. In-room amenities include bathrobes, hair dryers, lighted cosmetic mirrors, and upscale toiletries. In the suites you will also find VCRs and CD players. In 1999, an adjoining building was renovated to add 25 rooms and 35 suites for clients who want state-of-the-art business amenities (each is soundproof and has an office equipped with fax machine, at least three telephones with two-line speakers, portable telephones, and headsets for private TV listening). These rooms are also larger than those in the main hotel. Three of the suites have kitchenettes. The renovation expanded the space and facilities of the health club, too (see below).

Dining/Diversions: The elegant and highly acclaimed Seasons is reviewed in chapter 6. The delightful Garden Terrace is bordered by tropical plants, ficus trees, and flower beds and has a wall of windows overlooking the canal. It's open for lunch, a lavish Sunday jazz brunch, and classic English-style afternoon teas.

Amenities: Twice-daily maid service, 24-hour room service and concierge, complimentary sedan service weekdays within the District, gratis newspaper of your choice, car windows washed when you park overnight, complimentary shoe shine, beauty salon, gift shop, jogging trail, business facilities, children's programs, extensive state-of-the-art fitness club and spa that includes personal trainers, a Vichy shower, hydrotherapy, and synchronized massage (two people work on you at the same time).

EXPENSIVE

The Georgetown Inn. 1310 Wisconsin Ave. NW, Washington, DC 20007. ☎ **202/ 333-8900.** Fax 202/333-8308. www.georgetowninn.com. 96 units. A/C TV TEL. Weekdays $200–$350 double in-season, $185–$300 double off-season. Weekend rates start at $165 double in-season and at $135 double off-season. Extra person $20. Children under 12 stay free. AE, CB, DC, DISC, MC, V. Valet parking $18. Metro: Foggy Bottom, with a 30-minute walk, or take a cab.

Like its sister inn, The Latham (see below), the Georgetown Inn is in the thick of Georgetown. Most guests are here on business, but come Memorial Weekend, the hotel is full of the proud parents of graduating Georgetown University students. (The hotel books up two years in advance for graduation weekend.)

The Georgetown is smaller than the Latham, but has larger rooms. Furnishings are handsome, emphasizing colonial styles. Half of the rooms hold twin double beds, although a few rooms have twin single beds, usually connecting with suites, helpful to families traveling with children. Ask for an "executive room" if you'd like a reading lamp over the bed, a coffeemaker, and a telephone in the bathroom. All rooms have a hair dryer and iron and ironing board. The bathrooms have only showers (some also have bidets), no tub. The beds are of the squishy mattress kind.

Dining/Diversions: The Daily Grill opened an outpost here in 1999, offering the same large portions of American food served at its first D.C. location, at 1200 18th St. NW (see chapter 6 for review).

Amenities: Room service during restaurant hours, concierge, computer data ports in most rooms, daily delivery of *Washington Post,* free use of a local fitness center and pool privileges at the Latham, a small meeting room, audiovisual services, and a Thrifty car rental agency is located across the driveway from the hotel.

The Latham. 3000 M St. NW, Washington, DC 20007. ☎ **800/528-4261** or 202/726-5000. Fax 202/337-4250. 143 units. A/C TV TEL. Weekdays $200–$350 double in-season, $185–$300 double off-season. Weekend rates start at $165 double in-season and at $135 double off-season. Extra person $20. Children under 12 stay free. AE, CB, DC, DISC, MC, V. Valet parking $18. Metro: Foggy Bottom, with a 20-minute walk, or take a cab.

The Latham is at the hub of Georgetown's trendy nightlife/restaurant/shopping scene, but since its accommodations are set back from the street, none of the noise of night-time revelers will reach your room. Charming earth-tone rooms are decorated in French-country motif, with pine furnishings and multipaned windows; cable TVs are housed in forest-green armoires. All rooms are equipped with large desks, hair dryers, and irons and ironing boards. Some 7th through 10th-floor rooms offer gorgeous canal views; 3rd-floor accommodations, all two-room suites, have windows facing a hallway designed to replicate a quaint Georgetown street. Most luxurious are the two-story carriage suites with cathedral ceilings and full living rooms. Fax printers are in a third of the rooms; CD players with headphones are in 3rd-floor and carriage suites.

Dining/Diversions: Michel Richard's highly acclaimed Citronelle, one of D.C.'s hottest restaurants, is on the premises (see chapter 6 for a review). And fronting the hotel is the country-French La Madeleine; another branch is fully described under Alexandria restaurants in chapter 10.

Amenities: Room service during restaurant hours, concierge, valet parking, free delivery of *Washington Post,* business services, express checkout, small (unheated) outdoor pool and bilevel sundeck, jogging and bike path along the C&O Canal, meeting rooms, and audiovisual services.

MODERATE

The Georgetown Dutch Inn. 1075 Thomas Jefferson St. NW (just below M St.), Washington, DC 20007. ☎ **800/388-2410** or 202/337-0900. Fax 202/333-6526. www.Utell.com. 47 units. A/C TV TEL. Weekdays $135–$195 1-bedroom suite for 2; $250–$320 2-bedroom duplex penthouse (sleeps 6); weekends $110–$130 1-bedroom suite for 2; $195–$250 penthouse suite. Rates include continental breakfast. Extra person $20. Children under 14 stay free. AE, CB, DC, DISC, MC, V. Very limited free parking for small to midsize cars. Metro: Foggy Bottom, with a 20-minute walk. Bus: 32, 34, and 36 go to all major Washington tourist attractions.

Many European and South American guests, usually embassy folks, stay at this inn. It's also a favorite for families here to celebrate weddings or graduations; they book several suites, or maybe a whole floor. Personalized service is a hallmark of the hotel, whose staff greet you by name and protect your privacy.

Accommodations are moderately sized one- and two-bedroom, apartmentlike suites, nine of them duplex penthouses with 1½ bathrooms; all have tiny but full kitchens (no microwaves). Amenities include irons and ironing boards; coffeemakers;

and three phones. You'll also find a cosmetic mirror in the bathroom; a hair dryer is provided on request.

Complimentary continental breakfast is served in the lobby each morning. Guests also enjoy free use of nearby state-of-the-art health clubs, one with indoor pool. The C&O Canal towpath, just down the block, is ideal for jogging and cycling, though be wary at night.

Georgetown Suites. 1111 30th St. NW (between K and M sts.), Washington, DC 20007. ☎ **800/348-7203** or 202/298-1600. Fax 202/333-2019. www.georgetownsuites.com. 136 units. A/C TV TEL. $139 studio suite (for 2); $149 1-bedroom suite (for up to 4); weekends $99 studio suite; $109 1-bedroom suite. Rollaways or sleeper sofa $10 extra. Rates include extended continental breakfast. AE, DC, MC, V. Limited parking $15. Metro: Foggy Bottom with a 15-minute walk.

This hotel, located on a Georgetown side street, was designed to meet the needs of business travelers making extended visits, but its casual atmosphere and suites with kitchens work well for families, too. The hotel also provides some space for kids to kick around: in the brick courtyard with flowering plants in terra-cotta pots and Victorian white wooden benches, or in the large lobby area, which resembles a student lounge— the TV's going; games, books, magazines, and daily newspapers lie scattered across table tops in front of loveseats and chairs; and a cappuccino machine rests on the counter. Tea and coffee are available throughout the day.

Accommodations have full kitchens, living rooms, and dining areas, all with large desks, hair dryers, and irons and ironing boards. The biggest, if not the best suites are probably the two-level, two-bedroom townhouses; each goes for $400 a night, less in off-season (the hotel's Web site tells you these townhouses have their own entrances on 29th Street, but this is no longer true). Among the on-premises facilities are coin-operated washers and dryers and a small exercise room. Hotel services include weekday delivery of the *Washington Post,* and food delivery from nearby restaurants. Local calls are free. M Street buses (a block away) will take you to most major D.C. attractions.

Georgetown Suites maintains another 78 suites (same phone number, rates, and amenities) close by, at 1000 29th St. NW, between K and M streets, though I would choose the 30th Street location first—the property on 29th Street adjoins the White-hurst Freeway and is much noisier.

INEXPENSIVE

Holiday Inn Georgetown. 2101 Wisconsin Ave. NW, Washington, DC 20007. ☎ **800/ HOLIDAY** or 202/338-4600. Fax 202/333-6113. www.eventsofmagic.com. 296 units. A/C TV TEL. $99 off-season to $179 high season. Extra person $10. Children under 19 stay free. Children under 12 eat free. AE, CB, DC, DISC, JCB, MC, V. Parking $15. Bus: 30, 32, and 34 travels between Georgetown and downtown.

This Holiday Inn does a brisk international business, stemming from its proximity to many embassies and the National Academy of Sciences, visited by scientists from around the world. Northwest Airlines attendants and pilots and the German airforce bunk here on layovers.

If you capture a cheap rate, say $99 to $125, you'll get a fairly good deal: a clean, though plain and rather small, room with either a king bed and sofa bed or two double beds (all have firm mattresses), and small bathrooms with thin towels. All rooms have a hair dryer, iron and ironing board, coffeemaker, and desk. Your kids may stay free in the room with you, and, if they are under 12, they may eat for free when you order a meal. To get the best rate, call the hotel directly and request the "promotional rate." But I wouldn't pay more than $130—you can get more for your money elsewhere. There's a fitness center and outdoor pool, a full-service restaurant, a sports bar, and a gift shop on the premises; room service is available during restaurant hours. You can do without a car, if you don't mind busing it or walking a bit—you're about a 10 to 15-minute walk from the center of Georgetown.

5 Adams-Morgan/North Dupont Circle

VERY EXPENSIVE

Washington Hilton & Towers. 1919 Connecticut Ave. NW (at T St.), Washington, DC 20009. ☎ **800/HILTONS** or 202/483-3000. Fax 202/797-5755. www.washington-hilton.com. 2,206 units. A/C MINIBAR TV TEL. Weekdays $230–$270 double, Towers rms $265–305 double; weekends (and selected weekdays and holidays) $119–$129 double, Towers rms $149–159 double. Extra person $20. Children 18 and under stay free. AE, CB, DC, DISC, JCB, MC, V. Self parking $12. Metro: Dupont Circle.

This superhotel/resort occupies seven acres and offers every imaginable amenity. The Hilton caters to group business travelers and is accustomed to coordinating meetings for thousands. Its vast conference facilities include the largest hotel ballroom on the East Coast between New York and Orlando (it accommodates nearly 4,000, theater-style). Besides conventions, the Hilton also hosts inaugural balls, debutante cotillions, and state banquets. Numerous smaller meeting rooms are available, and a business center is open during regular business hours.

Guest rooms are cheerful and attractively furnished; the artwork on the walls was commissioned by local artists. All have a coffeemaker, iron and ironing board, and hair dryer. Eighty-two suites have kitchenettes. From the fifth floor up, city-side, you'll have panoramic views of Washington (as well as a view of the Olympic-size pool). The newly renovated 10th floor is a concierge level called the Towers. The 9th and 10th floors are the executive levels, where rooms have two telephones with data ports.

Dining/Diversions: The handsome mahogany-paneled 1919 Grill specializes in steaks, seafood, and pasta. The Capital Café, for buffet meals and full restaurant fare, has a wall of windows overlooking the pool. A poolside eatery serves light fare under a striped tent top in season. The clubby McClellan's is a handsome brass-railed mahogany bar lounge. Capital Court, an elegant lobby lounge, features a nightly piano bar.

Amenities: Concierge; room service during restaurant hours; transportation/sightseeing desk; daily delivery of *USA Today;* express checkout; extensive health club facilities; Olympic-size, lighted, and heated outdoor pool; children's pool; three lighted tennis courts; shuffleboard; lobby shops; comprehensive business center.

EXPENSIVE

Hotel Sofitel. 1914 Connecticut Ave. NW, Washington, DC 20009. ☎ **800/424-2464** or 202/797-2000. Fax 202/462-0944. www.sofitel.com. 144 units. A/C MINIBAR TV TEL. Weekdays $199–$259 double, weekends $139–$159 double. Extra person $20. Children under 12 stay free. AE, CB, DC, MC, V. Valet parking $17, $9 for the day. Metro: Dupont Circle.

The front desk greets you with "Bonjour"; your room amenities include a bottle of Evian and Roger Gallet toiletries; the hotel's Trocadero restaurant serves French bistro food; and you get a fresh baguette at checkout. Guess what, the Sofitel is part of a French hotel chain. The 1906 building, a registered historic property, sits on a hill a short walk from lively Dupont Circle; its elevated position allows for great city views from rooms on the upper level, Connecticut Avenue–side of this eight-floor hotel. You're also just a short walk from trendy Adams-Morgan: Cross Connecticut and walk up Columbia Road. Rooms, in muted shades of champagnes and peach, are spacious, each with a breakfast/study alcove and many with sitting areas. Thirty-six suites have kitchenettes. A multilingual staff sees to the needs of an international clientele of diplomats, foreign delegations, and corporate travelers. If you're looking for a romantic getaway at a reasonable rate, ask about the hotel's "Romantic Rendezvous" and

Adams-Morgan & Dupont Circle Accommodations

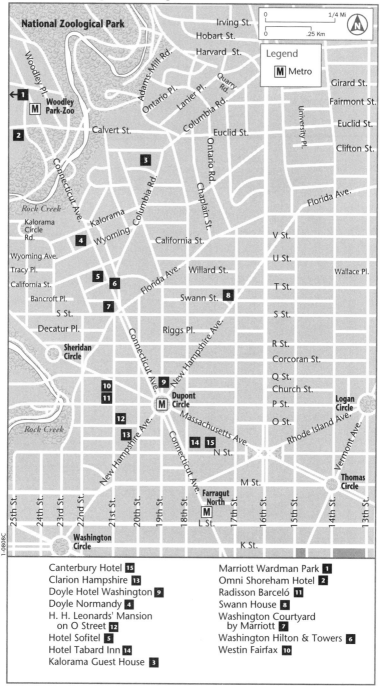

Canterbury Hotel **15**
Clarion Hampshire **13**
Doyle Hotel Washington **9**
Doyle Normandy **4**
H. H. Leonards' Mansion
    on O Street **12**
Hotel Sofitel **5**
Hotel Tabard Inn **14**
Kalorama Guest House **3**

Marriott Wardman Park **1**
Omni Shoreham Hotel **2**
Radisson Barceló **11**
Swann House **8**
Washington Courtyard
    by Marriott **7**
Washington Hilton & Towers **6**
Westin Fairfax **10**

"Weekend Superbe" packages. The Romantic Rendezvous gets you a suite, champagne, flutes, roses, and breakfast in bed for $199. The Weekend Superbe upgrades your room and provides continental breakfast in bed, for $125.

Dining/Diversions: The Trocadero is open for breakfast, lunch, and dinner; the Pullman Lounge bar adjoins the restaurant.

Amenities: Full-service concierge, 24-hour room service, dry cleaning and laundry, major national and European newspapers available in lobby or delivered to your door upon request, twice daily maid service, baby-sitting, secretarial services including faxing and copying, express checkout, fitness center with Nautilus and other equipment, conference rooms.

MODERATE

Washington Courtyard by Marriott. 1900 Connecticut Ave. NW (at Leroy Place), Washington, DC 20009. ☎ **800/842-4211** or 202/332-9300. Fax 202/328-7039. www.courtyard.com. 147 units. A/C TV TEL. $99–$195 double. Extra person $15. Children under 18 stay free. AE, DC, DISC, MC, V. Parking $10. Metro: Dupont Circle.

A major renovation in 1994 and another in 1997 maintain the Courtyard's European feel and well-heeled look. Waterford crystal chandeliers hang in the lobby and in the restaurant, and you may hear an Irish lilt from time to time (an Irish management company owns the hotel). Guests tend to linger in the comfortable lounge off the lobby, where coffee is available all day and cookies each afternoon.

The very comfortable and bright guest rooms, located off charming hallways, have coffeemakers; hair dryers; and phones with modem jacks. Accommodations on the 7th to 9th floors, facing the street, provide panoramic views. Especially nice are the corner "executive king" rooms, which are a little larger and are equipped with marble bathrooms, a refrigerator, terry robes, pants press, and fax machine.

In addition to an outdoor pool and sundeck, facilities include Claret's, serving American fare at breakfast and dinner. (Room service is available during restaurant hours.) Bailey's, a clubby bar, adjoins. *USA Today* is available for free at the front desk. A small exercise room and a meeting room are on site. For a fee, guests can use the well-equipped Washington Sports Club just across the street.

INEXPENSIVE

✪ **Doyle Normandy.** 2118 Wyoming Ave. NW (at Connecticut Ave.), Washington, DC 20008. ☎ **800/424-3729** or 202/483-1350. Fax 202/387-8241. www.doyle-hotels.ie. 75 units. A/C TV TEL. $79–$155 double. Extra person $10. Children under 18 stay free. AE, DC, DISC, MC, V. Parking $10 plus tax. Metro: Dupont Circle.

This gracious small hotel is a gem. Situated in a neighborhood of architecturally impressive embassies, the hotel receives many embassy-bound guests (the French Embassy is the Normandy's largest customer). You may discover this for yourself on a Tuesday evening, when guests gather in the charming Tea Room to enjoy complimentary wine and cheese served from the antique oak sideboard. This is also where continental breakfast is available daily (for $7), complimentary coffee and tea throughout the day, and cookies after 3pm. You can lounge or watch TV in the conservatory or, in nice weather, you can move outside to the garden patio.

The six-floor Normandy has small but pretty twin and queen guest rooms (all remodeled in 1998), with tapestry-upholstered mahogany and cherry-wood furnishings in 18th-century styles, and pretty floral-print bedspreads covering firm beds. Amenities include minifridges; coffeemakers; iron and ironing boards, in-room safes; hair dryers; access to the neighboring Washington Courtyard's pool and exercise room; and complimentary *Washington Post*. The Normandy is an easy walk from both Adams-Morgan and Dupont Circle. The Irish company that owns the Normandy also owns the Doyle Washington (see mention in Dupont Circle) and the Washington Courtyard by Marriott (see above).

Kalorama Guest House. 1854 Mintwood Place NW (between 19th St. and Columbia Rd.), Washington, DC 20009. ☎ **202/667-6369.** Fax 202/319-1262. 30 units (13 with bathroom). 5 suites. A/C. $45–$75 double with shared bathroom, $65–$105 double with bathroom; $95–$135 suite ($5 each additional occupant). Rates include continental breakfast. AE, DC, DISC, MC, V. Limited parking $7. Metro: Woodley Park–Zoo or Dupont Circle.

This San Francisco–style B&B was so successful, it expanded in a short time from a six-bedroom Victorian townhouse (at 1854 Mintwood) to include four houses on Mintwood Place and two on Cathedral Avenue NW in Woodley Park (☎ **202/ 328-0860;** fax 202/328-8730).

The cozy common areas and homey guest rooms are furnished with finds from antique stores, flea markets, and auctions. Students, Europeans, and conferees are usually your fellow guests.

Over at 1854 is the cheerful breakfast room with plant-filled windows. The morning meal includes bagels, croissants, and English muffins. There's a garden behind the house with umbrella tables. At each location, you have access to laundry and ironing facilities, a refrigerator, a seldom-used TV, and a phone (local calls are free; incoming calls are answered around the clock, so people can leave messages for you). It's customary for the innkeepers to put out sherry, crackers, and cheese on Friday and Saturday afternoons. Magazines, games, and current newspapers are available. Some of the houses are no-smoking.

The Mintwood Place location is near Metro stations, dozens of restaurants, nightspots, and shops. And the Cathedral Avenue houses, even closer to the Woodley Park–Zoo Metro, offer proximity to Rock Creek Park and the National Zoo. The Adams-Morgan location includes a small, two-room apartment with a kitchen, cable TV, telephone, and fax machine.

6 Dupont Circle

VERY EXPENSIVE

✪ **Westin Fairfax.** 2100 Massachusetts Ave. NW, Washington, DC 20008. ☎ **800/ 325-3589** or 202/293-2100. Fax 202/293-0641. www.luxurycollection.com. 206 units. A/C MINIBAR TV TEL. Weekdays $209–$289 double; weekends $139–$209 double (includes breakfast). Suites $350–$2,500 (for presidential suite). Children under 18 stay free. AE, CB, DC, MC, V. Valet parking $23. Metro: Dupont Circle.

This former Ritz-Carlton goes by a new name under new ownership, but don't worry, it's as distinctively debonair as ever. The hotel was built in 1927 and has served ever since as a D.C. haunt of the rich and famous. (Al Gore lived here as a kid.) You might see anyone here, from Bill Cosby to Uma Thurman.

From its canopied entrance, angled on Embassy Row, to the rich, walnut-paneled lobby, to pristine Oriental-carpeted hallways and lovely rooms, the Westin Fairfax maintains its top-drawer appearance. Best of all, you're guaranteed a good night's sleep. New as of 1999, each room features a "Heavenly Bed," created by the company that owns the Westin Fairfax; the bed features a feather-topped mattress that is firm but incredibly comfortable, and a feather duvet covering. Rooms are otherwise handsomely appointed with traditional dark-wood pieces; rich, brocade draperies; and French architectural watercolor renderings. Front-of-the-house rooms overlook Embassy Row. Some 6th- to 8th-floor rooms at the back of the house give you a glimpse of the Washington Monument and Georgetown. In-room amenities include coffeemakers with Starbucks coffee, iron and ironing board, safes, three phones, and terry robes. Gorgeous marble bathrooms are equipped with hair dryers and upscale toiletries (some also have small black-and-white TVs). The 7th floor of the eight-story hotel is the Club level, with its own lounge and concierge.

Dining/Diversions: The Jockey Club is one of Washington's most prominent restaurants (see chapter 6 for a review). The Fairfax Bar, with a working fireplace, is an intimate setting for cocktails, light fare, and piano music. On Friday and Saturday nights, the back room of the bar becomes an exclusive dance club.

Amenities: Weekday delivery of *USA Today* or the *New York Times,* complimentary shoe shine, 24-hour concierge and room service, twice daily maid service, express checkout, dry-cleaning and laundry service, meeting rooms, ballroom, and 24-hour fitness room with Stairmasters, Lifecycles, treadmills, sauna, massage, and separate locker areas.

EXPENSIVE

Canterbury Hotel. 1733 N St. NW, Washington, DC 20036. ☎ **800/424-2950** or 202/393-3000. Fax 202/785-9581. 99 units. A/C MINIBAR TV TEL. Weekdays $160–$400 double (most are under $200), weekends and off-season weekdays $119–$140 double. Rates include continental breakfast. Extra person $35. Children under 12 stay free. AE, CB, DC, DISC, MC, V. Parking $15. Metro: Dupont Circle.

Located on a lovely residential street, this small, European-style hotel is close to many tourist attractions.

Each individually decorated room is actually a junior suite. All have a sofa/sitting area, separate dressing room, and separate kitchenette or full kitchen. Attractively decorated, these spacious accommodations sport 18th-century mahogany English-reproduction furnishings (a few have four-poster beds). Among the amenities: cable TVs with CNN and pay-movie stations; iron and ironing board; coffeemakers; electronic locks; and phones with voice mail. Bathrooms have cosmetic mirrors; hair dryers; phones; and baskets of fine toiletries.

Dining/Diversions: The hotel's wonderful restaurant, Brighton (see chapter 6 for details), serves American-regional fare at all meals. And the Tudor-beamed Union Jack Pub, complete with dartboard and a menu featuring fish-and-chips, is the perfect place to relax after a busy day on the town. English beers on tap are served in pint mugs.

Amenities: Room service during restaurant hours, daily delivery of the *Washington Post,* complimentary *Wall Street Journal* available in lobby and restaurant, express checkout, secretarial services, meeting space for up to 75 people. Guests enjoy free use of the nearby YMCA/National Capital Health Center's extensive workout facilities, including an indoor lap pool.

H. H. Leonards' Mansion on O Street. 2020 O St. NW, Washington, DC 20036. ☎ **202/ 496-2020.** Fax 202/659-0547. www.erols.com/mansion. 6 suites and a 5-bedroom guest house. A/C TV TEL. $150–$1,000 (from $125 for room with shared bath, to $150 for the "Safari Room" to $500 for the log cabin suite, to $1,000 for the 5-bedroom guest house). Government and nonprofit rates available. Except for the guest house, rates include breakfast. AE, MC, V. Parking $15 on the premises, by reservation. Metro: Dupont Circle.

A legend in her own time, H. H. Leonards operates this Victorian property, made up of three five-story townhouses, as a museum with rotating exhibits, an event space, an art gallery, an antiques emporium, and—oh, yeah—a B&B. If you stay here, you may find yourself buying a sweater, a painting, or (who knows?) an antique bed. Everything's for sale. Guest rooms are so creative they'll blow you away; most breathtaking is a log cabin loft suite, with a bed whose headboard encases an aquarium. The art deco–style penthouse takes up an entire floor and has its own elevator, 10 phones, and seven televisions. The International Room has a nonworking fireplace and four TVs. All rooms have king-size beds and computer-activated telephones that can hook you up to the Internet; most have a whirlpool, and some have kitchens. Elsewhere on the property are an outdoor pool; eight office/conference spaces; 21 far-out bathrooms; art and antiques everywhere; an exercise room; and thousands and thousands of books. Full business services are available, including multiline phones, fax machines, IBM and Mac computers, LCD projectors, and satellite feeds. The Light House (guest house) has a separate entrance and five bedrooms, all white walls with light streaming in from windows and skylights; rates include maid service.

Radisson Barceló Hotel. 2121 P St. NW, Washington, DC 20037. ☎ **800/333-3333** or 202/293-3100. Fax 202/857-0134. www.radisson.com. 301 units. A/C TV TEL. Weekdays $199–$265 double, weekends $99–$169 double; $265–$750 suite weekdays in-season, $205–500 weekends and off-season. Extra person $20. Children under 18 stay free. AE, CB, DC, DISC, MC, V. Parking $16. Metro: Dupont Circle.

The first American venture for a Mallorca-based firm, the 10-story Barceló offers friendly European-style service, an unbeatable location midway between Dupont Circle and Georgetown, and a superb restaurant. The Barceló's art deco–style, marble-floored lobby is inviting, and its accommodations (formerly apartments) are larger than most (the standard room is 500 square feet). All offer workspaces with desks and living room areas containing sofas and armchairs. In-room amenities include cable TVs with HBO and more than 200 pay-movie options; three phones with voicemail and modem jacks; marble bathrooms with hair dryers and shaving mirrors; irons and ironing boards; coffee and coffeemakers. Each room also has a sofabed. *Note:* Ask about weekend "bed-and-breakfast" packages on Friday and Saturday nights in summer—they can go as low as $109 per night for a double, including breakfast for two.

Dining/Diversions: Gabriel features first-rate Latin American/Mediterranean cuisine (see chapter 6 for a review); its pleasant bar/lounge (featuring tapas and sherry) is popular with the after-work crowd.

Amenities: Concierge, room service (6:30am to 11pm), complimentary *Washington Post* in the morning at the front desk, faxing and other secretarial services, express checkout, rooftop sundeck, swimming pool in the courtyard, sauna, small fitness room, gift shop.

MODERATE

Clarion Hampshire Hotel. 1310 New Hampshire Ave. NW (at N St.), Washington, DC 20036. ☎ **800/368-5691** or 202/296-7600. Fax 202/293-2476. 87 suites. A/C MINIBAR TV TEL. Weekdays $119–$199 suite, weekends and off-season weekdays $99–$129 per suite. Extra person $20. Children under 12 stay free. AE, CB, DC, DISC, JCB, MC, V. Parking $12 plus tax. Metro: Dupont Circle.

The Clarion Hampshire is within easy walking distance of Georgetown and 2 blocks from Dupont Circle, convenient to numerous restaurants, nightspots, and offices. The hotel serves mostly an association, corporate, and government clientele, so you should inquire about low summer rates.

Spacious, junior-suite accommodations are furnished with 18th-century reproductions and offer lots of closet space, big dressing rooms, couches, coffee tables, and desks. Fifty of the 87 rooms have kitchenettes, which come with microwaves and coffeemakers; some have cooking ranges. Balconies at the front of the hotel (the New Hampshire Avenue side) offer city views. Amenities include a hair dryer; chocolates on arrival; data port–equipped phones; in-room safety deposit box; daily delivery of the *Washington Post.* Guests also receive free passes to the large YMCA health club with indoor pool, 10 minutes away.

At press time, the hotel's restaurant was serving only breakfast; plans were in the works to install a new restaurant serving American cuisine.

۞ Doyle Hotel Washington. 1500 New Hampshire Ave. NW, Washington, DC 20036. ☎ **800/42-DOYLE** or 202/483-6000. Fax 202/232-2230. www.doyle-hotels.ie. 314 units.

A/C MINIBAR TV TEL. Low season $135 to high season $185. Extra person $15. Children 17 and under stay free. AE, DC, DISC, MC, V. Parking $15. Metro: Dupont Circle.

Newly opened in 1999, this hotel gets high marks for convenience (it's located right on Dupont Circle), service, and comfort. A friend of mine arrived at 10am on a busy, high-season weekday, and was shown to her room immediately, though check-in is set at 3pm. The large rooms are furnished with two double beds with firm mattresses, an armoire with TV, desk, wet bar alcove, and a small but attractive bathroom. Decor is art-decoish, with lots of light wood furniture, a circular mirror, and purple plaid and stripe fabrics. Despite its prime location in a sometimes raucous neighborhood, the hotel's rooms are insulated from the noise. In-room amenities include Bath & Body Works toiletries, coffeemakers, hair dryer, iron and ironing board, safe, and on-demand movies. *USA Today* arrives free at your door weekdays. The comfortable and attractive hotel pub, Biddy Mulligan's, proudly features a bar imported from Ireland. Claddaghs serves a full Irish breakfast every morning and American fare with an Irish flair at other meals; room service is available daily 6:30am to midnight. Also on site is an exercise room with treadmills, stationary bikes, and Stairmasters.

Hotel Tabard Inn. 1739 N St. NW, Washington, DC 20036. ☎ **202/785-1277.** Fax 202/785-6173. 40 units (13 with shared bathroom). A/C TEL. Weekdays and weekends $90–$110 double with shared bathroom, $114–$170 double with private bathroom. Extra person $15. $10 for crib. Inquire about reduced summer rates. Rates include continental breakfast. AE, DC, MC, V. Street parking, $14 valet parking. Metro: Dupont Circle.

In 1914, three Victorian townhouses were joined to form the Tabard Inn, named for the famous hostelry in Chaucer's *Canterbury Tales*. The inn's owners live on the West Coast, but their son manages the Tabard, with the help of a chummy, peace-love-and-understanding sort of staff who clearly cherish the inn.

The heart of the ground floor is the dark, paneled lounge, with worn furniture, a wood-burning fireplace, original beamed ceiling, and bookcases. This is a favorite place for Washingtonians to come for a drink, especially in winter, or to linger before or after dining in the charming Tabard Inn restaurant (see chapter 6 for a review).

From the lounge, the inn leads you through nooks and crannies to guest rooms: Can you dig chartreuse? How about aubergine? Rooms are painted in these unconventional colors and decorated in similar style. Each is different, though N Street–facing rooms are largest and brightest, and some have bay windows. Furnishings are a mix of antiques and flea-market finds. Perhaps the most eccentric room is the top floor "penthouse," which has skylights, exposed brick walls, its own kitchen, and a deck accessed by climbing out a window.

✪ **Swann House.** 1808 New Hampshire Ave. NW, Washington, DC 20009. ☎ **202/265-7677.** Fax 202/265-6755. www.swannhouse.com. 10 units. A/C TV TEL. $110–$250 depending on unit and season. Extended stay and government rates available. Extra person $20. Rates include expanded continental breakfast. Limited off-street parking $10 per night. AE, MC, V. Metro: Dupont Circle.

This stunning 1883 mansion, standing prominently on a corner 4 blocks north of Dupont Circle, has ten exquisite guest rooms, two with private entrances. The coolest is the Blue Sky Suite, which has the original rose-tiled (working) fireplace, a queen-size bed and sofa bed, a gabled ceiling, and its own roof deck. The most romantic room is probably the Il Duomo, with Gothic windows, cathedral ceiling, working fireplace, and a turreted bathroom with angel murals. The Jennifer Green Room has a queen-size bed, another working fireplace, an oversize marble steam shower, and a private deck overlooking the pool area and garden. The Regent Room has a king-size bed in front of a carved working fireplace, a whirlpool, double shower, outdoor hot tub, TV, VCR, and stereo. There are three suites, each with a kitchen. The beautiful window treatments and bed coverings throughout are the handiwork of innkeeper Mary Ross. You'll want to spend some time on the main floor of the mansion, which has 12-foot ceilings, fluted woodwork, inlaid wood floors, a turreted living room, columned sitting room, and a sunroom (where breakfast is served) leading through three sets of French doors to the garden and pool. Laundry facilities, meeting space, and business services are available.

7 Foggy Bottom/West End

VERY EXPENSIVE

Washington Monarch Hotel. 2401 M St. NW, Washington, DC 20037. ☎ **877/ 222-2266** or 202/429-2400. Fax 202/457-5010. www.washingtonmonarch.com. 415 units. A/C MINIBAR TV TEL. Weekdays $289 double, weekends $159 double; $700–$1,700 suite. Extra person $30. Children under 18 stay free. AE, CB, DC, DISC, JCB, MC, V. Valet parking $19. Metro: Foggy Bottom.

A $12 million renovation completed in 1999 has given the guest rooms new bed linens, carpets, curtains, and replaced the tile in the bathrooms with Italian marble. Also spruced up are the function rooms and the interior courtyard, known as the "Colonnade." Best rooms in the house are the 146 that overlook the Colonnade, which, by the way, is a popular local spot for wedding receptions.

Amenities in guest rooms include large writing desks, terry robes, iron and ironing board, three phones (one in the bathroom) with voice mail, safes, and Caswell Massey toiletries. The ninth floor is a secured executive club level, popular with many of the business travelers who stay here (guests on this level pay no health club fee). The hotel has nine ADA-approved rooms to help disabled guests. Ask about summer weekend packages for best values.

The 17,500-square-foot Fitness Company West End Center includes an indoor pool and spa facilities, squash and racquetball courts, and every kind of exercise equipment. When in town, this is where Arnold Schwarzenegger stays, and where other visiting celebrities come to work out, even if they don't stay here. Guests pay $10 a day to use exercise equipment or to take aerobics classes but may use the pool, sauna, steam room, and whirlpool for free.

Dining/Diversions: Sunday brunch in the Colonnade is among the best in Washington. The Bistro serves contemporary American cuisine with a Mediterranean flair; cocktails, coffee, and pastries are available in the Lobby Lounge.

Amenities: 24-hour room service, concierge, dry cleaning and laundry service, twice daily maid service, express checkout, valet parking, complimentary shoe shine, business center, 5,500-square-foot ballroom, 90 fixed-seat auditorium, more than 29,000 square feet of meeting space.

Park Hyatt. 1201 24th St. NW, Washington, DC 20037. ☎ **202/789-1234.** Fax 202/457-8823. www.hyatt.com. 223 units. A/C MINIBAR TV TEL. Weekdays $255–$320 double, $295–$360 suite; weekends $179–$199 double, $202–$224 suite. Extra person $25. Children under 17 free. AE, CB, DC, DISC, JCB, MC, V. Valet parking $20 weekdays, $8 weekends. Metro: Foggy Bottom or Dupont Circle.

This luxury hotel, across the street from the Washington Monarch, also underwent a comprehensive renovation in 1999. The large guest rooms now have goosedown duvets on the beds, and new furniture, wall coverings, and fabrics. Specially commissioned artwork hangs throughout the hotel. The 143 suites now have dressing rooms with full vanities. Every room has an iron and ironing board, and each bathroom has a TV and radio, telephone, hair dryer, and makeup mirror. The 12-year-old, 10-story hotel prides itself on going the extra mile to please a customer, even if it means taking out a wall to enlarge a suite, as the Park Hyatt did for Lily Tomlin, right after the hotel opened. Guests include big names, royal families (who use the Presidential Suite, with its fireplace and grand piano), lobbyists, and tour bus travelers. Executive suites have separate living and dining areas, fax machines, and a second TV. Rooms are handsome and service is superb. Use of the fitness center is free.

Dining/Diversions: Melrose's bright and lovely dining room offers four-star cuisine with an emphasis on seafood (see chapter 6 for a review); look for the amiable chef, Brian McBride, who's been known to pop into the dining room from time to time to make sure all is well. From Thursday through Sunday, afternoon tea is served ($16.95), including finger sandwiches, scones, Devon cream, and pastries. Adjoining Melrose is a bar; outdoors is lovely cafe.

Amenities: 24-hour concierge, room service, business center, valet/laundry service, foreign currency exchange, shoe shine, twice-daily maid service, delivery of *Washington Post* daily, express checkout, gift shop. Hair and skin salon, health club including indoor pool, heated whirlpool, sauna and steam rooms, and extensive exercise room.

✪ **Swissôtel Washington—The Watergate.** 2650 Virginia Ave. NW, Washington, DC 20037. ☎ **800/424-2736** or 202/965-2300. Fax 202/337-7915. www.swissotel.com. 232 units. A/C MINIBAR TV TEL. $275–$450 double; from $650–$5,000 suite. Weekend rates sometimes lower. Extra person $25. Children under 17 stay free. AE, CB, DC, DISC, JCB, MC, V. Parking $20 (valet only). Metro: Foggy Bottom.

Don't confuse the immense Watergate condo and office complex—site of the notorious 1972 break-in that brought down the Nixon administration—with the elegantly intimate hotel housed within the complex. The Watergate's clientele includes high-level diplomats, business travelers, and Kennedy Center performers (the Kennedy Center is adjacent), such as Placido Domingo and Patti LaBelle. Hotel spa facilities, indoor lap pool and sundeck, state-of-the-art health club, entertainment options, and dozens of adjacent shops are popular with sophisticated travelers, including couples in search of a romantic weekend.

An extensive renovation in 1999 replaced all bed linens, wall coverings, carpeting, and so on, and each bathroom was remodeled to separate the shower stall from the bathtub. Rooms and suites are spacious—suites are said to be the largest in the city. River-facing rooms have splendid views of the Potomac, and of these, all but the 8th- and 14th-floor rooms have balconies. All rooms have writing desks and fax machines, and most have wet bars; most executive suites have kitchenettes. TVs offer Showtime movies and more than 50 cable stations. In your bathroom you'll find Gilchrist & Soames toiletries (although the brand may change with the renovation), a cosmetic mirror, hair dryer, phone, and terry robes.

Dining/Diversions: Aquarelle wins accolades for its Euro-American cuisine. The elegant Potomac Lounge serves British-style afternoon teas Tuesday through Sunday, while a pianist plays.

Amenities: 24-hour room service and concierge, full business services, complimentary shoe shine, daily newspaper of your choice, complimentary weekday morning limo to downtown, complimentary coffee in Potomac Lounge. Jacuzzi, steam, sauna, massage and spa treatments; barber/beauty salon (Zahira's, the stylist to three presidents), 10 meeting rooms, gift shop, ballroom overlooking the Potomac, and, in the adjacent complex, dozens of shops including jewelers, designer boutiques, a supermarket, drugstore, and post office.

EXPENSIVE

Hotel Lombardy. 2019 Pennsylvania Ave. NW, Washington, DC 20006. ☎ **800/424-5486** or 202/828-2600. Fax 202/872-0503. www.hotellombardy.com. 125 units. A/C MINIBAR TV TEL. Weekdays $140–$219 double, $179–$359 suite for 2; weekends (and sometimes off-season weekdays) $99–$219 double, $119–$359 suite for 2. Extra person $20. Children under 16 stay free in parents' room. AE, CB, DC, DISC, MC, V. Self-parking $17. Metro: Farragut West or Foggy Bottom.

From its handsome walnut-paneled lobby with carved Tudor-style ceilings to its old-fashioned manual elevator, the 11-story Lombardy offers a lot of character and comfort for the price and location (about 5 blocks west of the White House). (About that elevator: you should know that if the elevator attendant is new, you're in for a bumpy ride; travelers with disabilities or those who may be a little unsteady should look elsewhere.) George Washington University's campus is just across Pennsylvania Avenue, which means this part of town remains vibrant at night, when other downtown neighborhoods have shut down. Peace Corps, World Bank, and corporate guests make up a large part of the clientele, but other visitors will also appreciate the Lombardy's warm, welcoming ambience and the attentive service of the multilingual staff.

Spacious rooms, entered via pedimented louver doors, differ slightly in decor from one another, but all share a 1930s northern Italian motif. Large desks, precious dressing rooms, roomy walk-in closets, refrigerators, coffeemakers, iron and ironing boards, terry-cloth robes, data ports, and hair dryers enhance. Some suites have full kitchens.

Dining/Diversions: Moderately priced and open for all meals, the Café Lombardy, a sunny, glass-enclosed restaurant, serves authentic northern Italian fare. You can also dine in the Venetian Room, an exquisitely decorated haven with velvet upholstery, antique lanterns, mother-of-pearl-inlaid Moorish cocktail tables, and a custom-made cherry-wood bar. The Venetian Room shares a menu with the cafe, or you may choose from a special menu of appetizers.

Amenities: Free overnight shoe shine, daily delivery of the *Washington Post,* access to health club one block away ($5 per visit), and two small meeting rooms.

MODERATE

✪ **The George Washington University Inn.** 824 New Hampshire Ave. NW, Washington, DC 20037. ☎ **800/426-4455** or 202/337-6620. Fax 202/298-7499. www.gwinn.com. 95 units. A/C TV TEL. Weekdays $130–$165 double, $140–$185 efficiency, $155–$220 1-bedroom suite; weekends $99–$135 double, $110–$155 efficiency, $125–$170 1-bedroom suite. Children under 12 stay free. AE, DC, MC, V. Limited parking $15. Metro: Foggy Bottom.

It is rumored that this eight-story, whitewashed brick inn, another former apartment building, was a favorite spot for clandestine trysts for high-society types. These days you're more likely to see Kennedy Center performers and visiting professors. The university purchased the hotel (formerly known as "The Inn at Foggy Bottom") in 1994 and renovated it.

Rooms are a little larger and corridors a tad narrower than those in a typical hotel, and each room includes a roomy dressing chamber. One-bedroom suites are especially spacious, with living rooms that hold a sleeper sofa and a TV hidden in an armoire (there's another in the bedroom). Guest rooms are equipped with a minifridge, a microwave, and a coffeemaker; efficiencies and suites have kitchens. The roominess and the kitchen facilities make this a popular choice for families and for long-term guests, and if it's not full, the inn may be willing to offer reduced rates. Mention prices quoted in the inn's *New York Times* ad, if you've seen it, or your affiliation with George Washington University, if you can. This is a fairly safe and lovely neighborhood, within easy walking distance to Georgetown, the Kennedy Center, and downtown. But keep an eye peeled—you must pass through wrought-iron gates into a kind of cul-de-sac to find the inn. Off the lobby is the well-received restaurant Zuki Moon, a Japanese "noodle house" designed like a tea garden. Amenities include complimentary *Washington Post* delivered Monday through Saturday, 24-hour message service, and same-day laundry/valet service. There's a coin-operated laundry on the premises, five rooms designed for guests with disabilities, and meeting room for 50.

○ **St. James Suites.** 950 24th St. NW (off of Washington Circle), Washington, DC 20037. ☎ **800/852-8512** or 202/457-0500. Fax 202/466-6484. www.stjamesuiteswdc.com. 195 suites. A/C MINIBAR TV TEL. Weekdays $165–$185 suite, weekends $109–$120 suite. Rates include breakfast. Extra person $20. Children under 17 stay free. AE, DC, DISC, MC, V. Parking $17. Metro: Foggy Bottom.

The St. James is a home away from home for many of its guests, a number of whom book these luxury suites for more than a month at a time. Most of the suites are one-bedroom, with separate living and sleeping areas, marble bathrooms, two-line telephones with modem capability, and kitchens equipped with everything from china and flatware to cooking utensils. (About 13 suites are studios and 2 suites have two bedrooms.) Each living room includes a full pullout sofa. Unlike other hotels in this residential neighborhood of old townhouses, the St. James is fairly new (13 years old), which means accessibility was a factor in its design: A ramp in the lobby leads to the reception area, and 10 suites are available for travelers with disabilities, one with roll-in shower. The St. James is near Georgetown, George Washington University, and the Kennedy Center. Corporate club members (pay an extra $20 to become one) receive extra perks, such as evening cocktails and hors d'oeuvres served in the club's pleasant second-floor quarters. Tip: For best rates, check the hotel's Web site or look for the hotel's ad in the *New York Times.*

Amenities include room service (11am to 11pm), dry cleaning, laundry service, the *Washington Post* and *New York Times* available in the breakfast room or delivered to room on request, concierge assistance, business services, and overnight shoe shine. There is also an outdoor pool, a 24-hour, state-of-the-art fitness center, nearby tennis courts and jogging/biking paths, and conference rooms.

8 Woodley Park

EXPENSIVE

Marriott Wardman Park. 2660 Woodley Rd. NW (at Connecticut Ave. NW), Washington, DC 20008. ☎ **800/325-3535** or 202/328-2000. Fax 202/234-0015. www.marriotthotels. com. 1,338 units. A/C TV TEL. Weekdays $189–$235 double, weekends $89–$149 double; $350–$1,200 suite. Extra person $30. Children under 17 stay free. AE, CB, DC, DISC, MC, V. Valet parking $17, self-parking $14. Metro: Woodley Park–Zoo.

This is Washington's biggest hotel, resting on 16 acres just down the street from the National Zoo and several good restaurants. Its size and location (the Woodley Park–Zoo Metro station is literally at its doorstep) make it a good choice for large and small conventions, tour groups, and individual travelers. Built in 1918, it is also one of Washington's oldest hotels. A just-completed $100 million renovation has replaced bed and bath linens, carpeting, and wall coverings in all the guest rooms, upgraded the ballroom and meeting rooms, restructured the outdoor pools, and revamped the restaurants.

The hotel feels like a college campus: There's an old part, whose entrance is overhung with stately trees, and a new part, whose entrance is preceded by a great green lawn. The oldest part of the Wardman Park is the nicest. The 81-year-old, redbrick Tower houses 201 guest rooms, each featuring high ceilings, ornate crown moldings, and an assortment of antique French and English furnishings. This was once an apartment building whose residents ranged from presidents Hoover, Eisenhower, and Johnson, to actor Douglas Fairbanks, Jr., and author Gore Vidal. Wardman Tower rooms, which include 54 suites, offer a few more amenities, such as minibars and terry robes, than the hotel's other, more conventional guest rooms. All rooms have voice-mail and data ports; hair dryers; complimentary Gourmet Bean coffee and tea service; and irons and ironing boards. The 10th floor of the Center Tower is the club level.

Dining/Diversions: New, as of the renovation, are Harry's Pub (named after developer Harry Wardman), Perle's (named after Perle Mesta who used to live in the Wardman Tower), which serves American cuisine throughout the day, and Medici, which serves fine Tuscan cuisine. Still going strong are the hotel's gourmet deli and pastry shop, Java's, and its Lobby Bar, which is open for drinks daily.

Amenities: Multilingual concierge, laundry and valet, daily delivery of *USA Today*, express check-in and checkout, gift shop, 78,000 square feet of exhibit space and 95,000 square feet of meeting space, full business center, post office, barbershop, florist, two outdoor heated pools with sundeck, fitness room, nearby jogging and bike paths, 61 rooms equipped for guests with disabilities.

Omni Shoreham. 2500 Calvert St. NW (at Connecticut Ave.), Washington, DC 20008. ☎ **800/843-6664** or 202/234-0700. Fax 202/265-7972. www.omnihotels.com. 834 units. A/C TV TEL. $109–$299 double, depending on availability. Extra person $22. Children under 18 stay free. AE, CB, DC, DISC, JCB, MC, V. Parking $15. Metro: Woodley Park–Zoo.

A massive, $74-million renovation of all guest rooms and the lobby was recently completed. The spacious guest rooms remain twice the size of normal hotel rooms, but their new decor restores a traditional, elegant look through the use of chintz fabrics, mahogany furnishings, and porcelain fixtures. The hotel sits on 11 acres overlooking Rock Creek Park and many of the rooms offer spectacular views. A new air-conditioning system has been installed throughout the hotel, the pool is restructured, and the already excellent health club now includes extras like a dry sauna and whirlpool.

The hotel is popular as a meeting and convention venue, whose business travelers appreciate the two-line telephones with voice mail and the ability to program one's own wake-up call. Leisure travelers should consider the Shoreham for its large outdoor swimming pool, its proximity to the National Zoo and excellent restaurants, and the immediate access to biking, hiking, and jogging paths through Rock Creek Park. The hotel is just down the street from the Woodley Park-Zoo Metro station. You can also walk to the hipper neighborhoods of Adams-Morgan and Dupont Circle from the hotel; the stroll to Dupont Circle, taking you over the bridge that spans Rock Creek Park, is especially nice. Built in 1930, the Shoreham has been the scene of inaugural balls for every president since FDR. Do you believe in ghosts? Ask about Room 870, the haunted suite (available for $3,000 a night).

Dining/Diversions: The elegant Monique's Cafe et Brasserie specializes in French cuisine. Rock Creek Park provides a fitting backdrop for the lushly planted cocktail lounge, which is housed under a 35-foot vaulted ceiling.

Amenities: Room service (24-hour), concierge, dry-cleaning and laundry service, express checkout, shops, travel/sightseeing desk, business center and conference rooms, 10 miles of jogging, hiking, and bicycle trails, health and fitness center, 1½-mile Perrier parcourse, 22 meeting rooms, 7 ballrooms.

INEXPENSIVE

Kalorama Guest House. 2700 Cathedral Ave. NW (entrance on 27th St.), Washington, DC 20008. ☎ **202/667-6369.** Fax 202/319-1262. 19 units, 12 with bathrooms. A/C. $45–$75 double with shared bathroom, $65–$105 double with private bathroom. Rates include continental breakfast. AE, DC, DISC, MC, V. Limited parking $7. Metro: Woodley Park–Zoo.

This is the Woodley Park location of the bed-and-breakfast based in Adams-Morgan—see listing under "Adams-Morgan/North Dupont Circle," above, for more information.

9 Near the Airports

The rooms at all the hotels listed below are quiet; either the rooms are soundproofed, or away from the flight path.

BALTIMORE-WASHINGTON INTERNATIONAL

Sheraton International Hotel. 7023 Elm Rd., MD. ☎ **800/325-3535** or 410/859-3300. Fax 410/859-4984. www.starwoodhotels.com. A/C TV TEL. 196 units. $129–$199 double. Rates include free parking. Extra person $15. Children under 18 free. AE, CB, DC, DISC, MC, V.

This is the only hotel on the grounds of BWI Airport. Most of the rooms have king-size beds (the rest have two doubles); some have views of planes taking off and arriving. All rooms have a coffeemaker; iron and ironing board; hair dryer, magnifying mirror and nightlight in bathroom; armchair and ottoman; and updated flight information available on the TV screen. Rooms are a little crowded. The hotel has two rooms equipped for disabled guests, one with roll-in shower. Also on site are a gift shop, outdoor Olympic-sized pool, meeting rooms, health club, two restaurants, and a "high-energy nightclub" frequented by locals as well as hotel guests. Room service is available 24 hours, as is a shuttle to the airport.

RONALD REAGAN WASHINGTON NATIONAL AIRPORT

Hyatt Regency Crystal City. 2799 Jefferson Davis Hwy., Arlington, VA 22202. ☎ **800/233-1234** or 703/418-1234. Fax 703/418-1289. www.hyatt.com. A/C TV TEL. 685 units. Weekdays $189–$239 double, weekends $105–$149 double. Extra person $25. Valet parking $16. Children under 18 stay free. AE, CB, DC, DISC, MC, V. Metro: Crystal City.

National Airport does not have a hotel on its grounds, but this hotel is only a few minutes away, whether you're driving, taking the free shuttle—which operates from 6am to midnight between the hotel and airport—or hopping on the Metro (the hotel is only one Metro stop past the airport, on the blue and orange lines, and the hotel runs a free van from the station to the hotel). Rooms renovated in 1997 are soundproof, have direct-dial phones with voicemail and data ports, video checkout, hair dryer, iron and ironing board, and coffeemakers. For an extra $20 you can sign up for the business plan, which gives you a room with a fax/printer/copier machine, free breakfast, and free local and 800-number calls. On site are a health club, outdoor pool, Jacuzzi, and meeting space. But the main reason I recommend this hotel, besides its great location and fine rooms, is its rooftop restaurant, the Chesapeake Grill (☎ **703/413-6700**), which offers that rare thing: good food and a fantastic view. Open for dinner only, Monday through Saturday, the restaurant serves superb regional cuisine; children can order half-portions at half-price. Out the windows is a panorama that takes in the Potomac River, the lights of Washington's monuments shimmering in the distance, and the arrival and departure of planes at National Airport.

WASHINGTON DULLES INTERNATIONAL AIRPORT

Washington Dulles Airport Marriott. 45020 Aviation Dr., Dulles, VA 20166. ☎ **800/228-9290** or 703/471-9500. Fax 703/661-8714. www.marriott.com. A/C TV TEL. 370 units. Weekdays $149, weekends $79 (weekend rate includes breakfast). Rates cover up to 5 people in a room. Free parking for guests. AE, CB, DC, DISC, MC, V.

Built in 1969, the hotel is currently undergoing a renovation of everything, from plumbing to bedspreads, to bring it up to date. The renovation is progressing a wing at a time, however, so you will still be able to reserve a room, and at a good rate, too, throughout the renovation. The hotel is the only one on the grounds of the airport, although no rooms overlook the airport. Most rooms overlook a lake or a courtyard. About half of the rooms have king beds, the other half have two double beds. These rooms are fairly large and are equipped with a hair dryer, iron and ironing board, reading lamps, and armchairs. The hotel offers a fitness center, tennis courts, an indoor and an outdoor pool, a picnic pavilion, meeting space, three restaurants, a business center, and a gift shop. Shuttles leave every 15 minutes for the airport, a stone's throw away. In the lobby are an ATM and monitors showing flight arrivals and departures.

Where to Dine in Washington, D.C.

6

So you've planned your trip to Washington, scoped out where you want to eat, and called ahead, as recommended, to reserve a table, only to find the place is booked! Sure, this happens in major cities all over the country; the economy is good and people are eating out. But guess what: According to a *Washington Post* article, Washingtonians are at the top of the list, with households spending 50% of their food budget on restaurant meals, or an average of about $1,047 annually, making them the biggest spenders per capita in the nation.

People eat out here because they do business over meals, are too busy or tired to come home from work and cook, and because, "why not?" they can afford it. Most of all, people in Washington dine at restaurants because we've got so many good ones, with new ones opening every season. Italian restaurants are probably the most prevalent and will always be popular, from Obelisk (in the Dupont Circle neighborhood) for serious foodies, to Il Radicchio (at locations throughout the city) for excellent pizza and pasta. French cuisine is making a comeback, whether it's in the form of classic bistro fare, as at Bistro Bis on Capitol Hill, or in American/French dishes or haute cuisine, as at Lespinasse, in the St. Regis Hotel. But the biggest rise is in the new American category, with great chefs adding their own twist to the cuisine. You can choose from American/Southern (Vidalia, Georgia Brown's), American with Southwestern accents (The Mark, Red Sage, Austin Grill), and American seafood (DC Coast, Pesce, Tabard Inn, Kinkead's), just to give you an idea. And by the way, seafood restaurants now proliferate in the capital, a huge change from just a few years ago when we had maybe one or two of any note.

Other trends: the restaurant as lounge. Some restaurants are now seating diners at couches and comfortable chairs. Mostly, these are places that double as nightlife options, for example, Eleventh Hour on 14th Street, or Felix, in Adams-Morgan. But the restaurant as lounge seems to be part of a larger trend of making restaurants as much about entertainment as about food. So more and more places are offering live jazz or other music during dinner, or dancing after dinner. Sometimes this all-in-one approach works admirably—Kinkead's is one example. Other times, a restaurant like Eleventh Hour seems to be suffering an identity crisis: Is it a place to eat? To drink and get rowdy? To hear good music? To dance? By the time you read this, the restaurant may have worked out those kinks.

Believe it or not, one of the newest hotspots for dining and nightlife is actually outside of the District in seemingly sedate Arlington, Virginia. See the box "Arlington Row," in chapter 10 for details.

Read over the reviews that follow to see what appeals. A few tips: It's always wise to book a reservation in advance; few places require men to wear jacket and tie, but those that do are so noted; if you're driving, check whether my listing indicates valet parking, complimentary or otherwise—on Washington's crowded streets, this service can be a true bonus; if your desired restaurant is booked, consider eating at the bar, sometimes a fun alternative, and often serving the same menu.

ABOUT THE PRICES

I've tried to present you with a range of menus and prices, in most every Washington neighborhood. The restaurants listed below are grouped first by location, then listed alphabetically by price category. Keep in mind that the price categories refer to dinner prices, but some very expensive restaurants offer affordable lunches, early-bird dinners, tapas, or bar meals. (Or consider something totally different, like high tea in the late afternoon—look for the box in this chapter listing swell places to swill tea.) The prices within each review refer to the cost of individual entrees, not the entire meal.

Note: A Metro station is indicated when it's within walking distance of a restaurant. If you need bus-routing information, call ☎ **202/637-7000.**

1 Restaurants by Cuisine

AMERICAN
America (Capitol Hill, *M*)
Brighton (Dupont Circle, *E*)
Capitol City Brewing Co. (Downtown East, *M*)
Cashion's Eat Place (Adams-Morgan, *E*)
Clyde's (Georgetown, *M*)
Daily Grill (Downtown West, *E*)
District Chophouse & Brewery (Downtown East, *M*)
DC Coast (Downtown East, *E*)
Eleventh Hour (U St., *M*)
Felix (Adams-Morgan, *E*)
Kinkead's (Foggy Bottom, *E*)
Melrose (Foggy Bottom, *VE*)
Mendocino Grille and Wine Bar (Georgetown, *E*)
The Monocle (Capitol Hill, *E*)
Morrison-Clark Inn (Downtown East, *E*)
Nora (Dupont Circle, *VE*)
Occidental Grill (Downtown East, *VE*)
Old Ebbitt Grill (Downtown East, *M*)
Reeves Restaurant & Bakery (Downtown East, *I*)

Restaurant at The Jefferson (Downtown West, *VE*)
Roof Terrace Restaurant (Foggy Bottom, *VE*)
Rupperts (Downtown East, *VE*)
Seasons (Georgetown, *VE*)
Sequoia (Georgetown, *M*)
1789 (Georgetown, *VE*)
Tabard Inn (Dupont Circle, *E*)
Tahoga (Georgetown, *E*)
Trio (Dupont Circle, *I*)
The Willard Room (Downtown East, *VE*)

ASIAN FUSION
Asia Nora (Foggy Bottom, *E*)
Oodles Noodles (Downtown West, *I*)
Raku (Dupont Circle, *I*)
Teaism (Dupont Circle, *I*)

BARBECUE
Old Glory (Georgetown, *I*)

CARIBBEAN
BET on Jazz (Downtown East, *E*)

CHINESE
Ching Ching Cha (Georgetown, *I*)

Key to Abbreviations: *VE* = Very Expensive; *E* = Expensive; *M* = Moderate; *I* = Inexpensive

City Lights of China (Dupont
   Circle, *I*)
Full Kee (Downtown East, *I*)
Hunan Chinatown (Downtown East,
   M)

ETHIOPIAN

Meskerem (Adams-Morgan, *I*)
Zed's (Georgetown, *I*)

FRENCH

Bistro Bis (Capitol Hill, *E*)
Bistrot Lepic (Georgetown, *M*)
Citronelle (Georgetown, *VE*)
El Catalan (Downtown East, *VE*)
The Jockey Club (Dupont Circle, *VE*)
La Colline (Capitol Hill, *E*)
La Fourchette (Adams-Morgan, *M*)
Lespinasse (Downtown West, *VE*)
Marcel's (Foggy Bottom, *E*)
MAX'S of Washington (Downtown
   West, *VE*)

GERMAN

Café Berlin (Capitol Hill, *M*)

INDIAN

Aditi (Georgetown, *M*)
Bombay Club (Downtown West, *E*)

INTERNATIONAL

Cities (Adams-Morgan, *E*)
New Heights (Woodley Park, *E*)
701 (Downtown East, *E*)

ITALIAN

Al Tiramisu (Dupont Circle, *E*)
Barolo (Capitol Hill, *E*)
Coppi's (U Street Corridor, *I*)
Galileo (Downtown West, *VE*)
I Ricchi (Downtown West, *VE*)
Il Radicchio (Dupont Circle, *I*)
Luigino (Downtown East, *E*)
Obelisk (Dupont Circle, *E*)
Osteria Goldoni (Foggy Bottom, *E*)
Pasta Mia (Adams-Morgan, *I*)
Pizzeria Paradiso (Dupont Circle, *I*)
Sostanza (Dupont Circle, *E*)

JAPANESE

Sushi-Ko (Glover Park, *M*)
Zuki Moon (Foggy Bottom, *I*)

LATIN

Café Atlantico (Downtown East, *M*)
Gabriel (Dupont Circle, *E*)

MEDITERRANEAN

BeDuCi (Dupont Circle, *M*)

MEXICAN

Coco Loco (Downtown East, *M*)
Mixtec (Adams-Morgan, *I*)

MIDDLE EASTERN

Lebanese Taverna (Woodley Park, *M*)

SEAFOOD

Georgetown Seafood Grill on 19th
   Street (Downtown West, *E*)
Legal Sea Foods (Downtown West, *E*)
McCormick & Schmick's (Downtown
   West, *E*)
Pesce (Dupont Circle, *M*)
The Sea Catch (Georgetown, *E*)

SOUTHERN/SOUTHWESTERN

Austin Grill (Glover Park, *I*)
B. Smith's (Capitol Hill, *E*)
Georgia Brown's (Downtown East, *E*)
The Mark (Downtown East, *E*)
Music City Roadhouse
   (Georgetown, *I*)
Red Sage (Downtown East, *VE*)
Vidalia (Downtown West, *E*)

SPANISH

El Catalan (Downtown East, *VE*)
Jaleo (Downtown East, *M*)
Taberna del Alabardero (Downtown
   West, *VE*)

STEAKHOUSES

Les Halles (Downtown East, *E*)
Morton's of Chicago (Georgetown, *VE*)
The Palm (Downtown West, *E*)
Prime Rib (Downtown West, *VE*)

THAI

Busara (Glover Park, *M*)
Haad Thai (Downtown East, *I*)
Sala Thai (Dupont Circle, *I*)

VIETNAMESE

Miss Saigon (Georgetown, *M*)

2 Capitol Hill

For information on eating at the Capitol and other government buildings, see "Dining at Sightseeing Attractions," later in this chapter.

EXPENSIVE

B. Smith's. Union Station, 50 Massachusetts Ave. NE. ☎ **202/289-6188.** Reservations recommended. Main courses mostly $10.95–$23. AE, CB, DC, DISC, MC, V. Mon–Sat 11:30am–4pm; Mon–Thurs 5–11pm, Fri–Sat 5pm–midnight; Sun 11:30am–8:30pm. Free validated parking for 2 hours. Metro: Union Station. TRADITIONAL SOUTHERN.

Union Station's most upscale restaurant is the creation of former model Barbara Smith; it occupies the room where presidents once greeted visiting monarchs and dignitaries. The dining room has 29-foot ceilings, imposing mahogany doors, white marble floors, gold-leafed moldings, and towering Ionic columns. Background music is mellow (Nat King Cole, Ray Charles, Sarah Vaughan). The restaurant features live jazz on Friday and Saturday evenings and at Sunday brunch. Chef James Oakley's menu offers such appetizers as jambalaya or red beans and rice studded with andouille sausage and tasso (spicy smoked pork). Among the main dishes are sautéed Virginia trout piled high with crabmeat/vegetable "stuffing" and served over mesclun with rice and a medley of roasted vegetables. A basket of minibiscuits, corn and citrus-poppyseed muffins, and sourdough rolls accompanies all dishes. Desserts include pecan sweet potato pie. An almost all-American wine list features many by-the-glass selections.

✪ **Barolo.** 223 Pennsylvania Ave. NW. ☎ **202/547-5011.** Reservations recommended. Lunch $12.50–$15.50, dinner $13.50–$24. AE, DC, MC, V. Mon–Fri 11:30am–2:30pm; Mon–Thurs 5:30–10pm, Fri–Sat 5:30–10:30pm. Free valet parking at dinner. Metro: Capitol South. ITALIAN.

This excellent upscale Italian restaurant is a much-needed addition to Capital Hill dining. Another jewel in Roberto Donna's restaurant crown, Barolo is situated above another Donna creation, the inexpensive Il Radicchio (see write-up for Dupont Circle location). The intimate main room is paneled and has wooden floors, a working fireplace, and well-spaced tables; encircling the upper reaches of the room is a charming, narrow balcony set with tables for two. Though the menu changes daily, you can expect Piedmontese-style cuisine that may include a white asparagus salad with fresh fava beans and slices of Parma prosciutto; saffron pappardelle with fresh sautéed lobster, asparagus, roasted garlic, and fresh basil; or roasted fillet of red snapper over sweet potato, rosemary, black olives, and fresh basil. You can also expect to see Washington notables dining here; among those we've spotted are Mary Bono and Jerry Lewis, both representatives of California, and the owner himself, Roberto Donna. The wine list is entirely Italian, focusing on Piedmont wines, with emphasis on those produced from the Barolo grape.

Bistro Bis. 15 E St. NW. ☎ **202/661-2700.** Reservations recommended. Breakfast $6.75–$12, lunch $8–$22, dinner $17.50–$22. AE, DC, DISC, MC, V. Daily 7–10:30am, 11:30am–2:30pm, and 5:30–10:30pm. Valet parking at dinner. Metro: Union Station. FRENCH.

Hotel George is the home for this excellent French restaurant, whose owner-chef, Jeff Buben, runs another winner, Vidalia (see listing under, "Downtown, 16th St. NW & West"). You can sit at tables in the bar area (though even without a crowd it's loud), on the balcony overlooking the bar, or at leather banquettes in the main dining room,

⊕   Family-Friendly Restaurants

Baby-boomer parents (and I am one) are so insistent upon taking their children with them everywhere that sometimes it seems all restaurants are, of necessity, family-friendly (though you may wish certain ones were not). Hotel restaurants, no matter how refined, usually welcome children, since they may be guests of the hotel. The cafeterias at tourist attractions (see section 12, later in this chapter) are always a safe bet, since they cater to the multitudes. Inexpensive ethnic restaurants tend to be pretty welcoming to kids, too. Aside from those suggestions, I offer these:

Old Glory Barbecue *(see p. 142)*   A loud, laid-back place where the waitstaff is friendly without being patronizing. Go early, since the restaurant becomes more of a bar as the evening progresses. There is a children's menu, but you may not need it; the barbecue, burgers, muffins, fries, and desserts are so good, everyone can order from the main menu.

Austin Grill *(see p. 144)*   Another easygoing, good-service joint, with great background music. Kids will probably want to order from their own menu here, and their drinks arrive in unspillable plastic cups with tops and straws.

Il Radicchio *(see p. 133)*   A spaghetti palace to please the most finicky, at a price that should satisfy the family budget.

America *(see p. 111)*   The cavernous restaurant with its voluminous menu offers many distractions for a restless brood. No children's menu, but why would you need one, when macaroni and cheese, peanut butter and jelly, pizza, and chicken tenders are among the selections offered to everyone?

where you can watch Buben and staff at work in the glass-fronted kitchen. (In warm weather, there's a sidewalk cafe.) The menu covers French classics like bouillabaisse, pistou, steak frites, as well as Buben's own take on grilled tuna au poivre, pan-seared red snapper, and seared scallops with tomatoes, garlic, olives and an eggplant custard. The restaurant has been popular from the day it opened, with hungry movers and shakers intermingling with us ordinary folk who just love good food. The wine list is mostly French. There's always a traditional plat du jour, for example, Dover sole on Wednesday, bouillabaisse every Friday, and so on.

✪ **La Colline.** 400 N. Capitol St. NW. ☎ **202/737-0400.** Reservations recommended. Breakfast $5–$8.75, lunch $8.75–$16.25, dinner $18.75–$21. AE, CB, DC, MC, V. Mon–Fri 7–10am and 11:30am–3pm; Mon–Sat 6–10pm. Free garage parking after 5pm. Metro: Union Station. FRENCH.

This is the perfect spot for the breakfast fundraiser. Hill people like La Colline for its convenience to the Senate side of the Capitol, the great bar, the four private rooms, the high-backed leather booths that allow for discrete conversations, and, last but not least, the food. You'll always get a good meal here. The regular menu offers an extensive list of French standards, including salade Niçoise, terrine of foie gras, and fish—poached, grilled, or sautéed. Almost as long is the list of daily specials—the soft shell crab is superb here in season. The wine list concentrates on French and California wines; wine-by-the-glass choices change with the season to complement the menu. Don't let the dessert cart roll past you; the apple pie is a winner. As is the restaurant, which has been in business for 18 years.

West End, Downtown, U St. & Capitol Hill Dining

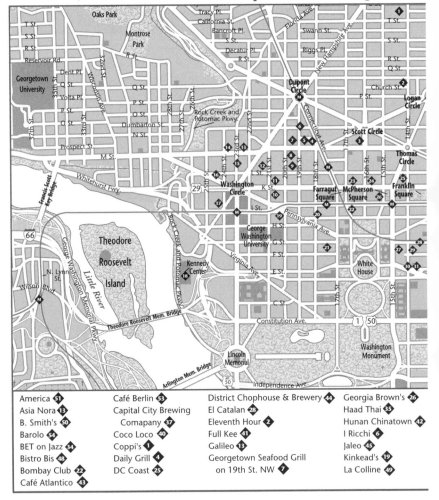

America **51**
Asia Nora **13**
B. Smith's **50**
Barolo **54**
BET on Jazz **34**
Bistro Bis **48**
Bombay Club **22**
Café Atlantico **43**

Café Berlin **53**
Capital City Brewing
  Comapany **37**
Coco Loco **40**
Coppi's **1**
Daily Grill **4**
DC Coast **25**

District Chophouse & Brewery **44**
El Catalan **28**
Eleventh Hour **2**
Full Kee **41**
Galileo **13**
Georgetown Seafood Grill
  on 19th St. NW **7**

Georgia Brown's **26**
Haad Thai **35**
Hunan Chinatown **42**
I Ricchi **6**
Jaleo **45**
Kinkead's **19**
La Colline **49**

The Monocle. 107 D St. NE. ☎ **202/546-4488.** Reservations recommended. Lunch $6.75–$15, dinner $15–$23. AE, CB, DC, MC, V. Mon–Fri 11:30am–midnight. Free valet parking. Metro: Union Station. AMERICAN.

A Capitol Hill institution, The Monocle has been around since 1960. This is a men-in-suits place, where the litter of briefcases resting against the too-close-together tables can make for treacherous navigating. But you might want to take a look at whose briefcase it is you're stumbling over, for The Monocle is the haunt of Supreme Court justices, members of congress, and senators. (The Monocle is close to both the Court and the Capitol.) The food is just OK, unless you order the hamburger, which is excellent or the penne with marinara and olives sauce (available only at lunch). Don't bother with the crab cakes. Service is old-style, all-male.

Legal Sea Foods ⓫	McCormick & Schmick's ㉓	Osteria Goldoni ⓯	Roof Terrace Restaurant ⓲
Les Halles ㉜	Melrose ⓮	The Palm ❺	Ruppert's ㊲
Lespinasse ㉔	The Monocle ㊼	Prime Rib ❿	701 ㊼
Luigino ㊱	Morrison-Clark Inn ㊳	Red Sage ㉙	Taberna del Alabardero ⓴
Marcel's ⓰	Occidental Grill ㉛	Reeve's ㉝	Vidalia ❽
The Mark ㊻	Old Ebbit Grill ㉗	Restaurant at the	Willard Room ㉚
MAX'S at Washington ㉑	Oodles Noodles ❾	Jefferson ❸	Zuki Moon ⓱

MODERATE

America. Union Station, 50 Massachusetts Ave. NE. ☎ **202/682-9555.** Reservations recommended. Main courses $6.95–$17.95; sandwiches, burgers, and salads $3.50–$13.95; brunch $7.25–$13.50. AE, DC, DISC, MC, V. Sun–Thurs 11:30am–midnight, Fri–Sat 11:30am–1am. Free validated parking for 2 hours. Metro: Union Station. AMERICAN REGIONAL.

Our helpful waiter gave us the lowdown: Candice Bergen, Justice Clarence Thomas, Newt Gingrich, and Alec Baldwin are among those who have eaten here at one time or another. People-watching is one reason to come to this vast, four-level restaurant, but sightseeing is another. Ask for a seat in the uppermost Capital Wine Room—if you look out the window, you see the Capitol dome; look the other direction (between the Roman legionnaire statues), and you've got a grand view of Union Station. (This area seats parties of up to four, not large groups.) Walls are decorated with WPA-style murals, a large painting of the American West, and a whimsical frieze depicting surfers, athletes, astronauts, and superheroes in outer space.

A vast American-classic menu comprises about 150 items, each with the name of the city, state, or region in which the dish supposedly originated: spaghetti and meatballs (Cleveland?), chili dogs (Fort Lee, New Jersey?). The B.L.T. (Newport) is a safe bet, the nachos (Eagle Pass, Texas) too greasy, and you'll definitely find better crab cakes (Ocean City, Maryland) elsewhere in the city.

✪ **Café Berlin.** 322 Massachusetts Ave. NE. ☎ **202/543-7656.** Reservations recommended. Main courses $11.95–$16.95 at lunch and dinner; soups, sandwiches, and salads $4.75–$6.95 at lunch. AE, CB, DC, MC, V. Mon–Thurs 11am–10pm, Fri–Sat 11am–11pm, Sun 4–10pm. Metro: Union Station. GERMAN.

You have to walk past the dessert display on your way to your table at Café Berlin, so forget your diet. These delicious, homemade confections are the best reason to come here. The vast spread might include a dense pear cheesecake, raspberry linzer torte, sour cherry crumbcake, or vanilla custard cake. Entrees feature things like the Rahm Schnitzel, which is a center-cut of veal topped with a light cream and mushroom sauce, or a wurstplatte of mixed sausages. Seasonal items highlight asparagus in spring, game in the fall, and so on. Lunch is a great deal: a simple chicken salad sandwich (laced with tasty bits of mandarin orange), the soup of the day, and German potato salad, all for $6.25. The owners and chef are German; co-owner Peggy Reed emphasizes that their dishes are "on the light side—except for the beer and desserts." The 13-year-old restaurant occupies two prettily decorated dining rooms on the bottom level of a Capitol Hill town house, whose front terrace serves as an outdoor cafe in warm weather.

3 Downtown, East of 16th Street NW

VERY EXPENSIVE

El Catalan. 1319 F St. NW. ☎ **202/628-2299.** Reservations recommended. Lunch $12–$18, dinner $18–$32. AE, DC, MC, V. Mon–Fri 11:30am–2:30pm; Mon–Thurs 5:30–10pm, Fri–Sat 5:30–11pm. Free valet parking at dinner. Metro: Metro Center. SPANISH/FRENCH PROVENÇAL.

This restaurant reinvented itself in 1999, so that its menu now offers two cuisines, Spanish and French Provençal. Typical dishes might include paella, veal chop with mushroom sauce, rabbit with potato gnocchi and basil sauce, Dover sole on a bed of lentils, and, for dessert, Catalan cream, a very rich crème brûlée. What has not changed is the decor: The front dining area, with a bar, is the more casual room, while the rear dining area is elegantly beautiful with, somehow, a Casablanca feel about it.

Occidental Grill. 1475 Pennsylvania Ave. NW. ☎ **202/783-1475.** Reservations recommended. Lunch $12.95–$20, dinner $12.95–$32.50; sandwiches, soups, and salads $4.95–$16.95; pretheater $28. AE, CB, DC, DISC, MC, V. Mon–Sat 11:30am–10pm, Sun noon–9:30pm. Free valet parking, when available at the Willard Hotel or the CarrPark on F St., between 14th and 15th sts. Metro: Metro Center or Federal Triangle. REGIONAL AMERICAN.

In the same complex as the Willard Hotel, the Occidental Grill was opened by the Willard family in 1906. Subsequent owner Gus Bucholz started, in the 1920s, the tradition of displaying autographed photographs of his customers, many of whom were famous. The restaurant closed in 1972, but when it reopened with the Willard in 1986, its walls in the lower dining room were covered with those photographs of past patrons—military, political, sports, even royal figures. They're the first thing you notice when you enter the clubby room, with dark wood paneling, a classic bar, and walls lined with booths. From April through October, you can sit at the outdoor patio on Pennsylvania Avenue, where you have a grand view of the Capitol. The upstairs dining room is more formal, with larger booths, a smaller bar, and no photos.

The menu favors traditional meat-and-potatoes fare along with grilled fish and nouvelle cuisine. Certain items are famous: onion crisps and the swordfish club sandwich. And certain ones that aren't famous should be: the black bean soup with grilled shrimp and lime cream and the grilled Atlantic salmon over crab and potato hash with saffron-fennel broth. The potato dishes are always good.

✪ **Red Sage.** 605 14th St. NW (at F St.). ☎ **202/638-4444.** Reservations recommended for main dining room, not accepted for chili bar and cafe. Lunch $12–$16, dinner $20–$30; Cafe/Chili Bar $5–$13. AE, CB, DISC, MC, V. Restaurant Mon–Thurs 11:30am–1:30pm and 5:30–9:45pm, Fri 11:30am–2pm and 5:30–10:30pm, Sat–Sun 5:30–10:30pm. Cafe/Chili Bar Mon–Thurs 11:30am–11:30pm, Fri–Sat 11:30am–12:30am, Sun 4:30–11pm. Metro: Metro Center. WESTERN/CONTEMPORARY AMERICAN.

Nationally renowned chef Mark Miller has created an elegantly whimsical Wild West fantasy. Downstairs, the main dining room is a warren of cozy, candlelit alcoves under a curved ponderosa-log–beamed ceiling. Upstairs are the more casually gorgeous Café and high-ceilinged Chili Bar.

When you look at the menu, think spicy. Red Sage is famous for its house-made sausages, its sautéed Virginia trout with grilled Maryland crab cakes, and for desserts like the dark chocolate praline tombstone with hazelnut crunch. The wine list is extensive and well researched. The Chili Bar and Cafe offer inexpensive light fare ranging from barbecued brisket quesadillas to mushroom and chicken enchiladas. Servers could use some fine tuning of their social skills.

✪ **Rupperts.** 1017 7th St. NW. ☎ **202/783-0699.** Reservations required. Main courses $25. AE, DC, MC, V. Thurs 11:30am–2:30pm; Tues–Thurs 6–10pm, Fri–Sat 6–11pm. Metro: Mount Vernon Square–UDC or Gallery Place–Chinatown. AMERICAN.

Within spitting distance of the D.C. Convention Center, Rupperts lies in a marginal neighborhood; thankfully, a boom in downtown development is rapidly bringing other restaurants and nightlife a little closer.

The restaurant's success is a tribute to the chef's simple but excellent preparations using seasonal produce. The menu changes daily, sometimes three times a day, to incorporate the freshest ingredients. You may see a foie gras and figs dish on the menu in late fall or soft-shell crabs and grilled rhubarb in spring. The food is not heavy, nor laden with sauces. With dinner come four different freshly baked breads. The wine list is eclectic, everything from a $225 bottle of Batard/Montrachet to a $15 Verdejo. Desserts, like truffle ice cream, are too hip for me.

This is a one-room, understated restaurant with a casual atmosphere. Patrons don't seem to fall into any identifiable group—most people are in business dress at lunch, less formal attire in the evening.

✪ **The Willard Room.** In the Willard Inter-Continental Hotel, 1401 Pennsylvania Ave. NW. ☎ **202/637-7440.** Reservations recommended. Breakfast $5.50–$12.50, American buffet $17.50, lunch $19–$28, prix fixe $32, spa lunch $27, dinner $24–$36, pretheater $36 fall-spring Mon–Sat 6–7pm. AE, DC, DISC, JCB, MC, V. Mon–Fri 7:30–10am and 11:30am–2pm; Mon–Sat 6–10pm. Jacket and tie preferred. Complimentary valet parking at dinner. Metro: Metro Center. AMERICAN REGIONAL/CLASSIC EUROPEAN.

Like the rest of the hotel (see chapter 5), The Willard dining room has been restored to its original turn-of-the-century splendor, with gorgeous carved oak paneling, towering scagliola columns, brass and bronze torchères and chandeliers, and a faux-bois beamed ceiling. Scattered among the statesmen and diplomats dining here are local couples seeking romance; the Willard has been the setting for more than one betrothal. The room has also been used in many movie shoots—look for it in *The Hollow Man.*

Chef de cuisine Gerard Madani changes the lunch menu daily, the dinner menu seasonally, and emphasizes lightness in cooking. Some examples: steamed Dover sole with a sorrel-flavored vermouth cream sauce, veal kidney with celery root mustard seed sauce, beef tenderloin with bordelaise sauce, and grilled whole Maine lobster. Two of the most popular desserts are the double-vanilla crème brûlée and the chocolate tears, which combines dark chocolate and white chocolate in a tear-shaped mousselike confection. The wine list offers more than 250 fine selections.

EXPENSIVE

BET on Jazz Restaurant. 730 11th St. NW. ☎ **202/393-0975.** Reservations recommended. Lunch $8–$17, dinner $16–$24, Sun brunch $26. AE, DC, DISC, MC, V. Mon–Fri 11:30am–2:30pm, Sun 11:30am–3pm; Mon–Thurs 5–10pm, Fri–Sat 5:30pm–midnight. Valet parking. Metro: Metro Center. AMERICAN/CARIBBEAN.

Dress up for a night at this art-decoish supper club, for if you're dressed too casually you won't get in. Black Entertainment Television (BET) Holdings, Inc., is the multimedia entertainment company that owns and operates the restaurant, and dining here is meant to be an event. The focus, naturally, is on jazz and fine cuisine. The menu is "New World Caribbean," meaning jerk chicken, red snapper ceviche, and Bahamian grilled black grouper fillet. This is a big place, with the second level looking down on the first, and the space broken up into booths and mingling areas. A huge screen shows jazz videos and live jazz is featured on Friday and Saturday nights and at Sunday brunch.

DC Coast. 1401 K St. NW. ☎ **202/216-5988.** Reservations recommended. Lunch $12–$18, dinner $16–$23, light fare $6–$8. AE, DC, DISC, MC, V. Mon–Thurs 11:30am–2:30pm and 5:30–10:30pm, Fri 11:30am–11pm, (light fare weekdays 2:30–5:30pm), Sat 5:30–11pm. Valet parking after 5:30pm $4. Metro: McPherson Square. AMERICAN.

The dining room is sensational: two stories high, glass-walled balcony, immense oval mirrors hanging over the bar, and a full-bodied stone mermaid poised to greet you at the entrance. Gather at the bar first to feel a part of the loud and trendy scene. This is one of the city's hottest restaurants, so call way ahead to book a reservation. The food's sometimes sensational. Chef Jeff Tunks has returned from stints in Texas, California, and New Orleans, and some of the dishes Washingtonians remember from his years at the River Club have returned with him: Chinese-style smoked lobster with fried spinach is the most famous. And it's still tasty. Other entrees to recommend: the "tower of crab" (a crab cake upon a fried soft-shell crab), and the fish fillet encrusted with portobello paste. Seafood is a big part of the menu, but there are plenty of meat dishes, too.

✪ Les Halles. 1201 Pennsylvania Ave. NW. ☎ **202/347-6848.** Reservations recommended. Lunch $11.75–$20, dinner $13.25–$22.50. AE, CB, DC, DISC, MC, V. Daily 11:30am–midnight. Complimentary valet parking after 6:30pm. Metro: Metro Center or Federal Triangle. FRENCH/STEAKHOUSE.

Anyone who believes that red meat is passé hasn't eaten here. At lunch and dinner, people are devouring the *onglet* (a boneless French cut hangar steak hard to find outside France), steak au poivre, steak tartare, New York sirloin, and other cuts—always accompanied by frites (fries), of course. The frites are a must. The menu isn't all beef, but it is classic French: cassoulet, confit de canard, escargots, onion soup, and such. I can never resist the frisée aux lardons, a savory salad of chicory studded with hunks of bacon and toasts smeared thickly with Roquefort.

Les Halles is big and charmingly French, with a French-speaking waitstaff providing breezy, flirtatious service. The banquettes, pressed tin ceiling, mirrors, wooden floor, and the side bar capture the feel of a brasserie. A vast windowfront overlooks Pennsylvania Avenue and the awning-covered sidewalk cafe, which is a superb spot to dine in warm weather. Every July 14, this is the place to be for the annual Bastille Day race, which Les Halles hosts. (See chapter 2, "Calendar of Events," for details.) Les Halles is a favorite hangout for cigar smokers, but the smoking area is well ventilated. Need a pick-me-up? Served all day at the bar and through the afternoon in the dining room are "les bouchies des Halles," (little mouthfuls), hors d'oeuvres that include a cheese plate, salmon tartare, canapés, and so on, each for under $4.

Luigino. 1100 New York Ave. NW. ☎ **202/371-0595.** Reservations recommended. Lunch $9.50–$14.50, dinner $12.50–$24.50; pretheater $22.50. AE, CB, DC, MC, V. Mon–Fri 11:30am–2:30pm; Mon–Thurs 5:30–10:30pm, Fri–Sat 5:30–11:30pm, Sun 5–10pm. Pretheater occasionally 5:30–7pm. Free validated parking for garage on 12th St. Metro: Metro Center. ITALIAN.

In the same building (an ex-bus station) that houses the Capitol City Brewing Company (see below) is this Italian restaurant, where elegance combines amusingly with informality. Starched white cloths lie upon traditional red-checked tablecloths, waiters wear colorful vests over their classic black pants and white shirts, a line of cushioned chairs (not stools) stretch the length of a bar overlooking the open kitchen, and rock and roll plays softly in the background.

The pizza is a bit greasy, but has a good, chewy thin crust. Grilled fish and meat specials are popular, but we find the fresh pasta dishes more satisfying, including the ravioli filled with crabmeat and braised vegetables, and the twists of pasta with diced green beans and potatoes topped with a basil pesto sauce. Among the wine list offerings are some affordable Italian wines.

The Mark. 401 Seventh St. NW. ☎ **202/783-3133.** Reservations suggested. Lunch $5–$14, dinner $13–$28, $4–$12 light fare weekdays 4–7pm at the bar. AE, CB, DC, DISC, MC, V. Mon–Sat 11:30am–3pm; Mon 5–9pm, Tues–Thurs 5–10:30pm, Fri–Sat 5–11pm, Mon–Fri Happy Hour 4–7pm. Valet parking at dinner. Metro: Gallery Place or Archives/Navy Memorial. AMERICAN REGIONAL.

I didn't like this place first time around—I was shown to the windowless back room, where my companion and I shared unremarkable lunch fare. Second time around went much better: We sat in the store-front window at rush hour counting the number of people walking by with a cellular phone to the ear (The Mark is in the middle of downtown, right near the MCI Center), as we munched on fried calamari, slurped up corn chowder with andouille sausage, and savored the Copper River salmon with fiddlehead ferns. Chef Allison Swope favors Southern and Southwestern cuisine, which you'll notice particularly in sauces like red chili butter sauce on salmon, and side dishes, which include garlic grits. Don't miss dessert; try the mocha pot de crème or chocolate hazelnut tart.

✪ **Morrison-Clark Inn.** Massachusetts Ave. NW (at 11th St.). ☎ **202/898-1200.** Reservations recommended. Lunch $12.75–$15.75, dinner $17.50–$23; 3-course Sun brunch (including unlimited sparkling wine) $30. AE, DC, DISC, MC, V. Mon–Fri 12:30–2pm; Mon–Sat 6–9:30pm. Complimentary valet parking. Metro: Metro Center. AMERICAN REGIONAL.

The Morrison-Clark restaurant is often mentioned as one of the best in the city in such publications as the *Washington Post* and *Gourmet* magazine. The dining room is a Victorian drawing room with ornately carved white marble fireplaces. At night, soft lighting emanates from Victorian brass candelabras, crystal chandeliers, and candles. During the day, sunlight streams through floor-to-ceiling, mahogany- and gilt-valanced windows. And, weather permitting, you can dine outdoors at courtyard umbrella tables.

Chef Susan McCreight Lindeborg's seasonally changing menus are elegant and inspired. An early spring menu may feature potato and leek soup with country ham toasts followed by sautéed salmon with risotto cakes and crimini mushroom butter sauce. The inn is known for its desserts, like the chocolate caramel tart topped with praline-studded whipped cream. Similar fare is available at lunch and brunch. A reasonably priced wine list offers a variety of premium wines by the glass, plus a nice choice of champagnes, dessert wines, and ports.

701. 701 Pennsylvania Ave. NW. ☎ **202/393-0701.** Reservations recommended. Main courses $12.50–$18.50 at lunch, $14.50–$22.50 at dinner; pretheater $22. AE, DC, MC, V. Mon–Fri 11:30am–3pm; Mon–Tues 5:30–10:30pm, Wed–Thurs 5:30–11pm, Fri–Sat 5:30–11:30pm, Sun 5–9:30pm. Free valet parking 5:30–11pm nightly. Metro: Archives–Navy Memorial. AMERICAN/INTERNATIONAL.

701 has gained renown for its extensive caviar and vodka selections. But don't disregard the main menu, which features sophisticated American fare and always includes a few vegetarian items. A signature soup with great texture and flavor is Iowa corn and shrimp chowder, with dry sack sherry and chives. Other dishes to recommend are the barbecue duck strudel and the fingerling potato custard with wild mushrooms. Artful presentation makes the food all the more enticing. Portions are generous, and service is marvelous.

This restaurant is literally steps away from the Archives–Navy Memorial Metro stop and a short walk from several theaters. Its plate-glass windows allow you to watch commuters, theatergoers, and tourists scurrying along Pennsylvania Avenue. Walls, glass partitions, and columns in the dining room create pockets of privacy throughout.

MODERATE

✪ **Café Atlantico.** 405 8th St. NW. ☎ **202/393-0812.** Reservations are a must. Lunch $4.95–$14.95, dinner $15.95–$21.95, light fare $4.50–$7.50 (weekdays 2:30–5:30pm), Latino dim sum $19.95 all you can eat (Sat 11:30am–2:30pm). AE, DC, MC, V. Mon–Fri 11:30am–2:30pm, Sun–Thurs 5:30–10pm, Fri–Sat 5:30–11pm. The bar stays open until 1am on weekends. Metro: Archives–Navy Memorial. LATIN AMERICAN/CARIBBEAN.

This place rocks on weekend nights, a favorite hot spot in Washington's burgeoning downtown. The colorful, three-tiered restaurant throbs with Latin, calypso, and reggae music, and everyone is having a good time—including, it seems, the waitstaff. If the place is packed, see if you can snag a seat at the second-level bar, where you can watch the genial bartender mix the potent drinks for which Café Atlantico is famous: the *caipirinha,* made of limes, sugar, and *cachacha* (sugar cane liqueur), or the *mojito,* a rum and crushed mint cocktail.

Seated at the bar or table, you get to watch the waiter make fresh guacamole right in front of you. As for the main dishes, you can't get a more elaborate meal for the price. The ceviche, Ecuadorean seared scallops, and Argentine ribeye are standouts, and tropical side dishes and pungent sauces produce a burst of color on the plate. The menu changes every week, so feel free to ask your waiter for guidance.

Capitol City Brewing Company. 1100 New York Ave. NW. ☎ **202/628-2222.** Reservations accepted for groups of 15 or more. Also at 2 Massachusetts Ave. NW. ☎ **202/**

842-2337. Reservations accepted for parties of 6 or more. Main courses $8.95–$18.95. AE, DC, DISC, MC, V. Sun–Thurs 11am–11pm, Fri–Sat 11am–midnight; the bar stays open until 1am. Metro: Metro Center. AMERICAN.

These two brew pubs are popular with singles, who enjoy swilling good beer in nicer-than-normal bar surroundings. The huge pubs are each situated within historic buildings: one across from the convention center and near the MCI Center, the other in the old City Post Office Building across from Union Station (upstairs from the National Postal Museum). Daily beer specials are posted on a chalkboard. The menu consists mostly of typical bar food, though here and there you find the odd item worth trying (like the grilled portobello mushroom). The burgers and the pan-seared, blackened catfish club sandwich are commendable. The service, however, is not. If you want to be waited on this year, sit at the bar. A basket of soft pretzels accompanied by a horseradish-mustard dip is complimentary.

✪ **Coco Loco.** 810 7th St. NW (between H and I sts.). ☎ **202/289-2626.** Reservations recommended. Tapas mostly $6–$12; churrascaria with antipasti bar $23 (dinner only); antipasti bar $6.95 lunch, $9.95 dinner. AE, MC, V. Mon–Fri 11:30am–2:30pm; Mon–Thurs 5:30–10pm, Fri–Sat 5:30–11pm. Metro: Gallery Place. BRAZILIAN/MEXICAN.

At 8pm on a Wednesday night, the floor is filled with young, well-dressed couples moving to the beats of salsa. Weekends, you can't even get in the joint. Besides the music and dancing, much of the action emanates from the open kitchen and the U-shaped bar. If you want a quieter setting, head for the window-walled front room or the garden patio. The exuberantly tropical interior space centers on a daily changing buffet table where cheeses, fresh fruits, salads (ranging from roasted tomatoes with mozzarella to garbanzos with figs), cold cuts, and other antipasti are temptingly arrayed on palm fronds and banana leaves.

An extensive selection of Mexican tapas includes interesting quesadillas and pan-roasted shrimp on chewy black (squid-infused) Chinese jasmine rice. Coco Loco's most popular dish is churrascaria, the Brazilian mixed grill. Waiters serve you chunks of sausage, chicken, beef, and pork from skewers. It comes with salsa, fried potatoes, and coconut-flavored rice, plus antipasti bar offerings. All this and Mexican chocoloate rice pudding for dessert, too. The wine list is small but well chosen.

District Chophouse & Brewery. 509 7th St. NW. ☎ **202/347-3434.** Reservations recommended. Lunch $6–$12, dinner $10–$25. AE, CB, DC, MC, V. Mon 11am–10pm, Tues–Sat 4–11pm, Sun 4–10pm. Metro: Gallery Place/Chinatown. AMERICAN.

Singles converge here after work most nights, because it's just that type of place: It's big; it's handsome; it plays loud music; it serves brewski's and plates of towering, thin-crisped onion rings, giant steaks, and big salads; plus it has pool tables, another bar, and couches on its upper level. But when the MCI Center, just up the street, has an event going on, watch out, the place practically bounces. Jocks feel especially at home here, but anyone might enjoy the fun—the goodtime feeling's contagious. Wouldn't expose the kids to it, though.

✪ **Georgia Brown's.** 950 15th St. NW. ☎ **202/393-4499.** Reservations recommended. Main courses $9–$19, Sun brunch $21.95. AE, DC, DISC, MC, V. Mon–Thurs 11:30am–10:30pm, Fri 11:30am–11:30pm, Sat 5:30pm–11:30pm, Sun 11:30am–4:30pm (brunch 11:30am–2:30pm) and 5:30–10:30pm. Valet parking after 6pm. Metro: McPherson Square. AMERICAN/SOUTHERN.

In Washington restaurants, seldom do you find such a racially diverse crowd. The harmony may stem from the waitstaff, whose obvious rapport results in gracious service, and certainly extends from the open kitchen, where the chef directs his multicultural staff. But in this large handsome room, whose arched windows overlook McPherson

Square, the food may capture all of your attention. A plate of corn bread and biscuits arrives, to be slathered with a butter that's been whipped with diced peaches and honey. The menu is heavily Southern, with the emphasis on the "low country" cooking of South Carolina and Savannah: collards, grits, and lots of seafood, especially shrimp dishes. The Carolina Perlau is a stewlike mix of duck, spicy sausage, jumbo shrimp, and rice, topped with toasted crumbs and scallions—it has bite without being terribly spicy.

Hunan Chinatown. 624 H St. NW. ☎ **202/783-5858.** Reservations recommended for 6 or more. Lunch $7.50–$15, dinner $9–$25. AE, CB, DC, DISC, MC, V. Mon–Thurs 11am–10pm, Fri–Sat 11am–11pm. Metro: Gallery Place–Chinatown. CHINESE.

Classical muzak playing in the background, comfortably cushioned chairs, and freshcut carnations on tabletops covered with pink and white tablecloths are several of the features that set this Chinatown restaurant apart from its neighbors. I liked the tea-smoked duck, the hot and sour soup (thick with shredded mushrooms), the fried wonton, fried dumplings, and shredded chicken in garlic sauce. Go here if you want good Chinese food in a calming atmosphere. The restaurant also operates a stand at the MCI Center, just around the corner.

✪ **Jaleo.** 480 7th St. NW (at E St.). ☎ **202/628-7949.** Reservations accepted until 6:30pm. Lunch $7.50–$10.75, dinner $10.50–$28, tapas $2.95–$7.50. AE, DC, DISC, MC, V. Mon–Sat 11:30am–2:30pm (with a limited tapas menu 2:30–5:30pm); Mon 5:30–10pm, Tues–Thurs 5:30–11:30pm, Fri–Sat 5:30pm–midnight, Sun 11:30am–3pm and 5:30–10pm. Valet parking $8 from 5:30pm. Metro: Archives or Gallery Place. SPANISH REGIONAL/TAPAS.

In theater season, Jaleo's dining room fills and empties each evening according to the performance schedule of the Shakespeare Theater, right next door. Lunchtime always draws a crowd from nearby office buildings and the Hill. This restaurant, which opened in 1993, may be credited with initiating the tapas craze in Washington. Among the menu items are mild but savory warm goat cheese served with toast points, a skewer of grilled chorizo sausage atop garlic mashed potatoes, and a delicious mushroom tart served with roasted red pepper sauce. Paella is among the few heartier entrees listed (feeds four). Spanish wines, sangrias, and sherries are available by the glass. Finish with a rum- and butter-soaked apple charlotte in bread pastry or a plate of Spanish cheeses. The casual-chic interior focuses on a large mural of a flamenco dancer inspired by John Singer Sargent's painting *Jaleo*. On Wednesday evenings at 8 and 9pm, flamenco dancers perform.

✪ **Old Ebbitt Grill.** 675 15th St. NW (between F and G sts.). ☎ **202/347-4801.** Reservations recommended. Breakfast $4.50–$7.95, brunch $5.95–$12.95, lunch $8.95–$18.95, dinner $10.95–$18.95; burgers and sandwiches $6.25–$10.95; raw bar $8.95–$18.50. AE, DC, DISC, MC, V. Mon–Fri 7:30am–1am, Sat 8am–1am, Sun 9:30am–1am. Bar Sun–Thurs to 2am, Fri–Sat to 3am. Raw bar open to midnight daily. Complimentary valet parking from 6pm Mon–Sat, from noon Sun. Metro: McPherson Square or Metro Center. AMERICAN.

Located 2 blocks from the White House, this is the city's oldest saloon, founded in 1856. Among its artifacts are animal trophies bagged by Teddy Roosevelt, and Alexander Hamilton's wooden bears—one with a secret compartment in which it's said he hid whiskey bottles from his wife. The Old Ebbitt is an attractive place, with Persian rugs strewn on beautiful oak and marble floors, beveled mirrors, flickering gaslights, etched-glass panels, and paintings of Washington scenes. The long, dark mahogany Old Bar area gives it the feeling of a men's saloon.

You may see preferential treatment given to movers and shakers, and you'll always have to wait for a table if you don't reserve ahead. The waitstaff is friendly and professional in a programmed sort of way; service could be faster. Menus change daily but always include certain favorites: burgers, the trout Parmesan (Virginia trout dipped in egg batter and Parmesan cheese, deep-fried), crab cakes, and oysters (there's an oyster bar). The tastiest dishes are usually the seasonal ones, whose fresh ingredients make the difference.

INEXPENSIVE

✪ **Full Kee.** 509 H St. NW. ☎ **202/371-2233.** Reservations accepted. Lunch $4.25–$9, dinner $6.95–$15. Cash only. Sun–Thurs 11am–1am, Fri–Sat 11am–3am. Metro: Gallery Place/Chinatown. CHINESE.

This is probably Chinatown's best restaurant, in terms of the actual food. Forget decor: Full Kee's two rooms are brightly lit and crammed with Chinese-speaking customers sitting on metal-legged chairs at plain rectangular tables. There's no such thing as a no-smoking section. A cook works in the small open kitchen at the front of the room, hanging roasted pig's parts on hooks and wrapping dumplings.

Chefs from some of Washington's best restaurants often congregate here after hours, and here's their advice. Order from the typed back page of the menu. Two selections are especially noteworthy: the jumbo breaded oyster casserole with ginger and scallions (I can second that) and the whole steamed fish. Check out the laminated tent card on the table and find the soups; if you love dumplings, order the Hong Kong-style shrimp dumpling broth: You get either eight shrimp dumplings or four if you order the broth with noodles. Bring your own wine or beer (and your own glasses in which to pour it) if you'd like to have a drink, since Full Kee does not serve any alcohol and accepts no responsibility for helping you imbibe.

Haad Thai. 1100 New York Ave. NW (entrance on 11th St. NW). ☎ **202/682-1111.** Reservations recommended. Lunch $6–$8, dinner $7–$11. AE, DC, MC, V. Mon–Fri 11:30am–2:30pm and 5–10:30pm, Sat noon–10:30pm, Sun 5–10pm. Metro: Metro Center. THAI.

The Washington area has lots of Thai restaurants, but not many are downtown. Fewer still offer food this good in such pretty quarters. Haad Thai is a short walk from the Convention Center, the MCI Center, and surrounding hotels. Plants and a pink and black mural of a Thai beach decorate the dining room. The standards are the best: pad thai, panang gai (chicken sautéed with fresh basil leaves in curry, with peanut sauce), and satays, although all dishes are flavorful and only mildly spicy; ask, if you want your food spicier.

Reeves Restaurant & Bakery. 1306 G St. NW. ☎ **202/628-6350.** Main courses $5.50–$8; sandwiches $3.50–$6; buffet breakfast $5.25 Mon–Fri, $6.25 Sat and holidays. MC, V. Mon–Sat 7am–6pm. Metro: Metro Center. AMERICAN.

There's no place like Reeves, a Washington institution since 1886, although in a new building since 1992. J. Edgar Hoover used to send a G-man to pick up chicken sandwiches, and Lady Bird Johnson and daughter Lynda Bird worked out the latter's wedding plans over lunch here. It's fronted by a long bakery counter filled with scrumptious pies and cakes. The original 19th-century wooden stools front the brass-railed counter. The ambience is cheerful, and much of the seating is in cozy booths and banquettes.

Everything is homemade with top-quality ingredients: the turkeys, chickens, salads, breads, desserts, even the mayonnaise. At breakfast, you can't beat the all-you-can-eat buffet: scrambled eggs, home fries, French toast, pancakes, doughnuts, corned-beef hash, grits, bacon, sausage, stewed and fresh fruit, biscuits with sausage gravy, and more. Hot entrees run the gamut from golden-brown Maryland crab cakes to country-fried chicken with mashed potatoes and gravy. Reeves pies are famous. No alcoholic beverages are served.

4 Downtown, 16th Street NW & West

VERY EXPENSIVE

✪ Galileo. 1110 21st St. NW. ☎ **202/293-7191.** Reservations recommended. Lunch $11–$19, dinner $17–$30. AE, CB, DC, DISC, MC, V. Mon–Fri 11:30am–2pm and 5:30–10pm, Sat 5:30–10:30pm, Sun 5–10pm. Complimentary valet parking in evening. Metro: Foggy Bottom. ITALIAN.

Food critics mention Galileo as one of the best Italian restaurants in the country and Roberto Donna as one of our best chefs. The likable Donna opened the white-walled, grottolike Galileo in 1984; since then, he has opened several other restaurants in the area, including Il Radicchio and Pesce (see Dupont Circle listings), has written a cookbook, and has established himself as an integral part of Washington culture.

Galileo features the cuisine of Donna's native Piedmont region, an area in northern Italy influenced by neighboring France and Switzerland—think truffles, hazelnuts, porcini mushrooms, and veal. The atmosphere is relaxed; diners are dressed in jeans and suits alike. For starters, munch on the Piedmont-style crostini—paper-thin toast dipped in pureed cannellini beans with garlic. Typical entrees include sautéed Chesapeake Bay oysters, served on a bed of leeks and porcini mushrooms; pansotti (a pasta) of truffled potatoes and crispy pancetta in a porcini mushroom sauce; and grilled rack of venison with a wild berry sauce. Finish with a traditional tiramisù or, better yet, the warm pear tart with honey vanilla ice cream and caramel sauce—spectacular. The cellar boasts more than 900 vintages of Italian wine (40% Piedmontese). Newly added is an interactive kitchen culinary center in the main dining room. There is also a terrace for warm weather dining.

I Ricchi. 1220 19th St. NW. ☎ **202/835-0459.** Reservations recommended. Lunch $10–$28, dinner $11.95–$32. AE, CB, DC, MC, V. Mon–Fri 11:30am–2pm; Mon–Sat 5:30–10pm. Free valet parking at dinner. Metro: Dupont Circle. ITALIAN.

This restaurant celebrated its 10th year in 1999, and it remains a popular and convivial place to enjoy Italian food à la Tuscany. An open kitchen with a blazing wood-burning grill creates a warming bustle in the large room. The daily specials are great, especially if you're into fish. I also liked the minestrone and the pastas, like one stuffed with spinach and ground veal, or the spaghettini covered with a thick tomato sauce, mushrooms, and crisp shrimp.

✪ Lespinasse. St. Regis Hotel, 923 16th St. NW. ☎ **202/879-6900.** Reservations recommended. Jacket required for men. Breakfast $8–$19; lunch prix fixe $36, à la carte $14–$20; tea $19; dinner prix fixe $48, à la carte $23–$32. AE, CB, DC, DISC, MC, V. Mon–Fri 7–10:30am, Sat–Sun 7–11am; Tues–Fri noon–2pm; Tues–Sat 6–10pm; tea (in lobby) Fri–Sun 3–5:30pm. Complimentary valet parking for lunch and dinner. Metro: Farragut North. FRENCH.

A $6-million renovation of Lespinasse's opulent dining room endowed it with a castle-like hand-stenciled wood beam ceiling, creamy gold-hued walls, royal blue stamped banquettes and floral carpeting, and comfortable yellow leather chairs. The china is Limoges, the crystal Riedel. You pay for the embellishments: This Washington branch of New York's Lespinasse is among the most expensive restaurants in town, although prices have come down considerably since it opened 2 years ago. St. Regis chef Sandro

In case you want to see the world.

At American Express, we're here to make your journey a smooth one. So we have over 1,700 travel service locations in over 130 countries ready to help. What else would you expect from the world's largest travel agency?

do more

Travel

In case you want to be welcomed there.

We're here to see that you're always welcomed at establishments everywhere. That's why millions of people carry the American Express® Card – for peace of mind, confidence, and security, around the world or just around the corner.

do more **Cards**

In case you're running low.

We're here to help with more than 190,000 Express Cash locations around the world. In order to enroll, just call American Express at 1 800 CASH-NOW before you start your vacation.

do more AMERICAN EXPRESS

Express Cash

And in case you'd rather be safe than sorry.

We're here with American Express® Travelers Cheques. They're the safe way to carry money on your vacation, because if they're ever lost or stolen you can get a refund, practically anywhere or anytime. To find the nearest place to buy Travelers Cheques, call 1 800 495-1153. Another way we help you do more.

do more

Travelers Cheques

Gamba commands the kitchen, turning out exquisite dishes such as shellfish ragout and cream of chestnut soup with truffles. Sommelier Vincent Feraud is the best, having presided at Jean-Louis (now closed). One unexpected twist to the wine list is that it offers a nice selection of reasonably priced good wines by the glass. Pastry chef Jill Rose is behind those delicious-looking and -tasting desserts, such as the persimmon pudding. A dinner at Lespinasse takes time—not because of the service, which is smooth and attentive, but because the kitchen is slow. But maybe that's for the good: The meal over which you linger becomes an event in itself.

MAX'S of Washington. 1725 F St. NW. ☎ **202/842-0070.** Reservations suggested. Lunch $9–$25, dinner $18–$35, light fare $5–$10 (weekdays 2:30–6pm). AE, DC, MC, V. Mon–Fri 11:45am–2:30pm; Mon–Sat 6–10pm. Happy Hour weekdays 4–7pm, 2-for-1 drinks. Complimentary valet parking after 5:30pm. Metro: Farragut West or Farragut North. FRENCH/AMERICAN.

The restaurant offers French in the grand old-fashioned way, with its dark-brown banquettes and starched white-linen covered tablecloths. MAX'S is, I believe, the closest restaurant to the White House and gets a lot of Administration traffic. The menu offers a mix of classic French and American dishes, from crab cakes to clams casino to lamb chops to lobster. The emphasis is on steaks, and these get high marks from *Washington Post* food critic Phyllis Richman. Side dishes include yummy creamed spinach and crispy latkes. Desserts—profiteroles, apple tart—do the kitchen proud.

✪ **Prime Rib.** 2020 K St. NW. ☎ **202/466-8811.** Reservations recommended. Lunch $11–$20, dinner $18–$39. AE, CB, DC, MC, V. Mon–Thurs 11:30am–3pm and 5–11pm, Fri 11:30am–3pm and 5–11:30pm, Sat 5–11:30pm. Jacket and tie required for men. Free valet parking after 5pm. Metro: Farragut West. STEAKS/CHOPS/SEAFOOD.

The Prime Rib has plenty of competition now, but it makes no difference. Beef lovers still consider this The Place. It's got a definite men's club feel about it: brass-trimmed black walls, leopard-skin carpeting, comfortable black leather chairs and banquettes. Waiters are in black tie, and a pianist at the baby grand plays show tunes and Irving Berlin classics.

The meat is from the best grain-fed steers and has been aged for 4 to 5 weeks. Steaks and cuts of roast beef are thick, tender, and juicy. For less carnivorous diners, there are about a dozen seafood entrees, including an excellent crab imperial. Mashed potatoes are done right, as are the fried potato skins.

✪ **The Restaurant at The Jefferson.** 1200 16th St. NW (at M St.). ☎ **202/833-6206.** Reservations recommended. Breakfast $8.50–$12, lunch $18 prix fixe, $13–$22 à la carte, dinner $23–$28; Sun brunch $19.50–$28, tea $15. AE, CB, DC, DISC, JCB, MC, V. Daily 6:30–11am, 11:30am–2pm, and 6–10:30pm; tea daily 3–5pm. Free valet parking. Metro: Farragut North. AMERICAN.

Cozy, rather than intimidatingly plush, the Jefferson Hotel's restaurant is actually pretty romantic (ask to be seated in "the snug," tables 39 or 40). The emphasis on privacy and the solicitous, but not imposing, service also make it a good place to do business.

Chef James Hudock changes his menus seasonally. Appetizers we enjoyed from a late winter menu included a baby spinach salad sprinkled with goat cheese and dressed with tangerine ginger dressing, and a warm artichoke heart salad with designer lettuce and scallops, resting upon a thin potato galette. Among the entrees were a caramelized black grouper with Kalamata olives, roasted peppers, English peas, and roasted potatoes, and perfectly done lamb chops. Our meal ended with a divine coffee crème brûlée. An extensive wine list includes many by-the-glass selections.

✪ **Taberna del Alabardero.** 1776 I St. NW (entrance on 18th St. NW). ☎ **202/429-2200.** Reservations recommended. Lunch $17.25–$20.75, dinner $19–$29.50; pretheater $30; tapas $5–$8.75. AE, DC, DISC, MC, V. Mon–Thurs 11:30am–2:30pm and 6–10pm, Fri 11:30am–2:30pm and 6–11pm, Sat 6–11pm; happy hour weekdays 4–6pm, half-price drinks. Jacket and tie required for men. Free valet parking at dinner. Metro: Farragut West. SPANISH.

Dress up to visit this truly elegant restaurant, where you receive royal treatment from the Spanish staff who are quite used to attending to the real thing: Spain's King Juan Carlos and Queen Sofia and their children regularly dine here when in Washington. In 1999, the Spanish ministry of agriculture named Taberna the best Spanish restaurant in the United States.

The dining room is old-world ornate, with lace covers placed over velvety banquettes and heavy brocadelike drapes framing the large front windows. Order a plate of tapas to start: lightly fried calamari, shrimp in garlic and olive oil, thin smoky ham, and marinated mushrooms. Although the à la carte menu changes with the seasons, four paellas (each requires a minimum of two people to order) are always available. The lobster and seafood paella served on saffron rice is rich and flavorful. (Ask to have the lobster de-shelled; otherwise, you do the cracking.) Another signature dish is Txangurro Gratinado (Basque-style crabmeat).

This is the only Taberna del Alabardero outside of Spain, where there are three. All are owned and operated by Father Luis de Lezama, who opened his first tavern outside the palace gates in Madrid in 1974, as a place to train delinquent boys for employment.

EXPENSIVE

Daily Grill. 1200 18th St. NW. ☎ **202/822-5282.** Reservations recommended. Lunch $7.95–$15, dinner $9–$23. AE, DC, DISC, MC, V. Mon–Thurs 11:30am–11pm; Fri–Sat 11:30am–midnight; Sun 10am–3pm (brunch), 3–5pm limited menu, and 5–10pm. Free valet parking from 5pm Mon–Sat and all day Sun. Metro: Farragut North or Dupont Circle. AMERICAN.

Step right in and get your Cobb salad, your chicken pot pie, your fresh fruit cobbler, your meat and potatoes. Talk about retro; in the case of the Daily Grill, retro means revisiting the food favorites of decades past. The California-based restaurant itself is not that old—about three years. It's a big space, with a nice bar at the front and windows on three sides. The winding bar offers an extensive selection: good wines, lots of single malts, tequilas, and small-batch bourbons. The Daily Grill is a favorite lunchtime spot—where else can you order eggs Benedict at noon on a weekday?

Like its chain siblings, the D.C. Grill is gaining a reputation for American-friendly service and large portions of grilled meats and fish. (The menu boasts a BLT made with "half a pound of bacon.") Favorite orders are the shortribs and the "Grill Combo" of tiny onion rings over skinny fries—a must for table-sharing. Another Daily Grill is located in the Georgetown Inn (1310 Wisconsin Ave. NW; ☎ **202/337-4900**).

✪ **Georgetown Seafood Grill on 19th St.** 1200 19th St. NW. ☎ **202/530-4430.** Reservations recommended. Lunch $5–$22, dinner $10–$24, salads and sandwiches $8.95–$12.95. AE, DC, DISC, MC, V. Mon–Thurs 11:30am–10pm, Fri 11:30am–11pm, Sat 5:30–11pm, Sun 5:30–10pm. Metro: Dupont Circle. SEAFOOD.

In the heart of downtown is this hint of the seashore. Two big tanks of lobsters greet you as you enter, and the decor is nautical throughout: aquariums set in walls, canoes fastened to the ceiling, models of tall ships placed here and there. Meanwhile, music from another era is heard—"Young at Heart," and the like. It's enough to make you forget what city you're in.

A bar and tables sit at the front of the restaurant, an open kitchen is in the middle, and tall wooden booths on platforms occupy the rear. The lobster Thermidor special is a mix of Pernod, scallions, mushrooms, and cream mixed with bits of lobster. But if you want really healthy chunks of lobster, order the lobster club, served on brioche with applewood bacon and mayo, or better yet, the fresh lobster delivered daily from Maine. As is the rule in many seafood restaurants, your best bets are the most simply prepared: Besides the lobster, you can choose from a list of at least eight "simply grilled" fish entrees. Raw bar selections list oysters from Canada, Virginia, and Oregon, and these may be the freshest in town. Service is excellent.

Legal Sea Foods. 2020 K St. NW. ☎ **202/496-1111.** Reservations recommended, especially at lunch. Lunch $8–$14 (sandwiches $6.95–$8.95), dinner $12–$20. AE, DC, DISC, MC, V. Mon–Thurs 11am–10pm, Fri 11am–10:30pm, Sat 5–10:30pm, Sun 4–9pm. Metro: Farragut North or Farragut West. SEAFOOD.

This famous family-run, Boston-based seafood empire, whose motto is "If it's not fresh, it's not Legal," made its Washington debut in August 1995. The softly lit dining room is plush, with terrazzo marble floors and rich cherrywood paneling. Sporting events, especially Boston games, are aired on a TV over the handsome marble bar/raw bar, and you can get a copy of the *Boston Globe* near the entrance. In 1998, the restaurant enclosed the bar area to allow for cigar smoking. As for the food, not only is everything fresh, but it's all from certified-safe waters.

Legal's buttery rich clam chowder is a classic. Other worthy appetizers include garlicky, golden-brown, farm-raised mussels au gratin and fluffy pan-fried Maryland lump crab cakes served with zesty corn relish and mayo-mustard sauce. Legal's signature dessert is a marionberry and blueberry cobbler with a brown-sugar, oatmeal-crisp crust; it's topped with a scoop of homemade vanilla ice cream. An award-winning wine list is a plus. At lunch, oyster po' boys and the shrimp roll are real treats. Another Legal Sea Foods is located in the new terminal at National Airport (☎ **703/413-9810**).

✪ **The Palm.** 1225 19th St. NW. ☎ **202/293-9091.** Reservations recommended. Lunch $9–$18, dinner $15–$50. AE, DC, MC, V. Mon–Fri 11:45am–10:30pm, Sat 6–10:30pm, Sun 5:30–9:30pm. Complimentary valet parking at dinner. Metro: Dupont Circle. STEAKHOUSE.

The Palm is one in a chain that started 77 years ago in New York—but here in D.C., it feels like an original. The Washington Palm is 28 years old; its walls, like all Palms, are covered with the caricatures of regulars, famous and not-so. (Look for my friend, Bob Harris.) If you think you see James Carville eating lunch at the bar, you're probably right; although sometimes he joins his better half, Mary Matalin, at a table. You can't go wrong with steak, whether it's the 36-ounce, dry-aged New York strip, or sliced in a steak salad. Oversize lobsters are a specialty, and certain side dishes are a must: creamed spinach, onion rings, Palm fries (something akin to deep-fried potato chips), and hash browns. Several of the longtime waiters like to kid with you a bit; service is always fast.

✪ **Vidalia.** 1990 M St. NW. ☎ **202/659-1990.** Reservations recommended. Lunch $6.75–$18.75, dinner $19.50–$27. AE, DC, DISC, MC, V. Mon–Fri 11:30am–2:30pm; Mon–Thurs 5:30–10pm, Fri–Sat 5:30–10:30pm, Sun 5–9:30pm (closed on Sundays July 4–Labor Day). Free valet parking at dinner. Metro: Dupont Circle. PROVINCIAL AMERICAN.

Down a flight of steps from the street, the charming Vidalia is a tiered dining room, with cream stucco walls hung with gorgeous dried-flower wreaths and works by local artists.

Chef Jeff Buben's "provincial American" menus (focusing on Southern-accented regional specialties) change frequently, but recommended constants include crisp East

Coast lump crab cakes, a fried grits cake with portobello mushrooms, and "the onion": a roasted whole Vidalia onion that's cut and opened up, like the leaves of a flower. Venture from the regular items, and you may delight in a timbale of roasted onion and foie gras.

A signature entree is the scrumptious sautéed shrimp on a mound of creamed grits and caramelized onions in a thyme and shrimp-cream sauce. Cornbread and biscuits with apple butter are served at every meal. Vidalia is known for its lemon chess pie, which tastes like pure sugar; I prefer the pecan pie. A carefully chosen wine list highlights American vintages.

MODERATE

۞ Bombay Club. 815 Connecticut Ave. NW. ☎ **202/659-3727.** Reservations recommended. Main courses $7.50–$18.50, Sun brunch $18.50; pretheater $24. AE, CB, DC, MC, V. Mon–Fri and Sun brunch 11:30am–2:30pm, Mon–Thurs 6–10:30pm, Fri–Sat 6–11pm, Sun 5:30–9pm. Free valet parking after 6pm. Metro: Farragut West. INDIAN.

Dine here and be prepared for Secret Service sweeps of the restaurant, in anticipation of visits by the Clintons or maybe Prince Bandar bin Sultan, the Saudi ambassador. (The White House is just across Lafayette Park.)

The Indian menu here ranges from fiery green chili chicken ("not for the faint-hearted," the menu warns) to the delicately prepared lobster malabar, a personal favorite. Tandoori dishes, like the chicken marinated in a yogurt, ginger, and garlic dressing, are specialties, as is the vegetarian fare—try the black lentils cooked overnight on a slow fire. Patrons are as fond of the service as the cuisine: Waitstaff seem straight out of Jewel in the Crown, attending to your every whim. This is one place where you can linger over a meal as long as you like. Slow-moving ceiling fans and wicker furniture accentuate the colonial British ambience.

McCormick & Schmick's. 1652 K St. NW (at corner of 17th St. NW). ☎ **202/861-2233.** Reservations suggested. Main courses $6.60–$19.95. AE, DC, DISC, MC, V. Mon–Thurs 11am–11pm, Fri 11am–midnight, Sat 5pm–midnight, Sun 5–10pm. Bar opens at 4pm Sat and Sun. Valet parking after 5pm. Metro: Farragut North and Farragut West. SEAFOOD.

In this branch of a Pacific Northwest–based restaurant, stained glass in the chandeliers and ceiling evince a patriotic theme. This huge place seats its patrons in booths, at a 65-foot bar, and at linen-laid tables. The vast menu offers selections of fresh fish from both nearby and Pacific waters—the more simply prepared, the better. Oyster lovers will choose happily from the half-dozen kinds stocked daily. For good value, look at the list of light entrees ranging from oyster stew to chicken picatta and costing $6.60 to $9.95. Or, head to the bar to enjoy a giant burger, fried calamari, quesadillas, fish tacos, and more, for only $1.95, Monday through Friday 3:30 to 6:30pm, Monday through Thursday 10:30pm to midnight, and Friday and Saturday 10pm to midnight. Friendly bartenders make you feel at home as they concoct "handmade from scratch" mixed drinks with freshly squeezed juices. A surf and turf version of McCormick & Schmick's, the M&S Grill, is located near the MCI Center, at 13th and F streets NW (☎ **202/347-1500**).

INEXPENSIVE

Oodles Noodles. 1120 19th St. NW. ☎ **202/293-3138.** Reservations recommended for 5 or more at dinner. Main courses $7–$9. AE, DC, MC, V. Mon–Fri 11:30am–3pm; Mon–Thurs 5–10pm, Fri–Sat 5–10:30pm. Metro: Dupont Circle or Farragut North. ASIAN.

Asian waiters, Asian background music, and calligraphy figures drawn on the walls put you in the right frame of mind for Pan-Asian noodle dishes. You can order dumplings, Szechuan dan dan noodles (egg noodles), Vietnamese vermicelli, and Thai drunken noodles, among others. Many of the items come in a soup, such as the Shanghai roast pork noodles soup and the Siam noodles soup, which is a spicy sweet and sour broth with shrimp, minced chicken, and squid.

But not everything is a noodle. Appetizers include satays, spring onion cakes, and vegetable spring rolls. Curry, teriyaki, and similar spicy non-noodle fare round out the menu.

Though Washington food critics give Oodles Noodles high marks, I find it hit or miss. My Noodles on the Boat (grilled marinated lemon chicken with rice vermicelli, bean sprouts, vegetables, peanuts, and fried onions) was bland, and my husband's Spices Chicken wasn't spicy at all. You can't beat the prices, though, and my children, at least, were content with their Chicken Wonton Soup and Ravioli.

5 U Street Corridor

MODERATE

Eleventh Hour. 1520 14th St. NW (between Church and P St. NW). ☎ **202/234-0886.** Reservations accepted for 6 or more only. Main courses $10–$22. Tues–Sun 5–10pm, Fri–Sat 5–11pm. Dancing nightly 11pm–3am. Free valet parking. Metro: Dupont Circle. AMERICAN.

It's loud, it's hip, and it's fun. A number of theaters are nearby—the Woolly Mammoth, the Source, and the Studio—so lots of people stop for a pretheater bite. But as the night goes on, it gets noisier and more crowded. The restaurant includes a dining room with french doors opening to the sidewalk cafe, a room for dancing, a room with a fireplace, a front bar, a back bar, colorfully painted walls, and loungy leather and funky furniture throughout.

The surprise is that you can eat well on choices like salt cod fritters, tempura shrimp, grilled pork with almond sauce, and asparagus risotto. The trouble is, Eleventh Hour wants to please everybody, and you know how that goes. Come here only for the food and you may be irritated by the bustle. But if you're ready to be flexible, you'll wind up having a pretty good meal and a fun time. The restaurant is actually about 6 blocks down from U Street.

INEXPENSIVE

Coppi's. 1414 U St. NW. ☎ **202/319-7773.** Reservations not accepted. Main courses $7–$11.50. AE, DC, DISC, MC, V. Mon–Thurs 5pm–midnight, Fri–Sat 5pm–1am, Sun 5–11pm. Metro: U St.–Cardoza. ITALIAN.

Crowded with neighborhood patrons and hungry clubgoers headed for one of the nearby music houses, Coppi's is a narrow room decorated with wooden booths and bicycle memorabilia from Italian bike races. The wood-burning oven turns out a mean pizza, a stiff competitor to that of topdog Pizzeria Paradiso (see below). The crust is chewy and your choice of toppings include quality ham, pancetta, cheeses, and vegetables. You can count on finding an extensive Italian wine list and entrees are all under $12. Another Coppi's, the larger **Coppi's Vigorelli,** is located in the Cleveland Park neighborhood, at 3421 Connecticut Ave. NW (☎ **202/244-6437**). Prices are a little higher, and hours are different, so call ahead.

6 Adams-Morgan

Though the action centers on just 2 or 3 blocks, Adams-Morgan is one of D.C.'s liveliest neighborhoods, filled with ethnic and trendy restaurants and happening nightclubs. At nighttime, it's best to come here via taxi, since parking is difficult and the closest Metro stop is a bit of a hike. (During the day, parking is usually not a problem.) If you do take the Metro, exit at Dupont Circle (the North exit) and walk uphill on Connecticut Avenue, picking up Columbia Road (where it forks off Connecticut Avenue), and follow it to Adams-Morgan. Or take the Metro to the Woodley

Park–Zoo stop, walk south on Connecticut Avenue to Calvert Street, turn left, and cross the Calvert Street bridge to Adams-Morgan.

EXPENSIVE

Cities. 2424 18th St. NW (near Columbia Rd.). ☎ **202/328-7194.** Reservations recommended. Main courses $16.50–$24.95. AE, CB, DC, DISC, MC, V. Sun–Thurs 6–11pm, Fri–Sat 6–1:30pm. Bar open Sun–Thurs 5pm–2am, Fri–Sat 5pm–3am. Valet parking $5. INTERNATIONAL.

Housed in a century-old former five-and-dime store, Cities is a restaurant-cum-travelogue. A recent $1.2 million renovation has dressed up the place, with additions like suede drapes, touches of mahogany and Italian leather, and soft lighting provided by hundreds of hanging filament bulbs. Once a year, the restaurant re-invents itself to reflect the cuisine, character, and culture of a different city. The music changes, and even the waiters are attired in native dress or some facsimile thereof. Until spring of 2000 or so, Cities is embracing Barcelona, with a menu that includes pan-seared fois gras with sautéed apples, Maine lobster salad with orange vinaigrette, and Mediterranean shellfish with fresh tomato juice and oregano. The wine and champagne list complements the menu; premium wines are offered by the glass. On the walls are photographs of Barcelona, taken by Francesco Catala-Roca. The bar, at the front of the restaurant, is upscale and loungy, and features light fare, starting around $7.50.

Upstairs is Privé at Cities, described by the restaurant as "a private club dedicated to the new age of self-indulgence, available to the restaurant's elite clientele and visiting celebrities." If you think you qualify, talk to your hotel concierge to arrange a visit.

✪ **Cashion's Eat Place.** 1819 Columbia Rd. NW (between 18th St. and Mintwood Place). ☎ **202/797-1819.** Reservations recommended. Brunch $6–$9, dinner $14–$21. MC, V. Tues 5:30–10pm, Wed–Sat 5:30–11pm, Sun 11:30am–2:30pm and 5:30–10pm. Valet parking $5. AMERICAN.

Owner/chef Ann Cashion has gained renown for her stints at Nora, Austin Grill, and Jaleo. Her menu features about eight entrees, split between seafood and meat, which could include grilled wild Chesapeake rockfish or rabbit stew with dumplings and vegetables. The side dishes that accompany each entree, such as spiced red cabbage and chestnuts and sautéed foie gras, are worth as much attention. Chocolate cinnamon mousse, lime tartalette, and other desserts are worth saving room for.

The pleasing dining room is centered around a slightly raised, curving bar. In warm weather, the glass-fronted Cashion's opens invitingly to the sidewalk, where you can also dine. But we were there on a frigid January day when each opening of the door blew a blast of cold air over those of us seated at the front of the restaurant; ask for a table in back during the winter.

Felix. 2406 18th St. NW. ☎ **202/483-3549.** Reservations recommended. Main courses $14–$24. AE, DC, MC, V. Sun–Thurs 5:30–10:30pm, Fri–Sat 5:30–11pm. Live music nightly Sun–Thurs until 1:30am, Fri–Sat until 2:30am. AMERICAN.

Felix and its patrons try hard to be hip. Customers down martinis at the bar and sometimes crush up against dining tables (the areas adjoin on the first floor). If you're here on a Friday evening, though, you'll be among regulars enjoying matzoh ball soup and beef brisket: Felix's Friday menu includes traditional Jewish fare. During Passover, staff will help you conduct your own seder, providing you with everything from gefilte fish to prayer books. (The regular menu is always available.)

Most nights, however, Felix feels like a party in a group house, an impression reinforced by the dimly lit living room setup in the back room and upstairs in the Loft

Lounge. You're afraid to peer too closely at what that couple in the corner is doing. (The Loft Lounge, by the way, is open Friday and Saturday nights only, as a bar and music club, not for dining.)

The food is quite good: Cream of mushroom soup is seasoned just right and delicately creamy; the pork chop, by contrast, is lean, huge, and hearty, and served with potato gallettes and sautéed spinach. A signature dish is the fresh yellowfin tuna panseared rare and presented with sticky rice, snow peas, and wasabi cream sauce. Desserts include bananas Foster sautéed in Jack Daniels.

MODERATE

La Fourchette. 2429 18th St. NW. ☎ **202/332-3077.** Reservations recommended on weekends. Main courses $8.95–$21.95. Mon–Thurs 11:30am–10:30pm; Fri 11:30am–11pm, Sat 4–11pm, Sun 4–10pm. AE, DC, MC, V. FRENCH.

Upstairs is no-smoking, but downstairs is where you want to be, among the French-speaking clientele and Adams-Morgan regulars. The waiters are suitably crusty and the ambience is as Parisian as you'll get this side of the Atlantic—as is the food. The menu lists escargots, onion soup, bouillabaisse, and mussels provencale, along with specials like the grilled salmon on spinach mousse and the shrimp Niçoise, ever-so-slightly crusted and sautéed in a tomato sauce touched with anchovy. A colorful mural covers the high walls; wooden tables and benches push up against bare brick walls. La Fourchette is Washington's Paris cafe.

INEXPENSIVE

Meskerem. 2434 18th St. NW (between Columbia and Belmont rds.). ☎ **202/462-4100.** Lunch $5–$10.50, dinner $8.50–$11.50. AE, CB, DC, DISC, MC, V. Sun–Thurs noon–midnight, Fri–Sat noon–2am. ETHIOPIAN.

Washington has a number of Ethiopian restaurants, but this is probably the best. It's certainly the most attractive; the three-level, high-ceilinged dining room (sunny by day, candlelit at night) has an oval skylight girded by a painted sunburst and walls hung with African art and musical instruments. On the mezzanine level, you sit at messobs (basket tables) on low carved Ethiopian chairs or upholstered leather poufs. Ethiopian music (including live bands after midnight on weekends) enhances the ambience.

Diners share large platters of food, which are scooped up with a sourdough crepe-like pancake called injera. Items listed as watt are hot and spicy; alitchas are milder and more delicately flavored. You might also share an entree—perhaps *yegeb kay watt* (succulent lamb in thick, hot berbere sauce)—along with a combination platter of five vegetarian dishes served with tomato and potato salads. Combination platters comprise an array of beef, chicken, lamb, and vegetables. There's a full bar, and the wine list includes Ethiopian wine and beer.

✪ **Mixtec.** 1792 Columbia Rd. (just off 18th St.). ☎ **202/332-1011.** Main courses $2.95–$9.95. MC, V. Sun–Thurs 11am–10:30pm, Fri–Sat 11am–11pm. MEXICAN REGIONAL.

This cheerful Adams-Morgan spot attracts a clientele of Hispanics, neighborhood folks, and D.C. chefs, all of whom appreciate the delicious authenticity of its regional Mexican cuisine. The kitchen is open, the dining room colorfully decorated, and the music is lively mariachi and other kinds of Mexican music.

Delicious made-from-scratch corn and flour tortillas enhance whatever they're stuffed with. Small dishes called antojitos ("little whims"), in the $2.50 to $4.95 range, include queso fundido (a bubbling hot dish of broiled Chihuahua cheese topped with shredded spicy chorizo sausage and flavored with jalapeños and cilantro). Also popular

are the enrollados mexicanos, which are large flour tortillas wrapped around a variety of fillings: grilled chicken, beef, vegetables, salmon. The freshly prepared guacamole is excellent. A house specialty, a full entree served with rice and beans, is mole Mexicano—broiled chicken in a rich sauce of five peppers (the kitchen uses some 200 different spices!), sunflower and sesame seeds, onions, garlic, almonds, cinnamon, and chocolate. Choose from 30 kinds of tequila, tequila-mixed drinks, Mexican beers, and fresh fruit juices.

Pasta Mia. 1790 Columbia Rd. NW. ☎ **202/328-9114.** Main courses $6.95–$9.95. V, MC. Mon–Sat 6:30pm–late. ITALIAN.

Right next door to Mixtec (see above) is another excellent inexpensive choice that stays busy all night. You might have to wait for a table, too, especially on a Friday or Saturday night, since the restaurant doesn't take reservations. But you'll agree it's worth it, after you dive into a plate heaped with one of the nearly 30 pasta dishes on the

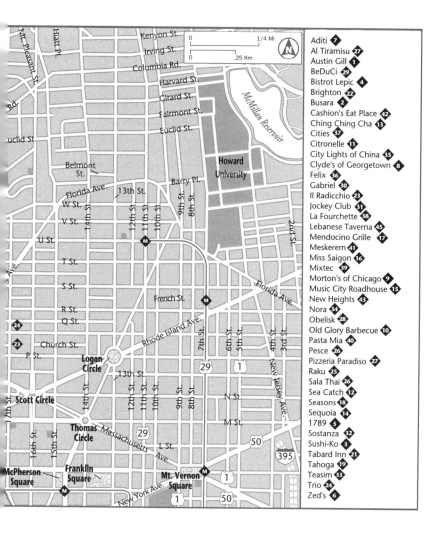

Aditi **7**
Al Tiramisu **27**
Austin Gill **1**
BeDuCi **29**
Bistrot Lepic **4**
Brighton **22**
Busara **2**
Cashion's Eat Place **42**
Ching Ching Cha **13**
Cities **37**
Citronelle **11**
City Lights of China **35**
Clyde's of Georgetown **8**
Felix **36**
Gabriel **30**
Il Radicchio **23**
Jockey Club **31**
La Fourchette **38**
Lebanese Taverna **45**
Mendocino Grille **17**
Meskerem **41**
Miss Saigon **16**
Mixtec **39**
Morton's of Chicago **9**
Music City Roadhouse **15**
New Heights **43**
Nora **34**
Obelisk **28**
Old Glory Barbecue **10**
Pasta Mia **40**
Pesce **26**
Pizzeria Paradiso **27**
Raku **25**
Sala Thai **26**
Sea Catch **12**
Seasons **18**
Sequoia **14**
1789 **5**
Sostanza **32**
Sushi-Ko **3**
Tabard Inn **21**
Tahoga **19**
Teasim **33**
Trio **24**
Zed's **6**

menu. Nine have meat sauces, three have seafood, and the remainder are vegetarian. I recommend the green fettuccine with cream-tomato sauce. Bread is made in-house, and appetizers, like the Caesar salad or white beans with fresh basil, are all flavorful. This place is as low-key as Washington gets, with a simple, bright-lit interior of red-checked covered tables packed together, and dishes served to a table as they are ready.

7 Dupont Circle

VERY EXPENSIVE

The Jockey Club. In the Westin Fairfax, Washington, D.C., 2100 Massachusetts Ave. NW. ☎ **202/835-2100.** Reservations required. Breakfast $10–$20, lunch $12–$30, dinner $24–$30. AE, DC, DISC, MC, V. Daily 6:30–11am, noon–2:30pm, and 6–10:30pm. Jacket and tie for men required at dinner. Free valet parking. Metro: Dupont Circle. FRENCH/CONTINENTAL.

The Jockey Club, Washington's longest-running power-dining enclave, opened in 1961 and immediately became a Kennedy clan favorite (it still is). JFK once quipped that when he wanted to reach a staff member, he first called their office, then their home, then The Jockey Club. Nancy Reagan and Barbara Bush were regulars. These days, it's a moneyed bunch who come here, and you're likely to see more than one whitehaired gentleman squiring about a much younger woman.

The dining room is cheerful and pubby, with red-leather banquettes, a random-plank oak floor, lanterns suspended from a low beamed ceiling (the subdued amber lighting is as cozy as the glow of a fireplace), and walls of stucco or aged oak paneling hung with English equestrian prints.

A new chef is in the kitchen, but the cuisine is the same as always: classic and continental. For instance, an appetizer of sautéed quail with California artichokes and green lentils is garnished with oba (Japanese basil). However, the signature dish is the big fluffy crab cakes meunière—more than 45,000 are ordered yearly. The pommes soufflés side dish has been on the menu since the restaurant opened.

Nora. 2132 Florida Ave. NW (at R St.). ☎ **202/462-5143.** Reservations recommended. Main courses $19–$30. DISC, MC, V. Mon–Thurs 6–10pm, Fri–Sat 6–10:30pm. Valet parking $5. Metro: Dupont Circle. ORGANIC AMERICAN.

Owner-chef Nora Pouillon brings haute panache to politically correct organic cookery in this charming restaurant. The main dining room is a converted stable, part of which is skylit, with a weathered-looking beamed pine ceiling, tables lit by shaded paraffin lamps, and a display of Amish and Mennonite patchwork crib quilts on the walls. The atmosphere is relaxed and cozy, and the dress code is anything goes. Journalists like to eat here, and so does Bill Clinton.

Don't expect brown rice and beans. Instead you'll find chemical-free, organically grown, free-range fare, some of which you won't ever have heard of, though you can bet they'll be extremely healthful. Nightly menus vary with the seasons. Recent popular dishes included sautéed Maine diver scallops in a soy-bacon vinaigrette and slow-roasted sesame salmon. A vegetarian entree, like green olive risotto, is always an option. Many desserts use fruits and nuts—for instance, orange-scented shortcake with fresh strawberries. An extensive wine list includes, but is not limited to, selections made with organically grown grapes.

EXPENSIVE

Al Tiramisu. 2014 P St. NW. ☎ **202/467-4466.** Reservations required. Lunch $11–$14, dinner $14–$20. AE, DC, MC, V. Mon–Fri noon–2:30pm; daily 5–11pm. Valet parking weekends. Metro: Dupont Circle. ITALIAN.

I called last minute for a reservation and the staff was kind enough to squeeze the four of us in, squeeze being the operative word: The tables are a little snug in this narrow but intimate restaurant. The charming servers have time to chat a little, and yet not keep you waiting. It was refreshing to have our waiter, without any discussion, hand the wine list to me, rather than to one of the men at the table. Make sure you give the menu due consideration; this is one place where the daily specials are not necessarily more superb, but certainly more expensive, than the restaurant's mainstays. Try the house-made spinach-ricotta agnolotti in mascarpone cream, the osso buco, or the grilled fish. Half-orders of pastas are allowed.

✪ **Brighton.** In the Canterbury Hotel, 1733 N St. NW. ☎ **202/296-0665.** Reservations recommended. Lunch $8–$12.50, dinner $14.50–$19.50. AE, CB, DC, DISC, MC, V. Mon–Fri 11:30am–2pm; Mon–Sat 6–10pm. Metro: Dupont Circle or Farragut North. AMERICAN.

Brighton lies below street level, and yet it is one of the brightest dining rooms you'll find. (If you want cozy, go upstairs to the Union Jack Pub.) Fabric colors are deep salmon and celery, the carpeting a grassy green, the walls lemon yellow. Little vases of fresh-cut yellow roses decorate each table. Locals tend to outnumber hotel guests.

The food is sublime. First comes a basket of biscuits, sweet bread, and crusty peasant bread. The appetizers and entrees that follow live up to their dramatically artistic presentation. For a starter, try the iron skillet–roasted mussels with shaved garlic and diced tomato in a Riesling Dijon broth. The macadamia nut–encrusted Chilean sea bass in a ginger, lime, and coconut sauce is an excellent entree. And for dessert, how about the banana, macadamia nut spring roll with ginger ice cream and chocolate sauce.

✪ **Gabriel.** In the Radisson Barceló Hotel, 2121 P St. NW. ☎ **202/956-6690.** Reservations recommended. Breakfast $7–$9.25, breakfast buffet $10; lunch $5.50–$12.25, $10.75 buffet; dinner $16.50–$22; tapas $3.75–$6.50; Sun brunch buffet $19.75, Wed–Fri happy-hour buffet $7.50. AE, DC, DISC, MC, V. Mon–Fri 6:30–11am, Sat 7–11am, Sun 7–10:30am; Mon–Fri 11:30am–2:30pm, Sun brunch 11am–3pm; Mon–Thurs 6–10pm, Fri–Sat 6–10:30pm, Sun 6–9:30pm; Happy hour Wed–Fri 5:30–8pm. Free valet parking. Metro: Dupont Circle. LATIN AMERICAN/MEDITERRANEAN.

Like Coco Loco (see above), Gabriel features Latin-accented fare and tapas; while the former is funky/hip, this is a more traditional setting. A large rectangular mahogany bar is the centerpiece of a convivial lounge area; outdoors is a small patio cafe with umbrella tables. Noted Washington chef Greggory Hill spent months studying with major chefs in various parts of Spain and Mexico before creating Gabriel's dazzlingly innovative and ever-changing menu.

Sample a variety of tapas at the bar or begin a meal with them—plump chorizo-stuffed black figs or gambas al ajillo (shrimp in garlic oil). Entrees might include lamb with mole and sweet potato plantain mash or pork tenderloin with black bean sauce on basmati rice. There's a well-chosen wine list, with several by-the-glass selections including dry and sweet sherries—the ideal complement to tapas. For dessert, sample the warm phyllo purse stuffed with papaya, pineapple, berries, and pistachio nuts, poised on cinnamon custard.

✪ **Obelisk.** 2029 P St. NW. ☎ **202/872-1180.** Reservations recommended. Prix-fixe 5-course dinner only: $45–$47. DC, MC, V. Tues–Sat 6–10pm. Metro: Dupont Circle. ITALIAN.

In this pleasantly spare room decorated with 19th-century French botanical prints and Italian lithographs, owner/chef Peter Pastan presents his small prix-fixe menus of simple, yet sophisticated Italian cuisine that uses the freshest possible ingredients. Pastan says his culinary philosophy is to "get the best stuff we can and try not to screw it up." Each night diners are offered two or three choices for each course. A recent dinner began with an antipasti of mushroom crostini, followed by a Tuscan bean soup, and an artfully arranged dish of pan-cooked cod with fried asparagus and green sauce. Rather than cheese, I enjoyed a dessert of pear spice cake. Breads and desserts are all baked in-house and are divine. Pastan's carefully crafted wine list represents varied regions of Italy, as well as California vintages. The $40-ish prix-fixe menu seems a deal, but the cost of wine and coffees can easily double the price per person.

✪ **Sostanza.** 1606 20th St. NW. ☎ **202/667-0047.** Reservations recommended. Main courses $15–$19. AE, CB, DC, MC, V. Mon–Sat 6–10pm. Metro: Dupont Circle. SEAFOOD/STEAKS/ITALIAN.

This is the sort of place you'd hope to stumble upon as a stranger in town. It's pretty, with a sophisticated but relaxed atmosphere, the food is excellent, and the service professional. And though the restaurant has changed its name repeatedly since it opened in 1980, (Vincenzo al Sole, Trattoria al Sole, and Vincenzo), it remains what it has always been, a reliable place to sample classic Italian cuisine. Conceived originally as an Italian steakhouse by owners Vince MacDonald and Roberto Donna, who now reigns over a small dynasty of his own restaurants (see Galileo, Barolo, Il Radicchio, Pesce), Sostanza's menu has expanded to offer classic Italian pastas, fish, chicken, and veal dishes. For steak, think alla siciliano: grilled with capers, olives, and sweet pickled peppers. The soft-shell crabs, in season in late spring, are a treat, lightly breaded and fried. Daily specials number about 18, half fish, half meat items. The antipasto selection is a holdover from the restaurant's early days, featuring roasted peppers with anchovies, stuffed zucchini, and the like.

Sostanza has a slate terrace at street level with umbrella tables, or go down a short flight of steps to reach the exquisite dining room; it resembles a trattoria with ochre and burnt sienna-toned walls, arched skylight, and tile floor. Across the long, narrow entry hall from the main dining room are the bar and more tables, where, if you're lucky, you can sit and shoot the breeze with owner Vince.

✪ **Tabard Inn.** 1739 N St. NW. ☎ **202/833-2668.** Reservations recommended. Breakfast $2.50–$7.50, lunch $9.50–$15, dinner $18–$28. AE, DC, MC, V. Mon–Fri 7–10am and 11:30am–2:30pm, Sat 8–10am and 11am–2:30pm, Sun 8–9:30am and 10:30am–2:30pm; Sun–Thurs 6–10pm, Fri–Sat 6–10:30pm. Metro: Dupont Circle. AMERICAN.

The restaurant here is only a shade more conventional than the inn in which it resides (see listing in chapter 5). From the cozy though tattered lounge, where you can enjoy a drink in front of a crackling fire, you enter a narrow room, where hanging plants dangle from skylights and a mural of a ponytailed waiter points the way to the kitchen. A small bar hugs one side of the passage, a series of small tables the other, and both lead to the main space. Or you can head up a set of stairs to another dining room and its adjoining courtyard. Restaurant staff, like inn staff, are disarmingly solicitous.

The food is fresh and seasonal, making use of the inn's own homegrown vegetables and herbs. Pastas, like the rigatoni with Bolognese meat sauce, are a sure thing, and so are desserts, like the house-made ice creams. Seafood dishes, supposedly the focus here, are not yet quite up to snuff.

MODERATE

BeDuCi. 2100 P St. NW. ☎ **202/223-3824.** Reservations recommended. Lunch $9.50–$20 (weekday lunch special $12.95), dinner $11.50–$22.95. AE, DC, DISC, MC, V. Mon–Thurs 11:30am–2:30pm and 5:30–10pm, Fri 11:30am–2:30pm and 5:30–10:30pm, Sat 5:30–10:30pm, Sun 5–9pm. Free valet parking at dinner. Metro: Foggy Bottom. MEDITERRANEAN.

Mediterranean cuisine continues to be trendy in Washington, and BeDuCi (Below Dupont Circle) has been serving it since opening seven years ago. Entrees range from pastas and couscous to paellas and vegetarian stews. Your best bets are the specials, whether you choose an appetizer (maybe cream of cauliflower soup with rock shrimp), or an entree (say, the duck breast with lemon zest, wrapped in bacon and figs). Desserts, like the pineapple cobbler, are wonderfully rich and made by Michele Miller, co-owner with Jean-Claude Garrat. A sun porch fronting the restaurant, turns into a covered outdoor cafe in warm weather. The three inside dining rooms are decorated simply with paintings and prints on white walls.

✪ **Pesce.** 2016 P St. NW. ☎ **202/466-3474.** Reservations accepted for lunch, 6 or more at dinner. Main courses $12.50–$18. AE, DC, DISC, MC, V. Mon–Fri 11:30am–2:30pm, Sat noon–2:30pm; Mon–Thurs 5:30–10pm, Thurs–Sat 5:30–10:30pm, Sun 5–9:30pm. Valet parking at dinner Thurs–Sat. Metro: Dupont Circle. SEAFOOD.

Nightly, from about 8:30 until 9:30, a line of people forms inside the cramped waiting area of this restaurant, sometimes trailing out the door, just to enjoy the marvelous grilled or sautéed fresh fish. This small, crowded restaurant has a convivial atmosphere, brought on, no doubt, by the collective anticipation of a pleasant meal. In a simple setting of exposed brick walls adorned with colorfully painted wooden fish, waiters scurry to bring you a basket of crusty bread, your wine selection, and the huge black-board menu. Among the many appetizers are bluepoint oysters on the half shell and several tasty salads. Entrees always list several pastas along with the differently prepared fish. The grilled monkfish was firm but tender, and delicious upon its bed of potato purée and wild mushroom ragoût. Owned by chefs Roberto Donna and Jean-Louis Palladin, Pesce bears their mark of excellence, even though neither actually works in the kitchen. Tip: Try ordering your wine by the glass; depending on which wine you choose, it may cost less for four people than by the bottle.

INEXPENSIVE

City Lights of China. 1731 Connecticut Ave. NW (between R and S sts.). ☎ **202/265-6688.** Reservations recommended. Lunch $4.50–$13, dinner $6.95–$11.95 (though some go as high as $26). AE, DC, DISC, MC, V. Mon–Thurs 11am–10:30pm, Fri 11:30am–11pm, Sat noon–11pm, Sun noon–10:30pm; dinner from 3pm daily. Validated parking after 5pm. Metro: Dupont Circle. CHINESE.

One of Washington's best Chinese restaurants outside of Chinatown, City Lights keeps getting bigger to accommodate its fans, who range from Mick Jagger to Jesse Jackson to Attorney General Janet Reno. White House workaholics frequently order takeout from here. Favorite dishes prepared by Taiwanese chef (and part owner) Kuo-Tai Soug include crisp-fried Cornish hen prepared in a cinnamon-soy marinade and served with a tasty dipping sauce, Chinese eggplant in garlic sauce, stir-fried spinach, crisp fried shredded beef, and Peking duck. The setting is pretty but unpretentious—a three-tiered dining room with much of the seating in comfortable pale-green leather booths and banquettes. Neat white-linened tables, cloth flower arrangements in lighted niches, and green neon track lighting complete the picture. There's a full bar.

✪ **Il Radicchio.** 1509 17th St. NW. ☎ **202/986-2627.** Reservations not accepted. Main courses $5.50–$15. AE, CB, DC, MC, V. Mon–Thurs 11:30am–10pm, Fri–Sat 11:30am–11pm; Sun 5–10:30pm. Metro: Dupont Circle, with a 10- to 15-minute walk. ITALIAN.

What a great idea: Order a replenishable bowl of spaghetti for the table at a set price of $6.50, and each of you chooses your own sauce from a long list, at prices that range from $1.50 to $4. Most are standards, like the carbonara of cream, pancetta, black pepper, and egg yolk, and the puttanesca with black olives, capers, garlic, anchovies, and tomato. It's a great deal.

The kitchen prepares daily specials, like Saturday's oven-baked veal stew with polenta, as well as sandwiches, and an assortment of 14 wood-baked pizzas, with a choice of 28 toppings. I'd stick with the pizza, pasta, and salad.

Ingredients are fresh and flavorful, the service quick and solicitous. This branch of the restaurant draws a neighborhood crowd to its long, warm, and cozy room deco-rated with wall murals of barnyard animals and radicchio leaves. The Georgetown Il Radicchio (1211 Wisconsin Ave. NW; ☎ 202/337-2627) tends to attract college students and families. Il Radicchio on Capitol Hill (223 Pennsylvania Ave. SE; ☎ 202/547-5114) caters to the overworked, underpaid Hill staffers who appreciate Il Radic-chio's food and the price.

✪ **Pizzeria Paradiso.** 2029 P St. NW. ☎ **202/223-1245.** Reservations not accepted. Pizzas $6.75–$15.95; sandwiches and salads $3.25–$6.25. DC, MC, V. Mon–Thurs 11:30am–11pm, Fri 11:30am–midnight, Sat 11am–midnight, Sun noon–10pm. Metro: Dupont Circle. PIZZA/PANINI.

Peter Pastan, master chef/owner of Obelisk, right next door, owns this classy, often crowded, 16-table pizzeria. An oak-burning oven at one end of the charming room produces exceptionally doughy but light pizza crusts. As you wait, you can munch on mixed olives and gaze up at the ceiling painted to suggest blue sky peeking through ancient stone walls. Pizzas range from the plain Paradiso, which offers chunks of toma-toes covered in melted mozzarella, to the robust Siciliano, a blend of nine ingredients including eggplant and red onion. Or you can choose your own toppings from a list of 29. As popular as pizza are the panini (sandwiches) of homemade focaccia stuffed with marinated roasted lamb and vegetables and other fillings, and the salads, such as tuna and white bean. Good desserts, but a limited wine list.

Raku. 1900 Q St. NW. ☎ **202/265-7258.** No reservations taken. All menu items $8.95–$13.50. AE, MC, V. Mon–Thurs and Sun 11:30am–10pm, Fri–Sat 11:30am–11am. Metro: Dupont Circle. ASIAN.

Raku's glass-fronted restaurant occupies a prominent people-watching corner near Dupont Circle. Spring through fall, the scene gets even better, when Raku's windowed walls open onto its sidewalk cafe. Inside, you find artfully tied bamboo poles and Japanese temple beams, shoji screens, and TV monitors airing campy videos (anything from Godzilla to instructions for using chopsticks), as background music plays Asian pop. A curvilinear bar overlooks the kitchen, where chefs prepare the street food of China, Japan, Korea, and Thailand. Try the skewers, like the soy-sesame–glazed chicken or the "squid sticks" (squid caramelized with a sweet ginger-soy glaze), and dumplings, especially "pork juicy buns" (stuffed with roast pork, cabbage, soy, and ginger, served with black bean sauce). But the noodle dishes are unreliable, bland one day and spicy the next, although the kowloon (roasted pork, shrimp, ham, and Peking duck dumplings in chicken broth full of bok choy, mustard greens, pea shoots, and thick noodles) may be worth taking a chance on. The Hunan chicken salad is wildly popular. Staff deliver each dish to your table as it is prepared, whether you're ready or not.

Sala Thai. 2016 P St. NW. ☎ **202/872-1144.** Reservations accepted for 5 or more. Lunch $6.25–$9, dinner $7.25–$13. AE, DC, MC, V. Mon–Fri 11:30am–3pm; Mon 5–10:30pm, Tues 5–11pm, Wed–Fri 5–11:30pm, Sat noon–11:30pm, Sun noon–10:30pm. Metro: Dupont Circle. THAI.

Sharing the same address as Pesce, Sala Thai lies downstairs. Decor is casual, like most Thai restaurants. With no windows to watch what's happening on P Street you're really here for the food, which is excellent and cheap. Even conventional pad thai doesn't dis-appoint. If you ask for something spicy, you'll get something really really spicy. (The waiter may try to caution you.)

Teaism. 2009 R St. NW (between Connecticut and 21st sts.). ☎ **202/667-3827.** All menu items 75¢–$7.75. AE, MC, V. Mon–Thurs 8am–10pm, Fri 8am–11pm, Sat 9am–11pm, Sun 9am–10pm. Metro: Dupont Circle. ASIAN TEAHOUSE.

Occupying a turn-of-the-century neoclassic building on a tree-lined street, Teaism has a lovely rustic interior such as you might find in the Chinese countryside. A display kitchen and tandoor oven dominate the sunny downstairs room, which offers counter seating along a wall of French windows, open in warm weather. Upstairs seating is on banquettes and small Asian stools at hand-crafted mahogany tables.

The impressive tea list comprises close to 50 aromatic blends, most of them from India, China, and Japan. Many have exotic names: golden water turtle, jasmine pearl. On the menu is light Asian fare served in lacquer lunch boxes (Japanese "bento boxes") or on stainless-steel plates. Dishes include salmon cured in lapsang souchong (a smoky Chinese tea) with chopped bok choy, tandoor-baked lamb kebabs, and stir-fried chicken with coconut. Baked goods, coconut ice cream, and lime shortbread cookies are among desserts. At breakfast you might try cilantro eggs and sausage with fresh tandoor-baked onion nan (chewy Indian bread). Everything's available for carryout. Tea pots, cups, and other gift items are for sale.

Trio. 1537 17th St. NW (at Q St.). ☎ **202/232-6305.** Main courses $5.75–$9.50, burgers and sandwiches $1.75–$5.75; full breakfasts $2.75–$5.95. AE, DISC, MC, V. Daily 7:30am–midnight. Metro: Dupont Circle (Q St. exit). AMERICAN.

This art-deco coffee shop's roomy red leather booths are filled each morning with local residents checking out the *Washington Post* over big platters of bacon and eggs. In warm weather, the awning-covered outdoor cafe is always packed. The four-decades-old Trio is run by George Mallios, son of the original owners, and is something of a Washington legend.

The food is fresh, and you can't beat the prices. The same menu is offered throughout the day, with low-priced specials, such as grilled pork chops with applesauce—all served with two side dishes (perhaps roasted new potatoes and buttered fresh carrots). The wine list has 36 offerings, all but the champagne available by the glass. The à la carte menu is extensive. A full bar offers everything from microbrews to Fuzzy Navels, and a soda fountain turns out hot-fudge sundaes and milkshakes.

8 Foggy Bottom/West End

VERY EXPENSIVE

✪ **Melrose.** In the Park Hyatt Hotel, 1201 24th St. NW (at M St.). ☎ **202/955-3899.** Reservations recommended. Breakfast $9–$18.50, lunch $15–$24, dinner $20–$28; pretheater $26.95; Sun brunch $36 ($39 with champagne). AE, CB, DC, DISC, JCB, MC, V. Mon–Sat 6:30–11am, Sun 6:30–10:30am; daily 11am–2:30pm and 5:30–10:30pm. Free valet parking all day. Metro: Foggy Bottom. AMERICAN.

Situated in an upscale hotel, this pretty restaurant offers fine cuisine presented with friendly flourishes. In nice weather, dine outdoors on the beautifully landscaped, sunken terrace whose greenery and towering fountain protect you from traffic noises. The glass-walled dining room overlooks the terrace and is decorated in accents of marble and brass, with more greenery and grand bouquets of fresh flowers.

Brian McBride is the beguiling executive chef who sometimes emerges from the kitchen to find out how you like the angel hair pasta with mascarpone and lobster, or his sautéed Dover sole with roasted peppers, forest mushrooms, and mache. McBride, like Bob Kinkead (see below), is known for his seafood, which makes up most of the entrees and nearly all of the appetizers. Specialities of the house include shrimp ravioli with sweet corn, black pepper, tomato, and lemongrass beurre blanc, and Melrose crab cakes with grilled vegetables in a remoulade sauce. Desserts, like the raspberry crème brûlée or the chocolate bread pudding with chocolate sorbet, are excellent. The wine list offers 30 wines by the glass. Friday nights, the restaurant dispenses with corkage fees; feel free to bring your own bottle. Saturday nights from 7 to 11pm, a quartet plays jazz, swing, and big band tunes; lots of people get up and dance.

Roof Terrace Restaurant/Hors d'Oeuvrerie. In the Kennedy Center, New Hampshire Ave. NW (at Rock Creek Pkwy.). ☎ **202/416-8555.** Reservations recommended for the Roof Terrace Restaurant, but not accepted for the Hors d'Oeuvrerie. Roof Terrace: Lunch $14–$26, dinner $25–$29, Sun prix-fixe buffet brunch $26.95 ($12.95 for children under 10). Hors d'Oeuvrerie, items mostly $9–$14. AE, CB, DC, MC, V. Roof Terrace, 11:30am–2pm matinee days and Sun; nightly 5:30–8pm. Hors d'Oeuvrerie, Sun and Tues–Wed 5pm–8pm; Thurs–Sat 5pm until half an hour after the last show ends. *Note:* The Roof Terrace is occasionally closed when there are few shows; call before you go. Metro: Foggy Bottom. AMERICAN REGIONAL.

Not only is a meal at the Roof Terrace convenient for theatergoers, it's also a gourmet experience in a glamorous dining room, where ornate crystal candelabra chandeliers hang from a lofty ceiling and immense windows provide panoramic views of the Potomac.

Executive chef Dan Storino changes the menu with the seasons, usually keeping the list to six or seven appetizers and seven to nine entrees, including one special. You might see a grilled salmon on celery root purée with port wine sauce or a grilled filet mignon with roasted garlic mashed potatoes and bordelaise sauce. In season (spring and summer), the Maryland crab cake is a constant among the appetizers. For dessert, look for the chocolate-pecan tart or flourless chocolate cake with vanilla ice cream. Many premium wines are offered by the glass. Every Sunday, the restaurant puts on its brunch buffet, a lavish spread that includes custom-made omelets, pastas, smoked meats and fish, fancy French toast, and tons of desserts; the $26.95 price entitles you to the buffet and either a glass of champagne, a mimosa, or a glass of fresh squeezed O.J.

After-theater munchies and cocktails are served in the adjoining and equally plush Hors d'Oeuvrerie. Stop here before or after a show for a glass of wine or champagne and a light supper—perhaps grilled shrimp, saffron risotto, oven-baked Maryland crab cakes, or the filet mignonette sandwich. It's gourmet snack fare. Desserts and coffee are also available.

EXPENSIVE

Asia Nora. 2213 M St. NW. ☎ **202/797-4860.** Reservations recommended. Main courses $18–$25. DISC, MC, V. Mon–Thurs 5:45–10pm, Fri–Sat 5:45–10:30pm. Valet parking $5. Metro: Dupont Circle or Foggy Bottom. ASIAN FUSION.

Everything's set at a slant here: the tables, the bar, the banquette at the back on the first floor, and the triangular cutaway balcony on the second. Museum-quality artifacts from Asia—batik carvings, Japanese helmets, and Chinese puppets—decorate the gold-flecked jade walls. It's intimate and exotic, a charged combination. Try sitting at the bar first, on the most comfortable bar stools in town. If you like good bourbons and single malt scotches, you're in luck.

Waitstaff dressed in black-satin pajamas serve Asian fusion cuisine, all prepared with organic ingredients, including a salad of smoked trout with field greens and Fuji apples, a "small dish" of crispy spinach and shitake spring rolls, and a main dish of banana leaf grilled sea bass. It actually sounds more far-out than it tastes.

✪ **Kinkead's.** 2000 Pennsylvania Ave. NW. ☎ **202/296-7700.** Reservations recommended. Lunch $10–$18, dinner $18–$26, Sun brunch $7.50–$13, light fare daily 2:20–5:30pm $4–$18. AE, DC, DISC, MC, V. Daily 11:30am–11pm. Free valet parking after 5:30pm. Metro: Foggy Bottom. AMERICAN/SEAFOOD.

When a restaurant has been as roundly praised as Kinkead's, you start to think no place can be that good—but Kinkead's is. An appetizer like grilled squid with creamy polenta and tomato fondue, leaves you with a permanent longing for squid. The signature dish, a pepita-crusted salmon with shrimp, crab, and chilies provides a nice hot crunch before melting in your mouth. Vegetables you may normally disdain—cabbage, for instance—taste delicious here.

The award-winning chef/owner Bob Kinkead is the star at this three-tier, 220-seat restaurant. He wears a headset and orchestrates his kitchen staff in full view of the upstairs dining room, where booths and tables neatly fill the nooks and alcoves of the townhouse. At street level is a scattering of tables overlooking the restaurant's lower level, the more casual bar and cafe, where a jazz group or pianist performs in the evening and at Sunday brunch. Beware: If the waiter tries to seat you in the "atrium," you should know that you'll be stuck at a table mall-side just outside the doors of the restaurant—yuk.

Kinkead's menu (which changes daily for lunch and again for dinner) features primarily seafood, but also includes at least one meat and one poultry entree. The wine list comprises more than 300 selections. You can't go wrong with the desserts either, like the chocolate dacquoise with cappucino sauce. If you're hungry but not ravenous in late afternoon, stop in for some delicious light fare: fish and chips, lobster roll, soups, and salads.

✪ **Osteria Goldoni.** 1120 20th St. NW. ☎ **202/293-1511.** Reservations recommended. Lunch $10–$19, dinner $16–$27. AE, CB, DC, DISC, MC, V. Mon–Fri 11:30am–2:30pm; Mon–Thurs 5:30–10pm, Fri–Sat 5–11pm; Sun 5–9:30pm. Free valet parking nightly, except Sunday, when street parking is easy. Metro: Farragut North or Farragut West. ITALIAN.

Osteria Goldoni occupies two floors: the downstairs more casual with a blue-tiled floor, long marble bar, and murals of circus performers; the upstairs main dining room red-carpeted and elegant. As dramatic as the decor is the food, which sometimes goes overboard in elaborateness—gnocchi drenched in sweet and sour veal sauce with pears? In general, lunch meals are simpler.

Still, most dishes are delicious, and service is executed with a flourish. Try the risotto with grapefruit, basil, and baby shrimp cradled in a grapefruit half; chef/owner Fabrizio Aielli's signature dish, grilled whole fish (we had rockfish, but snapper, sea bass, and others may be available), served on a huge platter with polenta and shitake mushrooms; or an excellent salad with radicchio, goat cheese, and ground walnuts. Sorbets are a specialty, as is the beautiful tiramisu (at a whopping $10!). Bring a party of people; Osteria Goldoni is a good spot for a celebration.

Marcel's. 2401 Pennsylvania Ave. NW. ☎ **202/296-1166.** Reservations recommended. Lunch $13–$21, dinner $19.50–$28. AE, MC, V. Mon–Fri 11:30am–2:30pm; Mon–Thurs 5:30–10:30pm, Fri–Sat 5:30–11pm. Free valet parking evenings. Metro: Foggy Bottom. FRENCH.

When you walk through the front door, look straight ahead into the exhibition kitchen and, chances are, you'll be staring directly into the eyes of owner/chef Robert Wiedmaier, formerly of Aquarelle, in what is now called the Swissotel Washington—Watergate Hotel. Wiedmaier is firmly at the helm here, creating French dishes that include nods to his Belgian training: pan-seared skate fish with hotchpot purée (a mix of winter vegetables); duck breast with roulade of duck confit; and for dessert, seasonal tarts such as spring pear tart with raspberry coulis. The French sommelier is expert.

Marcel's, named after Wiedmaier's young son, occupies the space that most recently was home to the restaurant Provence. When Wiedmaier took it over in spring 1999, he kept that restaurant's winning country French decor: panels of rough-hewn stone framed by rustic shutters, antique hutches displaying provincial pottery, and so on. To the right of the exhibition kitchen is a spacious bar area.

INEXPENSIVE

Zuki Moon Noodles. 824 New Hampshire Ave. NW. ☎ **202/333-3312.** Entrees $9–$17. AE, DC, MC, V. Mon–Fri 11:30am–2:30pm, Mon–Sat 5–11pm, Sun 5–10pm. Valet Parking. Metro: Foggy Bottom. JAPANESE.

Chef and co-owner Mary Richter, who gained a strong following from her days at Cities, has only acquired more fans since opening Zuki Moon in the George Washington University Inn. Her menu features Japanese soups filled with soba, udon, or somen noodles and grilled or roasted meats or seafood; delicately done shrimp tempura; grilled squid; spring rolls; and rich sorbets and ice cream for dessert. Soups, sake, and tea come in beautiful handmade pottery. The restaurant is steps away from the George Washington University, but students tend to go elsewhere (Burrito Brothers, for example). People from the neighborhood, hotel guests, office workers and theater-goers (the Kennedy Center is close by) are the ones who dine here.

9 Georgetown

VERY EXPENSIVE

✪ **Michel Richard's Citronelle.** In the Latham Hotel, 3000 M St. NW. ☎ **202/625-2150.** Reservations recommended. Breakfast $3.75–$14 (buffet $12.50), lunch $8–$16, dinner $24–$32. AE, DC, MC, V. Daily 6:30–10:30am, Mon–Fri noon–2pm, Sun–Thurs 5:30–10pm, Fri–Sat 5:30–10:30pm. Jacket and tie preferred at dinner. Free valet parking at dinner. CONTEMPORARY FRENCH.

In March 1998, Citronelle reopened after a $2 million renovation, with much fanfare provided by the enthusiastic Washington foodies establishment and Citronelle's ebullient chef/owner Michel Richard. Although Richard originally returned to his flagship restaurant, the famed Citrus, in Los Angeles, after opening Citronelle in 1992, the Frenchman has now moved to Washington, happy to please the palates of Washingtonians, whose tastes he believes to be more sophisticated than Los Angelenos.

In terms of decor, the Citronelle transformation includes a wall that changes colors, a state-of-the-art wine cellar (a glass-enclosed room that encircles the dining room, displaying its 8,000 bottles and a collection of 18th and 19th century corkscrews), and a Provençale color scheme of mellow yellow and a raspberry red.

Emerging from the bustling kitchen are appetizers like the fricassée of escargots, sweetbreads, porcinis, and crunchy pistachios, and entrees like the crispy lentil-coated salmon. The dessert of choice: Michel Richard's rich, layered chocolate "bar" with sauce noisette. Citronelle's extensive wine list offers many premium by-the-glass selections, but with all those bottles staring out at you from the wine cellar, you may want to spring for a full bottle.

Morton's of Chicago. 3251 Prospect St. NW. ☎ **202/342-6258.** Reservations recommended. Main courses $19.95–$30. AE, DC, MC, V. Mon–Sat 5:30–11pm, Sun 5–10pm. Free valet parking. STEAKS/CHOPS/SEAFOOD.

Arnie Morton, a flamboyant former Playboy Enterprises executive, created this empire of Morton's steakhouses, of which Washington now has three (the newest is at the corner of Connecticut Avenue and L Street NW (☎ **202/955-5997**), which is open for lunch weekdays and dinner every night). You'll see politicos, media types, and regular folks sitting upon comfortable cream-colored leather booths at white-linened tables lit by pewter oil lamps in the shape of donkeys or elephants. (Morton's was one of the many restaurants frequented by Monica Lewinsky and her erstwhile lawyer William Ginsburg, before she threw him out during special prosecutor Ken Starr's investigation.)

Morton's is known for its huge—some say grotesquely large—portions of succulent USDA prime midwestern beef and scrumptious side dishes. Start off with an appetizer such as smoked Pacific salmon or a lump-crabmeat cocktail served with mustard-mayonnaise sauce. Steaks (ribeye, double filet mignon, porterhouse, or New York sirloin) are perfectly prepared to your specifications. Other entree choices include veal or lamb chops, fresh swordfish steak in sauce béarnaise, and baked Maine lobster. Side orders of flavorfully fresh al dente asparagus served with hollandaise or hash browns are highly recommended. Consider taking home a doggie bag if you want to leave room for dessert—perhaps a soufflé Grand Marnier or fresh raspberries in sabayon sauce.

Seasons. In the Four Seasons Hotel, 2800 Pennsylvania Ave. NW. ☎ **202/944-2000.** Reservations recommended. Breakfast $4.75–$17.25, lunch $13.75–$23, dinner $21–$34. AE, DC, DISC, JCB, MC, V. Mon–Fri 7–11am and noon–2:30pm, Sat–Sun 8am–noon, nightly 6–10:30pm. Free valet parking. Metro: Foggy Bottom. AMERICAN.

Although Seasons is the signature restaurant of one of Washington's most upscale hotels, and a major celebrity haunt, it takes a casual approach to formal dining: relaxed atmosphere, no dress code, friendly service. Seasons is candlelit at night, sunlit during the day, with windows overlooking the C&O Canal.

Scottish chef William Douglas McNeill's cuisine focuses on fresh market fare. Stellar entrees range from seared tuna with shitake mushroom-mashed potatoes and peppercorn sauce, to mustard seed–encrusted roast rack of lamb served with Provençale veggies. A basket of scrumptious fresh-baked breads might include rosemary flat bread or sun-dried tomato bread drizzled with Parmesan. For dessert, consider a caramelized ginger crème brûlée. For the 11th consecutive year, Wine Spectator magazine has named Seasons's vast and carefully researched wine cellar one of the 100 best worldwide.

1789. 1226 36th St. NW (at Prospect St.). ☎ **202/965-1789.** Reservations recommended. Main courses $18–$32; prix-fixe pretheater menu $25. AE, DC, DISC, MC, V. Sun–Thurs 5–10pm, Fri–Sat 5–11pm. Jackets required. Free valet parking. AMERICAN REGIONAL.

The restaurant 1789 is cozy but formal. Housed in a Federal townhouse, its intimate dining areas are typified by the John Carroll Room, where the walls are hung with Currier and Ives prints and old city maps, a log fire blazes in the hearth, and a gorgeous flower arrangement is displayed atop a hunting-themed oak sideboard. Throughout, silk-shaded brass oil lamps provide romantic lighting. You might spot anyone from cabinet members and senators to Sharon Stone at the next table.

Noted chef Ris Lacoste varies her menus seasonally. Appetizers might include macadamia-crusted grilled shrimp. Typical entrees range from osso buco with risotto Milanese to roast rack of lamb with creamy feta potatoes au gratin in a red pepper purée–infused merlot sauce. A memorable dessert was the delicate tuile (crisp, rounded cookie) filled with chocolate, orange, and pistachio mascarpone on a bitter orange sauce. The wine list is long and distinguished. A great bargain here: The pretheater menu offered nightly through 6:45pm includes appetizer, entree, dessert, and coffee for just $25!

EXPENSIVE

✪ **Mendocino Grille and Wine Bar.** 2917 M St. NW. ☎ **202/333-2912.** Reservations recommended. Lunch $6.75–$18.75, dinner $15.75–$24.75. AE, DC, DISC, MC, V. Mon–Sat 11:30am–3pm; Sun–Thurs 5:30–10pm, Fri–Sat 5:30–11pm. Valet parking after 6:30pm. Metro: Foggy Bottom. AMERICAN/CALIFORNIAN.

Rough-textured slate walls alternate with painted patches of Big Sur sky to suggest a West Coast winery in California's wine-growing region. The wall sconces resemble rectangles of sea glass and the dangling light fixtures look like turned over wineglasses. The California-casual works, and so does the food.

Grilled seafood is the highlight: yellowfin tuna presented on wilted spinach and roasted pepper purée, Chilean sea bass on a warm salad of french beans. Non-seafood choices include free-range chicken served on roasted red bliss potatoes and sugar snap peas, and grilled tenderloin of beef. Ever in search of the perfect crab cake, I found a close call here in the form of the jumbo lump crabmeat and smoked-salmon cake appetizer.

All 150 wines on the list are highly rated West Coast selections. Waitstaff are knowledgeable about the wines, so don't hesitate to ask questions. California casual doesn't mean cheap: Prices range from $20 to $400, although most hover around $50 a bottle.

The Sea Catch. 1054 31st St. NW (just below M St.). ☎ **202/337-8855.** Reservations recommended. Lunch $10–$16, dinner $15–$25. AE, CB, DC, DISC, JCB, MC, V. Mon–Sat noon–3pm and 5:30–10:30pm. Free valet parking. SEAFOOD.

Before the recent onslaught of seafood restaurants in Washington, there was The Sea Catch. Since 1988 it has sat on the bank of the C&O Canal, with an awning-covered wooden deck from which you can watch ducks, punters, and mule-drawn barges glide by while you dine. Inside, the innlike main dining room has a working fireplace and rough-hewn walls made of fieldstone dug from Georgetown quarries. There's also a handsome white Carrara-marble raw bar and a deluxe brasserie. Classic jazz tapes play in the background.

For openers, plump farm-raised oysters, clams, house-smoked fish, and other raw-bar offerings merit consideration. Daily fresh fish and seafood specials may include big, fluffy jumbo lump crab cakes served with crunchy Oriental-style napa cabbage slaw or grilled marinated squid with fennel and basil aioli. The kitchen willingly pre-pares dishes to your specifications, including live lobster from the tanks. An extensive wine list highlights French, Italian, and American selections. Fresh-baked desserts usu-ally include an excellent Key lime pie.

Tahoga. 2815 M St. NW. ☎ **202/338-5380.** Reservations suggested. Lunch $7.50–$11, dinner $18–$22. AE, DC, MC, V. Mon–Fri 11:30am–2pm, Sun–Thurs 5:30–10pm, Fri–Sat 5:30–11pm. Valet parking at dinner. Metro: Foggy Bottom, with a 15-minute walk. AMER-ICAN.

Even if the food and the sparkling atmosphere didn't recommend Tahoga, two other unique features would: its hidden, brick-walled garden patio reached through French doors, and its lunchtime offering of every wine, by the bottle or glass, at half price. The modern American dishes are heavy on seafood in summer, with more meat dishes added in winter. Consider: pan-seared crayfish cakes; steamed clams with cilantro, line and chorizo; roasted halibut with morels and white green asparagus; stripped beef with crayfish mashed potatoes; and a simply prepared herb-roasted chicken. The curving bar beyond the main dining room is a comfortable spot for even a woman alone to have a drink.

MODERATE

Aditi. 3299 M St. NW. ☎ **202/625-6825.** Reservations recommended. Lunch $4.25–$9.95, dinner $5.95–$14.99. AE, DC, DISC, MC, V. Daily 11:30am–2:30pm and 5:30–10 or 10:30pm. INDIAN.

This charming, two-level restaurant provides a serene setting in which to enjoy first-rate Indian cooking to the tune of Indian music. A must here is the platter of assorted appetizers—bhajia (a deep-fried vegetable fritter), deep-fried cheese-and-shrimp pakoras, and crispy vegetable samosas stuffed with spiced potatoes and peas. Favorite entrees include lamb biryani, which is a basmati rice pilaf tossed with savory pieces of lamb, cilantro, raisins, and almonds; and the skewered jumbo tandoori prawns, chicken, lamb, or beef—all fresh and fork tender—barbecued in the tandoor (clay oven). Sauces are on the mild side, so if you like your food fiery, inform your waiter. A kachumber salad, topped with yogurt and spices, is a refreshing accompaniment to entrees. For dessert, try kheer, a cooling rice pudding garnished with chopped nuts. There's a full bar.

✪ Bistrot Lepic. 1736 Wisconsin Ave. NW. ☎ **202/333-0111.** Reservations suggested. Lunch $9–$12.25, dinner $14–$18. AE, CB, DC, DISC, MC, V. Tues–Sun 11:30am–2:30pm; Tues–Thurs 5:30–10pm, Fri–Sat 5:30–10:30pm, Sun 5:30–9:30pm. FRENCH.

Tiny Bistrot Lepic is the real thing, a charming French restaurant like you might find on a Parisian side street. The atmosphere is bustling and cheery, and you hear a lot of French spoken—not just by the waitstaff and the young proprietress, Cecile Fortin (her husband Bruno is chef), but by customers. The Bistrot is a neighborhood place, and you'll often see diners waving hellos across the room to each other, or even leaving their table to visit with those at another.

This is traditional French cooking, updated. The seasonal menu offers such entrees as grilled rockfish served with green lentils du Puy and aged balsamic sauce, and roasted rack of lamb with Yukon gold mashed potatoes and garlic juice. We opted for specials: rare tuna served on fennel with a citrusy vinaigrette, and grouper with a mildly spicy lobster sauce upon a bed of spinach.

The modest French wine list offers a fairly good range, but the house wine, Le Pic Saint Loup, is a nice complement to most menu choices and priced at less than $20 a bottle.

Clyde's of Georgetown. 3236 M St. NW. ☎ **202/333-9180.** Reservations recommended. Lunch/brunch mostly $6.50–$14 at lunch/brunch, dinner $6.50–$19 (most under $12); burgers and sandwiches under $7 all day. AE, DC, DISC, MC, V. Sun–Thurs 11:30am–midnight, Fri 11:30am–1am, Sat 10am–1am, Sun 9am–1am; brunch Sat 10am–4pm, Sun 9am–4pm. AMERICAN.

Clyde's has been a favorite watering hole for an eclectic mix of Washingtonians since 1963. You'll see university students, Capitol Hill types, affluent professionals, Washington Redskins, romantic duos, and well-heeled "ladies who lunch." A 1996 renovation transformed Clyde's from a saloon to a theme park, whose dining areas include a cherry-paneled front room with oil paintings of sport scenes, and an atrium with vintage model planes dangling from the glass ceiling and a 16th-century French limestone chimneypiece in the large fireplace.

Clyde's is known for its burgers, chili, and crab-cake sandwich. Appetizers are a safe bet, and the Clyde's take on the classic Niçoise is also recommended: chilled grilled salmon with greens, oven-roasted Roma tomatoes, green beans, and grilled new potatoes in a tasty vinaigrette. Sunday brunch is a tradition (brunch is also served on Saturday). The menu is reassuringly familiar—steak and eggs, omelettes, waffles—with variations thrown in for good measure. Among bar selections are at least ten draft beers and seven microbrews. *Note:* If you drive, park in the underground Georgetown Park garage; after your meal, stop at the concierge desk in the mall and show your meal receipt to receive parking ticket validation allowing you to pay $1 for two hours, a deal in Georgetown.

Miss Saigon. 3057 M St. NW. ☎ **202/333-5545.** Reservations recommended, especially weekend nights. Lunch $5.50–$7.95, dinner $6.95–$22.95. AE, DC, MC, V. Mon–Fri 11:30am–11pm (lunch menu served until 3pm), Sat–Sun noon–11pm (dinner menu served all day). VIETNAMESE.

This is a charming restaurant, with tables scattered amid a "forest" of tropical foliage, and twinkly lights strewn upon the fronds of the potted palms and ferns.

The food here is delicious and authentic, though the service can be a trifle slow when the restaurant is busy. To begin, there is the crispy calamari, a favorite of Madeline Albright. House specialties include steamed flounder, caramel salmon, and "shaking beef" (Vietnamese steak): cubes of tender beef, marinated in wine, garlic, butter, and soy sauce, then sautéed with onions and potatoes and served with rice and salad. There's a full bar. Desserts range from bananas flambé au rhum to ice cream with Godiva liqueur. Not to be missed is drip pot coffee, brewed tableside and served iced over sweetened condensed milk.

Sequoia. 3000 K St. NW (at Washington Harbour). ☎ **202/944-4200.** Reservations recommended (not accepted for outdoor seating). Main courses $6.95–$28.95; salads and sandwiches $6.95–$12.95. AE, DISC, MC, V. Mon–Thurs 11am–midnight, Fri 11am–1am, Sat–Sun 11am–3:30pm and 5:30pm–1am. Paid parking at the Harbour discounted after 5pm weekdays and on weekends. AMERICAN REGIONAL.

In the Washington-restaurant-with-a-view category, no setting is more spectacular than Sequoia's terrace, where umbrella-shaded tables overlook the boat-filled Potomac between two bridges. If outside tables are taken, you can enjoy the same river vista from the window-walled interior. The restaurant is huge and often the setting for large parties, so don't look for intimacy. It's especially popular as a place to come for drinks after work.

The varied and extensive menu runs the gamut from burgers, sandwiches, pastas, and pizzas to mint-marinated lamb chops with garlic smashed potatoes and napa cabbage. Save room for one of Sequoia's excellent desserts, perhaps toasted pecan/whiskey pie. Many wines are offered by the glass, and regional beers and ales are featured.

INEXPENSIVE

Ching Ching Cha. 1063 Wisconsin Ave. NW. ☎ **202/333-8288.** Reservations recommended. Tea meal $10, appetizers $1.50–$4.50. AE, CB, DC, DISC, MC, V. Daily 11:30am–10pm. CHINESE.

Located just below M Street, this skylit Chinese tearoom offers a pleasant respite from the crowds. You can sit on pillows at low tables or on chairs set at rosewood tables. Choices are simple: individual items like a tea-and-spice boiled egg, puff pastry stuffed with lotus seed paste, or five-spice peanuts; or the tea meal, which consists of miso soup, three marinated cold vegetables, rice, a salad, and tastings of either soy-ginger chicken, salmon with mustard-miso sauce, or steamed teriyaki-sauced tofu. Tea choices include several different green, black, medicinal, and oolong teas, plus a Fujian white tea and a ginseng brew.

Music City Roadhouse. 1050 30th St. NW. ☎ **202/337-4444.** Reservations recommended. Family-style meal $12.95, $5.95 for children 6–12, children under 6 can share with adults; brunch $12.95. AE, CB, DC, DISC, MC, V. Tues–Sat 4:30–10pm (Thurs to midnight, Fri–Sat to 1am), Sun 10:30am–9pm (brunch 10:30am–2pm). Free garage parking with validation. SOUTHERN/AMERICAN.

The downstairs of Music City Roadhouse is a large and raucous two-room bar with pool tables. Upstairs is the restaurant where live, mostly blues, bands play while you pig out on fried and barbecued chicken, barbecued spare ribs, fried catfish, pot roast, and country fried steak. The deal is, for $12.95 each, you may choose up to three entrees and three side dishes for your table. The sides, such as mashed regular and sweet potatoes, coleslaw, greens, and green beans with bacon, are replenishable. Another great deal for big eaters: a $12.95 all-you-can-eat rib dinner.

The music is great, but so loud it overwhelms conversation, and the small tables are packed together (most seating is family style, at long tables). In good weather, try to sit out on the terrace, which overlooks the C&O Canal. The food is plentiful and tastes of the true South (that is, the greens are soggy). *Note:* If you've got kids, make sure they go to the bathroom before you get here. The only restroom is downstairs in the bar, which, at 6:30 on a Saturday night is already noisy and jammed with beer-guzzling behemoths.

✪ **Old Glory Barbecue.** 3139 M St. NW. ☎ **202/337-3406.** Reservations for 6 or more Sun–Thurs, reservations not accepted Fri–Sat. Main courses $6.50–$17; late night entrees $5.25–$6.75; brunch buffet $11.95, $5.95 for kids 11 and under. AE, DC, DISC, MC, V. Sun–Thurs 11:30am–1am, Fri–Sat 11:30am–3am; Sun brunch 11am–3pm. Metro: Foggy Bottom. AMERICAN/BARBECUE.

Raised wooden booths flank one side of the restaurant; an imposing, old-fashioned dark wood bar with saddle-seat stools extends down the other. Blues, rock, and country songs play in the background. Thursday, Friday, and Saturday nights the music is live (R&B, soul and swing music.) Old Glory boasts the city's "largest selection of single-barrel and boutique bourbons," a claim which two buddies at the bar appear to be confirming firsthand. In a few hours, the two-story restaurant will be packed with the hard-drinkin' young and restless.

In early evening, though, Old Glory is prime for anyone—singles, families, an older crowd, although it's almost always noisy. Come for the messy, tangy, delicious spare ribs; hickory smoked chicken; tender, smoked beef brisket; or marinated, wood-fried shrimp. Six sauces are on the table, the spiciest being the vinegar-based East Carolina and Lexington. My Southern-raised husband favored the Savannah version, which reminded him of that city's famous Johnny Harris barbecue sauce. The complimentary corn muffins and biscuits, side dishes of collard greens, succotash, and potato salad, and desserts like apple crisp and coconut cherry cobbler all hit the spot.

Zed's. 3318 M St. NW. ☎ **202/333-4710.** Reservations accepted for parties of more than 5 people. Lunch $7.25–$10.75, dinner mostly $7.75–$13.50. AE, CB, DC, DISC, MC, V. Daily 11am–11pm. ETHIOPIAN.

Though Ethiopian cuisine has long been popular in Washington, few restaurants can match Zed's truly authentic, high-quality fare. Zed's is a trilevel, charming little place with indigenous paintings, posters, and artifacts adorning pine-paneled walls. Tables are set with fresh flowers, and Ethiopian music enhances the ambience.

Diners use a sourdough crepelike pancake called injera to scoop up food. Highly recommended are the doro watt (chicken stewed in a tangy, hot red chili pepper sauce), the infillay (strips of tender chicken breast flavored with seasoned butter and honey wine and served with a delicious chopped spinach and rice side dish), flavorful lamb dishes and the deep-fried whole fish. Vegetables have never been tastier. Consider ordering more of the garlicky chopped collard greens, red lentil purée in spicy red pepper sauce, or a chilled purée of roasted yellow split peas mixed with onions, peppers, and garlic. There's a full bar, and, should you have the inclination, there are Italian pastries for dessert.

10 Glover Park

MODERATE

Busara. 2340 Wisconsin Ave. NW. ☎ **202/337-2340.** Reservations recommended. Lunch $6–$9, dinner $8.25–$22.95. AE, DC, DISC, MC, V. Mon–Fri 11:30am–3pm, Sat–Sun 11:30am–4pm; Sun–Thurs 5–11pm, Fri–Sat 5pm–midnight. Valet parking. THAI.

Like many Thai restaurants, Busara gives you big portions for a pretty good price. The pad thai is excellent, less sweet than most, the satays are well marinated, and an appetizer called "shrimp bikini" serves up not-at-all-greasy deep-fried shrimp in a thin spring-roll covering.

Busara's dining room is large, with a picture window overlooking Wisconsin Avenue, modern art on the neon blue walls, and dimly set track lighting angled this way and that. Service is solicitous, but not pushy. If the dining room is full, you can eat at the bar (at dinner only), which is in a separate, rather inviting room. In warm weather, Busara also serves diners in its oriental garden.

✪ **Sushi-Ko.** 2309 Wisconsin Ave. NW. ☎ **202/333-4187.** Reservations recommended. Main courses $10.50–$18. AE, MC, V. Tues–Fri noon–2:30pm; Mon–Thurs 6–10:30pm, Fri 6–11pm, Sat 5:30–11pm, Sun 5:30–10pm. Valet parking for dinner. JAPANESE.

Sushi-Ko was Washington's first sushi bar when it opened 20 years ago and it remains the best in town. People know this, so sometimes there's a wait for tables. The sushi choppers are fun to watch, so try to sit at the sushi bar. You can expect superb versions of sushi and sashimi standards, but the best items are daily specials: sometimes sea trout napoleon

Taking a Break: Afternoon Tea

I've always appreciated the concept of high tea. What is it, after all, but an excuse to gorge on sweet pastries at a time of day when you really ought to be finishing up some task or other before the dinner hour arrives? When you think about it, afternoon tea might well have been designed with tourists in mind. At 3 in the afternoon, you may find yourself longing for a sightseeing break, but not wanting to return to your hotel room. You may feel it's too late to embark on some new adventure, yet too early to start sipping cocktails. (For those of you who think it's never too early for cocktails, see chapter 9, the box "Cheap Eats: Happy Hours to Write Home About.") You're thinking that you wouldn't mind having a little something to eat, something that wouldn't ruin your appetite for dinner. Well, here are some delicious possibilities.

The St. Regis Hotel, 923 16th St. NW, ☎ **202/879-6900.** You take tea in the exquisite lobby, where you sink down into a comfy armchair, admire the ornate decor, and observe the comings and goings of guests. A silver tiered-stand bears light currant scones with house-made strawberry jam and clabbered cream; tiny, crustless tea sandwiches layered thinly with smoked salmon, roast beef, cucumber and the like; and those pastries: miniature fruit tarts and cakes, a macaroon, a madeleine, and then a larger tart, perhaps of raspberries and almonds. Seven pure teas, seven blends, and six herbal and fruit teas are offered; champagne and sherry are available at a surcharge. Tea is served Friday to Sunday 3 to 5:30pm, $19 per person, with reservations suggested.

The Four Seasons Hotel, M St. NW, ☎ **202/342-0444.** This popular tea is served in the ✪ **Garden Terrace,** where a little forest of ficus trees and fern fronds and babbling fountains keep the seating arrangements separate and the conversations private. One wall of windows overlooks the C&O Canal. The Garden Terrace serves drinks and light fare, as well as tea, so expect a mix of business people, couples, and families. This is the only place where a children's tea is offered: a choice of tea, milkshake, or soda, with a brownie, PB&J sandwich, chocolate chip cookie, and strawberries dipped in chocolate. Adults get one scone with double Devon cream and both raspberry and blueberry jam, and a variety of finger sandwiches, tartlets, teacakes, and cookies that change day to day. Among the 16 teas are some herbal and decaffeinated brews; champagne and sherries are available at a surcharge. A pianist plays Tuesday through Sunday,

(diced sea trout layered between rice crackers), tuna tartare, seared Maine diver scallops with uni butter and forest mushrooms, or grilled Alaskan halibut with morels, fiddleheads and wild leeks. The tempuras and teriyakis are also excellent. And there's a long list of sakis.

INEXPENSIVE

✪ **Austin Grill.** 2404 Wisconsin Ave. NW. ☎ **202/337-8080.** Reservations not accepted. Main courses $6–$15. AE, DC, DISC, MC, V. Mon 11:30am–10:30pm, Tues–Thurs 11:30am–11pm, Fri 11:30am–midnight, Sat 11am–midnight, Sun 11am–10:30pm. TEX-MEX.

Owner Rob Wilder opened his grill in 1988 to replicate the easygoing lifestyle, Tex-Mex cuisine, and music he'd loved when he lived in Austin. The good food and festive atmosphere make this a great place for the kids, a date, or a group of friends. Austin

starting at 4pm. Tea is served Monday to Saturday, 3 to 5pm, Sun 3:30 to 5pm; $18 per adult and $9 per child; reservations suggested.

Hay-Adams Hotel, 16th and H sts. NW, ☎ **202/638-6600.** This very proper English tea is served in the hotel's elegant, light-filled main dining room, Lafayette, whose windows overlook Lafayette Square and the White House. You can choose from eight brewed teas to accompany your meal of four different finger sandwiches: cucumber, smoked salmon, tomato, and egg; the obligatory but delightfully rich scone and thick cream, and a variety of ever-changing doll-size pastries, tarts, and cookies. Wednesday through Sunday a pianist plays. If you're going to be in town for Mother's Day, ask about a special Mother's Day tea and tour event (it is not held every year, so be sure to inquire), which combines high tea at the Hay Adams with a tour of the nearby historic Decatur House. Champagne and sherries served at a surcharge. Tea served daily 3 to 4:30pm, $18.95 per person, reservations suggested. Dress nicely.

Park Hyatt Hotel, 1201 24th St. NW, ☎ **202/789-1234.** It's mostly well-dressed ladies who come here for a tea that includes finger sandwiches (cheese, cucumber, spinach, tomato), French pastries (eclairs and fruit tarts), scones with Devon cream and raspberry preserves, and a choice of 12 teas. The hotel's lounge, with many windows and greenery, is the setting, and a pianist plays background music. Tea is served Thursday to Sunday 3 to 5pm; traditional tea is $16.95, with champagne cocktail $20; reservations are suggested.

Washington National Cathedral, Massachusetts and Wisconsin aves. NW, ☎ **202/537-8993.** This tea begins with a tour of the world's sixth largest cathedral (see chapter 7), or, in May and September, a choice of either a garden or cathedral tour, and winds up on the seventh floor of the West tower, whose arched windows take in a stunning view of the city and beyond to the Sugarloaf Mountains in Maryland. Tea consists of scones and jam; sandwich triangles of egg salad or smoked salmon, or maybe pastry cups of tarragon chicken salad; tiny pastries; and brewed tea. During the school year, you can descend from the tower in time to enjoy evensong services performed at 4pm by the Youth Choir. Tea is served every Tuesday and Wednesday at 1:30pm; $18 per person; reserve as far in advance as possible (the cathedral accepts reservations up to 6 months ahead).

Grill is loud; as the night progresses, conversation eventually drowns out the sound of the taped music (everything from Ry Cooder to Natalie Merchant).

Fresh ingredients are used to create outstanding crabmeat quesadillas, "Lake Travis" nachos (tostidas slathered with chopped red onion, refried beans and cheese), a daily fish special (like rockfish fajitas), Key lime pie, and excellent versions of standard fare (chicken enchiladas, guacamole, pico de gallo, and so on). The margaritas are awesome.

Austin Grill's upstairs overlooks the abbreviated bar area below. An upbeat decor includes walls washed in shades of teal and clay and adorned with whimsical coyotes, cowboys, Indians, and cacti. Arrive by 6pm weekends if you don't want to wait; weekdays are less crowded. This is the original Austin Grill; another District Austin Grill is located near the MCI Center at 750 E St. NW (☎ **202/393-3776**). Suburban locations are in Old Town Alexandria (see chapter 10) and West Springfield, Virginia, and in Bethesda, Maryland.

11 Woodley Park

EXPENSIVE

✪ **New Heights.** 2317 Calvert St. NW. ☎ **202/234-4110.** Reservations recommended. Brunch $7.75–$11.50, dinner $16–$25. AE, CB, DC, DISC, MC, V. Sun–Thurs 5:30–10pm, Fri–Sat 5:30–11pm; Sun brunch 11am–2:30pm. Free valet parking. Metro: Woodley Park–Zoo. AMERICAN/INTERNATIONAL.

This attractive second-floor dining room has a bank of windows looking out over Rock Creek Park, and walls hung with the colorful works of local artist Lisa Williamson. New Heights attracts a casually upscale clientele, who fill the room every night. Certain features, like the excellent black bean pâté with smoked tomato and green onion sauces or the heavenly buttermilk fried oysters with corn, chiles, and lime, are fixtures. But new chef John Wabeck is responsible for innovations such as foie gras with mango salsa and the crisp-surfaced fish with spinach or quinoa-corn salad. An almond torte dessert proves a perfect antidote.

MODERATE

Lebanese Taverna. 2641 Connecticut Ave. NW. ☎ **202/265-8681.** Reservations accepted for before 6:30pm. Main courses $8–$14 at lunch, $11.50–$16 at dinner. AE, CB, DC, DISC, MC, V. Mon–Fri 11:30am–2:30pm, Sat 11:30am–3pm; Mon–Thurs 5:30–10:30pm, Fri–Sat 5:30–11pm, Sun 5:30–10pm. Free underground parking. Metro: Woodley Park–Zoo. LEBANESE.

This family-owned restaurant gives you a taste of Lebanese culture—its cuisine, decor, and music. It's very popular on weekends, so expect to stand in line (reservations are accepted for seating before 6:30pm only). Diners, once seated in the courtyard-like dining room, where music plays and prayer rugs hang on walls, hate to leave. The wood-burning oven at back bakes the pita breads and several appetizers. Order a demi mezze, with pita for dipping, and you get 12 sampling dishes, including hummus, tabbouleh, baba ghanoush, and pastry-wrapped spinach pies (fatayer bi sabanikh), enough for dinner for two, or hors d'oeuvres for four. The wealth of meatless dishes will delight vegetarians, while rotisserie items, especially the chicken and the char-grilled kebabs of chicken and shrimp, will please all others.

12 Dining at Sightseeing Attractions

With so many great places to eat in Washington, I have a hard time recommending those at sightseeing attractions. Most of these are overpriced and too crowded, even if they are convenient. A few, however, are worth mentioning—for their admirable cuisine, noteworthy setting, or both.

Head for the Capitol's numerous restaurants for a chance to rub elbows with your senators and representatives. But keep in mind these spots are usually open only for lunch and can get very crowded; to lessen the chances of a long wait, try going about 30 minutes before the posted closing time. You'll find the **House of Representatives Restaurant** (also called the "Members' Dining Room") in Room H118, at the South end of the Capitol (☎ **202/225-6300**). This fancy, chandelier-and-gilt-framed dining room is open to the public but doesn't take reservations (it's also open for breakfast). When the house is in session however, the dining room closes to the public from 11am to 1:30pm. Senators frequent the **Senate Dining Room,** but you'll need a letter from your senator to eat here (jacket and tie required for men, no jeans for men or women). More accommodating is the **Refectory,** first floor, Room S112, Senate side of the Capitol (☎ **202/224-4870**), which serves sandwiches and other light luncheon fare.

Most Hill staffers eat at places like the **Longworth Building Cafeteria,** Independence Avenue and South Capitol Street SE (☎ **202/225-4410**), where they can just grab a bite from a fairly nice food court. But by far the best deal for visitors is the **Dirksen Senate Office Building South Buffet Room,** First and C streets NE (☎ **202/224-4249**). For just $9.95 per adult, $6.50 per child (including a nonalcoholic drink and dessert), you can choose from a buffet that includes a carving station and eight other hot entrees. It's often crowded, but they will take reservations for parties of more than 10.

In the same neighborhood, two institutions offering great deals and views (of famous sites or people) are the **Library of Congress**'s Cafeteria (☎ **202/707-8300**), and its more formal Montpelier Room (☎ **202/707-8300**), where the buffet lunch is only $8.50; and the **Supreme Court**'s Cafeteria (☎ **202/479-3246**), where you'll likely spy a justice or two enjoying the midday meal.

Among museum restaurants, the ones that shine are the **Corcoran Gallery of Art**'s Café des Artistes (☎ **202/639-1786**); the new, six-story Atrium Cafe in the **National Museum of Natural History** (☎ **202/357-2700**); the **National Gallery of Art**'s Terrace Café (☎ **202/216-2492**) and Garden Café (☎ **202/216-5966**); and the **Phillips Collection**'s snug Café (☎ **202/387-2151**).

7

What to See & Do in Washington, D.C.

Big things are happening in Washington: The Washington Monument is nearing the end of its 2-year restoration, the National Gallery of Art now has a beautiful 6.1-acre Sculpture Garden, and the Smithsonian's National Museum of Natural History opened its Discovery Center with a six-story-high screen for showing 2-D and 3-D films. Two Smithsonian museums are closed for repairs: the National Museum of American Art and the National Portrait Gallery. The U.S. Botanic Garden hasn't finished its renovation yet, but it's getting there. And more memorials are planned: to honor World War II soldiers, Martin Luther King, Jr., Thomas Paine, George Mason, black Revolutionary War patriots, and Mahatma Gandhi.

But for all its changes, the capital stays wonderfully the same, offering visitors a menu that includes the three houses of government, scores of museums, more than 100 memorials, an abundance of historic houses and federal buildings, acres and acres of gorgeous parkland, and as many outdoor activities to match.

Read over this chapter and figure out what appeals to you most. If you have Internet access, you may want to check out the Web sites of individual attractions. Also, look at the National Park Service site, **www.nps.gov/nacc**, to learn about many of the NPS attractions reviewed on these pages, including the presidential memorials, Rock Creek Park, and the C&O Canal. The Smithsonian Institution (see section 3) also has its own Web site, **www.si.edu**, which will help get you to the home pages of its individual museums.

Now, are you feeling overwhelmed? At long last, the city has a walk-in visitor center, complete with maps, visitor guides, interactive information kiosks, brochures, and information specialists, to help you get a grip. In May 1999, the **Washington, D.C., Visitor Information Center** opened in the brand-new Ronald Reagan Building and International Trade Center, at 1300 Pennsylvania Ave. NW (☎ **202/ 328-4748 [DC-VISIT]**), just 1 block from the White House Visitor Center. Because the building is so enormous (largest federal building after the Pentagon), you may have trouble finding the entrance: Head for the corner of 13th Street and Pennsylvania Avenue, enter the building, then go down the hall and to the left, and you'll see the center. If you're arriving by Metro, exit the Federal Triangle station and cross Wilson Plaza to the visitor center, whose entrance lies directly across from the station. The center is open Monday to Saturday 8am to 6pm, and Sunday noon to 5pm.

Impressions

It has a damp, wheezy, Dickensian sort of winter hardly equalled by London, and a steaming tropical summer not surpassed by the basin of the Nile.

—Alistair Cooke

Take an umbrella, an overcoat, and a fan, and go forth.

—Mark Twain

Suggested Itineraries

If You Have 1 Day

Make the Mall your destination, visiting whichever museums appeal to you the most. Then take a breather: If you have young children, let them ride the carousel across from the Smithsonian's Arts and Industries Building. With or without kids, stroll across the Mall to the new National Gallery Sculpture Garden, where you can get a bite to eat in the cafe or sit and relax next to the reflecting pool. Rest up, dine in the Dupont Circle neighborhood, stroll Connecticut Avenue, then take a taxi to visit the Lincoln Memorial at night.

If You Have 2 Days

On your first day, take a narrated tour of the city (see list of tours at end of this chapter) for an overview of the city's attractions, stopping at the Jefferson, FDR, Lincoln, and Vietnam Veterans Memorials, and at the Washington Monument. Use the tour to determine which mall museums you'll want to visit. After taking in the Washington Monument, walk up 15th Street to the Old Ebbitt Grill for lunch (expect a wait unless you made a reservation). Following lunch, visit your top-pick museums on the Mall. Start your second day by visiting the Capitol, followed by a tour of the Supreme Court. Walk to Massachusetts Avenue for lunch at Café Berlin, then spend the afternoon visiting the Library of Congress, the Folger Shakespeare Library, and, if you have time, Union Station and the National Postal Museum.

Have dinner in Georgetown and browse the shops.

If You Have 3 Days

Spend your first 2 days as described above. On the morning of your third day, tour the White House and the National Archives. In the afternoon, ride the bus (an N bus from Dupont Circle, or a 30-series bus from Georgetown) to visit the Washington National Cathedral, or take in some of the non-Mall art museums, for example, the National Museum of Women in the Arts. Enjoy a pretheater dinner at one of the many restaurants that offer these good deals (some suggestions: 1789 in Georgetown, the Bombay Club near the White House), then head to the Kennedy Center for a performance.

If You Have 4 Days or More

Spend your first three days as suggested above.

On the fourth day, get an early start on the FBI tour, and, if your morning isn't shot, head to the Discovery Channel Retail Store (in the MCI Center) to view the 15-minute film, "Destination DC." Follow up the film with a DC Heritage Tour (departs from the Center weekdays at 10:30am, Sat–Sun at 1:30pm; you **must** call ahead to reserve your space on the tour (☎ **202/639-0908**), which gives you an inside look at

Washington in the 19th century as you walk through Chinatown and other parts of this downtown neighborhood. Have lunch at one of the many good restaurants here, then go to Ford's Theatre to see where Lincoln was shot. Use the rest of the afternoon for outdoor activities—go to the zoo or for a hike along the C&O Canal. Alternatively, you might visit the U.S. Holocaust Memorial Museum (not recommended for children under 12); this will require most of a day to see. Have dinner in Adams-Morgan, followed by club-hopping up and down 18th Street. (Or try jazz at one of the clubs; see chapter 9 for suggestions.)

On the fifth day, consider a day trip to Alexandria, Virginia. Or board a boat for Mount Vernon, and spend most of the day touring the estate, with the afternoon set aside for seeing sights you've missed. Have dinner downtown at one of the 7th Street district restaurants, then go on to see Shakespeare performed at the Lansburgh, or head to Coco Loco to practice your samba.

1 The Three Major Houses of Government

Three of the most visited sights in Washington are the buildings housing the executive, legislative, and judicial branches of the U.S. government. All are stunning and offer fascinating lessons in American history and government.

✪ **The White House.** 1600 Pennsylvania Ave. NW (visitor entrance gate at E St. and E. Executive Ave.). ☎ **202/456-7041** or 202/208-1631; www.whitehouse.gov. Free admission. Tues–Sat 10am–noon. Closed some days for official functions; check by calling the 24-hour number. Metro: McPherson Square (if you are going straight to the White House), Federal Triangle (if you are getting tour tickets from the White House Visitor Center).

If you think you're going to get the Monica Lewinsky tour, think again. Whether you visit the White House on a VIP guided tour or go through self-guided, you will see just what your escorts (Secret Service agents, by the way) want you to see, and that doesn't include the Oval Office. So forget the scandal, if you can, and soak up the history of this house that has served as a residence, office, reception site, and world embassy for every U.S. president since John Adams.

WHITE HOUSE TOURS AND TICKETS Tickets to tour the White House are only required in peak season, between mid-March and Labor Day and the month of December. If you're planning to visit the White House at any other time, you simply proceed to the southeast gate of the White House, at E Street and East Executive Avenue NW, and join the line. If you're in line by noon, you should gain admittance.

In peak or off-peak season, you should know a few things before heading out to the president's home. Try first to allow time to tour the **White House Visitor Center,** 1450 Pennsylvania Ave., in the Department of Commerce Building, between 14th and 15th streets (see listing below for more information). White House tours take place mornings only, Tuesday through Saturday. There are no public rest rooms or telephones in the White House, and picture-taking and videotaping are prohibited. (The Visitor Center has rest rooms, another reason to stop here first.)

For those visiting the White House during peak season, you must obtain tickets, which can be done in one of two ways: You can obtain advance tickets from your congressperson or senator months in advance (see box below). Or, if you don't have these VIP tour tickets, you can pick up free tickets at the White House Visitor Center.

Tickets are timed for tours between 10am and noon and are issued on the day of the tour on a first-come, first-serve basis starting at 7:30am. During the busy season, people start lining up outside the Visitor Center as early as 4am to snag one of the approximately 4,500 tickets distributed daily. A National Park ranger stamps the hand and takes down the name of each person in line and the number of tickets, up to four,

How to Obtain Advance Tickets for White House Tours

Tuesday through Saturday between 8:15am and 8:45am, the doors of the White House are open for special VIP tours to those with tickets. To obtain these tickets, contact the local or Washington office of your congressman or senator—at least 6 months in advance, because each senator and congressperson receives no more than 10 tickets a week to distribute. These early tours ensure entrance during the busy tourist season when thousands line up during the 2 hours daily that the White House is open to the public. The VIP tours are no more extensive than the regular tours, it's just that your Secret Service guides provide commentary as you proceed through the ground floor and state floor rooms. You should still expect to stand in line to get in, and you will still be one among many (70 or 80). The VIP tour lasts about 25 or 35 minutes and you're not allowed to ask questions until the tour is over.

the person wants. To gain admittance on the tour, someone in your party must have the magic stamp and the right name. (This is to prevent scalpers from obtaining free tickets, then turning around and selling them to unsuspecting tourists.) The ticket counter closes when the supply for that day is gone. Tickets are valid only for the date and time issued.

After obtaining your tickets, you'll probably have quite a bit of time to spare before your scheduled tour; consider enjoying a leisurely breakfast at **Reeve's Restaurant & Bakery** or the **Old Ebbitt Grill,** both close by (see chapter 6 for details).

Both the VIP tour and the not-so-VIP tour go through the same rooms; on the 25–35–minute VIP tour, a Secret Service agent guides you and answers questions at the end; on the 15–20–minute, self-guided tour, a Secret Service agent posted in each room will answer any questions you have along the way. Highlights of the tour include the following rooms:

The Gold-and-White East Room   This room has been the scene of presidential receptions, weddings of presidents' daughters (Lynda Bird Johnson, for one), and other dazzling events. This is where the president entertains visiting heads of state and the place where seven of the eight presidents who died in office (all but Garfield) laid in state. It was also the scene of Nixon's resignation speech. The room is decorated in the early 20th-century style of the Theodore Roosevelt renovation; it has parquet Fontainebleau oak floors and white-painted wood walls with fluted pilasters and classical relief inserts. Note the famous Gilbert Stuart portrait of George Washington that Dolley Madison saved from the British torch during the War of 1812.

The Green Room   Thomas Jefferson's dining room is today used as a sitting room. He designed a revolving door with trays on one side, so servants could leave dishes on the kitchen side. Then he would twirl the door and allow guests to help themselves, thus retaining his privacy. Green watered–silk fabric covers walls hung with notable paintings by Gilbert Stuart and John Singer Sargent, and early 19th-century furnishings attributed to the famous cabinetmaker Duncan Phyfe, decorate the room.

The Oval Blue Room   This room, decorated in the French Empire style chosen by James Monroe in 1817, is where presidents and first ladies have officially received guests since the Jefferson administration. It was, however, Van Buren's decor that began the "blue room" tradition. The walls, on which hang portraits of five presidents (including Rembrandt Peale's portrait of Thomas Jefferson and G. P. A. Healy's of Tyler), are covered in reproductions of early 19th-century French and American wallpaper. Grover Cleveland, the only president to wed in the White House, was married in the Blue Room; the Reagans, Nancy wearing symbolic yellow, greeted here the

53 Americans liberated after being held hostage in Iran for 444 days; and every year it's the setting for the White House Christmas tree.

The Red Room   Several portraits of past presidents, plus Albert Bierstadt's *View of the Rocky Mountains* and a Gilbert Stuart portrait of Dolley Madison, hang here. It's used as a reception room, usually for afternoon teas. The satin-covered walls and most of the Empire furnishings are red.

The State Dining Room   Modeled after late-18th-century neoclassical English houses, this room is a superb setting for state dinners and luncheons. Theodore Roosevelt, a big-game hunter, hung a large moose head over the fireplace and other trophies on the walls. Below G. P. A. Healy's portrait of Lincoln is an inscription written by John Adams on his second night in the White House (FDR had it carved into the mantel): "I Pray Heaven to Bestow The Best of Blessings on THIS HOUSE and on All that shall here-after Inhabit it. May none but Honest and Wise Men ever rule under This Roof."

A BRIEF HISTORY OF THE WHITE HOUSE   Irishman James Hoban submitted the winning design for the structure, beating out 52 other entries in a contest held by George Washington. Although Washington picked the winner, he was the only president never to live in the White House, or president's palace, as it was called before whitewashing brought the name "White House" into use. The White House took eight years to build, starting in 1792, when its cornerstone was laid, and its facade is made of the same stone as that used to construct the Capitol. In 1814, during the War of 1812, the British set fire to the White House, gutting the interior; the only reason the exterior endured is because a rainstorm extinguished the fire. What you see today is Hoban's basic creation: a building modeled after an Irish country house; in fact, Hoban had in mind the house of the duke of Leinster in Dublin.

Alterations over the years have incorporated the South Portico in 1824, the North Portico in 1829, and electricity in 1891, during Benjamin Harrison's presidency. In 1902, repairs and refurnishings of the White House cost nearly $500,000. No other great change took place until Harry Truman added his controversial "balcony" inside the columns of the South Portico. Also in 1948, after the leg of Margaret Truman's piano cut through the dining room ceiling, nearly $6 million was allotted to reconstruct the building. The Trumans lived at Blair House across the street for nearly four years while the White House interior was shored up with steel girders and concrete. It's as solid as Gibraltar now.

In 1961, Jacqueline Kennedy formed a Fine Arts Committee to help restore the famous rooms to their original grandeur.

Note: All visitors, even those with VIP congressional tour passes, should call ☎ **202/456-7041** before setting out in the morning; occasionally the White House is closed to tourists on short notice because of unforeseen events.

The White House Visitor Center. 1450 Pennsylvania Ave., NW. (in the Department of Commerce Building, between 14th and 15th sts.) ☎ **202/208-1631** or 202/456-7041 for recorded information. Daily 7:30am–4pm. Closed Thanksgiving, Christmas, and New Year's Day. Metro: Federal Triangle.

The Visitor Center opened in 1995 to provide extensive interpretive data about the White House (as well as other Washington tourist attractions) and serve as a ticket-distribution center. It is run under the auspices of the National Park Service, and the staff is particularly well informed. Try to catch the 30-minute video about the White House, *Within These Walls,* which provides interior views of the presidential precincts and features footage with both the president and Hillary Clinton (it runs continuously throughout the day). Before you leave the visitor center, pick up a copy of the National

Park Service's brochure on the White House, which tells you a little about what you see in the eight rooms you tour and a bit about the history of the White House. The White House Historic Association runs a small shop here. The association operates an informative Web site, **www.whitehousehistory.org**, although much of it seems designed to make you order something.

Before you leave the Visitor Center, take a look at the exhibits, which include:

Architectural History of the White House, including the grounds and extensive renovations to its structure and interior that have taken place since its cornerstone was laid in 1792.

Symbol and Image, showing how the White House has been portrayed by photographers, artists, journalists, political cartoonists, and others.

First Families, with displays about the people who have lived here (such as prankster Tad Lincoln, who once stood in a window above his father and waved a Confederate flag at a military review).

The Working White House, focusing on the vast staff of servants, chefs, gardeners, Secret Service people, and others who maintain this institution.

Ceremony and Celebration, depicting notable White House events from a Wright Brothers' aviation demonstration in 1911 to a ballet performance by Baryshnikov during the Carter administration.

White House Interiors, Past and Present, including photographs of the ever-changing Oval Office as decorated by administrations from Taft through Clinton.

✪ **The Capitol.** At the east end of the Mall, entrance on E. Capitol St. and 1st St. NW. ☎ **202/225-6827,** www.senate.gov, or www.house.gov. Free admission. Mar–Sept daily 9am–8pm; guided tours Mon–Fri 9:30am–7pm and Sat 9:30am–3:30pm, guides posted to assist but not guide you Sun 1–4:30pm. Sept–Feb daily 9am–4:30pm; guided tours Mon–Sat 9am–3:45pm. Closed Jan 1, Thanksgiving Day, and Dec 25. Parking at Union Station or on neighborhood streets. Metro: Union Station or Capitol South.

TOUR INFORMATION   For all tours, whether during peak season (March through August) or the slow season (September through February), find the east front side of the Capitol, whose sidewalks extend from the Capitol steps and plaza to 1st Street, across from the Library of Congress and Supreme Court. If you are visiting the Capitol in the off-season, you probably will be able to enter the Capitol without waiting in line: Walk up the long driveway and climb the central grand steps of the Capitol. After you pass through the security-check just inside the doors, you enter the Rotunda, where a (red-jacketed) Capitol Service Guide will direct you where to stand if you're interested in a guided tour, or hand you the self-guiding brochure if you want to tour on your own.

During the peak season, you have three options if you'd like a guided tour of the Capitol. If you are part of a group of more than 15 people, you can call ☎ **202/224-4910** to reserve a guided tour time, thus avoiding a wait in line. Reservations are very limited, so call months in advance. When you make your reservation, you will be told to come to the east front side of the Capitol and look for any guide in the official red jacket, who will escort you off to the far right side, away from the other lines, and then take you inside for the tour. If you are touring as individuals or as a family, you can try to arrange ahead (try 6 months in advance for spring through August tours) to obtain VIP tour tickets from the office of your representative or senator for the morning tours (departing at intervals between 8 and 8:30am). For these tours, you enter the Capitol through the Law Library door on the east front side of the Capitol, facing the Supreme Court, on the ground level, just to the right of the grand staircase. A Capitol Guide will meet you inside and take you on the tour.

Most people opt for just showing up at the Capitol, and if this is your plan, find the east front side of the Capitol and look for the signs posted at the end of either sidewalk flanking the Capitol. One sign designates the line for guided tours, the other denotes the self-guided tours line. Guided tours in peak season take place every 30 minutes and admit 50 people at a time. You may have a long wait, especially if you arrive in the morning. Your best bet is midday, late afternoon, or early evening. If you'd rather walk through on your own, you will also have to wait in line in peak season, but this queue moves a little faster. All tours are free, the guided tours last 20 to 30 minutes, and the self-guided tours last as long as you like. Whether you are self-guided or Capitol Guide Service–guided, you must have a ticket to enter the Capitol during the peak season, every day but Sunday; the tickets, which do not specify time and date, are handed to you just before you climb the steps and enter the Capitol, which means you're stuck in line and can't go and grab a bite to eat or tour another site in the interim.

The House and Senate galleries are always open to visitors, but passes are required when these galleries are in session. After 6pm, however, you may enter either gallery without a pass and watch the session to its conclusion. Once obtained, the passes are good through the remainder of the Congress. To obtain visitor passes in advance, contact your representative or senator. If you don't receive visitor passes in the mail (not every senator or representative sends them), they're obtainable at your senator's office on the Constitution Avenue side of the building or your representative's office on the Independence Avenue side. (Visitors who are not citizens can obtain a gallery pass by presenting a passport at the Senate or House appointments desk, located on the first floor of the Capitol). Call the Capitol switchboard at ☎ **202/224-3121** to contact the office of your senator or congressperson. You'll know the House and/or the Senate is in session if you see flags flying over their respective wings of the Capitol, or you can check the weekday "Today in Congress" column in the *Washington Post* for details on times of the House and Senate sessions and committee hearings. This column also tells you which sessions are open to the public, allowing you to pick one that interests you. To visit the Hall of the House of Representatives Gallery, enter the Capitol through the south door at the end of the building facing Independence Avenue; to visit the

Getting Around Underground

If you are going to be visiting your representative or senator, find out the building name and room number of the member's House or Senate office and then travel from the Capitol Building like those in-the-know do: underground. All six of the government buildings in the Capitol complex are accessible beneath the street, either by foot or train. Just stop a Capitol Hill police officer or Capitol Guide Service guide and ask for directions to the subway (not the Metro) that runs to the House side, or to the Senate side, depending on who you're visiting. One train runs between the Rayburn House Office Building and the House side of the Capitol; one runs between the Hart Senate Office Building and the Senate side of the Capitol, stopping in each direction at the Dirksen Senate Office Building, and one train runs directly between the Russell Senate Office Building and the Senate side of the Capitol. (The Cannon and Longworth House Office buildings are not on the train route, but you can continue your journey by walking, either at street level or along the underground passageway.) Since the train system was installed purposely to get members quickly to the House and Senate floors to vote, the trains offer good opportunities for political celebrity-sightings. Just don't get in their way.

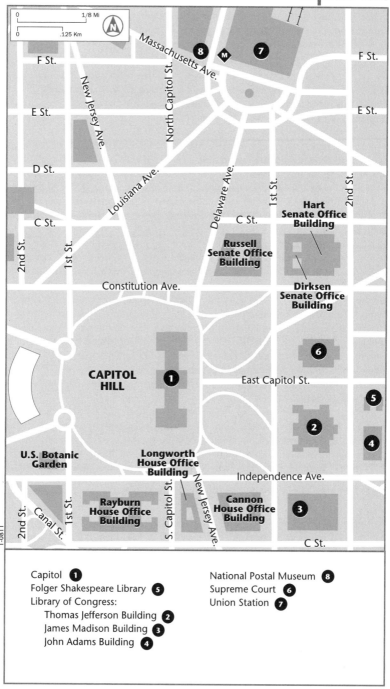

Capitol ❶
Folger Shakespeare Library ❺
Library of Congress:
   Thomas Jefferson Building ❷
   James Madison Building ❸
   John Adams Building ❹

National Postal Museum ❽
Supreme Court ❻
Union Station ❼

Senate Chamber Gallery, enter the building through the Law Library door on the east front side of the Capitol facing the Supreme Court, on the ground level, just to the right of the central grand staircase.

A Brief History of the Capitol   The Capitol is as awesome up close at it is from afar. As the place where our elected representatives formulate, debate, and pass into law our country's policies and principles, the Capitol is perhaps the most important edifice in the United States. For 135 years it sheltered not only both houses of Congress but the Supreme Court, and for 97 years the Library of Congress as well. When you tour the Capitol, you'll learn about America's history as you admire the place in which it unfolded. Classic architecture, interior embellishments, and hundreds of paintings, sculptures, and other artworks are integral elements of the Capitol.

On the massive bronze doors leading to the **Rotunda** are portrayals of events in the life of Columbus. The Rotunda—a huge, 96-foot-wide, circular hall that is capped by a 180-foot-high dome—is the hub of the Capitol. The dome was completed, at Lincoln's direction, while the Civil War was being fought. Nine presidents have lain in state here; when Kennedy's casket was displayed, the line of mourners stretched 40 blocks. On the circular walls are eight immense oil paintings of events in American history, such as the presentation of the Declaration of Independence and the surrender of Cornwallis at Yorktown. In the dome is an allegorical fresco masterpiece by Constantino Brumidi, *Apotheosis of Washington,* a symbolic portrayal of George Washington surrounded by Roman gods and goddesses watching over the progress of the nation. Brumidi was known as the "Michelangelo of the Capitol" for the many works he created throughout the building. Take another look at the dome and find the woman poised directly below Washington; the triumphant Armed Freedom figure is said to be modeled after Lola Germon, a young and beautiful actress with whom the 60-year-old Brumidi had a child. Beneath the dome is a trompe-l'oeil frieze that depicts events in American history from Columbus through the Wright brothers' flight at Kitty Hawk.

Newly added to the Rotunda is the sculpture of suffragists Elizabeth Cady Stanton, Susan B. Anthony, and Lucretia Mott. Until recently, the ponderous monument had been relegated to the Crypt, one level directly below the Rotunda. Women's groups successfully lobbied for its more prominent position in the Rotunda.

National Statuary Hall was originally the chamber of the House of Representatives. In 1864, it became Statuary Hall, and the states were invited to send two statues each of native sons and daughters to the hall. As the room filled up, statues spilled over into the Hall of Columns, corridors, and any space that might accommodate the bronze and marble artifacts. Many of the statues honor individuals who played important roles in American history, such as Henry Clay, Ethan Allen, Daniel Webster, and even a woman or two, like Jeannette Rankin (the first woman to serve in Congress).

The south and north wings are occupied by the House and Senate chambers, respectively. The House of Representatives chamber is the largest legislative chamber in the world. The president delivers his annual State of the Union address here. Before you leave, visit the Capitol's two museum rooms, the **Old Senate Chamber** and the **Old Supreme Court Chamber,** both of which have been restored to their mid-19th-century appearance. The Old Senate Chamber was the site of hotly debated issues, from slavery to territorial expansion; the Old Supreme Court Chamber is where Chief Justice John Marshall established the foundations of American constitutional law. (If you've seen the movie *Amistad,* you'll be interested to know that it was in this chamber that John Quincy Adams argued the Amistad case before the Supreme Court.) Keep your eyes peeled for senators and representatives as you walk around, because you're likely to see several.

An Art-Full Tour of the Capitol

One glance at the Capitol's grand architecture is enough to tell you that the building is about more than history and politics. The place is also about art. In addition to its superb design, the Capitol contains more than 800 artworks, from gilded 19th-century frames and the grand paintings they encase, to frescoes, ornamental bronze stair railings, and stained-glass windows. Take a guided tour of the Capitol, if you like, and sit in on a session of Congress, but try to save some time to explore on your own. Here are some special things to look for:

- For more of Constantino Brumidi's art, find the first floor of the Senate wing. Covering the vaulted ceilings and the crescent-shaped spaces over doorways are Brumidi's decorative paintings of 40 different kinds of birds, plus flowers, fruits, and animals; and portraits of famous Americans and Revolutionary War leaders.

- An immense 20-by-30-foot painting in the east staircase of the Senate wing is William Powell's *1873 Battle of Lake Erie,* depicting the moment during the War of 1812 when Oliver Hazard Perry (known for his victorious pronounce-ment "We have met the enemy and they are ours.") transfers the colors of his flagship to one in better shape.

- Another huge painting is the 20-by-30-foot fresco by Emanuel Leutze, better known for his *Washington Crossing the Delaware,* than for this *Westward the Course of Empire Takes its Way,* which covers the wall over the west stairway of the House wing. The 1862 painting is a tumultuous display of covered wagons and hopeful immigrants making their way over the Rocky Mountains to the West. It's as colorful as the artist, who was known to drink with his subjects as he worked.

- Albert Bierstadt's works hang in illustrious places, like the White House, the Corcoran Gallery of Art . . . and here, on a private stairway landing in the House wing. It's hard to find it, and when you do, you'll need to peer up from the steps, but it's worth it. Bierstadt was one of the country's best 19th-century landscape painters: *Entrance Into Monterey, 1770* is the name of this superb painting.

✪ **The Supreme Court of the United States.** One 1st St. NE (between E. Capitol St. and Maryland Ave. NE). ☎ **202/479-3000.** Free admission. Mon–Fri 9am–4:30pm. Closed weekends and all federal holidays. Metro: Capitol South or Union Station.

The highest tribunal in the nation, the Supreme Court is charged with deciding whether actions of Congress, the president, the states, and lower courts are in accord with the Constitution, and with applying the Constitution's enduring principles to novel situations and a changing country. It has the power of "judicial review"—authority to invalidate legislation or executive action that conflicts with the Constitu-tion. Out of the 6,500 cases submitted to it each year, the Supreme Court hears only about 100 cases, many of which deal with issues vital to the nation. The Court's rul-ings are final, reversible only by another Supreme Court decision, or in some cases, an Act of Congress or a constitutional amendment.

Until 1935 the Supreme Court met in the Capitol. Architect Cass Gilbert designed the stately Corinthian marble palace that houses the Court today. The building was considered rather grandiose by early residents: One justice remarked that he and his colleagues ought to enter such pompous precincts on elephants.

If you're in town when the Court is in session, try to see a case being argued (call ☎ 202/479-3211 for details). The Court meets Monday through Wednesday from 10am to noon and, on occasion, from 1 to 2pm, starting the first Monday in October through late April, alternating, in approximately 2-week intervals, between "sittings," to hear cases and deliver opinions, and "recesses," for consideration of business before the Court. Mid-May to late June, you can attend brief sessions (about 15 minutes) at 10am on Monday, when the justices release orders and opinions. You can find out what cases are on the docket by checking the *Washington Post*'s "Supreme Court Calendar." Arrive at least an hour early—even earlier for highly publicized cases—to line up for seats, about 150 of which are allotted to the general public.

At 10am the entrance of the justices is announced by the marshal, and all present rise and remain standing while the justices are seated following the chant: "The Honorable, the Chief Justice and Associate Justices of the Supreme Court of the United States. Oyez! Oyez! Oyez! [French for "Hear ye!"] All persons having business before the Honorable, the Supreme Court of the United States, are admonished to draw near and give their attention, for the Court is now sitting. God save the United States and this Honorable Court!" There are many rituals here. Unseen by the gallery is the "conference handshake"; following a 19th-century tradition symbolizing a "harmony of aims if not views," each justice shakes hands with each of the other eight when they assemble to go to the bench. The Court has a record before it of prior proceedings and relevant briefs, so each side is allowed only a 30-minute argument.

You might consider contacting your senator or congressperson—at least two months in advance—to arrange for a guided tour of the building led by a Supreme Court staff member. (Or go on a self-guided tour, though you won't be able to go everywhere the guided tour does.) Call the Supreme Court information line to find out days and times that court arguments will take place. You may view these on a first come, first serve basis, choosing between the three-minute line, which ushers visitors in and out of the court every three minutes, or the "regular" line, which admits visitors who wish to stay for the entire argument.

The Supreme Court is cloaked in mystery, purposefully. You can't take cameras or recording devices into the courtroom. The justices never give speeches or press conferences. The media reports that Justice Thomas is famously silent, Justice Scalia argumentative, and Justice Ginsburg talkative; all of the justices tend to be intimidating. See for yourself.

If the Court is not in session during your visit, you can attend a free lecture in the courtroom about Court procedure and the building's architecture. Lectures are given every hour on the half hour from 9:30am to 3:30pm.

After the talk, explore the Great Hall and go down a flight of steps to see the 20-minute film on the workings of the Court. On the same floor is an exhibit highlighting "History of High Courts Around the World," on display through mid-2000, at least. There's also a gift shop and a cafeteria that's open to the public and serves good food.

2　The Presidential Memorials

Tributes to American presidents appear in various guises all over the city, and the most recent additions honor Ronald Reagan: the immense Ronald Reagan Building and International Trade Center at 1300 Pennsylvania Ave. NW and the Ronald Reagan National Airport (known until winter of 1998 as the Washington National Airport). Far fewer in the capital are presidential memorials intended as national shrines to honor the chief executive. In fact, there are four: the Washington Monument, Lincoln

Memorial, Jefferson Memorial, and the Franklin Delano Roosevelt Memorial. Unfortunately, none of these lies directly on a Metro line, so you can expect a bit of a walk from the specified station, or you can go by Tourmobile (see "Organized Tours," near the end of this chapter).

Washington Monument. Directly south of the White House (at 15th St. and Constitution Ave. NW). ☎ **202/426-6841.** Free admission. Early Apr–Labor Day, daily 8am–midnight; Labor Day–Apr, daily 9am–5pm. Last elevators depart 15 minutes before closing (arrive earlier). Closed Dec 25, open till noon July 4. Metro: Smithsonian, then a 10-minute walk.

TICKET INFORMATION   Tickets are required for admission to the Washington Monument. The ticket booth is located at the bottom of the hill from the monument, on 15th Street NW between Independence and Constitution Avenues. The tickets grant admission at half-hour intervals between the stated hours. You can obtain tickets on the day of the tour; if you want to save yourself the trouble and get them in advance (up to six tickets per person), call Ticketmaster (☎ **800/505-5040**), but you'll pay $1.50 per ticket plus a 50¢ service charge per transaction.

Don't be alarmed when you catch sight of the Washington Monument under wraps. Underneath its radical chic, transparent blue sheath (designed by celebrated architect Michael Graves), the 555-foot marble obelisk is undergoing exterior renovation to restore and clean its mortar and masonry. The interior was renovated in 1998 and the monument was closed for tours for some months, as workers refurbished the elevator, installed a new climate-control system, scrubbed the 897 steps, and polished the 193 carved commemorative stones (see below). In early winter of 1998–1999, workers erected 37 miles-worth of aluminum tube scaffolding around the outside of the obelisk, which will remain in place until the restoration is complete, July 4, 2000.

If you were here anytime during the erection of the scaffolding, you may have felt as many Washingtonians did: transfixed by the sight of the crisscross of metal gradually making its way to the top of the monument. In our appreciation for what we could see was painstaking work by skilled workmen performing the restoration, we appreciated, perhaps for the first time, what effort must have gone into the original creation. If you are planning a trip to the capital during the first half of the year 2000, you will find the Washington Monument still scaffold-enshrouded, a sight that is especially dazzling at night, when it is bathed in light. (The National Park Service reports that some tourists prefer the wrapped version of the Washington Monument.)

The repair work is the monument's first major restoration since it opened in 1888. The restoration has received a lot of attention and brought to light a number of mysterious truths about the obelisk: For example, rangers and workmen have heard it sing as the wind whistles through cracks at the top, and, oddly, the more inferior building materials lie at the base of the monument and the best materials on top. But don't worry: The world's tallest, freestanding masonry work is structurally sound.

HISTORY   The idea of a tribute to George Washington first arose 16 years before his death, at the Continental Congress of 1783. But the new nation had more pressing problems, and funds were not readily available. It wasn't until the early 1830s, with the 100th anniversary of Washington's birth approaching, that any action was taken. Then there were several fiascoes. A mausoleum was provided for Washington's remains under the Capitol Rotunda, but a grand-nephew, citing Washington's will, refused to allow the body to be moved from Mount Vernon. In 1830, Horatio Greenough was commissioned to create a memorial statue for the Rotunda. He came up with a bare-chested Washington, draped in classical Greek garb; a shocked public claimed he looked as if he were "entering or leaving a bath," and so the statue was relegated to the Smithsonian. Finally, in 1833, prominent citizens organized the Washington National

Washington, D.C. Attractions

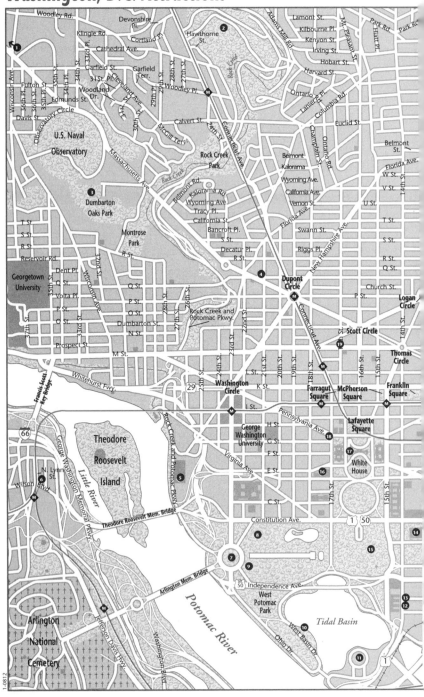

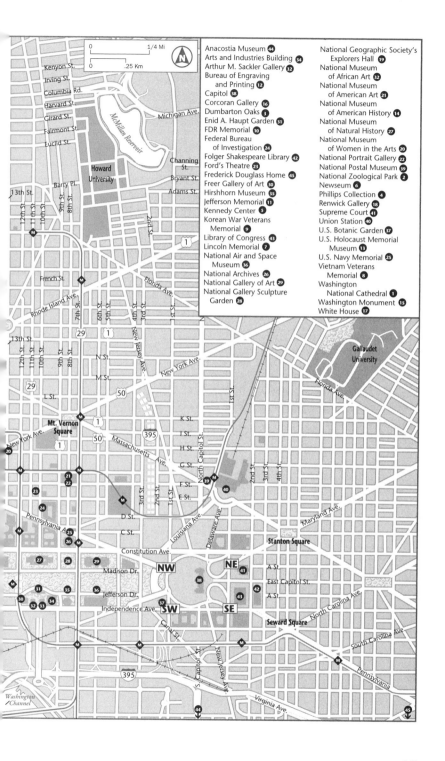

Monument Society. Treasury Building architect Robert Mills's design (originally with a circular colonnaded Greek temple base, which was later discarded for lack of funds) was accepted. The cornerstone was laid on July 4, 1848, and for the next 37 years, watching the monument grow, or not grow, was a local pastime. Declining contributions and the Civil War brought construction to a halt at an awkward 150 feet. The unsightly stump remained until 1876, when President Grant approved federal monies to complete the project. Dedicated in 1885, it was opened to the public in 1888.

VISITING THE WASHINGTON MONUMENT   But you want to know, will the monument be open for tours when you go there? The answer is, I can't tell you for sure, at the time of this writing. The best thing to do is to call the number listed above. Once the exterior work is completed, crews will renovate the observation levels, which will require the monument to be closed for some time. While all of the repair work has a July 4, 2000 end-date, it's a safe bet that it will take longer.

That doesn't mean you shouldn't visit the Washington Monument at all, though. The fabulous Washington Monument Interpretive Center opened at the base of the monument in February 1999 and will remain open until Labor Day 2000. The Discovery Channel donated the center, which uses hands-on exhibits to introduce Washington—the man, the city, and the monument—with a fourth gallery providing a rundown of important events in American history, for example, Vietnam War protests and Martin Luther King's "I Have a Dream" speech, over which the Washington Monument stood as witness. Even if the monument is open for tours, you should stop here. And if the monument is closed for tours, you can come here to operate the touch-screen monitors that simulate the view you get from the top of the Washington Monument, and to learn about the origin and history of each of the 193 commemorative stones.

If you get to the top of the monument while the scaffolding is up, you'll see that it does impede the spectacular view, but you should still be able to pick out the major sites. To the east are the Capitol and Smithsonian Buildings; to the north, the White House; to the west, the Lincoln and Vietnam Memorials, and Arlington National Cemetery beyond; and to the south, the gleaming-white shrine to Thomas Jefferson and the Potomac River. It's a marvelous orientation to the city.

Climbing the 897 steps is verboten, but the large elevator whisks visitors to the top in just 70 seconds. If, however, you're avid to see more of the interior, "Down the Steps" tours are given, subject to staff availability, weekends at 10am and 2pm. For details, call before you go or ask a ranger on duty. On this tour you'll learn more about the building of the monument and get to see the 193 carved stones inserted into the interior walls. The stones are gifts from foreign countries, all 50 states, organizations, and individuals. The most expensive stone was given by the state of Alaska in 1982—it's pure jade and worth millions. There's a stone from Siam (now Thailand), a stone from the Cherokee Nation, and a stone from the Sons of Temperance.

Light snacks are sold at a snack bar on the grounds, where you'll also find a few picnic tables. There's limited, free, 2-hour parking at the 16th Street Oval.

Impressions

May the spirit which animated the great founder of this city descend to future generations.

—John Adams

✪ **Lincoln Memorial.** Directly west of the Mall in Potomac Park (at 23rd St. NW, between Constitution and Independence aves.). ☎ **202/426-6842.** Free admission. Daily 8am–midnight, except Dec 25. Metro: Foggy Bottom, then about a 30-minute walk.

The Lincoln Memorial attracts millions of visitors annually. It's a beautiful and moving testament to a great American, its marble walls seeming to embody not only the spirit and integrity of Lincoln, but all that has ever been good about America.

Like its fellow presidential memorials, this one was a long time in the making. Although it was planned as early as 1867, 2 years after Lincoln's death, it was not until 1912 that Henry Bacon's design was completed, and the memorial itself was dedicated in 1922.

A beautiful neoclassical templelike structure, similar in architectural design to the Parthenon in Greece, the memorial has 36 fluted Doric columns representing the states of the Union at the time of Lincoln's death, plus two at the entrance. On the attic parapet are 48 festoons symbolizing the number of states in 1922, when the monument was erected. Hawaii and Alaska are noted in an inscription on the terrace. To the west, the Arlington Memorial Bridge crossing the Potomac recalls the reunion of North and South. To the east is the beautiful Reflecting Pool, lined with American elms and stretching 2,000 feet toward the Washington Monument and the Capitol beyond.

The memorial chamber, under 60-foot ceilings, has limestone walls inscribed with the Gettysburg Address and Lincoln's Second Inaugural Address. Two 60-foot murals by Jules Guerin on the north and south walls depict, allegorically, Lincoln's principles and achievements. On the south wall, an Angel of Truth freeing a slave is flanked by groups of figures representing Justice and Immortality. The north-wall mural depicts the unity of North and South and is flanked by groups of figures symbolizing Fraternity and Charity. Most powerful, however, is Daniel Chester French's 19-foot-high seated statue of Lincoln in deep contemplation. Its effect is best evoked by the words of Walt Whitman: "He was a mountain in grandeur of soul, he was a sea in deep undervoice of mystic loneliness, he was star in steadfast purity of purpose and service and he abides."

Acting on Lincoln's legacy, on several occasions those who have been oppressed have expressed their plight to America and the world at the steps of his shrine. Most notable was a peaceful demonstration of 200,000 people on August 28, 1963, at which another freedom-loving American, Dr. Martin Luther King, Jr., proclaimed "I have a dream."

An information booth and bookstore are on the premises. Rangers present 20- to 30-minute programs as time permits throughout the day, year-round. Limited free parking is available along Constitution Avenue and south along Ohio Drive.

Jefferson Memorial. South of the Washington Monument on Ohio Dr. (at the south shore of the Tidal Basin). ☎ **202/426-6841.** Free admission. Daily 8am–midnight, except Dec 25. Metro: Smithsonian, with 20- to 30-minute walk, or by Tourmobile.

President John F. Kennedy, at a 1962 dinner honoring 29 Nobel Prize winners, told his guests they were "the most extraordinary collection of talent, of human knowledge, that has ever been gathered together at the White House, with the possible exception of when Thomas Jefferson dined alone." A fascinating and passionate man, Jefferson penned the Declaration of Independence and served in America's government as George Washington's secretary of state, John Adams's vice president, and our third president. He spoke out against slavery, although, like many of his countrymen, he kept slaves himself. (And, as we all know now, Jefferson fathered a child with his slave, Sally Hemings.) In addition, he established the University of Virginia and pursued

> ### ❷ Did You Know?
>
> - Architect Pierre L'Enfant's bill for designing Washington came to $95,000; scoffed at by Congress, he died a pauper.
> - When The Washington Post sponsored a public music competition, John Philip Sousa was asked to compose a march for the awards ceremony; the result was the "Washington Post March," for which Sousa earned the grand sum of $35.
> - The only presidential inauguration ceremony to be held in the White House was that of Franklin D. Roosevelt, in 1941.
> - Ambassadors to Washington in the early days were given "hardship pay" for having to endure the inconveniences of living here.
> - Since 1800, when it was first occupied by John Adams, the White House has seen 1 presidential wedding, 5 first-family weddings, 11 births, 7 presidential funerals, and 2 presidential impeachments.

wide-ranging interests, including architecture, astronomy, anthropology, music, and farming.

The site for the Jefferson Memorial, in relation to the Washington and Lincoln Memorials, was of extraordinary importance. The Capitol, the White House, and the Mall were already located in accordance with L'Enfant's plan, and there was no spot for such a project if the symmetry that guided L'Enfant was to be maintained. So the memorial was built on land reclaimed from the Potomac River, now known as the Tidal Basin. Franklin Delano Roosevelt, who laid the cornerstone in 1939, had all the trees between the Jefferson Memorial and the White House cut down, so he could see the memorial every morning and draw inspiration from it.

It's a beautiful memorial, a columned rotunda in the style of the Pantheon in Rome, whose classic architecture Jefferson himself introduced to this country (he designed his home, Monticello, and the earliest University of Virginia buildings, in Charlottesville, Virginia). On the Tidal Basin side, the sculptural group above the entrance depicts Jefferson with Benjamin Franklin, John Adams, Roger Sherman, and Robert Livingston, all of whom worked on drafting the Declaration of Independence. The domed interior of the memorial contains the 19-foot bronze statue of Jefferson standing on a 6-foot pedestal of black Minnesota granite. The sculpture is the work of Rudolph Evans, who was chosen from more than 100 artists in a nationwide competition. Jefferson is depicted wearing a fur-collared coat given to him by his close friend, the Polish general Tadeusz Kosciuszko. Inscriptions from Jefferson's writing is engraved on the interior walls.

Rangers present 20- to 30-minute programs throughout the day as time permits, year-round. Spring through fall, a refreshment kiosk at the Tourmobile stop offers snacks. A gift shop and bookstore are located on the bottom floor of the memorial. There's free 1-hour parking.

✪ **Franklin Delano Roosevelt Memorial.** In West Potomac Park, about midway between the Lincoln and Jefferson Memorials, on the west shore of the Tidal Basin. ☎ **202/426-6841.** Free admission. Ranger staff on duty 8am–midnight daily, except Dec 25. Free parking along W. Basin and Ohio drs. Metro: Smithsonian, with a 30-minute walk or Tourmobile.

The Franklin Delano Roosevelt Memorial has proven to be the most popular of the presidential memorials since it opened in 1997, attracting twice as many visitors as any

Parking Near the Mall

Don't drive, use the Metro. If you're hell-bent on driving on a weekday, though, set out early to nab one of the Independence or Constitution avenues spots that become legal at 9:30am, when rush hour ends. Arrive about 9:15 and just sit in your car until 9:30am (to avoid getting a ticket), then hop out and stoke the meter. So many people do this, that if you arrive at 9:30 or later, you'll find most of the street parking spots gone.

other. Its popularity has to do as much with the design as the man it honors. This is a 7½-acre, outdoor memorial that lies beneath a wide-open sky. It stretches out, rather than rising up, across the stone-paved floor. Granite walls define the four "galleries," each representing a different term in FDR's presidency, from 1933 to 1945. Architect Lawrence Halprin's design includes waterfalls, sculptures (by Leonard Baskin; John Benson; Neil Estern; Robert Graham; Thomas Hardy; and George Segal), and Roosevelt's own words carved into the stone. These quotes continue to awe and inspire.

I had read much about the memorial before visiting it and nowhere did I read that the memorial is noisy, which it is. Planes on their way to or from nearby Reagan National Airport zoom overhead, and the many displays of cascading water can sound thunderous. All that water tempts both children and adults on warm days (the memorial is unsheltered and unshaded), and, when the memorial first opened, people arrived in bathing suits with towels and splashed around. The park rangers don't allow that anymore, whether out of a sense of propriety or because the structures were not built to withstand so much weight. The rangers do allow you to dip your feet in the various pools, though. A favorite time to visit is at night, when dramatic lighting reveals the waterfalls and statues against the dark parkland.

Conceived in 1946, the FDR Memorial has been in the works for 50 years. Part of the delay in its construction can be attributed to the president himself. FDR had told his friend, Supreme Court Justice Felix Frankfurter, "If they are to put up any memorial to me, I should like it to be placed in the center of that green plot in front of the Archives building. I should like it to consist of a block about the size of this," he said, as he pointed to his desk. In fact, such a plaque sits in front of the National Archives Building. Friends and relatives struggled to honor Roosevelt's request to leave it at that, but Congress and national sentiment overrode them.

On May 2, 1997, President Clinton officiated at the memorial dedication ceremony. The memorial lies directly across the Tidal Basin from the Washington Monument, on a sight line between the Jefferson and Lincoln Memorials, in a spot that the McMillan Commission reserved in 1901 for a presidential memorial, not knowing whose it would be. As with other presidential memorials, this one opened to some controversy. Advocates for people with disabilities were incensed that the memorial sculptures did not show the president in a wheelchair, which he used from the age of 39 after he contracted polio. President Clinton asked Congress to allocate funding for an additional statue portraying a wheelchair-bound FDR; in the works (if not in place by the time you read this) is a bronze relief of FDR in a wheelchair, placed at the front of the memorial. Step inside the gift shop to view a replica of Roosevelt's wheelchair, as well as one of the rare photographs of the president sitting in a wheelchair. The memorial is probably the most accessible tourist attraction in the city; as at most of the National Park Service locations, wheelchairs are available for free use on-site.

If you don't see a posting of tour times, look for a ranger and request a tour; the rangers are happy to oblige.

3 The Smithsonian Museums

The Smithsonian's collection of nearly 141 million objects encompasses the entire world and its history, its peoples and animals (past and present), and our attempts to probe into the future. The sprawling institution comprises 14 museums (9 of them on the Mall), as well as the National Zoological Park in Washington, D.C., plus two additional museums in New York City.

It all began with a $500,000 bequest from James Smithson, an English scientist who had never visited this country. When he died in 1829, he willed his entire fortune to his nephew, stipulating that should the nephew die without heirs (which he did in 1835), the estate should go to the United States to found "at Washington . . . an establishment for the increase and diffusion of knowledge. . . ." In 1846, Congress created a corporate entity to carry out Smithson's will, and the federal government agreed to pay 6% interest on the bequeathed funds in perpetuity. Since then, other munificent private donations have swelled Smithson's original legacy many times over. Major gallery and museum construction through the years stands as testament to thoughtful donors.

In 1987, the Sackler Gallery (Asian and Near Eastern art) and the National Museum of African Art were added to the Smithsonian's Mall attractions. The National Postal Museum opened in 1993. And future plans call for moving the National Museum of the American Indian (currently in New York) here in 2001.

To find out information about any of the Smithsonian museums, you call the same number: ☎ **202/357-2700** or TTY 202/357-1729. The information specialists who answer are very professional and always helpful. As mentioned earlier, you can also access the Smithsonian Institution Web site at www.si.edu, which will get you to the individual home pages for each of the museums.

Smithsonian Information Center (the "Castle"). 1000 Jefferson Dr. SW. ☎ **202/ 357-2700** or TTY 202/357-1729. www.si.edu. E-mail: info@info.si.edu. Daily 9am–5:30pm, info desk 9am–4pm. Closed Dec 25. Metro: Smithsonian.

Make your first stop the impressively high-tech and very comprehensive Smithsonian Information Center, located in the institution's original Norman-style red sandstone building, popularly known as the "Castle."

The main information area here is the Great Hall, where a 20-minute video overview of the institution runs throughout the day in two theaters. There are two large schematic models of the Mall (as well as a third in Braille), and two large electronic maps of Washington allow visitors to locate nearly 100 popular attractions and Metro and Tourmobile stops. Interactive videos, some at children's heights, offer extensive information about the Smithsonian and other capital attractions and transportation (the menus seem infinite).

The entire facility is accessible to persons with disabilities, and information is available in a number of foreign languages. Daily Smithsonian events appear on monitors; in addition, the information desk's volunteer staff can answer questions and help you plan a Smithsonian sightseeing itinerary. Most of the museums are within easy walking distance of the facility. While you're here, notice the charming vestibule, which has

Information, Please

If you want to know what's happening at any of the Smithsonian museums, just get on the phone; **Dial-a-Museum** (☎ **202/357-2020,** or 202/633-9126 for Spanish), a recorded information line, lists daily activities and special events. For other information, call ☎ **202/357-2700.**

been restored to its turn-of-the-century appearance. It was originally designed to display exhibits at a child's eye level. The gold-trimmed ceiling is decorated to represent a grape arbor with brightly plumed birds and blue sky peeking through the trellis. The Castle Commons Room is the location of a Sunday brunch, 11am to 3pm, open to the public. The price is $18.95 for adults, $8.95 for children (ages 6 to 10) and you must make reservations by calling ☎ **202/357-2957.** The Commons Room is also open to the public on Saturday, 11am to 2:30pm, for lunch.

Anacostia Museum. 1901 Fort Place SE (off Martin Luther King Jr. Ave.). ☎ **202/ 357-2700.** www.si.edu/anacostia. Free admission. Daily 10am–5pm. Closed Dec 25. Metro: Anacostia, then take a W1 or W2 bus directly to the museum.

This unique Smithsonian establishment was created in 1967 as a neighborhood museum. Expanding its horizons over the years, the museum today is devoted to the identification, documentation, protection, and interpretation of the African-American experience, focusing on Washington, D.C., and the Upper South. The permanent collection includes about 7,000 items, ranging from videotapes of African-American church services to art, sheet music, historic documents, textiles, glassware, and anthropological objects. In addition, the Anacostia produces a number of shows each year and offers a comprehensive schedule of free educational programs and activities in conjunction with exhibit themes. To complement an exhibition called "The African-American Presence in American Quilts," the museum featured a video about artist/quilt maker Faith Ringgold, quilting workshops for adults and children, talks by local quilting societies, and storytelling involving quilts.

Call for an events calendar (which always includes children's activities) or pick one up when you visit.

Arthur M. Sackler Gallery. 1050 Independence Ave. SW. ☎ **202/357-2700.** www. si.edu/asia. Free admission. Daily 10am–5:30pm; in summer, museum stays open Thursdays until 8pm, but call to confirm. Closed Dec 25. Metro: Smithsonian.

Opened in 1987, the Sackler, a national museum of Asian art, presents traveling exhibitions from major cultural institutions in Asia, Europe, and the United States. In the recent past, these have focused on such wide-ranging areas as 15th-century Persian art and culture; contemporary Japanese woodblock prints and ceramics; photographs of Asia; and art highlighting personal devotion in India. Art from the permanent collection supplements the traveling shows: It includes Khmer ceramics; ancient Chinese jades, bronzes, paintings, and lacquerware; 20th-century Japanese ceramics and works on paper; ancient Near Eastern works in silver, gold, bronze, and clay; and stone and bronze sculptures from South and Southeast Asia. Since the museum's opening, 11th-to 19th-century Persian and Indian paintings, manuscripts, calligraphies, miniatures, and bookbindings from the collection of Henri Vever have enhanced Sackler's original gift.

The Sackler is part of a museum complex that also houses the National Museum of African Art. And it shares its staff and research facilities with the adjacent Freer Gallery, to which it is connected via an underground exhibition space.

The Sackler offers museum programs (including many wonderful experiences for children and families); free highlight tours given daily (highly recommended); films; events; and temporary exhibits.

Arts & Industries Building. 900 Jefferson Dr. SW (on the south side of the Mall). ☎ **202/ 357-2700.** www.si.edu/ai. Free admission. Daily 10am–5:30pm. Closed Dec 25. Metro: Smithsonian.

Am I the only person who confuses this building with the one known as "the Castle"? (See the Smithsonian Information Center, above.) The Arts & Industries Building lies to the left of said Castle, when you're approaching Mall-side, to the right from the Independence Avenue side. Completed in 1881 as the first U.S. National Museum, this redbrick and sandstone structure was the scene of President Garfield's Inaugural Ball. From 1976 through the mid-1990s, it housed exhibits from the 1876 United States International Exposition in Philadelphia—a celebration of America's centennial that featured the latest advances in technology. Some of these Victorian tools, products, art, and other objects are on permanent display, along with rotating exhibits, such as "Speak to My Heart: Communities of Faith and Contemporary African American Life," on view through February 28, 2001.

Singers, dancers, puppeteers, and mimes perform in the **Discovery Theater** (open all year except August, with performances weekdays and on selected Saturdays). Call ☎ **202/357-1500** for show times and ticket information; admission of about $5 is charged. Don't miss the charming Victorian-motif shop on the first floor. Weather permitting, a 19th-century carousel operates across the street, on the Mall.

✪ **Freer Gallery of Art.** On the south side of the Mall (at Jefferson Dr. and 12th St. SW). ☎ **202/357-2700.** www.si.edu/asia. Free admission. Daily 10am–5:30pm; in summer, hours are extended Thurs to 8pm, but call to confirm. Closed Dec 25. Metro: Smithsonian (Mall or Independence Ave. exit).

Charles Lang Freer, a collector of Asian art and American art from the 19th and early 20th centuries, gave the nation 9,000 of these works for the Freer Gallery's opening in 1923. Freer's original interest was, in fact, American art, but his good friend James McNeill Whistler encouraged him to collect Asian works as well. Eventually the latter became predominant. Freer's gift included funds to construct a museum and an endowment to add objects of the highest quality to the Asian collection only, which now numbers more than 28,000 objects. It includes Chinese and Japanese sculpture, lacquer, metalwork, and ceramics; early Christian illuminated manuscripts; Iranian manuscripts, metalwork, and miniatures; ancient Near Eastern metalware; and South Asian sculpture and paintings.

Among the American works are more than 1,200 pieces (the world's largest collection) by Whistler, including the famous **Peacock Room.** Originally a dining room designed by an architect named Thomas Jeckyll for the London mansion of F. R. Leyland, the Peacock Room displayed a Whistler painting called *The Princess from the Land of Porcelain.* But after his painting was installed, Whistler was dissatisfied with the room as a setting for his work. When Leyland was away from home, Whistler painted over the very expensive leather interior, and embellished it with paintings of golden peacock feathers. Not surprisingly, a rift ensued between Whistler and Leyland. After Leyland's death, Freer purchased the room, painting and all, and had it shipped to his home in Detroit. It is now permanently installed here. Other American painters represented in the collections are Thomas Wilmer Dewing; Dwight William Tryon; Abbott Henderson Thayer; John Singer Sargent; and Childe Hassam.

Housed in a recently renovated granite-and-marble building that evokes the Italian Renaissance, the pristine Freer has lovely skylit galleries. The main exhibit floor centers on an open-roof garden court. An underground exhibit space connects the Freer to the neighboring Sackler Gallery, and both museums share the **Meyer Auditorium,** which is used for free chamber music concerts, dance performances, Asian feature

Freeze Frame

About 90% of the American works in the Freer are in their original frames, many of them designed by architect Stanford White or painter James McNeil Whistler.

films, and other programs. Inquire about these, as well as children's activities and free tours given daily, at the information desk.

Hirshhorn Museum & Sculpture Garden. On the south side of the Mall (at Independence Ave. and 7th St. SW). ☎ **202/357-2700.** www.si.edu/hirshhorn. Free admission. Daily 10am–5:30pm; in summer, hours are extended on Thurs to 8pm, but call to confirm. Sculpture Garden 7:30am–dusk. Closed Dec 25. Metro: L'Enfant Plaza (Smithsonian Museums/Maryland Ave. exit).

This museum of modern and contemporary art is named after Latvian-born Joseph H. Hirshhorn, who, in 1966, donated his vast art collection—more than 4,000 drawings and paintings and some 2,000 pieces of sculpture—to the United States "as a small repayment for what this nation has done for me and others like me who arrived here as immigrants." At his death in 1981, Hirshhorn bequeathed an additional 5,500 art-works to the museum, and numerous other donors have since greatly expanded his legacy.

Constructed 14 feet aboveground on sculptured supports, the museum's contemporary cylindrical concrete-and-granite building shelters a verdant plaza courtyard where sculpture is displayed. The light and airy interior follows a simple circular route that makes it easy to see every exhibit without getting lost in a honeycomb of galleries. Natural light from floor-to-ceiling windows makes the inner galleries the perfect venue for viewing sculpture, second only, perhaps, to the beautiful tree-shaded sunken Sculpture Garden across the street (don't miss it). Paintings and drawings are installed in the outer galleries, along with intermittent sculpture groupings.

A rotating show of about 600 pieces is on view at all times. The collection features just about every well-known 20th-century artist and touches on most of the major trends in Western art since the late 19th century, with particular emphasis on our contemporary period. Among the best-known pieces are Rodin's *The Burghers of Calais* (in the Sculpture Garden); Hopper's *First Row Orchestra;* de Kooning's *Two Women in the Country;* and Warhol's *Marilyn Monroe's Lips.*

Pick up a free calendar when you enter to find out about free films, lectures, concerts, and temporary exhibits. An outdoor cafe is open during the summer. Free tours of the collection are given daily; call about these, and about tours of the Sculpture Garden.

✪ **National Air & Space Museum.** On the south side of the Mall (between 4th and 7th sts. SW), with entrances on Jefferson Dr. or Independence Ave. ☎ **202/357-2700** or 202/357-1686 for IMAX ticket information. www.nasm.si.edu. Free admission. Daily 10am–5:30pm. In summer, hours are extended daily 9:30am–6pm, but call to confirm. Free 1½-hour highlight tours daily at 10:15am and 1pm. Closed Dec 25. Metro: L'Enfant Plaza (Smithsonian Museums/Maryland Ave. exit).

The National Air & Space Museum is the most visited museum in the world. The museum chronicles the story of our mastery of flight, from Kitty Hawk to outer space, in 23 galleries filled with exciting exhibits. Plan to devote at least three or four hours to exploring these exhibits and, especially during the tourist season and on holidays, arrive before 10am to make a rush for the film-ticket line when the doors open. The not-to-be-missed IMAX films shown in the Samuel P. Langley Theater here, on a screen five stories high and seven stories wide, are immensely popular, and tickets sell out quickly (although the first show seldom sells out). You can purchase tickets up to two weeks in advance; tickets are available only at the Langley Theater box office on the first floor. Five or more films play each day, most with aeronautical or space-exploration themes: *To Fly, Cosmic Voyage, Wildfire: Feel the Heat,* and *Everest,* are four. Tickets cost $5.50 for adults, $4.25 for ages 2 to 21 and seniors 55 and older; they're free for children under 2. You can also see IMAX films most evenings after closing (call for details and ticket prices, which are higher than daytime prices). At the same time, purchase tickets for a show at the Albert Einstein Planetarium.

In between shows, you can view the exhibits; audio tours are also available for rental. Interactive computers and slide and video shows enhance the exhibits throughout.

Highlights of the first floor include famous airplanes (such as the *Spirit of St. Louis*) and spacecraft (the *Apollo 11* Command Module); the world's only touchable moon rock; numerous exhibits on the history of aviation and air transportation; galleries in which you can design your own jet plane and study astronomy; and rockets, lunar-exploration vehicles, manned spacecraft, and guided missiles. (See box, this chapter, about attractions that highlight women's achievements.)

"How Things Fly," a gallery that opened in 1996 to celebrate the museum's 20th anniversary, includes wind and smoke tunnels, a boardable Cessna 150 airplane, and dozens of interactive exhibits that demonstrate principles of flight, aerodynamics, and propulsion. All the aircraft, by the way, are originals.

Kids love the "walk-through" **Skylab orbital workshop** on the second floor. Other galleries here highlight the solar system; U.S. manned space flights; sea-air operations; aviation during both world wars; and artists' perceptions of flight. An important exhibit is **"Beyond the Limits: Flight Enters the Computer Age,"** illustrating the primary applications of computer technology to aerospace.

An attractive cafeteria and a restaurant, Flight Line and the Wright Place, respectively, are on the premises.

National Museum of African Art. 950 Independence Ave. SW. ☎ **202/357-4600.** www.si.edu/nmafa. Free admission. Daily 10am–5:30pm; in summer, hours are extended Thurs to 8pm, but call to confirm. Closed Dec 25. Metro: Smithsonian.

Founded in 1964, and part of the Smithsonian since 1979, the National Museum of African Art moved to the Mall in 1987 to share a subterranean space with the Sackler Gallery (see above) and the Ripley Center. Its aboveground domed pavilions reflect the arch motif of the neighboring Freer.

The museum collects and exhibits ancient and contemporary art from the entire African continent, but its permanent collection of more than 7,000 objects (shown in rotating exhibits) highlights the traditional arts of the vast sub-Saharan region. Most of the collection dates from the 19th and 20th centuries. Also among the museum's holdings are the **Eliot Elisofon Photographic Archives,** comprising 300,000 photographic prints and transparencies and 120,000 feet of film on African arts and culture. Permanent exhibits include **"The Ancient West African City of Benin, A.D. 1300–1897"**; **"The Ancient Nubian City of Kerma, 2500–1500 B.C."** (ceramics, jewelry, and ivory animals); **"The Art of the Personal Object"** (everyday items such as chairs, headrests, snuffboxes, bowls, and baskets); and **"Images of Power and Identity."**

Inquire at the desk about special exhibits, workshops (including excellent children's programs), storytelling, lectures, docent-led tours, films, and demonstrations. A comprehensive events schedule provides a unique opportunity to learn about the diverse cultures and visual traditions of Africa.

National Museum of American Art. 8th and G sts. NW. ☎ **202/357-2700.** www.nmaa. si.edu. Free admission. Daily 10am–5:30pm. Closed Dec 25. Metro: Gallery Place–Chinatown.

This museum and the adjoining National Portrait Gallery will be closed for a major renovation beginning January 2000 and continuing for at least 2 years. Check its Web site for updates about renovation progress. What you're missing: the National Museum of American Art's more than 37,500 works representing 2 centuries of the nation's national art history. It is the largest collection of American art in the world.

A Liberal & Enlightened Donor

Wealthy English scientist **James Smithson** (1765–1829), the illegitimate son of the duke of Northumberland, never explained why he willed his vast fortune to the United States, a country he had never visited. Speculation is that he felt a new nation, lacking established cultural institutions, stood in greatest need of his bequest. Smithson died in Genoa, Italy, in 1829. Congress accepted his gift in 1836; two years later, a shipment of 105 bags of gold sovereigns (about half a million dollars' worth—a considerable sum in the 19th century) arrived at the U.S. Mint in Philadelphia. For the next 8 years, Congress debated the best possible use for these funds. Finally, in 1846, James Polk signed an act into law establishing the Smithsonian Institution and providing "for the faithful execution of said trust, according to the will of the liberal and enlightened donor." It authorized a board to receive "all objects of art and of foreign and curious research, and all objects of natural history, plants, and geological and mineralogical specimens . . . for research and museum purposes."

In addition to the original Smithson bequest—which has been augmented by many subsequent endowments—the Smithsonian is also supported by annual congressional appropriations. Today it comprises a complex of 16 museums in Washington, D.C., and New York, plus the National Zoological Park. Its holdings, in every area of human interest, range from a 3.5-billion-year-old fossil to part of a 1902 Horn and Hardart Automat. Thousands of scientific expeditions sponsored by the Smithsonian have pushed into remote frontiers in the deserts, mountains, polar regions, and jungles.

✪ **National Museum of American History.** On the north side of the Mall (between 12th and 14th sts. NW), with entrances on Constitution Ave. and Madison Dr. ☎ **202/357-2700.** www.si.edu/nmah. Free admission. Daily 10am–5:30pm. In summer, hours are extended daily to 7:30pm, but call to confirm. Closed Dec 25. Metro: Smithsonian or Federal Triangle.

The National Museum of American History deals with "everyday life in the American past" and the external forces that have helped to shape our national character. Its massive contents range from General George Washington's Revolutionary War tent to Archie Bunker's chair.

Exhibits on the **first floor** (enter on Constitution Avenue) explore the development of farm machinery, power machinery, transportation, timekeeping, phonographs, and typewriters. The **Palm Court** on this level includes the interior of Georgetown's Stohlman's Confectionery Shop as it appeared around 1900 and part of an actual 1902 Horn and Hardart Automat, where you can stop and have an ice cream. You can have your mail stamped "Smithsonian Station" at a post office that had been located in Headsville, West Virginia, from 1861 to 1971, when it was brought, lock, stock, and barrel, to the museum. An important first-floor exhibit, **"A Material World,"** deals with the changing composition of artifacts—from predominantly natural materials such as wood and stone to the vast range of synthetics we have today. **"Information Age"** considers the ways information technology has changed society during the past 150 years. And **"Science in American Life"** analyzes the impact of science on society from the 1870s to the present.

If you enter from the Mall, you'll find yourself on the second floor. Until late 1998, you would have seen hanging in an alcove here, the huge, original Star-Spangled Banner, 30 by 42 feet, that inspired Francis Scott Key to write the U.S. national anthem in 1814. The flag is undergoing restoration work and will return to its niche by late 2001; in the meantime, you should be able to watch the conservators at work behind a glass wall on this floor.

The museum holds many other major exhibits. **"After the Revolution"** focuses on the everyday activities of ordinary 18th-century Americans. **"Field to Factory"** tells the story of African-American migration, south to north, between 1915 and 1940. The **J Foucault Pendulum** is a copy of the original model that was exhibited in Paris in 1851 with the accompanying teaser, "You are invited to witness the earth revolve." (The pendulum vibrates in a single plane, tracing in sand what seems to be a scattered series of lines, but what is actually the proof of the Earth's rotation.) Don't miss it!

One of the most popular exhibits on the second floor is **"First Ladies: Political Role and Public Image,"** which displays the first ladies' gowns and tells you a bit about each of these women. Infinitely more interesting, I think, is the neighboring exhibit, **"From Parlor to Politics: Women and Reform in America, 1890–1925,"** which chronicles the changing roles of women as they've moved from domestic to political and professional pursuits. (See box, this chapter, about attractions that highlight women's achievements.)

Head for the third floor if you want less of a crowd. Here are a vast collection of ship models, uniforms, weapons, and other military artifacts; major exhibits focus on the experiences of GIs in World War II (and the postwar world) as well as the wartime internment of Japanese Americans. Other areas include Money and Medals, Textiles, Printing and Graphic Arts, and Ceramics. Here, too, is the first American flag to be called Old Glory (1824).

Inquire at the information desk about highlight tours, films, lectures, and concerts, and hands-on activities for children and adults. The gift shop is vast—it's the largest of the Smithsonian shops.

✪ **National Museum of Natural History.** On the north side of the Mall (at 10th St. and Constitution Ave. NW), with entrances on Madison Dr. and Constitution Ave. ☎ **202/357-2700** or 202/633-7400 for information about IMAX films. www.mnh.si.edu. Free admission. Daily 10am–5:30pm. In summer, hours are extended to 7:30pm daily, but call to confirm. Closed Dec 25. Free highlight tours Mon–Thurs 10:30am and 1:30pm, Fri 10:30am. Metro: Smithsonian or Federal Triangle.

Children refer to this Smithsonian showcase as the dinosaur museum (there's a great dinosaur hall), or sometimes the elephant museum (a huge African bush elephant is the first amazing thing you see if you enter the museum from the Mall). Whatever you call it, the National Museum of Natural History is the largest of its kind in the world, and one of the most visited museums in Washington. It contains more than 120 million artifacts and specimens, everything from Ice Age mammoths to the legendary Hope Diamond.

A **Discovery Room,** filled with creative hands-on exhibits "for children of all ages," is on the first floor. Call ahead or inquire at the information desk about hours.

On the Mall Level, off the Rotunda, is the **fossil collection,** which traces evolution back billions of years and includes a 3.5-billion-year-old stromatolite (blue-green algae clump) fossil—one of the earliest signs of life on Earth—and a 70-million-year-old dinosaur egg. **"Life in the Ancient Seas"** features a 100-foot-long mural depicting primitive whales, a life-size walk-around diorama of a 230-million-year-old coral reef, and more than 2,000 fossils that chronicle the evolution of marine life. The **Dinosaur Hall** displays giant skeletons of creatures that dominated the Earth for 140 million years before their extinction about 65 million years ago. Suspended from the ceiling over Dinosaur Hall are replicas of ancient birds, including a life-size model of the pterosaur, which had a 40-foot wingspan. Also residing above this hall is the jaw of an ancient shark—the *Carcharodon megalodon,* which lived in our oceans 5 million years ago. A monstrous 40-foot-long predator, its teeth were 5 to 6 inches long, and it could have consumed a Volkswagen "bug" in one gulp! Here, too, you'll find a spectacular living coral reef in a 3,000-gallon tank, a second 1,800-gallon tank housing a subarctic sea environment typical of the Maine coast, and a giant squid exhibit focusing on the world's largest invertebrates.

Upstairs is the popular **O. Orkin Insect Zoo,** where kids will enjoy looking at tarantulas, centipedes, and the like, and crawling through a model of an African termite mound. The **Ocean Planet** exhibit gives a video tour of what lies beneath the ocean surface, and teaches you about ocean conservation. The **Hope Diamond** is also on display on the second floor, where a renovation of the Gems and Minerals Hall has ended after years of work. The new hall, the **Janet Annenberg Hooker Hall of Geology, Gems, and Minerals,** includes all you want to know about earth science, from volcanology to the importance of mining in our daily lives. Interactive computers, animated graphics, and a multimedia presentation of the "big picture" story of the Earth are some of the things that have brought the exhibit and museum up to date. Additional exhibits include **"South America: Continent and Culture,"** with objects from the Inca civilization, among others, and **"Origin of Western Culture,"** from about 10,000 years ago to A.D. 500.

New as of May 1999 are a Discovery Center, funded by the Discovery Channel, and featuring an IMAX theater with a six-story high screen for 2-D and 3-D movies (*Africa's Elephant Kingdom* and *Galapagos* were the first two movies to be shown); a six-story Atrium Cafe offering a food court; and expanded museum shops. The theater box office is located on the first floor of the museum; purchase tickets as early as possible, or at least 30 minutes before the screening. The box office is open daily from 9:45 through the last show. Films are shown continuously throughout the day. Ticket prices are $5.50 for adults and $4.50 for children (2 to 17) and seniors (adults over 55).

National Portrait Gallery. 8th and F sts. NW. ☎ **202/357-2700.** www.npg.si.edu. Free admission. Daily 10am–5:30pm. Closed Dec 25. Metro: Gallery Place–Chinatown.

Beginning January 2000 and continuing for at least two years, this museum and the National Museum of American Art will be closed for renovations. Check the museum Web site to keep abreast of renovation progress. The gallery enshrines those who have made "significant contributions to the history, development, and culture of the United States" in paintings, sculpture, photography, and other forms of portraiture.

✪ **National Postal Museum.** 2 Massachusetts Ave. NE (at 1st St.). ☎ **202/357-2700.** www.si.edu/organize/museums/postal. Free admission. Daily 10am–5:30pm. Closed Dec 25. Metro: Union Station.

Bring your address book, and you can send postcards to the folks back home, through an interactive exhibit that issues a cool postcard and stamps it. That's just one feature that makes the museum visitor-friendly. Many of its exhibits involve easy-to-understand activities, like postal-themed video games. Despite our increasing use of e-mail, fax machines, and cellular phones for communicating, the act of writing and receiving letters still holds a special appeal.

The museum documents America's postal history from 1673 (about 170 years before the advent of stamps, envelopes, and mailboxes) to the present. (*Fun fact:* Did you know that a dog sled was used to carry mail in Alaska until 1963 when it was replaced by an airplane?) In the central gallery, titled **"Moving the Mail,"** three planes that carried mail in the early decades of the 20th century are suspended from a 90-foot atrium ceiling. Here, too, are a railway mail car, an 1851 mail/passenger coach, a Ford Model A mail truck, and a replica of an airmail beacon tower. In **"Binding the**

Nation," historic correspondence illustrates how mail kept families together in the developing nation. Several exhibits deal with the famed Pony Express, a service that lasted less than two years but was romanticized to legendary proportions by Buffalo Bill and others. In the Civil War section you'll learn about Henry "Box" Brown, a slave who had himself "mailed" from Richmond to a Pennsylvania abolitionist in 1856. **"The Art of Cards and Letters"** gallery displays rotating exhibits of personal (sometimes wrenching, always interesting) correspondence taken from different periods in history, as well as greeting cards and postcards. And an 800-square-foot gallery called **"Artistic License: The Duck Stamp Story,"** focuses on federal duck stamps (first issued in 1934 to license waterfowl hunters), with displays on the hobby of duck hunting and the ecology of American water birds. In addition, the museum houses a vast research library for philatelic researchers and scholars, a stamp store, and a museum shop. Inquire about free walk-in tours at the information desk.

Opened in 1993, this most recent addition to the Smithsonian complex occupies the lower level of the palatial beaux arts quarters of the City Post Office Building, which was designed by architect Daniel Burnham and is situated next to Union Station. This museum is, somewhat surprisingly, a hit for everyone in the family.

National Zoological Park. Adjacent to Rock Creek Park, main entrance in the 3000 block of Connecticut Avenue NW. ☎ **202/673-4800** (recording) or 202/673-4717. www.si. edu/natzoo. Free admission. Daily May to mid-Sept (weather permitting): grounds 6am–8pm, animal buildings 10am–6pm. Daily mid-Sept to May: grounds 6am–6pm, animal buildings 10am–4:30pm. Closed Dec 25. Metro: Woodley Park–Zoo or Cleveland Park.

Established in 1889, the National Zoo is home to several thousand animals of some 500 species, many of them rare and/or endangered. A leader in the care, breeding, and exhibition of animals, it occupies 163 beautifully landscaped and wooded acres and is one of the country's most delightful zoos. Among the animals you'll see are cheetahs, zebras, camels, elephants, Hsing-Hsing (the rare giant panda from China), tapirs, antelopes, brown pelicans and other waterfowl, kangaroos, hippos, rhinos, giraffes, apes, orangutans, reptiles, invertebrates, lions, tigers, spectacled bears, beavers, hummingbirds and monkeys (in Amazonia, a rain forest habitat), seals, and sea lions.

Pointers: Consider calling ahead (allow three weeks and call during weekday business hours) for a **free 90-minute highlights tour** (☎ **202/673-4954**). Not recommended for kids under 4. The tour guide will tell you how to look at the animals; where, why, and when to look; and fill your visit with lots of surprises. Enter the zoo at the Connecticut Avenue entrance; you will be right by the Education Building, where you can pick up a map and find out about feeding times and any special activities. Note that from this main entrance, you're headed downhill; the return uphill walk can prove trying if you have young children and/or it's a hot day. As noted below, the zoo does rent strollers and offers plenty of refreshment stands.

The zoo animals live in large, open enclosures—simulations of their natural habitats—along two easy-to-follow numbered paths, **Olmsted Walk** and the **Valley Trail.** You can't get lost, and you won't unintentionally miss anything.

You can hang out for an hour in **Amazonia** peering up into the trees and you still won't spy the sloth—do yourself a favor and ask the attendant where it is. However, if your whole purpose is to see the **rare giant panda,** Hsing-Hsing, go at feeding time, 11am or 3pm, because otherwise the moody panda seems to hide just to spite you. If Hsing-Hsing isn't cooperating, look next door for the red panda, not as rare but pretty cute.

Zoo facilities include stroller-rental stations; a number of gift shops; a bookstore; and several paid-parking lots. The lots fill up quickly, especially on weekends, so arrive early or take the Metro. Snack bars and ice-cream kiosks are scattered throughout the park.

Renwick Gallery of the National Museum of American Art. Pennsylvania Ave. and 17th St. NW. ☎ **202/357-2700.** www.nmaa.si.edu. Free admission. Daily 10am–5:30pm. Closed Dec 25. Metro: Farragut West or Farragut North.

A department of the National Museum of American Art (though nowhere near it), the Renwick, a showcase for American creativity in crafts, is housed in a historic mid-1800s landmark building of the French Second Empire style. The original home of the Corcoran Gallery, it was saved from demolition by First Lady Jacqueline Kennedy in 1963, when she recommended that it be renovated as part of the Lafayette Square restoration. In 1965, it became part of the Smithsonian and was renamed for its architect, James W. Renwick, who also designed the Smithsonian Castle. Although the setting—especially the magnificent Victorian Grand Salon with its wainscoted plum walls and 38-foot skylight ceiling—evokes another era, the museum's contents are mostly contemporary. The rich and diverse displays boast changing crafts exhibits and contemporary works from the museum's permanent collection. Typical exhibits range from **"Uncommon Beauty: The Legacy of African-American Craft Art"** to **"Calico and Chintz: Antique Quilts from the Patricia Smith Collection."** The above-mentioned **Grand Salon** on the second floor, furnished in opulent 19th-century style, displays paintings by 18th- and 19th-century artists. (The great thing about this room, besides its fine art and grand design, is its cushiony, velvety banquettes, perfect resting stops for the weary sightseer.)

The Renwick offers a comprehensive schedule of crafts demonstrations, lectures, and films. Inquire at the information desk. And check out the museum shop near the entrance for books on crafts, design, and decorative arts, as well as craft items, many of them for children. *Note:* It is the main branch of the National Museum of American Art that is closed for renovation, not this offshoot.

4 Elsewhere on the Mall

National Archives. Constitution Ave. NW (between 7th and 9th sts.; enter via Constitution Ave.). ☎ **202/501-5000** for information on exhibits and films or 202/501-5400 for research information. www.nara.gov. Free admission. Exhibition Hall Apr–Aug, daily 10am–9pm; Sept–Mar, daily 10am–5:30pm. Free tours weekdays 10:15am and 1:15pm by appointment only; call (way ahead) ☎ **202/501-5205.** Call for research hours. Closed Dec 25. Metro: Archives/Navy Memorial.

Keeper of America's documentary heritage, the National Archives display our most cherished treasures in appropriately awe-inspiring surroundings. Housed in the **Rotunda of the Exhibition Hall** are the nation's three charter documents—the Declaration of Independence, the Constitution of the United States, and the Bill of Rights, as well as the 1297 version of the Magna Carta—each on permanent display to the public.

High above and flanking the documents are two larger-than-life murals painted by Barry Faulkner. One, entitled *The Declaration of Independence,* shows Thomas Jefferson presenting a draft of the Declaration to John Hancock, the presiding officer of the Continental Congress; the other, entitled *The Constitution,* shows James Madison submitting the Constitution to George Washington and the Constitutional Convention. In the display cases on either side of the Declaration of Independence are exhibits that rotate over a 3-year period, for instance, **"American Originals,"** which features 26 compelling American historical documents ranging from George Washington's Revolutionary War expense account to the Louisiana Purchase Treaty signed by Napoléon. There are also temporary exhibits in the **Circular Gallery.**

The Archives serve as much more than a museum of cherished documents. Famous as a center for genealogical research—Alex Haley began his work on *Roots* here—it is sometimes called "the nation's memory." This federal institution is charged with sifting through the accumulated papers of a nation's official life—billions of pieces a year—and determining what to save and what to destroy. The Archives' vast accumulation of census figures, military records, naturalization papers, immigrant passenger lists, federal documents, passport applications, ship manifests, maps, charts, photographs, and motion picture film (and that's not the half of it) spans 2 centuries. And it's all available for the perusal of anyone age 16 or over (call for details). If you're casually thinking about tracing your roots, stop by Room 400 where a staff member can advise you about the time and effort that will be involved, and, if you decide to pursue it, exactly how to proceed.

Even if you have no research project in mind, the National Archives merit a visit. The neoclassical building, designed by John Russell Pope in the 1930s (also architect of the National Gallery of Art and the Jefferson Memorial), is an impressive example of the beaux arts style. Seventy-two columns create a Corinthian colonnade on each of the four facades. Great bronze doors herald the Constitution Avenue entrance, and allegorical sculpture centered on *The Recorder of the Archives* adorns the pediment. On either side of the steps are male and female figures symbolizing guardianship and heritage, respectively. *Guardians of the Portals* at the Pennsylvania Avenue entrance represent the past and the future, and the theme of the pediment is destiny.

Pick up a schedule of events (lectures, films, genealogy workshops) when you visit.

✪ **National Gallery of Art.** Fourth St. and Constitution Ave. NW, on the north side of the Mall (between 3rd and 7th sts. NW). ☎ **202/737-4215.** www.nga.gov. Free admission. Mon–Sat 10am–5pm, Sun 11am–6pm. Closed Jan 1 and Dec 25. Metro: Archives, Judiciary Square, or Smithsonian.

Most people don't realize it, but the National Gallery of Art is not part of the Smithsonian complex.

Housing one of the world's foremost collections of Western painting, sculpture, and graphic arts from the Middle Ages through the 20th century, the National Gallery has a dual personality. The original West Building, designed by John Russell Pope (architect of the Jefferson Memorial and the National Archives), is a neoclassic marble masterpiece with a domed rotunda over a colonnaded fountain and high-ceilinged corridors leading to delightful garden courts. It was a gift to the nation from Andrew W. Mellon, who also contributed the nucleus of the collection, including 21 masterpieces from the Hermitage, two Raphaels among them. The ultramodern East Building, designed by I. M. Pei and opened in 1978, is composed of two adjoining triangles with glass walls and lofty tetrahedron skylights. The pink Tennessee marble from which both buildings were constructed was taken from the same quarry; it forms an architectural link between the two structures.

The West Building: On the main floor of the West Building, about 1,000 paintings are always on display. To the left (as you enter off the Mall) is the **Art Information Room,** housing the **Micro Gallery,** where those so inclined can design their own tours of the permanent collection and enhance their knowledge of art via user-friendly computers. Continuing to the left of the rotunda are galleries of 13th- through 18th-century Italian paintings and sculpture, including what is generally considered the finest Renaissance collection outside Italy; here you'll see the only painting by

---

Avoiding the Crowds at the National Gallery of Art

The best time to visit the National Gallery is Monday morning; the worst is Sunday afternoons.

Leonardo da Vinci housed outside Europe, *Ginevra de' Benci*. Paintings by El Greco, Ribera, and Velázquez highlight the Spanish galleries; Grünewald, Dürer, Holbein, and Cranach can be seen in the German; Van Eyck, Bosch, and Rubens in the Flemish; and Vermeer, Steen, and Rembrandt in the Dutch. To the right of the rotunda, galleries display 18th- to 19th-century French paintings (including one of the world's greatest impressionist collections), paintings by Goya, works of late-18th- and 19th-century Americans—such as Cole, Stuart, Copley, Homer, Whistler, and Sargent—and of somewhat earlier British artists, such as Constable, Turner, and Gainsborough. Room decor reflects the period and country of the art shown: Travertine marble heralds the Italian gallery, and somber oak panels define the Dutch galleries. Down a flight of stairs are prints and drawings; 15th- through 20th-century sculpture (with many pieces by Daumier, Degas, and Rodin); American naive 18th- and 19th-century paintings; Chinese porcelains; small Renaissance bronzes; 16th-century Flemish tapestries; and 18th-century decorative arts.

On May 23, 1999, the long-awaited National Gallery Sculpture Garden, just across 7th Street from the West Wing, opened to the public. The park takes up two city blocks and features open lawns; a central pool with a spouting fountain (the pool is converted into an ice rink in winter); an exquisite, glassed-in pavilion housing a cafe; 17 sculptures by renowned artists, like Roy Lichtenstein and Ellsworth Kelly (and Scott Burton, whose "Six-Part Seating," you're welcome to sit upon); and informally landscaped shrubs, trees, and plants. It was an instant hit.

The East Building: This wing was conceived as a showcase for the museum's collection of 20th-century art, including Picasso, Miró, Matisse, Pollock, and Rothko; and to house the art history research center. Always on display are the massive aluminum Calder mobile dangling under a seven-story skylight and an exhibit called **"Small French Paintings,"** which I love.

Pick up a floor plan and calendar of events at an information desk to find out about National Gallery exhibits, films, tours, lectures, and concerts. Highly recommended are the free highlight tours (call for exact times) and audio tours. The gift shop is a favorite. The gallery offers several good dining options, the best being the Terrace Café, which sometimes tailors its menu to complement a particular exhibit.

✪ **United States Holocaust Memorial Museum.** 100 Raoul Wallenberg Place (formerly 15th St. SW; near Independence Ave., just off the Mall). ☎ **202/488-0400.** www. ushmm.org. Free admission. Daily 10am–5:30pm. Closed Yom Kippur and Dec 25. Metro: Smithsonian.

When this museum opened in 1993, officials thought perhaps 500,000 people might visit annually. In fact, 2 million come here every year. On a daily basis, the number is 1,650, which is the maximum number of free timed tickets the museum gives out each day to visitors who come to tour the permanent exhibit. The museum opens its doors at 10am and the tickets are usually gone by 10:30am. It's best to get in line early in the morning (around 8am). Most visitors—80%—are not Jewish, 14% are foreigners, and 18% are repeats.

Holocaust Museum Touring Tips

Because so many people want to visit the museum, tickets specifying a visit time (in 15-minute intervals) are required. Reserve them via **Protix** (☎ **800/400-9373**). There's a small service charge. You can also get them at the museum beginning at 10am daily (lines form earlier).

The noise and bustle of so many visitors can be disconcerting and certainly at odds with the experience that follows, when you first enter the lobby of the United States Holocaust Museum, our national institution for the documentation, study, and interpretation of Holocaust history. The museum also serves as a memorial to the 6 million Jews and millions of others (including gypsies, homosexuals, physically challenged, and political prisoners) who were murdered during the Holocaust. But things settle down as you begin your tour.

You will spend most of your time—anywhere from one to five hours—in the permanent exhibit, which takes up three floors, presenting the information chronologically. When you enter, you will be issued an identity card of an actual victim of the Holocaust. By 1945, 66% of those whose lives are documented on these cards were dead. The tour begins on the fourth floor, where exhibits portray the events of 1933 to 1939, the years of the Nazi rise to power. On the third floor (documenting 1940 to 1944), exhibits illustrate the narrowing choices of people caught up in the Nazi machine. You board a Polish freight car of the type used to transport Jews from the Warsaw ghetto to Treblinka and hear recordings of survivors telling what life in the camps was like. This part of the museum documents the details of the Nazis' "Final Solution" for the Jews.

The second floor recounts a more heartening story: It depicts how non-Jews throughout Europe, by exercising individual action and responsibility, saved Jews at great personal risk. Denmark—led by a king who swore that if any of his subjects wore a yellow star, so would he—managed to hide and save 90% of its Jews. Exhibits follow on the liberation of the camps, life in Displaced Persons camps, emigration to Israel and America, and the Nuremberg trials. A highlight at the end of the permanent exhibition is a 30-minute film called *Testimony,* in which Holocaust survivors tell their personal stories. The tour concludes in the hexagonal Hall of Remembrance, where you can meditate on what you've experienced and light a candle for the victims.

Chartered by a unanimous Act of Congress in 1980 and located adjacent to the Mall, the museum strives to broaden public understanding of Holocaust history. In addition to its permanent and temporary exhibitions, the museum has a Resource Center for educators, which provides materials and services to Holocaust educators and students; an interactive computer learning center; and a registry of Holocaust survivors, a library, and archives, which researchers may use to retrieve historic documents, photographs, oral histories, films, and videos.

The museum recommends not bringing children under 11; for older children, it's advisable to prepare them for what they'll see. There's a cafeteria and museum shop on the premises.

You can see some parts of the museum without tickets. These include two special exhibit areas on the first floor and concourse: **"Daniel's Story: Remember the Children"** and the **Wall of Remembrance** (Children's Tile Wall), which commemorates the 1.5 million children killed in the Holocaust, and the **Wexner Learning Center.**

5 Other Government Agencies

Bureau of Engraving & Printing. 14th and C sts. SW. ☎ **202/874-3188** or 202/874-2330. www.bep.treas.gov. Free admission. Mon–Fri 9am–2pm (last tour begins at 1:40pm). Extended hours in summer 5–6:40pm. Closed Dec 25–Jan 1 and federal holidays. Metro: Smithsonian (Independence Ave. exit).

This is where the cash is. A staff of 2,600 works around the clock churning it out at the rate of about 22.5 million notes a day. Everyone's eyes pop as they walk past rooms overflowing with fresh green bills. But although the money draws everyone in, it's not the whole story. The bureau prints many other products, including 25 billion postage stamps per year, presidential portraits, and White House invitations.

As many as 5,000 people line up each day to get a peek at all that moola, so arriving early, especially during the peak tourist season, is essential. Consider securing VIP tickets from your senator or congressperson; VIP tours are offered weekdays at 8am and 8:15am, with an additional 4pm tour added in summer, and last about 45 minutes. Write at least 3 months in advance for tickets. Tickets are required daily, all year long. Obtain a same-day ticket specifying a tour time from the ticket booth on Raoul Wallenburg Place to enter the building at its 14th Street entrance. Booth hours are 8am to 2pm all year long, and reopening in summer from 4 to 6:30pm.

The 40-minute guided tour begins with a short introductory film. Then you'll see, through large windows, the processes that go into the making of paper money: the inking, stacking of bills, cutting, and examination for defects. Most printing here is done from engraved steel plates in a process known as "intaglio," the hardest to counterfeit, because the slightest alteration will cause a noticeable change in the portrait in use. Additional exhibits include bills no longer in use, counterfeit money, and a $100,000 bill designed for official transactions (since 1969, the largest denomination printed for the general public is $100).

After you finish the tour, allow time to explore the **Visitor Center,** open 8:30am to 3:30pm (until 7:30pm in summer), where exhibits include informative videos, money-related electronic games, and a display of $1 million. Here, too, you can buy gifts ranging from bags of shredded money—no, you can't tape it back together—to copies of documents such as the Gettysburg Address.

Federal Bureau of Investigation. J. Edgar Hoover FBI Building, E St. NW (between 9th and 10th sts.). ☎ **202/324-3447.** Free admission. Mon–Fri 8:45am–4:15pm. Closed Jan 1, Dec 25, and other federal holidays. Metro: Metro Center or Federal Triangle.

More than half a million visitors (many of them kids) come here annually to learn why crime doesn't pay. Tours begin with a short videotape presentation about the priorities of the bureau: organized crime; white-collar crime; terrorism; foreign counterintelligence; illegal drugs; and violent crimes. En route, you'll learn about this organization's history (it was established in 1908) and its activities over the years. You'll see some of the weapons used by big-time gangsters such as Al Capone, John Dillinger, Bonnie and Clyde, and "Pretty Boy" Floyd; and an exhibit on counterintelligence operations. There are photographs of the 10 most-wanted fugitives (2 were recognized at this exhibit by people on the tour, and 10 have been located via the FBI-assisted TV show *America's Most Wanted*).

Other exhibits deal with white-collar crime, organized crime, terrorism, drugs, and agent training. On display are more than 5,000 weapons, most confiscated from criminals; they're used for reference purposes.

FBI Touring Tips

To beat the crowds, arrive before 8:45am or write to a senator or congressperson for a scheduled reservation as far in advance as possible. Guided congressional tours take place at 9:45am, 11:45am, 1:45, and 3:15pm, with an additional 2:45pm tour added in summer. Contact your senator or representative at least three months ahead to schedule an appointment for constituent groups of six or fewer. Tours last one hour and are conducted every 20 to 30 minutes, depending upon staff availability. The building closes at 4:15pm, so you must arrive at least one hour before closing if you want to make the last tour (arrive even earlier in high season). Once inside, you'll undergo a security check.

You'll also visit the **DNA lab** (the very same where tests did indeed conclude that the stains on Monica Lewinsky's blue Gap dress were a) semen and b) "to a reasonable degree of scientific certainty" genetically linked to Bill Clinton). Other stops include the **Firearms Unit** (where agents determine whether a bullet was fired from a given weapon); the **Material Analysis Unit** (where the FBI can deduce the approximate make and model of a car from a tiny piece of paint); the unit where hairs and fibers are examined; and a **Forfeiture and Seizure Exhibit**—a display of jewelry, furs, and other proceeds from illegal narcotics operations. The tour ends with a bang, lots of them in fact, when an agent gives a sharpshooting demonstration and discusses the FBI's firearm policy and gun safety.

At the height of the season, say mid-April, you might be standing in line with 300 people at 8 in the morning to tour the FBI Building, and not get in. If you're coming anytime between April and August, try to arrange for tickets ahead of time; even so, the tour office might tell you that they won't confirm your tickets until a week before your visit.

✪ **Library of Congress.** 1st St. SE (between Independence Ave. and E. Capitol St.). ☎ **202/707-8000.** www/loc.gov/. Free admission. Madison Building Mon–Fri 8:30am–9:30pm, Sat 8:30am–6pm. Jefferson Building Mon–Sat 10am–5:30pm. Closed Sun and all federal holidays. Stop at the information desk inside the Jefferson Building's west entrance on 1st Street to obtain same-day, free tickets to tour the Library. Tours of the Great Hall Mon–Sat 11:30am, and 1, 2:30, and 4pm. Metro: Capitol South.

The question most frequently asked by visitors to the Library of Congress is: "Where are the books?" The answer is: on the 532 miles of shelves located throughout the library's three buildings. Established in 1800, "for the purchase of such books as may be necessary for the use of Congress," the library today serves the nation, with holdings for the visually impaired (for whom books are recorded on cassette and/or translated into braille), research scholars, and college students. Its first collection of books was destroyed in 1814 when the British burned the Capitol (where the library was then housed) during the War of 1812. Thomas Jefferson then sold the institution his personal library of 6,487 books as a replacement, and this became the foundation of what would grow to become the world's largest library. Today, the collection contains a mind-boggling 113 million items. Its buildings house, among many other things, more than 17 million catalogued books; over 49 million manuscripts; the letters of George Washington; over 13 million prints and photographs; more than 2 million audio holdings (discs, tapes, talking books, and so on); more than 700,000 movies and videotapes; musical instruments from the 1700s; and the papers of everyone from Freud to Groucho Marx. The library offers a year-round program of free concerts, lectures, and poetry readings, and houses the Copyright Office.

As impressive as the scope of the library's effects and activities is its original home, the ornate Italian Renaissance–style Thomas Jefferson Building, which reopened to the public May 1, 1997, after an $81.5 million, 12-year overhaul of the entire library. The Jefferson Building was erected between 1888 and 1897 to hold the burgeoning collection and establish America as a cultured nation with magnificent institutions equal to anything in Europe. Fifty-two painters and sculptors worked for 8 years on its interior. There are floor mosaics of Italian marble; allegorical paintings on the overhead vaults; more than 100 murals; and numerous ornamental cornucopias, ribbons, vines, and garlands within. The building's exterior has 42 granite sculptures and yards of bas-reliefs. Especially impressive are the exquisite marble **Great Hall** and the **Main Reading Room,** the latter under a 160-foot dome. Originally intended to hold the fruits of at least 150 years of collecting, the Jefferson was, in fact, filled up in 13. It is now supplemented by the James Madison Memorial Building and the John Adams

Building. On permanent display in the Jefferson Building's Great Hall is an exhibit called **"Treasures of the Library of Congress,"** which rotates a selection of more than 200 of the rarest and most interesting items from the library's collection—like Thomas Jefferson's rough draft of the Declaration of Independence with notations by Benjamin Franklin and John Adams in the margins, and the contents of Lincoln's pockets when he was assassinated.

If you have to wait for a tour, take in the 12-minute orientation film in the Jefferson's new visitors' theater or browse in its new gift shop. Pick up a calendar of events when you visit. Free concerts take place in the Jefferson Building's elegant Coolidge Auditorium; find out more about them on the LOC concert Web site: **lcweb.loc.gov/rr/perform/concert**. **The Madison Building** offers interesting exhibits and features classic, rare, and unusual films in its Mary Pickford Theater. It also houses a cafeteria and the more formal Montpelier Room restaurant, both of which are open for lunch weekdays.

Anyone over high school age may use the library's collections, but first you must obtain a user card with your photo on it. Go to Room G-22 (ground floor level of the Jefferson Building) and present a driver's license or passport, complete a brief, self-registration procedure, and receive your user card. Then head to the Information Desk in either the Jefferson or Madison Buildings to find out about the research resources available to you, and how to use them. Most likely, you will be directed to the Main Reading Room. All books are used on-site; when you know which books you need, and their call numbers, you complete a "call" slip, and submit it to a staff person, who enters your request into a computer. The clerk receiving the request retrieves the books from the stacks and sends them up to the central desk, where you pick them up.

6 War Memorials & Cemeteries

Arlington National Cemetery. Just across the Memorial Bridge from the base of the Lincoln Memorial. ☎ **703/607-8052.** Free admission. Apr–Sept, daily 8am–7pm; Oct–Mar, daily 8am–5pm. Metro: Arlington National Cemetery. If you come by car, parking is $1.25 an hour for the first 3 hours, $2 an hour thereafter. The cemetery is also accessible via Tourmobile.

Upon arrival, head over to the Visitor Center, where you can view exhibits, pick up a detailed map, use the rest rooms (there are no others until you get to Arlington House), and purchase a Tourmobile ticket ($4.75 per adult, $2.25 for children 4 to 11) allowing you to stop at all major sights in the cemetery and then reboard whenever you like. Service is continuous, and the narrated commentary is informative; this is the only guided tour of the cemetery offered. If you've got plenty of stamina, consider doing part or all of the tour on foot. Remember as you go that this is a memorial frequented not just by tourists but by those visiting the graves of beloved relatives and friends who are buried here.

This shrine occupies approximately 612 acres on the high hills overlooking the capital from the west side of the Memorial Bridge. It honors many national heroes and more than 240,000 war dead, veterans, and dependents. Many graves of the famous at Arlington bear nothing more than simple markers. Five-star General John J. Pershing's is one of those. Secretary of State John Foster Dulles is buried here. So are President William Howard Taft and Supreme Court Justice Thurgood Marshall. Cemetery highlights include:

The Tomb of the Unknowns, containing the unidentified remains of service members from both world wars, the Korean War, and, until three years ago, the Vietnam War. In 1997, the remains of the unknown soldier from Vietnam were identified as those of Lt. Michael Blassie, whose A-37 was shot down in South Vietnam in 1962.

Women Who Have Made a Difference— Places in Washington Celebrating Women & Their Accomplishments

All you have to do to be reminded that this is still very much a man's world is to visit a legislative session of Congress and notice how many more men there are than women (58 out of 435 representatives, 9 out of 100 senators, at press time). But women have done and are doing great things, even if these great things often go unacknowledged, especially in post-Impeachment Washington. Fortunately, the city includes a number of sites that recognize women and their achievements, varied as they are:

Even **The Capitol,** at E. Capitol St. and 1st St. NW (☎ **202/225-6827;** www. senate.gov or www.house.gov), that bastion of maleness, offers tribute to the achievements of women. In the Rotunda, look for Adelaide Johnson's large 1921 Portrait Monument to suffragists Lucretia Mott, Elizabeth Cady Stanton, and Susan B. Anthony. The background stonework within the sculpture was left unfinished on purpose, to represent the work in the women's movement that remained unfinished. To the left of the suffragists is a life-size marble statue of Abraham Lincoln by the self-taught sculptor Vinnie Ream, who was only 19 when she received the commission and 23 when she completed it. Ream was the first woman to receive a federal art commission. You can see her craftsmanship in National Statuary Hall, too, where her statues of politician Samuel Jordan Kirkwood of Iowa and Cherokee leader Sequoya of Oklahoma reside. While you're in Statuary Hall, seek out the (few) statues on display here honoring prominent women in American history, including that of Jeannette Rankin, the first woman to serve in Congress; Mother Joseph, a 19th-century nun and architect; and Frances Willard, an Illinois educator and suffragist.

See "The Three Major Houses of Government" earlier in the chapter for detailed information about touring the Capitol.

The **Mary McLeod Bethune House,** 1318 Vermont Ave., NW. (☎ **202/ 673-2402;** www.nps.gov/mamc; Metro: McPherson Square), was the last official Washington residence of African-American activist/educator Bethune, who was a leading champion of black and women's rights during the Roosevelt administration. Today, the house presents and preserves African-American women's history. Open Monday to Saturday 10am to 4pm.

At the **National Air and Space Museum,** between 4th and 7th streets SW, with entrances on the Mall and Independence Ave. (☎ **202/357-2700;** www. nmas.si.edu), head first to the Early Flight Gallery, on the first floor. At the far right front corner is the display, "Women Pilots in America," which, to be truthful, could be a lot better. But at least you can learn a little about women like Blanche Stuart Scott, the first woman in America to fly solo, in September 1910, and Harriet Quimby, who was the first American woman to earn a pilot's license and the first woman to fly solo across the English Channel.

Upstairs, in the Pioneers of Flight Gallery, check out Bessie Coleman, profiled as part of "The American Black in Aviation" exhibit. In 1922, Coleman was the first licensed African-American pilot, male or female, in the United States. After she trained in France, Coleman returned to America to pursue a career as a barnstormer. She died in 1926 at the age of 33 in an aircraft accident.

In this same gallery is the bright-red Lockheed Vega 5B plane that our most famous female aviator, Amelia Earhart, flew in her nonstop solo flight across the Atlantic Ocean in 1932. Earhart was the first woman to fly solo across the Atlantic and the first woman to fly solo nonstop across the United States. She and her navigator Fred Noonan disappeared in the Pacific, July 2, 1937, while attempting an around-the-world flight.

Downstairs in the Space Race Exhibition, you can view the flight suit worn by Sally Ride, America's first woman in space. A model of the space shuttle is also here. See "The Smithsonian Museums," above, for further information.

Head into the East Wing of the **National Museum of American History,** between 12th and 14th streets NW, with entrances on the Mall and Constitution Avenue NW (☎ **202/357-2700;** www.nmah.si.edu), to view the First Ladies' exhibit (one of the Smithsonian's most popular), and then "From Parlor to Politics, 1890–1925," which connects with the First Ladies' exhibit. Much of the exhibit displays the inaugural gowns worn and the china used by our first ladies. Their individual personalities, public images, and realms of influence are also explored.

"From Parlor to Politics" traces the struggles and strides of women who gradually grew politically active after years of associating with each other in clubs formed for charitable, literary, or social purposes. These clubs formed the springboard for reforms in temperance, labor, suffrage, children's health, and immigration policy. See "The Smithsonian Museums," above, for more information.

The **National Museum of Women in the Arts** celebrates women artists and their works, over 2,000 of them; see "More Museums," below, for further information.

The **Sewall-Belmont House,** 144 Constitution Ave. NE (☎ **202/546-3989;** www.natwomanparty.org), is one of the oldest houses on Capitol Hill, constructed in 1799 to 1800 for Robert Sewall. Since 1929, the house has served as headquarters for the National Woman's Party. That party's founder, Alice Paul, lived here for more than four decades, and the house is filled with art and artifacts that tell the story of the suffragist movement.

The Sewall-Belmont House is open Tuesday through Friday from 10am to 3pm, and on Saturday from noon to 4pm. A donation of $2 to $3 is requested.

In Arlington, Virginia, The **Women in Military Service for America Memorial** pays tribute to women military heroes; and the **Newseum** chronicles women in the field of journalism. (See "Further Afield: Arlington" below for details.)

After visiting these sites, why not continue the theme by dining at a restaurant whose chef is a woman? Washington has quite a number of them:

At **Cafe Berlin,** the menu is German, and the desserts are sublime. Chef Susan McCreight Lindeborg has won national attention for her seasonally changing menus of American regional fare at the **Morrison-Clark Inn.** Chef Ann Cashion, a local favorite, serves innovative American fare in comfortable surroundings at Cashion's Eat Place; also check out her latest venture, **Johnny's Half-Shell,** for raw bar and other seafood specialties. See chapter 6 for details.

Blassie's family, who had reason to believe that the body was their son's, had beseeched the Pentagon to exhume the soldier's remains and conduct DNA testing to determine if what the family suspected was true. Upon confirmation, the Blassies buried Michael in his hometown of St. Louis. The crypt honoring the dead but unidentified Vietnam War soldiers remains empty for the time being.

The entire tomb is an unembellished massive white-marble block, moving in its simplicity. Inscribed are the words: "Here rests in honored glory an American Soldier known but to God." A 24-hour honor guard watches over the tomb, with the changing of the guard taking place every half-hour April to September, every hour on the hour October to March, and every two hours at night.

A 20-minute walk, all uphill, from the Visitor Center is **Arlington House** (☎ **703/ 557-0613**). For 30 years (1831–61) this was the legal residence of Robert E. Lee, where he and his family lived off and on until the Civil War. Lee married the great-granddaughter of Martha Washington, Mary Anna Randolph Custis, who inherited the estate upon the death of her father. It was at Arlington House that Lee, having received the news of Virginia's secession from the Union, decided to resign his commission in the U.S. Army. During the Civil War, the estate was taken over by Union forces, and troops were buried here. A year before the defeat of the Confederate forces at Gettysburg, the U.S. government bought the estate. A fine melding of the styles of the Greek Revival and the grand plantation houses of the early 1800s, the house has been administered by the National Park Service since 1933.

You tour the house on your own; park rangers are on-site to answer your questions. About 30% of the furnishings are original. Slave quarters and a small museum adjoin. Admission is free. It's open daily 9:30am to 4:30pm but is closed January 1 and December 25.

Pierre Charles L'Enfant's grave was placed near Arlington House at a spot that is believed to offer the best view of Washington, the city he designed.

Below Arlington House, an 8-minute walk from the visitor center, is the **Gravesite of John Fitzgerald Kennedy.** Simplicity is the key to grandeur here, too. John Carl Warnecke designed a low crescent wall embracing a marble terrace, inscribed with memorable words of the 35th U.S. president, including his famous utterance, "And so my fellow Americans, ask not what your country can do for you, ask what you can do for your country." Jacqueline Kennedy Onassis rests next to her husband, and Senator Robert Kennedy is buried close by. The Kennedy graves attract streams of visitors. Arrive close to 8am to contemplate the site quietly; otherwise, it's mobbed. Looking north, there's a spectacular view of Washington.

About 1½ miles from the Kennedy graves, the **Marine Corps Memorial,** the famous statue of the marines raising the flag on Iwo Jima, stands near the north (or Orde & Weitzel Gate) entrance to the cemetery as a tribute to marines who died in all wars. On Tuesday evenings in summer, there are military parades on the grounds at 7pm.

Close to the Iwo Jima statue is the **Netherlands Carillon,** a gift from the people of the Netherlands, with 50 bells. Every spring thousands of tulip bulbs bloom on the surrounding grounds. Carillon concerts take place from 2 to 4pm on Saturday during May and September; and from 6 to 8pm on Saturday June through August. (Sometimes the hours change; call ☎ **703/289-2530** before you go.) Visitors are permitted to enter the tower to watch the carillonneur perform and enjoy the panoramic views of Washington.

In October 1997, the ✪ **Women in Military Service for America Memorial** (☎ **800/222-2294** or 703/533-1155; www.womensmemorial.org), was added to Arlington Cemetery to honor the more than 1.8 million women who have served in the armed forces from the American Revolution to the present. The impressive new memorial lies just beyond the gated entrance to the cemetery, a 3-minute walk from the Visitor Center. What you see as you approach the memorial is a large, circular reflecting pool, perfectly placed within the curve of the granite wall rising behind it. Arched passages within the 226-foot-long wall lead to an upper terrace and dramatic views of Arlington National Cemetery and the monuments of Washington; an arc of large glass panels (which form the roof of the memorial hall) contains etched quotations from servicewomen (and a couple from men). Currently, only 11 quotations appear, including this one from American Red Cross founder Clara Barton: "From the storm-lashed Mayflower . . . to the present hour, woman has stood like a rock for the welfare and the glory of the history of the country, and one might well add . . . unwritten, unrewarded, and almost unrecognized." Behind the wall and completely underground is the **Education Center,** housing a **Hall of Honor,** a gallery of exhibits tracing the history of women in the military, a theater, and a computer register of servicewomen, which visitors may access for information about individual military women, past and present. Hours are October through March 8am to 5pm and April through September 8am to 7pm. Stop at the reception desk for a brochure that details a self-guided tour through the memorial. The memorial is open every day but Christmas.

The Korean War Veterans Memorial. Just across from the Lincoln Memorial (east of French Dr., between 21st and 23rd sts. NW). ☎ **202/426-6841.** Free admission. Rangers on duty 8am–midnight daily except Dec 25. Ranger-led interpretive programs are given throughout the day. Metro: Foggy Bottom.

This privately funded memorial founded in 1995 honors those who served in Korea, a 3-year conflict (1950–53) that produced almost as many casualties as Vietnam. It consists of a circular "Pool of Remembrance" in a grove of trees and a triangular "Field of Service." The latter is highlighted by lifelike statues of 19 infantrymen, who appear to be trudging across fields, their expressions and stances suggesting that their enemies lurk nearby. The scene is wholly compelling. In addition, a 164-foot-long black granite wall depicts the array of combat and combat support troops that served in Korea (nurses, chaplains, airmen, gunners, mechanics, cooks, and others); a raised granite curb lists the 22 nations that contributed to the UN's effort there; and a commemorative area honors KIAs, MIAs, and POWs. Limited parking is available along Ohio Drive. If you don't mind a walk, try to snag a spot along W. Basin Drive near the FDR Memorial; the Korean War and the Vietnam Veterans memorials (see below), as well as the Lincoln Memorial, are then all within reach.

United States Navy Memorial and Naval Heritage Center. 701 Pennsylvania Ave. NW. ☎ **800/723-3557** or 202/737-2300. www.lonesailor.org. Free admission. Mon–Sat 9:30am–5pm. Closed Thanksgiving, New Year's Day, and Dec 25. Metro: Archives–Navy Memorial.

Authorized by Congress in 1980 to honor the men and women of the U.S. Navy, this memorial comprises a 100-foot-diameter circular plaza bearing a granite world map flanked by fountains and waterfalls salted with waters from the seven seas. A statue of *The Lone Sailor* watching over the map represents all who have served in the navy. And two sculpture walls adorned with bronze bas-reliefs commemorate navy history and related maritime services.

The building adjoining the memorial houses a naval heritage center. The center's museum includes interactive video kiosks proffering a wealth of information about navy ships, aircraft, and history; the **Navy Memorial Log Room,** a computerized record of past and present navy personnel; the **Presidents Room,** honoring the six U.S. presidents who served in the navy and the two who became secretary of the navy; the **Ship's Store,** filled with nautical and maritime merchandise; and a wide-screen 70mm Surroundsound film called *At Sea,* which lets viewers experience the grandeur of the ocean and the adventure of going to sea on a navy ship. The 35-minute film plays every Monday through Saturday at 11am, 1pm, and 3pm; admission is $4 for adults, $3 for seniors and students 18 and under.

Guided tours are available from the front desk, subject to staff availability. The plaza is the scene of many free band concerts in spring and summer; call for details.

✪ **The Vietnam Veterans Memorial.** Just across from the Lincoln Memorial (east of Henry Bacon Dr. between 21st and 22nd sts. NW). ☎ **202/426-6841.** Free admission. Rangers on duty 8am–midnight daily except Dec 25. Ranger-led programs are given throughout the day. Metro: Foggy Bottom.

The Vietnam Veterans Memorial is possibly the most poignant site in Washington: two long, black granite walls inscribed with the names of the men and women who gave their lives, or remain missing, in the longest war in our nation's history. Even if no one close to you died in Vietnam, it's wrenching to watch visitors grimly studying the directories at either end to find out where their husbands, sons, and loved ones are listed. The slow walk along the 492-foot wall of names—it names close to 60,000 people, many of whom died very young—powerfully evokes the tragedy of all wars. It's also affecting to see how much the monument means to Vietnam veterans who visit it. Because of the raging conflict over U.S. involvement in the war, Vietnam veterans had received virtually no previous recognition of their service.

The memorial was conceived by Vietnam veteran Jan Scruggs and built by the Vietnam Veterans Memorial Fund, a nonprofit organization that raised $7 million for the project. The VVMF was granted a 2-acre site in tranquil Constitution Gardens to erect a memorial that would make no political statement about the war and would harmonize with neighboring memorials. By separating the issue of the wartime service of individuals from the issue of U.S. policy in Vietnam, VVMF hoped to begin a process of national reconciliation.

Yale senior Maya Ying Lin's design was chosen in a national competition open to all citizens over 18 years of age. It consists of two walls in a quiet, protected park setting, angled at 125° to point to the Washington Monument and the Lincoln Memorial. The wall's mirrorlike surface reflects surrounding trees, lawns, and monuments. The names are inscribed in chronological order, documenting an epoch in American history as a series of individual sacrifices from the date of the first casualty in 1959 to the last death in 1975.

The wall was erected in 1982. In 1984, a life-size sculpture of three Vietnam soldiers by Frederick Hart was installed at the entrance plaza. He describes his work this way: "They wear the uniform and carry the equipment of war; they are young. The contrast between the innocence of their youth and the weapons of war underscores the poignancy of their sacrifice. . . . Their strength and their vulnerability are both evident." Near the statue a flag flies from a 60-foot staff. Another sculpture, the *Vietnam Veterans Women's Memorial,* which depicts three servicewomen tending a wounded soldier, was installed on Veterans Day 1993.

The park rangers at the Vietnam Veterans Memorial are very knowledgeable and are usually milling about—be sure to seek them out if you have any questions. Limited parking is available along Constitution Avenue.

7 More Museums

✪ **Corcoran Gallery of Art.** 500 17th St. NW (between E St. and New York Ave.). ☎ **202/ 639-1700.** www.corcoran.org. Free admission. Wed and Fri–Mon 10am–5pm, Thurs 10am–9pm. Suggested contribution $3 adults, $1 students and senior citizens, $5 for families; children 12 and under are free. Free 45-minute tours daily at noon, Thurs 7:30, Sat–Sun 10:30am and 12:30pm. Closed Tues, Jan 1, and Dec 25. Some street parking. Metro: Farragut West or Farragut North.

This elegant art museum is a favorite party site in the city, hosting everything from MTV's ball during the 1996 presidential inauguration (2,800 turned out, twice the number expected, everyone from Sheryl Crow to Lauren Bacall), to wedding receptions for the wealthy. In 1997, the Corcoran made the papers as the site of a standoff between Russian and American sponsors of a Romanov jewels exhibit. The Russians parked a large truck outside the museum, refusing to budge until the American committee returned the jewels to them. The Russians eventually capitulated and the jewels continued on to the next stop on their traveling tour.

The first art museum in Washington (and one of the first in the nation), the Corcoran Gallery was housed from 1869 to 1896 in the redbrick and brownstone building that is now the Renwick. The collection outgrew its quarters and was transferred in 1897 to its present beaux arts building, designed by Ernest Flagg.

The collection, shown in rotating exhibits, focuses chiefly on American art. A prominent Washington banker, William Wilson Corcoran was among the first wealthy American collectors to realize the importance of encouraging and supporting this country's artists. Enhanced by further gifts and bequests, the collection comprehensively spans American art from 18th-century portraiture to 20th-century moderns like Nevelson, Warhol, and Rothko. Nineteenth-century works include Bierstadt's and Remington's imagery of the American West; Hudson River School artists; expatriates like Whistler, Sargent, and Mary Cassatt; and two giants of the late 19th century, Homer and Eakins.

The Corcoran is not exclusively an American art museum. On the first floor is the collection from the estate of Senator William Andrews Clark, an eclectic grouping of Dutch and Flemish masters; European painters; French impressionists; Barbizon landscapes; Delft porcelains; a Louis XVI *salon dore* transported in toto from Paris; and more. Clark's will stated that his diverse collection, which any curator would undoubtedly want to disperse among various museum departments, must be shown as a unit. He left money for a wing to house it, and the new building opened in 1928. Don't miss the small, walnut-paneled room known as "Clark Landing," which showcases 19th-century French impressionist and American art; a room of exquisite Corot landscapes; another of medieval Renaissance tapestries; and numerous Daumier lithographs donated by Dr. Armand Hammer.

Pick up a schedule of events—temporary exhibits, gallery talks, concerts, art auctions, and more. Families should inquire about the Corcoran's series of Saturday Family Days and Sunday Traditions. (Family Days are especially fun and always feature great live music.) Both programs are free, but you need to reserve a slot for the Sunday events. The charming Café des Artistes is open for lunch Monday through Saturday 11am to 3pm, for dinner on Thursday, and for Sunday brunch 11am to 2pm (reservations accepted for parties of 6 or more), which costs $18.95 per adult, $8.50 per child, and includes live gospel music singers; call ☎ **202/639-1786** for more information. The Corcoran has a nice gift shop.

Dumbarton Oaks. 1703 32nd St. NW (entrance to the collections on 32nd St., between R and S sts.; garden entrance at 31st and R sts.). ☎ **202/339-6401.** www.doaks.com. Garden Apr–Oct $4 adults, $3 children under 12 and senior citizens, Nov–Mar free admission; collections year-round suggested donation $1. Garden Apr–Oct, daily 2–6pm, Nov–Mar, daily (weather permitting) 2–5pm; collections year-round Tues–Sun 2–5pm. Gardens and collections are closed national holidays and Dec 24. Street parking.

Fun Fact

Displayed on the second floor of the Corcoran is the white-marble female nude, *The Greek Slave,* by Hiram Powers, considered so daring in its day that it was shown on alternate days to men and women.

Many people associate Dumbarton Oaks, a 19th-century Georgetown mansion named for a Scottish castle, with the 1944 international conference that led to the formation of the United Nations. Today the 16-acre estate is a research center for studies in Byzantine and pre-Columbian art and history, as well as landscape architecture. Its yards, which wind gently down to Rock Creek Ravine, are magical, modeled after European gardens. The pre-Columbian museum, designed by Philip Johnson, is a small gem, and the Byzantine collection is a rich one.

This unusual collection originated with Robert Woods Bliss and his wife, Mildred. In 1940 they turned over their estate, their extensive Byzantine collection, a library of works on Byzantine civilization, and 16 acres (including 10 acres of exquisite formal gardens) to Mr. Bliss's alma mater, Harvard, and provided endowment funds for continuing research in Byzantine studies. In the early 1960s they also donated their pre-Columbian collection and financed the building of a wing to house it, as well as a second wing for Mrs. Bliss's collection of rare books on landscape gardening. The Byzantine collection includes illuminated manuscripts, a 13th-century icon of St. Peter, mosaics, ivory carvings, a 4th-century sarcophagus, jewelry, and more. The pre-Columbian works, displayed chronologically in eight marble- and oak-floored glass pavilions, feature Olmec jade and serpentine figures, Mayan relief panels, textiles from 900 B.C. to the Spanish Conquest, funerary pottery, gold necklaces made by the lost-wax process, and sculptures of Aztec gods and goddesses.

The historic music room, furnished in European antiques, was the setting for the 1944 Dumbarton Oaks Conversations about the United Nations. It has a beamed, painted 16th-century French-style ceiling and an immense 16th-century stone fireplace. Among its notable artworks is El Greco's *The Visitation.*

Pick up a self-guiding brochure to tour the staggeringly beautiful formal gardens, which include an Orangery; a Rose Garden (final resting place of the Blisses amid 1,000 rose bushes, newly brought back to life after near extinction); wisteria-covered arbors; herbaceous borders; groves of cherry trees; and magnolias. Exit at R Street, turn left, cross an honest-to-goodness Lovers' Lane, and proceed next door to Montrose Park, where you can picnic.

The Folger Shakespeare Library. 201 E. Capitol St. SE. ☎ **202/544-7077** or 202/544-4600. www.folger.edu. Free admission. Mon–Sat 10am–4pm. Closed federal holidays. Free walk-in tours daily 11am. Metro: Capitol South or Union Station.

"Shakespeare taught us that the little world of the heart is vaster, deeper, and richer than the spaces of astronomy," wrote Ralph Waldo Emerson in 1864. A decade later, Amherst student Henry Clay Folger was profoundly affected by a lecture Emerson gave similarly extolling the bard. Folger purchased an inexpensive set of Shakespeare's plays and went on to amass a prodigious mass—by far the world's largest—of his printed works, today housed in the Folger Shakespeare Library. By 1930, when Folger and his wife, Emily (whose literary enthusiasms matched his own), laid the cornerstone of a building to house the collection, it comprised 93,000 books, 50,000 prints and engravings, and thousands of manuscripts. The Folgers gave it all as a gift to the American people.

The building itself has a marble facade decorated with nine bas-relief scenes from Shakespeare's plays; it is a striking example of art deco classicism. A statue of Puck stands in the west garden, and quotations from the bard and from contemporaries such as Ben Jonson adorn the exterior walls. An Elizabethan garden on the east side of the building is planted with flowers and herbs of the period, many of them mentioned in the plays. Inquire about docent-led tours scheduled on certain Saturdays, April to October. The garden is also a quiet place to have a picnic.

The facility, which houses some 250,000 books, 100,000 of which are rare, is an important research center not only for Shakespearean scholars, but for those studying any aspect of the English and continental Renaissance. And the oak-paneled **Great Hall,** reminiscent of a Tudor long gallery, is a popular attraction for the general public. It has an intricate plaster ceiling decorated with Shakespeare's coat of arms, fleurs-de-lis, and other motifs. On display are rotating exhibits from the permanent collection: books, paintings, playbills, Renaissance musical instruments, and more.

At the end of the Great Hall is a theater designed to suggest an Elizabethan inn-yard where plays, concerts, readings, and Shakespeare-related events take place (see chapter 9 for details).

Ford's Theatre & Lincoln Museum. 517 10th St. NW (between E and F sts.). ☎ **202/426-6925.** www.nps.gov/foth. Free admission. Daily 9am–5pm. Closed Dec 25. Metro: Metro Center.

On April 14, 1865, President Abraham Lincoln was in the audience of Ford's Theatre, one of the most popular playhouses in Washington. Everyone was laughing at a funny line from Tom Taylor's celebrated comedy, *Our American Cousin,* when John Wilkes Booth crept into the president's box, shot the president, and leapt to the stage, shouting "Sic semper tyrannis" (Thus ever to tyrants). With his left leg broken from the vault, Booth mounted his horse in the back alley and galloped off. Doctors carried Lincoln across the street to the house of William Petersen, where the president died the next morning.

After Lincoln's assassination, the theater was closed by order of Secretary of War Edwin M. Stanton. For many years afterward it was used as an office by the War Department. In 1893, 22 clerks were killed when three floors of the building collapsed. It remained in disuse until the 1960s, when it was remodeled and restored to its appearance on the night of the tragedy. Except when rehearsals or matinees are in progress (call before you go), visitors can see the theater and trace Booth's movements on that fateful night. Free 15-minute talks on the history of the theater and the story of the assassination are given throughout the day. Be sure to visit the Lincoln Museum in the basement, where exhibits—including the Derringer pistol used by Booth and a diary in which he outlines his rationalization for the deed—focus on events surrounding Lincoln's assassination and the trial of the conspirators. The theater stages productions most of the year (see chapter 9 for information).

The House Where Lincoln Died (the Petersen House). 516 10th St. NW. ☎ **202/426-6830.** Free admission. Daily 9am–5pm. Closed Dec 25. Metro: Metro Center.

After the shooting, the doctors attending Lincoln carried him out into the street, where boarder Henry Safford, standing in the open doorway of his rooming house, gestured for them to bring the president inside. So Lincoln died in the home of William Petersen, a German-born tailor. Now furnished with period pieces, the dark, narrow townhouse looks much as it did on that fateful April night. It takes about 5 minutes to troop through the building. You'll see the front parlor where an anguished Mary Todd Lincoln spent the night with her son, Robert. Her emotional state was such that she was banned from the bedroom because she was creating havoc. In the back parlor, Secretary of War Edwin M. Stanton held a Cabinet meeting and began questioning witnesses. From this room, Stanton announced at 7:22am on April 15, 1865, "Now he belongs to the ages." Lincoln died, lying diagonally because he was so tall, on a bed the size of the one you see here. (The Chicago Historical Society owns the actual bed and other items from the room.)

Twelve years after Lincoln's death, the house was sold to Louis Schade, who published a newspaper called the *Washington Sentinel* in its basement for many years. In

Museums of Special Interest

In addition to the many superb museums described within this chapter, many other lesser-known, but wonderful, ones exist around the city. Often these museums focus on one select subject, architecture, perhaps, or the life of the historic figure who lived within. Peruse the following list to see whether one of these sites covers a topic that happens to be of special interest to you, and then call for further information. Don't try to drop in without calling, because most of these museums are not open daily and some require appointments.

Art Museum of the Americas. 201 18th St. NW (☎ **202/458-3000**), within the Organization of American States. Permanent collection of 20th-century Latin American art. Metro: Farragut West, then walk south about 6 blocks.

B'Nai B'rith Klutznick Museum. 1640 Rhode Island Ave. NW (☎ **202/857-6583**). Jewish history and culture. Metro: Farragut North.

Capital Children's Museum. 800 3rd St. NW (☎ **202/675-4120**). Hands-on educational complex. Metro: Union Station.

Daughters of the American Revolution (DAR) Museum. 1776 D St. NW (☎ **202/879-3254**). Early American furnishings and decorative arts. Metro: Farragut West, then walk south about 5 blocks.

Decatur House. 748 Jackson Place (☎ **202/842-0920**). Historic house museum with permanent collection of Federalist and Victorian furnishings. Metro: Farragut West or McPherson Square.

Dumbarton House. 2715 Q St. NW (☎ **202/337-2288**). Another historic house museum (also featured in Walking Tour 2, later in the chapter), with permanent collection of 18th- and 19th-century English and American furniture and decorative arts. Metro: Dupont Circle, with a 20-minute walk along Q Street.

Frederick Douglass Home. 1411 W St. SE (☎ **202/426-5961**). Last residence of famous African-American, 19th-century abolitionist. Metro: Anacostia, then catch bus no. B2, which stops right in front of the house.

Historical Society of Washington. 1307 New Hampshire Ave. NW (☎ **202/785-2068**). The 1899 Christian Heurich mansion, resplendent in late Victoriana (see Walking Tour 1, later in the chapter, for a detailed description). Metro: Dupont Circle, 19th Street exit.

Interior Department Museum. 1849 C St. NW (☎ **202/208-4743**). Permanent exhibits relating to American historical events and locales, including murals

---

1896, the government bought the house for $30,000, and it is now maintained by the National Park Service.

National Geographic Society's Explorers Hall. 17th and M sts. NW. ☎ **202/857-7588.** www.nationalgeographic.com. Free admission. Mon–Sat and holidays 9am–5pm, Sun 10am–5pm. Closed Dec 25. Metro: Farragut North (Connecticut Ave. and L St. exit).

I don't know that I'd come here if I didn't have kids. Whatever, as my 12-year-old says. The truth is, anyone over 8 will find something fascinating or enjoyable at Explorers Hall.

The National Geographic Society was founded in 1888 for "the increase and diffusion of geographic knowledge." At Explorers Hall, dozens of fascinating displays, most

by prominent Native American artists, newly on view on the 9th floor. Metro: Farragut West, then walk about 6 blocks south.

Kreeger Museum. 2401 Foxhall Rd. NW (☎ 202/337-3050). Permanent collection of impressionist, Postimpressionist, expressionist, and African paintings and sculpture. No convenient Metro or bus stop; best to drive or take a taxi.

National Aquarium. Within the Department of Commerce Building, on 14th St. NW, between Pennsylvania and Constitution aves. NW (☎ 202/482-2825). The nation's first public aquarium, tiny but interesting. Metro: Federal Triangle.

National Building Museum. 401 F. St. NW (☎ 202/272-2448). Housed within a historic building of mammoth proportions is this museum devoted to architecture, building, and historic preservation. Metro: Judiciary Square.

Octagon. 1799 New York Ave. NW (☎ 202/638-3105). Another historic house museum, it also features exhibits on architecture (its neighbor is the American Institute of Architects headquarters). Metro: Farragut West.

Sewall-Belmont House. 144 Constitution Ave. NE (☎ 202/546-3989). A must for those interested in women's history (see box, this chapter, highlighting women's achievements), the historic house displays memorabilia of the women's suffragette movement, which got its start here. Metro: Union Station.

Textile Museum. 2320 S St. NW (☎ 202/667-0441). Historic and contemporary handmade textile arts, housed in historic John Russell Pope mansion (also featured on Walking Tour 1, later in this chapter). Metro: Dupont Circle, Q Street exit, then walk a couple of blocks up Massachusetts Avenue until you see S Street.

Treasury Department. 15th St. and Pennsylvania Avenue NW (☎ 202/622-0896). An immense building with marvelous architecture and fascinating history. Metro: Metro Center or Federal Triangle.

Tudor Place. 1644 31st St. NW (☎ 202/965-0400). An 1816 mansion with gardens, home to Martha Washington's descendants until a decade ago. (See Walking Tour 2, later in this chapter.) Metro: Dupont Circle, with a 25-minute walk along Q Street.

Woodrow Wilson House. 2340 S St. NW (☎ 202/387-4062). Former home of this president, preserved the way it was when he lived here (see description in Walking Tour 1, later in this chapter). Metro: Dupont Circle, then walk a couple of blocks up Massachusetts Avenue until you reach S Street.

---

of them using interactive videos, put that knowledge at your fingertips. In **Geographica,** on the north side of the hall, you can touch a tornado; find out what it's like inside the Earth; and explore the vast Martian landscape. The major exhibit here is **Earth Station One,** an interactive amphitheater (centered on an immense free-floating globe) that simulates an orbital flight. You can also peer into a video microscope that zooms in clearly on slides showing such specimens as a hydra (a simple multicellular animal) or mosquito larva.

Other displays include a scale model of Jacques Cousteau's diving saucer, in which he descended to 25,000 feet; the flag and dog sled, among other equipment, of Admiral Robert E. Peary, the first man to reach the North Pole; an *Aepyornis maximus*

Exhibits Scheduled at Museums in 2000

The following listing, though not comprehensive, is enough to give you an idea about upcoming or current exhibits at major Washington museums. Because schedules sometimes change, it's always a good idea to call ahead. See individual entries in this chapter for phone numbers and addresses.

Arthur M. Sackler Gallery "Imaging the Word: New Selections of Calligrapahy from the Islamic World" (November 17, 1999–May 7, 2000) highlights Islamic calligraphy from the 9th to the 20th centuries. These works on paper are shown together with inscribed textiles, coins, and other objects to display the art of writing in its many applications.

Corcoran Gallery of Art "Norman Rockwell: Pictures for the American People" (June 17–September 10) is the first major exhibit of this artist's works in 30 years. Includes 70 paintings and 322 *Saturday Evening Post* covers.

Freer Gallery of Art "Court Arts of the Ming Dynasty" (January–July) displays paintings and objects of porcelain, lacquer, cloisonne, and gold that were produced under imperial patronage during the Ming dynasty (1368–1644).

Hirshhorn Museum & Sculpture Garden "Salvador Dalí Optical Illusions" (April 20–June 25) features 60 paintings covering Dalí's career, with emphasis on visual trickery and surrealist inventions.

National Gallery of Art "The Impressionists at Argenteuil" (May 28–August 20) shows off more than 50 Impressionist paintings by 6 artists: Eugene Boudin, Gustave Caillebotte, Edouard Manet, Claude Monet, Auguste Renoir, and Alfred Sisley, all of whom used the town of Argenteuil, France as subject and inspiration.

National Museum of African Art "The Art of African Money" (December 19, 1999–March 19, 2000) explores the use of special objects and tokens often used in Africa to facilitate trade and measure wealth. Objects on display include cowrie shells, beads, and fabric.

---

egg, from Madagascar's extinct 1,000-pound flightless "elephant bird"; and the world's largest freestanding globe. Also on view are a full-size replica of a giant Olmec stone head dating from 32 B.C. from La Venta, Mexico and a 3.9 billion-year-old moon rock. Video excerpts from the society's TV specials are shown in the National Geographic Television Room. The hall offers an ongoing series of lectures and temporary exhibits.

National Museum of Women in the Arts. 1250 New York Ave. NW (at 13th St.). ☎ **202/783-5000.** www.nmwa.org. Suggested contribution: $3 adults, $2 students and senior citizens. Mon–Sat 10am–5pm, Sun noon–5pm. Closed Jan 1, Thanksgiving Day, and Dec 25. Metro: Metro Center, 13th St. exit.

Celebrating "the contribution of women to the history of art," this relatively new museum is Washington's 72nd but a national first. Its 10th anniversary in 1997 saw the opening of the **Elizabeth A. Kasser Wing,** which adds 5,300 square feet and two new galleries to the museum. Founders Wilhelmina and Wallace Holladay, who donated the core of the permanent collection—more than 200 works by women from the 16th through the 20th century—became interested in women's art in the 1960s. After discovering that no women were included in H. W. Janson's *History of Art,* a standard text (this, by the way, did not change until 1986!), the Holladays began collecting art by women, and the concept of a women's art museum (to begin correcting the inequities of underrepresentation) soon evolved.

National Museum of American History "Nobel! One Hundred Years of the Prize" (October 2000–January 2002) profiles the lives of Nobel laureates around the world and the life of the man after whom the prize is named, Alfred Nobel. Scientific equipment, photographs, and computer interactives are included.

National Museum of Natural History "Vikings: The North Atlantic Saga" (April 29–September 4), commemorates the 1000-year anniversary of the Viking arrival in North America and explores the historical impact of new archaeological finds that have redefined what we know of early North American and Scandinavian life. Exhibit includes Viking Age jewelry, wooden carvings, grave goods, medieval church carvings, and other items.

National Postal Museum "Posted Aboard the R.M.S. *Titanic*" (September 17–closing date to be set) tells the moving story of five sea post clerks who perished aboard the ill-fated ship. Also "As Precious as Gold" (through September 30, 2000), which examines the great Klondike/Alaska Gold Rush and the role of mail carriers in keeping those who panned for gold in contact with their families far away.

The Phillips Collection "Honore Daumier" (February 19–May 14) will be the first major exhibition dedicated to the artist in the United States. This complete retrospective of Daumier's work features 67 paintings, 67 drawings and watercolors, 38 sculptures, and 70 lithographs.

Renwick Gallery "The Renwick Invitational: Five Women in Craft" (March 31–August 20) features the work of ceramicist Janel Jacobson, fiber artist Consuelo Jimenez Underwood, basketmaker Mary Jackson, jewelry designer Sondra Sherman, and metalsmith Myra Mimlitsch Gray. Also "Spirited Objects: Traditional Craft for the 21st Century" (October 6, 2000–January 21, 2001) presents contemporary examples of traditional American crafts.

Since its opening, the collection has grown to more than 2,000 works by artists including Rosa Bonheur, Frida Kahlo, Helen Frankenthaler, Barbara Hepworth, Georgia O'Keeffe, Camille Claudel, Lila Cabot Perry, Mary Cassatt, Elaine de Kooning, Käthe Kollwitz, and many other lesser known but notable artists from earlier centuries. You will discover here, for instance, that the famed Peale family of 19th-century portrait painters included a very talented sister, Sarah Miriam Peale. The collection is complemented by an ongoing series of changing exhibits.

The museum is housed in a magnificent Renaissance Revival landmark building designed in 1907 as a Masonic temple by noted architect Waddy Wood. Its sweeping marble staircase and splendid interior make it a popular choice for wedding receptions.

✪ **Phillips Collection.** 1600 21st St. NW (at Q St.). ☎ **202/387-2151.** www.phillipscollection.org. Admission Sat–Sun $6.50 adults, $3.25 seniors and students, free for children 18 and under; contribution suggested Tues–Fri. Special exhibits may require an additional fee. Sept–May Tues–Wed and Fri–Sat 10am–5pm, Thurs 10am–8:30pm, Sun noon–5pm; June–Aug, noon–7pm. Free tours Wed and Sat 2pm. Closed Jan 1, July 4, Thanksgiving Day, and Dec 25. Metro: Dupont Circle (Q St. exit).

Conceived as "a museum of modern art and its sources," this intimate establishment, occupying an elegant 1890s Georgian Revival mansion and a more youthful wing, houses the exquisite collection of Duncan and Marjorie Phillips, avid collectors and proselytizers of modernism. Carpeted rooms with leaded- and stained-glass windows, oak paneling, plush chairs and sofas, and frequently, fireplaces, establish a comfortable, homelike setting. Today the collection includes more than 2,500 works. Among the highlights: superb Daumier, Dove, and Bonnard paintings; some splendid small Vuillards; five van Goghs; Renoir's *Luncheon of the Boating Party;* seven Cézannes; and six works by Georgia O'Keeffe. Ingres, Delacroix, Manet, El Greco, Goya, Corot, Constable, Courbet, Giorgione, and Chardin are among the "sources" or forerunners of modernism represented. Modern notables include Rothko, Hopper, Kandinsky, Matisse, Klee, Degas, Rouault, Picasso, and many others. It's a collection no art lover should miss. The museum presents an ongoing series of temporary shows, supplementing works from the Phillips with loans from other museums and private collections.

A full schedule of events includes gallery talks, lectures, and free concerts in the ornate music room. (Concerts take place every Sunday at 5pm, September through May; arrive early. Although the concert is free, admission to the museum on weekends costs $6.50.) On Thursdays, the museum stays open until 8:30pm for **Artful Evenings** with music, gallery talks, and a cash bar; admission is $5.

On the lower level, a charming little restaurant serves light fare.

8　Other Attractions

John F. Kennedy Center for the Performing Arts. New Hampshire Ave. NW (at Rock Creek Pkwy.). ☎ **800/444-1324** or 202/416-8341 for information or tickets. kennedy-center.org. Free admission. Daily 10am–midnight. Free guided tours Mon–Fri 10am–5pm, Sat–Sun between 10am and 1pm. Metro: Foggy Bottom (there's a free shuttle service from the station). Bus: no. 80 from Metro Center.

Opened in 1971, the Kennedy Center is both our national performing arts center and a memorial to John F. Kennedy. Carved into the center's river facade are several Kennedy quotations, including, "the New Frontier for which I campaign in public life can also be a New Frontier for American art." Set on 17 acres overlooking the Potomac, the striking $73-million facility, designed by noted architect Edward Durell Stone, encompasses an opera house, a concert hall, two stage theaters, a theater lab, and a film theater. The best way to see the Kennedy Center, including restricted areas, is to take a free 50-minute guided tour (see above for schedule). You can beat the crowds by writing in advance to a senator or congressperson for passes for a VIP tour, which are given year-round Monday through Saturday at 9:30am and 4:30pm, with a 9:45am tour added April through September. These tours are free, but you must have a letter from your senator or congressperson. Call ☎ **202/416-8303** for details.

The tour begins in the **Hall of Nations,** which displays the flags of all nations diplomatically recognized by the United States. Throughout the center you'll see gifts from more than 40 nations, including all the marble used in the building (3,700 tons), which Italy donated. First stop is the **Grand Foyer,** scene of many free concerts and programs and the reception area for all three theaters on the main level; the 18 crystal chandeliers are a gift from Sweden. You'll also visit the **Israeli Lounge** (where 40 painted and gilded panels depict scenes from the Old Testament); the **Concert Hall,** home of the National Symphony Orchestra; the **Opera House;** the **African Room** (decorated with beautiful tapestries from African nations); the **Eisenhower Theater;** the **Hall of States,** where flags of the 50 states and four territories are hung in the order they joined the Union; the **Performing Arts Library;** and the **Terrace Theater,** a Bicentennial gift from Japan. Your guide will point out many notable works of art along the way. If rehearsals are being held, visits to the theaters are omitted.

If you'd like to attend performances during your visit, call the toll-free number above and request the current issue of *Kennedy Center News Magazine,* a free publication that describes all Kennedy Center happenings and prices.

After the tour, walk around the building's terrace for a panoramic view of Washington and plan a meal in one of the Kennedy Center restaurants (see chapter 6). See chapter 9 for specifics on theater, concert, and film offerings. There is limited parking below the Kennedy Center during the day at $3 for the first hour, $6 for 2 hours, and a flat $8 starting at 2pm weekdays and all day weekends and holidays.

✪ **Union Station.** 50 Massachusetts Ave. NE. ☎ **202/371-9441.** www.unionstation.com. Free admission. Daily 24 hours. Shops Mon–Sat 10am–9pm, Sun 10am–6pm. Garage parking: $5 for up to 1 hour, $8 for 1 to 2 hours, $10 for 2 to 16 hours, and $12 for 16 to 24 hours. You get 2 hours free parking with store or restaurant's stamped validation. Metro: Union Station.

In Washington, D.C., the very train station where you arrive is itself a noteworthy sightseeing attraction. Union Station, built between 1903 and 1907 in the great age of rail travel, was painstakingly restored in the 1980s at a cost of $160 million. The station was designed by noted architect Daniel H. Burnham, who modeled it after the Baths of Diocletian and Arch of Constantine in Rome.

When it opened in 1907, this was the largest train station in the world. The Ionic colonnades outside were fashioned from white granite. The facade contains 100 eagles. In the front of the building, a replica of the Liberty Bell and a monumental statue of Columbus hold sway. Six carved fixtures over the entranceway represent Fire, Electricity, Freedom, Imagination, Agriculture, and Mechanics. You enter the station through graceful 50-foot Constantine arches, and walk across an expanse of white marble flooring. The **Main Hall** is a massive rectangular room with a 96-foot barrel-vaulted ceiling and a balcony adorned with 36 Augustus Saint-Gaudens sculptures of Roman legionnaires. Off the Main Hall is the **East Hall,** shimmering with scagliola marble walls and columns, a gorgeous hand-stenciled skylight ceiling, and stunning murals of classical scenes inspired by ancient Pompeian art. Today it's the station's plushest shopping venue.

In its heyday, this "temple of transport" witnessed many important events. President Wilson welcomed General Pershing here in 1918 on his return from France. South Pole explorer Rear Admiral Richard Byrd was also feted at Union Station on his homecoming. And Franklin D. Roosevelt's funeral train, bearing his casket, was met here in 1945 by thousands of mourners.

But after the 1960s, with the decline of rail travel, the station fell on hard times. Rain damage caused parts of the roof to cave in, and the entire building—with floors buckling, rats running about, and mushrooms sprouting in damp rooms—was sealed in 1981. That same year, Congress enacted legislation to preserve and faithfully restore this national treasure.

Today, Union Station is once again a vibrant entity patronized by locals and visitors alike. Every square inch of the facility has been cleaned, repaired, and/or replaced according to the original design. About 100 retail and food shops on three levels offer a wide array of merchandise. And you'll be happy to find that most of the offerings in the Food Court are not fast-food joints, but an eclectic mix of restaurants. The skylit **Main Concourse,** which extends the entire length of the station, is the primary shopping area as well as a ticketing and baggage facility. A nine-screen cinema complex has been installed on the lower level. The remarkable restoration, which involved hundreds of European and American artisans using historical research, bygone craft techniques, and modern technology, is meticulous in every detail.

Stop by the visitor kiosk in the Main Hall. See chapter 6 for information on Union Station restaurants and chapter 8 for information about shops.

✪ **Washington National Cathedral.** Massachusetts and Wisconsin aves. NW (entrance on Wisconsin Ave.). ☎ **202/537-6207.** www.cathedral.org. Admission $3 adults, $1 children, plus fees for specialty tours (see information below). Cathedral daily 10am–4:30pm; May 1– Labor Day, the nave level stays open weeknights until 9pm. Gardens open daily until dusk. Tours Mon–Sat 10–11:30am and 12:45–3:15pm, and Sun 12:30–2:45pm; suggested donation $2 per adult, $1 per child. No tours are given on Thanksgiving, Christmas, Palm Sunday, or Easter, or during services. Worship services vary throughout the year but you can count on a daily Evensong service at 4pm, a noon service Mon–Sat, and an 11am service every Sun; call for other service times. Metro: Tenleytown, then about a 20-minute walk. Bus: Any N bus up Massachusetts Ave. from Dupont Circle or any 30-series bus along Wisconsin Ave. Also, this is a stop on the Old Town Trolley Tour.

Pierre L'Enfant's 1791 plan for the capital city included "a great church for national purposes," but possibly because of early America's fear of mingling church and state, more than a century elapsed before the foundation for Washington National Cathedral was laid. Its actual name is the Cathedral Church of St. Peter and St. Paul. The church is Episcopal, but it has no local congregation and seeks to serve the entire nation as a house of prayer for all people. It has been the setting for every kind of religious observance from Jewish to Serbian Orthodox.

A church of this magnitude—it's the sixth-largest cathedral in the world—took a long time to build. Its principal (but not original) architect, Philip Hubert Frohman, worked on the project from 1921 until his death in 1972. The foundation stone was laid in 1907 using the mallet with which George Washington set the Capitol cornerstone. Construction was interrupted by both world wars and by periods of financial difficulty. The cathedral was completed with the placement of the final stone atop a pinnacle on the west front towers on September 29, 1990, 83 years to the day it was begun.

English Gothic in style (with several distinctly 20th-century innovations, such as a stained-glass window commemorating the flight of *Apollo 11* and containing a piece of moon rock), the cathedral is built in the shape of a cross, complete with flying buttresses and gargoyles. It is, along with the Capitol and the Washington Monument, one of the dominant structures on the Washington skyline. Its 57-acre landscaped grounds have two lovely gardens (the lawn is ideal for picnicking); four schools, including the College of Preachers; an herb garden; a greenhouse; and two gift shops (one in the cathedral basement, the other in the Herb Cottage).

Over the years the cathedral has seen much history. Services to celebrate the end of World Wars I and II were held here. It was the scene of President Wilson's funeral (he and his wife are buried here), as well as President Eisenhower's. Helen Keller and her companion, Anne Sullivan, were buried in the cathedral at her request. And during the Iranian crisis, a round-the-clock prayer vigil was held in the Holy Spirit Chapel throughout the hostages' captivity. When they were released, the hostages came to a service here, and tears flowed at Colonel Thomas Shaefer's poignant greeting, "Good morning, my fellow Americans. You don't know how long I've been waiting to say those words."

The best way to explore the cathedral and see its abundance of art, architectural carvings, and statuary is to take a 30- to 45-minute guided tour; they leave continually, from the west end of the nave. You can also walk through on your own, using a self-guiding brochure available in several languages. Call about group and special-interest tours, both of which require reservations (☎ **202/537-6207**). Special-interest tours cover topics ranging from the cathedral's architecture to its stained glass, and generally cost $4 per person.

Allow additional time to tour the grounds or "close" and to visit the Observation Gallery where 70 windows provide panoramic views. Tuesday and Wednesday afternoon tours are followed by a high tea in the Observation Gallery—for $18 per person, reservations required.

The cathedral hosts numerous events: organ recitals, choir performances, an annual flower mart, calligraphy workshops, jazz, folk, and classical concerts, and the playing of the 53-bell carillon. Check the cathedral's Web site for upcoming events and other information at **www.cathedral.org**.

9 Further Afield: Arlington

The land that today comprises Arlington County was originally carved out of Virginia as part of the nation's new capital district. In 1847, the land was returned to the state of Virginia, although it was known as Alexandria County until 1920, when the name was changed to avoid confusion with the city of Alexandria.

The county was named to honor Arlington House (inside Arlington National Cemetery, see entry earlier in this chapter), built by George Washington Parke Custis, whose daughter married Robert E. Lee. The Lees lived in Arlington House on and off until the onset of the Civil War in 1861. After the first Battle of Bull Run, at Manassas, several Union soldiers were buried here; the beginnings of Arlington National Cemetery date from that time. The Arlington Memorial Bridge leads directly from the Lincoln Memorial to the Robert E. Lee Memorial at Arlington House and symbolizes the joining of the figures of Lincoln, representing the North, and Lee, representing the South, into one Union, following the Civil War.

Arlington has long been a residential community, with most people commuting into Washington to work and play. In recent years, however, the suburb has come into its own, booming with business, restaurants, and nightlife, giving residents reasons to stay put and tourists more of an inducement to visit (see the box, "Arlington Row," in chapter 9). Here are a couple of sites worth seeing:

The Newseum & Freedom Park. 1101 Wilson Blvd. (at N. Kent St.). ☎ **888-NEWSEUM** or 703/284-3544. www.newseum.org. Newseum Wed–Sun 10am–5pm. Freedom Park daily dawn–dusk. Limited parking is available in the building. Metro: Rosslyn.

Kids love this place because they can ham it up as a pretend newscaster, view themselves broadcasting up on the screen, and then talk mom and dad into plunking down $7 so they can take home the videotaped performance.

The Newseum opened on April 18, 1997, and is the world's first museum dedicated exclusively to news. The 72,000 square feet of space occupies an existing office building, reconfigured into exhibit halls and a 220-seat theater topped by an immense dome. Using state-of-the-art multimedia presentations and interactive exhibits, the museum explores the history of news dissemination and the influence of the First Amendment, granting Americans the freedom of speech and of the press. Highlights include a geodesic globe constructed of stainless steel plates and bearing the names of every existing American daily newspaper and many from around the world; a two-story-high, block-long Video Newswall displaying, via satellite and fiber optics, more up-to-the-minute news feeds than any other site in the world; a theater featuring a signature presentation about news; a news forum/TV studio where visitors can view broadcast productions in progress and discuss news events and issues; and a walk-through history of news gathering from the ancient preprint oral traditions to the latest electronic developments. In the news history gallery, look for intriguing artifacts, such as a 1455 Gutenberg Bible and a pen that belonged to Charles Dickens. The museum hosts a series of three photography exhibits during the year. The News Byte Cafe offers snack fare; the gift shop sells T-shirts, hats, and other souvenir items.

Pentagon Touring Tips

Tourists under 16 must be accompanied by an adult. Those 16 and older must bring a current photo ID that includes a signature and expiration date (driver's license, passport, college ID, international student ID, and so on) to be admitted. You'll have to go through a metal detector and have your bags X-rayed before the tour.

Adjoining the museum, **Freedom Park,** which opened in the summer of 1996 and sits atop a never-used elevated highway, celebrates the spirit of freedom and the struggle to preserve it. Here, too, are many intriguing exhibits: segments of the Berlin Wall; stones from the Warsaw Ghetto; a bronze casting of a South African ballot box; a headless statue of Lenin (one of many that were pushed over and beheaded when the Soviet Union collapsed in 1991); and a bronze casting of the Birmingham, Alabama, jail-cell door that enclosed Martin Luther King, Jr. The glass-and-steel Freedom Forum Journalists Memorial (honoring more than 900 journalists killed while on assignment) rises above the Potomac, offering views of the Washington Monument, the Lincoln and Jefferson Memorials, and the National Cathedral.

The Pentagon. Off I-395. ☎ **703/695-1776.** Free admission. Guided tours Mon–Fri 9:30am–3:30pm, every 30 minutes. Closed federal holidays and weekends. Metro: Pentagon.

The immense five-sided headquarters of the American military establishment was built during the early years of World War II. It's the world's largest office building, housing approximately 24,000 employees. For their convenience, it contains a complete indoor shopping mall, including two banks, a post office, an Amtrak ticket office, a beauty salon, a dry cleaner, and more. It's a self-contained world. There are many mind-boggling statistics to underscore the vastness of the Pentagon—for example, the building contains enough phone cable to gird the globe three times!

You can take a free 75-to-90 minute tour of certain corridors, covering the distance of a mile. It departs from the registration booth in the Concourse area at the Pentagon Metro entrance. During the tourist season, try to arrive by 9am, when the booth opens. Groups of 10 or more must make reservations.

The tour begins with an explanation of the Department of Defense hierarchy and a short introductory film about the development of the Pentagon. Then a military guide takes you around. You'll visit:

The Air Force Art Collection, which commemorates historic events involving the U.S. Air Force, including cartoons drawn by Walt Disney when he was an ambulance driver during World War I.

The Air Force Executive Corridor, where, as you might have guessed, air force executives have their offices.

The POW Alcove, hung with artists' conceptions of life in POW camps such as the "Hanoi Hilton."

The Marine Corps Corridor, with a small display, because the marines are actually headquartered in the Navy Annex a quarter of a mile away. Did you know that marines are called "leathernecks" because they used to wear leather collars to protect their necks from fatal sword blows?

The Navy Executive Corridor, lined with portraits of former secretaries and undersecretaries of the navy. Glass cases display models of ships and submarines in the navy's current fleet, and the solid oak doors in this corridor are modeled after old ship captain's doors.

The Army Executive Corridor, or Marshall Corridor, named for General George C. Marshall, the first military man to receive a Nobel Peace Prize (for the Marshall Plan that helped Europe recover after World War II). Displayed here are army command and divisional flags and 172 army campaign streamers dating from 1775 through the Gulf War.

The Time-Life Art Collection Corridor. During World War II Time-Life hired civilian artists to paint battle scenes at the front line. Most affecting is *Two-Thousand Yard Stare,* showing a soldier suffering from battle fatigue.

The MacArthur Corridor honors General Douglas MacArthur. His career spanned 52 years, during which he served in three wars under nine presidents.

The Hall of Heroes is where Medal of Honor recipients (3,409 to date) are commemorated. The medal is given out only during wartime and usually posthumously.

The Military Women's Corridor documents the role of women throughout U.S. armed services history.

The Navaho Code Talkers Corridor tells the story of the code language developed for military communications after the Japanese bombed Pearl Harbor during World War II. The U.S. military recruited the help of 400 Navahos, all marines, to create an indecipherable means of communication from the Navaho language.

The Flag Corridor displays state and territorial flags, from the first Union Jack to the 50-star flag of today. This is where the tour concludes.

Note: The best way to get to the Pentagon is via Metro's blue or yellow lines. If you must drive, call for directions.

10 More Than a Pedestrian Experience: Two Walking Tours

So much of Washington sightseeing focuses on larger-than-life buildings, events, and people. And that's how it should be. Monumental accomplishments deserve monumental recognition. By visiting the Capitol, the White House, the Supreme Court, and the presidential and war memorials, you begin to understand the tremendous achievements of American history. By touring the Smithsonian and other large museums, you come to appreciate the beauty and significance of arts and sciences from the dawn of man to the present.

It can be overwhelming, though. So much history and culture, such a grand scale. If you find yourself suffering from edifice complex, try a more manageable approach to sightseeing, the walking tour. This section presents two that are each very specific and personal in scope. They take you in and out of historic houses in a particular neighborhood, allowing you to learn about the long-ago lives of individual Washingtonians, some famous, others not so.

Walking Tour 1
Dupont Circle's Historic Homes

Start: 1307 New Hampshire Ave. NW (Dupont Circle Metro station).

Finish: 2320 S St. NW (Dupont Circle Metro station).

Time: Approximately 4 to 5 hours, including tours and breaks.

Best Times: If you want to see all the houses, you should start mid-morning, Wednesday through Saturday.

Worst Times: Before 10am, in late afternoon, and Sunday through Tuesday, when the houses are closed or getting ready to close.

The neighborhood you cover in this tour is Washington at its most cosmopolitan. At its center is Massachusetts Avenue, the main thoroughfare known as ✪ **"Embassy Row"** because of the number of embassies located along the avenue and on its side streets. Many of the embassies occupy magnificent mansions built in the early part of the 20th century for the city's wealthy, so it is a treat to stroll here.

From the Dupont Circle Metro station, 19th Street exit, cross 19th Street, continue around the circle to New Hampshire Avenue, and turn left. Follow New Hampshire Avenue to its juncture with 20th Street. Here is the:

1. **Heurich House Museum,** 1307 New Hampshire Ave. NW (☎ **202/785-2068;** www.hswdc.org). This four-story, brownstone and brick, turreted Victorian castle was built as a residence in 1894 for wealthy German businessman and brewer Christian Heurich and his family. (Heurich's grandson, Gary, revived the business in 1986; you may notice his Foggy Bottom Ale delivery trucks around Washington). Old Heurich was a character, as you'll learn by touring three floors of the mansion. He was more than cautious: He constructed the house of poured concrete, making it the city's first fireproof dwelling. And though Heurich installed 17 grand fireplaces throughout, he permitted no one to use them; to this day, the fireplaces remain virginal. The proud brewer incorporated his favorite drinking mottoes into the murals painted on the walls of his basement Bierstube (tavern room): "He who has never been drunk is not a brave man" and "There is room in the smallest chamber for the biggest hangover." As you tour, be on the lookout for Heurich's ghost, who has been spotted here "wearing a blue seersucker-like jacket and looking like Colonel Sanders."

Whether or not you spy any ghosts, your jaw may drop at the sight of Heurich's heavy-handed decorating, reflective of Victorian times and the man's indomitable personality. Elaborate embellishments adorn every conceivable space throughout the 31 principal rooms. Allegorical paintings cover the ceilings; decorative brass grilles hide the radiators; intricately carved wood panels encase the fireplaces; gilding gelds the bathroom tiles. The foyer recalls a medieval castle, with its standing suit of armor, mosaic floor, and silvered plaster medallions on the stucco walls. A Victorian garden (open to picnickers weekdays 11am to 3pm) and brick patio lie off the back of the house. The mansion serves as headquarters for the Historical Society of Washington, D.C., whose offices and library are on the second and third floors.

Tours, Hours & Admission: Tours are walk-in, self-guided, Monday through Saturday 10am to 4pm. Admission is $3 for adults, $1.50 for seniors and students, free for children under 6. Docents also lead guided tours that highlight varied themes, from technology of the time, to women's history viewed through domestic life, to servants' stories. Call in advance for a schedule and reservations for the guided tours, which cost $5. The gift shop stocks Victorian and turn-of-the-century items, as well as jewelry and decorative arts crafted by local artisans. Closed federal holidays.

☕ **TAKE A BREAK**   Is it too soon for lunch? Cross New Hampshire Avenue at the corner to reach 20th Street, then cross 20th Street. Walk up 20th Street to P Street NW and turn left. The 2 blocks of P Street, from 20th to 22nd Street, but especially that first block, hold one good restaurant after another: **Johnny's Half Shell** (☎ **202/296-2021**) for inexpensive raw bar and seafood eating, **Al Tiramisu,** 2014 P St. NW (☎ **202/467-4466**) for excellent pasta; **Pesce,** 2016 P St. NW (☎ **202/466-3474**) for sophisticated seafood dishes in a laid-back atmosphere; **Sala Thai,** 2016 P St. NW (☎ **202/872-1144**) for great

Walking Tour 1—Dupont Circle's Historic Homes

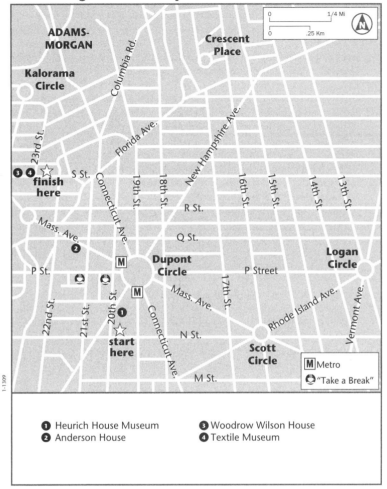

0 .... 1/4 Mi

0 .... .25 Km

ADAMS-MORGAN

Crescent Place

Kalorama Circle

Columbia Rd.

Florida Ave.

New Hampshire Ave.

23rd St.

19th St.

18th St.

16th St.

15th St.

14th St.

13th St.

S St.

❸❹ ☆ **finish here**

Connecticut Ave.

R St.

Q St.

Mass. Ave.

❷

P St.

Ⓜ **Dupont Circle**

Logan Circle

P Street

22nd St.

21st St.

20th St.

Ⓜ

17th St.

Mass. Ave.

❶

Connecticut Ave.

N St.

start here ☆

Rhode Island Ave.

Vermont Ave.

Scott Circle

M St.

| Ⓜ Metro |
| ☕ "Take a Break" |

1-1309

❶ Heurich House Museum
❷ Anderson House

❸ Woodrow Wilson House
❹ Textile Museum

Thai food at good prices; and **BeDuCi,** 2100 P St. NW (☎ **202/223-3824**), which serves Mediterranean cuisine in a sunporch-fronted dining room that opens to the outdoors in warm weather. Across P Street are more restaurants. See chapter 6 for full descriptions.

Back outside, return to the corner of 21st and P Streets, cross P Street, and walk up 21st Street to Massachusetts Avenue NW. Turn left at the Westin Fairfax and proceed to the "house" next door.

2. **Anderson House,** 2118 Massachusetts Ave. NW (☎ **202/785-2040**). It took three years, from 1902 to 1905, to build this palatial beaux arts mansion, which was the winter residence of Larz Anderson and his heiress wife, Isabel. Isabel's $17 million inheritance from her grandfather, shipping magnate William Fletcher Weld, helped pay for Anderson House. Anderson was a career diplomat who served as ambassador to Japan in 1912 and 1913. In 1937, following her husband's death, Isabel gave the house and much of its original art and furnishings to the Society of the Cincinnati, to which Larz had belonged. Anderson was

descended from an original member of this society, which was founded in 1783 by Continental officers who had served in the American Revolution. (George Washington was its president-general from 1783 until 1799.) A $6.1 million renovation was completed to preserve, not alter, the magnificent castle. The mansion's 50 rooms stagger the imagination, and include an immense ballroom with a 30-foot-high coffered ceiling and ornate, Louis XV–style French and English parlors embellished in 23-karat gold leaf. Anderson belongings are on display throughout, including Belgian and Flemish tapestries, 17th-century wood choir stalls from Naples, and Asian and European paintings and antiquities. A solarium (with gilt-accented door frames and ceilings) leads through French doors to a lovely courtyard-garden. Open by appointment is the Society of the Cincinnati Library, which houses more than 40,000 works focused on the American Revolution and the "art of war" in the 18th century.

Tours, Hours & Admission: Tours are walk-in, self-guided, Tuesday through Saturday 1 to 4pm. Admission is free. Closed on national holidays. Call about free concert series.

From Anderson House, turn left on Massachusetts Avenue NW, away from Dupont Circle, cross Q Street, proceed down Massachusetts Avenue, cross Florida Avenue, and then cross Massachusetts Avenue. Walk up Massachusetts Avenue and around Sheridan Circle to 24th Street and turn right. Go half a block to S Street NW, turn right, and walk a few yards to the:

3. Woodrow Wilson House, 2340 S St. NW (☎ 202/387-4062). Woodrow Wilson wasn't just our 28th president, he was also a lovesick suitor who married his second wife, Edith Galt, after a whirlwind courtship. He was a prolific writer, whose 19 books include a popular biography of George Washington. Here you'll learn about the personal as well as the political sides of Wilson's life.

Wilson served two terms in the White House, then retired to this Georgian Revival home in 1921 with Edith, whom he had courted and married while in the White House, following the death of his first wife. During 1-hour tours given continuously throughout the day, docents describe Wilson's career and character: He had been a mediocre lawyer, but successful president of Princeton University, then governor of New Jersey, before becoming president. You are reminded that this is the president best remembered for his international outlook, and that his efforts to promote the League of Nations contributed to a stroke and declining health until his death in 1924.

The house is preserved much as it was when the Wilsons lived here in the 1920s. The drawing room is furnished with wedding presents, including a Gobelin tapestry given to the couple by the French ambassador; and it was at the drawing room window that Wilson stood to acknowledge the crowd that had gathered in the street below to honor him on Armistice Day in 1923. Among the items you see in the family room/library are Wilson's desk chair from the White House and the screen that the Wilsons pulled down to watch silent movies by Charlie Chaplin (their favorite) and other stars. Unlike today, when Wilson was president no laws restricted him from keeping the gifts he received while in office. Throughout the house, you'll notice beautiful tapestries and other gifts that foreign governments bestowed on him. When you reach the dining room, the docent tells you that Wilson insisted that guests at dinner "wear black tie and refrain from discussing religion and politics." Edith died in 1961, bequeathing the house and its belongings to the National Trust for Historic Preservation. The Woodrow Wilson House is the only presidential museum in the capital.

Tours, Hours & Admission: The house is open Tuesday through Sunday 10am to 4pm. Admission is $5 for adults, $4 for seniors, $2.50 for students, free for children age 7 and under. Closed on federal holidays. Call about special events and exhibits. There's also a gift shop.

Now turn right from the entrance and go right next door to:

4. The Textile Museum, 2320 S St. NW (☎ **202/667-0441;** www.textilemuseum. org). The Textile Museum occupies two buildings, the first designed by John Russell Pope, architect of the Jefferson Memorial and the West Wing of the National Gallery, and the adjoining structure designed by Waddy B. Wood, architect for the Woodrow Wilson House.

A man named George Hewitt Myers founded The Textile Museum in 1925, in what was then his home (one of several). Myers was a wealthy man, the founder of Merganthaler Linotype and of the investment firm Y.E. Booker & Co., which is still in operation in Baltimore. His interest in textiles began in 1896, when Myers purchased an Oriental rug for his Yale dormitory room. By 1925, his collection included 275 rugs and 60 related textiles. When he died in 1957, Myers's collection encompassed not only Oriental carpets, but also textiles from Africa, Asia, and Latin America.

Today, the Textile Museum holds more than 15,500 textiles and carpets, dating as far back as 3,000 B.C. They include Turkish rugs and Peruvian tunics, Suzani embroideries from central Asia, and tapestries from Egypt. Not all are on display, of course. The museum rotates exhibits from its permanent collection in high-ceilinged rooms that are dimly lighted to preserve the fabrics. One of the exhibit areas holds a computer loaded with design software that visitors, especially kids, are invited to use. Friendly interns assist.

Tours, Hours & Admission: Introductory tours take place September through May, Wednesday, Saturday, and Sunday at 2pm. Or you can call two weeks in advance to reserve a spot on a docent-led tour. You may also walk in and tour the place on your own: The museum is open year-round Monday through Saturday 10am to 5pm, Sunday 1 to 5pm. Closed on federal holidays and Christmas Eve. Donation of $5 suggested. Call about special lectures and workshops. Poke around the garden and intriguing gift shop.

To get back to the Metro, return to Massachusetts Avenue, turn left, and follow the avenue back around Sheridan Circle, keeping to the odd-numbered side of the street until it meets 20th Street, where you'll find the entrance to the Dupont Circle Metro station.

Walking Tour 2
Georgetown's Historic Homes

Start: 3051 M St. NW (Foggy Bottom Metro station).

Finish: 1703 32nd St. NW (Dupont Circle Metro station).

Time: Approximately 5 hours, including tours and breaks.

Best Times: If you want to see all the houses, you should start first thing in the morning, Wednesday through Saturday, because two of the houses close in midafternoon.

Worst Times: In August, when Dumbarton House is closed, and in late afternoon, when two of the houses are closed.

The Georgetown area famous for its shops, restaurants, and bars is not the Georgetown you'll see on this walking tour. Instead, the circuit will take you along quiet streets lined with charming houses and stately trees that bespeak the town's age and history. The town of George, comprising 60 acres and named for the king of England, was officially established in 1751. It assumed new importance in 1790, when George Washington specified a nearby site on the Potomac River for America's new capital city.

From the Foggy Bottom Metro station, walk up 23rd Street NW to Washington Circle, and go left around the circle to Pennsylvania Avenue. Continue on Pennsylvania Avenue until you reach M Street NW.

TAKE A BREAK   Seasons, Four Seasons Hotel, 2800 Pennsylvania Ave. NW (☎ **202/342-0810**). Before you start walking, give yourself something to walk off. Breakfast here is sumptuous but pricey: $7.75 for blueberry pancakes, $11.50 for continental breakfast, and so on. For a quicker, cheaper fix, stop at the **Starbucks** at 3122 M St. NW.

Once you are satiated, head to the:

1. **Old Stone House,** 3051 M St. NW (☎ **202/426-6851**). Located on one of the busiest streets in Washington, the unobtrusive Old Stone House offers a quiet look back at pre-Revolutionary times, when its first owner, a carpenter, used the ground floor as a workshop. The house dates from 1765, making it the only surviving pre-Revolutionary building in the city. Acquired by the National Park Service in 1926, the House's four small rooms are furnished as they would have been in the late 18th century, during the period when Georgetown was a significant tobacco and shipping port. Park rangers provide information and sometimes demonstrate cooking on an open fireplace, spinning, and making pomander balls. Beyond the house is a pretty, terraced lawn and 18th-century–style English flower garden, a spot long frequented by Georgetown shop and office workers seeking a respite.

    Tours, Hours & Admission: The Old Stone House is open to the public Wednesday to Sunday 10am to 4pm. Admission is free. Closed federal holidays.

    From the Old Stone House, head to Dumbarton House. First, though, you may want to take a short detour to the **Georgetown Post Office,** around the corner on 31st Street. Recently renovated to the tune of $2.1 million, the 140-year-old building was designed with Italian Renaissance palaces in mind. Step inside to admire the grand space, with its high ceiling, gilded capitals, and cast-iron columns. When you're through, walk back down to M Street, follow it to 28th Street, and turn left. Follow 28th Street to Q Street and turn right, where you'll have no trouble finding:

2. **Dumbarton House,** 2715 Q St. NW (☎ **202/337-2288**). This stately mansion lies behind a long brick wall and dominates the block. Begun in 1799 and completed in 1805, the house is exemplary of Federal-period architecture, meaning its rooms are exactly symmetrical, below and above stairs, and are centered around a large hall. The house is filled with Federal-period furnishings, like the dining room's late-18th-century sideboard, over which hangs a painting by Charles Willson Peale.

    On guided, 45-minute tours, you learn a bit of the history of the house. For example, one of its first owners was Joseph Nourse, first Register of the U.S. Treasury, who lived here with his family from 1805 to 1813. Recent research has confirmed that Dolley Madison stopped here for a cup of tea during her escape from the burning White House in 1812, before crossing by ferry into Virginia.

Walking Tour 2—Georgetown's Historic Homes

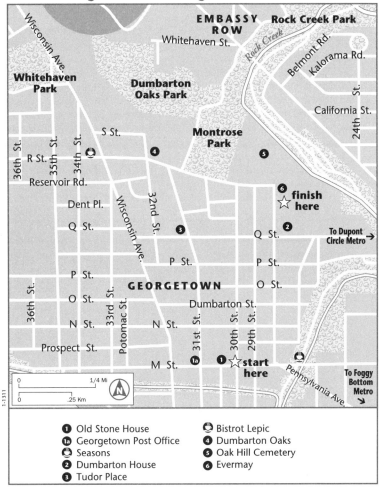

- **1** Old Stone House
- **1a** Georgetown Post Office
- **Seasons**
- **2** Dumbarton House
- **3** Tudor Place
- **Bistrot Lepic**
- **4** Dumbarton Oaks
- **5** Oak Hill Cemetery
- **6** Evermay

Tours, Hours & Admission: Dumbarton House serves as headquarters for the Colonial Dames of America, who restored the house. It is open for guided tours only, Tuesday through Saturday starting at 10:15am, with the last tour at 12:15pm. A $3 donation is requested; students are free. Groups of 10 or more need a reservation. Dumbarton House is closed August 1 through Labor Day, Thanksgiving holiday weekend, and December 25 through January 1.

Turn right when you exit the house, and follow Q Street as far as 31st Street. This is a quiet and pleasant stroll, along wide, brick-laid sidewalks, past old town houses with turrets and other examples of Georgetown's fine architecture. For some reason, many of these streets bear no street signs. Fortunately, 31st Street is not only marked, but a sign tells you to turn right on 31st Street to reach Tudor Place. So, turn right and walk to the grand gates at mid-block and press the buzzer to gain entry.

3. Tudor Place, 1644 31st St. NW (☎ **202/965-0400;** www.tudorplace.org). Occupying an entire city block, Tudor Place is a 5.5-acre estate of sloping green lawns and exquisite gardens. At its summit is the magnificent, Palladian-style manor house designed by Dr. William Thornton, the first architect of the U.S. Capitol. Martha Custis Peter, Martha Washington's granddaughter, purchased Tudor Place in 1805 with an $8,000 legacy left her by her step-grandfather, George Washington. Martha Custis Peter was married to Georgetown mayor Thomas Peter; their descendants lived here until 1984.

The house is architecturally exceptional—note the clever pull-up windows to the domed portico overlooking the south lawn, a feature found in another Thornton creation, the Octagon. Many of the furnishings were inherited or were purchased at auction from Mount Vernon. On your tour, you'll have the chance to scan a loving letter written by George Washington to Martha on June 18, 1775, upon receiving command of the Revolutionary Army: ". . . I should enjoy more real happiness and felicity in 1 month with you, at home, than I have the most distant prospect of reaping abroad . . . ."

Henry Clay, Daniel Webster, and John Calhoun visited Tudor Place. The Marquis de Lafayette attended a reception held here in his honor in 1824. Robert E. Lee was a close friend of the family, who were Confederate sympathizers.

Tours, Hours & Admission: If you arrive between the normal tour times of Tuesday through Friday at 10am, 11:30am, 1pm, and 2:30pm, and Saturday on the hour, 10am to 3pm, take the opportunity to visit the delightful 5-acre Federal-period garden, which includes centuries-old boxwoods, a lily pond, a bowling green, pear trees, ivy-covered arbors, and intimate seating alcoves. You tour the Tudor Place mansion by guide only, in 45-minute sessions. Tudor Place offers several tours on specific subjects, for instance, the "19th-Century Mistresses of Tudor Place," tour. Donations of $6 per adult, $5 for seniors, $3 for students are requested. The gardens are open Monday through Saturday 10am to 4pm for self-guided tours; a $2 per person donation is requested. A map guides you through the gardens. Tudor Place is closed for major holidays.

From Tudor Place, turn left on 31st Street, away from the direction you came, and follow 31st Street to R Street and turn left again. Walk along R Street for about 2 blocks, and you reach Wisconsin Avenue. Cross Wisconsin Avenue and walk the few steps to:

TAKE A BREAK   Bistrot Lepic, 1736 Wisconsin Ave. NW (☎ **202/333-0111**). The very French Bistrot Lepic is a small place with a large following. Because of the restaurant's petite size and great popularity, it's best to reserve a table in advance if you want to sample its traditional (onion tart) and nouvelle (grape leaves stuffed with crab) cuisine. See chapter 6 for details.

Now retrace your steps, crossing Wisconsin Avenue again to return to R Street. Turn right and walk a block to 32nd Street, turning left. Go to the imposing double doors and enter at:

4. Dumbarton Oaks, 1703 32nd St. NW (☎ **202/339-6401;** www.doaks.org). The oldest part of this grand mansion dates from 1800. Since then, the house has undergone considerable change, most notably at the hands of a couple named Robert and Mildred Bliss.

The wealthy Blisses retired here in 1933, ending Robert's 33-year career in the Foreign Service. Over the years, the Blisses amassed collections of Byzantine and pre-Columbian art and books relating to those studies, as well as to landscape architecture. Their move into Dumbarton Oaks began a remodeling of the mansion to accommodate the collections and the library, which now occupy the entire building. When the Blisses relocated in 1940, they conveyed the house, gardens, and Byzantine art collection to Harvard University, Robert's alma mater. In 1963, two new wings were completed, one to house the pre-Columbian works, the other to hold Mrs. Bliss's gardening books.

You may guide yourself through the exhibit rooms to view these unique artworks, from Byzantine illuminated manuscripts, jewelry, and mosaic icons to pre-Columbian Olmec jade figures (the Olmec is the earliest known civilization in Mexico) and Mayan pottery. Pre-Columbian works are displayed chronologically in an octet of glass pavilions.

In 1944, Dumbarton Oaks hosted two international conferences that cemented the principles later incorporated into the United Nations charter. The conferences took place in the Music Room, which you should visit to see the immense, 16th-century stone chimneypiece, 18th-century parquet floor, and antique French, Italian, and Spanish furniture, as well as the El Greco painting, *The Visitation.*

Today, Dumbarton Oaks is a research center for studies in Byzantine and pre-Columbian art and history and in landscape architecture. Most Washingtonians know Dumbarton Oaks for its magnificent 10-acre terraced garden, which includes an orangery; wisteria-covered arbors; groves of cherry trees; magnolias; and herbaceous borders. You can't picnic here, though; for that, you must go down the block to Montrose Park.

Hours & Admission: Dumbarton Oaks' collections are open Tuesday through Sunday 2 to 5pm ($1 donation suggested). The gardens (entrance on R Street) are open November to March, daily 2 to 5pm for no charge; April to October, daily 2 to 6pm for a charge of $4 per adult, $3 per senior citizen and children under 12. Both gardens and collections are closed on national holidays and Dec. 24; the gardens may also close during inclement weather.

You can wind down your tour by walking away from Wisconsin Avenue on R Street, passing Montrose Park and:

5. **Oak Hill Cemetery,** the 25-acre Victorian landscaped burial place founded in 1850 and whose graves include those of William Wilson Corcoran (of the Corcoran Gallery of Art), Edwin Stanton (Lincoln's secretary of war), and Dean Acheson (secretary of state under Truman). If you want to stroll, purchase a map of the graves at the gatehouse, 3001 R St. NW, itself a beautiful brick and sandstone Italianate structure built in 1850. The cemetery is open weekdays 10am to 4pm.

As you leave, note the beautiful house across the street at 2920 R St.: It's the home of *Washington Post* publisher Katherine Graham.

Follow the brick sidewalk and iron fence as it curves down 28th Street to:

6. **Evermay,** 1623 28th St. NW, which you can't visit—it's a private residence—but which you can ogle from the gate. You also can't see much of it, because the brick ramparts and foliage hide it so well, but what's on view is impressive. As the plaque on the estate wall tells you, Evermay was built in 1792–94 by Scotsman Samuel Davidson, with the proceeds Davidson made from the sale of lands he owned around the city, including part of the present-day White House and Lafayette Square property.

Note: From here, believe it or not, you are only about a 15- or 20-minute walk from the Dupont Circle part of town—and the Metro. Walk down to Q Street NW, turn left, and follow Q Street across the Dumbarton Bridge to Massachusetts Avenue NW. Walk along Massachusetts Avenue to 20th Street NW and turn left. Continue another block, and you're at the Dupont Circle Metro station.

11 Parks & Gardens

Like most cities, Washington intersperses manicured pockets of green between office buildings and traffic-laden streets. Unlike most cities, it's also extensively endowed with vast natural areas all centrally located within the District: thousands of parkland acres; two rivers; the mouth of an 185-mile-long, tree-lined canalside trail; an untamed wilderness area; and a few thousand cherry trees. And there's much more just a stone's throw away.

GARDENS

Enid A. Haupt Garden. 10th St. and Independence Ave. SW. ☎ **202/357-2700.** Free admission. Late May–Aug daily 7am–8pm; Sept to mid-May daily 7am–5:45pm. Closed Dec 25. Metro: Smithsonian.

Named for its donor, a noted supporter of horticultural projects, this stunning garden presents elaborate flower beds and borders; plant-filled turn-of-the-century urns; 1870s cast-iron furnishings; and lush baskets hung from reproduction 19th-century lampposts. Although on ground level, the garden is really a 4-acre rooftop garden above the subterranean Sackler and African Art museums. A magnolia-lined parterre, framed by four floral swags, centers on a floral bed patterned after the rose window in the Commons of the Castle; it is composed of 30,000 green and yellow Alternanthera, supplemented by seasonal displays of spring pansies, begonias, or cabbage and kale. An "Island Garden" near the Sackler Gallery, entered via a 9-foot moongate, has benches backed by English boxwoods under the shade of weeping cherry trees; half-round pieces of granite in its still pool are meant to suggest ripples. A "Fountain Garden" outside the African Art Museum provides granite seating walls shaded by hawthorn trees, with tiny water channels fed by fountains and a waterfall or "chadar" inspired by the gardens of Shalimar. Three small terraces, shaded by black sour-gum trees, are located near the Arts & Industries Building. And five majestic linden trees shade a seating area around the Downing Urn, a memorial to American landscapist Andrew Jackson Downing. Additional features include wisteria-covered dome-shaped trellises, clusters of trees (Zumi crabapples, ginkgoes, and American hollies), a weeping European beech, and rose gardens. Elaborate cast-iron carriage gates made according to a 19th-century design by James Renwick, flanked by four red sandstone pillars, have been installed at the Independence Avenue entrance to the garden.

✪ United States Botanic Garden. 100 Maryland Ave. at 1st St. SW (at the east end of the Mall). ☎ **202/225-8333.** Free admission. Daily 9am–5pm. Metro: Federal Center SW.

Well, you're out of luck. The Botanic Garden is currently undergoing a major renovation and won't reopen until about 2001. Keep up with its progress by checking the Web site at **www.nationalgarden.org**. You *can* visit the garden annex across the street, **Bartholdi Park.** The park is about the size of a city block, with a stunning cast-iron classical fountain created by Frédéric Auguste Bartholdi, designer of the Statue of Liberty. Charming flower gardens bloom amid tall ornamental grasses, benches are sheltered by vine-covered bowers, and a touch and fragrance garden contains such herbs as pineapple-scented sage.

United States National Arboretum. 3501 New York Ave. NE. ☎ **202/245-2726.** www.ars-grin.gov/ars/Beltsville/na. Free admission. Daily 8am–5pm; bonsai collection 10am–3:30pm. 40-minute, open-air, tram tour Apr–Oct, weekends 10:30 (may be pre-sold to

Alert

The U.S. Botanic Garden is closed for renovations and is not expected to reopen until the year 2001 or later.

groups), 11:30am, 1, 2, 3, and 4pm (only in peak season); $3 per adult, $2 members and seniors, $1 children 4–16. Closed Dec 25. Free parking. Metro: Stadium Armory, then take bus no. B2 to Bladensburg Rd. and R St. NE (or hop in a taxi; it's only a few dollars).

A research and educational center focusing on a vast variety of landscape plants, the U.S. National Arboretum is a must-see for the horticulturally inclined. Its 9½ miles of paved roads meander through 444 hilly acres of azaleas (the most extensive plantings in the nation), magnolias, hollies, dwarf conifers, and boxwoods. One highlight is the National Bonsai and Penjing Museum, which includes a Bicentennial gift from Japan of 53 beautiful miniature trees, some of them more than 3 centuries old. Each one is an exquisite work of art. The exhibit was augmented by a gift of 35 Chinese Penjing trees in 1986, and again in 1990 by the American Bonsai Collection of 56 North American plants; in 1993, a conservatory for tropical bonsai was erected. This area also includes a Japanese Garden and an American plants garden. The Herbarium contains 600,000 dried plants for reference purposes. The Herb Garden, another highlight, includes a historic rose garden (150 old-fashioned fragrant varieties), a contemporary interpretation of a 16th-century English-style "knot" garden, and 10 specialty gardens: a dye garden, a medicinal garden, and a culinary garden among them. Along **Fern Valley Trail** is the **Franklin Tree,** a species now extinct in the wild, discovered in 1765 by a botanist friend of Benjamin Franklin. And a magnificent sight is the arboretum's acropolis, 22 of the original U.S. Capitol columns designed by Benjamin Latrobe in a setting created by the noted English landscape artist Russell Page. The **American Friendship Garden** is a collection of ornamental grasses and perennials, with brick walkways, terraces, and a statue of Demeter, the Greek goddess of agriculture. Its colorful spring bulb plants include a wide variety of narcissi and irises plus small flowering and fruiting trees and interesting shrubs. Carefully placed teak benches provide a place for quiet contemplation. This garden also features an extensive collection of perennials and bulb plants. And the **Asian Collections,** in a landscaped valley, include rare plants from China and Korea.

Magnolias and early bulbs bloom in late March or early April; azaleas, daffodils, and flowering cherry trees in mid-April; rhododendrons and peonies in May; daylilies and crape myrtles in summer. In autumn, the arboretum is ablaze in reds and oranges as the leaves change color.

On the open-air tram tour, a guide tells you about the history and highlights of the arboretum. Purchase tickets at the ticket kiosk (located in the parking lot next to the administration building) for the day of the tour only.

A relatively new feature of the National Arboretum is the monthly moonlit tour, a strenuous 5-mile hike through the Arboretum grounds as you make your way by the light of the full moon. These tours have proven so popular that if you're thinking you might be interested, you should call now (☎ **202/245-4521**) to reserve your spot. The tours take place September to May, include a maximum of 30 people per tour, and cost $7 per person. In addition, the arboretum offers lectures and workshops (including bonsai classes), and a comprehensive guidebook is available in the gift shop.

PARKS
POTOMAC PARK

West and East Potomac Parks, their 720 riverside acres divided by the Tidal Basin, are most famous for their spring display of cherry blossoms and all the hoopla that goes with it. So much attention is lavished on Washington's cherry blossoms, that the National Park Service devotes a home page to the subject: **www.nps.gov/nacc/cherry**. You can access this site to find out forecasts for the blooms and assorted other details. You can also call the National Park Service (☎ **202/485-9880**) for details.

In all, there are 3,363 cherry trees planted along the Tidal Basin, with another 337 blooming on the grounds of the Washington Monument and in other pockets of the city. To get to the Tidal Basin by car (not recommended in cherry blossom season), you want to get on Independence Avenue and follow the signs posted near the Lincoln Memorial that show you where to turn to find parking and the FDR Memorial. If you're walking, you'll want to cross Independence Avenue where it intersects with W. Basin Drive (there's a stoplight and crosswalk), and follow the path to the Tidal Basin. There is no convenient Metro stop near here.

West Potomac Park has 1,628 trees bordering the Tidal Basin, some of them Akebonos with delicate pink blossoms, but most Yoshinos with white cloudlike flower clusters. The blossoming of the cherry trees is the focal point of a weeklong celebration, including the lighting of the 300-year-old Japanese Stone Lantern near Kutz Bridge, presented to the city by the governor of Tokyo in 1954. The trees bloom for a little less than two weeks beginning somewhere between March 20 and April 17; April 5 is the average date. Planning your trip around the blooming of the cherry blossoms is an iffy proposition, and I wouldn't advise it. All it takes is one good rain and those cherry blossoms are gone. And the cherry blossoms are not illuminated at night, so if you think you're going to beat the crush of tourists touring the Tidal Basin during the day by going at night, you'll be out of luck. See the calendar of events in chapter 2 for further details on cherry blossom events.

East Potomac Park has 1,681 cherry trees in 11 varieties. The park also has picnic grounds, tennis courts, three golf courses, a large swimming pool, and biking and hiking paths by the water, all of which are described in "Outdoor Activities," below.

West Potomac Park encompasses Constitution Gardens; the Vietnam, Korean, Lincoln, Jefferson, and FDR Memorials; a small island where ducks live; and the Reflecting Pool.

ROCK CREEK PARK

Created in 1890, ☼ **Rock Creek Park** (www.nps.gov/rocr) was purchased by Congress for its "pleasant valleys and ravines, primeval forests and open fields, its running waters, its rocks clothed with rich ferns and mosses, its repose and tranquillity, its light and shade, its ever-varying shrubbery, its beautiful and extensive views." A 1,750-acre valley within the District of Columbia, extending 12 miles from the Potomac River to the Maryland border (another 4,700 acres), it's one of the biggest and finest city parks in the nation. Parts of it are still wild; it's not unusual to see a deer scurrying through the woods in more remote sections.

The park's offerings include the **Old Stone House** (see description in Walking Tour 1), **Carter Barron Amphitheater** (see chapter 9); playgrounds; an extensive system of beautiful hiking and biking trails; sports facilities, for which there are detailed listings in "Outdoor Activities," below; remains of Civil War fortifications; and acres and acres of wooded parklands. See also our entry in "More Museums," above, on the formal gardens at Dumbarton Oaks, which border Rock Creek Park in upper Georgetown.

For full information on the wide range of park programs and activities, visit the Rock Creek Nature Center and Planetarium, 5200 Glover Rd. NW (☎ **202/ 426-6829**), Wednesday to Sunday 9am to 5pm; or Park Headquarters, 6545 Williamsburg Rd. NW (☎ **202/282-1063**), weekdays 7:45am to 4:15pm. To get to the Nature Center by public transportation, take the Metro to Friendship Heights and transfer to bus no. E2 or E3 to Military Road and Oregon Avenue/Glover Road.

The Nature Center and Planetarium itself is the scene of numerous activities, including weekend planetarium shows for kids (minimum age 4) and adults; nature films; crafts demonstrations; live animal demonstrations; guided nature walks; plus a

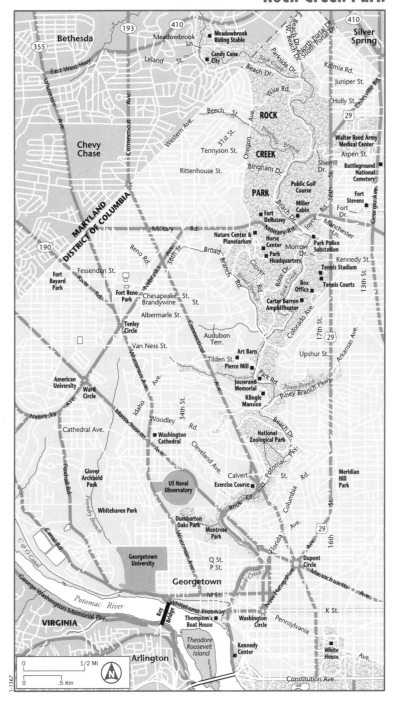

Rock Creek Park

Bethesda

355

193

410

Meadowbrook Ln.

Meadowbrook Riding Stable

Candy Cane City

Leland St.

East West Hwy.

Beach Dr.

North Portal Dr.
W. Beach Dr.
Parkside Dr.
South Portal Dr.

410

Silver Spring

Chevy Chase

Western Ave.

Beech St.

Oregon Ave.

Wise Rd.

ROCK

Kalmia Rd.

Juniper St.

Holly St.

29

Coleswille Rd.

Tennyson St.

31st St.

CREEK

Walter Reed Army Medical Center

Rittenhouse St.

Bingham Dr.

Aspen St.

Sherrill Dr.

Battleground National Cemetery

MARYLAND
DISTRICT OF COLUMBIA

190

PARK

Public Golf Course

Miller Cabin

Beach Dr.

Fort Stevens

Fort Dr.

16th St.

Georgia Ave.

Military Rd.

Reno Rd.

36th St.

Nebraska Ave.

Broad

Fort DeRussey

Nature Center & Planetarium

Military Rd.

Horse Center

Park Headquarters

Morrow Dr.

Park Police Substation

Kennedy St.

13th St.

Fort Bayard Park

Fessenden St.

River Rd.

Fort Reno Park

Chesapeake St.
Brandywine St.

Broad Branch Rd.

Clover Rd.

Ross Dr.

Rock Creek

Tennis Stadium

Tennis Courts

Box Office

Albermarle St.

Tenley Circle

Carter Barron Amphitheater

Colorado Ave.

17th St.

29

Arkansas Ave.

Van Ness St.

Wisconsin Ave.

Connecticut

Audubon Terr.

Tilden St.

Art Barn

Pierce Mill

Upshur St.

American University

Ward Circle

Idaho Ave.

34th St.

Woodley Rd.

Jusserand Memorial

Klingle Mansion

Park Rd.

Piney Branch

Piney Branch Pkwy.

Nebraska Ave.

Massachusetts Ave.

Cathedral Ave.

Washington Cathedral

Cleveland Ave.

National Zoological Park

Beach Dr.

Glover Archbold Park

Foxhall Rd.

Whitehaven Park

Calvert St.

US Naval Observatory

Exercise Course

Rock Cr. and Potomac Pkwy.

Columbia Rd.

16th St.

Meridian Hill Park

Foundry Branch

Canal Rd.

Georgetown University

Dumbarton Oaks Park

Montrose Park

Wisconsin Ave.

Q St.

P St.

Florida Ave.

29

16th St.

Dupont Circle

Massachusetts Ave.

C & O Canal

George Washington Memorial Pky.

Potomac River

Georgetown

Key Bridge

Whitehurst Freeway

Thompson's Boat House

M St.

Rock Creek

New Hampshire Ave.

Washington Circle

Pennsylvania

K St.

VIRGINIA

Theodore Roosevelt Island

Kennedy Center

White House

Ave.

Arlington

0   1/2 Mi

0   .5 Km

N

Constitution Ave.

1-1367

daily mix of lectures, films, and other events. A calendar is available on request. Self-guided nature trails begin here. All activities are free, but for planetarium shows you need to pick up tickets a half hour in advance. There are also nature exhibits on the premises. The Nature Center is closed on federal holidays.

Not far from the Nature Center is Fort DeRussey, one of 68 fortifications erected to defend the city of Washington during the Civil War. From the intersection of Military Road and Oregon Avenue, you walk a short trail through the woods to reach the fort, whose remains include high earth mounds with openings where guns were mounted, surrounded by a deep ditch/moat.

At Tilden Street and Beach Drive, you can see a water-powered 19th-century grist-mill grinding corn and wheat into flour (☎ **202/426-6908**). It's called **Pierce Mill** (a man named Isaac Pierce built it), and it's open to visitors Wednesday to Sunday 9am to 5pm. Pierce's old carriage house is now the **Art Barn** (☎ **202/244-2482**), where works of local artists are shown; it's open Thursday to Sunday 11am to 4:30pm (closed federal holidays and one month in summer, either July or August).

Call ☎ **202/673-7646** or 202/673-7647 for details, locations, and group reservations at any of the park's 30 picnic areas, some with fireplaces. A brochure available at Park Headquarters or the Nature Center also provides details on picnic locations.

Poetry readings and workshops are held during the summer at **Miller's Cabin,** the one-time residence of High Sierra poet Joaquin Miller, Beach Drive north of Military Road. Call ☎ **202/426-6829** for information.

There's convenient free parking throughout the park.

THEODORE ROOSEVELT ISLAND

A serene, 88-acre wilderness preserve, Theodore Roosevelt Island is a memorial to our 26th president, in recognition of his contributions to conservation. An outdoor enthusiast and expert field naturalist, Roosevelt once threw away a prepared speech and roared, "I hate a man who would skin the land!" During his administration, 150 million acres of forest land were reserved, and 5 national parks, 51 bird refuges, and 4 game refuges were created.

Theodore Roosevelt Island was inhabited by Native American tribes for centuries before the arrival of English explorers in the 1600s. Over the years, it passed through many owners before becoming what it is today, an island preserve of swamp, marsh, and upland forest that's a haven for rabbits, chipmunks, great owls, fox, muskrat, turtles, and groundhogs. It's a complex ecosystem in which cattails, arrow arum, and pickerelweed grow in the marshes, and willow, ash, and maple trees root on the mud-flats. You can observe these flora and fauna in their natural environs on 2½ miles of foot trails.

In the northern center of the island, overlooking an oval terrace encircled by a water-filled moat, stands a 17-foot bronze statue of Roosevelt. From the terrace rise four 21-foot granite tablets inscribed with tenets of his conservation philosophy.

To get to the island, take the George Washington Memorial Parkway exit north from the Theodore Roosevelt Bridge. The parking area is accessible only from the northbound lane; from there, a pedestrian bridge connects the island with the Virginia shore. You can also rent a canoe at Thompson's Boat Center (see "Outdoor Activities," below) and paddle over, or walk across the pedestrian bridge at Rosslyn Circle, two blocks from the Rosslyn Metro station. Picnicking is permitted on the grounds near the memorial.

For further information, contact the District Ranger, Theodore Roosevelt Island, George Washington Memorial Parkway, c/o Turkey Run Park, McLean, VA 22101 (☎ **703/289-2530**). Or check the Web site, at www.nps.gov/gwmp.

ACTIVITIES ON THE C&O CANAL

One of the great joys of living in Washington is the **C&O Canal** (www.nps.gov/choc) and its unspoiled 184½-mile towpath. One leaves urban cares and stresses behind while hiking, strolling, jogging, cycling, or boating in this lush, natural setting of ancient oaks and red maples, giant sycamores, willows, and wildflowers. But the canal wasn't always just a leisure spot for city people. It was built in the 1800s, when water routes were considered vital to transportation. Even before it was completed, the Canal was being rendered obsolete by the B&O Railroad, which was constructed at about the same time and along the same route. Today, perhaps, it serves an even more important purpose as a cherished urban refuge.

Headquarters for canal activities is the Office of the Superintendent, C&O Canal National Historical Park, P.O. Box 4, Sharpsburg, MD 21782 (☎ **301/739-4200**). Another good source of information is the National Park Service office at **Great Falls Tavern Visitor Center,** 11710 MacArthur Blvd., Potomac, MD 20854 (☎ **301/ 299-3613**). At this 1831 tavern, you can see museum exhibits and a film about the canal; there's also a bookstore on the premises. The park charges an entrance fee, $4 per car, $2 per walker or cyclist. And April to November, Wednesday to Sunday, the **Georgetown Information Center,** 1057 Thomas Jefferson St. NW (☎ **202/653-5190**), can also provide maps and information. Call ahead for hours at all of the above.

Hiking any section of the flat dirt towpath or its more rugged side paths is a pleasure. There are picnic tables, some with fire grills, about every 5 miles beginning at **Fletcher's Boat House** (☎ **202/244-0461**) (about 3.2 miles out of Georgetown) on the way to Cumberland. Enter the towpath in Georgetown below M Street via Thomas Jefferson Street. If you hike 14 miles, you'll reach **Great Falls,** a point where the Potomac becomes a stunning waterfall plunging 76 feet. Or drive to Great Falls Park on the Virginia side of the Potomac.

Stop at Fletcher's Boat House, described below in "Outdoor Activities," to rent bikes or boats or purchase bait and tackle (and a license) for fishing. A snack bar and picnic area are on the premises.

Much less strenuous than hiking is a mule-drawn 19th-century canal boat trip led by Park Service rangers in period dress. They regale passengers with canal legend and lore and sing period songs. These boats depart mid-April to early November; departure times and tickets are available at the Georgetown Information Center (see above). The Georgetown barge ride lasts 45 minutes and the Great Falls barge ride lasts 1 hour. In Georgetown, you pay $5.50 per adult, $4.50 per senior over 61, and $3.50 per child ages 3 to 14; at Great Falls, you pay $7.50 per adult, $6 per senior, and $4 per child.

Call any of the above information numbers for details on riding, rock climbing, fishing, bird-watching, concerts, ranger-guided tours, ice skating, camping, and other canal activities (or consult "Outdoor Activities," below).

12 Especially for Kids

Who knows what kids might enjoy in Washington better than other kids? So, I asked my own children, Caitlin (12) and Lucy (7); my nieces, Sarah (10) and Annie (8), and my nephew, Nick (4), what sites in Washington they would recommend to friends and cousins visiting from out of town. Here are some of their suggestions (with translations where needed—refer to mentions in this chapter for details):

Caitlin: "I liked the DC Ducks boat, because it was fun to go from land to water and to see all the sights from the water, and wave to people on land. And it was fun to drive it." [Yes, parents, be prepared for the captain of this amphibious vessel to turn the wheel over to your youngsters when you're out on the Potomac.]

Sarah: "The Newseum is fun because you can make your own video of you pretending to be a news reporter while you stand in front of a camera and hold a microphone and read the news. My friend Helen and I reported a story on an elephant and they put the zoo in the background. You can also play a lot of games using computers, like the one where you have to pick the front page stories and edit them."

Annie: "I like the Phillips because there are lots of good paintings and because there's one called *Night Baseball* that I like; the fans look like dots in the picture. [Annie's a baseball player and fan.] Also I like the Canal, because you can take rides in a barge pulled by a mule and the people on the barge were dressed in costumes and they told us stories."

Lucy: "I liked going to the theater where there was a puppet show and it was funny because first the people came out to introduce themselves and then they went on with the show. I think it was called "New Clothes for the King." [Lucy is talking about the Discovery Theater in the Smithsonian's Arts and Industries Building; the puppet show we saw was "The Emperor's New Clothes."]

Nick: "The Zoo, because it has animals in it and I like the white tiger. And the Civil War fort we saw in Rock Creek Park." [Fort DeRussey].

For more ideas, consult the Friday "Weekend" section of the *Washington Post,* which lists numerous activities (mostly free) for kids: special museum events, children's theater, storytelling programs, puppet shows, video-game competitions, and so forth. Call the Kennedy Center, the Lisner, and National Theatre to find out about children's shows; see chapter 9 for details. Also read the write-up of Discovery Theater, within the Smithsonian's Arts & Industries Building, earlier in this chapter.

I've checked out hotels built with families in mind in chapter 5's "Family-Friendly Hotels"; that hotel pool may rescue your sanity for an hour or two. Public swimming pools are another option—see the swimming listing, and other suggestions for outdoor activities, below. The "Organized Tours" section may also be your saving grace when you've either run out of steam or need a jump start to your day.

FAVORITE CHILDREN'S ATTRACTIONS

Check for special children's events at museum information desks when you enter. As noted within the listings for individual museums, some children's programs are also great fun for adults. I recommend the programs at the Corcoran Gallery of Art, the Folger Shakespeare Library, and the Sackler Gallery in particular. (The gift shops in most of these museums have wonderful toys and children's books.) Call ahead to find out which programs are running. Here's a rundown of the biggest kid-pleasers in town (for details, see the full entries earlier in this chapter):

National Air & Space Museum. Spectacular IMAX films (don't miss), planetarium shows, missiles, rockets, and a walk-through orbital workshop.

National Museum of Natural History. A Discovery Room just for youngsters, an insect zoo, shrunken heads, and dinosaurs, and the new IMAX theater showing 2-D and 3-D films.

National Museum of American History. The Foucault pendulum, locomotives, Archie Bunker's chair, and an old-fashioned ice-cream parlor.

Federal Bureau of Investigation. Gangster memorabilia, crime-solving methods, espionage devices, and a sharp-shooting demonstration.

Bureau of Engraving and Printing. Kids enjoy looking at immense piles of money as much as you do.

National Zoological Park. Kids always love a zoo, and this is an especially good one.

Ford's Theatre and Lincoln Museum and the House Where Lincoln Died.
Booth's gun and diary, the clothes Lincoln was wearing the night he was assassinated, and other such grisly artifacts. Kids adore the whole business.

National Geographic Society's Explorers Hall. A moon rock, the egg of an
extinct "elephant bird" (if hatched, it would weigh 1,000 pounds), numerous
interactive videos. The magazine comes alive.

Washington Monument. Easy to get them up there, hard to get them down. If
only they could use the steps, they'd be in heaven. Also the new interactive
center has lots of interesting ways for kids to learn about Washington.

Lincoln Memorial. Kids know a lot about Lincoln and enjoy visiting his
memorial. A special treat is visiting it after dark (the same goes for the Washington Monument and Jefferson Memorial).

Newseum. Kids can ham it up as an ace news reporter, then take home the
videotaped performance to show to their friends.

13 Organized Tours

BY FOOT

TOUR de Force (☎ **703/525-2948**) is historian and raconteur Jeanne Fogel's 16-
year-old company. She offers a variety of walking and bus tours around the city,
revealing little-known anecdotes and facts about neighborhoods, historic figures, and
the most visited sites. Fogel's tours are custom-designed, for groups, not individuals.
Call for rates.

TourDC, Walking Tours of Georgetown (☎ **301/588-8999;** www.tourdc.com)
conducts 90-minute ($12) walking tours of Georgetown, telling about the neighbor-
hood's history up to the present and taking you past the homes of notable residents.

✪ **Weekend Walks in Georgetown** (☎ **301/294-9514**) offers 2-hour walks
through the streets of Georgetown, Adams-Morgan, and other locations, guided by
author/historian Anthony S. Pitch. Rates are $10 per person, seniors and students $6.

D.C. Heritage Tours (☎ **202/639-0908**), co-sponsored by the D.C. Heritage
Tourism Coalition and the Discovery Store, depart from the MCI Center weekdays at
10:30am and Saturday and Sunday at 1:30pm; but call ahead to reserve your space on
the tour. During this walking tour, a costumed guide whisks you in and out of historic
spots for 90 minutes, as he or she offers a view of 19th century Washington, revealing
on the way the house where John Wilkes Booth plotted Lincoln's assassination, the halls
where Walt Whitman cared for the Civil War wounded, and so on. Tour costs $7.50
per adult, $5 per child under 6 and per senior 55 and older. Before the tour starts, you
might want to see the 15-minute film *Destination DC,* shown on the top floor of the
Discovery store; the charge is $2.50 per adult, $1.50 per child under 6 and seniors.

BY BUS

If you're looking for an easy-on/easy-off tour of major sites, consider ✪ **Tourmobile
Sightseeing** (☎ **202/554-5100** or 888/868-7707; www.tourmobile.com), whose
comfortable red, white, and blue sightseeing trams travel to as many as 25 sites, as far
out as Arlington National Cemetery and even (with coach service) Mount Vernon.
(Tourmobile is the only narrated sightseeing shuttle tour authorized by the National
Park Service.)

WASHINGTON/ARLINGTON CEMETERY TOUR   You can take the Wash-
ington/Arlington Cemetery tour or tour only Arlington Cemetery. The former stops

at 21 different sites on or near the Mall and four sights at Arlington Cemetery: the Kennedy grave sites, the Tomb of the Unknowns, Arlington House, and the Women in Military Service Memorial.

Here's how the system works: You can board a Tourmobile at 24 different locations—the White House, the Washington Monument, the Arts and Industries Building/Hirshhorn Museum, the National Air and Space Museum, Union Station/National Postal Museum, the East Face of the Capitol/Library of Congress/Supreme Court, the West Face of the Capitol, Ford's Theater/FBI Building, The White House Visitor Center, the Old Post Office Pavilion, the U.S. Navy Memorial/National Archives, the National Gallery of Art, the National Museum of Natural History, the National Museum of American History, the Bureau of Engraving and Printing/U.S. Holocaust Memorial Museum; the Jefferson Memorial; the Franklin D. Roosevelt Memorial, the Kennedy Center, the Lincoln/Vietnam Veterans/Korean War Veterans Memorials, the National Law Enforcement Memorial Visitor's Center/National Portrait Gallery/National Museum of American Art/MCI Center, and Arlington National Cemetery.

You pay the driver when you first board the bus (you can also purchase a ticket at the booth at the Washington Monument or inside the Arlington National Cemetery Visitor Center or, for a small surcharge, order your ticket in advance from Ticketmaster (☎ **800/551-SEAT**). Along the route, you may get off at any stop to visit monuments or buildings. When you finish exploring each area, step aboard the next Tourmobile that comes along without extra charge (as long as you can show your ticket). The buses travel in a loop, serving each stop about every 15 to 30 minutes. One fare allows you to use the buses for a full day. The charge for the Washington/Arlington Cemetery tour is $16 for anyone 12 and older, $7 for children 3 to 11. For Arlington Cemetery only, those 12 and older pay $4.75, children $2.25. Children under 3 ride free. Buses follow figure-eight circuits from the Capitol to Arlington Cemetery and back. You can also buy an advance ticket after 2pm June 15–Labor Day or after 1pm the rest of the year, that is valid for the rest of the afternoon plus the following day; these tickets cost $18 per adult, $8 for children 3 to 11. Well-trained narrators give commentaries about sights along the route and answer questions.

Tourmobiles operate daily year-round, except Christmas. From June 15 to Labor Day, they ply the Mall between 9am and 6:30pm. After Labor Day, the hours are 9:30am to 4:30pm. In Arlington Cemetery, between November and March, they start at 8:30am and end at 4:30pm; April through October, the hours are 8:30am to 6:30pm.

OTHER TOURMOBILE TOURS   April through October, Tourmobiles also run round-trip to Mount Vernon. Coaches depart from the Arlington National Cemetery Visitor Center at 10am, noon, and 2pm, with a pickup at the Washington Monument shortly thereafter. The price is $22 for those 12 and older, $11 for children ages 3 to 11, and includes admission to Mount Vernon. A combination tour of Washington, Arlington Cemetery, and Mount Vernon (good for 2 days) is $40 for anyone 12 and older, $18.50 for children ages 3 to 11. Another offering (June 15 to Labor Day) is the Frederick Douglass National Historic Site Tour, which includes a guided tour of Douglass's home, Cedar Hill, located in southeast Washington. Departures are from Arlington National Cemetery at noon, with a pickup at the Washington Monument shortly thereafter. Those 12 and older pay $7, and children ages 3 to 11 pay $3.50. A 2-day Combination Frederick Douglass Tour and Washington/Arlington National Cemetery Tour is also available at $32 for those 12 and older, $14 for children ages 3 to 11. For both the Mount Vernon and Frederick Douglass tours, you must reserve in person at either Arlington Cemetery or the Washington Monument at least a half-hour in advance. Tourmobile's newest offering is a Twilight Tour that departs each evening at 7:30pm June 15 through Labor Day from Union Station, stopping at the Jefferson, FDR, and Lincoln Memorials, the White House, and the Capitol, before returning to Union Station. The tour lasts nearly 3 hours, includes narrated touring on the bus and at each site, and costs $16 per adult, $7 children ages 3 to 11.

OLD TOWN TROLLEY   A service similar to Tourmobile's is Old Town Trolley Tours of Washington (☎ 202/832-9800; www.historictours.com). For a fixed price, you can get on and off these green-and-orange vehicles as often as you like for an entire loop around the city. The trolleys stop at 19 locations in the District, including Georgetown; they also go out to Arlington National Cemetery. They operate daily from 9am to 4pm all year round. The cost is $24 for adults, $12 for children 4 to 12, free for children under 4. The full tour, which is narrated, takes 2½ hours, and trolleys come by every 30 minutes or so. Stops are made at Union Station, the Hyatt Regency Hotel (near the National Gallery), the Pavilion at the Old Post Office, National Museum of Women in the Arts, Chinatown/MCI Center, the FBI Building/Ford's Theatre, Freedom Plaza/National Aquarium, the Hotel Washington (near the White House), the Capital Hilton, the Renaissance Mayflower Hotel (near the National Geographic Society), the Washington Hilton (near the Phillips Collection and Adams-Morgan restaurants), the Washington Park Gourmet (near the National Zoo), Washington National Cathedral, the Georgetown Park Mall, Arlington Cemetery, Lincoln Memorial, the Washington Monument/U.S. Holocaust Memorial Museum/Smithsonian Castle, the Air and Space Museum, and the U.S. Capitol/Library of Congress. You can board without a ticket and purchase it en route.

Old Town Trolley also offers a 2½-hour "Washington After Hours" tour of illuminated federal buildings and memorials all year long, weather permitting. Rates are $25 per adult and $13 per child.

THE GRAY LINE   This company (☎ 202/289-1995) offers a variety of tours, among them: "Washington After Dark" (3 hours; $25 per adult, $12 per child), focusing on night-lit national monuments and federal buildings; the "Washington, D.C., All-Day Combination Tour" ($42 per adult, $21 per child), which includes major Washington sights plus Arlington National Cemetery, Mount Vernon, and Alexandria; and the full-day "Interiors of Public Buildings" ($36 per adult, $18 per child), which covers Ford's Theatre, the Jefferson Memorial, the Museum of American History, the Capitol, the Supreme Court, the National Air & Space Museum, and the National Archives. There are also trips as far afield as Colonial Williamsburg ($65 per adult, $55 per child), Gettysburg ($55 per adult, $35 per child), and Charlottesville ($65 per adult or child). Most tours depart from Gray Line's Union Station terminal, with pickups at most major hotels, but call to confirm. Headsets and tour tapes in certain foreign languages are available for certain afternoon tours, at $30 per adult, $15 per child.

All About Town, 519 6th St. NW (☎ 202/393-3696; fax 202/393-2006), offers a similar range of tours at rates running from $22 to $66 per adult. Pickup is offered at 102 hotels in the Washington area.

BY BOAT

Since Washington is a river city, why not see it by boat? Potomac cruises allow sweeping vistas of the monuments and memorials, Georgetown, the Kennedy Center, and other Washington sights. Read the information carefully, since not all boat cruises offer guided tours.

Some of the following boats leave from the Washington waterfront and some from Old Town Alexandria:

Spirit of Washington Cruises, Pier 4 at 6th and Water Streets SW (☎ **202/ 554-8000;** www.spiritcruises.com; Metro: Waterfront), offers a variety of trips daily from early March through October, including evening dinner, lunch and brunch, and moonlight dance cruises, as well as a half-day excursion to Mount Vernon and back. Lunch and dinner cruises include a 40-minute, high-energy musical revue. Prices range from $26.50 for a sightseeing (no meals) excursion to Mount Vernon, which takes 5½ hours in all, including a 2-hour tour break, to $72.45 for a Saturday dinner cruise, drinks not included. Call to make reservations in advance.

The *Spirit of Washington* is a luxury harbor climate-controlled cruise ship with carpeted decks and huge panoramic windows designed for sightseeing. There are three well-stocked bars on board. Mount Vernon cruises are aboard an equally luxurious sister ship, the *Potomac Spirit.*

Potomac Party Cruises (☎ **703/683-6076;** www.dandydinnerboat.com) has been operating for about 20 years. Its boat, *The Dandy,* is a climate-controlled, all-weather, glassed-in, floating restaurant that operates year-round. Lunch, evening dinner/dance, and special charter cruises are available daily. You board *The Dandy* in Old Town Alexandria, at the Prince Street pier, between Duke and King Streets (Metro: Waterfront). Trips range from $32.32 for a 2½-hour weekday lunch cruise to $78 for a 3-hour Saturday dinner cruise, including tax and service charges but not drinks.

Odyssey III (☎ **800/946-7245;** www.odysseycruises.com) was designed specifically to glide under the bridges that cross the Potomac. The boat looks like a glass bullet, with its snub-nosed port and streamlined, 240-foot-long glass body. The wraparound see-through walls and ceiling allow for great views. Like *The Dandy,* the *Odyssey* operates all year. You board the *Odyssey* at the Gangplank Marina, on Washington's waterfront, at 6th and Water streets SW (Metro: Waterfront). Cruises available include lunch, Sunday brunch, and dinner excursions, with live entertainment provided during each cruise. It costs $42.24 for a 2-hour weekday lunch cruise and $106.24 for a 3-hour Saturday dinner cruise; prices include tax and gratuity, but not drinks.

The ✪ **Potomac Riverboat Company** (☎ **703/548-9000)**offers three sightseeing tours April through October, aboard: the *Matthew Hayes,* on a 90-minute tour past Washington monuments and memorials; the *Admiral Tilp,* on a 40-minute tour of Old Town Alexandria's waterfront; and the *Miss Christin,* which cruises to Mount Vernon, where you hop off and reboard after you've toured the estate. You board the boats at the pier behind the Torpedo Factory in Old Town Alexandria, at the foot of King Street (Metro: Waterfront); or, for the Washington monuments and memorials tour, the Georgetown Harbour. *Matthew Hayes* tickets are $15 for adults, $7 for children ages 2 to 12; *Admiral Tilp* tickets are $8 for adults, $4 for children ages 2 to 12; and *Miss Christin* tickets are $24 for adults, $12 for children (6–10), and include admission to Mount Vernon. A concession stand selling light refreshments and beverages is open during the cruises.

The **Capitol River Cruise's** *Nightingale II* (☎ **800/405-5511** or 301/460-7447) is a historic 65-foot steel riverboat that can accommodate up to 90 people. The *Nightingale II*'s narrated jaunts depart Georgetown's Washington Harbour every hour on the hour, from noon until 8pm weekdays and 9pm weekends, April through October. The 50-minute narrated tour travels past the monuments and memorials as you head to National Airport and back. A snack bar on board sells light refreshments, beer, wine, and sodas; you're welcome to bring your own picnic aboard. The price is $10 per adult, $5 per child ages 3 to 12. To get here, take the Metro to Foggy Bottom and then walk into Georgetown, following Pennsylvania Avenue, which becomes M Street. Turn left on 31st Street NW, which dead-ends at the Washington Harbour complex.

A BOAT ON WHEELS   Old Town Trolley also operates the **DC Ducks** (☎ 202/966-3825; www.historictours.com), which feature unique land and water tours of Washington aboard the red, white, and blue *DUKW,* an amphibious army vehicle (boat with wheels) from World War II that accommodates 30 passengers. Ninety-minute guided tours aboard the open-air canopied craft include a land portion taking in major sights—the Capitol, Lincoln Memorial, Washington Monument, the White House, and Smithsonian museums—and a 30-minute Potomac cruise. Tickets can be purchased inside Union Station at the information desk; you board the vehicle just outside the main entrance to Union Station. There are departures daily during tour season (April to November); hours vary, but departures usually follow an 11am, 1, and 3pm schedule. Tickets cost $24 for adults, $12 for children 5 to 12, children under 5 free.

BIKE TOURS

Bike the Sites, Inc. (☎ 202/966-8662; www.bikethesites.com), offers a more active way to see Washington. The company has designed several different biking tours of the city, including an Early Bird Fun Ride, which is a 1-hour, moderately paced ride costing $25 per person, and the Capital Sites Ride (the most popular), which takes three hours, covers many sites along a 10-mile stretch, and costs $35 per person. Bike the Sites provides you with a 21-speed Trek Hybrid bicycle fitted to your size, bike helmet, handlebar bag, water bottle, light snack, and two guides to lead the ride. Guides impart historical and anecdotal information as you go. The company will customize bike rides to suit your tour specifications.

14 Outdoor Activities

BIKING   First see listings for **Fletcher's Boat House** and **Thompson's Boat Center** under "Boating," below; these two sites rent both bikes and boats.

As does **Big Wheel Bikes,** 1034 33rd St. NW, right near the C&O Canal just below M Street (☎ 202/337-0254). The rate is $5 per hour, with a 3-hour minimum, or $25 for the day. Shop opens at 10am daily, closing times vary. There's another Big Wheel shop on Capitol Hill at 315 7th St. SE (☎ 202/543-1600); call for hours. Photo ID and a major credit card are required to rent bicycles.

On Fridays, the *Washington Post* "Weekend" section lists cycling trips. Rock Creek Park has an 11-mile paved bike route from the Lincoln Memorial through the park into Maryland. On weekends and holidays, a large part of it is closed to vehicular traffic. The C&O Canal and the Potomac Parks, described earlier in "Parks & Gardens," also have extended bike paths. A new 7-mile path, the **Capital Crescent Trail,** takes you from Georgetown to the suburb of Bethesda, Maryland, following a former railroad track that parallels the Potomac River part of the way and passes by old trestle bridges and pleasant residential neighborhoods.

BOATING   **Thompson's Boat Center,** 2900 Virginia Ave. at Rock Creek Parkway NW (☎ 202/333-4861 or 202/333-9543; Metro: Foggy Bottom with a 10-minute walk), rents canoes, kayaks, rowing shells (recreational and racing), and bikes. They also offer sculling and sweep-rowing lessons. Photo ID and a credit card are required for rentals. They're open for boat and bike rentals usually from March through November, daily 8am to 6pm. Boat rentals range from $6 an hour for a canoe to $32 for a day's rental of a doubles-kayak. Bike rentals range from $4 per hour for a single-speed cruiser to $22 for a day's rental of an all-terrain, 15-speed bike.

Late March to mid-September, you can rent paddleboats on the north end of the Tidal Basin off Independence Avenue (☎ 202/479-2426). They rent four-seaters for

$14 an hour or two-seaters for $7 an hour. Hours are 10am to about an hour before sunset daily.

Fletcher's Boat House, Reservoir and Canal Roads (☎ 202/244-0461; www.fletchersboathouse.com), is right on the C&O Canal, about 3.2 wonderfully scenic miles from Georgetown. The same family has owned it since 1850! Open March to mid-November, daily from about sunrise to dusk, Fletcher's rents canoes, rowboats, and bikes (bikes: $8 for 2 hours, or $12 for the day; boats: $8 for 1 hour, or $16 for the day; you aren't allowed to leave the canal area), and sells fishing licenses, bait, and tackle. Identification is required (a driver's license or major credit card). A snack bar and rest rooms here are welcome facilities. There are also picnic tables (with barbecue grills) overlooking the Potomac. You don't have to walk to Fletcher's; it's accessible by car (west on M Street to Canal Road) and has plenty of free parking.

CAMPING There are numerous camping areas on the C&O Canal starting at **Swain's Lock,** 16 miles from Georgetown. Use of campsites is on a first-come, first-serve basis.

FISHING The Potomac River around Washington holds an abundant variety of fish, some 40 species, all perfectly safe to eat. Good fishing is possible from late February to November, but mid-March to June (spawning season) is peak. Perch and catfish are the most common catch, but during bass season a haul of 20 to 40 is not unusual. The Washington Channel offers good bass and carp fishing year-round.

To make sure you abide by local restrictions, pick up a free regulations book on fishing, available at **Fletcher's Boat House** (☎ 202/244-0461; details above). You can also obtain the required fishing license here. Cost for nonresidents is $7.50 a year, $3 for a 14-day permit. Residents pay $5. Bring your own fishing equipment.

GOLF There are dozens of public courses within easy driving distance of the D.C. area, but within the District itself **East Potomac Park** and **Rock Creek Park** have the only public courses; check out the Web site www.golfdc.com. Fees run from $9 weekdays for 9 holes to $19 weekends for 18 holes. The 18-hole Rock Creek Golf Course and clubhouse, at 16th and Rittenhouse Streets NW (☎ 202/882-7332), is open to the public daily year-round from dawn to dusk. You will find a snack bar on the premises, and you can rent clubs and carts.

East Potomac Park has one 18-hole, par-72 layout, and two 9-hole courses. For details, call ☎ 202/554-7660.

HIKING Check the *Washington Post* Friday "Weekend" section for listings of hiking clubs; almost all are open to the public for a small fee. Be sure to inquire about the difficulty of any hike you plan to join and the speed with which the group proceeds; some hikes are fast-paced, allowing no time to smell the flowers.

There are numerous hiking paths. The C&O Canal offers 184½ miles; Theodore Roosevelt Island has more than 88 wilderness acres to explore, including a 2½-mile nature trail (short but rugged); and in Rock Creek Park there are 20 miles of hiking trails for which maps are available at the Visitor Information Center or Park Headquarters.

HORSEBACK RIDING There are stables at the **Rock Creek Park Horse Center,** near the Nature Center on Glover Road NW (☎ 202/362-0117). One-hour guided trail rides are offered Tuesday through Thursday at 3pm, weekends at noon, 1:30, and 3pm; they cost $21. Call for reservations or information on riding instruction.

ICE SKATING If you have your own skates, you can skate on the C&O Canal (call ☎ 301/299-3613 for information on ice conditions). If you need to rent skates, head to one of these three locations: the National Gallery Sculpture Garden Ice Rink, on the Mall at 7th Street and Constitution Avenue NW (call the National Gallery's main number, ☎ 202/737-4215, for information); the Pershing Park outdoor rink, at 14th Street and Pennsylvania Avenue NW (☎ 202/737-6938); and a huge hockey-size indoor facility, the Fort Dupont Ice Arena, at 3779 Ely Place SE, at Minnesota Avenue in Fort Dupont Park (☎ 202/584-5007). The Sculpture Garden rink is open from late October to mid-March; the Pershing Park rink from about Thanksgiving to February, weather permitting; Fort Dupont, from Labor Day to the end of April. Call for hours and admission prices.

JOGGING A parcourse jogging path, a gift from Perrier, opened in Rock Creek Park in 1978. Its 1½-mile oval route, beginning near the intersection of Calvert Street NW and Rock Creek Parkway (directly behind the Omni Shoreham Hotel), includes 18 calisthenics stations with instructions on prescribed exercises. There's another Perrier parcourse, with only four stations, at 16th and Kennedy Streets NW. Other popular jogging areas are the C&O Canal and the Mall.

SWIMMING There are 44 swimming pools in the District run by the D.C. Department of Recreation Aquatic Program (☎ 202/576-6436). They include the **Capitol East Natatorium,** an indoor pool with sundeck and adjoining baby pool at 635 North Carolina Ave. SE (☎ 202/724-4495 or 202/724-4496); the outdoor pool in East Potomac Park (☎ 202/863-1309); a large outdoor pool at 25th and N Streets NW (☎ 202/727-3285); and the Georgetown outdoor pool at 34th Street and Volta Place NW (☎ 202/282-2366). Indoor pools are open year-round; outdoor pools, from mid-June to Labor Day. Thirty-nine of the District pools are free; the remaining five charge about $3 per adult, $1 per child. Call for hours and details on other locations.

TENNIS The D.C. Department of Recreation and Parks, 3149 16th St. NW, Washington, DC 20010 (☎ 202/673-7660 or 202/673-7665), maintains 57 outdoor tennis courts throughout the District (25 of them lighted for night play). Court use is on a first-come, first-serve basis. Call or write for a list of locations. Most courts are open year-round, weather permitting. At **Rock Creek,** there are 15 soft-surface (clay) and 10 hard-surface tennis courts at 16th and Kennedy Streets NW (☎ 202/722-5949). From April to mid-November you must make a reservation in person at Guest Services on the premises to use them. Six additional clay courts are located off Park Road, just east of Pierce Mill. **East Potomac Park** has 24 tennis courts, including five indoors and three lighted for night play (☎ 202/554-5962). Fees vary with court surface and time of play; call for details.

15 Spectator Sports

Sports venues in Washington, D.C. are new, state of the art, and some of the nicest around. And you pay for it. A Washington Redskins ticket for a game at Jack Kent Cooke Stadium sells at the highest average price ($52.92) in the National Football League; a Wizards ticket for a game at the MCI Center sells at the second highest average price ($51.63) in the National Basketball Association; a Baltimore Orioles ticket for a game at Camden Yards sells for the fourth highest average price ($15.66) in Major League Baseball; and a Washington Capitals ticket for a game at the MCI Center sells for the fifth highest average price ($50.36) in the National Hockey League. But if you're a sports fan, it may be worth it.

TICKETS For tickets to most events, call ☎ 800/551-SEAT or 202/432-SEAT.

BASEBALL Lovely 48,000-seat Camden Yards, 333 W. Camden St. (between Howard and Conway streets), Baltimore (☎ 410/685-9800), is home to the American League's Baltimore Orioles. Unlike recent ultramodern sports stadiums and ugly domes, Camden Yards is an old-fashioned ballpark, unafraid to incorporate features of its urban environment, such as the old B&O Railroad yards. A renovated brick ware-house serves as a striking visual backdrop beyond the right-field fence.

It was here on September 6, 1995, that Cal Ripken broke Lou Gehrig's legendary consecutive-game record; he took a lap around the field and was acclaimed with a 22-minute standing ovation and a citywide celebration.

Tickets (which range from $9 to $35) were once impossible to get; now it's possible but still tough, so call ☎ **800/551-SEAT** or 410/481-SEAT well in advance if you want to catch a game. There are usually scalpers outside the stadium before a game; use your judgment if you try this option. And there's a D.C. ticket office as well, at 914 17th St. NW (☎ **202/296-2473**). From Union Station in Washington, take a MARC train to Baltimore, where you are let off right at the ballpark. If you're driving, take I-95 north to Exit 53.

BASKETBALL   The Washington Wizards (née Bullets), the Washington Mystics (our women's team), and the Georgetown Hoyas play home games at the MCI Center (☎ **202/628-3200**), at 7th and F Streets NW, adjacent to the Gallery Place Metro station in downtown Washington. Tickets cost around $20 to $65 for the Wizards, $8 to $65 for the Mystics, and $5 to $16 for the Hoyas.

FOOTBALL   The Washington Redskins played their last home game at RFK Sta-dium in 1997 and now play at the Jack Kent Cooke Stadium, 1600 Raljohn Rd., Raljohn, MD 20785 (☎ **301/276-6050;** Metro: Addison Road, with bus shuttle to stadium). Tickets for Redskins games have been sold out since Lyndon Johnson was in the White House, so forget about getting your hands on one, unless you're willing to shell out $250 for a club-level seat.

The Baltimore Ravens (formerly the Cleveland Browns, until Art Modell moved the team and broke the city's heart) started off the 1998–1999 season in their new home, the PSINet Stadium, right next to Camden Yards. Tickets cost $17 to $75; for more information, call ☎ **410/261-7283.**

HOCKEY   Home ice for the NHL's Washington Capitals is now the MCI Center (☎ **202/628-3200**), at 7th and F streets NW, adjacent to the Gallery Place Metro sta-tion. Tickets cost about $19 to $50.

SOCCER   D.C. United, the champions of Major League Soccer in 1996, play at RFK Stadium (☎ **202/547-9077;** Metro: Stadium-Armory). Tickets to their games range from $13 to $34. The Washington Warthogs indoor soccer team plays its games at the US Airways Arena (☎ **301/350-3400**) in Landover, Maryland. Tickets cost $12.50 to $15.50.

Shopping the District 8

A shopping mecca, Washington is not. Meaning only that people generally don't travel to the capital solely to shop. But maybe they should. We've got it all, from The Gap to Chanel, from one of the most popular discount malls in the world (Potomac Mills), to the country's oldest jewelry store (Galt's, established in 1801). We're known for our numerous bookstores and for stores selling political memorabilia and government spoof gifts (where else would you find baseball caps with "CIA" and "DEA" printed on their bills, or guest towels with the White House insignia on them? See Made in America listing under "Gifts/Souvenirs," below.) And if you go home without stopping in a Smithsonian gift shop then you've missed an opportunity for finding the perfect memento.

1 The Shopping Scene

But it's not just the Smithsonian museums that have gift shops. In fact, there is no tourist attraction in Washington too small to hold a little store. So if you worry about cramming in shopping with sightseeing, don't: Just make sure you hit each site's boutique on the way out and you'll do fine. Tourist attraction stores often offer good buys in terms of novel gifts, if not cheap prices. Bargain hunters may be interested in the annual Smithsonian warehouse sale, typically held in May at a suburban location (the 1999 sale was held in Chantilly, Virginia, near Dulles International Airport), and offering merchandise at 50% to 80% off the original price. Also consider the discount stores listed within this chapter. Washington area stores are usually open daily from 10am to 5pm or 6pm Monday through Saturday, with one late night (usually Thursday), when hours extend to 9pm, and with Sunday hours from noon to 5pm or 6pm. Exceptions are the malls, which are open late nightly, and antiques stores and art galleries, which tend to keep their own hours. Play it safe and call ahead, if there's a store you really want to get to. Sales tax on merchandise is 5.75% in the District, 5% in Maryland, and 4.5% in Virginia. Most gift, arts, and crafts stores, including those at the Smithsonian museums, will handle shipping for you; clothes stores generally do not.

GREAT SHOPPING AREAS

Adams-Morgan   This lively part of town spills over with the sounds, sights, and smells of different cultures intermixing. Defined by 18th Street and Columbia Road, NW, Adams-Morgan is a neighborhood of ethnic eateries interspersed with the odd secondhand bookshop and eclectic collectibles store. Though Adams-Morgan has more nightclubs and bistros than actual stores, it's still a fun area for walking and shopping. Parking is possible during the day, but impossible at night, simple as that. Closest Metro: Dupont Circle; exit at Q Street NW and walk up Connecticut Avenue NW to Columbia Road NW.

Connecticut Avenue/Dupont Circle   Running from the mini-Wall Street that is K Street north to S Street, Connecticut Avenue NW is a main thoroughfare, where you'll find traditional clothing at Brooks Brothers, Talbots, and Burberry's, casual duds at The Gap and Liz Claiborne, discount items at Filene's Basement and Hit or Miss, and haute couture at Rizik's. The closer you get to Dupont Circle, the fewer businesstypes you see. People are younger, mellower, and sport more pierced body parts. This pedestrian-friendly section of the avenue is studded with coffee bars and neighborhood restaurants, as well as art galleries, book and record shops, and gay and lesbian boutiques. Metro: Farragut North, at one end, Dupont Circle at the other.

Downtown   The area bounded east and west by 7th and 14th streets NW, and north and south by New York and Pennsylvania avenues NW is in a frenzy of development. Stores already here include the tony Chanel and Harriet Kassman, both located within the Willard Inter-Continental Hotel's courtyard, and the Shops at National Place, a four-level mall whose stores include Washington Kids (mostly clothes), Casual Corner, and Filene's Basement. New kids on the block are expected: a huge Borders bookstore at 14th and F streets NW, in the grand old Garfinckel's building; and a large retail and residential space at 11th and F streets NW, housed within another beloved former department store, the old Woodward & Lothrop. (At this writing, it's too early to know the names of specific stores opening here.) Hecht's, at 12th and G streets, continues as the sole carrier of the department store flag downtown. Metro: Metro Center.

Meanwhile, back on Pennsylvania Avenue at 11th Street, the Pavilion at the Old Post Office is worth a visit, if only to admire the architecture or view the city from the top of the 315-foot-high clock tower. The pavilion's three lower levels contain 30 or so touristy shops and kiosks selling mostly souvenirs, novelty items, and food. Metro: Federal Triangle.

Georgetown   Georgetown is the city's perennial favorite shopping area, with stores lining Wisconsin Avenue and M Street NW at the heart of it, and fanning out along side streets from the central intersection. You'll find both chain and one-of-a-kind shops, chic as well as thrift. But you may come away with a headache from trying to make your way along its crowded streets, sidewalks, and shops. Weekends, especially, bring out all kinds of yahoos, who are mainly here to drink. Visit Georgetown on a weekday morning, if you can. Weeknights are another good time to visit, for dinner and strolling afterwards. On afternoons, early evenings, and weekends, traffic is heavy, and parking can be tough. Consider taking a bus or taxi—the closest Metro stop is at Foggy Bottom, a good 20- to 30-minute walk away. If you drive, you'll find parking lots expensive and tickets even more so, so be careful where you plant your car.

Old Town Alexandria   Old Town is becomingly increasingly like Georgetown, warts (heavy traffic, crowded sidewalks, difficult parking) and all. Weekdays are a lot tamer than weekends. It's always a nice place to visit, though; the drive alone is worth the trip. From Memorial Bridge, near the Lincoln Memorial, you follow the George Washington Parkway alongside the Potomac River (the same route that takes you to National Airport) about 14 miles, where the parkway becomes Washington Street. Look for a parking spot on King Street or a side street, and then walk. Shops run the length of King Street, from the waterfront up to Washington Street, and from Washington Street west to the Masonic Temple. You can also take the Metro to King St. See chapter 10, which includes Alexandria as one of its "Side Trips from Washington."

Union Station   Not a neighborhood, but a legitimate "shopping area" nonetheless. The only one on Capitol Hill, it has more than 100 specialty shops, selling jewelry, apparel, and gifts, and over 25 eateries.

Upper Wisconsin Avenue Northwest   In a residential section of town known as Friendship Heights on the D.C. side and Chevy Chase on the Maryland side, is a quarter-mile shopping district that extends from Saks Fifth Avenue at one end to Roche Bobois at the other. In between lie Lord & Taylor, Nieman-Marcus, and Hecht Company department stores; a bevy of top shops, such as Tiffany's and Versace; two malls, the Mazza Gallerie and its younger, hipper sister, the Chevy Chase Pavilion; and several stand-alone staples, such as Banana Republic. The street is too wide and traffic always too snarled to make this a strolling kind of district, although teenagers do love to loiter here. Generally speaking, people head for particular stores and leave. Drive here if you want; the Mazza Gallerie and the Hecht's Store parking lot offer two hours of free parking with validation. Or Metro it; the strip is right on the Red Line, with the "Friendship Heights" exits leading directly into each of the malls and into Hecht's.

2 Shopping A to Z

ANTIQUES

While you won't find many bargains in Washington area antique stores, you will see beautiful and rare decorative furniture, silver, jewelry, art, and fabrics, from Amish quilts to Chinese silks. Antique shops dot the greater Washington landscape, with the richest concentrations found in Old Town Alexandria; Capitol Hill; Georgetown; Adams-Morgan; and Kensington, Maryland.

Antique Row. Howard and Connecticut aves., Kensington, Maryland.

A few miles north of the city is not far to go for the good deal or true bonanza you're likely to discover among these 40-odd antiques and collectibles shops. The stores, lined up along Howard Avenue, offer every sort of item in a wide variety of styles, periods, and prices. If you don't drive or catch a cab, you'll have to take an L2 bus from Dupont Circle. Get a transfer from the driver and ask him to let you know when you reach the transfer point for the L8 bus. When you reach that juncture, board the L8 bus and ask to be let off at Connecticut and Knowles avenues. Howard Avenue is one block north of Knowles.

✪ **Antiques-on-the-Hill.** 701 North Carolina Ave. SE. ☎ **202/543-1819.** Metro: Eastern Market.

A Capitol Hill institution since the 1960s, this place sells silver, furniture, glassware, jewelry, porcelain, and lamps.

✪ **The Brass Knob Architectural Antiques.** 2311 18th St. NW. ☎ **202/332-3370.** www.brassknob.com. Metro: Dupont Circle.

When early homes and office buildings are demolished in the name of progress, these savvy salvage merchants spirit away saleable treasures, from chandeliers to wrought-iron fencing. Cross the street to its other location: The Brass Knob's Back Doors Warehouse, 2329 Champlain St. NW (☎ **202/265-0587**).

Cherishables. 1608 20th St. NW. ☎ **202/785-4087.** www.washingtonpost.com/yp/cherishables. Metro: Dupont Circle.

An adorable shop specializing in 18th- and 19th-century American furniture, folk art, quilts, and decorative accessories. The store is known for a world-renowned line of Christmas ornaments designed each year around a new theme: the garden, architecture, and breeds of dogs are some from years past.

Georgetown Antiques Center. 2918 M St. NW. Metro: Foggy Bottom, with a 20-minute walk.

The Cherub Antiques Gallery (☎ 202/337-2224) specializes in art nouveau and art deco, art glass (signed Tiffany, Steuben, Lalique, and Gallé), Liberty arts and crafts, and Louis Icart etchings. Sharing the premises is Michael Getz Antiques (☎ 202/ 338-3811), which sells American, English, and continental silver; porcelain lamps; and many fireplace accessories.

GKS Bush. 2828 Pennsylvania Ave. NW. ☎ 202/965-0653. Metro: Foggy Bottom.

In business for 16 years selling antique American paintings, furniture, and decorative accessories.

Gore-Dean. 1529 Wisconsin Ave. NW. ☎ 202/625-1776. Metro: Foggy Bottom, then a 25-minute walk, or take one of the 30-series buses (nos. 30, 32, 34, 36, 38B) from downtown into Georgetown.

The name is somewhat of a misnomer. Though its offerings include some American pieces, the store specializes in 18th- and 19th-century European furnishings, decorative accessories, paintings, prints, and porcelains.

Millennium. 1528 U St. NW. ☎ 202/483-1218. Metro: U St.–Cardozo.

This is antique shopping for the TV generation, where anything made between the 1930s and the 1970s is considered collectible. The shop works with 18 dealers and stock changes weekly. Funky wares run from bakelite to Heywood-Wakefield blond-wood beauties to used drinking glasses.

Old Print Gallery. 1220 31st St. NW. ☎ 202/965-1818. www.oldprintgallery.com. Metro: Foggy Bottom, with a 20-minute walk.

This gallery carries original American and European prints from the 18th and 19th centuries, including British political cartoons, maps, and historical documents. It's one of the largest antique print and map shops in the United States.

Susquehanna Antiques. 3216 O St. NW. ☎ 202/333-1511. Metro: Foggy Bottom, with a 25-minute walk.

This Georgetown store specializes in American, English, and European furniture and paintings, with most furniture dating from pre-1840.

ART GALLERIES

Art galleries abound in Washington, but are especially prolific in the Dupont Circle and Georgetown neighborhoods, and along 7th Street, downtown. For a complete listing of local galleries, get your hands on a copy of "Galleries," a monthly guide to major galleries and their shows; the guide is available free at many hotel concierge desks and at each of the galleries listed in the publication. Here's a selection of top places.

DUPONT CIRCLE

For all galleries listed below, the closest Metro stop is Dupont Circle.

✪ **Addison/Ripley Gallery, Ltd.** 9 Hillyer Court NW. ☎ 202/328-2332.

This gallery displays contemporary paintings, sculpture, and drawings by Americans, some but not all by locals. Edith Kuhnle, Richard Hunt, and Wolf Kahn are a few of the artists represented here. Second location at 1670 Wisconsin Ave. NW (☎ 202/ 333-3335).

Affrica. 2010 R St. NW. ☎ 202/745-7272. www.affrica.com.

African masks, figures, and artifacts. The gallery's clients include major museums and private collectors from around the world.

Anton Gallery. 2108 R St. NW. ☎ **202/328-0828.**

Expect to find contemporary American paintings, with maybe a little sculpture or photography. Nearly all of the artists shown live locally but hail from around the world.

Fondo del Sol Visual Arts and Media Center. 2112 R St. NW. ☎ **202/483-2777.**

This is a lively gallery in a picturesque town house, showcasing the art and cultures of Latin American, Native American, Caribbean, and African-American artists.

H. H. Leonards' Mansion on O Street. 2020 O St. NW. ☎ **202/496-2000.** Open by appointment only.

Not an art gallery in the usual sense, H. H. Leonards' consists of three Victorian town houses joined together and decorated throughout with more than 5,000 antiques and artworks, in styles ranging from art deco to avant garde. Everything's for sale. This is the Leonards' home, a special events spot, and a luxurious B&B to boot. (Christie Brinkley, Alec Baldwin, and Kim Basinger are among her clients.) H. tells you to help yourself to champagne or coffee in the kitchen and then wander around on your own, which you could do for hours. Parking is such a problem that neighbors are trying to shut her down.

Kathleen Ewing Gallery. 1609 Connecticut Ave. NW. ☎ **202/328-0955.** www.artline. com (click on Galleries).

This gallery shows photography, from 19th century works up to the present.

Very Special Arts Gallery. 1300 Connecticut Ave. NW. ☎ **202/628-2800.** www.vsarts.org.

This one-of-a-kind gallery represents about 800 American artists with disabilities who have created astounding works that include folk art, paintings, and sculptures.

GEORGETOWN

If you're not driving, take a cab, a "30" series bus, or the Metro. If you Metro it, hop off at the Foggy Bottom station, walk up to Washington Circle, turn left and follow Pennsylvania Avenue, which becomes M Street, into Georgetown.

Govinda Gallery. 1227 34th St. NW. ☎ **202/333-1180.** www.govindagallery.com.

You read about this one in the newspaper a lot since it often shows artwork by famous musicians (like the 1999 exhibit of paintings and prints by Rolling Stones guitarist Ronnie Wood) and pictures of celebrity musicians taken by well-known photographers.

Guarisco Gallery, Ltd. 2828 Pennsylvania Ave. NW (in the courtyard). ☎ **202/333-8533.**

Its display of 19th- and early-20th-century oil paintings and sculptures by the likes of H. Herzog, John Singer Sargent, and H. Lebasque, make this gallery as much a museum as a shop.

Spectrum Gallery. 1132 29th St. NW (just below M St.). ☎ **202/333-0954.**

A cooperative venture since 1968, in which 30 professional Washington area artists, including painters, potters, sculptors, photographers, collagists, and printmakers, share in shaping gallery policy, maintenance, and operation. The art is reasonably priced.

SEVENTH STREET ARTS CORRIDOR

A couple of these galleries predate the renaissance taking place in this downtown neighborhood. To get here, take the Metro to either the Archives/Navy Memorial (Blue-Orange line) or Gallery Place/Chinatown/MCI Center (Red-Yellow line) stations.

406 Art Galleries. 406 7th St. NW, between D and E sts.

Several first-rate art galleries, some interlopers from Dupont Circle, occupy this historic building, with its 13-foot-high ceilings and spacious rooms. They include: **David Adamson Gallery** (☎ 202/628-0257; www.artnet.com/adamsonexhibitions), which is probably the largest gallery space in D.C., with two levels featuring the works of contemporary artists, like locals Kevin MacDonald and Renee Stout, and national artists KiKi Smith and William Wegman; and **Touchstone Gallery** (☎ 202/347-2787), which is a self-run co-op of 15 artists who take turns exhibiting their work.

Mickelson Gallery. 707–709 G St. NW. ☎ **202/628-1734.**

Around the corner from the Seventh Street gang, this is one of the oldest D.C. galleries, approaching 40 years, with a framing business going back 89 years. The gallery shows mostly contemporary American and some European artists. For sale by appointment are M. C. Escher works, as well as a large selection of works by George Bellows. (Some Bellows works do hang in the gallery.)

✪ **Zenith Gallery.** 413 7th St. NW. ☎ **202/783-2963.** www.zenithgallery.com.

Across the street from the 406 Group, this 22-year-old gallery shows diverse works by contemporary artists, most American, about half of whom are local. You can get a good deal here, paying anywhere from $50 to $50,000 for a piece. Among other things you'll find here are annual humor shows, neon exhibits, realism, abstract expressionism, and landscapes.

BOOKS

Washingtonians are readers, so bookstores constantly pop up throughout the city. An increasingly competitive market means that chain bookstores do a brisk business, even in a town that can claim more general interest, independent bookstores than any other city. Here are my favorite bookstores in general, used, and special interest categories. *Note:* Web sites for chain bookstores are for the chain, itself, not individual stores.

GENERAL

Barnes & Noble. 3040 M St. NW. ☎ **202/965-9880.** www.barnesandnoble.com. Metro: Foggy Bottom, then a 20-minute walk.

This wonderful three-story shop discounts all hardcovers by 10%, *New York Times* hardcover bestsellers by 30%, and *New York Times* paperback bestsellers by 20%. It has sizable software, travel book, and children's title sections. A cafe on the second level hosts concerts. Other area locations of this discount bookstore and cafe include 4801 Bethesda Ave., in Bethesda, Maryland (☎ **301/986-1761**); 12089 Rockville Pike, in Rockville, Maryland (☎ **301/881-0237**); 3651 Jefferson Davis Highway, in Alexandria, Virginia (☎ **703/299-9124**); and 6260 Seven Corners Center, in Falls Church, Virginia (☎ **703/536-0774**).

B. Dalton. Union Station. ☎ **202/289-1750.** (Web site is same as Barnes & Noble's.) Metro: Union Station.

Your average all-round bookstore, heavy on the bestsellers. They sell magazines, too. Other locations: Shops at National Place (☎ **202/393-1468**) and Chevy Chase Pavilion (☎ **202/686-6542**). See entries under "Malls" for more specific information about each of these locations.

Borders Books & Music. 1800 L St. NW. ☎ **202/466-4999.** www.borders.com. Metro: Farragut North.

With its overwhelming array of books, records, videos, and magazines, this outpost of the rapidly expanding chain has taken over the town. Most hardcovers are 10% off; *New York Times* and the *Washington Post* hardcover bestsellers are 30% off. People hang out here, hovering over the magazines or sipping espresso in the cafe as they read their books. The store often hosts performances by local musicians.

Other Borders stores in the District include 5333 Wisconsin Ave. NW (☎ **202/686-8270**), in upper northwest D.C., and Hamilton Square, at 14th and F streets, NW (phone number not available at this writing). Other area Borders stores include those in North Bethesda, Maryland, at White Flint Mall, 11301 Rockville Pike (☎ **301/816-1067**); Arlington, Virginia, 1201 Hays St. (☎ **703/418-0166**); Bailey's Crossroads, Virginia, 5871 Crossroads Center Way (☎ **703/998-0404**); and Vienna, Virginia, 8311 Leesburg Pike, Virginia (☎ **703/556-7766**).

Bridge Street Books. 2814 Pennsylvania Ave. NW. ☎ **202/965-5200.** Metro: Foggy Bottom.

A small, serious shop with a good selection of current fiction, literary criticism, and publications you won't find elsewhere. Bestsellers and discounted books are not its raison d'être.

Chapters Literary Bookshop. 1512 K St. NW. ☎ **202/347-5495.** Metro: McPherson Square or Farragut North.

Chapters is strong in new and backlisted fiction, and is always hosting author readings. No discounts. Tea is always available, and on Friday afternoons they break out the sherry and cookies.

Crown Books. 11 Dupont Circle. ☎ **202/319-1374.** Metro: Dupont Circle.

Crown has the best discounts but not the best selection: 10% off all paperbacks, 15% off all hardcovers, 40% off hardcover bestsellers, and 25% off *New York Times* paperback bestsellers.

Kramerbooks & Afterwords Café. 1517 Connecticut Ave. NW. ☎ **202/387-1400.** Metro: Dupont Circle.

The first bookstore/cafe in the Dupont Circle area, this place has launched countless romances. It's jammed and often noisy, stages live music Wednesday through Saturday evenings, and is open all night weekends. Paperback fiction takes up most of its inventory, but the store carries a little of everything. No discounts.

✪ **Olsson's Books and Records.** 1239 Wisconsin Ave. NW, between M and N sts. ☎ **202/338-9544.** www.olssons.com. Metro: Foggy Bottom, then a 20-minute walk.

This 26-year-old, independent, quality bookstore chain has about 60,000 to 70,000 books on its shelves. Members of its helpful staff know what they're talking about and will order books they don't have in stock. Discounts given include: 25% off *Washington Post* hardcover bestsellers, 20% off certain other hardcover books. Similar discounts exist for tapes and CDs, and their regular prices are pretty good

Besides the Georgetown branch, there are three other District locations: at 418 Seventh St. NW (☎ **202/638-7610**), at 12th and F streets NW (☎ **202/347-3686**) and at 1307 19th St. NW (☎ **202/785-1133**). In the suburbs are three other Olsson's: in Bethesda, Maryland, at 7647 Old Georgetown Rd. (☎ **301/652-3336**); in Old Town Alexandria, Virginia, at 106 S. Union St. (☎ **703/684-0077**) and in Arlington, Virginia, 2111 Wilson Blvd. (☎ **703/525-4227**). The store on Seventh Street has a creditable cafe called Footnotes, known for its loungy atmosphere, made-in-house selections, and artistic crowd.

⭐ **Politics and Prose Bookstore.** 5015 Connecticut Ave. NW. ☎ **202/364-1919.** Metro: the closest is Van Ness–UDC, but you'll have to walk about a half-mile from there.

This is a two-story shop in a residential part of town. A devoted neighborhood clientele helped move this shop, book by book, across the street to larger quarters in 1990 (it's expanded again since then). It has vast offerings in literary fiction and nonfiction alike, with the largest psychology section in the city (possibly on the East Coast), and an excellent children's department. A warm, knowledgeable staff will help you find what you need. Downstairs is a cozy coffeehouse. Twenty percent off staff-recommended books, otherwise discounts available only to members.

Trover Shop. 227 Pennsylvania Ave. SE. ☎ **202/543-8006.** Metro: Capitol South.

The only general interest bookstore on Capitol Hill, Trover's strengths are its political selections and its magazines. The store discounts 20% on the top 10 *Washington Post* hardcover fiction and nonfiction bestsellers.

Waldenbooks. Georgetown Park Mall. ☎ **202/333-8033.** Metro: Foggy Bottom, with a 20-minute walk.

Borders owns this general-selection chain bookstore; this location offers discounts ranging from 10% to 50% on selected merchandise at any one time.

OLD & USED BOOKS

Booked Up. 1204 31st St. NW. ☎ **202/965-3244.** Metro: Foggy Bottom, with a 20-minute walk, or take one of the 30-series buses (30, 32, 34, 36, 38B) from downtown into Georgetown.

An antiquarian bookstore (owned by author Larry McMurtry) in Georgetown where you can stumble upon some true collectors' items; specializes in travel and literature.

Idle Time Books. 2410 18th St. NW. ☎ **202/232-4774.** Metro: Woodley Park–Zoo or Dupont Circle.

A dusty two-story treasure trove of used books in Adams-Morgan; strong on politics.

Second Story Books. 2000 P St. NW. ☎ **202/659-8884.** secondstorybooks.com. Metro: Dupont Circle.

If it's old, out-of-print, custom-bound, or a small-press publication, this is where to find it. The store also specializes in used CDs and vinyl, and has an interesting collection of antique French and American advertising posters.

SPECIAL-INTEREST BOOKS

ADC Map and Travel Center. 1636 I St. NW. ☎ **800/544-2659** or 202/628-2608.

This newly renovated store sells street maps and atlases for the East Coast from Philadelphia to Atlanta, and carries an extensive collection of maps and guidebooks for the entire world. Globes and atlases are also for sale.

American Institute of Architects/Rizzoli Bookstore. 1735 New York Ave. NW. ☎ **202/626-7475.** Metro: Farragut West.

This store carries books and gifts related to architecture.

Back Stage. 2101 P St. NW. ☎ **202/775-1488.** Metro: Dupont Circle.

This is the headquarters for Washington's theatrical community, which buys its books, scripts, trades, and sheet music here.

Franz Bader Bookstore. 1911 I St. NW. ☎ **202/337-5440.** Metro: Farragut West or Farragut North.

This store stocks books on art, art history, architecture, photography, as well as exhibition catalogues.

Lambda Rising. 1625 Connecticut Ave. NW. ☎ **202/462-6969.** Metro: Dupont Circle.

It was a big deal when this gay and lesbian bookstore opened with a plate glass window revealing its interior to passersby. Now it's an unofficial headquarters for the gay/lesbian/bi community, carrying every gay/lesbian and bisexual book in print, plus videos, music, and gifts.

MysteryBooks. 1715 Connecticut Ave. NW. ☎ **800/955-2279** or 202/483-1600. Metro: Dupont Circle.

The name of the store should give you a clue. Here's where to find out whodunit. It has more paperbacks than hardcovers.

National Museum of American History Giftshop. Constitution Ave. between 12th and 14th sts. NW. ☎ **202/357-1784.** Metro: Federal Triangle or Smithsonian.

Within the National Museum of American History's giftshop, you'll find this wonderful selection of books on American history and culture, including some for children.

Travel Books & Language Center. 4437 Wisconsin Ave. NW. ☎ **800/220-2665** or 202/237-1322. Metro: Tenleytown.

Its move in November 1997 to new digs tripled the space of this 15-year-old travel bookstore, which has the best-in-the-area assortment of guidebooks and maps covering the entire world, as well as language dictionaries and learning tapes, travel diaries, memoirs, and novels famous for their evocation of particular places.

CAMERAS & FILM DEVELOPING

Photography is a big business in this image-conscious tourist town. A wide range of services and supplies, from inexpensive point-and-shoot cameras to deluxe German and Japanese equipment, is available at competitive prices. Some shops offer repair services and have multilingual staff.

✪ **Penn Camera Exchange.** 915 E St. NW. ☎ **202/347-5777.** www.penncamera.com. Metro: Gallery Place or Metro Center.

Across the street from the FBI Building, Penn Camera does a brisk trade with professionals and concerned amateurs. The store offers big discounts on major brand-name equipment, such as Olympus and Canon. Penn has been owned and operated by the Zweig family since 1953; its staff is quite knowledgeable, its inventory wide-ranging. Their specialty is quality equipment and processing—not cheap, but worth it. Also at 1015 18th St. NW (☎ **202/785-7366**).

Ritz Camera Centers. 1740 Pennsylvania Ave. NW. ☎ **202/466-3470.** Metro: Farragut West.

This place sells camera equipment for the average photographer and offers 1-hour film processing. Call for other locations—there are many throughout the area.

CRAFTS

✪ **A mano.** 1677 Wisconsin Ave. NW. ☎ **202/298-7200.** Metro: Foggy Bottom, then a 30-minute walk, or take one of the 30-series buses (nos. 30, 32, 34, 36, 38B) from downtown into Georgetown.

This shop sells unique handmade imported French and Italian ceramics and linens that owner Adam Mahr brings back from his frequent forages to Europe.

✪ **American Hand Plus.** 2906 M St. NW. ☎ **202/965-3273.** Metro: Foggy Bottom, with a 20-minute walk.

This store features exquisite contemporary handcrafted American ceramics and jewelry, plus international objets d'art.

Appalachian Spring. 1415 Wisconsin Ave. NW, at P Street. ☎ **202/337-5780.** Metro: Foggy Bottom, then a 25-minute walk, or take one of the 30-series buses (nos. 30, 32, 34, 36, 38B) from downtown into Georgetown.

Here you'll find country crafts in citified Georgetown. They sell pottery, jewelry, newly made pieced and appliqué quilts, stuffed dolls and animals, candles, rag rugs, hand-blown glassware, an incredible collection of kaleidoscopes, glorious weavings, and wooden kitchen ware. Everything in the store is made by hand in the USA. There's another branch in Union Station (☎ **202/682-0505**).

Corso De-Fiori. 801 Pennsylvania Ave. NW (entrance at 8th and D sts.) www.corso.com. ☎ **202/628-1929.** Metro: Navy Memorial/Archives.

This Sydney, Australia-based store sells its own line of furniture, made of forged iron or wood in Spanish colonial style, as well as upholstered pieces; beautiful handpainted ceramics imported from Deruta, Italy, a village dating from the 15th century and known for its handcrafted ceramics; and Haddonstone limestone English garden accessories.

Indian Craft Shop. Department of the Interior, 1849 C St. NW, Room 1023. ☎ **202/208-4056.** Weekday hours only. Metro: Farragut West or Foggy Bottom.

The Indian Craft Shop has represented authentic Native American artisans since 1938, selling their handwoven rugs and handcrafted baskets, jewelry, figurines, paint-ings, pottery, and other items. You need a photo ID to enter the building.

✪ **The Phoenix.** 1514 Wisconsin Ave. NW. ☎ **202/338-4404.** Metro: Foggy Bottom, with a 30-minute walk, or take one of the 30-series buses (nos. 30, 32, 34, 36, 38B) from down-town into Georgetown.

Around since 1955, The Phoenix still sells those embroidered Mexican peasant blouses popular in hippie days; Mexican folk and fine art; handcrafted, sterling silver jewelry from Mexico and all over the world; clothing in natural fibers from Mexican and American designers like Eileen Fisher and Flax; collectors' quality masks; and decora-tive doodads in tin, brass, copper, and wood.

Random Harvest. 1313 Wisconsin Ave. NW. ☎ **202/342-1922.** Metro: Foggy Bottom, with a 25-minute walk, or take one of the 30-series buses (nos. 30, 32, 34, 36, 38B) from downtown into Georgetown.

This pretty shop holds home and garden furnishings, including antiques and archi-tectural, pine and decorative accessories.

✪ **Torpedo Factory Art Center.** 105 North Union St. ☎ **703/838-4565.** Metro: King Street, then take the DASH bus (AT2 or AT5), eastbound to the waterfront.

This three-story, converted munitions factory houses more than 83 working studios and the works of about 160 artists, who tend to their crafts before your very eyes, pausing to explain their techniques or to sell their pieces, if you so desire. Artworks include paintings, sculpture, ceramics, glasswork, and textiles.

CRYSTAL/SILVER/CHINA
Neiman-Marcus (see "Department Stores," below) and **Tiffany's** (see "Jewelry," below) sell many of these items. First, though, consider visiting these two Georgetown landmarks:

✪ **Little Caledonia.** 1419 Wisconsin Ave. NW. ☎ **202/333-4700.** Metro: Foggy Bottom, then a 25-minute walk, or take one of the 30-series buses (nos. 30, 32, 34, 36, 38B) from downtown into Georgetown.

This delightful rabbit warren of tiny rooms is filled with indoor and outdoor furnish-ings (18th- and 19th-century mahogany reproductions are featured), ceramic figures, exquisite upholstery and drapery fabrics, candles, tablecloths, wallpapers, lamps, and much, much more. It's been here for 60 years.

Martin's of Georgetown. 1304 Wisconsin Ave. NW. ☎ **202/338-6144.** Metro: Foggy Bottom, then a 20-minute walk.

This shop has been proffering exquisite wares since 1929. Come in and feast your eyes on Martin's selection of Lalique vases, Christofle silver, hand-painted Herend china, and Limoges boxes, along with other fine lines of china, silver, crystal, flatware, and dinnerware. Martin's is a prestigious bridal registry (both the Nixon and Johnson daughters were registered here). You'll find stuffed animals, baby gifts, picture frames, and other quality gift items here, too. Georgetown Inn, next door, validates parking.

DEPARTMENT STORES

Bloomingdale's. White Flint Mall, North Bethesda, MD. ☎ **301/984-4600.** Metro: White Flint.

This outpost of the famous New York–based chain features trendsetting fashions for men, women, and children, as well as shoes, accessories, household goods, furnishings, and cosmetics. Don't look for the same variety and selection found in New York, however, since the Washington version seems restrained by comparison.

Hecht's. Metro Center, 1201 G St. NW. ☎ **202/628-6661.** Metro: Metro Center.

Everything from mattresses to electronics, children's underwear to luggage, can be bought at this mid-priced emporium.

Lord & Taylor. 5255 Western Ave. NW. ☎ **202/362-9600.** Metro: Friendship Heights.

This is another lesser version of a New York chain, although lately the store has vastly improved its selections. The staff, too, seems more professional and helpful than in the past. Its women's clothing and accessories departments are probably its strong suit; go elsewhere for gadgets and gifts.

Macy's. Fashion Center at Pentagon City, 1000 S. Hayes St., Arlington, VA. ☎ **703/418-4488.** Metro: Pentagon City.

A household name for many East Coasters, this Macy's (though nowhere near the size of its Manhattan counterpart) hopes to fulfill the same role for Washington customers. Expect mid- to upscale merchandise and prices.

Neiman-Marcus. Mazza Gallerie, 5300 Wisconsin Ave. NW. ☎ **202/966-9700.** Metro: Friendship Heights.

The legendary Texas institution's catalogs and "his-and-hers" Christmas gifts are exercises in conspicuous consumption. Look for remarkably good bargains at their "Last Call" half-yearly sales; otherwise, this store is pretty pricey. It sells no furniture or home furnishings, except for exquisite china and crystal.

Nordstrom. Fashion Center at Pentagon City. 1400 S. Hayes St., Arlington, VA. ☎ **703/415-1121.** Metro: Pentagon City.

This Seattle-based retailer's reputation for exceptional service is well deserved. In keeping with the store's beginnings as a shoe store, this location has three entire departments devoted to women's shoes (designer, dressy, and just plain fun); if you can't find your size or color, they'll order it.

Saks Fifth Avenue. 5555 Wisconsin Ave., Chevy Chase, MD. ☎ **301/657-9000.** Metro: Friendship Heights.

If you can make it past the cosmetics counters without getting spritzed by a makeup-masked woman brandishing a perfume bottle, you've accomplished something special.

On other levels, you'll find designer and tailored men's and women's clothing, and some for children.

DISCOUNT SHOPPING

Discount shops in Washington are few and far between. Stores like JCPenney's and K-Mart are all in the far 'burbs. This list includes the best of the D.C. bunch, followed by a sampling of thrift, secondhand, and consignment stores, where inventory may be eclectic, but the prices often low. Also check out the listing of flea markets, below.

DISCOUNT SHOPS

Filene's Basement. 1133 Connecticut Ave. NW. ☎ **202/872-8430.** www.filenesbasement. com. Metro: Farragut North.

This Boston-based store is a hit in Washington, selling designer and famous-name clothes and accessories at this downtown location and two others in the District: 529 14th St. NW, in the Shops at National Place complex (☎ **202/638-4110**) and in the Mazza Gallerie in upper northwest Washington, 5300 Wisconsin Ave. NW (☎ **202/ 966-0208**). Filene's also has suburban locations.

Hit or Miss. The Shops at National Place, 14th and F sts. NW. ☎ **202/347-0280.** Metro: Metro Center.

Here you'll find a mixture of professional and casual clothes for women at bargain prices. Other locations include 1140 Connecticut Ave. NW (☎ **202/223-8231**), 1701 K St. NW (☎ **202/833-8344**), and 900 19th St. (☎ **202/785-2226**).

Potomac Mills Mall. 25 miles south on I-95. Accessible by car, or by shuttle bus leaving from designated places throughout the area, including Dupont Circle and Metro Center. Call ☎ **800/VA-MILLS** or 703/490-5948 for information about Potomac Mills; call ☎ **703/ 551-1050** for information about the shuttle bus service. www.potomacmills.com.

When you are stuck in the traffic that always clogs this section of I-95, you may wonder if a trip to Potomac Mills is worth it. Believe it or not, this place attracts more visitors than any other site in the Washington area, and twice as many as the next top draw, the Smithsonian's National Air and Space Museum. It's the largest indoor outlet mall around, with more than 220 shops such as New York's Barney's, DKNY, Nordstrom Rack, IKEA, Royal Doulton Outlet, and Emanuel Ungaro.

THRIFT/CONSIGNMENT/SECOND-HAND SHOPS

Christ Child Opportunity Shop. 1427 Wisconsin Ave. NW. ☎ **202/333-6635.** Metro: Foggy Bottom, with a 20-minute walk.

Proceeds from merchandise bought here go to children's charities. Among the first-floor items, all donations, are the usual thrift shop jumble of jewelry, clothes, shoes, hats, and odds and ends. Upstairs, higher quality merchandise is left on consignment; it's more expensive, but if you know antiques, you might find bargains in jewelry, silver, china, quilts, and other items. Closed in August.

Secondhand Rose. 1516 Wisconsin Ave. NW, between P St. and Volta Place. ☎ **202/ 337-3378.** Metro: Foggy Bottom, with a 20-minute walk.

This upscale second-floor consignment shop specializes in designer merchandise. Creations by Chanel, Armani, Donna Karan, Calvin Klein, Yves Saint-Laurent, Ungaro, Ralph Lauren, and others are sold at about a third of the original price, like a gorgeous Scaasi black velvet and yellow satin ball gown for $400 (it was $1,200 new) and Yves Saint-Laurent pumps in perfect condition for $45. Everything is in style, in season, and in excellent condition. Secondhand Rose is also a great place to shop for gorgeous furs, designer shoes and bags, and costume jewelry.

Secondi Inc. 1702 Connecticut Ave. NW. ☎ **202/667-1122.** Metro: Dupont Circle.

On the second floor of a building right next to a Starbucks is this "high style" consignment shop that sells clothing and accessories, including designer suits, evening wear, and more casual items, with nothing older than 2 years.

FARMERS & FLEA MARKETS

Alexandria Farmers' Market. 301 King St., at Market Sq. in front of the city hall, in Alexandria. ☎ **703/838-4770.** Metro: King Street, then take the DASH bus (AT2 or AT5) eastbound to Market Square.

The oldest continuously operating farmers' market in the country (since 1752), this market offers the usual assortment of locally grown fruits and vegetables, along with delectable baked goods, cut flowers, and plants. Open Saturday from 5:30 to 9:30am.

✪ **Eastern Market.** 225 7th St. SE, between N. Carolina Ave. and C St. SE. ☎ **202/546-2698.** Metro: Eastern Market.

This is the one everyone knows about, even if they've never been here. Located on Capitol Hill, Eastern Market is an inside/outside bazaar of stalls, where greengrocers, butchers, bakers, farmers, artists, crafts people, florists and other merchants vend their wares on weekends. Saturday morning is the best time to go. On Sundays, the food stalls become a flea market. Open Saturday and Sunday from 10am to 5pm.

✪ **Georgetown Flea Market.** In a parking lot bordering Wisconsin Ave., between S and T sts. NW. ☎ **202/223-0289.** Metro: Foggy Bottom, with a 30- to 40-minute walk, or take one of the 30-series buses (nos. 30, 32, 34, 36, 38B) from downtown into Georgetown.

Grab a coffee at Starbucks across the lane and get ready to barter. The Georgetown Flea Market is frequented by all types of Washingtonians looking for a good deal—they often get it—on antiques, painted furniture, vintage clothing, and decorative garden urns. Nearly 100 vendors sell their wares here. Open Sundays from 8:30am to 5pm March through December.

Montgomery County Farm Woman's Cooperative Market. 7155 Wisconsin Ave., in Bethesda. ☎ **301/652-2291.** Metro: Bethesda.

Vendors set up inside every Saturday, year-round from 7am to about 3:30pm, to sell preserves, homegrown veggies, cut flowers, slabs of bacon and sausages, and mouthwatering pies, cookies, and breads; there's an abbreviated version on Wednesdays. Outside, on Saturdays and Wednesdays, are flea market vendors selling rugs, tablecloths, furniture, sunglasses, everything.

FASHION

See also "Discount Shopping," "Vintage Clothing," and "Shoes."

CHILDREN'S CLOTHES

Gap Kids. 1267 Wisconsin Ave. NW. ☎ **202/333-2411.** Metro: Foggy Bottom, with a 20-minute walk.

You can pick up anything here from a pretty sweater to a rain poncho to underwear to jellies, if you've left any such necessities at home. Other location: 2006 Pennsylvania Ave. NW (☎ **202/429-8711**).

Gymbaby. Union Station. ☎ **202/408-2696.** Metro: Union Station.

The only children's clothing store in Union Station, Gymbaby sells togs for the very youngest, from newborn through 3 years.

Kid's Closet. 1226 Connecticut Ave. NW. ☎ **202/429-9247.** Metro: Dupont Circle.

Its storefront display of cute kids' clothes stands out among the bank and restaurant facades in this downtown block; inside are clothes and accessories mostly with brand names like Osh Kosh and Little Me.

Washington Kids. 1331 Pennsylvania Ave. NW, in the lobby of the J. W. Marriott Hotel, within the Shops at National Place. ☎ **202/737-5151.** Metro: Metro Center.

Good for clothes with Osh Kosh, Little Me, Jolene and other labels. Some gifts, too.

MEN'S CLOTHES

Banana Republic. Wisconsin and M sts. ☎ **202/333-2554.** Metro: Foggy Bottom, with a 20-minute walk.

All Banana Republic labels–casual to dressy: wool gabardine and wool crepe pants, khakis, shorts, vests, and jackets. Mid- to high prices. Women's clothes, too. Another location is at F and 13th streets NW (☎ **202/638-2724**).

Beau Monde. International Sq., 1814 K St. NW. ☎ **202/466-7070.** Metro: Farragut West.

This boutique sells all Italian-made clothes, some double-breasted traditional suits, but mostly avant-garde.

Britches of Georgetown. 1247 Wisconsin Ave. NW. ☎ **202/338-3330.** Metro: Foggy Bottom, then 20-minute walk.

See where Washington men go for that straight-laced look. Britches sells moderately priced to expensive dress apparel, both designer wear and from its own label. You'll find Donna Karan, Hickey Freeman, and Zegna, among others. Another location is at 1776 K St. NW (☎ **202/347-8994**).

Brooks Brothers. 1201 Connecticut Ave. NW. ☎ **202/659-4650.** Metro: Dupont Circle or Farragut North.

This is where to go for the K Street/Capitol Hill pinstriped power look. Brooks sells the fine line of Peal's English shoes. This store made the news as the place where Monica Lewinsky bought a tie for President Clinton. Other locations are at Potomac Mills (see "Malls," below) and at 5500 Wisconsin Ave., in Chevy Chase, Maryland (☎ **301/654-8202**).

Burberry's. 1155 Connecticut Ave. NW. ☎ **202/463-3000.** Metro: Farragut North.

Here you'll find those plaid-lined trenchcoats, of course, along with well-tailored but conservative English clothing for men and women.

Eddie Bauer. 3040 M St. NW. ☎ **202/965-9880.** Metro: Foggy Bottom, then a 20-minute walk.

This handsome two-level emporium specializes in outdoorsy sportswear for men and women. Come here for fly-fishing equipment (and books about fishing), backpacks, English Barbour jackets, hunter's caps, Stetson hats, luggage, flashlights, binoculars, hiking boots, Swiss Army knives, and other accoutrements of the adventurous lifestyle.

Urban Outfitters. 3111 M St. NW. ☎ **202/342-1012.** Metro: Foggy Bottom, with a 20-minute walk.

For the latest in casual attire, from fatigue pants to tube tops. The shop has a floor of women's clothes, a floor of men's clothes, as well as housewares, inflatable chairs, books, cards, and candles.

WOMEN'S CLOTHES

If Washington women don't dress well, it isn't for lack of stores. The following boutiques range in styles from baggy grunge to the crisply tailored, from Laura Ashley to black leather. Also see listings in "Men's Clothes," above.

Ann Taylor. Union Station. ☎ **202/371-8010.** Metro: Union Station.

Specializes in American-look, chic clothing, Joan and David and other footwear, and accessories. Other locations include 1720 K St. NW (☎ **202/466-3544**), 600 13th St. NW (☎ **202/737-0325**), and Georgetown Park, 3222 M St. NW (☎ **202/338-5290**).

Betsy Fisher. 1224 Connecticut Ave. NW. ☎ **202/785-1975.** Metro: Dupont Circle.

A walk past the store is all it takes to know that this shop is a tad different. Its windows and racks show off whimsically feminine fashions by new American designers.

Betsey Johnson. 1319 Wisconsin Ave. NW. ☎ **202/338-4090.** Metro: Foggy Bottom, then a 20-minute walk.

New York's flamboyant flower-child designer has a Georgetown shop. She personally decorated the bubble-gum pink walls. Her sexy, offbeat play-dress-up styles are great party and club clothes for the young and the still-skinny young at heart.

Chanel Boutique. 1455 Pennsylvania Ave. NW, in the courtyard of the Willard Inter-Continental Hotel. ☎ **202/638-5055.** Metro: Metro Center.

A modest selection of Chanel's signature designs, accessories, and jewelry, at immodest prices.

♻ **Commander Salamander.** 1420 Wisconsin Ave. NW. ☎ **202/337-2265.** Metro: Foggy Bottom, with a 20-minute walk.

Loud music, young crowd, and funky clothes. Commander Salamander has a little bit of everything, including designer items, some of which are quite affordable: Anna Sui and Moschino dresses, $1 ties, and handmade jackets with Axl jewelry sewn on. Too cool.

Giotto. Georgetown Park. ☎ **202/338-6223.** Metro: Foggy Bottom, with a 20-minute walk.

You'll find Italian designer sports and dress wear here.

Pirjo. 1044 Wisconsin Ave. NW, in Georgetown. ☎ **202/337-1390.** www.pirjo.com. Metro: Foggy Bottom, with a 20-minute walk.

The funky, baggy, and pretty creations of designers like Finnish Marimekko, Bettina, Flax, and VIP. Styles range from casual to dressy; Pirjo sells elegant jewelry to boot.

Rizik Brothers. 1100 Connecticut Ave. NW. ☎ **202/223-4050.** Metro: Farragut North.

In business since 1908, this downtown high fashion store sells designs by Caroline Herrara, Oscar de la Renta, and their ilk.

Saks-Jandel. 5510 Wisconsin Ave., Chevy Chase, MD. ☎ **301/652-2250.** Metro: Friendship Heights.

This store displays elegant afternoon and evening wear by major European and American designers—Giorgio Armani, Hervé Leger, Vera Wang, Louis Féraud, Christian Dior, Sonia Rykiel, Yves Saint-Laurent, Isaac Mizrahi (this was the site of the designer's promo for his movie, *Unzipped*), John Galliano, and many others. Saks-Jandel has an international clientele.

Talbots. 1227 Connecticut Ave. NW. ☎ **202/887-6973.** Metro: Farragut North.

Talbots sells career and casual clothes with a decidedly conservative bent, and accessories to go with them. Another branch is at Georgetown Park, 3222 M St. NW (☎ **202/338-3510**).

Toast & Strawberries. 1608 Connecticut Ave. NW. ☎ **202/234-2424.** Metro: Dupont Circle.

You'll see clothes from around the world here and some by local designers, too. Many in the collection are one-of-a-kind; some are casual and some ethnic, but all are fun to wear. The shop also sells accessories.

Victoria's Secret. Union Station. ☎ **202/682-0686.** Metro: Union Station.

Washington women really like the chain's feminine, sexy line of lingerie, so you'll find you're never too far from one of the shops. Other locations at Connecticut and L streets NW (☎ **202/293-7530**) and Georgetown Park (☎ **202/965-5457**).

GOOD FOOD TO GO
Demanding jobs and hectic schedules leave Washingtonians less and less time to prepare their own meals. Or so they say. At any rate, a number of fine-food shops and bakeries are happy to come to the rescue. Even the busiest bureaucrat can find the time to pop into one of these gourmet shops for a moveable feast.

The Bread Line. 1751 Pennsylvania Ave. NW. ☎ **202/822-8900.** Metro: Farragut West or Farragut North.

Owner Mark Furstenberg is credited with revolutionizing bread baking in Washington (he started the Marvelous Market chain, though he has since bowed out; see below). At The Bread Line, he concentrates on selling freshly baked loaves of wheat bread, flatbreads, baguettes, and more; sandwiches like the roast pork bun or the muffaletta; tasty soups; and desserts such as bread puddings, pear tarts, and delicious cookies. Seating available.

Dean & Deluca. 3276 M St. NW. ☎ **202/342-2500.** Metro: Foggy Bottom.

This famed New York store has set down roots in Washington, in a historic Georgetown building that was once an open-air market. Though it is now closed in, this huge space still feels airy with its high ceiling and windows on all sides. You'll pay top prices, but the quality is impressive—charcuterie, fresh fish, produce, cheeses, prepared sandwiches and cold pasta salads, and the hot-ticket desserts, like crème brûlée and tiramisù. Also on sale are housewares; on site is an espresso bar/cafe. In addition, the chain has two other cafe locations, where you can sit and eat, or take out: 1299 Pennsylvania Ave. NW (☎ **202/628-8155**) and 19th and I streets NW (☎ **202/296-4327**).

Firehook Bakery. 1909 Q St. NW. ☎ **202/588-9296.** Metro: Dupont Circle.

Known for its sourdough baguettes, apple-walnut bread, fresh fruit tarts, and, at its Farragut Square store, 912 17th St. NW (☎ **202/429-2253**), for sandwiches like smoked chicken on sesame-semolina bread. A third D.C. location is at 3411 Connecticut Ave. NW (☎ **202/362-2253**).

Lawson's Gourmet. 1350 Connecticut Ave. NW. ☎ **202/775-0400.** Metro: Dupont Circle.

Sitting at this Lawson's cluster of outside tables and chairs, you will see all of Washington pass by, from sharply dressed lawyers to bohemian artistes and panhandlers. You can buy elaborate sandwiches made to order and very nice desserts, wines, breads, and salads. Other locations include 1350 I St. (☎ **202/789-0800**), 1776 I St. (☎ **202/296-3200**), and Metro Center, 601 13th St. NW (☎ **202/393-5500**).

Marvelous Market. 1511 Connecticut Ave. NW. ☎ **202/332-3690.** Metro: Dupont Circle.

First there were the breads: sourdough, baguettes, olive, rosemary, croissants, scones. Now, there are things to spread on the bread, including smoked salmon mousse and tapenade; pastries to die for, from gingerbread to flourless chocolate cake; and prepared foods, such as soups, empanadas, and pasta salads. The breakfast spread on Sunday mornings is sinful, and individual items, like the croissants, are tastier and less expensive here than at other bakeries. The location is grand, with 18th century chandeliers, an antique cedar bar, and a small number of tables. Another store is at 5035 Connecticut Ave. NW (☎ **202/686-4040**).

Reeves Bakery. 1305 G St. NW. ☎ **202/628-6350.** Metro: Metro Center.

Razed to the ground in 1988 to make way for yet another office building, this dieter's nightmare took more than 3 years to find a new home 2 blocks away. Meanwhile, fans pined for the famous strawberry pie, the pineapple dream cake, the blueberry doughnuts, and chicken salad sandwiches. The offerings here are 1950s-style, tasty but not elegant. See chapter 6 for further information.

Uptown Bakers. 3313 Connecticut Ave. NW. ☎ **202/362-6262.** Metro: Cleveland Park.

If you're visiting the zoo and need a sweets fix, walk down the street to this bakery for a muffin, sweet tart, or a delicious "Vicki" bun, a cinnamon roll named for the long-gone worker who invented it. Coffee, sandwiches, and a wide range of breads are also available.

GIFTS/SOUVENIRS

Chocolate Moose. 1800 M St. NW. ☎ **202/463-0992.** Metro: Farragut North.

Here's where to go when you need a surprising and unexpected gift. They stock wacky cards; a range of useful, funny, and lovely presents; candies; eccentric clothing; and jewelry.

Discovery Channel Store: Destination DC. 601 F St. NW. ☎ **202/639-0908.** Metro: Gallery Place/MCI Center.

This flagship store for the Discovery Channel is purposely designed to resemble a museum as much as a store, with interactive displays, like the virtual dinosaur "dig," that invite participation. The idea is, once you've become involved, you'll want to buy. And there's plenty to buy. The store arranges merchandise according to theme for each of its four levels, from Paleo World (fossils, jewelry, gems, minerals), to Ocean Planet (cermics, clothing, games), to Wild World Cultures (books, home decorating, music, gardening), to Sky Science (science kits, telescopes, and globes). Make sure you make it to the top floor to see the 15-minute film, *Destination DC.*

Made in America. Union Station. ☎ **202/842-0540.** Metro: Union Station.

Union Station is full of gifts shops, actually, but stop here if you want to pick up one of those baseball caps with a "DEA," "CIA," or "Police SWAT" insignia on its bill; White House guests towels; and for other impress-the-folks-back-home items.

MUSEUM SHOPS

The gift stores in the Smithsonian's 14 Washington museums are terrific places to shop, with wares related to the focus of the individual museums. The largest Smithsonian store is in the **National Museum of Natural History.** The one in the Smithsonian's **Arts and Industries Building** sells all of the items offered in the museum catalogs. Smithsonian's museum shop buyers travel the world for unusual items, many of which are made exclusively for its shops. Call ☎ **202/357-2700** for more information; the Smithsonian shops ship items by UPS.

The Smithsonian doesn't corner the market on museum merchandise, however. Here's a sample of smaller museum gift shops and some of the unique gifts that make them worth a stop. (See chapter 7 for museum locations and hours.)

The **National Gallery of Art** gift shop, 4th Street and Constitution Avevue NW (☎ 202/842-6446; Metro: Archives or Judiciary Square), is not so small, actually. Its wares include printed reproductions, stationery, and jewelry, whose designs are all based on works in the gallery's permanent collections or from special exhibitions. The shop also has one of the largest selections of books on art history and architecture in the country, and a generous offering of children's products (books, art kits, games, and so on), too.

The gift shop at the **Textile Museum,** 2320 St. NW (☎ 202/667-0441; Metro: Dupont Circle) offers an extensive selection of books on carpets and textiles, as well as Indian silk scarves, kilim pillows, Tibetan prayer rugs, and other out-of-the-ordinary items.

Washington National Cathedral's main shop, Massachusetts and Wisconsin avenues NW (☎ 202/537-6207), in the crypt of the Gothic cathedral, sells books, stained glass, and tapes. The Herb Cottage is a delightful oasis, selling dried herbs and garden gifts. The Greenhouse shop is one of the best and certainly most charming places in town to buy flowering plants and live herbs.

JEWELRY

Beadazzled. 1507 Connecticut Ave. NW. ☎ 202/265-BEAD. Metro: Dupont Circle.

The friendly staff helps you assemble your own affordable jewelry from an eye-boggling array of beads and artifacts.

Charles Schwartz & Son. Willard Hotel, 1401 Pennsylvania Ave. NW. ☎ 202/737-4757. Metro: Metro Center.

In business since 1888, Charles Schwartz specializes in diamonds and sapphires, rubies and emeralds, and is one of the few distributors of Baccarat jewelry. The professional staff also repairs watches and jewelry. There's another branch at the Mazza Gallerie (☎ 202/363-5432; Metro: Friendship Heights).

✪ **Galt & Brothers.** 607 15th St. NW. ☎ 202/347-1034. Metro: Metro Center.

In existence since 1801, Galt's is the capital's oldest business and America's oldest jewelry store. The shop sells and repairs high-quality jewelry, diamonds, and all manner of colored gems. Gifts of crystal, silver, and china are also sold.

✪ **Tiffany and Company.** 5500 Wisconsin Ave., Chevy Chase, MD. ☎ 301/657-8777. Metro: Friendship Heights.

Tiffany's is known for exquisite diamonds and other jewelry that can cost hundreds of thousands of dollars, but what you may not know is that the store carries less expensive items, as well: $35 candlesticks, for example. Tiffany's will engrave, too. Other items include tabletop gifts and fancy glitz: china, crystal, flatware, and bridal registry service.

✪ **Tiny Jewel Box.** 1147 Connecticut Ave. NW. ☎ 202/393-2747. Metro: Farragut North.

The first place Washingtonians go for estate and antique jewelry.

MALLS

Chevy Chase Pavilion. 5345 Wisconsin Ave. NW. ☎ 202/686-5335. Metro: Friendship Heights.

This is a manageably sized mall with about 50 stores and restaurants, anchored by an Embassy Suites Hotel. The inside is unusually pretty, with three levels winding around a skylit atrium. Giant palm trees, arrangements of fresh flowers, and seasonal events add panache. Stores include The Limited, a two-level Pottery Barn, a Bath and Body shop, and a Joan and David shoe store. A small food court, the Cheesecake Factory, and the California Pizza Kitchen are among the eating options.

Fashion Center at Pentagon City. 1400 S. Hayes St., Arlington, VA. ☎ **703/415-2400.** Metro: Pentagon City.

Nordstrom's and Macy's are the biggest attractions in this block-long, five-story, elegant shoppers' paradise that also houses a Ritz-Carlton Hotel (where Ken Starr nabbed Monica Lewinsky), office suites, multiplex theaters, and a sprawling food court. Villeroy and Boch, Crate & Barrel, and Eddie Bauer are among the nearly 167 shops.

Mazza Gallerie. 5100 Wisconsin Ave. NW. ☎ **202/966-6114.** Metro: Friendship Heights.

Undergoing a renovation scheduled for completion in 1999, the mall is looking down at its heels right now, despite the presence of Neiman-Marcus. With sprucing up, the Mazza should return as an attractive shopping center, with its skylit atrium and stores like Ann Taylor and Harriet Kassman. There are theaters on the lower level, and there is access to Chevy Chase Pavilion, the subway, and to the Hecht's department store via the Metro tunnel. Parking is free with validated ticket.

The Pavilion at the Old Post Office. 1100 Pennsylvania Ave. NW. ☎ **202/289-4224.** Metro: Federal Triangle.

This is mainly a tourist trap holding souvenir shops and a food court. Noontime concerts are a draw, as is the view of the city from the building's clock tower, 315 feet up.

Potomac Mills. See "Discount Shopping," above.

The Shops at Georgetown Park. 3222 M St. NW. ☎ **202/342-8180.** Metro: Foggy Bottom, then a 20-minute walk.

This four-story complex of about 100 shops belongs, architecturally, to two worlds: outside, quietly Federal, in keeping with the character of the neighborhood; inside, flamboyantly Victorian, with a huge skylight, fountains, and ornate chandeliers.

This is a deluxe mall, where you'll see the beautiful people shopping for beautiful things. You could spend hours here exploring branches of the nation's most exclusive specialty stores, including Ann Taylor, Caché, J. Crew, and Polo/Ralph Lauren. Also featured are many gift/lifestyle boutiques such as Circuit City Express, Sharper Image, Crabtree & Evelyn, and the fascinating Gallery of History (framed collector historical documents). If you have kids, take them to F.A.O. Schwarz and Learningsmith (billing itself as "the general store for the curious mind," it has many interactive facilities for children).

An Old Town Trolley ticket booth (see chapter 7) is on the premises. There are several restaurants, including Clyde's (see chapter 6 for details), gourmet emporium/cafe Dean and Deluca, and the parklike Canal Walk Café Food Court. An archaeological exhibit of artifacts found during the complex's excavation can be viewed on Level 2. Georgetown Park maintains a full-service Concierge Center offering gift wrapping, worldwide shipping, postal/fax/photocopy services, gift certificates, even sightseeing information. Validated parking in the underground garage is available with minimum $10 purchase.

The Shops at National Place. 1331 Pennsylvania Ave. NW. ☎ **202/662-1250.** Metro: Metro Center.

You can enter through the J. W. Marriott Hotel or at F Street, between 13th and 14th streets. National Place has more than 75 specialty shops and eateries, including Casual Corner, Filene's Basement discount department store, and an international food court.

Tyson's Corner Center. 9160 Chain Bridge Rd., McLean, VA. ☎ **703/893-9400.** Tyson's Corner II, The Galleria, 2001 International Dr., McLean, VA. ☎ **703/827-7700.** Metro: West Falls Church, take shuttle.

Facing each other across Chain Bridge Road, these two gigantic malls could lead to shopper's overload. Tyson's Corner Center, the first and less expensive, has Nordstrom's, Bloomingdale's, and JCPenney, and specialty stores, such as Abercrombie & Fitch and Crabtree & Evelyn. The Galleria has Macy's, Saks Fifth Avenue, and more than 100 upscale boutiques.

✪ **Union Station.** 50 Massachusetts Ave. NE. ☎ **202/371-9441.** Metro: Union Station.

After the National Air & Space Museum, this is the next most popular stop within Washington itself. The architecture is magnificent. Its more than 120 shops include The Nature Company, Brookstone, and Appalachian Spring; among the places to eat are America, B. Smith, and an international food court. There's also a nine-screen movie theater complex.

White Flint Mall. 11301 Rockville Pike, Kensington, MD. ☎ **301/468-5777.** Metro: White Flint, then take the free "White Flint" shuttle, which runs every 12 to 15 minutes.

Another Bloomingdale's, another long trip in the car or on the Metro, but once you're there, you can shop, take in a movie, and dine cheaply or well. Notable stores include Lord & Taylor's, a huge Borders Books & Music, Ann Taylor, and The Coach Store.

MISCELLANEOUS

Al's Magic Shop. 1012 Vermont Ave. NW. ☎ **202/789-2800.** Metro: McPherson Square.

This first-rate novelty shop is presided over by prestidigitator and local character Al Cohen, who is only too happy to demonstrate his latest magic trick or practical joke.

Ginza, "Things Japanese." 1721 Connecticut Ave. NW. ☎ **202/331-7991.** Metro: Dupont Circle.

Everything Japanese, from incense and kimonos to futons to Zen rock gardens.

Grafix. 2904 M St. NW. ☎ **202/342-0610.** Metro: Foggy Bottom, then a 20-minute walk.

This shop carries a noteworthy collection of vintage posters (mostly French), 16th- to 20th-century maps, 19th-century prints, vintage magazines from the turn of the century through the 1930s, and other collectibles.

Hats in the Belfry. 1237 Wisconsin Ave. NW. ☎ **202/342-2006.** Metro: Foggy Bottom, then a 25-minute walk.

In business for 22 years now, this hat store features designer hats, floppy hats, straw hats, panama hats, all sorts of hats, for men and women, some for children, and some handbags. Go ahead, try some on.

MUSIC

Borders Books & Music. 1800 L St. NW. ☎ **202/466-4999.** Metro: Farragut North. (See other locations under "Books," above.)

Besides being a great bookstore, Borders offers the best prices in town for CDs and tapes, and a wide range of music.

DCCD. 2423 18th St. NW. ☎ **202/588-1810.** Metro: Woodley Park, with a 10- to 15-minute walk.

This store sells new and used CDs, new records, and new and used video games. Known best as Washington's independent rock record store, DCCD features in-store performances by local and national bands.

Primping for a Night on the Town: Salons

With a few exceptions, the best salons are in Georgetown and cater to both men and women. But expect to spend a little money.

Bogart, 1063 Wisconsin Ave. NW (☎ **202/333-6550;** Metro: Foggy Bottom, with a 20-minute walk, or take one of the 30-series buses—nos. 30, 32, 34, 36, 38B—from downtown into Georgetown), is favored by certain local TV news anchors and specializes in "corrective color." Facials cost $60; haircuts range between $30 and $75 for women, between $25 and $50 for men.

Gloria (Interiano) has been cutting my husband's hair for 21 years now and mine about half that time at **Interiano Salon,** 1025 31st St. NW (☎ **202/333-3455;** Metro: Foggy Bottom, with a 20-minute walk). In her cozy den on the second floor of a Georgetown townhouse, Gloria and her staff make you feel at home. Rates: $35 for men, $60 for women.

IPSA for Hair, 1629 Wisconsin Ave. NW (☎ **202/338-4100;** Metro: Foggy Bottom, with a 30-minute walk, or take one of the 30-series buses—nos. 30, 32, 34, 36, 38B—from downtown into Georgetown) won the most votes for favorite hair styling salon in a local count, but it only does hair. Haircuts average $65 for women, $45 for men.

✪ **Okyo,** 2903 M St. NW (☎ **202/342-2675;** Metro: Foggy Bottom, with a 10-minute walk, or take one of the 30-series buses—nos. 30, 32, 34, 36, 38B—from downtown into Georgetown) only does hair, but at surprisingly reasonable rates: cuts start at $60 for women, $35 for men. Owner Bernard Portelli used to color Catherine Deneuve's hair in France, which means he's so booked that he isn't taking any new clients.

HMV. 1229 Wisconsin Ave. NW. ☎ **202/333-9292.** Metro: Foggy Bottom, with a 20-minute walk.

This London-based record and tape store is fun to visit for its party atmosphere and listening stations with headphones. But you can get a better deal almost anywhere else.

Melody Record Shop. 1623 Connecticut Ave. NW. ☎ **202/232-4002.** Metro: Dupont Circle, Q St. exit.

CDs, cassettes, and tapes are discounted 10% to 20% here, new releases 20% to 30%. Melody offers a wide variety of rock, classical, jazz, pop, show, and folk music, as well as a vast number of international selections. This is also a good place to shop for discounted portable electronic equipment, blank tapes, and cassettes. Its knowledgeable staff is a plus.

Olsson's Books & Records. See entry under "Books," above for other locations.

Tower Records. 2000 Pennsylvania Ave. NW. ☎ **202/331-2400.** Metro: Foggy Bottom.

When you need a record at midnight on Christmas Eve, you go to Tower. The large, funky store, across the street from George Washington University, has a wide choice of records, cassettes, and CDs in every category—but the prices are high.

12" Dance Records. 2010 P St. NW, 2nd floor. ☎ **202/659-2010.** www.12inchdance.com. Metro: Dupont Circle.

Disco lives. If you ever moved to it on a dance floor, Wresch Dawidjian and his staff of DJs have it, or they can get it. There's always a DJ mixing it up live in the store, and they pump the beats out into the street.

POLITICAL MEMORABILIA

Capitol Coin and Stamp Co. Inc. 1701 L St. NW. ☎ **202/296-0400.** Metro: Farragut North.

A museum of political memorabilia—pins, posters, banners—and all of it is for sale. This is also a fine resource for the endangered species of coin and stamp collectors.

✪ **Political Americana.** Union Station. ☎ **202/547-1685.** Metro: Union Station.

This is another great place to pick up souvenirs. The store sells political novelty items, books, bumper stickers, old campaign buttons, and historical memorabilia. Another location is at 14th Street and Pennsylvania Avenue NW (☎ **202/737-7730**).

SHOES

Brooks Brothers. See entry under "Men's Clothes," above.

Comfort Zone Shoes. 1630 Connecticut Ave. NW. ☎ **202/328-3141.** Metro: Dupont Circle.

Despite its unhip name, this store sells a great selection of popular styles for both men and women: Doc Martens to Birkenstocks to Ecco. You can always find something that actually feels comfortable. Lots of locations: 1617 Connecticut Ave. NW (☎ **202/667-5300**), 3222 M St. NW (☎ **202/667-5300**), and 1706 Eye St. NW (☎ **202/331-8870**), to name several.

Foot Locker. Union Station. ☎ **202/289-8364.** Metro: Union Station.

This chain sells sports shoes for men, women, and children. Lots of other locations: 3221 M St. NW (☎ **202/333-7640**) and 1331 Pennsylvania Ave. NW (The Shops at National Place) (☎ **202/783-2093**), to name two.

Nine West. Union Station. ☎ **202/216-9490.** Metro: Union Station.

Dress and casual shoes for women. Other locations: 1008 Connecticut Ave. NW (☎ **202/452-9163**) and 1227 Wisconsin Ave. NW (☎ **202/337-7256**).

Steve Madden. 3109 M St. NW. ☎ **202/333-2224.** Metro: Foggy Bottom, then a 20-minute walk.

The music's so loud, you may not be able to hear a word the salesperson says, but this is Washington's only Steve Madden location, the women's shoe store that's really popular among the college-age crowd for its chunky platforms, sandals, and thongs.

TOYS

Discovery Channel Store. See entry under "Miscellaneous," above.

Flights of Fancy. Union Station. ☎ **202/371-9800.** Metro: Union Station.

Picture books, Playmobil toys, board games, and assorted other toys and amusements cram this small store.

Learningsmith. 3222 M St. NW (shops at Georgetown Park Mall). ☎ **202/337-0800.** Metro: Foggy Bottom, with a 20-minute walk.

This store carries educational toys and games for the 10 and younger set.

VINTAGE CLOTHING

Check out entries under "Farmers & Flea Markets," above, and see "Discount Shopping," above, in addition to this store:

Glorious Revivals. 1749 Connecticut Ave. NW. ☎ **202/232-5416.** Metro: Dupont Circle.

This is an antiques store that has a room devoted to vintage clothing and accessories, from turn-of-the-century through the '60s.

WINE & SPIRITS

Calvert Woodley Liquors. 4339 Connecticut Ave. NW. ☎ **202/966-4400.** Metro: Van Ness–UDC.

This is a large store with a friendly staff, nice selections, and good cheeses (about 300 to choose from) and other foods to go along with your drinks.

✪ **Central Liquor.** 917 F St. NW. ☎ **202/737-2800.** Metro: Gallery Place–9th and G St. NW/Smithsonian exit.

This is like a clearinghouse for liquor: Its great volume allows the store to offer the best prices in town on wines and liquor.

MacArthur Liquor. 4877 MacArthur Blvd. NW. ☎ **202/338-1433.** Bus: D4 from Dupont Circle.

With a knowledgeable and enthusiastic staff, and because an extensive and reasonably priced selection of excellent wines, both imported and domestic, this shop is always busy.

9

Washington, D.C., After Dark

For a long time, Washington has suffered the indignity of being compared to other cities, mainly New York and Los Angeles. People seem to think we're stuffy and a bit dull. When the North Atlantic Treaty Organization (NATO) celebrated its 50th anniversary in Washington in April 1999, stories ran in the newspapers quoting diplomats, like the Belgian Defense Minister's spokesman, who remarked, "In comparison with New York, Washington seems, if you allow me to say, quite provincial."

This would be worrisome, except that, well, comparisons are odious. If you want New York, go to New York. If you like Los Angeles, go to Los Angeles. That's one response Washingtonians make. The other is to note all that the capital offers, its unique features, and its many charms—that's the point of this whole book, obviously. (And just for the record, when NATO came to town, the town shut down, because of security measures.)

And when it comes to nightlife, Washington is "happening," if not round-the-clock hip. Theater and performing arts are diverse and first-rate. Ditto the live music scene. And as far as free or inexpensive cultural opportunities are concerned, I doubt that any other city comes close to what Washington proffers. As for the bar and club scene—a virtual renaissance is taking place.

Exclusive clubs, a fixture in New York and L.A. nightlife, have arrived here. Never mind that in Washington, the ultimate coup de grace has always been receiving an invitation to that most exclusive of events, the White House dinner. For those of us who are still waiting, Washington offers other select venues where we can hope to pass muster at the door to frolic among the anointed, famous, rich, beautiful, or otherwise "important." These VIP rooms and restricted-access clubs are increasingly popular in Washington, and I have included some of them in this chapter, if you are so inclined.

All the signs are that Washington is loosening up. You can see this in the explosion of lounge-bars (as opposed to bar-lounges), where decor includes lots of comfy furniture arranged haphazard, the better to encourage conversation and relaxation (slouching to Gommorrah?). And suddenly people are dancing. A few dance clubs have always been around, but now bars, like Politiki on Capitol Hill, are making room for dancing. New nightclubs are opening, like 2:K:9 and Zanzibar, and going all out with decor and even gimmicks (2:K:9 has dancing women in cages), to get people shakin' and groovin'. Clubs are offering dance lessons, and by golly, people are taking them.

And for those of you looking for just a pleasant spot to have a drink, don't worry, we'll always have plenty of those.

In addition to the listings below, check the Friday "Weekend" section of the *Washington Post,* which will inform you about children's theater, sports events, flower shows, and all else. The *City Paper,* available free at restaurants, bookstores, and other places around town, is another good source.

TICKETS

TICKETplace, Washington's only discount, day-of-show ticket outlet, has one location: in the Old Post Office Pavilion, 1100 Pennsylvania Ave. NW (Metro: Federal Triangle). Call ☎ **202/TICKETS** for information. On the day of performance only (except Sunday and Monday, see below), you can buy half-price tickets (with cash, select debit and credit cards, or traveler's checks) to performances with tickets still available at most major Washington area theaters and concert halls, not only for dramatic productions, but for opera, ballet, and other events as well. TICKETplace is open Tuesday to Saturday from 11am to 6pm; half-price tickets for Sunday and Monday shows are sold on Saturday. Though you purchase the ticket for half price, you will have to pay a service charge, 10% of the full face value of the ticket.

Full-price tickets for most performances in town can be bought through Ticketmaster (☎ **202/432-SEAT**) at Hecht's Department Store, 12th and G streets NW, and at George Washington University's Marvin Center, across from Lisner Auditorium, at 21st Street and H Street NW (Metro: Foggy Bottom). These locations are open 10am to 8pm. You can purchase tickets to Washington theatrical, musical, and other events before you leave home by calling ☎ **800/551-SEAT.** Another similar ticket outlet is Protix (☎ **800/955-5566** or 703/218-6500).

1 Theater

D.C.'s theatrical productions are first-rate and varied. Almost anything on Broadway has either been previewed here or will eventually come here. The city also has several nationally acclaimed repertory companies and a theater specializing in Shakespearean productions. Additional theater offerings, including those at the Kennedy Center, are listed under "Other Performing Arts" later in this chapter.

Arena Stage. 6th St. and Maine Ave. SW. ☎ **202/488-3300.** www.arenastage.org. Tickets $26–$45; discounts available for students, people with disabilities, groups, and senior citizens. A limited number of $10 tickets, called HOTTIX, are available 90 minutes before most performances (call for details). $5 reserved parking onsite and satellite lots, as well as street parking. Metro: Waterfront.

Founded by the brilliant Zelda Fichandler, the Arena Stage, now in its fifth decade, is home to one of the oldest acting ensembles in the nation. Several works nurtured here have moved to Broadway, and many graduates have gone on to commercial stardom, among them Ned Beatty, James Earl Jones, Robert Prosky, Jane Alexander, and George Grizzard.

Arena presents eight productions annually on two stages: the Fichandler (a theater-in-the-round) and the smaller, fan-shaped Kreeger. In addition, the Arena houses the Old Vat, a space used for new play readings and special productions.

The 1999 to 2000 September-to-June season includes productions of *Dinah Was,* by Oliver Goldstick; *The Miracle Worker,* by William Gibson; *Blue,* by Charles Randolph-Wright; *All My Sons,* by Arthur Miller; *The Royal Family,* by George S. Kaufman and Edna Ferber; and *Guys and Dolls,* starring Maurice Hines.

Should you have any questions, call the number above. Arena Stage staff and volunteers are remarkable for their genial courtesy and helpfulness. The theater has always championed new plays and playwrights and is committed to producing the works of playwrights from diverse cultures. Molly D. Smith is the Arena Stage's new artistic director.

Ford's Theatre. 511 10th St. NW (between E and F sts.). ☎ **202/347-4833,** TDD 202/347-5599 for listings, 800/955-5566 or 703/218-6500 to charge tickets. www.fordstheatre. org. Tickets $27–$40; discounts available for families, also for senior citizens at matinee performances and any time on the "day of" for evening shows; students with ID can get "rush" tickets an hour before performances if tickets are available. Metro: Metro Center or Gallery Place.

This is the actual theater where, on the evening of April 14, 1865, actor John Wilkes Booth shot President Lincoln. The assassination marked the end of what had been John T. Ford's very popular theater; it remained closed for more than a century. In 1968, Ford's reopened, completely restored to its 1865 appearance, based on photographs, sketches, newspaper articles, and samples of wallpaper and curtain material from museum collections. The presidential box is decorated and furnished as it was on that fateful night, including the original crimson damask sofa and framed engraving of George Washington.

Ford's season is more or less year-round (it's closed for a while in the summer). Several of its productions have gone on to Broadway and off-Broadway. Recent shows have included Steve Martin's *Picasso at the Lapin Agile* and *Eleanor: An American Love Story.*

A big event here is the nationally televised "A Festival at Ford's," which is a celebrity-studded bash usually held in the fall, and attended by the president and first lady. A Washington tradition is the holiday performance of Dickens' *A Christmas Carol.*

National Theatre. 1321 Pennsylvania Ave. NW. ☎ **202/628-6161,** or 800/447-7400 to charge tickets by phone. www.nationaltheatre.org. Tickets $30–$75; discounts available for students, senior citizens, military personnel, and people with disabilities. Metro: Metro Center.

The luxurious, Federal-style National Theatre, elegantly renovated to the tune of $6.5 million in 1983, is the oldest continuously operating theater in Washington (since 1835) and the third-oldest in the nation. It's exciting just to see the stage on which Sarah Bernhardt, John Barrymore, Helen Hayes, and so many other notables have performed. The 1,672-seat National is the closest thing Washington has to a Broadway-style playhouse. Managed by New York's Shubert Organization, it presents star-studded hits, often pre- or post-Broadway, most of the year. The 1999 season included productions of *Bring in Da Noise, Bring in Da Funk* and *Les Miserables.*

The National also offers free public-service programs: Saturday-morning children's theater (puppets, clowns, magicians, dancers, and singers) and Monday-night show-cases of local groups and performers September through May, plus free summer films. Call ☎ 202/783-3372 for details.

Shakespeare Theatre. 450 7th St. NW (between D and E sts.). ☎ **202/547-1122.** www.shakespearedc.org. Tickets $17.50–$56, $10 for standing-room tickets sold 1 hour before sold-out performances; discounts available for students, groups, and senior citizens. Metro: Archives–Navy Memorial or Gallery Place.

This internationally renowned classical ensemble company, which for 2 decades performed at the Folger Shakespeare Library, moved to larger quarters at the above address in 1992. Under the artistic direction of Michael Kahn, it offers five productions, usually three Shakespearean and two modern classics each September-to-June season. The 1999–2000 season includes *King Lear, A Midsummer Night's Dream, The Two Gentleman of Verona,* and Noel Coward's *Design for Living.* (The schedule may have changed slightly by the time you read this.) This is top-level theater. Furthermore, the company offers one admission-free, 2-week run of a Shakespeare production at the Carter Barron Amphitheatre in Rock Creek Park (see listing for Carter Barron below, under "Outdoor Pavilions & Stadiums").

Source Theatre Company. 1835 14th St. NW (between S and T sts.). ☎ **202/462-1073** for information or 301/738-7073 to charge tickets. Tickets $20–$25, OFF HOURS shows $15, Washington Theatre Festival shows $8–$15.

Washington's major producer of new plays, the Source also mounts works by established playwrights—for example, David Mamet's *The Cherry Orchard,* Arthur Miller's *A View from the Bridge,* and A. R. Gurney's *A Cheever Evening.* It presents top local artists in a year-round schedule of dramatic and comedy plays, both at the above address and, during the summer, at various spaces around town. The theater is also used for an OFF HOURS series of productions geared to a contemporary urban audience. Annual events here include the Washington Theatre Festival each July, a 4-week showcase of about 50 new plays. The Source, which produces many African-American works, welcomes original scripts from unknowns.

Studio Theatre. 1333 P St. NW. ☎ **202/332-3300.** www.studiotheatre.org. Tickets $19.50–$36.50. Discounts available for groups of 15 or more, students, and senior citizens. Metro: Dupont Circle, McPherson Square, or U St.–Cardozo.

Under artistic director Joy Zinoman, the Studio has consistently produced interesting contemporary plays, nurtured Washington acting talent, and garnered numerous Helen Hayes Awards for outstanding achievement. Many plays come here from off-Broadway. Past seasons have included August Wilson's *Seven Guitars* and Terrence McNally's *Love! Valour! Compassion!* On the books for the 1999–2000 season are *India Ink,* by Tom Stoppard, *Master Harold and the Boys,* by Athol Fugard, and *Sideman,* by Warren Leight. The Studio also houses Secondstage, a 50-seat space on the third floor where emerging artists, directors, and actors can showcase their work. The season runs year-round. A $4.5 million renovation completed in 1997 remodeled the main theater and added a wonderful new one, the Milton. Street parking is easy to find, and there's a pay lot at P Street between 14th and 15th streets.

Woolly Mammoth Theatre Company. 1401 Church St. NW (between P and Q sts.) ☎ **202/393-3939.** For tickets, call Protix ☎ **800/955-5566** or 703/218-6500. Tickets $15–$28. They offer a range of ticket discounts, including reduced prices for seniors and those under 25, and pay-what-you-can nights; inquire at the box office. Free parking across the street. Metro: Dupont Circle, about 5 blocks away. You might prefer to take a cab from there; on request, they'll call a cab for you after the show.

Established in 1980, the Woolly Mammoth offers as many as six productions each year-long season, specializing in new, offbeat, and quirky plays. "I'm not interested in theater where people sit back and say, 'That was nice. I enjoyed that,'" says artistic director Howard Shalwitz. "I only look for plays that directly challenge the audience in some important way." Recent plays included *The Last Orbit of Billy Mars,* by Robert Alexander and Friedrich Durrenmatt's comedy *The Marriage of Mr. Mississippi.* This company has garnered more than 14 Helen Hayes Awards, among other accolades, and is consistently reviewed by the *New York Times.*

2 Other Performing Arts

The following listings are a potpourri of places offering a mixed bag of theater, opera, classical music, headliners, jazz, rock, dance, and comedy. Here you'll find some of the top entertainment choices in the District.

MULTICULTURAL FACILITIES

DAR Constitution Hall. 18th and D sts. NW. ☎ **202/628-4780;** 800/551-SEAT or 202/432-SEAT to charge tickets. Tickets $15–$50. Metro: Farragut West.

Housed within a beautiful, turn-of-the-century beaux-arts–style building is this fine, 3,746-seat auditorium. Its excellent acoustics have supported an eclectic group of performers—the Boston Symphony, Britney Spears, John Hiatt, Count Basie Orchestra, Los Angeles Philharmonic, Lee Greenwood, Diana Ross, Jay Leno, Ray Charles, Buddy Guy, The Temptations, Trisha Yearwood, Roy Clark, Kathleen Battle, and Marilyn Horne.

The Folger Shakespeare Library. 201 E. Capitol St. SE. ☎ **202/544-7077.** www.folger.edu. Students and seniors receive discounts with proof of ID. Call for information about ticket prices, which can range from $8–$50, depending upon the event. Metro: Capitol South or Union Station.

The Folger Shakespeare Library is open year-round, featuring exhibits and tours of its Tudor-style great rooms (see chapter 7 for details). In its 23rd season at the Folger is the Folger Consort, an early music ensemble, which performs medieval, Renaissance, and baroque music, troubadour songs, madrigals, and court ensembles; between October and May, they give 30 concerts over the course of seven weekends.

The Folger presents plays and musical performances, lectures, readings, and other events in its Elizabethan Theatre, which is styled after the inn yard theatre of Shakespeare's time.

On selected evenings, readings feature such poets as W. S. Merwin, Jorie Graham, Seamus Heany, Gwendolyn Brooks, Michael Ondaatje, and John Ashbery. Another exciting program is the Friday-night PEN/Faulkner series of fiction readings by noted authors such as John LeCarre, Joyce Carol Oates, Ann Beattie, Susan Power, Albert Murray, Joan Didion, and Richard Ford. And the Folger offers Saturday programs for children, ranging from medieval treasure hunts to preparing an Elizabethan feast.

✪ **John F. Kennedy Center for the Performing Arts.** At the southern end of New Hampshire Ave. NW and Rock Creek Pkwy. ☎ **800/444-1324** or 202/467-4600. kennedy-center.org. 50% discounts are offered (for most attractions) to students, seniors 65 and over, people with permanent disabilities, enlisted military personnel, and persons with fixed, low incomes (call ☎ **202/416-8340** for details). Garage parking $8. Metro: Foggy Bottom (though it's a fairly short walk, there's a free shuttle between the station and the Kennedy Center, departing every 15 minutes from 7pm to midnight). Bus: 80 from Metro Center.

Our national performing arts center, the hub of Washington's cultural and entertainment scene, is actually made up of six different theaters. You can find out what is scheduled during your stay (and charge tickets) before leaving home by calling the above toll-free number.

The Kennedy Center's free concert series, known as "Millennium Stage," features daily performances by area musicians, staged each evening at 6pm in the center's Grand Foyer. These free performances are so popular (as many as 7,000 people have shown up at a time, although 400 is a more typical number), that in 1999 the Kennedy Center expanded the Millennium Stage area to include two new spaces and debuted broadcasts of the nightly performances on the Internet: http://kennedy-center.org/stage/millennium. The Friday "Weekend" section of the *Washington Post* lists the free performances scheduled for the coming week. Also call about "pay what you can" performances, scheduled throughout the year on certain days, for certain shows.

In line with its focus on the millennium, the Kennedy Center has launched "Kennedy Center 2000: The Legacy and Promise of the Performing Arts." This plan commits the center to producing at least 100 new works during the first decade of the millennium, and 600 productions in all, including 267 on the main stages.

The 28-year-old center is in the middle of a $50 million overhaul scheduled to continue until the year 2007. The Concert Hall was the first to be renovated; following 10 months of work, the hall reopened in October 1997 with improvements that include wheelchair accessibility for 4% of the seats and enhanced acoustics.

Opera House   This plush red-and-gilt 2,300-seat theater is designed for ballet, modern dance, musical comedy, and opera, and it's also the setting for occasional gala events such as the Kennedy Center Honors, which you've probably seen on TV (Neil Simon, B. B. King, Lauren Bacall, and Bob Dylan have been honorees). Other offerings have included performances by the Joffrey Ballet, the Bolshoi Ballet, the Kirov Ballet, the Royal Ballet, and the American Ballet Theatre. The Washington Opera (http://www/dc-opera.org) stages many of its performances here and in the Eisenhower Theater. Among the dance performances scheduled for the year 2000 are the American Ballet Theatre's *Swan Lake* and the Alvin Ailey American Dance Theatre. Tickets often sell out before the season begins.

Concert Hall   This is the home of The National Symphony Orchestra, which presents concerts from September to June. Tickets are available by subscription and for individual performances. Guest artists have included Itzhak Perlman, Vladimir Ashkenazy, Zubin Mehta, Pinchas Zukerman, André Previn, Jean-Pierre Rampal, and Isaac Stern. Headliner entertainers such as Ray Charles, Patti LuPone, Bill Cosby, and Harry Belafonte also appear here. Among the year 2000 performances are the National Symphony Orchestra's Piano 2000 Festival in June and *Faust,* a musical being written by Randy Newman.

Terrace Theater   Small chamber works, choral recitals, musicals, comedy revues, cabarets, and theatrical and modern-dance performances are among the varied provinces of the 500-seat Terrace Theater, a Bicentennial gift from Japan. It's been the setting for solo performances by violinist Eugene Fodor, pianists Santiago Rodriguez and Peter Serkin, soprano Dawn Upshaw, and jazz singer Barbara Cook. Performance artists Laurie Anderson and Michael Moschen have performed here, and jazz evenings have included tributes to Count Basie, Louis Armstrong, and Duke Ellington. More recently, a production of Athol Fugard's *The Captain's Tiger* took the stage here. Every spring the Terrace (along with the Theater Lab) hosts productions of six finalists in the American College Theatre Festival competition.

Eisenhower Theater   A wide range of dramatic productions can be seen here. Coming in 2000: the Tony-Award-winning play, *Art,* and *Electra,* adapted from the Sophocles work by Frank McGuinness. The Eisenhower is also the setting for smaller productions of the Washington Opera from December to February, solo performances by the likes of Harry Belafonte, dance presentations by the Paul Taylor Dance Company, and others. Tickets for most theatrical productions are in the $25 to $70 range. Prices for opera seats tend to soar higher.

Theater Lab & More   By day, the Theater Lab is Washington's premier stage for children's theater. Evenings it becomes a cabaret, now in a long run of *Shear Madness,* a comedy whodunit (tickets are $25 to $29). Elsewhere at the center, there are family concerts by the National Symphony Orchestra several times each year, not to mention clowns, jugglers, dance troupes, improvisational theater, storytellers, and films. Many events are scheduled around the Christmas and Easter holidays.

Limited underground parking at the Kennedy Center is $8 for the entire event after 2pm; if that lot is full, go to the Columbia Plaza Garage at 2400 Virginia Ave. NW, which runs a free shuttle back to the facility.

Lincoln Theater. 1215 U St. NW. ☎ **202/328-6000.** Tickets range in price from $10 to $25 and are available at the theater box office and through Ticketmaster outlets or by calling ☎ 800/551-SEAT or 202/432-SEAT to charge tickets. Metro: U St.–Cardozo.

In the heart of happening U Street, the Lincoln was once a movie theater, vaudeville house, and nightclub featuring black stars like Louis Armstrong and Cab Calloway. The theater closed in the 1970s and reopened in 1994 after a renovation restored the theater to its former elegance. Today the theater books jazz, R&B, gospel, and comedy acts, and events like the D.C. Film Festival.

Lisner Auditorium. On the campus of George Washington University, 21st and H sts. NW. ☎ **202/994-1500.** www.gwu.edu/~Lisner. Tickets range from $15–$75 depending upon event; some are free. Tickets are available through Protix (☎ 703/218-6500) and Ticket-master (☎ 800/551-SEAT or 202/432-SEAT). Discounts may be available. Metro: Foggy Bottom.

One of my favorite places to hear good music, Lisner is small, only 1,500 seats, and you always feel close to the stage. Bookings sometimes include musical groups like Los Lobos and Siouxsie and the Banshees, comedians like "Weird Al" Yankovic, and children's entertainers like Raffi, but are mostly cultural shows, everything from a Pakistani rock group to the Washington Revels' annual romp at Christmas.

Warner Theatre. 1299 Pennsylvania Ave. NW (entrance on 13th St., between E and F sts.). ☎ **202/783-4000** for information; 800/551-SEAT, 202/783-4000, or 202/432-SEAT to charge tickets. www.warnertheatre.com. Tickets $20–$60. Metro: Metro Center. Parking is available in the Warner Building PMI lot on 12th St. NW.

Opened in 1924 as the Earle Theatre (a movie/vaudeville palace) and restored to its original appearance in 1992 at a cost of $10 million, this stunning neoclassical-style theater features a gold-leafed grand lobby and auditorium. Everything is plush and magnificent, from the glittering crystal chandeliers to the gold-tasseled velvet draperies. It's worth coming by just to see its ornately detailed interior. The 2,000-seat auditorium offers year-round entertainment, alternating dance performances (from Baryshnikov to the Washington Ballet's Christmas performance of *The Nutcracker*) and Broadway/off-Broadway shows (the fabulous *Stomp* and *Jelly's Last Jam*) with headliner entertainment (Sheryl Crow, k.d. lang, Natalie Merchant, Chris Isaak, Wynton Marsalis). Call ahead for a schedule of events taking place during your visit.

HUGE ARENAS

Ticket prices for arena performances vary widely, based on the type of event being held—from trade fairs to popular sports events to sold-out rock concerts. So it's best to call for ticket price information.

Baltimore Arena. 201 W. Baltimore St., Baltimore, MD. ☎ **410/347-2020;** 800/551-SEAT or 410/481-SEAT for tickets. www.sunspot.net/citysearch/baltimorearena.

This 13,500-seat arena, a few blocks from Baltimore's Inner Harbor and around the corner from Camden Yards, is home to several local sports teams. When they're not playing, the arena hosts big-name concerts and family entertainment shows. The Beatles appeared here back in the 1960s. More recently, they've presented Sesame Street Live, Ringling Brothers and Barnum & Bailey Circus, Disney on Ice, and headliners such as New Edition, Alan Jackson, Reba McEntire, Brooks & Dunn, Paul Simon, Liza Minnelli, Luther Vandross, and Vince Gill.

To get here by car, take I-95 north to I-395 (stay in the left lane) to the Inner Harbor exit and follow Howard Street to the Arena. You can also take a MARC train from Union Station.

MCI Center. 601 F St. NW, where it meets 7th St. ☎ **202/628-3200.** www.mcicenter.com. To charge tickets by phone, call ☎ 800/551-SEAT or 202/432-SEAT. Very limited parking on site; surface lots and garages in neighborhood, but your best bet is the Metro: Gallery Place (stop lies just beneath the building).

Set on 5 acres of prime downtown real estate, the MCI Center is the new home of the Washington Wizards (formerly the Bullets), the Washington Mystics (women's basketball), the Georgetown Hoyas basketball team, and the Washington Capitals hockey team, with seats for 20,600 fans. This is also the site for the world championship figure skating competition and the Franklin National Bank Classic college basketball tournament. See chapter 7 for more information about sports events.

The center also hosts rock and country concerts and business conferences. The Rolling Stones played here in 1999. Within the three-story complex are a 25,000 square-foot Discovery Channel, Destination D.C. retail store; a National Sports Gallery (an interactive sports museum); and three restaurants.

The Patriot Center. George Mason University, 4400 University Dr., Fairfax, VA. ☎ **703/ 993-3000;** 800/551-SEAT or 202/432-SEAT to charge tickets. The facility has 4,000 free parking spaces.

This 10,000-seat facility hosts major headliners. Performers here have included Randy Travis, David Copperfield, Gloria Estefan, Tom Petty, Natalie Cole, Sting, Counting Crows, and Phish. There are family events such as *Sesame Street Live* here, too. To get here by car, take the I-495 to Braddock Road West, and continue about 6 miles to University Drive. It's difficult to get here by public transportation: From D.C., take the blue/orange line Metro to the Vienna station, where you transfer to a Fairfax City "Cue" bus for a 40-minute ride to George Mason University. At the university, you have to ask someone for directions across campus to the Patriot Center, which is a 20-minute walk from the bus stop.

OUTDOOR PAVILIONS & STADIUMS

When summer comes to Washington, much of the entertainment moves outdoors. As city theaters go dark or cut back on performance schedules in July and August to catch their breath and gear up for a new season, a handful of Washington area amphitheaters pick up the slack. Performers who might have appeared indoors from fall through spring now show up on the stages listed below. It's a happy arrangement for everyone.

Carter Barron Amphitheater. 16th St. and Colorado Ave. NW. ☎ **202/260-6836.** Take Metro to Silver Spring, transfer to S2 or S4 bus, with "Federal Triangle" destination sign, and let the driver know you wish to hop off at the 16th St. bus stop nearest the Carter Barron; the amphitheater is a 5-minute walk from that stop.

Way out on 16th Street (close to the Maryland border) is this 4,250-seat amphitheater in Rock Creek Park. Summer performances include a range of gospel, blues, and classical entertainment. You can always count on Shakespeare: The **Shakespeare Theatre Free For All** takes place at the Carter Barron usually for 2 weeks in June, Tuesday through Sunday evenings; the free tickets are available the day of performance only, on a first-come, first-serve basis (call ☎ 202/334-4790 for details). The 1999 Free For All featured *The Merry Wives of Windsor.*

Merriweather Post Pavilion. 10475 Little Patuxent Pkwy. (just off Rte. 29 in Columbia, MD). ☎ **410/730-2424** for information; 800/955-5566, 410/481-6500, or 703/218-6500 to charge tickets. Tickets $17.50–$65 pavilion, $15–$25 lawn.

During the summer there's quality entertainment almost nightly at the Merriweather Post Pavilion, about 40 minutes by car from downtown D.C. There's reserved seating

Music for the Masses: Free Shows

In D.C., some of the best things at night are free—or very cheap. See chapter 7 for information about free entertainment offered year-round by individual museums and historic sites; see information earlier in this chapter about the free performances staged by the Kennedy Center, the Shakespeare Theatre, and the Carter Barron Amphitheater.

The city comes especially alive in summer with numerous outdoor concerts performed around town. Choose a night, any night, and you will find a **military band** playing at one of three locations in Washington, D.C.: the U.S. Capitol, the Sylvan Theater on the grounds of the Washington Monument, and the Navy Memorial Plaza. These bands perform jazz, show tunes, blues, music for strings—you name it. The concerts begin at 8pm and continue every night June through Labor Day. For details about military events, call the individual branches: the U.S. Army Band, "Pershing's Own" (☎ **703/696-3399**); the U.S. Navy Band (☎ **202/433-2525** for a 24-hour recording, or 202/433-6090); the U.S. Marine Band, "The President's Own" (☎ **202/433-4011** for a 24-hour recording, or 202/433-5809); and the U.S. Air Force Band, "America's International Musical Ambassadors" (☎ **202/767-5658** for a 24-hour recording, or 202/767-4310).

On the southeast side of town, you'll find renowned Washington blues and jazz artists doing their thing at the **Fort Dupont Summer Theatre,** Minnesota Avenue SE at Randle Circle, in Fort Dupont Park (☎ **202/426-7723** or 202/619-7222), every Friday and Saturday at 8:30pm from sometime in July to the end of August. Bring a blanket and a picnic dinner; arrive early to get a good spot on the lawn. Fort Dupont features both talented local performers and nationally known acts such as Marion Meadows, Miles Jaye, The Sensational Nightingales, Pieces of a Dream, and Roy Ayers. No tickets required; admission is free.

Concerts at the Capitol, an **American Festival,** is sponsored jointly by the National Park Service and Congress. It's a series of free summer concerts performed by the **National Symphony Orchestra** at 8pm on the west side of the Capitol on Memorial Day, July 4, and Labor Day. Seating is on the lawn, so bring a picnic. Major guest stars in past years have included Ossie Davis (a narrator and host), Leontyne Price, Johnny Cash, Rita Moreno, Mary Chapin Carpenter, and Mstislav Rostropovich. The music ranges from light classical to country to show tunes. For further information call ☎ **202/619-7222.**

Two only-in-Washington, not-to-be-missed outdoor events are the Smithsonian's annual **Festival of American Folklife,** which offers a potpourri of musical and cultural performances; and the **National Independence Day Celebration on the Mall;** for more information, see chapter 2's calendar for June and July.

Finally, the Washington National Cathedral and its grounds are a magnificent setting for the cathedral's annual **Summer Festival** series of musical events, which include a weekly carillon recital ("best heard from the Bishop's Garden," according to a staff member). Call ☎ **202/537-6200** for details.

in the open-air pavilion (overhead protection provided in case of rain) and general-admission seating on the lawn (no refunds for rain) to see such performers as James Taylor, Tina Turner, Van Halen, the Beach Boys, Liza Minnelli, Sting, Julio Iglesias, Phish, Joan Rivers, Hootie and the Blowfish, Jimmy Buffett, Elton John, Al Jarreau, and Lilith Fair. If you choose the lawn seating, bring blankets and picnic fare (beverages must be bought on the premises).

Nissan Pavilion at Stone Ridge. 7800 Cellar Door Dr. (off Wellington Rd. in Bristow, VA). ☎ **800/455-8999** or 703/754-6400 for concert information; 800/551-SEAT or 202/432-SEAT to charge tickets. Tickets $25–$62 pavilion, $9.50–$29.

With a capacity of 22,500 seats (10,000 under the roof, the remainder on the lawn), this immense state-of-the-art entertainment facility, just 25 minutes from the Beltway, features major acts varying from classical to country. Since its opening in the summer of 1995, featured performers have included Yanni, Dave Matthews Band, Rush, Melissa Etheridge, Phish, Shania Twain, The Cranberries, James Taylor, Van Halen, Jimmy Buffett, David Bowie, Nine Inch Nails, Hanson, R.E.M., and Spice Girls. The action is enhanced by giant video screens inside the pavilion and on the lawn. To get here by car, take I-66 west to Exit 43B, turn left on Route 29, continue half a mile, and turn left onto Wellington Road; the Nissan Pavilion is about a mile down on your right.

Robert F. Kennedy Memorial Stadium/D.C. Armory. 2400 E. Capitol St. SE. ☎ **202/547-9077;** 800/551-SEAT or 202/432-SEAT to charge tickets. Metro: Stadium-Armory.

Until 1998, RFK was the home stadium for the Washington Redskins, who now play at the new Jack Kent Cooke facility in Raljohn, MD. The stadium continues as a spring, summer, fall event facility, packing crowds of 55,000-plus into its seats for concert festivals and to watch D.C. United Major League soccer and college football.

The D.C. Armory, right next door, is a year-round venue for the Ringling Brothers Barnum & Bailey Circus, antiques shows, and other large-scale events.

Wolf Trap Farm Park for the Performing Arts. 1551 Trap Rd., Vienna, VA. ☎ **703/255-1868,** or Protix (☎ 703/218-6500) to charge tickets. www.wolf-trap.org. Filene Center seats $16–$70, lawn $7–$20; Barns tickets average $14–$20.

The country's only national park devoted to the performing arts, Wolf Trap, just 30 minutes by car from downtown D.C., offers a star-studded Summer Festival Season from late May to mid-September. The 1999 season featured performances by the National Symphony Orchestra (it's their summer home), adopted daughter Mary Chapin Carpenter, Natalie Merchant, Shawn Colvin, Dwight Yokam, and the Joffrey Ballet.

Performances take place in the 7,000-seat Filene Center, about half of which is under the open sky. You can also buy cheaper lawn seats on the hill, which is sometimes the nicest way to go. If you do, arrive early (the lawn opens 90 minutes before the performance), and bring a blanket and a picnic dinner; it's a tradition.

Wolf Trap also hosts a number of very popular festivals. The park features a daylong Irish music festival in May; the Louisiana Swamp Romp Cajun Festival and a weekend of jazz and blues in June; and the International Children's Festival each September.

From late fall until May, the 350-seat Barns of Wolf Trap, just up the road at 1635 Trap Rd., features jazz, pop, country, folk, bluegrass, and chamber musicians. The Barns are the summer home of the Wolf Trap Opera Company, which is the only entertainment booked here May through September. Call ☎ **703/938-2404** for information.

By car, take I-495 (the Beltway) to Exit 12W (Dulles Toll Road); follow the signs and exit (after paying a 50¢ toll) at the Wolf Trap ramp. Stay on the local exit road (you'll see a sign) until you come to Wolf Trap. The park is also accessible from Exit 67 off I-66 West. There's plenty of parking. In summer only, you can get to Wolf Trap by taking the Metro to the West Falls Church stop; the Wolf Trap Shuttle ($3.50 round-trip) runs every 20 minutes starting 2 hours before performance time and (return trip) 20 minutes after the performance ends or 11pm (whichever comes first).

3 The Club & Music Scene

You don't have to go to an enormous auditorium or a fancy concert hall to enjoy live entertainment in the capital. If you're looking for a tuneful night on the town, Washington offers smoky jazz clubs, lively bars, warehouse ballrooms, places where you sit back and listen, places where you can get up and dance, even a roadhouse or two. If you're looking for comic relief, Washington can take care of that, too (the pickings are few but good).

A lot of nightlife sites fall into more than one category: For example, the Black Cat is a bar and a dance club, offering food and sometimes poetry readings; Coco Loco is a hot Brazilian restaurant and an even hotter nightclub on weekend nights. So I've listed each nightspot according to the type of music it features, and included the details in its description.

The best nightlife districts are Adams-Morgan; the area around U and 14th streets NW, a still developing district that's in a somewhat dangerous part of town; the 7th Street NW corridor near Chinatown and the MCI Center; and Georgetown. If you don't mind venturing into the suburbs, you should know about Arlington's hot spots—see the box called "Arlington Row." As a rule, while club-hopping—even in Georgetown—stick to the major thoroughfares and steer clear of deserted side streets. The best source of information about what's doing at bars and clubs is *City Paper,* which is available free at bookstores, movie theaters, drugstores, and other locations.

COMEDY

In addition to the list below, large auditoriums, like DAR Constitution Hall, also feature big-name comedians from time to time.

Chelsea's. 1055 Thomas Jefferson St. NW (in the Foundry Building on the C&O Canal). ☎ **202/298-8222.** $50 for dinner and show, $33.50 for show alone. Fri and Sat nights. Complimentary parking in building garage. Metro: Foggy Bottom, with a 10-minute walk.

This nightclub in the Foundry Building on the C&O Canal is home base for the Capitol Steps comedy satire troupe, whose claim to fame is poking fun at Washington institutions through song. You may have heard of them via their many albums and national TV appearances. And they certainly know their material: The Steps are ex-Congressional staffers, well acquainted with the crazy workings of government. Their shows are at 5:30pm Saturday, 6pm Friday. See Chelsea's listing under "International Sounds," this chapter, for information about Latino and Arabic music and dancing nights here.

The Improv. 1140 Connecticut Ave. NW (between L and M sts.). ☎ **202/296-7008.** www.dcimprov.com. Cover $12 Sun–Thurs, $15 Fri–Sat, plus a 2-drink minimum (waived if you dine). Metro: Farragut North. Parking garage next door $4.

The Improv features top performers on the national comedy club circuit as well as comic plays and one-person shows. Saturday Night Live performers Ellen Cleghorne, David Spade, Chris Rock, and Adam Sandler have all played here, as have comedy bigs Ellen DeGeneres, Jerry Seinfeld, David Alan Grier, Robin Williams, Rosie O'Donnell, and Brian Regan. Shows are about 1½ hours long and include three comics (an emcee, feature act, and headliner). Show times are 8:30pm from Sunday to Thursday, 8:30 and 10:30pm on Friday and Saturday. The best way to snag a good seat is to have dinner here (make reservations), which allows you to enter the club as early as 7pm. Dinner entrees ($9.95 to $14.95) include prime rib, sandwiches, and pasta selections. Drinks average $4.95. You must be 18 to get in.

POP/ROCK

Nation. 1015 Half St. SE (at K St.). ☎ **202/554-1500.** www.cellardoor.com. Cover Fri–Sat $9–12; other nights $8–$30, depending on the performer. Metro: Navy Yard.

A $2 million renovation in 1999 transformed the "Ballroom" into a more functional concert/dance space, with separate areas for live music, dance music, and lounging, and a three-tiered outdoor patio. (The building used to be a boiler-company warehouse.) This is primarily a Gen-X mecca (though some performers attract an older crowd). It's also D.C.'s largest club, accommodating about 2,000 people a night. Friday night features DJs playing techno, house, and jungle music from 10pm to 6am. Saturday night is devoted to swing until late night, when a gay dance party takes over. The rest of the week is given over to live concerts, mostly featuring nationally known acts (such as 311, David Bowie, Tool, The Artist-formerly-known-as-Prince), and, occasionally, local groups. You can buy tickets in advance via Ticketmaster (☎ **202/ 432-SEAT**). The Ballroom is all ages for concerts; for dancing you must be 18 to get in. The game room and state-of-the-art lighting/laser/sound systems are a plus. The Nation is in a pretty bad neighborhood, so make sure you have good directions to get there; the building itself is very secure.

Black Cat. 1831 14th St. NW (between S and T sts.). ☎ **202/667-7960.** Cover $5–$10 for concerts; no cover in the Red Room. Metro: U St.–Cardozo.

This comfortable, low-key bar draws a black-clothed crowd to its large, funky, red-walled living-roomy lounge with booths, tables, a red-leather sofa, pinball machines, a pool table, and a jukebox stocked with a really eclectic collection. A college crowd collects on weekends, but you can count on seeing a 20-to-30-something bunch here most nights, including members of various bands who like to stop in for a drink. There's live music in the adjoining room, essentially a large dance floor (it accommodates about 400 people) with stages at both ends. Entertainment is primarily alternative rock (mostly locals, but some bigger names such as Squirrel Nut Zippers, Blur, Morphine, Foo Fighters, The Offspring, and The Cramps), with a little jazz, swing, folk, and occasional poetry readings thrown in. The Red Room Bar is open until 2am from Sunday to Thursday, and until 3am Friday and Saturday. Concerts take place 4 or 5 nights a week, beginning at about 8:30pm (call for details). Light fare, such as kebob dinners, is available, and the bar has European and microbrew beers on tap.

Chief Ike's Mambo Room. 1725 Columbia Rd. NW. ☎ **202/332-2211.** www.greatidea.com/chiefike. Cover $3–$5 Wed–Sat. Open from 4pm to 2am or 3am nightly. Metro: Woodley Park–Zoo, with a 20-minute walk.

In early 1998, Chief Ike's served as a location shot for a scene in Will Smith's movie, *Enemy of the State.* Its more usual role though is as a party scene, with live music (jazz, blues, rock) playing Wednesday and Thursday, and a DJ on weekends. Chief Ike's, unlike other clubs, sets great store by its grub: regional American. Happy hour lasts weeknights from 4 to 8pm. The crowd is (for the most part) young, with lots of politicos and local artists stopping in. Downstairs is where you'll find the dancing, upstairs is good for kibitzing and pool-playing.

Metro Café. 1522 14th St. NW. ☎ **202/518-7900.** Shows start at 9:30pm, nightly. For advance tickets, call ☎ 202/884-0060. Cover $5 until 12:30am. Free parking across the street. Metro: Dupont Circle, about 5 blocks away.

The Metro holds about 100 people in a room with a big stage, an L-shaped bar, red velvet curtains, and tall ceilings. Acts range from hip-hop to good local rock bands to national acts like Andy Summers, one-time guitarist for The Police. The club attracts all ages, everyone in black. Like several other nightclubs, State of the Union for one (see below), the Metro is also into drama, presenting short plays on various nights.

9:30 Club. 815 V St. NW. ☎ **202/393-0930.** Tickets $5–$40, depending on the performer. Metro: U St.–Cardozo.

Housed in yet another converted warehouse, this major live-music venue hosts frequent record company parties and features a wide range of top performers. In 1998, the concert trade publication, *Pollstar,* named the 9:30 the nightclub of the year. You might catch Sheryl Crow, the Wallflowers, Smashing Pumpkins, Shawn Colvin, and even Tony Bennett. It's only open when there's a show on (call ahead), and, obviously, the crowd varies with the performer. The sound system is state of the art. There are four bars, two on the main dance-floor level, one in the upstairs VIP room (anyone is welcome here unless the room is being used for a private party), and another in the distressed-looking cellar. The 9:30 Club is a standup place, literally; there are no seats. Tickets to most shows are available through Protix (☎ **800/955-5566** or 703/218-6500).

Polly Esther's. 605 12th St. NW. ☎ **202/737-1970.** Thurs 9pm–2am, Fri 5pm–3:30am, Sat 8pm–4am. Cover $8 Fri, $10 Sat. Metro: Metro Center.

Seventies decor and music reign here, with artifacts from that decade hanging on the walls (a John Travolta memorial, anything to do with the Brady Bunch), and disco music (think "YMCA," ABBA, the BeeGees) blaring from the sound system. Another dance floor features '90s music. And downstairs is more culture-clubish, where you dance to '80s tunes by artists like Madonna and Prince.

State of the Union. 1357 U St. NW. ☎ **202/588-8810.** Cover generally $5–$7. Open through 2am Sun–Thurs, 3am Fri–Sat. Metro: U St.–Cardozo.

DJ and live music highlight reggae, hip-hop, and acid jazz sounds in this nightclub that plays on a Soviet Union theme: hammer and sickle sconces, a bust of Lenin over the bar, and a big painting of Rasputin on a back wall. The hip crowd is diverse ("different every half hour," says a bartender), ranging from mid-20s to about 35, interracial, and international. The music, both live and DJ-provided, is cutting edge. On Friday and Saturday nights, live bands play 9pm to 11pm, followed by renowned D.C. DJs playing rare grooves, funk, soul, hip-hop, and house; Wednesday there's live reggae; Monday from 10pm to 2am is live jazz night; and other nights there's live entertainment, generally, straight, funk, and acid jazz. You might also happen upon a poetry reading. Weather permitting, the back room has an open-air screen (actually more like a cave wall). There's an interesting selection of beers and over 30 flavored vodkas.

2:K:9. 2009 Eighth St. NW. ☎ **202/575-2009.** www.2k9.com. Cover $10–$15 after 9pm (women are free). Thurs–Fri 5pm–3am, Sat 9pm–3am. Metro: U St.–Cardozo.

Not far from the 9:30 Club is this huge and grandiose, two-level club with concrete dance floor, VIP lounge, two raised cages where women dancers undulate, a bar and a DJ booth. And that's just the first floor. The second floor, not finished at this writing, will feature live acts and fake snow-generating machines. If it sounds all too Studio 54-ish it may be because one of that club's designers had a hand in the design here. Put on your funkiest outfit to dance to hip-hop, techno beats, and international sounds.

JAZZ/BLUES

BET on Jazz Restaurant. 730 11th St. NW. ☎ **202/393-0975.** No cover. Metro: Metro Center.

Despite its name, BET on Jazz is primarily a restaurant. But stop here on a Friday or Saturday night, from 8pm to midnight, and you'll be treated to good Caribbean cuisine and

D.C. Boogie

"Where can we go to dance? It's the question asked most frequently by my readers," says Eric Brace, who reports on the city's nightlife for the *Washington Post*. (See his column, "Nightwatch," which appears every Friday in the Post's Weekend section.) And fortunately, says Brace, "I can tell them there are more places opening all the time."

Dance places do exist in D.C., and the following suggestions will help you figure out where to go and what to expect. For clubs not already listed within this chapter, I provide an address and phone number; otherwise, refer back to full entries within the main text to find out information.

To begin with, let me tell you that one clear deficiency is the absence of a dinner-dance club. If that's the kind of thing you have in mind, you might want to try either **Marley's Lounge** at the Henley Park Hotel, 926 Massachusetts Ave. NW (☎ **202/414-0500**), for live jazz standards Friday and Saturday nights, or **the Melrose Bar,** at the Park Hyatt Hotel, 1201 24th St. NW (☎ **202/ 955-3899**), for dinner and swing dancing to live jazz Friday and Saturday nights.

Latin jazz continues to be popular in Washington and one of the best places to salsa and rhumba is Adams-Morgan's **Habana Village.** Habana Village, which is Brace's top spot ("It's small and sweaty, but it's a lot of fun"), is open Wednesday through Saturday evenings for both lessons and dancing. Other choices include **Latin Jazz Alley,** also in Adams-Morgan, the downtown **Coco Loco,** and Georgetown's **Chelsea's.**

Adams-Morgan, in general, is a convenient street to travel if you're in a dancing mood. Stop in at **Chief Ike's** for disco-driven dance music, and at **Madam's Organ,** if live jazz, blues, or R&B turns you on. And speaking of blues, another location near Adams-Morgan to recommend for live performances is the **New Vegas Lounge,** which really isn't a dance club, but sure turns into one when the music's hot.

A number of one-stop entertainment places have opened up in the past year, so that if you visit **Eleventh Hour,** on 14th Street, or **Zanzibar,** on the waterfront, you can dine well, dance to live music, lounge, sip and listen, or sip and talk; both feature a different kind of music every night.

Dance venues, where the emphasis is on live bands playing current music, include **Nation, Black Cat, Metro Café, State of the Union,** and, in Arlington, **IOTA** (see box on Arlington Row, for more selections there). Alas, the live rock-dance scene is one category that remains woefully underrepresented in Washington.

Now, if you're into DJ-spun dance music, you're in luck, since this is the most prevalent option. All but the Metro, from the paragraph above, have DJs on certain nights. In addition, you might consider the swank **2:K:9** (a Studio 54 for the millennium), the waterfront **Zanzibar,** or **Chief Ike's** (as previously mentioned), for choices ranging from alternative to hip-hop; **Polly Esther's** for '80s retro; and **Nathans, Club Zei,** 1415 Z Alley, between H and I sts. NW (☎ **202/842-2445**), and **Sesto Senso,** 1214 18th Sts. NW (☎ **202/785-9525**) for a combination of international, Euro, and Top 40.

the sounds of say, Brazilian jazz. This is an elegant place (see review, chapter 6) and you must dress up to get in. But let's hope the owners host more acts as time goes by.

Blues Alley. 1073 Wisconsin Ave. NW (in an alley below M St.). ☎ **202/337-4141.** Cover $15–$40, plus $7 food or drink minimum, plus $1.75 surcharge.

Blues Alley, in Georgetown, has been Washington's top jazz club since 1965, featuring such artists as Nancy Wilson, McCoy Tyner, Sonny Rollins, Flora Purim, Herbie Mann, Wynton Marsalis, Charlie Byrd, Ramsey Lewis, Rachelle Ferrell, and Maynard Ferguson. There are usually two shows nightly at 8 and 10pm; some performers also do midnight shows on weekends. Reservations are essential (call after noon); since seating is on a first-come, first-serve basis, it's best to arrive no later than 7pm and have dinner. Entrees on the steak and creole-seafood menu are in the $14 to $22 range; snacks and sandwiches are $5.25 to $9, and drinks are $5.35 to $9. The decor is of the classic jazz club genre: exposed-brick walls, beamed ceiling, and small candlelit tables. Sometimes well-known visiting musicians get up and jam with performers; one night when Jerry Lewis was in the audience, he got up on stage and told a few jokes.

City Blues. 2651 Connecticut Ave. NW. ☎ **202/232-2300.** Cover $5 Thurs–Sat. Metro: Woodley Park–Zoo.

This is a neighborhood club that offers live entertainment 7 nights a week, mostly blues and some jazz, performed by locals, with big names sitting in from time to time. Look for groups like the Mary Ann Redmond Band. The 7-year-old club is a cozy den of three interconnected rooms on one floor of a converted townhouse. Seating is at tables and at the bar. The full menu features American cuisine, with a few pastas and Cajun dishes.

Columbia Station. 2325 18th St. NW. ☎ **202/462-6040.** No cover but $6 minimum. Open weeknights until 1:30am, 2am on weekends. Metro: Dupont Circle (North exit) or Woodley Park-Zoo, with a 20- to 30-minute walk.

Another fairly intimate club in Adams-Morgan, this one showcases live blues and jazz nightly. The performers are pretty good, which is amazing, considering there's no cover. Columbia Station is also a bar/restaurant, with the kitchen usually open until midnight, serving semi-Cajun cuisine.

Madam's Organ Restaurant and Bar. 2461 18th St. NW. ☎ **202/667-5370.** Cover $2–$5. Sun–Thurs 5pm–2am, Fri–Sat 5pm–3am. Metro: Dupont Circle (North exit) or Woodley Park-Zoo, with a 20- to 30-minute walk.

This beloved Adams-Morgan hangout fulfills owner Bill Duggan's definition of a good bar: great sounds and sweaty people. The great sounds feature fusion jazz on Mondays, bluesman Ben Andrews on Tuesdays, bluegrass open mike on Wednesday, and live R&B, including the likes of Bobby Parker, Fridays and Saturdays; you provide the sweat. Thursday is Ladies Night: women's drinks are $1. The club includes a wide open bar decorated eclectically with a 150-year-old gilded mirror, stuffed fish and animal heads, and paintings of nudes. The second-floor bar is called Big Daddy's Love Lounge & Pick-Up Joint, which tells you everything you need to know. Other points to note: You can play darts, and redheads pay half-price for drinks.

New Vegas Lounge. 1415 P St. NW. ☎ **202/483-3971.** Cover $7–$10. Tues–Thurs until 2am, Fri–Sat until 3am. Metro: Dupont Circle.

When the Vegas Lounge is good, it's very good. When it's bad, it's laughable. This dark, one-room joint is crowded with tables filled with a mix of Washingtonians, black and white, college kids and their elders. If you're lucky, you might find a blues band out of Chicago covering Otis Redding so well that everyone's on their feet dancing.

On other nights, you're likely to hear a neighborhood group who has no business appearing in public. Thursdays are college nights.

One Step Down. 2517 Pennsylvania Ave. NW. ☎ **202/955-7141.** Cover $5 Mon–Thurs, typically $12.50 or $13.50 Sat–Sun, with 2-drink minimum every night. Metro: Foggy Bottom.

This quintessential, hole-in-the-wall jazz club is the constant on this stretch of Pennsylvania Avenue just outside of Georgetown. After 36 years, One Step Down has seen its neighbors change names and owners too many times to count. The One Step showcases the talents of names you often recognize, and some you don't: sax player Paul Bollenbeck, the Steve Wilson Quartet, Ronnie Wells, and Ron Elliston. Blues night the last Thursday of every month (cover $5). Every Saturday and Sunday, from 3:30 to 7:30pm, the club stages a jam session; no cover. Live music plays here 6 nights a week; the club is open from 5:30pm to 1am Monday through Thursday, until 2am on weekends. The people who come to the One Step tend to be heavy jazz enthusiasts who stay quiet during the sets.

Twins Lounge. 5516 Colorado Ave. NW. ☎ **202/882-2523.** No cover, but a $7 minimum weeknights; variable cover weekends, plus a $10 minimum. Take a taxi or drive.

Four blocks from the Carter Barron Amphitheater (see listing above) on the outskirts of town is this intimate jazz club, which offers live music every night. On weeknights you'll hear local artists (open mike on Wednesday nights); weekends you'll hear out-of-town acts, such as Bobby Watson, Gil Scott Heron, and James William. Sunday night is a weekly jam session attended by musicians from all over town. Menu features Italian, Ethiopian, and Caribbean dishes. Crowd is mixed, "75% white, ages 25 to 90," according to the staff.

Utopia. 1418 U St. NW. ☎ **202/483-7669.** No cover. Sun–Thurs until 2am, Fri and Sat until 3am. Metro: U St.–Cardozo.

Unlike most music bars, the arty New York/Soho–style Utopia is serious about its restaurant operation. A moderately priced international menu features entrees ranging from lamb couscous to blackened shrimp with creole cream sauce, not to mention pastas and filet mignon béarnaise. There's also an interesting wine list and a large selection of beers and single-malt scotches. The setting is cozy and candlelit, with walls used for a changing art gallery show (the bold, colorful paintings in the front room are by Moroccan owner Jamal Sahri). The eclectic crowd here varies with the music, ranging from early 20s to about 35, for the most part, including South Americans and Europeans. On Thursday there's live Brazilian jazz; Friday, for the time being, it's jukebox only—everything from Algerian Ray to the Gypsy Kings (but call, because live music is sometimes scheduled); and on Sunday, bluesy jazz singer Pam Bricker takes the stage. There's no real dance floor, but people find odd spaces to move to the tunes.

INTERNATIONAL SOUNDS

Chelsea's. 1055 Thomas Jefferson St. NW. (in the Foundry Building on the C&O Canal). ☎ **202/298-8222.** Cover $10. Complimentary parking in the building garage. Metro: Foggy Bottom, with a 10-minute walk.

Wednesday, 10pm to 2am, is Arabic night, featuring an Arabic band and a belly dancer. Sunday is Persian night, and Thursday through Saturday nights are devoted to Latino music, with a DJ playing disco Latino tunes Thursday 10:30pm to 2am, and bands playing live music 10:30pm to 4am Friday and Saturday nights.

Chi Cha Lounge. 1624 U St. NW. ☎ **202/234-8400.** Cover $8. Sun–Thurs 5:30pm–1:30am, Fri–Sat 5:30pm–2:30am. Metro: U St.–Cardozo.

You can sit around on couches, eat Ecuadoran tapas, and listen to live Latin music, featured Sunday to Wednesday. Or you can sit around on couches and smoke Arabic tobacco through a 3-foot-high arguileh pipe. Anyway, the point is, you sit around. It's a neighborhood place, and it's popular.

Coco Loco. 810 7th St. NW (between H and I sts.). ☎ **202/289-2626.** Cover $10 Fri–Sat. Metro: Gallery Place.

This is one of D.C.'s liveliest clubs, heralded by marquee lights. Friday and Saturday nights, come for a late tapas or mixed-grill dinner (see chapter 6 for details) and stay for international music and dancing, with occasional live bands. On Friday and Saturday nights, the entertainment includes a sexy 11pm floor show featuring Brazilian exhibition dancers who begin performing in feathered and sequined Rio Rita costumes and strip down to a bare minimum. Laser lights and other special effects enhance the show, which ends with a conga line and a limbo contest. Dancing to DJ music follows the show, Latin music in one room, and international music in the other—until 3am. Come here on Thursday nights at 9pm for a free salsa lesson, followed by dancing until 2am. Coco Loco draws an attractive, upscale, international crowd of all ages, including many impressively talented dancers. It's great fun.

Eleventh Hour. 1520 14th St. NW. ☎ **202/234-0886.** Cover $10 Fri–Sat. Metro: Dupont Circle.

This is one that falls into the one-stop entertainment category, since it's a good restaurant (see review, chapter 6) serving French-influenced American food; a dance club with different music every night, mainly DJ; and a comfortably decorated bar/lounge—leather couches, whimsical bar stools, a fireplace, and colorful furniture. The theater crowd stops in before and after shows (four theaters are nearby); otherwise patrons are a mix.

Habana Village. 1834 Columbia Rd. NW. ☎ **202/462-6310.** Cover $5 Fri–Sat after 9:30pm, and only for men. Wed–Thurs 6:30pm–1am, Fri–Sat 6:30pm–3am. Metro: Dupont Circle, with a 15-minute walk, or Woodley Park-Zoo, with a 20-minute walk.

This two-story nightclub holds a bar/restaurant on the first floor, and a dance floor and bar on the second level. Salsa and merengue lessons are given every Wednesday and Thursday evenings, from 7:30pm to 9:30pm, tango lessons every Friday and Saturday evening, same time; each lesson is $10. Otherwise, a DJ plays danceable Latin jazz tunes.

Latin Jazz Alley. 1721 Columbia Rd. NW, on the 2nd floor of the El Migueleno Cafe. ☎ **202/328-6190.** Wed–Thurs 6pm–midnight, Fri–Sat 6pm–3am. $5 for dance lessons; 2-drink minimum. Metro: Dupont Circle, with a 15-minute walk, or Woodley Park-Zoo, with a 20-minute walk.

This is another place to get in on Washington's Latin scene, this one in Adams-Morgan. At the Alley, you can learn to dance: salsa on Wednesday, Friday, and Saturday nights at 8pm; and mambo, rumba, and chachacha on Thursday nights at 7:30pm. Friday and Saturday nights, from about 10pm to 2am, a DJ plays Latin jazz. Dinner is served until midnight (the food comes from El Migueleno, the Salvadorean/Mexican restaurant on the first floor).

Zanzibar on the Waterfront. 700 Water St. SW. ☎ **202/554-9100.** Cover typically $10. Metro: Waterfront.

One day Washington will get its act together and develop the waterfront neighborhood in which you find Zanzibar. In the meantime, this area is pretty deserted at night, except for a handful of restaurants and Arena Stage. It really doesn't matter, though, because inside the nightclub, you're looking out at the Potomac. Yes, this is a club with windows. In keeping with current trends, Zanzibar has lots of couches and chairs arranged just so. A Caribbean and African menu is available and you can dine while listening to both live and DJ music. Every night brings something different, from jazz and blues to oldies. An international, African and Caribbean crowd gathers here to dance or just hang out.

GAY CLUBS

Dupont Circle is the gay hub of Washington, D.C., with at least 10 gay bars within easy walking distance of one another. At either of the two Dupont Circle locales listed below, you'll find natives happy to tell you about (or take you to) the others.

J.R.'s. 1519 17th St. NW (between P and Q sts.). ☎ **202/328-0090.** No cover. Sun–Thurs until 2am, Fri–Sat until 3am. Metro: Dupont Circle.

This casual and intimate all-male Dupont Circle club draws a crowd that is friendly, upscale, and very attractive. The interior—not that you'll be able to see much of it, because J.R.'s is always sardine-packed—has a 20-foot-high, pressed-tin ceiling and exposed-brick walls hung with neon beer signs. The big screen over the bar area is used to air music videos, showbiz singalongs on Mondays, and favorite TV shows on Wednesdays. Thursday is all-you-can-drink for $5, from 5:30–8pm; at midnight you get free shots. The balcony, with a pool table, is a little more laid-back. No food is served.

Tracks. 1111 1st St. SE. ☎ **202/488-3320.** Cover $5–$15. Thurs–Sun 8pm–late. Metro: Navy Yard.

This vast, high-energy club (a converted auto dealership, with 21,000 square feet inside and a 10,000-square-foot patio) is a favorite place to dance in D.C. Its more-chic-than-funky interior houses a main dance floor with a mirrored ball, another with a zigzag display of video monitors, and a great sound and light system. DJs provide the music, and the crowd is uninhibited. Thursday nights there's progressive house, techno, and industrial video for a predominantly straight crowd (there's an open bar from 9 to 10pm, and pitchers of beer are $4 all night; some nights there are rave parties). Friday also draws a straight crowd for progressive and house music. Saturday is a gay night (mostly men but some women and a sprinkling of straights), with high-energy house in the main room, deep underground and club house in the video room. Gay country-and-western tea dances are featured Sunday afternoons. On warm nights, much of the action centers on the outdoor deck, which has a volleyball court! Other pluses: a pool table, video games, and a snack bar. Liquor is available through 2am Thursday and Friday, till 3am Saturday and Sunday; the club often stays open until 6am.

4 The Bar Scene

Washington has a thriving and varied bar scene. But just when you think you know all the hotspots, a spate of new ones pop up. Travel the triangle formed by the intersections of Connecticut Avenue, 18th Street, and M Street, in the Dupont Circle neighborhood, and you'll find the latest bunch, Dragonfly and MCCXXIII among them (see below).

If you're in the mood for a sophisticated setting, seek out a bar in one of the nicer hotels, like The Jefferson, the Willard, the St. Regis, or the Westin Fairfax (see chapter 5 for more information and suggestions). If you want a convivial atmosphere and decent grub, try bars that are known as much for their food as for their good time. Refer to chapter 6 for details about these in particular: Capital City Brewing Company, Clyde's, Music City Roadhouse, Old Ebbitt Grill, Old Glory, and Sequoia.

But if you're looking for the more typical, drink and mingle, drink and converse, or drink and get rowdy spot, try these:

Washington, D.C. Clubs & Bars

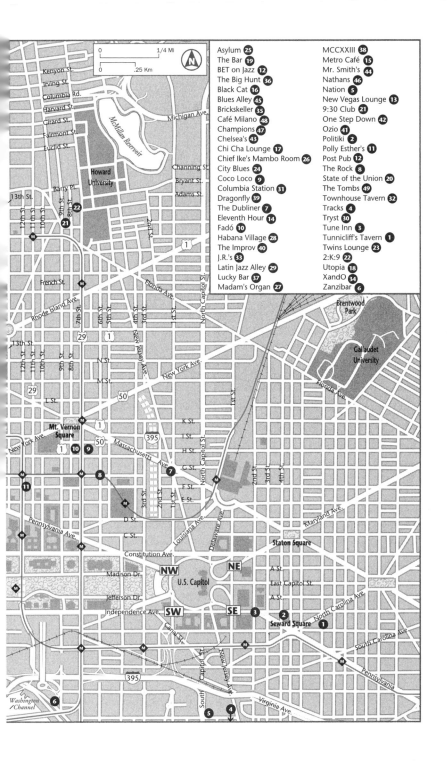

Asylum **25**
The Bar **19**
BET on Jazz **12**
The Big Hunt **36**
Black Cat **16**
Blues Alley **45**
Brickskeller **35**
Café Milano **48**
Champions **47**
Chelsea's **43**
Chi Cha Lounge **17**
Chief Ike's Mambo Room **26**
City Blues **24**
Coco Loco **9**
Columbia Station **31**
Dragonfly **39**
The Dubliner **7**
Eleventh Hour **14**
Fadó **10**
Habana Village **28**
The Improv **40**
J.R.'s **33**
Latin Jazz Alley **29**
Lucky Bar **37**
Madam's Organ **27**

MCCXXIII **38**
Metro Café **15**
Mr. Smith's **44**
Nathans **46**
Nation **5**
New Vegas Lounge **13**
9:30 Club **21**
One Step Down **42**
Ozio **41**
Politiki **2**
Polly Esther's **11**
Post Pub **12**
The Rock **8**
State of the Union **20**
The Tombs **49**
Townhouse Tavern **32**
Tracks **4**
Tryst **30**
Tune Inn **3**
Tunnicliff's Tavern **1**
Twins Lounge **23**
2:K:9 **22**
Utopia **18**
XandO **34**
Zanzibar **6**

Asylum. 2471 18th St. NW. ☎ **202/319-8353.** No cover. Sun–Tues 8pm–2am, Wed–Thurs 5pm–2am, Fri 5pm–3am, Sat 7pm–3am. Metro: Dupont Circle, with a 15-minute walk, or Woodley Park-Zoo, with a 20-minute walk across the Calvert St. Bridge.

This below-street joint has room for about 100 people, plays rock CDs, has a pool table, tables for sitting and drinking, a heavy Goth decorative scheme, and a stream of underage youth trying to get served at the bar.

The Bar. 1416 U St. NW. ☎ **202/588-7311.** No cover. Tues–Thurs 5:30pm–2am, Fri–Sat 5:30pm–3am. Metro: U St.–Cardozo.

The Bar is a mellow place to get comfortable and listen to good music. It's cozy, with candles, sofas, and mural-covered brick walls. Musicians, usually jazz, funk, or Latin, set up in the front window. The bartender is amiable and the food isn't bad.

The Big Hunt. 1345 Connecticut Ave. NW (between N St. and Dupont Circle). ☎ **202/785-2333.** No cover. Sun–Thurs until 2am, Fri–Sat until 3am. Metro: Dupont Circle.

This casual and comfy Dupont Circle hangout for the twentysomething-to-thirtysomething crowd—billing itself as a "happy hunting ground for humans"—has a kind of Raiders of the Lost Ark/jungle theme. A downstairs room (where music is the loudest) is adorned with exotic travel posters and animal skins; another area has leopard-skin–patterned booths under canvas tenting. Amusing murals grace the balcony level, which adjoins a room with pool tables. The candlelit basement is the spot for quiet conversation. The menu offers typical bar food; and the bar offers close to 30 beers on tap, most of them microbrews. An outdoor patio lies off the back pool room.

Brickskeller. 1523 22nd St. NW. ☎ **202/293-1885.** No cover. Mon–Thurs 11:30am–2am, Fri 11:30am–3am, Sat 6pm–3am, Sun 6pm–2am. Metro: Dupont Circle or Foggy Bottom.

If you like beer and you like choice, head for Brickskeller, which has been around for nearly 40 years and offers about 1,000 beers from the world over. If you can't make up your mind, ask one of the waiters, who tend to be knowledgeable about the brews. The tavern draws students, college professors, embassy types, and people from the neighborhood. Brickskeller is a series of interconnecting rooms filled with gingham table-clothed tables; upstairs rooms are only open weekend nights. The food is generally OK; more than OK are the burgers, which include the excellent Brickburger, topped with bacon, salami, onion, and cheese.

Café Milano. 3251 Prospect St. NW. ☎ **202/333-6183.** No cover. Daily noon–1am. Metro: Foggy Bottom, with a 25-minute walk.

Located just off Wisconsin Avenue in lower Georgetown, Café Milano has gained a reputation for attracting beautiful people. You might see a few glamorous faces—or just see a bunch of people on the prowl for glamorous faces. My husband and I saw secretary of state Madeline Albright, and an intimidating pack of security types when we stopped here on a summer Saturday afternoon. It's often crowded, especially Thursday through Saturday nights. The food is rather good; salads and pastas are excellent.

Champions. 1206 Wisconsin Ave. NW (just north of M St.). ☎ **202/965-4005.** No cover. Sun–Thurs 6pm–2am, Fri–Sat 6pm–3am. Metro: Foggy Bottom, with a 20-minute walk.

Smells like beer. This is a sports bar, where both sports fans and athletes—Redskins players among them—like to hang out. Champions lies at the end of an alley off Wisconsin Avenue—be careful at night. The two-story bar is a clutter of sports paraphernalia, with TV monitors airing nonstop sporting events. Conversation has two themes: sports and pickup lines. Champions is often packed and doesn't take reservations; in the evening, you can expect to wait for a table, so arrive early.

Cheap Eats: Happy Hours to Write Home About

Even the diviest of bars puts out some free nibbles to complement your drink—peanuts or pretzels at the very least. And then there are those bars that go all out: certain fine restaurants and hotels around town that set out gourmet food during happy hour, either at no cost or for an astonishingly low price. Sometimes they also offer specially priced drinks, and often entertainment, during specified hours on weekdays. Here are a few that many Washingtonians don't even know about:

Gabriel, 2121 P St. NW, in the Radisson Barceló Hotel (☎ **202/956-6690**). Perhaps the best value in town. Wednesday, Thursday, and Friday evenings, from 5:30pm to 8pm, a mere $7.50 entitles you to an all-you-can-eat buffet, with a choice of about seven scrumptious tapas, quesadillas made to order, and reduced drink prices, including microbrew drafts for $2.50. A more extensive lunch buffet (weekdays 11:30am to 2pm, $9.50) offers a similar array plus marvelous salads, cheeses, and entrees such as paella and cassoulet.

McCormick & Schmick's, 1652 K St. NW., at corner of 17th St. NW (☎ **202/861-2233**). Available in the bar area only: a choice of giant burger, fried calamari, quesadillas, fish tacos, and more, for only $1.95 each, Monday through Friday 3:30pm to 6:30pm, Monday through Thursday 10:30pm to midnight, and Friday and Saturday 10pm to midnight. Friendly bartenders make you feel at home as they concoct mixed drinks with juice they squeeze right at the bar (the drinks, alas, are not discounted).

Town and Country Lounge, in the Renaissance Mayflower Hotel, 1127 Connecticut Ave. NW (☎ **202/347-3000**). This clubby, mahogany-paneled pub is the setting weeknights, from 5:30pm to 7:30pm, for complimentary cocktail-hour hors d'oeuvres that change from night to night: slices of roast beef on toasts, chicken/beef fajitas, pastas, and so on. Here, you also have the pleasure of watching the personable bartender Sambonn Lek at work, whether mixing drinks or performing magic tricks. Drinks are regular price.

Pullman Lounge, in the Hotel Sofitel, 1914 Connecticut Ave. NW (☎ **202/797-2000**). Weeknights, from 6pm to 7pm, this lounge offers complimentary buffet of hot hors d'oeuvres, mostly French whimsies: canapés, mini croque monsieurs, and the like. Beer is $1.50, mixed drinks and wine $3 each.

Taberna del Alaberdero, 1776 I St. NW (☎ **202/429-2200**). Surprisingly, one of the most elegant restaurants in town hosts a happy hour weeknights from 4 to 6pm, with drinks at half-price, and a menu of tapas available for $5 to $8.75 a piece. Dress presentably.

Dragonfly. 1215 Connecticut Ave. NW. ☎ **202/331-1775.** No cover. Mon–Thurs 5:30pm–12:45am, Fri–Sat 5:30pm–1:45am, Sun 6pm–12:45am. Metro: Dupont Circle or Farragut North.

Lines wait to get in here and at other hip clubs along this stretch of Connecticut. Dragonfly is a club, with music playing, white walls glowing, white leather chairs beckoning, and people in black vogue-ing. And Dragonfly is a restaurant, with serious aspirations to please sushi-lovers. But Dragonfly is not a dance club, so put on your cool clothes and leave your dance shoes at home.

The Dubliner. In the Phoenix Park Hotel, at 520 N. Capitol St. NW, with its own entrance on F St. NW. ☎ **202/737-3773.** No cover. Sun–Thurs 11am–1am, Fri–Sat 11am–2:30am. Metro: Union Station.

This is your old Irish pub, the port you can blow into in any storm, personal or weather-related. It's got the dark wood paneling and tables, the etched-and-stained glass windows, Irish-accented staff from time to time, and, most importantly, the Auld Dubliner Amber Ale. You'll probably want to stick to drink here, but you can grab a burger, grilled chicken sandwich, or roast duck salad. The Dubliner is frequented by Capitol Hill staffers and journalists who cover the Hill. Irish music groups play nightly.

Fadó. 808 7th St. NW. ☎ **202/789-0066.** No cover. Open daily until 2am. Metro: Gallery Place/Chinatown.

Another Irish pub, this one a kind of Ireland as theme park. It's gotten a lot of attention from its opening in 1998, partly because it was designed and built by the Irish Pub Company of Dublin, who shipped everything—the stone for the floors, the etched glass, the milled wood—from Ireland. The pub has separate areas, including an old Irish "bookstore" alcove and a country-cottage bar. Authentic Irish food, like potato pancakes, is served with your Guinness. Fadó, Gaelic for "long ago," doesn't take reservations, which means that hungry patrons tend to hover over your table, waiting for you to finish.

Lucky Bar. 1221 Connecticut Ave. NW. ☎ **202/331-3733.** No cover. Mon–Thurs 3pm–2am, Fri–Sat noon–3am, Sun noon–3pm. Metro: Dupont Circle or Farragut North.

Lucky Bar is a good place to kick back and relax. But, in keeping with the times, it also features dance lessons: salsa on Monday nights and swing on Saturday nights. Sometimes the music is live, sometimes it's a DJ. Other times the juke box plays, but never so loud that you can't carry on a conversation. The bar has a front room overlooking Connecticut Avenue, and a back room, which is decorated with good luck signs, couches, hanging TVs, booths, and a pool table.

MCCXXIII. 1223 Connecticut Ave. NW. ☎ **202/822-1800.** No cover. Sun–Thurs until 2am, Fri–Sat until 3am. Metro: Dupont Circle or Farragut North.

This is about as swank and New York as Washington gets: hipsters lined up at the velvet rope, a dress code (but really an excuse for the doorman to decide whether you measure up for admittance), outrageously high prices (drink and food charges are written in Roman numerals, so some people are taken aback when settling up), a soaring ceiling and opulent interior, beautiful women servers who purr at you, more beautiful people milling about. It's something else, I'm telling you, but will it last? We'll see.

Mr. Smith's of Georgetown. 3104 M St. NW. ☎ **202/333-3104.** No cover. Sun–Thurs 11:30am–1:30am, Fri–Sat 11:30am–2:30am. Metro: Foggy Bottom, with a 15-minute walk.

Mr. Smith's bills itself as "The Friendliest Saloon in Town," but the truth is that it's so popular among regulars, you're in danger of being ignored if the staff doesn't know you. The bar, which opened about 30 years ago, has a front room with original brick walls, wooden seats, and a long bar, at which you can count on finding pairs of new-found friends telling obscene jokes, loudly. At the end of this room is a large piano around which customers congregate each night to accompany the pianist. An interior, light-filled garden room adjoins an outdoor garden area.

Nathans. 3150 M St. NW. ☎ **202/338-2600.** No cover. Mon–Thurs 2pm–2am, Fri–Sat 2pm–3am, Sun 11am–2am. Metro: Foggy Bottom, with a 20-minute walk.

Nathans is on the corner of M Street and Wisconsin Avenue in the heart of Georgetown. If you pop in here in mid-afternoon, it's a quiet place to grab a beer or glass of wine and watch the action out on the street. (I know someone who uses Nathans as an in-town office for his suburban business.) Visit at night, though, and it's the more typical bar scene, crowded with locals, out-of-towners, students, and a sprinkling of couples in from the 'burbs. That's the front room. The back room at Nathans is a civilized, candlelit restaurant serving classic American fare. Once dinner is over Thursday through Saturday, this room turns into a dance hall, playing DJ music and attracting the 20-somethings Thursday and Friday nights, and an older crowd Saturday nights.

Ozio, Martini and Cigar Lounge. 1835 K St. NW. ☎ **202/822-6000.** Cover $20 (men only) Fri–Sat after 10:30pm. Mon–Thurs 11:30am–2am, Fri 11:30am–3am, Sat 6:30pm–3am. Happy hour weekdays 4–7pm. Metro: Farragut West or Farragut North.

Winston Churchill's rule of life reigns here: "Smoking cigars and drinking of alcohol before, after, and if need be, during all meals, and intervals between them." Ozio has a whimsical/upscale art-deco interior, with distressed-look walls and columns, Persian rugs strewn on concrete floors, and comfortable seating in plush armchairs, sofas, and banquettes. The lighting is loungy, and the music mellow (light jazz, blues, Sinatra, Tony Bennett). People dance wherever they can find a space. Ozio is the kind of place where limos are parked out front, and the suit-and-tie crowd is comprised of senators, hotshot professionals, and local sports figures. Exotic-looking cigar men (the stogie equivalents of sommeliers) come by during the evening with humidors. Vodka and gin martinis are favorites, as are single malt scotches (choose from a list of 20). The menu ranges from tapas and pastas to filet mignon.

Politiki. 319 Pennsylvania Ave. SE. ☎ **202/546-1001.** No cover. Daily 4pm–1:30am. Metro: Capitol South.

This funny, funky bar with a Polynesian theme is a welcome addition to the more traditional pubs along this stretch of Capitol Hill. It's a theme you can build upon: think Scorpion Bowl and Pina Colada drinks, pu-pu platters, and hula dancer figurines. The basement has pool tables, a bar, and a lounge area (behind beaded curtains); the street level has booths and a bar; and the top floor occasionally features live music, dance lessons, and a promised Don Ho night. Now's your chance to wear your Hawaiian shirt.

Post Pub. 1422 L St. NW. ☎ **202/628-2111.** No cover. Mon–Fri 11am–midnight, Sat 11am–8pm. Metro: McPherson Square.

This joint fits into the "comfortable shoe" category. Situated between Vermont and 15th streets, across from the offices of the *Washington Post,* the pub gets busy at lunch, grows quiet in the afternoon, and picks up again in the evening. Post Pub has two rooms furnished with old-fashioned black banquettes, faux wood paneling, mirrored beer insignias, juke boxes, cigarette machines, and a long bar with tall stools. There are different happy hour specials every night, like the 5 to 9pm Thursday "Anything Absolute," which offers drinks made with Absolut vodka for $2.50 each. The food is homey and inexpensive (under $10)—onion rings, sandwiches, chicken parmigiana, and the like.

The Rock. 717 6th St. NW. ☎ **202/842-7625.** No cover. Mon–Thurs 3pm–2am, Fri–Sat noon–3am, Sun noon–2am. Metro: Gallery Place.

The Rock has the best location a sports bar could have: across the street from the MCI Center. The three-floor bar fills a former warehouse, its decor a montage of preexisting exposed pipes and concrete floors, and TV screens, pool tables, and sports memorabilia. The most popular spot is the third floor, where the pool tables and a cigar lounge are located. In good weather, folks head to the rooftop bar.

Arlington Row

As unlikely as it seems, one of the hottest spots for Washington nightlife, suddenly, is a stretch of suburban street in Arlington, VA. I'm talking about a section of Wilson Boulevard in the Clarendon neighborhood, roughly between Highland and Danville streets. For many years, people referred to this area as "Little Vietnam," for the many Vietnamese cafes and grocery stores that have flourished here. Now some are calling it "the new Adams-Morgan," with some pretty good nightclubs and several well-reviewed restaurants joining the still-strong Vietnamese presence.

Let's get one thing straight: It isn't Adams-Morgan. Adams-Morgan is urban, ethnic, and edgy. Black clothes, body piercings, colorful hair, tattoos, and bad attitudes, are de rigueur. Arlington Row is a lot tamer, attracting, so far anyway, a mostly white crowd of all ages, dressed, usually, for comfort. In one respect, Arlington Row clubs are more accepting: You don't feel like your presence has to make a statement. Certainly, the clubs are more accessible: Metro stops are nearby, parking is easier, streets are safer, clubs front the streets with picture windows and aren't as exclusive.

But I wouldn't even be recommending you visit Arlington Row if it weren't for one key element: the music. It's live, it's good (most of the time), and it's here almost nightly in greater supply than in Adams-Morgan, believe it or not. So take the Metro to the Clarendon stop and walk down Wilson, or drive up Wilson from Key Bridge, turn left on Edgewood Road and park in the vast (and free) lot where the street dead-ends. Then walk to these spots. Food is served at each.

Galaxy Hut. 2711 Wilson Blvd. ☎ **703/525-8646.** No cover. Smallest of the bunch, Galaxy Hut's a comfortable bar weeknights, with far-out art on the walls and a patio in the alley. Live alternative rock on weekends.

The Tombs. 1226 36th St. NW. ☎ **202/337-6668.** Cover sometimes on Tues nights, never more than $5. Open Mon–Fri 11:30am–1:30am, Sat 11am–1:30am, Sun 10:30am–1:30am. Metro: Foggy Bottom, with a 40- to 45-minute walk.

Housed in a converted 19th-century Federal-style home, the Tombs, which opened in 1962, is a favorite hangout for students and faculty of nearby Georgetown University. (Bill Clinton came here during his college years.) GU types tend to congregate at the central bar and surrounding tables, while local residents head for "the Sweeps," the room that lies down a few steps and has red leather banquettes.

Directly below the upscale 1789 Restaurant (see chapter 6 for details), the Tombs benefits from 1789 chef Riz Lacoste's supervision. The menu offers burgers, sandwiches, and salads, as well as more serious fare.

Townhouse Tavern. 1637 R St. NW. ☎ **202/234-5747.** Mon–Thurs 2pm–2am, Fri 2pm–3am, Sat noon–3am, Sun noon–2am. Metro: Dupont Circle, with a short walk.

Anytime you go by this place, it's busy. It appears to be a home away from home for much of the neighborhood. You can sit outside at a sidewalk table or move indoors, either to the basement bar, with a fantastic CD jukebox, pool table, and pinball machines; or to the upstairs bar with its TV turned to a sports event. Owners and bartenders R.T. Smith and Doug Edgerton are known to many from their stints at Fox and Hounds, nearby. Bar food at the tavern is a cut above: black bean soup, cajun popcorn, and lamb chops.

IOTA. 2832 Wilson Blvd. ☎ 703/522-8340. Cover: If there's a cover it runs about $4, but can be as high as $12 when the band is really good. Here, up and coming local bands take the stage nightly in a setting with minimal decor (cement floor, exposed brick walls, and wood-beamed ceiling); there's a patio in back. Live music weeknights and weekends.

Whitlow's on Wilson. 2854 Wilson Blvd. ☎ 703/276-9693. Cover $3 Thurs–Sat after 9pm. This is the biggest spot on the block, spread throughout three rooms, the first showcasing the music, usually blues, with anything from surfer music to rock thrown in. The place has the appearance of a diner, from formica table-booths to soda fountain, and serves retro diner food. The other rooms hold coin-operated pool tables, dartboards, and air-hockey.

Clarendon Grill. 1101 N. Highland St. ☎ 703/524-7455. Cover $2–$5 Tues–Sat. This one wins a best decor award for its construction theme: murals of construction workers, building materials displayed under glass-covered bar, and so on. Music is a mix of modern rock, jazz, and reggae.

Now, get in your car, hop the Metro, or get out your rambling shoes to visit one other place, about one mile south of this stretch of Wilson:

Rhodeside Grill. 1835 Wilson Blvd. ☎ 703/243-0145. Cover averages $3 Thurs–Sat, starting at 9:30pm. Rhodeside Grill (3 blocks from the Courthouse Metro stop) is a well-liked American restaurant on its first floor, with a rec-room-like bar downstairs, which features excellent live bands playing roots rock, jazz funk, Latin percussion, country rock, blues, you name it.

Tryst. 2459 18th St. NW. ☎ 202/232-5500. No cover. Mon–Thurs 7am–2am, Fri–Sat 7am–3am, Sun 8am–11pm. Metro: Dupont Circle, with a 15-minute walk, or Woodley Park-Zoo, with a 20-minute walk across the Calvert St. Bridge.

This is the most relaxed of the new lounge bars. The room is surprisingly large for Adams-Morgan, and it's jam packed with worn armchairs and couches, which are usually occupied, no matter what time of day. People come here to have coffee or a drink, get a bite to eat, read a book, meet a friend. Sort of like a student lounge on a college campus, only alcohol is served.

The Tune Inn. 33½ Pennsylvania Ave. SE. ☎ 202/543-2725. No cover. Sun–Thurs 8am–2am, Fri–Sat 8am–3am. Metro: Capitol South.

Capitol Hill has a number of bars that qualify as "institutions," but the Tune Inn is probably the most popular. Capitol Hill staffers and their bosses, apparently at ease in dive surroundings, have been coming here since it opened in 1955. Or maybe it's the cheap beer and greasy burgers that draw them. Anyway, stop in.

Tunnicliff's Tavern. 222 7th St. SE. ☎ 202/546-3663. Daily noon–2am. Metro: Eastern Market.

Directly across from Eastern Market, this Capitol Hill institution is named after the original, circa-1796 Tunnicliff's Tavern. (This Tunnicliff's opened in 1988.) An out-door cafe fronts the tavern, which includes a great bar and a partly enclosed dining room. You're likely to see Hill people here; the last time I was there, Louisiana Senator John Breaux and his wife stopped by. Proprietress Lynne Breaux, though not related to the senator, hails from New Orleans and cultivates a Mardi Gras atmosphere that includes live music (no cover) on Saturday nights. The menu features some standard New Orleans items, like po'boys, gumbo, and fried oysters, as well as nachos and other bar fare. Breaux likes to make everyone feel welcome, including families, and has toys and coloring books at the ready.

XandO. 1350 Connecticut Ave. NW. ☎ **202/296-9341.** No cover. Mon–Thurs 6:30am–1am, Fri 6:30am–2am, Sat 7am–2am, Sun 7am–1am. Metro: Dupont Circle, South exit.

Popular from the start, XandO (pronounced "zando") is a welcoming place in the morning for a coffee drink, and even more inviting for a cocktail later in the day. Men, you'll see a lot of cute girls hanging here, drawn perhaps by the s'mores (you get to make them), and other delicious desserts. XandO also serves sandwiches and soups. The music is loud, the decor a cross between bar and living room.

Side Trips from Washington, D.C.

10

Just across the Potomac River from Washington is the picturesque enclave of Old Town Alexandria, where George Washington dined and hung out with friends. Travel a little further and you'll reach our first president's home, Mount Vernon. For history and appeal, these two destinations are unbeatable, and they are so close to Washington that the two sites make easy day-trips, even half-day trips from downtown D.C. Make sure your excursion allows time for eating and shopping in Old Town, which has many good restaurants, arts and antiques stores, and other shops. But don't expect to find Mount Vernon and Old Town less crowded than Washington these days; their abundant charms and proximity draw locals and tourists alike.

1 Mount Vernon

No visit to Washington would be complete without a trip to Mount Vernon, George Washington's estate. Only 16 miles south of the capital, this southern plantation dates from a 1674 land grant to a certain Washington—the president's great-grandfather.

ESSENTIALS
GETTING THERE If you're going by car, take any of the bridges over the Potomac into Virginia to the George Washington Memorial Parkway (Route 1) going south; the parkway ends at Mount Vernon.

Tourmobile buses (☎ **202/554-5100**) depart daily, April through October only, from Arlington National Cemetery and the Washington Monument. The round-trip fare is $22 for adults, $11 for children 3 to 11 (free for children under 3) and includes the admission fee to Mount Vernon. You must reserve your space in person at either Arlington Cemetery or the Washington Monument at least 30 minutes in advance. Gray Line bus tours (☎ **202/289-1995**) go to Mount Vernon daily, leaving from the bus's terminal at Union Station at 8:30am and returning by 12:30pm. The cost is $25 per adult and $12 per child.

Boat tours to Mount Vernon include the Spirit of Washington Cruises' (☎ **202/554-8000**) *Potomac Spirit,* which leaves from the Washington waterfront every day except Monday, early March through October, at 9am, returning by 2:30pm, and costs $26.50 per adult, $17 per child (ages 6 to 11). The Potomac Riverboat Company's (☎ **703/548-9000**) *Miss Christin,* a two-level vessel, departs for

Special Activities at Mount Vernon

There's an ongoing schedule of events at Mount Vernon, especially in summer. For adults, these might include tours focusing on 18th-century gardens, slave life, colonial crafts, or archaeology; for children there are hands-on history programs and treasure hunts. Call to find out if anything is on during your visit.

Mount Vernon from the pier adjacent to the Torpedo Factory, at the bottom of King Street in Old Town Alexandria, and costs $24 per adult and $12 per child. Bus and boat tour prices include price of admission to Mount Vernon.

See chapter 7's section on "Organized Tours" for details about Tourmobile, Gray Line, and boat tours to Mount Vernon.

If you're in the mood for exercise in a pleasant setting, rent a bike (see "Outdoor Activities" in chapter 7 for rental locations) and hop on the pathway that runs along the Potomac. In Washington, this is the Rock Creek Park Trail; once you cross Memorial Bridge into Virginia, the name changes to the Mount Vernon Trail, which, as it sounds, is a straight shot to Mount Vernon. The trail takes you past National Airport and through Old Town Alexandria. The section from Memorial Bridge to Mount Vernon is about 19 miles in all.

TOURING THE ESTATE

Mount Vernon. South George Washington Pkwy. (no house number). (Mailing address is Mount Vernon, P.O. Box 110, Mount Vernon, VA 22121.) ☎ **703/780-2000.** www.mountvernon.org. Admission $8 adults, $7.50 senior citizens, $4 children 6–11, children under 6 free. Apr–Aug 8am–5pm, Mar, Sept and Oct daily 9am–5pm, Nov–Feb daily 9am–4pm. Allow at least 2 hours to tour.

Mount Vernon was purchased for $200,000 in 1858 by the Mount Vernon Ladies' Association from John Augustine Washington, great-grandnephew of the first president. Without the group's purchase, the estate might have crumbled and disappeared, for neither the federal government nor the Commonwealth of Virginia had wanted to buy the property when it was earlier offered for sale. The restoration is an unmarred beauty; many of the furnishings are original pieces acquired by Washington, and the rooms have been repainted in the original colors favored by George and Martha.

Mount Vernon's mansion and grounds are stunning. Some 500 of the original 8,000 acres (divided into five farms) owned by Washington are still intact. Washington delighted in riding horseback around his property, directing planting and other activities; the Bowling Green entrance is still graced by some of the trees he planted. The American Revolution and his years as president took Washington away from his beloved estate most of the time. He finally retired to Mount Vernon in 1797, just two years before his death, to "view the solitary walk and tread the paths of private life with heartfelt satisfaction." He is buried on the estate. Martha was buried next to him in May 1802. Public memorial services are held at the estate every year on the third Monday in February, the date commemorating Washington's birthday; admission is free that day.

Mount Vernon has been one of the nation's most-visited shrines since the mid–19th century. Today more than a million people tour the property annually. There's no formal tour, but attendants stationed throughout the house and grounds provide brief orientations and answer questions. Maps of the property are available at the entrance. The best time to visit is off-season; during the heavy tourist months, avoid weekends and holidays if possible, and year-round, arrive early to beat the crowds.

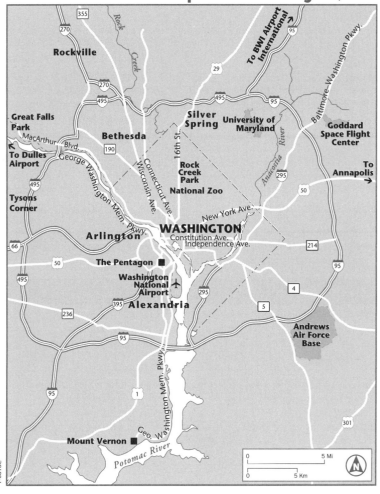

The house itself is interesting not only for its former owner, but as an outstanding model of colonial architecture and a window into the aristocratic lifestyle of the 18th century. There are a number of family portraits, and the rooms are appointed as if actually in day-to-day use.

After leaving the house, you can tour the outbuildings: the kitchen, slave quarters, storeroom, smokehouse, overseer's quarters, coachhouse, and stables. A 4-acre exhibit area called "George Washington, Pioneer Farmer" includes a replica of Washington's 16-sided barn and fields of crops that he grew (corn, wheat, oats, and so forth). Docents in period costumes demonstrate 18th-century farming methods. A museum on the property exhibits Washington memorabilia, and details of the restoration are explained in the museum's annex; there's also a gift shop. You'll want to walk around the grounds (most pleasant in nice weather), and see the wharf, the slave burial ground, the greenhouse, the tomb containing George and Martha Washington's sarcophagi (24 other family members are also interred here), the lawns, and the gardens.

WHERE TO DINE

At the entrance to Mount Vernon you'll find a snack bar serving light fare, and there are picnic tables outside. If a picnic is what you have in mind, drive a mile north on the parkway to Riverside Park, where you can lunch at tables overlooking the Potomac.

Mount Vernon Inn. Near the entrance to Mount Vernon. ☎ **703/780-0011.** Reservations recommended at dinner. Main courses $4.50–$8.50 at lunch, $12–$24 at dinner; prix-fixe dinner $14. AE, DISC, MC, V. Daily 11am–3:30pm and Mon–Sat 5–9pm. AMERICAN.

Lunch or dinner at the inn is an intrinsic part of the Mount Vernon experience. It's a quaint and charming colonial-style restaurant, complete with period furnishings and three working fireplaces. The waitstaff is in 18th-century costume. Be sure to begin your meal with the homemade peanut and chestnut soup (usually on the lunch menu). Lunch entrees range from colonial turkey pye (a sort of Early American quiche served in a crock with garden vegetables and a puffed pastry top) to a 20th-century–style burger and fries. There's a full bar, and premium wines are offered by the glass. At dinner, tablecloths and candlelight make this a more elegant choice. Happily, a prix-fixe dinner means that it is also affordable. The meal includes soup (perhaps broccoli cheddar) or salad, an entree such as Maryland crab cakes or roast venison with peppercorn sauce, homemade breads, and dessert (like Bavarian parfait or English trifle).

2 Alexandria

Founded by a group of Scottish tobacco merchants, the seaport town of Alexandria came into being in 1749 when a 60-acre tract of land was auctioned off in half-acre lots. Colonists came from miles around, in ramshackle wagons and stately carriages, in sloops, brigantines, and lesser craft, to bid on land that would be "commodious for trade and navigation and tend greatly to the ease and advantage of the frontier inhabitants. . . ." The auction took place in Market Square (still intact today), and the surveyor's assistant was a capable lad of 17 named George Washington.

Today, the original 60 acres of lots in George Washington's hometown (also Robert E. Lee's) are the heart of Old Town, a multimillion-dollar urban-renewal historic district. Many Alexandria streets still bear their original colonial names (King, Queen, Prince, Princess, Royal—you get the drift), while others like Jefferson, Franklin, Lee, Patrick, and Henry are obviously post-Revolutionary.

In this "mother lode of Americana," the past is being restored in an ongoing archaeological and historical research program. And though the present can be seen in the abundance of shops, boutiques, art galleries, and restaurants capitalizing on tourism, it's still easy to imagine yourself in colonial times by listening for the rumbling of horse-drawn vehicles over cobblestone (portions of Prince and Oronoco streets are still cobblestone); dining on Sally Lunn bread and other 18th century grub in the centuries-old Gadsby's Tavern; and learning about the lives of our forefathers during walking tours that take you in and out of their houses.

ESSENTIALS

GETTING THERE   Old Town Alexandria is about 5 miles south of Washington. If you're traveling by car, take the Arlington Memorial or the 14th Street Bridge to the George Washington Memorial Parkway south, which becomes Washington Street in Old Town Alexandria. Washington Street intersects with King Street, Alexandria's main thoroughfare. Turn left from Washington Street onto one of the streets before or after King Street (southbound left turns are not permitted from Washington Street onto King Street), and you'll be heading toward the waterfront and the heart of Old Town. Turn right onto King Street and you'll find an avenue of shops and restaurants.

Old Town Alexandria

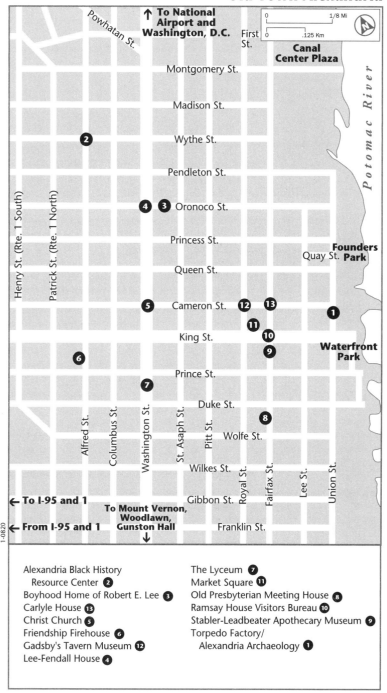

To National Airport and Washington, D.C.

Powhatan St.

First St.

Canal Center Plaza

Potomac River

Montgomery St.

Madison St.

Wythe St.

Pendleton St.

Oronoco St.

Princess St.

Queen St.

Quay St.

Founders Park

Cameron St.

King St.

Waterfront Park

Prince St.

Duke St.

Wolfe St.

Wilkes St.

Gibbon St.

Franklin St.

Henry St. (Rte. 1 South)

Patrick St. (Rte. 1 North)

Alfred St.

Columbus St.

Washington St.

St. Asaph St.

Pitt St.

Royal St.

Fairfax St.

Lee St.

Union St.

← To I-95 and 1

← From I-95 and 1

To Mount Vernon, Woodlawn, Gunston Hall

1-0820

Alexandria Black History
   Resource Center **2**
Boyhood Home of Robert E. Lee **3**
Carlyle House **13**
Christ Church **5**
Friendship Firehouse **6**
Gadsby's Tavern Museum **12**
Lee-Fendall House **4**

The Lyceum **7**
Market Square **11**
Old Presbyterian Meeting House **8**
Ramsay House Visitors Bureau **10**
Stabler-Leadbeater Apothecary Museum **9**
Torpedo Factory/
   Alexandria Archaeology **1**

You can obtain a free parking permit from the Visitors Association (see below), or park at meters or in garages.

The easiest way to make the trip may be the Metro's Yellow Line to the King Street station. From there, you can catch an eastbound AT2 or AT5 blue-and-gold DASH bus (☎ **703/370-DASH**), marked either "Old Town" or "Braddock Metro," which will take you up King Street, dropping you at City Hall, across from the Visitors Association. The fare is 85¢, and you'll need exact change. Or you can walk into Old Town, although it's about a mile from the station into the center of Old Town. The town is compact, so you won't need a car once you arrive.

VISITOR INFORMATION   The Alexandria Convention and Visitors Association, located at Ramsay House, 221 King Street, at Fairfax Street (☎ **800/388-9119** or 703/838-4200; fax 703/838-4683; www.funside.com) is open daily from 9am to 5pm (closed January 1, Thanksgiving, and December 25). Here you can obtain a map/self-guided walking tour and brochures about the area; learn about special events that might be scheduled during your visit and get tickets for them; and receive answers to any questions you might have about accommodations, restaurants, sights, or shopping. The association supplies materials in five languages.

If you come by car, get a free 1-day parking permit here for complimentary parking at any 2-hour meter for up to 24 hours; when you park, put money in the meter to cover yourself until you post your permit. The permit can be renewed for a second day.

ORGANIZED TOURS   Though it's easy to see Alexandria on your own by putting yourself in the hands of colonial-attired guides at the various attractions, you might consider taking a comprehensive walking tour. Among those offered are:

Doorways to Old Virginia (☎ **703/548-0100**). Weather permitting, **Doorways** leads its "Footsteps of George Washington" tour daily March through November, leaving from the Stabler-Leadbeater Apothecary Museum at 105 S. Fairfax St., at 11am Monday through Saturday and at 2pm Sunday; you can purchase the $4 adult tickets (children 11 and under are free) at Ramsay House.

Doorways also conducts "Ghost and Graveyard" tours Friday and Saturday evenings spring through October (weather permitting), departing from Ramsay House at 7:30pm and again at 9pm Friday; the cost is $5 for adults, $3 for children ages 7 to 17, free for children 6 and younger. You purchase tickets from the guide.

Alexandria Tours (☎ **703/329-1122**). This company offers daily 1-hour **Overview Tours** Friday, Saturday and Sunday at 2pm for $5 per person (ages 6 and under free); and nightly 1-hour **Ghosts, Legends, and Folklore Tours** beginning at Market Square, at 8pm, for $5 per person. Call ahead to reserve your tour; you pay the guide when you arrive.

The Old Town Experience (☎ **703/836-0694**). On this guided tour of Alexandria's historic district, you learn about Alexandria's hospitality symbols, merchant houses, flounder houses, busybodies, and more, as you walk along cobblestone streets and visit the Gadsby's Tavern Museum, Carlyle House, and the Stabler-Leadbeater Apothecary Shop. Call ahead; the tours are by appointment only.

CITY LAYOUT   Old Town is very small. It's helpful to know, when looking for addresses, that Alexandria is laid out in a grid. At the center is the intersection of Washington Street and King Street. Streets that run parallel to Washington Street, running north and south, are identified according to which side of King Street they lie, so that Alfred Street, for example, is North Alfred Street on the side of King Street closest to the city of Washington; once it crosses King Street, it becomes South Alfred Street. Understand? Take a look at the map and these instructions should become clear.

SPECIAL EVENTS

Major events follow. If you're planning to participate in any of them, book your accommodations far ahead and contact the Visitors Association for details and advance tickets. Whenever you come, you're sure to run into some activity or other—a jazz festival, tea garden or tavern gambol, quilt exhibit, wine tasting, or organ recital. Be sure to checkout the Alexandria Convention and Visitors Association Web site, www.funside.com, which lists a calendar of events, updated from time to time.

January   The birthdays of **Robert E. Lee** and his father, Revolutionary War Colonel "Light Horse Harry" Lee, are celebrated together at the Lee-Fendall House and Lee's Boyhood Home the third Sunday of the month. The party features period music, refreshments, and house tours.

February   Alexandria celebrates **George Washington's Birthday,** on Presidents' Weekend, which precedes the federal holiday, usually the third Monday in February. Festivities typically include a colonial-costume or black-tie banquet, followed by a ball at Gadsby's Tavern, a 10-kilometer race, special tours, a Revolutionary War encampment at Fort Ward Park (complete with uniformed troops engaging in skirmishes), the nation's largest George Washington Birthday Parade (50,000 to 75,000 people attend each year), and 18th-century comic opera performances.

March   On the first Saturday in March, King Street is the site of a popular **St. Patrick's Day Parade.**

April   Alexandria celebrates **Historic Garden Week in Virginia** with tours of privately owned local (usually historic) homes and gardens the third Saturday of the month.

June   The **Red Cross Waterfront Festival,** the second weekend in June, honors Alexandria's historic importance as a seaport and the vitality of its Potomac shoreline today with a display of historic tall ships, ship tours, boat rides and races, nautical art exhibits, waterfront walking tours, fireworks, children's games, an arts and crafts show, food booths, and entertainment. Admission is charged.

July   Gather with the clans for **Virginia Scottish Games,** a 2-day Celtic festival the fourth weekend of the month that celebrates Alexandria's Highland heritage. Activities include athletic events (such as the caber toss, in which competitors heave a 140-pound pole in the air), musicians (playing reels, strathspeys, and laments), fiddling and harp competitions, a parade of clan societies in tartans, a Celtic crafts fair, storytelling, Highland dance performances and competitions, booths selling Scottish foods and wares, dog trials featuring Scottish breeds, and a Scottish Country Dance Party. Admission is charged; you can get a small discount on tickets purchased in advance at the Ramsay House Visitors Center.

September   Chili enthusiasts can sample "bowls of red" at the **Hard Times Chili Cookoff** in Waterfront Park. Contestants from almost every U.S. state and territory compete, and for an admission charge of a few dollars, you can taste all their creations. Proceeds go to charity. Fiddling contests, jalapeño-eating contests, and country music are part of the fun.

October   October is Arts Month in Alexandria and two events celebrate the arts, both taking place the first Saturday in October. **Alexandria Arts Safari** includes archeological and arts tours, and interactive events, all over Old Town; **Art on the Avenue** takes over Mount Vernon Avenue, about a mile northwest of Old Town, with art displays up and down the street. Both of these events are free.

   Also: Explore the ghosts and graveyards of Alexandria on a **Halloween Walking Tour** with a lantern-carrying guide in 18th-century costume. The tour focuses on eerie

Alexandria legend, myth, and folklore. See "Organized Tours," above, for phone numbers and costs.

November   The Historic Alexandria **Antiques Show,** on the third weekend of the month, features several dozen dealers from many states displaying an array of high-quality antiques, including jewelry, silver, rare books, rugs, paintings, folk art, furniture, pottery, and decorative objects. Admission is charged; proceeds help restore historic sites. Pricier activities include a gala opening party (about $75 admission) and a champagne brunch with a featured speaker (about $40).

There's a **Christmas Tree Lighting** in Market Square the Friday after Thanksgiving; the ceremony, which includes choir singing, puppet shows, dance performances, and an appearance by Santa and his elves, begins at 7pm. The night the tree is lit, thousands of tiny lights adorning King Street trees also go on.

December   Holiday festivities continue with the **Annual Scottish Christmas Walk** on the first Saturday in December. Activities include kilted bagpipers, Highland dancers, a parade of Scottish clans (with horses and dogs), caroling, fashion shows, storytelling, booths (selling crafts, antiques, food, hot mulled punch, heather, fresh wreaths, and holly), and children's games. Admission is charged for some events.

The **Old Town Christmas Candlelight Tour,** the second week in December, visits seasonally decorated historic Alexandria homes and an 18th-century tavern. There are colonial dancing, string quartets, madrigal and opera singers, and refreshments, too. Purchase tickets at the Ramsay House Visitors Center.

There are so many holiday season activities, the Visitors Association issues a special brochure about them each year. Pick one up to learn about decorations, workshops, walking tours, tree lightings, concerts, bazaars, bake sales, crafts fairs, and much more.

WHAT TO SEE & DO

In addition to the annual events mentioned above, there's much more to see and do.

Tip: Available at Ramsay House (see "Visitor Information," above) is a money-saving block ticket for admission to at least three historic Alexandria properties: Gadsby's Tavern, the Carlyle House, and Stabler-Leadbeater Apothecary Shop. The ticket, which can also be purchased at any of the buildings, costs $9 for adults, $5 for children ages 11 to 17; children under 11 enter free. By the time you read this, it may also be possible to purchase a block ticket that includes the Boyhood Home of Robert E. Lee and the Lee-Fendall House. In any case, I would recommend that you visit all five attractions, as well as the others mentioned here.

Alexandria Museums are on the Web at ci.alexandria.va.us/oha.

Alexandria Black History Resource Center. 638 N. Alfred St. (at Wythe St.). ☎ **703/ 838-4356.** Free admission (donations accepted). Tues–Sat 10am–4pm.

In a 1940s building that originally housed the black community's first public library, the center exhibits historical objects, photographs, documents, and memorabilia relating to African-American Alexandrians from the 18th century forward. In addition to the permanent collection, the museum presents rotating exhibits and other activities. If you're interested in further studies, check out the center's Watson Reading Room.

✪ **Boyhood Home of Robert E. Lee.** 607 Oronoco St. (between St. Asaph and Washington sts.). ☎ **703/548-8454.** Admission $4 adults, $2 children 11–17, free for children under 11. Tours given Mon–Sat 10am–3:30pm, Sun 1–3:30pm. Closed Easter, Thanksgiving, and Dec 15–Jan 31 (except for the Sun closest to Jan 19, Robert E. Lee's birthday).

Revolutionary War cavalry hero Henry "Light Horse Harry" Lee brought his wife, Ann Hill Carter, and five children to this early Federal-style mansion in 1812, when Robert, destined to become a Confederate military leader, was just 5 years old. A tour of the house, built in 1795, provides a glimpse into the gracious lifestyle of Alexandria's gentry. George Washington was an occasional guest of two earlier occupants, John Potts (the builder of the house) and Col. William Fitzhugh. In 1804 the Fitzhughs' daughter, Mary Lee, married Martha Washington's grandson, George Washington Parke Custis, in the drawing room. And the Custises' daughter, Mary Ann Randolph, married Robert E. Lee.

General Lafayette honored Ann Hill Carter Lee with a visit to the house in October 1824 in tribute to her husband, "Light Horse Harry" Lee, who had died in 1818. Lafayette had been a comrade-in-arms with Lee during the American Revolution. The drawing room today is called the Lafayette Room to commemorate that visit.

On a fascinating tour, you'll see the nursery with its little canopied bed and toy box; Mrs. Lee's room; the Lafayette Room, furnished in period antiques, with the tea table set up for use; the morning room, where The Iliad translated into Latin reposes on a gaming table (both "Light Horse Harry" and Robert were classical scholars); and the winter kitchen. The furnishings are of the Lee period but did not belong to the family. The house was occupied by 17 different owners after the Lees left. It was made into a museum in 1967.

✪ **Carlyle House.** 121 N. Fairfax St. (at Cameron St.). ☎ **703/549-2997.** Admission $4 adults, $2 children 11–17, free for children under 11; or buy a block ticket. Tues–Sat 10am–4:30pm, Sun noon–4:30pm.

Not only is Carlyle House regarded as one of Virginia's most architecturally impressive 18th-century houses, it also figured prominently in American history. In 1753 Scottish merchant John Carlyle completed the mansion for his bride, Sarah Fairfax of Belvoir, a daughter of one of Virginia's most prominent families. It was designed in the style of a Scottish/English manor house and lavishly furnished. Carlyle, a successful merchant, had the means to import the best furnishings and appointments available abroad for his new Alexandria home.

When it was built, Carlyle House was a waterfront property with its own wharf. A social and political center, the house was visited by numerous great men of the time, including George Washington. But its most important moment in history occurred in April 1755 when Maj. Gen. Edward Braddock, commander-in-chief of his majesty's forces in North America, met with five colonial governors here and asked them to tax colonists to finance a campaign against the French and Indians. Colonial legislatures refused to comply, one of the first instances of serious friction between America and Britain. Nevertheless, Braddock made Carlyle House his headquarters during the campaign, and Carlyle was less than impressed with him. He called the general "a man of weak understanding. . . very indolent. . . a slave to his passions, women and wine. . . as great an Epicure as could be in his eating, tho a brave man." Possibly these were the reasons his unfinanced campaign met with disaster. Braddock received, as Carlyle described it, "a most remarkable drubbing."

A tour of Carlyle House takes about 40 minutes. Two of the original rooms, the large parlor and the adjacent study, have survived intact; the former, where Braddock met the governors, still retains its original fine woodwork, paneling, and pediments. The house is furnished in period pieces; however, only a few of Carlyle's possessions remain. In an upstairs room an architecture exhibit depicts 18th-century construction methods with hand-hewn beams and hand-wrought nails. Tours are given every half hour on the hour and half hour.

Planning Note

Many Alexandria attractions are closed on Monday.

Christ Church. 118 N. Washington St. (at Cameron St.). ☎ **703/549-1450.** Suggested donation $2 per person. Mon–Fri 9am–4pm, Sun 2–4:30pm. Closed all federal holidays.

This sturdy redbrick Georgian-style church would be an important national landmark even if its two most distinguished members had not been Washington and Lee. It has been in continuous use since 1773.

There have, of course, been many changes since Washington's day. The bell tower, church bell, galleries, and organ were added by the early 1800s, the "wineglass" pulpit in 1891. But much of what was changed later has since been restored to its earlier state. The pristine white interior with wood moldings and gold trim is colonially correct, though modern heating has obviated the need for charcoal braziers and hot bricks. For the most part, the original structure remains, including the handblown glass in the windows. The town has grown up around the building that was first called the "Church in the Woods" because of its rural setting.

Christ Church has had its historic moments. Washington and other early church members fomented revolution in the churchyard, and Robert E. Lee met here with Richmond representatives to discuss assuming a command of Virginia's military forces at the beginning of the Civil War. You can sit in the pew where George and Martha sat with her two Custis grandchildren, or in the Lee family pew.

It's a tradition for U.S. presidents to attend a service here on a Sunday close to Washington's birthday and sit in his pew. One of the most memorable of these visits took place shortly after Pearl Harbor, when Franklin Delano Roosevelt attended services with Winston Churchill on the World Day of Prayer, January 1, 1942.

Of course, you're invited to attend a service. There's no admission, but donations are appreciated. A guide gives brief lectures to visitors. The old Parish Hall today houses a gift shop and an exhibit on the history of the church. Walk out to the weathered graveyard, Alexandria's first and only burial ground until 1805; its oldest marked grave is that of Isaac Pearce, who died in 1771. The remains of 34 Confederate soldiers are also interred here.

Fort Ward Museum & Historic Site. 4301 W. Braddock Rd. (between Rt. 7 and Seminary Rd.). ☎ **703/838-4848.** Free admission. Park, daily 9am–sunset; museum, Tues–Sat 9am–5pm, Sun noon–5pm. Call for information regarding special holiday closings. From Old Town, follow King St. west, go right on Kenwood Ave., then left on West Braddock Rd.; continue for ¾ mile to the entrance on the right.

A short drive from Old Town is a 45-acre museum, historic site, and park that take you on a leap forward in Alexandria history to the Civil War. The action here centers, as it did in the early 1860s, on an actual Union fort that Lincoln ordered erected. It was part of a system of Civil War forts called the "Defenses of Washington." About 90% of the fort's earthwork walls are preserved, and the Northwest Bastion has been restored with six mounted guns (originally there were 36). A model of 19th-century military engineering, the fort was never attacked by Confederate forces. Self-guided tours begin at the Fort Ward ceremonial gate.

Visitors can explore the fort and replicas of the ceremonial entrance gate and an officer's hut. There's a museum of Civil War artifacts on the premises where changing exhibits focus on subjects such as Union arms and equipment, medical care of the wounded, and local war history.

There are picnic areas with barbecue grills in the park surrounding the fort. Concerts are presented on selected evenings June to mid-August in the outdoor amphitheater. A living-history program takes place in mid-August (call for details).

Friendship Firehouse. 107 S. Alfred St. (between King and Prince sts.). ☎ **703/838-3891.** Free admission. Fri–Sat 10am–4pm, Sun 1–4pm.

Alexandria's first fire-fighting organization, the Friendship Fire Company, was established in 1774. In the early days, the company met in taverns and kept its fire-fighting equipment in a member's barn. Its present Italianate-style brick building dates from 1855; it was erected after an earlier building was, ironically, destroyed by fire. Local tradition holds that George Washington was involved with the firehouse as a founding member, active firefighter, and purchaser of its first fire engine, although research does not confirm these stories. Fire engines and fire fighting paraphernalia are on display.

✪ **Gadsby's Tavern Museum.** 134 N. Royal St. (at Cameron St.). ☎ **703/838-4242.** Admission $4 adults, $2 children 11–17, free for children under 11; or buy a block ticket. Tours given Apr–Sept, Tues–Sat 10am–5pm, Sun 1–5pm; Oct–Mar, Tues–Sat 11am–4pm, Sun 1–4pm. Closed all federal holidays except Veterans Day.

Alexandria was at the crossroads of 18th-century America, and its social center was Gadsby's Tavern, which consisted of two buildings (one Georgian, one Federal) dating from circa 1770 and 1792, respectively. Innkeeper John Gadsby combined them to create "a gentleman's tavern," which he operated from 1796 to 1808; it was considered one of the finest in the country. George Washington was a frequent dinner guest; he and Martha danced in the second-floor ballroom and it was here that Washington celebrated his last birthday. The tavern also saw Thomas Jefferson, James Madison, and the Marquis de Lafayette. It was the scene of lavish parties, theatrical performances, small circuses, government meetings, and concerts. Itinerant merchants used the tavern to display their wares, and traveling doctors and dentists treated a hapless clientele (these were rudimentary professions in the 18th century) on the premises.

The rooms have been restored to their 18th-century appearance with the help of modern excavations and colonial inventories. On the 30-minute tour, you'll get a good look at the Tap Room, a small dining room; the Assembly Room, the ballroom; typical bedrooms; and the underground icehouse, which was filled each winter from the icy river. Tours depart 15 minutes before and after the hour. Inquire about a special "living history" tour called Gadsby's Time Travels, which is given four or five times a year. Cap off the experience with a meal at the restored colonial-style restaurant (see "Where to Dine," below).

✪ **Lee-Fendall House Museum.** 614 Oronoco St. (at Washington St.). ☎ **703/548-1789.** Admission $4 adults, $2 children 11–17, free for children under 11. Tues–Sat 10am–3:45pm, Sun 1–3:45pm. Tours given on the hour, 10am to 3pm. Closed mid-December through Jan 1 and Thanksgiving.

This handsome Greek Revival–style house is a veritable Lee family museum of furniture, heirlooms, and documents. "Light Horse Harry" Lee never actually lived here, though he was a frequent visitor, as was his good friend, George Washington. He did own the original lot, but sold it to Philip Richard Fendall (himself a Lee on his mother's side), who built the house in 1785. Fendall married three Lee wives, including Harry's first mother-in-law and, later, Harry's sister.

Thirty-seven Lees occupied the house over a period of 118 years (1785 to 1903), and it was from this house that Harry wrote Alexandria's farewell address to Washington, delivered when he passed through town on his way to assume the presidency. (Harry also wrote and delivered, but not at this house, the famous funeral oration to Washington that contained the words: "First in war, first in peace, and first in the hearts of his countrymen.") During the Civil War, the house was seized and used as a Union hospital.

Thirty-minute guided tours interpret the 1850s era of the home and provide insight into Victorian family life. You'll also see the colonial garden with its magnolia and chestnut trees, roses, and boxwood-lined paths. Much of the interior woodwork and glass is original.

The Lyceum. 201 S. Washington St. (off Prince St.). ☎ **703/838-4994.** Free admission. Mon–Sat 10am–5pm, Sun 1–5pm. Closed Jan 1, Thanksgiving, and Dec 25.

This Greek Revival building houses a museum depicting Alexandria's history from the 17th through the 20th century. It features changing exhibits and an ongoing series of lectures, concerts, and educational programs.

Information is also available here about Virginia state attractions, especially Alexandria attractions. You can obtain maps and brochures, and a knowledgeable staff will be happy to answer your questions.

But even without its many attractions, the brick and stucco Lyceum merits a visit. Built in 1839, it was designed in the Doric temple style to serve as a lecture, meeting, and concert hall. It was an important center of Alexandria's cultural life until the Civil War, when Union forces appropriated it for use as a hospital. After the war it became a private residence, and still later it was subdivided for office space. In 1969, however, the city council's use of eminent domain prevented The Lyceum from being demolished in favor of a parking lot.

Old Presbyterian Meeting House. 321 S. Fairfax St. (between Duke and Wolfe sts.). ☎ **703/549-6670.** www.opmh.org. Free admission. Mon–Fri 9am–3pm, Sun services at 8:30am and 11am, with a 10am service added mid-June through mid-Sept.

Presbyterian congregations have worshiped in Virginia since the Rev. Alexander Whittaker converted Pocahontas in Jamestown in 1614. This brick church was built by Scottish pioneers in 1775. Although it wasn't George Washington's church, the Meeting House bell tolled continuously for four days after his death in December 1799, and memorial services were preached from the pulpit here by Presbyterian, Episcopal, and Methodist ministers. According to the Alexandria paper of the day, "The walking being bad to the Episcopal church the funeral sermon of George Washington will be preached at the Presbyterian Meeting House." Two months later, on Washington's birthday, Alexandria citizens marched from Market Square to the church to pay their respects.

Many famous Alexandrians are buried in the church graveyard, including John and Sarah Carlyle, Dr. James Craik (the surgeon who treated—some say killed—Washington, dressed Lafayette's wounds at Brandywine, and ministered to the dying Braddock at Monongahela), and William Hunter, Jr., founder of the St. Andrew's Society of Scottish descendants, to whom bagpipers pay homage on the first Saturday of December. It is also the site of a Tomb of an Unknown Revolutionary War Soldier. Dr. James Muir, minister between 1789 and 1820, lies beneath the sanctuary in his gown and bands.

The original Meeting House was gutted by a lightning fire in 1835, but parishioners restored it in the style of the day a few years later. The present bell, said to be recast from the metal of the old one, was hung in a newly constructed belfry in 1843, and a new organ was installed in 1849. The Meeting House closed its doors in 1889, and for 60 years it was virtually abandoned. But in 1949 it was reborn as a living Presbyterian U.S.A. church, and today the Old Meeting House looks much as it did following its first restoration. The original parsonage, or manse, is still intact. There's no guided tour, but there is a recorded narrative in the graveyard.

Stabler-Leadbeater Apothecary Museum. 105–107 S. Fairfax St. (near King St.). ☎ **703/836-3713.** Admission $2.50 adults, $2 children 11–17, free for children under 11; or buy a block ticket. Mon–Sat 10am–4pm, Sun 1–5pm. Closed major holidays.

When its doors closed in 1933, this landmark drugstore was the second oldest in continuous operation in America. Run for five generations by the same Quaker family (beginning in 1792), its famous early patrons included Robert E. Lee (he purchased the paint for Arlington House here), George Mason, Henry Clay, John C. Calhoun, and George Washington. Gothic Revival decorative elements and Victorian-style doors were added in the 1840s.

Today the apothecary looks much as it did in colonial times, its shelves lined with original handblown gold-leaf–labeled bottles (actually the most valuable collection of antique medicinal bottles in the country), old scales stamped with the royal crown, patent medicines, and equipment for bloodletting. The clock on the rear wall, the porcelain-handled mahogany drawers, and two mortars and pestles all date from about 1790. Among the shop's documentary records is this 1802 order from Mount Vernon: "Mrs. Washington desires Mr. Stabler to send by the bearer a quart bottle of his best Castor Oil and the bill for it."

There are tours Sundays from 1 to 5pm; other times a 10-minute recording will guide you around the displays. The adjoining gift shop uses its proceeds to maintain the apothecary.

✪ **Torpedo Factory.** 105 N. Union St. (between King and Cameron sts. on the waterfront). ☎ **703/838-4565.** Free admission. Daily 10am–5pm; archaeology exhibit area, Tues–Fri 10am–3pm, Sat 10am–5pm, Sun 1–5pm. Closed Easter, July 4, Thanksgiving, Dec 25, and Jan 1.

This block-long, three-story building, once a torpedo shell-case factory, now accommodates some 160 professional artists and craftspeople who create and sell their own works on the premises. Here you can see artists at work in their studios: potters, painters, printmakers, photographers, sculptors, and jewelers, as well as those who make stained-glass windows and fiber art.

On permanent display here are exhibits on Alexandria history provided by Alexandria Archaeology (☎ **703/838-4399**), which is headquartered here and engages in extensive city research. A volunteer or staff member is on hand to answer questions.

SHOPPING

Old Town has hundreds of charming boutiques, antique stores, and gift shops selling everything from souvenir T-shirts to 18th-century reproductions. Some of the most interesting are at the sites, but most are clustered on King and Cameron streets and their connecting cross streets. A guide to antique stores is available at the Visitors Association. Also see chapter 8, which includes some Alexandria shops.

WHERE TO DINE

There are so many fine restaurants in Alexandria that Washingtonians often drive over just to dine here and stroll the cobblestone streets.

EXPENSIVE

Landini Brothers. 115 King St. (between Lee and Union sts.). ☎ **703/836-8404.** Reservations recommended. Main courses $10–$13 at lunch, $17–$25 at dinner. AE, CB, DC, DISC, MC, V. Mon–Sat 11:30am–11pm, Sun 4–10pm. NORTHERN ITALIAN.

The classic, delicate cuisine of Tuscany is featured at this rustic, almost grottolike restaurant with stone walls, a flagstone floor, and rough-hewn beams overhead. It's especially charming by candlelight. Everything is homemade: the pasta, the desserts, and the crusty Italian bread. At lunch you might choose a cold seafood salad or spinach and ricotta-stuffed agnolotti in buttery Parmesan cheese sauce. At dinner, try the prosciutto and melon, the shrimp sautéed in garlic with tangy lemon sauce, or maybe the prime aged beef tenderloin medallions sautéed with garlic, mushrooms, and rosemary in a Barolo wine sauce. Dessert choices include tiramisù and custard-filled fruit tarts.

✪ **Le Refuge.** 127 N. Washington St. (1 block from King St.). ☎ **703/548-4661.** Reservations recommended. Main courses $9–$14 at lunch, $15–$22 at dinner; pretheater $16.95. AE, DC, DISC, MC, V. Mon–Sat 11:30am–2:30pm and 5:30–10pm. FRENCH.

Housed in a cramped, but still appealing, space, Le Refuge is dark and busy and inexorably French. The food is mostly old fashioned: onion soup, bouillabaisse, rack of lamb, and chicken in mustard cream sauce. Perfectly prepared vegetables surround all entrees. Desserts, like everything here, are homemade and include fruit tarts, crème brûlée, and profiteroles.

MODERATE

Bilbo Baggins. 208 Queen St. (at Lee St.). ☎ **703/683-0300.** Main courses $7.50–$12 at lunch/brunch, $15–$18 at dinner. AE, DC, DISC, MC, V. Mon–Fri 11:30am–2:30pm, Sat 11:30am–5:30pm, Sun 11am–2:30pm; Mon–Sat 5:30–10:30pm, Sun 4:30–9:30pm. AMERICAN/CONTINENTAL.

Named, in case you didn't know, for a character in The Hobbit, Bilbo Baggins is a charming two-story restaurant offering scrumptious fresh and homemade fare. Plants flourish in the sunlight throughout the rustic downstairs area and among the stained-glass windows and murals of scenes from The Hobbit upstairs. Candlelit at night, it becomes an even cozier setting. The restaurant adjoins a skylit wine bar with windows overlooking Queen Street.

The restaurant offers many pasta dishes, such as tortellini stuffed with crabmeat, fresh salmon, and dill, in an apple-ginger Chardonnay cream sauce. Other entrees range from grilled salmon and scallops in lemon-dill vinaigrette to chicken breast stuffed with feta cheese, accompanied by potato croquettes or seasonal vegetables. An extensive wine list is available (32 boutique wines are offered by the glass), as are 10 microbrewery draft beers, and out-of-this-world homemade desserts such as the Lord of the Rings—seven layers of raspberry-filled white and chocolate cake topped with chocolate ganache.

East Wind. 809 King St. (between Columbus and Alfred sts.). ☎ **703/836-1515.** Reservations recommended. Main courses $6–$8 at lunch, $8–$14 at dinner; prix-fixe lunch $7. AE, CB, DC, DISC, MC, V. Mon–Fri 11:30am–2:30pm; Mon–Thurs 5:30–10pm, Fri–Sat 5:30–10:30pm, Sun 5:30–9:30pm. VIETNAMESE.

An East Wind meal might begin with an appetizer of cha gio (delicate Vietnamese spring rolls) or a salad of shredded chicken and vegetables mixed with fish sauce. A favorite entree is bo dun: beef tenderloin strips marinated in wine, honey, and spices, rolled in fresh onions, and broiled on bamboo skewers. Also excellent are the grilled lemon chicken or charcoal-broiled shrimp and scallops served on rice vermicelli. Vegetarians will find many appealing selections on East Wind's menu. There's refreshing ginger ice cream for dessert. A good bargain is the prix-fixe lunch, which includes soup, an entree, and coffee or tea.

Gadsby's Tavern. 138 N. Royal St. (at Cameron St.). ☎ **703/548-1288.** Reservations recommended. Main courses $7–$10 at lunch/brunch, $15–$23 at dinner. Half-price portions available on some items for children 12 and under. AE, CB, DC, DISC, MC, V. Mon–Sat 11:30am–3pm, Sun 11am–3pm; nightly 5:30–10pm. COLONIAL AMERICAN.

In the spirit of history, pass through the portals where Washington often came to dine and dance and where he reviewed his troops for the last time. The famous Gadsby's Tavern evokes the 18th century authentically, with period music, wood-plank floors, hurricane-lamp wall sconces, and a rendition of a Hogarth painting over the fireplace (one of several).

Servers are dressed in traditional colonial attire. A strolling violinist entertains Sunday and Monday nights and at Sunday brunch. Tuesday through Saturday night an "18th-century gentleman" regales guests with song and tells the news of the day (200 years ago). When the weather's nice, you can dine in a flagstone courtyard edged with flower beds.

All the fare is homemade, including the sweet Sally Lunn bread baked daily. You might start off with soup from the stockpot served with homemade sourdough crackers, followed by an entree of baked ham and cheese pye (a sort of Early American quiche), or hot roast turkey with giblet gravy and bread and sage stuffing on Sally Lunn bread, or George Washington's favorite: slow-roasted crisp duckling served with fruit dressing and Madeira sauce. For dessert, try the English trifle or creamy buttermilk-custard pye with a hint of lemon. Colonial "coolers" are also available: scuppernong, Wench's Punch, and such. The Sunday brunch menu adds such items as thick slices of toast dipped in a batter of rum and spices, with sausage, hash browns, and hot cinnamon syrup. And a "desserts and libations" menu highlights such favorites as Scottish apple gingerbread and bourbon apple pye, along with a wide selection of beverages.

INEXPENSIVE

The Deli on the Strand. 211 The Strand #5 (entrance on S. Union St. between Duke and Prince sts.). ☎ **703/548-7222.** Sandwiches $2.75–$7. AE, MC, V. Daily 8am–7pm. DELI.

Who could refuse a sunlit picnic in Fort Ward Park (described above); in the Old Town at Founders Park, bordering the Potomac at the foot of Queen Street; or in the Market Square? Buy the fixings at the Deli on the Strand and grab a plot of grass. The divine aroma of baking bread wafts through the air, and you can get reasonably priced cold-cut sandwiches on it, as well as muffins, brownies, and (on the weekend) bagels. Also available are homemade seafood or pasta salads, cheeses, beer, wine, and champagne. There are a few picnic tables outside under an awning.

✪ **Hard Times Café.** 1404 King St. (near S. West St.). ☎ **703/683-5340.** Reservations not accepted. Main courses $4–$7. AE, MC, V. Sun–Thurs 11am–10pm, Fri–Sat 11am–11pm. AMERICAN/SOUTHWESTERN.

Will Rogers once said he "always judged a town by the quality of its chili." He would have loved Alexandria, where the fabulous Hard Times Café serves up top-secret-recipe homemade chilis and fresh-from-the-oven cornbread. It's a laid-back hangout where waiters and waitresses wear jeans and T-shirts; country music is always playing on the 100-CD jukebox; and the Texas decor features Lone Star flags, a longhorn steer hide overhead, and historic photos of the Old West on the walls. The chili comes in three varieties: Texas, Cincinnati (cooked with sweeter spices, including cinnamon), and vegetarian. Try it Texas-style: coarse-ground chuck simmered for 6 hours with special spices in beef sauce. If chili isn't your thing, order grilled chicken breast, a burger, or salad. Wash it all down with one of the menu's 30 beers, including a Hard Times label and many selections from western microbreweries. The Hard Times has garnered many a chili cookoff award, and CHILI-U.S.A., a resolution before Congress "to make chili the official food of this great nation," was conceived by Oklahoma lobbyists over a "bowl of red" here. The Colorado flag overhead was brought in by a senator from that state.

La Madeleine. 500 King St. (at S. Pitt St.). ☎ **703/739-2854.** Main courses $3–$8 at lunch, $7–$11 at dinner. AE, DISC, MC, V. Sun–Thurs 7am–10pm, Fri–Sat 7am–11pm. FRENCH CAFE.

Part of a self-service chain, this place is charming nonetheless. Its French-country interior has a beamed ceiling, bare oak floors, a wood-burning stove, and maple hutches displaying crockery and pewter mugs. The walls are hung with copper pots and antique farm implements.

Come in the morning for fresh-baked croissants, Danish, scones, muffins, and brioches, or a heartier bacon-and-eggs plate. Throughout the day, there are delicious salads (such as roasted vegetables and rigatoni), sandwiches (including a traditional croque monsieur), and hot dishes ranging from quiche and pizza to rotisserie chicken with a Caesar salad. After 5pm, additional choices include pastas and specials such as beef bourguignonne and salmon in dill cream sauce, both served with a crispy potato galette and sautéed broccoli. There are about 2 dozen fabulous fresh-baked French desserts, including yummy fruit tarts and a chocolate, vanilla, and praline triple-layer cheesecake with graham-cracker crust. Wine and beer is served.

✪ **South Austin Grill.** 801 King St. (at S. Columbus St.). ☎ **703/684-8969.** Reservations not accepted. $8–$15. AE, DC, DISC, MC, V. Mon–Thurs 11:30am–11pm, Fri 11:30am–midnight, Sat 11am–midnight, Sun 11am–10pm. TEX-MEX.

One of five Austin Grills in the area, this one is larger than the original outpost in Glover Park. The two dining floors are cheerfully decorated, with roomy booths and walls hung with Austin music club posters and other Tex-Mex-abilia. A corner location permits lots of sunlight to stream in.

Otherwise, menu, music, and ambience are the same as at the Glover Park location; see chapter 6 listing for that information.

The Tea Cosy. 119 S. Royal St. (between King and Prince sts.). ☎ **703/836-8181.** Reservations not accepted. Tea cakes and sandwiches $2–$5; full afternoon tea $10.50; main courses $4–$10. DISC, MC, V. Sat–Thurs 10am–6pm, Fri 10am–7pm. BRITISH TEAROOM.

This authentic British tearoom has posters advertising Bovril and Colman's Mustard on whitewashed walls, a beamed ceiling, and a magazine rack stocked with British periodicals and newspapers. Tables are set with pretty floral-patterned place mats. A shop in the back sells archetypal British foodstuffs: digestive biscuits, ginger wine, Irish oatmeal, chutney, and such.

Come in for a full afternoon tea, including assorted tea sandwiches and oven-fresh scones (date/pecan, lemon, raisin, apricot, or cheese) served with jams and Devonshire cream. Crumpets, shortbread, and trifle are also à la carte options. For heartier meals, your choices include steak-and-kidney pie, shepherd's pie, Cornish pasty, cheese-and-vegetable pasty, Scottish sausage rolls, and bangers and mash. Everything, including vegetables, is fresh and homemade. There are daily dessert specials such as apple-blackberry pie with custard. British ales and beers, hard cider, and a soft drink called orange quosh are served.

Appendix A:
Washington, D.C., in Depth

Two hundred years ago, the world wondered why America had chosen this swampy locale as its capital. It took its first hundred years for Washington to evolve from bumpkin backwater status to an international hub of power, diplomacy and beauty. Today, Washington has fully commanded center-stage in both literature and film. This section will provide an overview of the history and culture associated with this bustling city.

1 History 101

A WANDERING CONGRESS It all began in 1783, when 250 Revolutionary War soldiers, understandably angered because Congress was ignoring their petitions for back pay, stormed the temporary capitol in Philadelphia to demand justice. The citizens of Philadelphia sympathized with the soldiers and ignored congressional pleas for protection; as the soldiers rioted outside, lawmakers huddled inside the State House behind locked doors. When the soldiers finally calmed down and returned to their barracks, Congress decided it would be prudent to move itself to Princeton. Lawmakers also decided they needed a capital city whose business was government and the protection thereof.

This decision to relocate was not a new one. Congress had been so nomadic during its first decade that when a statue of George Washington was commissioned in 1783, satirist Francis Hopkinson suggested putting it on wheels so it could follow the government around. Before permanently settling in Washington, Congress convened in New York, Baltimore,

Dateline

- **1608** Capt. John Smith sails up Potomac River from Jamestown; for the next 100 years, Irish-Scotch settlers colonize the area.
- **1783** Continental Congress proposes new "Federal Town"; both North and South vie for it.
- **1790** A compromise is reached: If the South pays off the North's Revolutionary War debts, the new capital will be situated in its region.
- **1791** French engineer Pierre Charles L'Enfant designs the capital city but is fired within a year.
- **1792** Cornerstone is laid for Executive Mansion.
- **1793** Construction begins on the Capitol.
- **1800** First wing of the Capitol completed; Congress moves from Philadelphia; Pres. John Adams moves into Executive Mansion.
- **1801** Library of Congress established.

continues

- **1812** War with England.
- **1814** British burn Washington.
- **1817** Executive Mansion rebuilt, its charred walls painted white; becomes known as White House.
- **1822** Population reaches 33,000.
- **1829** Smithsonian Institution founded for the "increase and diffusion of knowledge."
- **1861** Civil War; Washington becomes North's major supply depot.
- **1865** Capitol dome completed; Lee surrenders to Grant April 8; Lincoln assassinated at Ford's Theatre April 14.
- **1871** Alexander "Boss" Shepherd turns Washington into a showplace, using many of L'Enfant's plans.
- **1900** Population reaches about 300,000.
- **1901** McMillan Commission plans development of Mall from Capitol to Lincoln Memorial.
- **1907** Union Station opens, largest train station in country.
- **1912** Cherry trees, a gift from Japan, planted in Tidal Basin.
- **1914** World War I begins.
- **1922** Lincoln Memorial completed.
- **1941** First plane lands at National Airport; United States declares war on Japan.
- **1943** Pantheon-inspired Jefferson Memorial and Pentagon completed.
- **1960** Population declines for first time, from 800,000 to 764,000.
- **1963** More than 200,000 March on Washington, hear Martin Luther King's "I Have a Dream" speech supporting civil rights.
- **1971** John F. Kennedy Center for Performing Arts opens.
- **1976** Metro, city's first subway system, opens in time for Bicentennial.
- **1982** Vietnam Veterans Memorial erected in Constitution Gardens.

continues

Philadelphia, Lancaster, Princeton, Annapolis, York, and Trenton.

A DEAL MADE OVER DINNER

When Congress proposed that a city be designed and built for the sole purpose of housing the government of the new nation, fresh difficulties arose. There was a general feeling that wherever the capital might be built, a great commercial center would blossom; therefore, many cities vied for the honor. Then, too, northerners were strongly opposed to a southern capital—and vice versa. Finally, after seven years of bickering, New Yorker Alexander Hamilton and Virginian Thomas Jefferson worked out a compromise over dinner one night in New York. The North would support a southern site for the capital in return for the South's assumption of debts incurred by the northern states during the Revolutionary War. As a further sop to the North, it was agreed that the seat of government would remain in Philadelphia through 1800 to allow suitable time for surveying, purchasing land, and constructing government buildings.

ENTER L'ENFANT TERRIBLE An act passed in 1790 specified a site "not exceeding 10 miles square" to be located on the Potomac. President and experienced surveyor George Washington, charged with selecting the exact site, chose a part of the Potomac Valley where the river becomes tidal and is joined by the Anacostia. Maryland gladly provided 69¼ square miles and Virginia 30¾ for the new Federal District. (In 1846, Virginia's territorial contribution was returned to the state.) The District today covers about 67 square miles.

President Washington hired French military engineer Pierre Charles L'Enfant to lay out the federal city. It has since been said that "it would have been hard to find a man better qualified artistically and less fitted by temperament" for the job. L'Enfant arrived in 1791 and immediately declared Jenkins Hill (today Capitol Hill) "a pedestal waiting for a monument." He surveyed every inch of the designated Federal District and began creating his vision by selecting dominant sites for major buildings. He designed broad, 160-foot-wide avenues radiating from squares and circles centered on monumental sculptures and fountains. The Capitol, the "presidential palace," and an equestrian statue—the last to be erected where the Washington Monument stands today—were to be the city's focal points. Pennsylvania Avenue would be the major thoroughfare, and the Mall was conceived as a bustling ceremonial avenue of embassies and other distinguished buildings.

L'Enfant's plan dismayed landowners who had been promised $66.66 per acre for land donated for buildings, while land for avenues was to be donated free; of the 6,661 acres to be included in the boundaries of the federal city, about half would be avenues and the 2-mile-long Mall.

A more personable man might have won over the reluctant landowners and commissioners, inspiring them with his dreams and his passion, but L'Enfant exhibited only a peevish and condescending secretiveness that alienated one and all. A year after he had been hired, L'Enfant was fired. Congress offered him $2,500 compensation for his year of work, and James Monroe urged him to accept a professorship at West Point. Insulted, he spurned all offers, suing the government for $95,500 instead. He lost and died a pauper in 1825. In 1909, in belated recognition of his services, his remains were brought to Arlington National Cemetery. Some 118 years after he had conceived it, his vision of the federal city finally had become a reality.

- **1991** Population drops to 600,000.
- **1993** U.S. Holocaust Memorial Museum opens near Mall.
- **1994** Marion Barry is elected to a fourth term as mayor, after serving time in prison.
- **1995** Korean War Veterans Memorial is dedicated. Pennsylvania Avenue closed to vehicular traffic in front of the White House on security grounds.
- **1996** The city goes through tough times, plagued by municipal and federal budget woes.
- **1997** Federal government offers aid package to save D.C. from bankruptcy. Franklin Delano Roosevelt Memorial is dedicated.
- **1998** White House beset by sex scandal. In December, the House of Representatives impeaches the president.
- **1999** Washington, DC, inaugurates Mayor Anthony Williams. In February, the Senate acquits the president.

HOME NOT-SO-SWEET HOME In 1800, government officials (106 representatives and 32 senators) arrived according to schedule, ready to settle into their new home. What they found bore little resemblance to a city. "One might take a ride of several hours within the precincts without meeting with a single individual to disturb one's meditation," commented one early resident. Pennsylvania Avenue was a mosquito-infested swamp, and there were fewer than 400 habitable houses. Disgruntled Secretary of the Treasury Oliver Wolcott wrote his wife, "I do not perceive how the members of Congress can possibly secure lodgings, unless they will consent to live like Scholars in a college or Monks in a monastery . . . ." The solution was a boom in boarding houses.

Abigail Adams was dismayed at the condition of her new home, the presidential mansion. The damp caused her rheumatism to act up, the main stairs had not yet been constructed, not a single room was finished, and there were not even enough logs for all the fireplaces. And since there was "not the least fence, yard, or other convenience," she hung the presidential laundry in the unfinished East Room. To attend presidential affairs or to visit one another, Washington's early citizens had to drive through mud and slush, their vehicles often becoming embedded in bogs and gullies—not a pleasant state of affairs, but one that would continue for many decades.

There were many difficulties in building the capital. Money, as always, was in short supply, as were materials and labor, with the result that the home of the world's most enlightened democracy was built largely by slaves. And always, in the background, there was talk of abandoning the city and starting over somewhere else.

REDCOATS REDUX   Then came the War of 1812. At first fighting centered on Canada and the West—both too far away to affect daily life in the capital. (In the early 1800s, it was a 33-hour ride from Washington, D.C., to Philadelphia—if you made good time.) In May 1813, the flamboyant British Rear Admiral Cockburn sent word to the Executive Mansion that "he would make his bow" in the Madisons' drawing room shortly. On August 23, 1814, alarming news reached the capital: The British had landed troops in Maryland. On August 24, James Madison was at the front, most of the populace had fled, and Dolly Madison created a legend by refusing to leave the President's mansion without Gilbert Stuart's famous portrait of George Washington. As the British neared her gates, she calmly wrote a blow-by-blow description to her sister:

> Our kind friend, Mr. Carroll, has come to hasten my departure, and is in a very bad humour with me because I insist on waiting until the large picture of General Washington is secured, and it requires to be unscrewed from the wall. This process was found too tedious for these perilous moments; I have ordered the frame to be broken, and the canvas taken out; it is done. . . . And now, dear sister, I must leave this house, or the retreating army will make me a prisoner in it, by filling up the road I am directed to take.

When the British arrived early that evening, they found dinner set up on the table (Dolly had hoped for the best until the end), and, according to some accounts, ate it before torching the mansion. They also burned the Capitol, the Library of Congress, and newly built ships and naval stores. A thunderstorm later that night saved the city from total destruction, while a tornado the next day added to the damage but daunted the British troops.

It seemed that the new capital was doomed. Margaret Bayard Smith, wife of the owner of the influential *National Intelligencer,* privately lamented, "I do not suppose the Government will ever return to Washington. All those whose property was invested in that place, will be reduced to general poverty. . . . The consternation about us is general. The despondency still greater." But the *Intelligencer* was among the printed voices speaking out against even a temporary move. Editorials warned that it would be a "treacherous breach of faith" with those who had "laid out fortunes in the purchase of property in and about the city." To move the capital would be "kissing the rod an enemy has wielded." Washingtonian pride rallied, and the city was saved once again. Still, it was a close call; Congress came within nine votes of abandoning the place!

In 1815, leading citizens erected a brick building in which Congress could meet in relative comfort until the Capitol was restored. The Treaty of Ghent, establishing peace with Great Britain, was ratified at Octagon House, where the Madisons were temporarily ensconced. And Thomas Jefferson donated his own books to replace the destroyed contents of the Library of Congress. Confidence was restored, and the city began to prosper. When the Madisons moved into the rebuilt presidential mansion, its exterior had been painted gleaming white to cover the charred walls. From then on, it would be known as the White House.

THE CITY OF MAGNIFICENT INTENTIONS   Between the War of 1812 and the Civil War, few people evinced any great enthusiasm for Washington. European visitors in particular looked at the capital and found it wanting. It was still a provincial backwater, with Pennsylvania Avenue and the

Mall remaining muddy messes inhabited by pigs, goats, cows, and geese. Many were repelled by the slave auctions openly taking place in the backyard of the White House. The best that could be said—though nobody said it—was that the young capital was picturesque. Meriwether Lewis kept the bears he captured during his 4,000-mile expedition up the Missouri in cages on the president's lawn. Native American chiefs in full regalia were often seen negotiating with the white man's government. Matching them in visual splendor were magnificently attired European court visitors.

The only foreigner who praised Washington was Lafayette, who visited in 1825 and was feted with lavish balls and dinners throughout his stay. Charles Dickens gave us the raspberry in 1842:

> It is sometimes called the City of Magnificent Distances, but it might with greater propriety be termed the City of Magnificent Intentions . . . Spacious avenues, that begin in nothing and lead nowhere; streets, miles long, that only want houses, roads, and inhabitants; public buildings that need but a public to be complete; and ornaments of great thoroughfares, which only lack great thoroughfares to ornament—are its leading features.

Tobacco chewing and sloppy senatorial spitting particularly appalled him:

> Both houses are handsomely carpeted, but the state to which these carpets are reduced by the universal disregard of the spittoon with which every honorable member is accommodated, and the extraordinary improvements on the pattern which are squirted and dabbled upon it in every direction, do not admit of being described. I will merely observe, that I strongly recommend all strangers not to look at the floor; and if they happen to drop anything . . . not to pick it up with an ungloved hand on any account.

But Dickens's critique was mild when compared with Anthony Trollope's, who declared Washington in 1860 "as melancholy and miserable a town as the mind of man can conceive."

A NATION DIVIDED During the Civil War, the capital became an armed camp. It was the principal supply depot for the Union Army and an important medical center. Parks became campgrounds, churches became hospitals, and forts ringed the town. The population doubled from 60,000 to 120,000, including about 40,000 former slaves who streamed into the city seeking federal protection. More than 3,000 soldiers slept in the Capitol building, and a bakery was set up in the basement. The streets were filled with the wounded, and Walt Whitman became a familiar figure, making daily rounds to succor the ailing soldiers. In spite of everything, Lincoln insisted that work on the incomplete Capitol be continued. "If people see the Capitol going on, it is a sign we intend the Union shall go on," he said. When the giant dome was finished in 1863 and a 35-star flag was flown overhead, Capitol Hill's field battery fired a 35-gun salute, honoring the Union's then 35 states.

There was joy in Washington and an 800-gun salute in April 1865, when news of the fall of the Confederacy reached the capital. The joy was short-lived, however. Five days after Appomattox, President Lincoln was shot at Ford's Theatre while attending a performance of *Our American Cousin*. Black replaced the festive tri-colored draperies decorating the town, and Washington went into mourning.

The war had enlarged the city's population while doing nothing to improve its facilities. Agrarian, uneducated ex-slaves stayed on, and poverty, unemployment, and disease were rampant. A red-light district remained, the parks were trodden bare, and tenement slums mushroomed within a stone's throw of the Capitol.

LED BY A SHEPHERD   Whereas L'Enfant had been aloof and introverted, his glorious vision was not forgotten, finally being implemented 70 years later by Alexander "Boss" Shepherd, a swashbuckling and friendly man. A real estate speculator who had made his money in a plumbing firm, Shepherd shouldered a musket in the Union Army and became one of General Ulysses S. Grant's closest intimates. When Grant became president, he wanted to appoint Shepherd governor, but blue-blooded opposition ran too high. Washington high society considered him a parvenu and feared his ambitions for civic leadership. In response, Grant named the more popular Henry D. Cooke (a secret Shepherd ally) governor and appointed Shepherd vice-president of the Board of Public Works. No one was fooled. Shepherd made all the governor's decisions, and a joke went around the capital: "Why is the new governor like a sheep? Because he is led by A. Shepherd." He became the official governor in 1873.

Shepherd vowed that his "comprehensive plan of improvement" would make the city a showplace. But an engineer he wasn't—occasionally, newly paved streets had to be torn up because he had forgotten to install sewers. But he was a first-rate politician who knew how to accomplish his goals. He began by hiring an army of laborers and starting them on projects all over town. Congress would have had to halt work on half-finished sidewalks, streets, and sewers throughout the District in order to stop him. It would have been a mess. The press liked and supported the colorful Shepherd; however, people forced out of their homes because they couldn't pay the high assessments for improvements hated him. Between 1871 and 1874, he established parks, paved and lighted the streets, installed sewers, filled in sewage-laden Tiber Creek, and planted more than 50,000 trees. He left the city bankrupt—more than $20 million in debt. But he got the job done.

L'ENFANT REBORN   Through the end of the 19th century, Washington continued to make great aesthetic strides. The Washington Monument, long a truncated obelisk and major eyesore, was finally dedicated in 1885. Pennsylvania Avenue was becoming the ceremonial thoroughfare L'Enfant had envisioned, and important buildings were completed one after another. Shepherd had done a great deal, but much was still left undone. In 1887, L'Enfant's "Plan for the City of Washington" was resurrected. In 1900, Michigan Senator James McMillan—a retired railroad mogul with architectural and engineering knowledge—determined to complete the job L'Enfant had started a century earlier. A tireless lobbyist for government-sponsored municipal improvements, he persuaded his colleagues to appoint an advisory committee to create "the city beautiful." At his personal expense, McMillan sent this illustrious committee—landscapist Frederick Law Olmsted (designer of New York's Central Park), sculptor Augustus Saint-Gaudens, and noted architects Daniel Burnham and Charles McKim—to Europe for 7 weeks to study the landscaping and architecture of that continent's great capitals. Assembled at last was a group that combined L'Enfant's artistic genius and Shepherd's political savvy.

"Make no little plans," counseled Burnham. "They have no magic to stir men's blood, and probably themselves will not be realized. Make big plans, aim high in hope and work, remembering that a noble and logical diagram once recorded will never die, but long after we are gone will be a living thing, asserting itself with ever growing insistency."

The committee's big plans—almost all of which were accomplished—included the development of a complete park system, selection of sites for government buildings, and the designing of the Lincoln Memorial, the Arlington Memorial Bridge, and the Reflecting Pool (the last inspired by Versailles). They also got to work on improving the Mall; their first step was to remove the tracks, train sheds, and stone depot constructed there by the Baltimore and Potomac Railroad. In return, Congress authorized money to build the monumental Union Station, whose design was inspired by Rome's Baths of Diocletian.

Throughout the McMillan Commission years, the House was under the hostile leadership of Speaker "Uncle Joe" Cannon of Illinois who, among other things, swore he would "never let a memorial to Abraham Lincoln be erected in that goddamned swamp" (West Potomac Park). Cannon caused some problems and delays, but on the whole the committee's prestigious membership added weight to their usually accepted recommendations. McMillan, however, did not live to see most of his dreams accomplished. He died in 1902.

By the 20th century, Washington was no longer an object of ridicule. The capital was coming into its own as a finely designed city of sweeping vistas studded with green parks and grand architecture. Congress's 1899 mandate limiting building heights in downtown Washington ensured the prominence of landmarks in their landscape. As the century progressed, the city seamlessly incorporated additional architectural marvels, including the Library of Congress, Union Station, and the Corcoran Gallery, which were all built around the turn of the century; several more Smithsonian museums and the Lincoln Memorial were completed in 1922. A Commission of Fine Arts was appointed in 1910 by President Taft to create monuments and fountains, and, thanks to Mrs. Taft, the famous cherry trees presented to the United States by the Japanese in 1912 were planted in the Tidal Basin. During the Great Depression in the 1930s, FDR's Works Progress Administration—WPA, We Do Our Part—put the unemployed to work erecting public buildings and artists to work beautifying them. By the 1930s, too, increasing numbers of automobiles—nearly 200,000—were traversing Washington's wide avenues, joining the electric streetcars that had been in use since about 1890.

Washington's population, meanwhile, continued to grow, spurred by the influx of workers remaining after each of the world wars. In 1950, the city's population reached a zenith of more than 800,000 residents, an estimated 60% of which were black. At the same time that Washington was establishing itself as a global power, the city was gaining renown among African-Americans as a hub of black culture, education, and identity. From the 1920s to the 1960s, Washington drew the likes of Cab Calloway, Duke Ellington, and Pearl Bailey, who performed at speakeasies and theaters along a stretch of U Street called the Black Broadway. (The reincarnated "New U," as it is dubbed, now attracts buppies, yuppies, and restless youth to its nightclubs and bars.) Howard University, created in 1867, distinguished itself as the nation's most comprehensive center for the higher education of blacks. And when the Civil Rights movement gained momentum throughout the country in the 1960s and '70s, Washington's large black presence (nearly 75% of the city's overall population) and activist spirit were instrumental in furthering the cause.

On August 28, 1963, black and white Washingtonians joined the ranks of the more than 200,000 who "Marched on Washington" to ensure passage of the Civil Rights Act. It was at this event that Rev. Martin Luther King, Jr., delivered his "I Have a Dream" speech at the Lincoln Memorial, where

41 years earlier, during the memorial's dedication ceremony, black officials were required to stand and watch across the road, segregated from the whites. When King was assassinated on April 4, 1968, rioting erupted here as it did in many cities around the country.

Ever since, black and white Washingtonians have continued to thrash out race relations in a city whose population has declined to a little more than 530,000, about 60% of which now is African-American. But Washington is on an upswing, as the section "Washington Today" details. Mayor Anthony Williams, an African-American, was inaugurated in January 1999, and has focused his efforts to improve the city, despite criticism that he acts unilaterally rather than collaboratively.

Washington, the federal city, proceeds apace, adding more jewels to its crown. In 1989, renovation of the city's magnificent Union Station was completed. Its brilliant architect, Daniel Burnham, also designed the palatial City Post Office Building which, in 1993, became part of the Smithsonian complex as the National Postal Museum. The same year saw the opening of the United States Holocaust Memorial Museum, adjoining the Mall. In 1995, the Korean War Veterans Memorial was dedicated. Washington's fourth presidential monument—and the first in more than half a century—was dedicated in May 1997, to honor Franklin Delano Roosevelt; it is the first memorial in Washington purposely designed to be totally wheelchair accessible. Finally, the Women in Military Service Memorial, next to Arlington Cemetery, was inaugurated in October 1997, followed, in June 1998, by a Civil War memorial recognizing the efforts of African-American soldiers who fought for the Union.

2 Hollywood on the Potomac

On a brisk April Saturday morning, police cars and orange cones block 15th Street NW, between Pennsylvania Avenue and G Street NW. It's early still, about 9am, but the sidewalks are already bustling with activity. Otherwise nondescript, T-shirt-and-jeans attired types strut about the sectioned-off area, talking into their headsets or walkie-talkies; roadies remove camera equipment from the backs of huge trucks parked along the curb. A huddle of brown canvas directors' chairs ("Director Mark Pellington, Producer Peter Samuelson") take up a corner of the sidewalk across from the Treasury Building at F Street, and this seems to be center stage, where men and women in black shades and jeans jackets are congregating, greeting each other with hugs, talking, and gesticulating. Out of this cluster of VIPs steps actor Jeff Bridges, who hops nimbly into a shiny black car as bystanders gather and gape. The car pulls away and people start waving to Bridges, who responds with a smile and a goofy wagging up-and-down of the wrist out the window.

It's a movie shoot: *Arlington Road,* whose plot centers on domestic terrorism, stars Jeff Bridges as a college professor who teaches history, including a class on terrorism, and Tim Robbins in the role of the mad domestic terrorist. If you've seen the movie, you may remember the chase scene, which takes in a sweeping view of the Hotel Washington, the imposing, block-long Treasury Building, and the Washington Monument. The scene, which lasts no more than a couple of minutes in the finished film, takes at least a day to shoot, and that is what is going on here.

Washingtonians, long used to stopped traffic and sectioned-off streets for political demonstrations, presidential cavalcades, and historic visits by world dignitaries, are now growing accustomed to traffic jams caused by movie shoots; *Arlington Road* is just one of many productions that are using

Washington as a location for movies, TV, commercials, music videos, documentaries, you name it. All in all, these projects create $42 million in revenue for the city annually, according to Crystal Palmer, director of The Washington, D.C., Office of Motion Picture and TV Development. Palmer reports that, on the average, 6 films and anywhere from 10 to 35 TV productions are shot here each year, although the number of films tends to go up in election years: 14 movies were made here in 1996, including *Mars Attacks, The People vs. Larry Flynt, Absolute Power,* and *Independence Day.* Among the films shot here in 1999 were *The Nutty Professor II, Rocky and Bulwinkle,* and *The Hollow Men.* When you are visiting Washington, you may well stumble upon a filming or taping in progress, especially since the capital's most famous tourist attractions are also producers' favorite backdrops. Nothing packs a Washington punch like a flash of the White House on the screen.

But if movie- and TV series–making are currently on the rise in Washington, the practice of using Washington—and politicians—as a subject for films has long been fashionable. Starting in 1915 with *Birth of a Nation,* the lineup includes *Mr. Smith Goes to Washington* (1939), *All the King's Men* (1949), *Advise and Consent* (1962), *Dr. Strangelove* (1963), *All the President's Men* (1976), *Broadcast News* (1987), *Bob Roberts* (1992), *Nixon* (1995), and *Contact* (1997), to name just a few.

Given Washington's popularity among TV and film producers, its sometime nickname, "Hollywood on the Potomac," seems apt. The funny thing is, though, that the appellation derives not from the capital's frequent use as a film location or subject, but from its magnetic appeal for Hollywood celebrities. Although Ronald Reagan was the actor-turn-president, the concept is firmly associated with our current president, Bill Clinton.

Barbra Streisand, music mogul David Geffen, and studio chairman Lew Wasserman are among those who have raised major bucks for Clinton's campaigns. The most honored friends of Bill ("FOBs") have been invited to spend the night in the Lincoln Bedroom (guests have included Candice Bergen and Richard Dreyfuss). Clinton's inaugural balls in 1993 and 1997 brought so many Hollywood types to Washington that for days it was difficult to wander anywhere in the city without spotting a star: Kim Basinger coming out of H.H. Leonards' B&B on O Street, Gregory Hines puffing on a cigar in the Fairfax Bar of the Ritz-Carlton (now the Westin Fairfax), Kevin Costner walking down a hallway of the Willard. Throughout the president's impeachment proceedings, no constituency was more vociferous in its support than the Hollywood crowd.

As much as Clinton has enjoyed hobnobbing with Hollywood stars and moguls, he never would have wished himself portrayed on screen in quite the ways Tinseltown has shown him. In 1998, the American public witnessed a truly surreal moment when the film *Wag the Dog,* about an administration's attempts to distract the American people from a scandal involving the president's dalliance with a young "Firefly Girl," was released only weeks before allegations about Clinton's affair with intern Monica Lewinsky hit the papers. The movie *Primary Colors,* based on the book about a womanizing Clinton-like governor running for president, seemed like old news when it opened shortly after *Wag the Dog,* which may explain why turnout was less than expected.

The phrase "Hollywood on the Potomac" also refers to another growing phenomenon, the use of "star" testimony on Capitol Hill. Depending on the type of hearings being held, you might see anyone as you tour the Capitol, from Andie MacDowell lobbying for more oil pipeline regulations, to Alec Baldwin pushing for federal funding of the arts.

Politicians, on the whole, rarely mind doing a star turn for the cameras. Next time you watch a movie or turn on the TV, be on the lookout. You may spot Sen. Barbara Boxer popping up in the movie *Deep Impact,* the James Carville-Mary Matalin duo playing themselves in American Express commercials, or even the likes of Gen. Colin Powell and Sen. John Glenn appearing, for some odd reason, on stage during the television presentation of the Academy Awards.

When you think about it, it's easy to see similarities between politics and moviemaking. Both businesses are about creating stars, wooing the public, building power bases, fanning egos. It's a connection that Hollywood impressarios and politicians themselves perceive. In a Maureen Dowd column that appeared last year in the *New York Times* on the subject of Warren Beatty's then-new film, *Bulworth,* Dowd quotes Beatty as saying: "Washington is Hollywood. The techniques and events and the people are the same. As though if the actors left the party, there'd be a more serious discussion? Dream on." Amid rumors of Beatty considering a run for the presidency himself in 2000, the line between politics and Hollywood blurs even more.

3 Recommended Reading

You can put yourself in the mood for a visit to Washington by reading some great novels set in Washington, memoirs and histories by some of the city's more famous residents, and other guide books whose topics supplement what you've learned in these pages.

Fiction-lovers might pick up books by Ward Just, including his collection of stories *The Congressman Who Loved Flaubert;* Ann Berne's *A Crime in the Neighborhood;* Marita Golden's *The Edge of Heaven;* Allen Drury's *Advise and Consent;* or one of the growing number of mysteries whose plot revolves around the capital, such as Margaret Truman's series (*Murder at the Smithsonian, Murder at the Kennedy Center,* and so on).

If you're keen on learning more about the history of the nation's capital and about the people who have lived here, try Arthur Schlesinger's *The Birth of the Nation,* F. Cary's *Urban Odyssey,* David Brinkley's *Washington at War,* former Washington Post publisher Katharine Graham's memoir, *Personal History,* and Paul Dickson's *On This Spot,* which traces the history of the city by revealing exactly what took place at specific locations—"on this spot"—in years gone by, neighborhood by neighborhood.

Finally, to find out more about the architecture of Washington, pick up a copy of the *AIA Guide to the Architecture of Washington, D.C.,* by Christopher Weeks; to discover information about Washington's parks, hiking trails, and other green spaces, look for *Natural Washington* by Richard Berman and Deborah Gerhard; and for a humorous read that, nevertheless, may send chills up your spine, purchase a copy of *Ghosts, Washington's Most Famous Ghost Stories* by John Alexander.

Appendix B: Useful Toll-Free Numbers & Web Sites

AIRLINES

Air Canada
☎ 800/776-3000
www.aircanada.ca

Air France
☎ 800/237-2747
wwwairfranc.com

American Airlines
☎ 800/433-7300
www.americanair.com

British Airways
☎ 800/247-9297
☎ 0345/222-111 in Britain
www.british-airways.com

Canadian Airlines International
☎ 800/426-7000
www.cdnair.ca

Continental Airlines
☎ 800/525-0280
www.flycontinental.com

Delta Air Lines
☎ 800/221-1212
www.delta-air.com

El Al Israel
☎ 800/223-6700
www.elal.co.il

KLM Royal Dutch
☎ 800/374-7747
www.klm.nl

Lufthansa
☎ 800/645-3880
www.lufthansa.com

Northwest Airlines
☎ 800/225-2525
www.nwa.com

Southwest Airlines
☎ 800/435-9792
www.southwest.com

Trans World Airlines (TWA)
☎ 800/221-2000
www2.twa.com

United Airlines
☎ 800/241-6522
www.ual.com

US Airways
☎ 800/428-4322
www.usairways.com

Virgin Atlantic Airways
☎ 800/862-8621 in
    Continental U.S.
☎ 0293/747-747 in Britain
www.fly.virgin.com

CAR-RENTAL AGENCIES

Alamo
☎ 800/327-9633
www.goalamo.com

Avis
☎ 800/331-1212 in
    Continental U.S.
☎ 800/TRY-AVIS in Canada
www.avis.com

Budget
☎ 800/527-0700
www.budgetrentacar.com

Dollar
☎ 800/800-4000
www.dollarcar.com

Enterprise
☎ 800/325-8007
www.pickenterprise.com

Hertz
☎ 800/654-3131
www.hertz.com

National
☎ 800/CAR-RENT
www.nationalcar.com

Thrifty
☎ 800/367-2277
www.thrifty.com

MAJOR HOTEL & MOTEL CHAINS

Clarion Hotels
☎ 800/CLARION
www.hotelchoice.com/cgi-bin/res/
　webres?clarion.html

Courtyard by Marriott
☎ 800/321-2211
www.courtyard.com

Hilton Hotels
☎ 800/HILTONS
www.hilton.com

Holiday Inn
☎ 800/HOLIDAY
www.holiday-inn.com

Hyatt Hotels & Resorts
☎ 800/228-9000
www.hyatt.com

ITT Sheraton
☎ 800/325-3535
www.sheraton.com

Marriott Hotels
☎ 800/228-9290
www.marriott.com

Radisson Hotels International
☎ 800/333-3333
www.radisson.com

Red Roof Inns
☎ 800/843-7663
www.redroof.com

Frommer's Online Directory

by Michael Shapiro

Michael Shapiro is the author of *Michael Shapiro's Internet Travel Planner* (The Globe Pequot Press).

Frommer's Online Directory is a new feature designed to help you take advantage of the Internet to better plan your trip. Part 1 lists general Internet resources that can make any trip easier, such as sites for booking airline tickets. In Part 2 you'll find some top online guides for Washington, D.C. Please keep in mind that this is not a comprehensive list, but rather a discriminating selection to get you started. We've awarded stars to the best sites, which are earned, not paid for. Finally, remember this is a press-time snapshot of leading Web sites—some undoubtedly will have evolved, changed, or moved by the time you read this.

1 The Top Travel-Planning Web Sites

Among the most popular travel sites are online travel agencies. The top agencies, including Expedia, Preview Travel, and Travelocity, offer an array of tools that are valuable even if you don't book online. You can check flight schedules, hotel availability, car rental prices, or even get paged if your flight is delayed.

While online agencies have come a long way over the past few years, they don't always yield the best price. Unlike a travel agent, for example, they're unlikely to tell you that you can save money by flying a day earlier or a day later. On the other hand, if you're looking for a bargain fare, you might find something online that an agent wouldn't take the time to dig up. Because airline commissions have been cut, a travel agent may not find it worthwhile spending half an hour trying to find you the best deal. On the Net you can be your own agent and take all the time you want.

Online booking sites aren't the only places to book airline tickets— all major airlines have their own Web sites and often offer incentives, such as bonus frequent flyer miles or Net-only discounts, for buying online. These incentives have helped airlines capture the majority of the online booking market. According to Jupiter Communications, online agencies such as Travelocity booked about 80% of tickets purchased online in 1996, but by 1999 airline sites (such as www.ual.com) were projected to own more than half of the online market, with online agencies' share of the pie dwindling each year.

WHEN SHOULD YOU BOOK ONLINE?

Online booking is not for everyone. If you prefer to let others handle your travel arrangements, one call to an experienced travel agent

---

Editor's Note: What You'll Find at Frommer's Site

We highly recommend **Arthur Frommer's Budget Travel Online** (**www. frommers.com**) as an excellent travel planning resource. Of course, we're a little biased, but you will find indispensable travel tips, reviews, monthly vacation give-aways, and online booking.

Subscribe to **Arthur Frommer's Daily Newsletter** (**www.frommers.com/ newsletters**) to receive the latest travel bargains and inside travel secrets in your mailbox every day. You'll read daily headlines and articles from the dean of travel himself, highlighting last-minute deals on airfares, accommodations, cruises, and package vacations. You'll also find great travel advice by checking our Tip of the Day or Hot Spot of the Month.

Search our **Destinations archive** (**www.frommers.com/destinations**) of more than 200 domestic and international destinations for great places to stay, tips for traveling there, and what to do while you're there. Once you've researched your trip, you might try our online reservation system (www.frommers.com/ booktravelnow) to book your dream vacation at affordable prices.

---

should suffice. But if you want to know as much as possible about your options, the Net is a good place to start, especially for bargain hunters.

The most compelling reason to use online booking is to take advantage of last-minute specials, such as American Airlines' weekend deals or other Internet-only fares that must be purchased online. Another advantage is that you can cash in on incentives for booking online, such as rebates or bonus frequent flyer miles. Online booking works best for trips within North America—for international tickets, it's usually cheaper and easier to use a travel agent or consolidator.

Online booking is certainly not for those with a complex international itinerary. If you require follow-up services, such as itinerary changes, use a travel agent. Though Expedia and some other online agencies employ travel agents available by phone, these sites are geared primarily for self-service.

And remember, the descriptions below are true at press time, but the pace of evolution on the Net is relentless, so you'll probably find some advancements by the time you visit these sites.

LEADING BOOKING SITES

Cheap Tickets. **www.cheaptickets.com**
Essentials: Discounted rates on domestic and international airline tickets and hotel rooms. Sometimes discounters such as Cheap Tickets have exclusive deals that aren't available through more mainstream channels. Registration at Cheap Tickets requires inputting a credit card number before getting started, which is one reason many

---

Factoid

Far more people look online than book online, partly due to fear of putting their credit cards through on the Net. Though secure encryption has made this fear less justified, there's no reason why you can't find a flight online and then book it by calling a toll-free number or contacting your travel agent. To be sure you're in secure mode when you book online, look for a little icon of a key (in Netscape) or a pad-lock (Internet Explorer) at the bottom of your Web browser.

> ### Note
>
> See the appendix on p. 299 for toll-free numbers and Web addresses for airlines, hotels, and rental car companies.

people elect to call the company's toll-free number rather than booking online. One of the most frustrating things about the Cheap Tickets site is that it will offer fare quotes for a route, and later show this fare is not valid for your dates of travel—other Web sites, such as Preview Travel, consider your dates of travel before showing what fares are available. Despite its problems, Cheap Tickets can be worth the effort because its fares can be lower than those offered by its competitors.

✪ Expedia.com. expedia.com

Essentials: Domestic and international flight, hotel, and rental car booking; late-breaking travel news, destination features and commentary from travel experts; deals on cruises and vacation packages. Free registration is required for booking.

Expedia makes it easy to handle flight, hotel, and car booking on one itinerary, so it's a good place for one-stop shopping. Expedia's hotel search offers crisp, zoomable maps to pinpoint most properties; click on the camera icon to see images of the rooms and facilities. But like many online databases, Expedia focuses on the major chains, such as Hilton and Hyatt, so don't expect to find too many one-of-a-kind resorts or B&Bs here.

Once you're registered (it's only necessary to do this once from each computer you use), you can start booking with the Roundtrip Fare Finder box on the home page, which expedites the process. After selecting a flight, you can hold it until midnight the following day or purchase online. If you think you might do better through a travel agent, you'll have time to try to get a lower price. And you may do better with a travel agent because Expedia's computer reservation system does not include all airlines. Most notably absent are some leading budget carriers, such as Southwest Airlines. (*Note:* At press time, Travelocity was the only major booking service that included Southwest.)

Expedia's World Guide, offering destination information, is a glaring weakness—it takes a lot of page views to get very little information. However, Expedia compensates by linking to other Microsoft Network services, such as its Sidewalk city guides, which offer entertainment and dining advice for many of the cities it covers.

Preview Travel. www.previewtravel.com

Essentials: Domestic and international flight, hotel and rental car booking; Travel Newswire lists fare sales; deals on cruises and vacation packages. Free (one-time) registration is required for booking. Preview offers express booking for members but at press time this feature was buried below the fold on Preview's reservation page.

Preview features the most inviting interface for booking trips, though the wealth of graphics involved can make the site somewhat slow to load. Use Farefinder to quickly find the lowest current fares on flights to dozens of major cities. Carfinder offers a similar service for rental cars, but you can only search airport locations, not city pick-up sites. To see the lowest fare for your itinerary, input the dates and times for your route and see what Preview comes up with.

In recent years Preview and other leading booking services have added features such as Best Fare Finder, so after Preview searches for the best deal on your itinerary, it will check flights that are a bit later or earlier to see if it might be cheaper to fly at a different time. While these searches have become quite sophisticated, they still occasionally overlook deals that might be uncovered by a top-notch travel agent. If you have the time, see what you can find online and then call an agent to see if you can get a better price.

With Preview's Fare Alert feature, you can set fares for up to three routes and you'll receive e-mail notices when the fare drops below your target amount. For example, you could tell Preview to alert you when the roundtrip fare between Los Angeles and Washington, D.C. drops below $350. If it does, you'll get an e-mail telling you the current fare.

Priceline.com. www.priceline.com
Even people who aren't familiar with too many Web sites have heard about Priceline.com. Launched in 1998 with a $10 million ad campaign featuring William Shatner, Priceline lets you "name your price" for domestic and international airline tickets and hotel rooms. In other words, you select a route and dates, guarantee with a credit card, and make a bid for what you're willing to pay. If one of the airlines in Priceline's database has a fare that's lower than your bid, your credit card will automatically be charged for a ticket.

You can't say what time you want to fly—you have to accept any flight leaving between 6am and 10pm on the dates you choose, and you may have to make one stopover. No frequent-flyer miles are awarded, and tickets are nonrefundable and can't be exchanged for another flight. So if your plans change, you're out of luck. Priceline can be good for travelers who have to take off on short notice (and who are thus unable to qualify for advance purchase discounts). But be sure to shop around first—if you overbid, you'll be required to purchase the ticket and Priceline will pocket the difference between what it pays for a ticket and what you bid.

Travelocity. www.travelocity.com
Essentials: Domestic and international flight, hotel, and rental car booking; deals on cruises and vacation packages. Travel Headlines spotlights latest bargain airfares. Free (one-time) registration is required for booking.

Travelocity almost got it right. Its Express Booking feature enables travelers to complete the booking process more quickly than they could at Expedia or Preview, but Travelocity gums up the works with a page called "Featured Airlines." Big placards of several featured airlines compete for your attention—if you want to see the fares for all available airlines, click the much smaller box at the bottom of the page labeled "Book a Flight."

Some have worried that Travelocity, which is owned by American Airlines' parent company AMR, directs bookings to American. This doesn't seem to be the case—I've booked there dozens of times and have always been directed to the cheapest listed flight, for example on Tower or ATA. But the "Featured Airlines" page seems to be Travelocity's way of trying to cash in with ads and incentives for booking certain airlines. (*Note:* It's hard to blame these booking services for trying to generate some revenue—many airlines have slashed commissions to $10 per domestic booking for online transactions so these virtual agencies are groping for revenue streams.) There are rewards for choosing one of the featured airlines. You'll get 1,500 bonus frequent flyer miles if you book through United's site, for example, but the site doesn't tell you about other airlines that might be cheaper. If the United flight costs $150 more than the best deal on another airline, it's not worth spending the extra money for a relatively small number of bonus miles.

On the plus side, Travelocity has some leading-edge techie tools for modern travelers. Exhibit A is Fare Watcher Email, an "intelligent agent" that keeps you informed of the best fares offered for the city pairs (round-trips) of your choice. Whenever the fare changes by $25 or more, Fare Watcher will alert you by e-mail. Exhibit B is Flight Paging: If you own an alphanumeric pager with national access that can receive e-mail, Travelocity's paging system can alert you if your flight is delayed. Finally, though Travelocity doesn't include every budget airline, it does include Southwest, the leading U.S. budget carrier.

FINDING LODGINGS ONLINE

While the services above offer hotel booking, it can be best to use a site devoted primarily to lodging because you may find properties that aren't listed on more general online travel agencies. Some lodging sites specialize in a particular type of accommodations, such as bed and breakfast inns, which you won't find on the more mainstream booking services. Other services, such as TravelWeb, offer weekend deals on major chain properties, which cater to business travelers and have more empty rooms on weekends.

Note: See the appendix on p. 299 for toll-free numbers and Web addresses for airlines, hotels and rental car companies.

All Hotels on the Web. www.all-hotels.com
Well, this site doesn't include all the hotels on the Web, but it does have tens of thousands of listings throughout the world. Bear in mind that each hotel listed has paid a small fee of ($25 and up) for placement, so it's not an objective list but more like a book of online brochures. Also see Hotels and Travel on the Net (**www. hotelstravel.com**) which claims to offer discount booking on more than 100,000 hotels and other lodgings in more than 120 countries.

Hotel Reservations Network. www.180096hotel.com
Bargain room rates at hotels in more than 2 dozen U.S. and international cities. The cool thing is that HRN pre-books blocks of rooms in advance, so sometimes it has rooms—at discount rates—at hotels that are "sold out." Select a city, input your dates, and you'll get a list of best prices for a selection of hotels. Descriptions include an image of the property and a locator map—to book online click the "Book Now" button. HRN is notable for some deep discounts, even in cities where hotel rooms are expensive. The toll-free number is printed all over this site; call it if you want more options than are listed online.

InnSite. www.innsite.com
B&B listings for inns in all 50 U.S. states and dozens of countries around the globe.

Find an inn at your destination, have a look at images of the rooms, check prices and availability, and then send e-mail to the innkeeper if you have further questions. This is an extensive directory of bed and breakfast inns but only includes listings if the proprietor submitted one (*Note:* it's free to get an inn listed). The descriptions are written by the innkeepers and many listings link to the inn's own Web sites, where you can find more information and images. Also see: Bed and Breakfast Channel (**bedandbreakfast.com**).

Places to Stay. www.placestostay.com
Mostly one-of-a-kind places in the U.S. and abroad that you might not find in other directories, with a focus on resort accommodations. Again, listing is selective—this isn't a comprehensive directory, but can give you a sense of what's available at different destinations.

Check E-mail at Internet Cafes While Traveling

Until a few years ago, most travelers who checked their e-mail while traveling carried a laptop, but this posed some problems. Not only are laptops expensive, but they can be difficult to configure, incur expensive connection charges, and are attractive to thieves. Thankfully, Web-based free e-mail programs have made it much easier to check your mail while traveling.

Just open an account at a freemail provider, such as **Hotmail** (hotmail.com) or **Yahoo! Mail** (mail.yahoo.com) and all you'll need to check your mail is a Web connection, easily available at Net cafes and copy shops around the world. After logging on, just point the browser to www.hotmail.com, enter your username and password and you'll have access to your mail.

Internet cafes have become ubiquitous, so for a few dollars an hour you'll be able to check your mail and send messages back to colleagues, friends and family. If you already have a primary e-mail account, you can set it to forward mail to your freemail account while you're away. Freemail programs have become enormously popular (Hotmail claims more than 10 million members), because they enable everyone, even those who don't own a computer, to have an e-mail address they can check wherever they log onto the Web.

Quikbook. www.quikbook.com
Though Quikbook lists hotels for only seven U.S. cities (including New York), it offers some good rates on these properties, such as rooms for under $200 at Manhattan's Omni, where the rack rate (top price) is as high as $389. Lists of amenities and expandable images of the hotel, room and lobby round out Quikbook's listings.

✪ TravelWeb. **www.travelweb.com**
TravelWeb lists more than 16,000 hotels worldwide, focusing on chains such as Hyatt and Hilton, and you can book almost 90% of these online. TravelWeb's Click-It Weekends, updated each Monday, offers weekend deals at many leading hotel chains. TravelWeb is the online home for Pegasus Systems, which provides transaction processing systems for the hotel industry.

LAST-MINUTE DEALS & OTHER ONLINE BARGAINS

There's nothing airlines hate more than flying with lots of empty seats (well, maybe they hate competition more but that's another story). The Net has enabled airlines to offer last-minute bargains to entice travelers to fill those seats. Most of these are announced on Tuesday or Wednesday and are valid for travel the following weekend, but some can be booked weeks or months in advance. You can sign up for weekly e-mail alerts at airlines' sites (for airline Web site addresses, see the appendix on airlines, hotels, and car rental companies) or check sites such as WebFlyer (see below) that compile lists of these bargains. To make it easier, visit a site (see below) that will round up all the deals and send them in one convenient weekly e-mail. But last-minute deals aren't the only online bargains—other sites can help you find value even if you can't wait until the eleventh hour.

✪ 1travel.com. **www.1travel.com**
Deals on domestic and international flights, cruises, hotels, and all-inclusive resorts such as Club Med. 1travel.com's Saving Alert compiles last-minute air deals so you don't have to scroll through multiple e-mail alerts. A feature called "Drive a little using low-fare airlines" helps map out strategies for using alternate airports to find lower

While most people learn about last-minute air specials from e-mail dispatches, it can be best to find out precisely when these deals become available and check airlines' Web sites at this time. To find out when deals become available, check the pages devoted to these specials on airlines' Web pages. Because these deals are limited, they can vanish within hours, sometimes even minutes, so it pays to log on as soon as they're available. An example: Southwest's specials are posted at 12:01am Tuesdays (Central time). So if you're looking for a cheap flight, stay up late and check Southwest's site at that time to grab the best new deals.

fares. And Farebeater searches a database that includes published fares, consolidator bargains, and special deals exclusive to 1travel.com. *Note:* The travel agencies listed by 1travel.com have paid for placement.

BestFares. www.bestfares.com
Budget seeker Tom Parsons lists some great bargains on airfares, hotels, rental cars, and cruises, but the site is poorly organized. News Desk is a long list of hundreds of bargains but they're not broken down into cities or even countries, so it's not easy trying to find what you're looking for. If you have time to wade through it, you might find a good deal. Some material is available only to paid subscribers.

Go4less.com. www.go4less.com
Specializing in last-minute cruise and package deals, Go4less has some eye-popping offers. You can avoid sifting through all this material by using the Search box and entering vacation type, destination, month and price.

LastMinuteTravel.com. www.lastminutetravel.com
Travel suppliers with excess inventory distribute unsold airline seats, hotel rooms, cruises, and vacation packages through this online agency.

Moment's Notice. www.moments-notice.com
As the name suggests, Moment's Notice specializes in last-minute vacation and cruise deals. You can browse for free, but if you want to purchase a trip you have to join Moment's Notice, which costs $25.

Smarter Living. www.smarterliving.com
Best known for its e-mail dispatch of weekend deals on 20 airlines, Smarter Living also keeps you posted about last-minute bargains on everything from Windjammer Cruises to flights to Iceland.

✪ WebFlyer. www.webflyer.com
WebFlyer is the ultimate online resource for frequent flyers and also has an excellent listing of last-minute air deals. Click on "Deal Watch" for a round-up of weekend deals on flights, hotels, and rental cars from domestic and international suppliers.

TRAVELER'S TOOLKIT
Veteran travelers usually carry some essential items to make their trips easier. Following is a selection of online tools to smooth your journey.

ATM LOCATORS
Visa. www.visa.com/pd/atm/
MasterCard. www.mastercard.com/atm
Find ATMs in hundreds of cities in the U.S. and around the world. Both include maps for some locations and both list airport ATM locations, some with maps. Remarkably, MasterCard lists ATMs on all seven continents (there's one at Antarctica's McMurdo

Station). *Tip:* You'll usually get a better exchange rate using ATMs than exchanging traveler's checks at banks.

✪ CultureFinder. **www.culturefinder.com**
Up-to-date listings for plays, opera, classical music, dance, film and other cultural events in more than 1,300 U.S. cities. Enter the dates you'll be in a city and get a list of events happening then—you can also purchase tickets online. Also see FestivalFinder (www.festivalfinder.com) for the latest on more than 1,500 rock, folk, reggae, blues, and bluegrass festivals throughout North America.

Intellicast. **www.intellicast.com**
Weather forecasts for all 50 states and cities around the world. Note that temperatures are in Celsius for many international destinations, so don't think you'll need that winter coat for your next trip to Athens.

✪ MapQuest. **www.mapquest.com**
Specializing in U.S. maps, MapQuest enables you to zoom in on a destination, calculate step-by-step driving directions between any two U.S. points, and locate restaurants, hotels and other attractions on maps.

Net Cafe Guide. **www.netcafeguide.com/mapindex.htm**
Locate Internet cafes at hundreds of locations around the globe. Catch up on your e-mail, log onto the Web and stay in touch with the home front, usually for just a few dollars per hour.

Tourism Offices Worldwide Directory. **www.towd.com**
An extensive listing of tourism offices, some with links to these offices' Web sites.

The Travelite FAQ. **www.travelite.org**
Tips on packing light, choosing luggage, and selecting appropriate travel wear.

Trip.com: Airport Maps and Flight Status. **www.trip.com**
A business travel site where you can find out when an airborne flight is scheduled to arrive. Click on "Guides and Tools" to peruse airport maps for more than 40 domestic cities.

2 The Top Web Sites for Washington, D.C.

CITY GUIDES

The District. **www.thedistrict.com**
While this site has all the requisite links to monuments and museums, it also connects to sites for getting around, recreation, and sports. Most of the information comes from the sites it links to.

Local Guys' Guide to Washington, D.C. **members.aol.com/localguys/ dcguide.html**
This offbeat look at the nation's capital offers some frank opinions about what to see and what not to bother with. Click on "Beyond the Mall" for topics including 10 Must-See Sights, Most Underrated Attractions, and Most Overrated Attractions, such as The White House ("A 3-hour wait for a 3-minute tour of three rooms of the White House").

✪ Sidewalk Washington D.C. **washington.sidewalk.msn.com**
Wondering where to dine, shop, or have a drink? Sidewalk is a leading entertainment guide, and also features listings describing Washington's top attractions. Click on "Places to Go" for an extensive archive of day trips, family outings, and timely features, such as coverage of the spring Cherry Blossom celebrations. Within the Places to Go

section is the Visitors Guide, listing lodgings, nightspots, cultural attractions and more.

✪ **Style Live (from the Washington Post and CitySearch). www.washingtonpost. com/wp-srv/style/front.htm**

Whether you're looking for a place to dine or are wondering about the latest exhibition at the National Portrait Gallery Archives, Style Live is a fine place to get up to date. This collaborative site from the Washington Post and CitySearch includes an events calendar, nightlife advice, theater and dance listings, and much more. The Visitors' Guide has a section called "What's Up" which includes daily rosters of Congressional hearings, House and Senate schedules for the week ahead, White House public events, and a weekly diplomacy report. News analysis and commentary from the Post is woven through the site.

TimeOut.com: Washington DC. www.timeout.com/washingtondc

This lively online magazine includes reviews and a calendar of events covering the latest happenings in the nation's capital. You won't find mammoth directories here; instead *TimeOut* selects a handful of worthy events and covers them in some detail.

Visit Washington D.C. www.dchomepage.net

A production of the D.C. Office of Tourism and Promotions, this site links to many popular Web pages for D.C. attractions. You'll also find links to information on lodging and the local transit system.

Washington DC: The American Experience. www.washington.org

A product of Washington's convention and visitors association, this site gives a broad overview of what to see and do in D.C. Click on "Vacation Planning" for tips on where to stay, dine, shop, and sightsee. To book a room here, click on the scrolling banner at the top. In the vacation planning section is an up-to-date calendar of events and a list of 101 Free Things to Do in D.C.

Washington D.C. for Visitors. godc.about.com

This site from About.com is a compendium of links—consider it a jumping-off point. About.com's guide for Washington does a pretty good job of culling lots of useful links for the capital. You'll also find features on some of Washington's top attractions, such as the White House.

✪ **Washingtonian Online. www.washingtonian.com**

Sure you'll find some nice articles from the print magazine of the same name, but there's much more here. Click on "Visitors Guide" or "Arts & Entertainment" for advice on where to stay and dine, and what to see. You'll find features such as "The 100 Best Bargain Restaurants" in the dining section, and "The Four-Hour Mall" in the Attractions and Events section. What's Happening is a monthly guide to what's going on at museums, theaters and other cultural showplaces around town.

✪ **WashingtonPost.com: Destination D.C. www.washingtonpost.com/ wp-srv/local/longterm/tours/guide2.htm**

True, this is a very long Web address, but it's worth entering for the rich content here. You'll find a clickable map of the Smithsonian and the Mall, a guide to the FDR monument, restaurant reviews, a tour of scandal sights, and a guide to Washington's theater productions. Scroll down to find a section called "Short Hops" where you can get ideas for day trips just outside the capital.

DINING & LODGING

Several city guides listed above include dining and lodging sections—below are a few sites that focus solely on dining or lodging.

Cuisine Net: Washington. www.cuisinenet.com/restaurant/washington
Each restaurant has a capsule review compiled by CuisineNet and ratings based on surveys received from site users. For many restaurants, only two or three people have bothered to submit ratings, so they may not be statistically significant. However, comments can be instructive, as CuisineNet's readers discuss service, parking, free birthday desserts and a host of other insightful observations. In addition to Washington, CuisineNet covers 15 other cities.

DiningWeb. dc.diningweb.com
Use this guide to find restaurants based on criteria you select, such as neighborhood and type of cuisine. Some restaurants have ratings from other restaurant-goers. You can also browse through the listings.

Washington D.C. Accommodations. www.dcaccommodations.com
A nicely designed site that recommends hotels suited for families, for women, for sightseers, and for business travelers. To reserve call the toll-free number or fill out the online form and send it via e-mail.

✪ **Zagat.com: Washington DC.** zagat.com
Famous for the print editions of its restaurant surveys, Zagat has gone online with reviews of Washington's restaurants. Using the same survey approach, the recommendations come from hundreds of restaurant-goers, as opposed to a few critics. To get to the Washington D.C. page, start at the home page and use the "Choose a Locale" menu to select Washington D.C. You'll find favorites listed by cuisine, decor, and service. In addition to the Washington survey, Zagat has pages for more than 20 other U.S. and international cities.

TOP ATTRACTIONS

Arlington National Cemetery. www.mdw.army.mil/cemetery.htm
Each year about 4 million people come to the cemetery to pay respects to President John F. Kennedy and the 250,000 military personnel buried there. The Web site includes fact sheets and a cemetery map.

FDR Memorial. www.nps.gov/fdrm/index2.htm
One of the newest tributes in Washington, the memorial to Franklin Delano Roosevelt has attracted visitors in droves since its recent unveiling. The Web site includes facts, descriptions, inscriptions, and links to FDR's speeches and biographical information.

Ford's Theater National Historic Site. www.nps.gov/foth/index2.htm
With a fascinating capsule history of Booth's assassination of Lincoln, this Web site is well worth visiting. You'll also find a gallery of images and general information for visitors (www.nps.gov/foth/index.htm).

Jefferson Memorial. www.nps.gov/thje/index2.htm
Learn about the history and symbolism of the Jefferson Memorial, and find out why FDR cut down all the trees between the White House and the memorial.

The Kennedy Center. www.kennedy-center.org
Find out what's playing at the center and listen to live broadcasts through the Net!

Library of Congress. www.loc.gov
Enjoy a sneak peak at some of the library's treasures in the online version of the American Treasures permanent exhibition. You can also learn about special exhibitions, as well as the history of the nation's library.

Lincoln Memorial. www.nps.gov/linc/index2.htm
There's an ineffable feeling you get when standing before the Lincoln Memorial. Though the Web site can't quite capture this feeling, it can certainly help you learn

Web Sites for Washington Area Spectator Sports Teams

Use the sites listed below for schedules, ticket information, and floor plans for arenas and stadiums.

Baltimore Orioles (Pro baseball)   **www.theorioles.com**

Baltimore Ravens (Pro football)   **www.theravens.com**

Washington Capitals (Pro hockey)   **www.washingtoncaps.com**

Washington Redskins (Pro football)   **www.redskins.com**

Washington Wizards (Pro basketball)   **www.nba.com/wizards**

about the architecture and history of the memorial, which will enhance your appreciation of it when you get there.

Mount Vernon. www.mountvernon.org
Click on "Visitor's Guide" for daily attractions and a calendar of events, as well as information on dining, shopping and school programs. For a sneak preview, click on "Mount Vernon Tour" to see images and descriptions of the master bedroom, dining room, slave memorial, and the Washingtons' tomb.

National Capital Parks Central. www.nps.gov/nacc
This site from the National Park Service includes links to about a dozen memorials and monuments maintained by the NPS. Among the links: the Washington Monument, Jefferson Memorial, National Mall, and Vietnam Veterans Memorial. Each page has a brief description of the memorial or monument, some images, and basic visitor information. You'll also find information of grand spectacles in the capital, such as the Fourth of July festivities.

National Gallery of Art. www.nga.gov
Enjoy an online tour or have a look at the permanent collection. You can also find out about current exhibitions and museum events.

The National Garden. www.nationalgarden.org
Enjoy an online preview of the National Garden (which incorporates the U.S. Botanical Garden). Created by the United States' Founding Fathers, the garden includes the Rose Garden, Water Garden, and the Environmental Learning Center. A visit to the National Garden can be a relaxing respite—see this site to learn more about visiting.

The Newseum. www.newseum.org
Located in nearby Arlington, Virginia, the Newseum chronicles the history of media, through historical newspapers, photographs, and other media. Learn about what's happening at the museum, sample the online exhibits, and find basic visitor information at this site.

The Pentagon. www.defenselink.mil/pubs/pentagon
Learn about the labyrinthine building named for how many sides it has, and find out about touring the facility. Requests for group tours can be made through this site.

✪ **Smithsonian Institution. www.nasm.si.edu**
There's nothing quite like the Smithsonian Institution. If you allow sufficient time, you can get a better education at the Smithsonian than you can at many American colleges—for a lot less money. The range of museums encompassed here is phenomenal; you can wander from the National Museum of the American Indian to the National Air and Space Museum. The Web site includes information about what's happening at each museum, and has updates on general Smithsonian events.

United States Holocaust Memorial Museum. www.ushmm.org
Learn about visiting this memorial to the 6 million who died during World War II.

U.S. House of Representatives. www.house.gov
Click on "Visiting the Nation's Capital" (www.house.gov/house/Visitor.html) to learn more about touring the Capitol building. From here, click on "The House Chamber" where you can get a view of the chamber where the House meets and learn whether the House is in Session.

U.S. Senate. www.senate.gov
Click on "Visiting the Senate" for an online virtual tour of the Capitol building and and information about touring the actual Senate Gallery. It takes a few seconds for the images to download, but it's worth the wait to enjoy the panoramic video tour. Also, find out when the Senate is in session.

✪ **Vietnam Veterans Memorial. www.nps.gov/vive/index2.htm**
This tremendously popular memorial has provided a catharsis for the nation after one of its least popular wars. Learn about the design of this tremendously popular memorial or find out more about the Vietnam Veterans Memorial Collection, which has been selected by citizens.

Washington Monument. www.nps.gov/wamo/index2.htm
Take a virtual tour of the monument and learn about the $4 million restoration effort that's refurbishing the towering edifice. The Web site contains a fascinating discussion of the Know Nothing party (not a bad name for either party these days) that delayed construction of the monument during the 1800s.

The White House. www.whitehouse.gov
Click on "Tour Information" to learn about seeing the White House and upcoming public events. You'll also find a link to Congressional Tours on this page. Also on the White House home page: recent presidential speeches and links for sending e-mail to the president or vice president.

GETTING AROUND

Metropolitan Washington Airports Authority. www.metwashairports.com
Ground transport, terminal maps, flight status, and airport facilities for Dulles International and Ronald Reagan (National) airports.

Washington Metropolitan Area Transit Authority. www.wmata.com
Timetables, maps, fares, and more for the buses and trains that serve the Washington D.C. metro area.

Index

See also Accommodations and Restaurant indexes, below.

General Index

General Index

Restaurant Index

FROMMER'S® COMPLETE TRAVEL GUIDES

Alaska
Amsterdam
Arizona
Atlanta
Australia
Austria
Bahamas
Barcelona, Madrid & Seville
Beijing
Belgium, Holland & Luxembourg
Bermuda
Boston
Budapest & the Best of Hungary
California
Canada
Cancún, Cozumel &
   the Yucatán
Cape Cod, Nantucket & Martha's Vineyard
Caribbean
Caribbean Cruises & Ports of Call
Caribbean Ports of Call
Carolinas & Georgia
Chicago
China
Colorado
Costa Rica
Denmark
Denver, Boulder & Colorado Springs
England
Europe
Florida
France
Germany
Greece
Greek Islands
Hawaii
Hong Kong
Honolulu, Waikiki & Oahu
Ireland
Israel
Italy
Jamaica & Barbados
Japan
Las Vegas
London
Los Angeles
Maryland & Delaware
Maui
Mexico
Miami & the Keys

Montana & Wyoming
Montréal & Québec City
Munich & the Bavarian Alps
Nashville & Memphis
Nepal
New England
New Mexico
New Orleans
New York City
Nova Scotia, New Brunswick &
   Prince Edward Island
Oregon
Paris
Philadelphia & the
   Amish Country
Portugal
Prague & the Best of the Czech Republic
Provence & the Riviera
Puerto Rico
Rome
San Antonio & Austin
San Diego
San Francisco
Santa Fe, Taos &
   Albuquerque
Scandinavia
Scotland
Seattle & Portland
Singapore & Malaysia
South Africa
Southeast Asia
South Pacific
Spain
Sweden
Switzerland
Thailand
Tokyo
Toronto
Tuscany & Umbria
USA
Utah
Vancouver & Victoria
Vermont, New Hampshire
   & Maine
Vienna & the Danube Valley
Virgin Islands
Virginia
Walt Disney World & Orlando
Washington, D.C.
Washington State

FROMMER'S® DOLLAR-A-DAY GUIDES

Australia from $50 a Day
California from $60 a Day
Caribbean from $70 a Day
England from $70 a Day
Europe from $60 a Day
Florida from $60 a Day

Hawaii from $70 a Day
Ireland from $50 a Day
Israel from $45 a Day
Italy from $70 a Day
London from $85 a Day
New York from $80 a Day

New Zealand from $50 a Day
Paris from $85 a Day
San Francisco from $60 a Day
Washington, D.C.,
    from $60 a Day

FROMMER'S® PORTABLE GUIDES

Acapulco, Ixtapa &
    Zihuatanejo
Alaska Cruises & Ports of Call
Bahamas
Baja & Los Cabos
Berlin
California Wine Country
Charleston & Savannah
Chicago

Dublin
Hawaii: The Big Island
Las Vegas
London
Maine Coast
Maui
New Orleans
New York City
Paris

Puerto Vallarta, Manzanillo
    & Guadalajara
San Diego
San Francisco
Sydney
Tampa & St. Petersburg
Venice
Washington, D.C.

FROMMER'S® NATIONAL PARK GUIDES

Family Vacations in the
    National Parks
Grand Canyon

National Parks of the
    American West
Rocky Mountain

Yellowstone & Grand Teton
Yosemite & Sequoia/
    Kings Canyon
Zion & Bryce Canyon

FROMMER'S® GREAT OUTDOOR GUIDES

New England
Northern California

Southern California & Baja
Washington & Oregon

FROMMER'S® MEMORABLE WALKS

Chicago
London

New York
Paris

San Francisco
Washington D.C.

FROMMER'S® IRREVERENT GUIDES

Amsterdam
Boston
Chicago
Las Vegas

London
Los Angeles
Manhattan

New Orleans
Paris
San Francisco

Seattle & Portland
Vancouver
Walt Disney World
Washington, D.C.

FROMMER'S® BEST-LOVED DRIVING TOURS

America
Britain
California

Florida
France
Germany

Ireland
Italy
New England

Scotland
Spain
Western Europe

THE UNOFFICIAL GUIDES®

Bed & Breakfast in
  New England
Bed & Breakfast in
  the Northwest
Beyond Disney
Branson, Missouri
California with Kids
Chicago

Cruises
Disneyland
Florida with Kids
The Great Smoky &
  Blue Ridge
  Mountains
Inside Disney
Las Vegas

London
Miami & the Keys
Mini Las Vegas
Mini-Mickey
New Orleans
New York City
Paris
San Francisco

Skiing in the West
Walt Disney World
Walt Disney World
  for Grown-ups
Walt Disney World
  for Kids
Washington, D.C.

SPECIAL-INTEREST TITLES

Born to Shop: France
Born to Shop: Hong Kong
Born to Shop: Italy
Born to Shop: New York
Born to Shop: Paris
Frommer's Britain's Best Bike Rides
The Civil War Trust's Official Guide
  to the Civil War Discovery Trail
Frommer's Caribbean Hideaways
Frommer's Europe's Greatest Driving Tours
Frommer's Food Lover's Companion to France
Frommer's Food Lover's Companion to Italy
Frommer's Gay & Lesbian Europe
Israel Past & Present
Monks' Guide to California

Monks' Guide to New York City
The Moon
New York City with Kids
Unforgettable Weekends
Outside Magazine's Guide
  to Family Vacations
Places Rated Almanac
Retirement Places Rated
Road Atlas Britain
Road Atlas Europe
Washington, D.C., with Kids
Wonderful Weekends from Boston
Wonderful Weekends from New York City
Wonderful Weekends from San Francisco
Wonderful Weekends from Los Angeles

FROMMER'S CITY-TO-GO

Keeping You Connected on the Road...

Frommer's and Palm Computing, Inc. have teamed up to bring you all the convenience of a Frommer's guide in the form of the Palm VII™ connected organizer.

Whether you're in New York City on business or wandering the streets of San Francisco for leisure, let Frommer's City-To-Go be your guide. With listings for the best restaurants, accommodations, nightlife, sightseeing and shopping highlights in most major U.S. cities at your fingertips, you'll have the ideal pocket-sized travel resource wherever you go.

For more information about Frommer's City-To-Go and the new Palm VII™ organizer, visit www.palm.com.

WHEREVER YOU TRAVEL, *H*ELP IS NEVER FAR AWAY.

From planning your trip to providing travel assistance along the way, American Express® Travel Service Offices are always there to help you do more.

Washington, D.C.

American Express Travel Service
1150 Connecticut Ave., N.W.
(202) 457-1300

American Express Travel Service
5300 Wisconsin Ave., N.W.
Garden Level, Mazza Galleria
(202) 362-4000

do more AMERICAN EXPRESS
Travel

www.americanexpress.com/travel

**American Express Travel Service Offices
are located throughout the United States.
For the office nearest you, call 1-800-AXP-3429.**